DATE DUE

Advertising Slogans of America

Compiled by Harold S. Sharp

The Scarecrow Press, Inc.
Metuchen, N.J. & London
1984

Library of Congress Cataloging in Publication Data

Sharp, Harold S.
    Advertising slogans of America.

    1. Slogans. 2. Advertising--United States.
I. Title.
HF6135.S53   1984   659.13'22   83-20431
ISBN 0-8108-1681-4

Lovingly dedicated
to the memory of my maternal grandmother,
Mrs. Teresa B. Spencer,
and her sister,
my great-aunt, Miss Agnes Brunstead--
two of the best friends a boy ever had.

FOREWORD

Advertising has been defined as "a collective term for public announcements designed to promote the sale of specific commodities or services." The concept of advertising began centuries ago and has burgeoned into a worldwide industry. Advertisers now spend in excess of fifteen billion dollars annually in the United States alone. This includes consumer advertising and trade advertising, the former being directed to the ultimate purchaser and the latter appealing to dealers and other middlemen.

Prior to the American Civil War few products were identifiable by brand name. In the decades that followed competition for the buyer's dollar intensified. The various manufacturers and service organizations assigned brand names to their products, advertising these in the media and coining slogans to accompany them. It was hoped that this would create a favorable image and hence a demand for the specific goods and services so advertised. Slogans thus became an integral part of advertisements.

The word "slogan" is an Anglicization of the Gaelic "slaughghairm" which means "army cry" or "war cry," formerly used by the Scottish clans. Its purpose was then to inspire the members of the clan to fight fiercely "for its protection or the extension of its glory." Today it is defined by one authority as "a relatively pithy phrase or sentence used repeatedly in advertisements by manufacturers and service organizations for the purpose of influencing the buying behavior of consumers."

v

Prior to the passage of the Lanham Act by Congress in the mid-1940s advertising slogans were not protected from infringement except when they were incorporated in trademarks and, as such, were registered with the United States Patent Office in Washington. Consequently a specific slogan could then be used legally by two or more separate advertisers. Thus, "Standard of the world" dealt with the Cadillac automobile, The American Blower Company and Bull Durham tobacco. "World's finest" was associated with the Autocar truck, Garrard phonograph record changer, J. A. Baldwin Manufacturing Co. and Phillipson Rod Co. The Lanham Act "does not protect slogans from infringement to the extent that the Patent Office accepts on the principal register only those which integrate the product name. Those slogans which identify or distinguish the products to which they refer are carried on the supplemental register."

Slogans have been used extensively in American advertising for over a century. From a comparatively staid beginning until the late 1870s advertising did not include "nonsense selling, rhyming or advertising cards." Then slogans began to appear. For example, in 1882 the maker of the Carpenter library organ stated in an advertisement that it was "something entirely new! The aesthetic taste gratified!" In the same decade other flamboyant claims were made for the James Means' $3 shoe ("Absolutely without a rival") and for the Unique Hair Crimper ("The best in the world. None can equal it!"). Many manufacturers of patent medicines touted their nostrums in a similar manner until they were forbidden to do so by the Federal Trade Commission some years later.

Advertising slogans can take many forms, some of which are described below.

Question. What good is paint if it's not good paint? (Pratt & Lambert paint).

Challenge. Hammer the hammer (Iver Johnson Arms & Cycle Works).

Originator. The original baby food for baby chicks (Pratt Food Co.).

Longevity. Since 1846 the quality of elegance underfoot (Philadelphia Carpet Co.).

Initialism. LS/MFT (Lucky Strike means fine tobacco) (Lucky Strike cigarettes).

Pun. The prince of ales (Busch pale dry ale).

Superlative. The greatest show on earth (Barnum & Bailey's circus).

Transferred epithet. Fly the friendly skies of United (United Air Lines).

Acrostic. Merit And Reliability Made Our Name (Marmon automobile).

Rhyme. Behind the fame of the Jarman name (Jarman shoes).

Alliteration. You'll love the look of your leg in Larkwood (Larkwood hosiery).

Metaphor. Like pearl temples behind the ears (No-Ease spectacles).

Single Word. Think (International Business Machines).

Contrived Word. Crunchycheweynuttysweet (Raisin Grape Nuts).

Simile. As unique as the person who drives one (Oldsmobile Toronado automobile).

Ungrammatical. (1) (Intentional) Nobody doesn't like Sara Lee (Sara Lee coffee cake). (2) (Unintentional) If anyone tells you Michelin is too expensive they're putting you on (Michelin tires).

Analogy. A piano is the soul of the home (Musette piano).

Allusion. Don't be a RUBBIT! (Brillo cleanser).

Hyperbole. Only the rich can afford poor windows (Anderson Corp.).

Chiasmus. The right business form for every form of business (Moore Business Forms, Inc.).

Personification. The pressure cooker people (Presto Industries, Inc.).

Statement of capabilities. Prepares for college or business while touring the world (Nautical Preparatory School).

Boast. The fastest growing battery business in America (Prest-O-Lite).

Statement of advantageous characteristic. Does not boil away (Prestone anti-freeze).

General Philosophizing. Priceless ingredient of every product is the honor and integrity of its maker (E. R. Squibb).

In some cases the slogan pertaining to a specific product, service or organization will mention the item to which it refers, thus: "When better automobiles are built, Buick will build them" (Buick automobile). In other instances that to which the slogan refers is not mentioned, as in the case of Ivory soap's "It floats" and Steinway piano's "The instrument of the immortals." Slogans range in length from those composed of a single word, as "Because" (Modess sanitary napkin) to thirteen or more words, as exemplified by Pepsodent tooth paste's "You'll wonder where the yellow went when you brush your teeth with Pepsodent."

The rhyming slogan, such as the one immediately above may, in some cases, be considered a jingle, defined as "a simple, repetitious, catchy rhyme or doggerel."

Some organizations have but one slogan; others have, over the years, used many. For example the Sharp-Moore Meat Co., in its advertising, spoke only of "Smoked meats that are treats." The Chevrolet automobile, on the other hand, has used at least twenty-five slogans and, no doubt, there are others which the compiler of this volume did not locate.

The slogans appearing in this collection were gathered from many sources. These include television and radio broadcasts, films, books depicting published advertisements of the past, newspapers, magazines, matchbook covers, truck panels, billboards, posters and other advertising signs, labels on cans, packages, boxes and similar containers, manufacturers' catalogs, metered mail envelopes showing company slogans, letterheads, handbills, sandwich boards and phonographic recordings. Approximately 15,000 slogans used by some 6,000 business and other organizations are listed.

In this book the slogans and the organizations using them and/or the products and services to which they pertain are shown in a single alphabetical listing. Each entry covering an organization, product or service appears once in the listing, with the slogan(s) dealing with it being shown immediately below. Each separate slogan is shown alphabetically within the listing, and the organization or product connected with it is indicated.

Examples

Organization entry:

Stewart-Warner Corporation
    Fluid handling is Stewart-Warner's
        business

SW- Symbol of excellence
Twelve million people are today
    using Stewart-Warner products

Slogan entries:

Fluid handling is Stewart-Warner's
        business
    Stewart-Warner Corporation

SW- Symbol of excellence
    Stewart-Warner Corporation

Twelve million people are today
        using Stewart-Warner
        products
    Stewart-Warner Corporation

Product entry:

Packer's Tar Soap
    Long ago distanced all
        competitors

Slogan entry:

Long ago distanced all
        competitors
    Packer's Tar Soap

    The names of magazines and newspapers are un-
derlined, as Saturday Evening Post and Chicago Tribune.
In cases of alternative spellings and non-inverted entries, "See also" and "See" references are used, as:

Kimball. See also:
    Kimble glass
    Miles Kimball mail order
        service
    W. W. Kimball Co.

Stuart. See:
    Stewart
    Stewart's

x

Where a product might be known by more than one name, cross-references between these have been used, thus:

Deviled Ham. <u>See</u>: Underwood's
    Original Deviled Ham

While this book was being compiled many people gave willing and helpful assistance. The reference librarians in the Fort Wayne and Allen County Public Library, the Indiana-Purdue University Library of Fort Wayne and the Indianapolis Public Library were particularly obliging. My sister-in-law, Mrs. Kenneth Sharp, who furnished me with a number of basic sources of slogan information and assisted me in other ways, was particularly helpful. I wish to thank these people at this time.

Harold S. Sharp

ADVERTISING SLOGANS OF AMERICA

-A-

A & P Coffee
    Right from the start
A & P Supermarket
    Favorite "meating" for partic-
        ular people
A & W Root Beer
    That frosty mug sensation
The ABC of radio satisfaction
    Ray-O-Vac batteries
A. B. C. Super Electric
    America's leading washing
        machine
A. C. Gilbert Co.
    Toys that are genuine
A. C. Laurence Leather Co.
    Fibre-sorted soles
A. C. Spark Plug Div., General
        Motors Corporation
    Master navigators through
        time and space
A. C. Spark Plug Div., General
        Motors Corporation
    See also: General Motors
        Corporation
A. C. Spark Plugs
    Grime does not pay
A. G. Becker & Co., Inc.
    The man from A. G. Becker
        is always worth listening
        to
A. G. Spalding & Dros.
    The ball that made baseball
A. H. Robins Co.
    Making today's medicines
        with integrity ... seek-
        ing tomorrow's with per-
        sistence
A. L. Mechling Barge Lines,
        Inc.
    Personalized service that
        makes the big difference
AM Jacquard Systems

Let's talk about facts and
    figures
AMF. See: American Machine &
    Foundry Co.
AO polaroid day lens
    If it's marked AO, it suits
        you so
    If it's marked AO, it's smart-
        ly styled, optically cor-
        rect
A-1 makes hamburgers taste like
        steakburgers
    A-1 Sauce
A-1 Sauce
    A-1 makes hamburgers taste
        like steakburgers
    The dash that makes the dish
    Makes today's hash as tasty
        as yesterday's roast
    Ze dash zat makes ze dish
A. P. Green Fire Brick Co.
    First name in refractories
    Serve the world's industries
    They last longer
A. P. Parts Corp. mufflers
    Sold by more dealers than any
        other brand
A.S.C.A.P. See: American Soci-
    ety of Composers, Authors
    and Publishers
A. Schrader's Son
    First name in tire valves for
        original equipment and
        replacement
A T & M advances centrifugal de-
    sign
    American Tool & Machine Co.
A. T. Cross Co.
    America's finest writing in-
        struments since 1846
A votre service
    Air France
Abbey Effervescent Co.
    Stay young as you grow old

1

Abbott-Detroit automobile
    Build for permanence and
        guaranteed for life
Abbott Laboratories
    Basic provider of chemicals in
        volume
Abex Corp.
    Abex means controls
Abex means controls
    Abex Corp.
Abilene Flour Mills
    Hot biscuits in a jiffy
    Just a minute, please
    Ninety golden brown biscuits
        from each package
    That ole southern flavor
Above all, dependable
    Universal motors
Above all, under all
    Dove Skin undies
Absence makes the meat grow
        tender
    Hotpoint Div., General Elec-
        tric Company
Absolutely non-explosive
    Adams & Westlake Oil Stove
Absolutely pure
    Royal Baking Powder
Absolutely unequaled
    Hoffman House cigar
Absolutely without a rival
    James Means' $3 shoe
Absorb shocks and jars
    Massagic Air Cushion shoes
The absorbent soft white toilet
        tissue
    ScotTissue
Absorbine, Jr.
    The antiseptic liniment
    Ditch the itch with Absor-
        bine, Jr.
    Oh, my aching back! Ah,
        my Absorbine, Jr!
    Quick relief for sunburn, too!
    She merely carried the daisy
        chain ... yet she has
        "Athlete's Foot!"
Abused children are helpless.
        Unless you help
    National Committee for Pre-
        vention of Child Abuse
Acason truck
    Every Acason is a good
        truck
Accent food flavor stimulant
    Wakes up food flavor

Accentuate the positive
    Fuel Oil Supply & Terminal-
        ing, Inc.
The accepted educational standard
    Compton's Encyclopedia
The accepted name for value
    Haskell, Inc.
Acclaimed by millions from coast to
        coast
    Dreft soap flakes
Acco Babcock, Inc.
    The material handling systems
        house
According to Hoytt
    Hoytt Construction Co.
Accuracy first in home and indus-
        try
    Taylor Instruments
Accuracy to seconds a month
    Pulsar watches
Accurate beyond comparison
    Warren telechron
Accurate to the very edge
    Tillyen lenses
Accustomed to the finest ... you'll
        find it in a Beechcraft
    Beech Aircraft Corp.
Ace combs
    Clean hair means a healthy
        scalp
Ace Hardware Stores
    Ace is the place for the help-
        ful hardware man
Ace is the place for the helpful
        hardware man
    Ace Hardware Stores
Ace of the eights
    Marmon automobile
Aces. See: The Seven Aces Or-
        chestra
Achievement. See: Junior
        Achievement, Inc.
Acknowledged the world's best pi-
        ano
    Knabe piano
Acme Appliance Mfg. Co.
    More doors fold on Fold-Aside
        than any other kind!
Acme Glove Corp.
    A love of a glove
Acme Life Products Co.
    Feather touch control
Acme motor truck
    The pinnacle of performance
    The truck of proved units
Acme National Refrigeration Co.

2

Where inches count
Acme Steel Co.
   Bound to get there
   For making shipments "bound
     to get there"
   Idea leader in storage sys-
     tems
   Idea leader in strapping
Acme White Lead & Color Works
   The sign of paint success
Acousticon hearing aid
   Sole makers of Acousticon
     since 1903
Across the Atlantic
   United American Lines
Across the continent in comfort
   Ford automobile
The Action Bank
   National Westminster
The action company
   Stat-Tab Computer Services
Action keeps on longer after the
   brushing stops
   Squibb toothpaste
The action line
   Evans Products Co.
Action people
   Bell System telephone direc-
     tory yellow pages
Action shoes for boys and girls
   Red Goose shoes
Action underwear for active men
   Munsingwear underwear
The active man's summer under-
   wear
   Porosknit
The active sulphur for soil
   Bacsul
Activision video games
   Puts you in the game
Acts well, tastes swell
   Ex-Lax laxative
Actual stories of actual people
   Secrets
Ad-Novelty Sales Co.
   The kit that hands you
     money
Adam. See: Frank Adam Elec-
   tric Co.
Adamite Gears
   Adamite Gears last for
     years
Adamite Gears last for years
   Adamite Gears
Adams. See also: Stacy Adams
   shoe

Adams & Westlake Oil Stove
   Absolutely non-explosive
Add a fiber from Celanese and
   good things get better
   Celanese Corp.
Add-A-Pearl Co.
   The gift that lives and grows
Add sparkle to your breakfast and
   sparkle to your day
   Sunsweet prunes
The added touch that means so
   much
   Lea & Perrin's Sauce
Addington Mfg. Co.
   The original Plaster and Stuc-
     co Fabric
Addressing society's major unmet
   needs as profitable busi-
   ness opportunities
   Control Data Corporation
Addressograph-Multigraph Corp.
   Cutting costs is our business
   Helping people communicate
   Prints from type
   You can't buy a Multigraph
     unless you need it
Adds comfort to every step
   Armstrong's Shoe Products
Adds magic to soap
   Klenzing Emulsion
Adds miles to tire life
   Tirometer Valve Corp.
Adds science to fisherman's luck
   True Temper Corp.
Adds 70% more nourishment to
   milk
   Cocomalt
Adds the finishing touch
   Linit laundry starch
Adds zest
   Snider's tomato products
Adel Precision Products Corp.
   Design simplicity and depend-
   ability
Adirondack Bats, Inc.
   The bat with the most on the
     ball
Adjusto-Lite
   It clamps everywhere
Adler elevator shoes
   Your personal pedestal
Adler socks
   Take to water like a duck
   Wash them any way you like,
     we guarantee the size
Administrative Management

The magazine of methods,
  personnel and equipment
Admiral Line. See: New York-
  Miami route, Admiral
  Line
Admiral radio receiver
  America's smart set
Admiral refrigerator
  Worth it's WAIT in gold
Admiral television sets
  Mark of quality throughout
  the world
Admiration cigar
  Best for half a century, bet-
  ter than ever today
  Everybody loves Admiration
  Little cigars that win
Admiration nylon stockings
  Priced from mill to Milady
Admiration soapless shampoo
  For springy-soft hair
  Wakes up your hair
Admits light, retards heat
  Owens-Illinois Glass Co.
Adohr Creamery Co.
  Highest continuous record in
  official scoring tests
  Quality you can taste
Adola brassiere
  Flatters where it matters
Adolph's meat tenderizer
  No ifs, ands or additives
Adolphus Hotel, Dallas, Texas
  Tune in your favorite tem-
  perature
Adorns your skin with the frag-
  rance men love
  Cashmere Bouquet soap
Adrian perfume
  As mischevious as a sidelong
  glance
Advance Pattern Co.
  There are many advance
  styles, but there is only
  one Advance pattern
  The third dimension pattern
  Tomorrow's styles today
Advanced Formula Sugar Twin
  It's sugar for your mouth
Advertise and realize
  Pencil Specialty Co.
Advertise for action
  Bell system telephone direc-
  tory yellow pages
Advertising Age
  Important to important peo-

ple
  The national newspaper of mar-
  keting
The Advertising Council
  Our teachers mold the nation's
  future
  Please! Only you can prevent
  forest fires
Advertising Federation of America
  Truth in advertising
Advertising is the power of an
  idea multiplied
  D'Arcy Advertising Co.
Advertising Supply Co.
  Printing with a personal ap-
  peal
Advertising that follows through to
  sales
  Lithographers National Asso-
  ciation
Advertising that makes sense makes
  dollars
  John A. Lane
Advertising with a basic idea
  J. Walter Thompson Co.
Aeolian-Vocalion
  The world's most wonderful
  phonograph
Aermore exhaust horn
  The Horn Harmonious
  Signal with a smile
Aero Mayflower Transit Co., Inc.
  America's most recommended
  mover
Aeromatic Koppers
  The propeller with a brain
  for your private plane
Aeronca aircraft
  Your personal plane is HERE
Aeroquip Corp.
  The lifeline of your equipment
Aeroshade Co.
  More home to the house
The aerospace company with its
  feet on the ground
  The Garrett Corporation
Aerospatiale Helicopter Corporation
  Sets performance standards
Aerowax
  Old floors to look new in six
  to nine minutes
Aetna Brewing Co.
  As tonic as sunshine itself
  A case of Aetna is a case of
  health
  That old-time ale with the

4

old-fashioned flavor
Aetna Explosives Co.
  It does the work
Aetna Insurance Co.
  Aetna is protecting your
    privacy
  Aetna-ize, according to your
    needs, as you prosper,
    as your obligations in-
    crease
  The Aetna-izer, a man worth
    knowing
  Aetna wants insurance to be
    affordable
  Are you Aetna-ized?
  Be wise, Aetna-ize
  The choice of businessmen
    lets you choose with
    confidence
  For your family and business
    --your auto, home and
    everything you own
  A man worth knowing
  Our concern is people
  P.S.--Personal service
Aetna is protecting your privacy
  Aetna Insurance Co.
Aetna-ize, according to your
    needs, as you prosper,
    as your obligations in-
    crease
  Aetna Insurance Co.
The Aetna-izer, a man worth
    knowing
  Aetna Insurance Co.
Aetna wants insurance to be af-
    fordable
  Aetna Insurance Co.
Affordable insurance is our busi-
    ness ... and yours
  American Insurance Associ-
    ation
African business is our business
  Farrell Lines, Inc.
After all, if smoking isn't a
    pleasure, why bother?
  Newport cigarettes
After all, ink makes the picture
  Sigmund Ullman & Co.
After all, life is to enjoy
  Buick automobile
After all, "The taste tells"
  Delrich Margarine
After every meal
  Wrigley's chewing gum
After sunset, Lightoliers

Lightolier, Inc.
Again a year ahead
  Zenith radio receiver
Aged extra long for extra flavor
  Breidt beer
Aged for 8
  Bell's Blended scotch whiskey
Aged for smoothness and taste
  Puerto Rican rums
Aged in natural rock caves
  Ebling beer
Aged in the wood
  Velvet Tobacco
An agency is known by the clients
    it keeps
  Gottschalk-Humphrey
Agfa-Gevaert, Inc.
  Pictures that satisfy or a new
    roll free
  World's second largest manu-
    facturer of cameras and
    films
Aglow with friendliness
  Hotel Fort Shelby, Detroit
Agree hair conditioner
  Helps stop the greasies
An agreeable chewing digestant
  Bi-Car chewing gum
Agricultural Publishers Assn.
  Prosperity follows the plow
  Safest to use the best
Ahh, the beer with the taste for
    food!
  Natural Light beer
Ahrend. See: D. H. Ahrend Co.
Aid-A-Walker shoes
  Moulded to your foot
Aids. See also: Ayds
Aids digestion
  Beechnut gum
The AIG Companies
  Let us take the risks
  Once again the answer is AIG
  We offer more kinds of insur-
    ance than anyone else in
    the business
Aim toothpaste
  Brush often with Aim
  Take Aim against cavities
Aint no reason to go anyplace
    else
  Wendy's fast food restaurants
Air Canada
  A friend of the family
Air change, not just air movement
  ILG Electric Ventilating Co.

5

Air conditioning for profit
    Kelvinator air conditioning
Air conditioning's first name
    Carrier Corporation
Air Express
    Gets there first
The air force in freight
    Emery Air Freight Co.
Air France
    A votre service
    The best of France to all
        the world
    Fly anywhere in Europe via
        Air France
    We know where you're going
    The world's largest airline
Air-freight specialists
    Flying Tiger Line, Inc.
Air-India
    The airline that treats you
        like a maharajah
Air King radio receiver
    The royalty of radio since
        1920
Air New Zealand
    The airline that knows the
        South Pacific best
The air of quality
    Rheem air conditioners
Air speed at truck rates
    Eastern Air-Freight
Air Step shoe
    More graceful stairsteps in
        magic Air Steps
    The shoe with the youthful
        feel
    Turns sidewalks into soft
        carpets
Air unlox to Magnavox
    Magnavox radio receiver
The air valve people
    Numatics, Inc.
Air-Way Sanitary System
    No cleaner bag or contain-
        er to empty
Airacobras for victory, future
    planes for peace
    Bell Airacobra
Airborne Freight Corp.
    World's most dependable
        air freight service
Airbus Industrie of North
    America
    Fly in the best of circles
    We did it our way
Aircraft Accessories Corpora-
tion
    Saflight means safety in flight
Aircraft Marine Products
    Precision engineering applied
        to the end of a wire
Airedale brick
    Airedale brick, like Airedale
        dogs, so darned ugly
        they are beautiful
    Airedale brick, like Airedale dogs,
        so darned ugly they are
        beautiful
    Airedale brick
Airline honey
    From flower to bee to you
The airline of the international
        business traveler
    Royal Dutch Airlines
Airline of the professionals
    American Airlines, Inc.
The airline run by flyers
    Transcontinental & Western
        Airline
The airline run by professionals
    Delta Air Lines, Inc.
An airline that goes to the world's
        most prestigious places
    Pan American World Airways,
        Inc.
The airline that knows the South
        Pacific best
    Air New Zealand
The airline that measures the mid-
        west in minutes
    Ozark Air Lines, Inc.
The airline that treats you like a
        maharajah
    Air-India
The airline with the big jets
    Delta Air Lines, Inc.
Airosol insecticide
    Jet that bug
The airplane feel of the Franklin
        opens the road to new
        motoring thrills
    Franklin automobile
Airplane transport
    We smile at miles
The airplanes that mean business
    North American Aviation,
        Inc.
Airstream motor coach
    The leader by design
Airtex Products, Inc.
    Number 1 in acceptance
    The only name for both fuel

6

and water pumps
Aiwa tape recorders
  Feature rich
Ajax cleanser
  Ajax, that foaming cleanser
  Bleaches out the toughest
    food stains fast
  Cleans like a white tornado!
Ajax laundry detergent
  Stronger than dirt
Ajax Rope Co.
  Strength in every length
Ajax, that foaming cleanser
  Ajax cleanser
Akro Agate Co.
  Dad played marbles, too
Akron-Selle Co.
  Forgings that stand the test
Alabama Power Co.
  The power that lights and
    moves Alabama
Aladdin Dye Soap
  Colors while it cleans
Aladdin Mfg. Co.
  Lighting over a million
    homes tonight
Aladdin prefabricated houses
  Home builders to the nation
  Protect yourself against the
    middleman
Alameda Plaza Hotel, Kansas
    City, Mo.
  Alameda Plaza: the hotel
    of Kansas City
  Kansas City's finest hotel
    at Kansas City's finest
    address
  Where short stays are long
    remembered
Alameda Plaza: The hotel of
    Kansas City
  Alameda Plaza Hotel, Kansas
    City, Mo.
Alamite. See also: Alemite
Alamite Dairy
  Paint your cheeks from the
    inside
Alaska Airlines, Inc.
  Golden nugget jet service
  Golden nugget jets
  The Alaska flag line
  Pacific Northern Airlines
Alaska Refrigerator Co.
  A life preserver for foods
Alaska Travel Div., Dept. of
  Economic Development

and Planning
  You haven't seen your country
    if you haven't seen Alaska
Alba dry milk product
  The only chocolate milk with
    no sugar added
Albert. See also:
  Elbert
  Prince Albert pipe and cigar-
    ette tobacco
Albert Ehlers, Inc.
  The cream of coffees
Albert soaps
  Best for you and baby, too
Alberthaw Construction Co.
  Built by Alberthaw
Alberto VO-5 beauty spray
  The natural beauty spray
Albolene cleansing cream
  And McKesson makes it
Alcoa. See: Aluminum Company
    of America
Alden radio sockets
  It's the contact that counts
Aldens mail order catalog
  America's most convenient
    shopping mall
Aldrich Pump Co.
  The tough pumping problems
    go to Aldrich
Alemite. See also:
  Alamite Dairy
  Horace Heidt and his Musical
    Knights orchestra
Alemite automobile lubrication sys-
    tem
  Alemite helps the world go
    'round
  Alemite means correct lubri-
    cation
  High pressure lubrication
  Specialized lubrication
Alemite helps the world go 'round
  Alemite automobile lubrication
    system
Alemite means correct lubrication
  Alemite automobile lubrication
    system
Alert Beverage Co.
  Be alert, bottle Alert
Alexander & Alexander insurance
    brokers
  From the client's point of
    view
Alexander pens and pencils
  Write around the world

7

Alexander Young Distilling Co.
  The whiskey that grew up
    with America
Alfred Hale Rubber Co.
  Prince of soles
Algoma Panel Co.
  Small cost for great richness
Alice. See: Allis
Alive with pleasure!
  Newport cigarettes
Alka-Seltzer
  Alkalize with Alka-Seltzer
  America's home remedy
  Good taste in a remedy
  I can't believe I ate the
    whole thing!
  Plop, plop! Fizz, fizz! Oh,
    what a relief it is!
  Relief is just a swallow away
  Speedy is its middle name
Alkaid
  The candy-mint alkalizer
The alkaline antiseptic
  Glyco-Thymoline
The alkaline dental cream
  Squibb toothpaste
Alkalize with Alka-Seltzer
  Alka-Seltzer
All along the line, Duz does
    everything
  Duz washing powder
The All-American ale
  Cleveland-Sandusky Brewing
    Corp.
The All-American beer
  Cleveland-Sandusky Brewing
    Corp.
All-American Premium Beer
  Ask your doctor
All-American Radio Corp.
  The largest-selling trans-
    former in the world
  Pioneers in the radio indus-
    try
  Radio builds for the years
    to come
All-American radio receiver
  The choice of noted music
    critics
  Radio built for the years to
    come
All-American since 1909
  Central Steel & Wire Com-
    pany
All around the world
  Western Union Interna-

tional, Inc.
  The all around whiskey
  Ancient Age whiskey
All-Crop Harvester
  Successor to the binder
All detergent
  Outcleans other leading pow-
    ders on tough, greasy,
    oily dirt
All Fiction Field
  Magazines of clean fiction
  Read by everybody, every-
    where
All fires are not alike, nor are all
    fire extinguishers
  Foamite-Childs Corp.
All-fluid drive belongs to Dodge,
    the results belong to you
  Dodge Div., Chrysler Corpor-
    ation
All fresh-fruit good!
  Kraft Foods Div., Kraftco
    Corp.
All goods worth price charged
  Lynchburg Hardware and Gen-
    eral Store
All in one piece; twist, it opens;
    twist, it closes
  Gem razor
All is not new that glitters
  Old Dutch Cleanser
All is vanity ... all is Vanity Fair
  Vanity Fair Mills, Inc.
The all-natural ice cream
  Breyer's ice cream
The all-new business jets
  Canadair Challenger jet aero-
    plane
All-out aid for a hungry man
  Campbell's condensed soups
All over the world BOAC takes
    good care of you
  British Overseas Airway Corp.
All over town
  Young Hat Co.
All phonographs in one
  Brunswick phonograph
The all-purpose cocoa
  Runkel Bros. cocoa
All-purpose film
  Kryptar Corp.
The all-purpose one-man crane
  Byers Crane
The all-star record
  Decca phonograph records
All steel and a car wide

Stewart-Warner bumpers
All-Steel Equipment, Inc.
   The choice when you want
      quality, too
All that is best in radio
   Eagle Radio Co.
All that its name implies
   True Shape Hosiery
All that the name implies
   General Electric vacuum
      cleaner
All that you like in a hat
   Mallory hats
All that's best at lowest cost
   Chevrolet automobile
All that's best at lowest price
   Chevrolet automobile
All the bank you'll ever need in
   Texas
      Texas National Bank of Com-
         merce of Houston
All the business news you need.
   When you need it
   Wall Street Journal
All the dirt, all the grit, Hoover
   gets it, every bit
   Hoover vacuum cleaner
All the facts, no opinion
   United States Daily
All the flexibility of a newspaper
   with the coverage of a
   national magazine
   United States Daily
All the good things wrapped up
   in one
   Tastykake
All the meat of the golden wheat
   Shredded Wheat
All the new ones all the time
   Rothschild Bros. Hat Co.
All the news that's fit to print
   New York Times
All the news while it is news
   Automotive Daily News
All the old-time flavor
   Atmore mince meat
All the shield you'll ever need
   Shelter LIfe Insurance Co.
All the taste without the waste
   Council Meats
All the way from the refinery
   to your farm
   Cities Service gasoline
All the way with Chevrolet
   Chevrolet automobile
All the wheat that's fit to eat

Wheatlet
All the world loves a happy
   BLENDING
   Calvert "Extra" whiskey
All there is in bearings
   Timken Roller Bearing Co.
All they're cracked up to be
   California Walnut Growers
      Assn.
All things considered, Hyatt hotels
   continue to be a touch
   above the rest
   Hyatt hotels
All through your beauty sleep your
   skin must stay awake
   Woodbury's Cold Cream
All trains vestibuled from end to
   end
   Baltimore & Ohio Railroad
All ways. See also: Always
All ways look to Linton for leader-
   ship!
   Linton Mfg. Co.
All work and no play
   Timken Roller Bearing Co.
All write with a Waterman's
   Waterman's Ideal Fountain Pen
All write with a Waterman's Ideal
   Fountain pen ... all wrong
   if you don't
   Waterman's Ideal Fountain Pen
All you can eat for a nickel
   Baby Ruth candy bar
All you have to lose is high com-
   missions
   Fidelity/Source Discount Brok-
      erage
All you need in a drug store ...
   more
   Hook's drug stores
All you need to know about paint
   Sherwin-Williams Co.
All you want for a nickel
   Baby Ruth candy bar
All your banking under one roof
   Mellon National Bank
Allan. See also:
   Allen
   Allen's
Allan Mfg. Co.
   First choice in fishing tackle
      hardware
Allcock's Porous Plasters
   Standard plasters of the
      world
   Used and preferred by all

9

Allegheny Airlines, Inc.
    Your air commuter service in
        12 busy states
Allegheny Industrial Chemical Co.
    The bright new silicates for
        industry
Allegheny International
    Special skills for special
        needs
Allen. See also:
    Allan
    Allen's
    S. L. Allen & Co.
Allen automobile
    In cars under $1000 the Al-
        len is without a pe_r
    The smaller fine car
Allen-Bradley Co.
    Quality electronic components
    Quality is the best tradition
    Quality motor control
Allen-Edmonds shoes
    A cut above the rest
    The hand crafted world of
        Allen-Edmonds. Step
        into it
    We hand craft the world's
        finest shoes for men
Allen parlor furnace
    Modern heat with oldtime
        fireside cheer
Allendale Mutual Insurance Com-
        pany
    Rethinking property con-
        servation from the ground
        up
Allen's. See also:
    Allan
    Allen
Allen's Foot-Ease
    Easy to use, just shake in
        your shoes
    Just a smile, all the while
    The man who put the EE's
        in FEET
Allentown Morning Call
    Ask us about advertiser's
        cooperation
The allergy medicine made for
        your eyes
    Visine eye drops
The Alliance Mfg. Co., Inc.
    Put Alliance in your appli-
        ance
Allied Chemical Corp.
    Ask Allied Chemical

Basic to America's progress
    Fine chemicals
    Producers of all basic ure-
        thane chemicals
Allied Products Corp. See: Ful-
        ton Cotton Mills Div., Al-
        lied Products Corp.
Allied Van Lines, Inc.
    America's number 1 mover
    Families that move the most
        call the world's largest
        mover
    We move families, not just
        furniture
Alligator cigarettes
    They respect your throat
Alligator raincoats
    Always ready, always dry
    Because it's sure to rain
    The best name in all-weather
        coats and rainwear
    A 'round the year coat
Allis. See also: Louis Allis Co.
Allis-Chalmers does its share to
        help you share in a bet-
        ter future
    Allis-Chalmers Mfg. Co.
Allis-Chalmers Mfg. Co.
    Allis-Chalmers does its share
        to help you share in a
        better future
    Allis-Chalmers, the tractor
        people
    Be sure to get a quote
    Biggest of all in range of in-
        dustrial products
    Freedom follows a furrow
    Fresh ideas to meet basic
        world needs
    From the tractor people who
        make the big ones
    The long line of construction
        machinery
Allis-Chalmers, the tractor people
    Allis-Chalmers Mfg. Co.
Allpeece Corp.
    The ribbon of 1000 uses
Allstate Insurance Co.
    Working to hold your insur-
        ance costs down
    You're in good hands with
        Allstate
Allsweet oleomargarine
    The brand they ask for first
    The most asked-for brand of
        all

Almadén Vineyards, Inc.
    California's premier wines
    Taste what experience can do
      for a wine
Almay cosmetics
    So glamorous you have to be
      told they're hypo-aller-
      genic
Almond Candies
    A favorite wherever buddies
      bunk
Almond Roca candy
    America's finest confection
    A name to remember
Alone in tone
    Magnavox radio receiver
Alonzo
    A precious bit more than a
      laxative
Alpagora
    Everything you ever wanted
      in a coat
Alpha-Bits cereal
    Alpha-Bits, the cereal that
      provides wholesome fun
      at breakfast
    Alpha-Bits, the cereal that pro-
      vides wholesome fun at
      breakfast
    Alpha-Bits cereal
ALPO beef flavored dog food
    ALPO dry: as much meat
      protein in this bag as
      10 lbs. of sirloin
    ALPO means more meat
    Doesn't your dog deserve
      ALPO?
ALPO dry: as much meat pro-
    tein in this bag as 10
    lbs. of sirloin
    ALPO beef flavored dog food
ALPO means more meat
    ALPO beef flavored dog food
Alps Brau beer
    Cool. Crisp. Clear
Alt. See:
    Anne Alt brassiere
    Ault
Alta Vineyards Co.
    Enjoy a sip of California
      Sunshine
    Make Alta your home port
Altman. See: B. Altman & Co.
Alton Box Board Co.
    Full circle packaging
    Packaging that builds and

    holds sales
Altos computer systems
    Packed with fresh ideas for
      business
Aluminum Company of America
    Change for the better with
      Alcoa Aluminum
    First in aluminum
    More people want more alumi-
      num for more uses than
      ever before
    We can't wait for tomorrow
    What next from Alcoa!
    Your guide to quality in alu-
      minum
The aluminum foil you can count
    on
    Reynolds aluminum foil wrap
The aluminum six with magnetic
    gear shift
    Premier automobile
Aluminum Ware Association
    The best cooks use aluminum
The aluminum ware with the
    smooth finish
    Buckeye Aluminum Co.
Always. See also: All ways
Always a good companion
    Dutch Masters cigar
Always a step ahead in style
    Connolly Shoe Co.
Always a year ahead
    Zenith radio receiver
Always accurate
    Guarantee Liquid Measure Co.
Always an adventure in good eat-
    ing
    Duncan Hines packaged foods
Always begin with a good finish
    Pemco glass colors
Always better, better all ways
    Philip Morris cigarettes
The always busy store
    Kahn's department store
Always buy Chesterfield
    Chesterfield cigarettes
Always churned from sweet cream
    June Dairy Products Co.
Always correct
    Eaton Paper Corp.
Always "correct" in style
    Simmons Chains
Always first, always fair
    Indianapolis Star
Always first quality
    J. C. Penney and Co.

Always first with all that's new
Winthrop shoes
Always first with the best
Polly-Flex Housewares
Always fresh
Jewel Tea Co., Inc.
Always fresh, wet-proof panties
Nata-Pax
Always in good company
Standard Brewing Co.
Always in good taste
Colonial Bakeries
Royal Blend Coffee
Always in the lead
Detroit News
Always makes good printing better
Northwest Paper Co.
Always on guard
Belknap automatic valve
Always on the beam
Spotlite handbags
Always on the level
The Liquidometer Corp.
Always one step ahead of the
weather
Rusco windows
Always reaches home
Newark Evening News
Always ready, always dry
Alligator raincoats
Always refreshing
Beechnut gum
Always reliable
Philadelphia Record
Always right on the job
The Bowdil Company
Always right with Wilsonite
Wilsonite sun glasses
Always save money in the end
Keith Furnace Co.
Always sharp, never sharpened
Eversharp mechanical pencil
Always smoother because it's
slow-distilled
Early Times bourbon whiskey
Always something new
Percy Kent bags
Always Springfield's greatest
newspaper
Illinois State Register
Always starts your engine--and
pumps your tires
Stewart starter for Ford
cars
Always the leader
Mack trucks

Always the right answer with a
Wayne
Wayne Pump Co.
Always the same, always good
Old Reliable Coffee
Always 2,000 pounds to the ton
Apex Coal Corp.
Always virgin wool
Pendleton Woolen Mills
Always worth par when misfortune
strikes
Fireman's Fund American In-
surance
Always writes all ways
W. A. Sheaffer Pen Co.
Amana Refrigeration, Inc.
Backed by a century-old tradi-
tion of fine craftsmanship
Ambassador Hotel, Los Angeles,
Calif.
The greatest hotel value in
America
In Los Angeles, why settle
for less?
Ambassador West hotel, Chicago,
Ill.
The intimate hotel on Chicago's
Gold Coast
Amberdent tooth paste
Leaves that clean taste in
your mouth
Amchem Products, Inc.
First name in herbicide re-
search
Amco. See: Ammco Tools, Inc.
Amelia Earhart luggage
If you have an instinct for
quality ...
Someone's always looking at
your luggage
Amerdent mouth wash
The sign of a healthy mouth
America appreciates good time
Ribaux watches
America for rent!
Taylor Rental Corporation
America Fore Insurance and In-
demnity Group
Sell protection, not policies
America has gone Budweiser
Budweiser beer
America lives in Dacron
Dacron fabric
America lives in R and K Originals
R and K Originals, Inc.
America looks to Lincoln for lead-

ership in luggage
Lincoln luggage
America marches forward on TIME
Hamilton Watch Co.
America reads TV Guide
TV Guide
America rides Monroe
Monroe shock absorbers
America runs on Bulova time
Bulova watches
America sparkles with Canada
Dry
Canada Dry ginger ale
American Ace
The flour of the nation
American Air Filter Co., Inc.
Better air is our business
American Airlines, Inc.
Airline of the professionals
America's leading airline
Coast to coast overnight
We're American Airlines do-
ing what we do best
American Appraisal
Knowing what it's worth can
be worth a lot
We know values
American artistry in glass
Turchin glass
American Asbestos Co.
The unseen giant of the
brakes
American automobile
The world's motor car
unique
American Baby
National magazine for moth-
ers of infants
American Banker
The only daily banking
newspaper
Where your advertising
earns extra interest
American Banker's Association
God of two faces
American Beauties
A story-telling pictorial of
stage, art, screen, hu-
mor
American Blower Co.
Standard of the world
American Bond & Mortgage Co.
An old responsible house
American Bosch automobile
media washion
More pleasure per mile

American Bosch Corp.
The best in radio
American Bosch Corp. See also:
Bosch
American Bottle Co.
The bottles of unequalled
strength
American Boy
Biggest, brightest, best
magazine for boys in all
the world
Keep your boy out of danger!
American Brake-Block Brake Lin-
ing
If you can't stop, don't start
American Brands, Inc.
Tobacco is our middle name
American Brass Co.
From mine to consumer
Think copper
American Brewing Co.
The brew for you
American Broadcasting Co.
Wide world of entertainment
American Broom & Brush Co.
A good broom sweeps cleaner
and lasts longer
A "Royal Blue" broom adds
life to the rug in your
room
American Can Co.
Canned food is grand food
American Can Co. See also:
Marathon Div., American
Can Co.
American Cancer Society
Give to conquer cancer
Share the cost of living
Stop excusing your life away
2,000,000 people fighting
cancer
American Chain and Cable Co.
See also: Page Steel
and Wire Div., American
Chain and Cable Co.
American Chain and Cable Co.
In business for your safety
American Chain Co.
Don't be a dead-eye Dick
The jack that saves your
back
The most profitable of all
accessories
No straps to stretch, fray or
rot
Overcome skidding, nerve

strain and muddy roads
Sensible protection, fore and
aft
There can be no compromise
with safety
They level the road as you
go
Use 'em yourself to sell 'em
You can put them on in a
moment
American Chewing Products Corp.
Be Chic-Chek chicks
Be Chic-Chew chicks
A grand slam favorite
Popular at contract or auc-
tion games
Refreshing as the rising sun
Served by modern hostesses
A sure winner
The welcome partner
American Coal Mining Industry
Coal--the modern energy
miracle that's as old as
the hills
American Coffee Co.
Every cup's a cup of joy
American Council of Life Insur-
ance
We're investing in a healthi-
er America
American Cranberry Exchange
The tonic fruit
American Credit Indemnity Com-
pany
Smart people, smart money
American Cyanamid Co.
Basic in catalyst chemistry
Color is the difference
Cyanamid serves the man
who makes a business
of agriculture
Headquarters for nitrogen
chemicals
In home, health, farm and
industry, science in ac-
tion for you
It's all color in all colors
It's all in the finish
Moulding the future through
chemistry
When it comes to color, come
to Cyanamid
When performance counts,
call on Cyanamid
American Cyclometer
The best on the market

American Dairy Association
Cheese: zest at its best
Cool it with milk, the fresher
refresher
First in foods
It's better with butter
Voice of the dairy farmer
When you see the "REAL"
seal you'll know it's real
Zest at its best
American dark chaser
American Gas Machine Co.
American Distilling Corp.
The crystal clear gin in the
crystal clear bottle
Distilled by the celebrated
Old English process
Distilled from selected grains
From the heart of the grain
country
The test that tells
American Engineering Co.
The electric hoist that oper-
ates in the minimum
American Export Isbrandtsen
Lines, Inc.
Sunlane cruises to Europe
The American Express Card
Don't leave home without
it
American Express credit card
American Express Company
The company for people who
travel
American Express credit card
The American Express card
Don't leave home without
it
American Express traveler's checks
Spendable everywhere
They're worth asking for by
name
American Face Brick Association
Use face brick, it pays
American Farming
The farm paper with a mis-
sion
American Flange & Mfg. Co., Inc.
Tri-sure the world over
American Forest Products Corp.
See: Tarter, Webster
and Johnson Div., Amer-
ican Forest Products
Corp.
American Fruit Growers Assn.
Blue Goose stands today, as

always, for quality
American Gas Accumulator Co.
  A signal for every traffic
    need
American Gas Association, Inc.
  Do it tomorrow's way ...
    with gas
  For commercial cooking ...
    gas is good business
  For heating and cooling ...
    gas is good business
  Gas makes a big difference
  Gas: the future belongs
    to the efficient
  If it's done with heat you
    can do it better with
    gas
  Live modern for less with
    gas
  You can do it better with
    gas
American Gas Machine Co.
  American dark chaser
  America's favorite camp
    stove
  America's most popular camp
    stove
  Chases darkness
  Complete gas service for
    every home
  Cozy comfort for chilly days
  Heat like the rays of the
    sun
  The lantern with the blue
    porcelain top
  The perfect reading light
  The world's fastest cook
    stove
American gentleman shoes de-
    signed for the American
    man
  Hamilton Brown Shoe Co.
An American gentleman's whiskey
    since 1860
  Hunter whiskey
American Girl Service
  Office help--temporary or
    permanent
American Grease Stick Co.
  For clean lubrication
  Penetrates, lubricates, cuts
    grease, prevents rust,
    will not gum
  Runs in, will not run out
American Hammer Corp.
  The hammer with a back-

bone
American Hammered Piston Ring
    Co.
  America's leading replacement
    ring
American Hardware Mutual Insur-
    ance Co.
  For a sure tomorrow--insure
    enough today!
American Heart Association
  Eat less saturated fat
  We're fighting for your life
American Home
  Reach her when home is on
    her mind
  An American institution
    Saturday Evening Post
  An American institution since 1840
    Park & Tilford candy
American Insulator Corp.
  Where everything is done in
    plastics
American Insurance Association
  Affordable insurance is our
    business ... and yours
American Insurance Co.
  With everything American,
    tomorrow is secure
American International Group.
  See: The AIG Companies
American La France Fire Engine
  Everything for fire preven-
    tion and fire protection
  Nothing talks like actual per-
    formance
American lady shoes designed for
    the American woman
  Hamilton Brown Shoe Co.
American Laundry Machine Indus-
    tries
  You get more from American
American Laundry Machinery Co.
  Clothes do help you win, dry
    clean them oftener
  Send it to the dry cleaner
  Send it to the laundry
An American leader in advanced
    systems of photo-optics
    for information process-
    ing
  Itek Corp.
American Leather Products, Inc.
  Nothing takes the place of
    leather
American Legion Monthly
  A magazine for all Americans

American Linen Companies
  It pays to keep clean
American Lung Association
  It's a matter of life and
    breath
American Machine & Foundry Co.
  And you thought all we made
    were weekends
  Bowl where you see the
    Magic Triangle
  Machinery specialists to the
    tobacco industry
American Machine & Foundry Co.
  See also: Lowerator
    Div., American Machine
    & Foundry Co.
American Machinist
  The most useful magazine in
    metalworking
American Magazine
  Magazine of today and to-
    morrow
  Merrily we bowl along
  Where important people turn
    to say important things
American Medical International
  The international health care
    services company
American Mercedes automobile
  The handsomest car in the
    world
American Mercedes automobile.
  See also: Mercedes-Benz
    automobile
American Metal Cap Co.
  A quarter turn to unseal,
    a quarter turn to seal
American Mono-Rail Co.
  Overhead handling reduces
    handling overhead
American Motors Corp.
  Dedicated to excellence
  Miles of smiles
  The sensible spectaculars
  Where quality is built in, not
    added on
American Mutual Insurance Com-
    panies
  Helping America make intel-
    ligent insurance deci-
    sions since 1887
  We want to keep you safe
    and sound
American Mutual Liability Insur-
    ance Co.
  Our savings are your

profits
  Protection for employer and
    employee
  Your helping hand when trou-
    ble comes
American National Bank and Trust
    Co. of Chicago
  We're the bank for business
American News Co.
  Covering a continent
American Nickeloid Co.
  America's pioneer manufactur-
    er of prefinished metals
American Oil Co. See: Standard
    Oil Div., American Oil
    Co.
American Optical Co.
  For better eyesight
  Products that extend and pro-
    tect man's physical senses
  Since 1883 ... better vision
    for better living
American Painter and Decorator
  A monthly magazine devoted
    to more profitable paint-
    ing
American Petroleum Institute
  See America best by car
American Photo Engravers Assn.
  Your story in pictures leaves
    nothing untold
American Photocopy Equipment Co.
  Copies for communication
    throughout the world
American Poultry Advocate
  The practical poultry paper
    for practical poultry peo-
    ple
American President Lines
  Cruising everywhere under
    the sun
  For 75 years, America's link
    with the Orient
  The world's supreme travel
    experience
American Press
  A better product deserves a
    better label
American Press Association
  Covers the country inten-
    sively
American Pulley Co.
  Light as wood and twice as
    good
  The power-wise group their
    drives

16

American Railroad Foundation
We've just made your production line 300,000 miles long
American Red Cross
The good neighbor is you.
Belong
Together, we can change things
We'll help. Will you?
American Red Cross. See also: Red Cross
American Register Co.
Flat folded stationery
American Republic LIne
See the Americas first
American Rice Products Co.
As good as it tastes
American Rolling Mill Co.
The purest iron made
American Rope Co.
Serving industry from A to Z
American Safety Razor Corp.
The little barber in a box
American Saint Gobain Corp.
Creative ideas in glass
American Satellite Company
Between heaven and earth there's little we can't do
American Saw & Mfg. Co.
The tools in the plaid box
American Seating Co.
Prevent schoolroom slouch
American Silversheet
It's the specification-finished surface that does it
American Slicing Machine Co.
The American way is the right way
American Society of Composers, Authors and Publishers
Justice for genius
American Solvents & Chemical Corp.
Continent-wide service
An American standard for the world
Cadillac automobile
American Standard, Inc.
Serving the nation's health and comfort
American Standard, Inc. See also: C. F. Church Div., American

Standard, Inc.
The American Stationery Company, Inc.
Finest personalized values since 1919
American Steel & Wire Co.
The post with the steel backbone
The steel backbone for concrete
American Steel Wool Mfg. Co.
My right hand in the home
American Tar & Chemical Co.
The builder's selection for unfailing protection
American Telephone & Telegraph Co.
One policy, one system, universal service
The voice with the smile wins
The voice with the smile wins the world over
American Telephone & Telegraph Co. See also: Bell Telephone System
American Thermos Products Co.
Foremost brand in outdoor living
American Tobacco Company
Sold American!
American Tool & Machine Co.
A T & M advances centrifugal design
Save time and space
American Tourister is beautiful under pressure
American Tourister luggage
American Tourister luggage
American Tourister is beautiful under pressure
An American tradition, growing with time
Simplex electronic time calculator
American Trucking Associations, Inc.
Today's trucking industry. It works for America
The truck stops here
The wheels that go everywhere
American United Life Insurance Co.
The company with the partnership philosophy
American Walnut Mfrs. Assn.

The cabinet-wood of the
elect
The noblest of all cabinet
woods
American Warehousemen's Associ-
ation
Our integrity is your secur-
ity
The American way is the right
way
American Slicing Machine Co.
The American way to get your
money's worth
Plymouth automobile
American Weekly
The national magazine with
local influence
The American whiskey for the
American taste
Frankfort Distilleries
American Window Glass Co.
The best glass
American Wine Co.
Renowned 'round the world
American Woman
The real magazine of the
small towns
American Wool Council
Well dressed/wool dressed
American Writing Paper Co.
The right paper for the
purpose
American Yarn & Process Co.
It's the yarn that counts
American Zinc Institute
Value engineering favors
zinc
America's airline to the world
Pan American World Airways,
Inc.
America's best cartons
Set Mfg. Corp.
America's best-dressed women
wear Coro jewelry
Coro jewelry
America's best fleet buy
Rambler automobile
America's best-known shoes
W. L. Douglas shoes
America's best-liked cereal as-
sortment
Kellogg Co.
America's best-liked junior wear
Donmoor Donbrook
America's best loved greeting
cards

Norcross greeting cards
America's best-managed city
Milwaukee, Wis.
America's best nutrition values are
at GNC
General Nutrition Centers
America's best read weekly
Liberty Magazine
America's best-selling window
weatherstrip for over 40
years
Mortite window weatherstrip
America's best tasting little cigar
Between the Acts cigars
America's best traveling companion
Mendel-Drucker trunks
America's beverage of moderation
U. S. Brewers Assn.
America's biggest home magazine
Better Homes & Gardens
America's biggest-selling brake
lining
Raybestos-Manhattan, Inc.
America's biggest selling weekly
magazine
TV Guide
America's biggest suburban home
market
Better Homes & Gardens
America's busiest buildings
Quonset huts
America's business address
Hilton Hotels Corp.
America's business gateway to the
world
Miami, Fla.
America's cities are Bergstrom's
forests
Bergstrom Paper Co.
America's distinguished timepiece
Harvel watches
America's driving machines
Dodge automobile
America's family magazine
Look Magazine
America's fastest growing fuel
Thermogas, Inc.
America's fastest-growing tire
company
Cooper Tire & Rubber Co.
America's fastest selling record
Perfect phonograph record
America's favorite
Tide laundry detergent
America's favorite bleach and
household disinfectant

18

Clorox bleach
America's favorite bookseller
B. Dalton
America's favorite bran flakes
Post's Bran Flakes
America's favorite camp stove
American Gas Machine Co.
America's favorite corn chip
Fritos corn chips
America's favorite fun car
Ford Mustang automobile
America's favorite mayonnaise
Best Foods mayonnaise
Hellmann's mayonnaise
America's favorite nuts
Beer Nuts confection
America's favorite pickles
Vlasic pickles
America's favorite vacation
Sea Pines Plantation
America's favorite way to fly
Eastern Air Lines, Inc.
America's fifth freedom is free
enterprise
Union Oil Company
America's fifth largest telephone
company (And growing
fast!)
Central Telephone & Utilities
America's finest basement door
Bilco Company
America's finest bread
Langendorf United Bakeries
America's finest campers
Highway Cruisers, Inc.
America's finest camping tents
Hoosier tents
America's finest chocolates
Miss Saylor's Chocolates
America's finest cigarette
Philip Morris cigarettes
America's finest cola drink
Lime Cola
America's finest confection
Almond Roca candy
Brown & Haley
America's finest cooking centers
Jenn-Air Corp.
America's finest fish lines
Sunset lines
America's finest fishing rods
Browning Arms Company
America's finest ginger ale
Anheuser-Busch ginger ale
America's finest mattress
Spring-Air mattress

America's finest mixer
White Rock club soda
America's finest motor car for
America's finest families
Pierce-Arrow automobile
America's finest pipe tobacco
Edgeworth Tobacco
America's finest power-loomed rug
Karastan Rug Mills Div.,
Field Crest Mills, Inc.
America's finest whiskey regardless
of age or price
Four Roses whiskey
America's finest writing instru-
ments since 1846
A. T. Cross Co.
America's first car
Haynes automobile
America's first choice for flavor
Armour and Co.
America's first cord tire
Goodrich Silvertown tire
America's first, finest, and favor-
ite pork and beans
Stokely-Van Camp, Inc.
America's first gin
Fleischmann's gin
America's first great liqueur
Wild Turkey liqueur
America's first name in formal
wear
Rudofker's Sons
America's first name in lighting
Lightolier, Inc.
America's first service magazine
Better Homes & Gardens
America's first truly fine small car
Marmon automobile
America's foremost leg specialists
Plastic Industries, Inc.
America's foremost manufacturer
of decorative accessories
since 1890
Syroco Div., Dart Industries,
Inc.
America's foremost producer of
custom steels
Sharon Steel Corp.
America's foremost school of com-
mercial art
Federal School
America's foremost tractor
Wallis tractor
America's getting the message
Code-a-phone telephone
answering equipment

America's grandest cereal
assortment
Kellogg Co.
America's greatest luggage value
Lady Baltimore luggage
America's greatest reference book
World Almanac
America's greatest truck
Mutual truck
America's handsomest desks
Nottingham desks
America's home remedy
Alka-Seltzer
America's home shoe polish
Shinola
America's investment weekly
Financial World
America's largest art supply dis-
tributor
Art Brown artist's supplies
America's largest builder of
camping trailers
Nimrod Ward Mfg. Co.
America's largest dairy magazine
The Dairy Farmer
America's largest discount brok-
erage firm
Charles Schwab & Co., Inc.
America's largest leasing system
Ford Authorized Leasing
System
America's largest manufacturer
of custom day beds and
sofa beds
M. Mittman Co.
America's largest manufacturer
of lighting reproduc-
tions
Ruby Lghting Corp.
America's largest Polish newspa-
per
Everybody's Daily
America's largest-selling ale
Ballantine ale
America's largest selling camping
trailer
Nimrod Ward Mfg. Co.
America's largest selling corn
oil margarines
Fleischmann's margarine
America's largest selling high
grade coffee
Maxwell House Master Blend
coffee
America's largest-selling im-
ported beer

Tecate beer
America's largest selling laxative
Ex-Lax laxative
America's largest selling residential
locksets
Kwikset Div., Emhart Corp.
America's leading airline
American Airlines, Inc.
America's leading bearing special-
ists since 1925
Detroit Aluminum & Brass
Corp.
America's leading energy company
Enco Div., Humble Oil and
Refining Co.
America's leading power boat maga-
zine
Power Boating
America's leading producer of
quality canvas products
Fulton Cotton Mills Div., Al-
lied Products Corp.
America's leading replacement ring
American Hammered Piston
Ring Co.
America's leading silversmiths
since 1831
Gorham Div., Textron, Inc.
America's leading washing machine
A. B. C. Super Electric
America's lowest-priced fine car
Pontiac automobile
America's luxury ham
Armour and Co.
America's luxury whiskey
Park & Tilford whiskey
America's magazine for the out-
doorsman
Field & Stream
America's most beautiful lamps
Art Lamp Mfg. Co.
America's most comprehensive
packaging service
Container Corp. of America
America's most convenient shop-
ping mall
Aldens mail order catalog
America's most copied radio
Zenith radio receiver
America's most customer-minded
oil company!
Sunray DX Oil Company
America's most distinguished cig-
arette holder
Kirsten Pipe Co.
America's most distinguished

20

motorcar
Lincoln Continental automobile
America's most distinguished
source for fine English
furniture
Wood and Hogan
America's most distinguished
timepiece
Elgin watches
America's most distinguished ver-
mouth
Tiara vermouth
America's most famous bouquet
Four Roses whiskey
America's most famous dessert
Jell-o gelatin dessert
America's most famous line of
baking mixes
Duff's ginger bread mix
America's most interesting state
Tennessee Dept. of Con-
servation
America's most luxurious mattress
Englander mattress
America's most modern cola
Diet-Rite Cola soft drink
America's most popular boats
Starcraft Company
America's most popular camp
stove
American Gas Machine Co.
America's most popular cigar
King Edward cigar
America's most popular nurser
Evenflo nursing nipple
America's most potent editorial
force
Life
America's most recommended
mover
Aero Mayflower Transit Co.,
Inc.
America's most used products
away from home
Fort Howard Paper Co.
America's most useful farm im-
plement
Staude Mak-a-Tractor
America's most useful personal
planes
Stinson aircraft
America's new breakfast banquet
of shredded whole wheat
Cubs cereal
America's No. 1 gasoline
Socony-Vacuum Oil Co.

America's #1 get well card
Blue Cross/Blue Shield
America's No. 1 heel
O'Sullivan rubber heel
America's #1 iron and vitamin sup-
plement
Geritol iron and vitamin sup-
plement
America's No. 1 low-calorie cola
Diet-Rite Cola soft drink
America's No. 1 mountain grown
coffee
Folger's ground coffee
America's number 1 mover
Allied Van Lines, Inc.
America's #1 news magazine
Time
America's No. 1 sports station
TV station WGN, Chicago
America's number one sportsman's
magazine
Field & Stream
America's No. 1 stain remover
Spray 'n' Wash
America's number one transporta-
tion/natural resources
company
CSX Corporation
America's No. 1 used car company
National Autofinders
America's oldest and largest show-
room distributor of fine
decorative furniture
Knapp and Tubbs, Inc.
America's only fire-brewed beer
Stroh's beer
America's only known-priced
clothes
Styleplus Clothes
America's only motor car designed
originally for both 4-
wheel brakes and balloon
tires
Rollin automobile
America's only un-sugar-coated
news magazine
U. S. News and World Re-
port
America's original sparkling malt
liquor
Champale
America's personal driving ma-
chine
Dodge 400 automobile
America's physic
Pluto Water

America's pioneer manufacturer
of prefinished metals
American Nickeloid Co.
America's pioneers in worm gears
Cleveland Worm & Gear Co.
America's popular year 'round
breakfast
Quaker Oats
America's premier banker's bank
Manufacturers Hanover Bank
America's premium quality beer
Falstaff beer
America's quality beer
Miller High Life beer
America's quality bicycle
Shelby bicycle
America's quality magazine of
discussion
Forum
America's quality mattress
Ostermoor mattress
America's resourceful railroad
Milwaukee Road
America's roast beef. Yes, sir!
Arby's roast beef restaur-
ants
America's sleepheart
Chesapeake and Ohio Rail-
way
America's smart set
Admiral radio receiver
America's smartest car
Ranier automobile
America's smartest resort hotel
Ritz-Carlton Hotel, Atlantic
City, N. J.
America's smartest walking shoes
Enna Jettick shoes
America's social-light whiskey
Ben Burk whiskey
America's sports newsweekly
Sports Illustrated
America's spunky spritzer
Mogen David wine
America's storyteller
Kodak cameras
America's supreme dessert
Richardson & Robbins plum
pudding
America's supreme ignition sys-
tem
Bosch ignition
America's thickest, best-tasting
ketchup
Heinz ketchup
America's truck. Built Ford-

tough
Ford motor trucks
America's true blue friend
Phillips' Milk of Magnesia
America's "wake-up" voice
Westclox Div., General Time
Corp.
Americore Soaps
Fine soaps--naturally
Amerikorn cereal
The nation's breakfast food
Amerio Contact Plate Freezers,
Inc.
It's the contacts that count
AmeriTrust Bank, Cleveland, Ohio
Making things happen in Mid-
America
The strong bankers
Amerock Corp.
Amerock makes it authentic
Amerock makes it authentic
Amerock Corp.
Ametek solar panels
Growing with solar energy
Amfac Hotels (Dallas/Fort Worth)
Bringing you life's little
things in a big way
One good idea after another
One well-placed idea after
another
Amherst. See: Jane Amherst
Food Products
Amho underwear
Means better underwear
Amity Leather Products Co.
There's a need-keyed billfold
for you
Ammco Tools, Inc.
Re-equip/equip and profit
Ammonite
Keep your hands youthful
Amoco Chemicals Corp.
Make it Amoco all the way
Where what's happening gets
its start
You expect more from Amoco
Amolin
The antiseptic deodorant
powder
Amorall automobile polish
Works like magic
Ampex Corporation
Ask anyone who knows
Amsterdam-Rotterdam Bank
Dutch, dependable and de-
veloping worldwide

Amway Corporation
    Home-care-know-how ...
        at your doorstep!
Anacin pain reliever
    Anacin relieves muscle pain
        headache tension fast
    Fight headache pain and win
    Fight pain and win with Ana-
        cin
    Get the Anacin difference
    Largest selling pain reliever
    Turn a frown to a grin with
        Anacin
Anacin relieves muscle pain head-
    ache tension fast
    Anacin pain reliever
Anaconda Company
    We grew up with the Old
        West
Analax
    Nothing acts like Analax
Anatomic energy
    Gold Center wheat cereal
Anchor Cap & Closure Corp.
    The strongest ally of the
        glass container
Anchor Hocking Glass Co.
    Everyday good ... glass
        with flair
    The greatest line in glass-
        ware!
    We set the table for America
    World's largest manufacturer
        of glass tableware
Anchor Line
    The lucky ones go Anchor
        Line
Ancient Age whiskey
    The all around whiskey
Anco windshield washing equip-
    ment
    To see your way clear
And an unbeatable flyaway price
    Hughes Helicopters, Inc.
And away go troubles down the
    drain
    Roto-Rooter Corp.
And McKesson makes it
    Albolene cleansing cream
And that's Hal at the piano!
    Hal Sharp's Golden Bears
        dance orchestra
And the bride lived happily
        ever after
    Community silverplate
And the world will approve

    your choice
    Cadillac automobile
And when you listen you'll buy
        this Westinghouse
    Westinghouse radio receiver
And who makes great skis? Head,
        of course
    Head Ski Co.
And you thought all we made were
        weekends
    American Machine & Foundry
        Co.
And you thought there was no
        such thing as miracles
    Helen Keller Centennial Fund
Andersen Corporation
    Only the rich can afford
        poor windows
    Window beauty is Andersen
Anderson. See also: E. L.
        Anderson whiskey
Anderson Chemical Co., Inc.
    Specialists in making water
        behave
André champagne
    For the holidays and all year
        long
Andrea radio receiver
    The standard of reception
Angelus lipstick
    For that "come hither" look
Angelus Marshmallows
    A message of purity
    One taste invites another
Anglo-California Trust Co.
    The personal service bank
Anglo-Swiss Milk Food
    33 million tins sold in 1883
Angostura Bitters
    It's terribly smart in a
        cherry tart
    It's what you put in to make
        the flavor come out
Anheuser-Busch ginger ale
    America's finest ginger ale
Anita of Paris perfume
    Regal scent to center atten-
        tion on lovely you
Ankle-fashioned shoes
    Nunn-Bush Shoe Co.
Anne Alt brassiere
    The difference makes the
        difference
Annette Kellermann health studios
    Reduce or increase your
        weight

Announcing a new RING champ
Super-X piston rings
Another carefree Johnson
Johnson Motors Div., Outboard Marine Co.
Another clinical-strength medication from Warner-Lambert
Warner-Lambert Pharmaceutical Co.
Another example of how Monsanto moves on many fronts to serve you
Monsanto Company
Another fine creation by Krueger
Krueger Metal Products Co.
Another idea whose time has come
Grumman Corporation
Another Nash
Nash automobile
Another volunteer
Mutual Benefit Life Insurance Company
Anson Weeks' dance orchestra
Let's go dancin' with Anson!
The answer is in the bottle
Teacher's Highland Cream Scotch whiskey
The answer is wool ... it costs less in the long run
Wool Carpets of America
Answer to a modern's prayer
Nescafe instant coffee
Anthracite Mining Assn.
To heat right, burn our anthracite
The anthracite that serves you right
Deering Coal & Wood Co.
The anti-freeze underwear for men and boys
Hanes underwear
Anticipating tomorrow's needs today
Enjay Chemical Co. Div., Humble Oil and Refining Co.
Antiphlogistine
Common sense about the common cold
The antiseptic baby oil
Mennen's baby oil
The antiseptic dental cream
Kolynos dental cream
The antiseptic deodorant powder

Amolin
The antiseptic liniment
Absorbine, Jr.
Antonio y Cleopatra cigars
The cigar that never lasts long enough
Antrol
Kills ants in the nest
Antron carpets
The beauty lasts
The fiber that carpets the country
Any mail for me?
Eaton Paper Corp.
Any metal worth painting is worth protecting
Rust-Oleum Corp.
Any mountains you want moved?
Association of American Railroads
Any Palizzio is better than no Palizzio
Palizzio, Inc.
Any price is too high if it can be reduced
International Harvester Co.
Any time is STANDARD time
Standard Brewing Co.
Anything can happen when you wear Fame
Fame perfume
Anything that sticks
Mystik adhesive products
Anywhere in the wide world
Hertz automobile rentals
Apex Coal Corp.
Always 2,000 pounds to the ton
Apex Smelting Co.
Consistently better
Apex vacuum cleaner
Peak of quality
Peak of quality for more than 30 years
Apollinaris carbonated water
Apollinaris mixes best with holiday spirits
Carbonated with its own natural gas
Apollinaris mixes best with holiday spirits
Apollinaris carbonated water
Apollo Magneto Corp.
Built for the best
Apollo satellite TV systems bring the world to you

National Microtech, Inc.
Apperson automobile
    The eight with eighty less
      parts
    The Jackrabbit
Appetites don't take vacations
    Campbell's condensed soups
An apple a day
    Washington State Apple Com-
      mission
An apple a day is Doc Apple's
    way
    Pacific Northwest Fruits,
      Inc.
Apple computers
    The most personal computer
    The personal computer
Appleton Electric Co.
    The handy light on a reel
    The original reel spotlight
Applied science of Elpeco re-
    frigeration
    Coolatronics
Applying advanced technology to
    bring you exciting new
    products
    Eaton Yale and Towne, Inc.
The appreciated chocolates
    Johnston's Chocolates
Approved by professional hair
    colorists
    Nestle Color Tint
Apri Apricot facial scrub
    Isn't your skin worth it?
April-fresh Downy
    Downy laundry washing aid
April Showers perfume
    The fragrance of youth
April Showers talcum powder
    Exquisite, but not expensive
Aqua-fresh toothpaste
    A complete toothpaste
Aqua Velva skin bracer
    Keeps your face fit
Arabian Eye Lotion
    Very effective, yet harmless
      to a baby
Arabian Joint Oil
    Used by gymnasts and acro-
      bats
Arabian nighties
    Arabian nightwear
Arabian nightwear
    Arabian nighties
Arbogast. See: Fred Arbogast
    Co., Inc.

Arby's piles it on!
    Arby's roast beef restaurants
Arby's roast beef restaurants
    America's roast beef. Yes,
      sir!
    Arby's piles it on!
The arcade game you can take
    home with you
    Coleco
Arcade toys
    Made by the tiny Arcadians
    They look real
    Tiny Arcadians
Arch Preserver Shoe
    Keep the foot well
    Keeps the foot well
Architectural and Engineering
    News
    It pays to be in the news
Architecture
    The service magazine
ARCO Atlantic Richfield Co.
    Making petroleum do more
      things for more people
    Making things happy with
      petroleum energy
    Remember what ARCO did
    There are no easy answers
Arco paint
    Lengthens your days
    Sprays on, stays on
Arcola is not only best but
    cheapest
    Arcola radiator
Arcola radiator
    Arcola is not only best but
      cheapest
Arcraft Brooms
    Of paramount importance to
      the housewife
Arctic electric fan
    When the mercury soars,
      keep happy
Arctic Lights cigarettes
    More menthol refreshment
      than any other low "tar"
      cigarette
Arcturus Radio Tube Co.
    The blue tube with the life-
      like tone
Arden. See:
    Elizabeth Arden
    June Arden
Are you Aetna-ized?
    Aetna Insurance Co.
Are you annoyed by a drip?

Peerless Plumbing Corp.
Are you man enough to try it?
  Brylcreem hair dressing
Are you pensioning your shirts
    too soon?
  Wings Shirts
Are you true to your type?
  Stetson hats
Are your cocktails such great
    shakes?
  Heublein's cocktails
Aren't you glad you use Dial?
    Don't you wish every-
    body did?
  Dial soap
Ar-ex Products, Inc.
  The lipstick without the dye
Argand wood-burning stoves
  The clinkerless grate
Argosy
  The No. 1 men's service
    magazine
Arid. See: Arrid
Aris Gloves
  Brand name of better gloves
The aristocrat of auto jacks
  Duff Mfg. Co.
Aristocrat of blended Scotch-type
    whiskey
  Royal Banquet whiskey
The aristocrat of building mate-
    rials
  Indiana Limestone Quarry-
    men's Association
The aristocrat of cigars
  Robert Burns cigar
The aristocrat of electric ranges
  Benjamin Electric Mfg. Co.
The aristocrat of fine corsetry
  Cordé de Parie, Inc.
The aristocrat of flavors
  Certified Extracts, Inc.
The aristocrat of ginger ales
  Saegertown Mineral Water
    Co.
The aristocrat of liqueurs
  Cherristock liqueur
The aristocrat of music magazines
  Singing
The aristocrat of pipe tobacco
  Old Briar pipe tobacco
The aristocrat of polyester
    neckwear
  Wembley neckties
The aristocrat of refrigerators
  Herrick refrigerator

The aristocrat of salad fruits
  Calavo Growers of California
The aristocrat of shirtings
  Sea Island Mills
The aristocrat of smokeless coals
  Red Jacket Coal Sales Co.
Aristocrat of summer suits
  Priestley's Nor-East
The aristocrat of the breakfast
    table
  Chivers & Sons marmalade
The aristocrat of the kitchen
  Rome kitchen ware
The aristocrat of tissues
  Golden Fleece tissue
The aristocrat of winter trains
  Atlantic Coast Line Railroad
Aristocrat slips
  Royalty in slips
An aristocratic beverage at a
    democratic price
  Hires' Improved Root Beer
Arizona Republican
  The state's greatest news-
    paper
Arkadelphia Milling Co.
  The heart of the grain plus
    the art of the grain
Arkatex Ceramic Corp.
  First with the finest
Arkograph Pen Co.
  Burn your name in metal
Arm & Hammer baking soda
  A pure and natural product
    for over 130 years
The armchair shopper's favorite
    for 48 years
  Miles Kimball mail order
    service
Armco Building Systems
  Armco Building Systems won't
    be undersold
Armco Building Systems won't be
    undersold
  Armco Building Systems
Armco Steel Corp.
  New steels are born at Armco
  Resists rust
Armour and Co.
  America's first choice for
    flavor
  America's luxury ham
  The best and nothing but
    the best is labeled Ar-
    mour
  The best lookin' cookin' in

town
Get better yields from your
fields with Armour
Let us help put Armour
Idea chemicals to work
for you
The meats that wear the
Armour star are the
meats the butcher brings
home
Tempt lazy summer appetites
Win yourself a halo for these
heavenly meals
Armour Grain Co.
Makes pancakes mother's way
You'll like the taste
Armour Star bacon
Banquet on bacon
Its wood-smoky fragrance
warms up appetites
Armour's Extract of Beef
Has that rich beefy flavor
Armour's Fertilizer
Makes every acre do its
best
Armour's Star Ham
The first name in ham, the
last word in flavor
The ham what am
Armour's Treet
Perfect platemates, Treet
and tomatoes
Serve this feast for four in
a thrifty jiffy
The arms that protect American
farms
Iver-Johnson shotguns
Armstrong. See also: Collin
Armstrong, Inc.
Armstrong Bros. Tool Co.
The Tool Holder People
Armstrong Cork Co.
Cork-lined houses make
comfortable houses
For favorable "first impres-
sions"
Heat-proof lining for walls
and roof
New ideas from the Arm-
strong world of interior
design
Armstrong flutes
The name to remember in
flutes
Armstrong linoleum
For every floor in the

house
For every room in the house
Armstrong S.S. Gentlemen's Gar-
ters
Made without rubber
Armstrong table stove
Cooks 3 things at once
Armstrong tires
Built to last
It's no accident that Amer-
ica's trucks set the
standards for safety
Armstrong's shoe products
Adds comfort to every step
Army. Be all you can be
U. S. Army Recruiting Serv-
ice
The army weekly
Yank
Arnheim's. See: Gus Arnheim's
dance orchestra
Arno Adhesive Tapes, Inc.
The best in tapes has "Able"
on the label
Arnold Bernhard & Co., Inc.
Serving the investment field
since 1931
Aromatic in the pack, aromatic
in the pipe
Holiday tobacco
Around the world on Dunlops
Dunlop Tire & Rubber Corp.
Arpege perfume
Promise her anything but
give her Arpege
Arrid anti-perspirant
Fights wetness and odor
Arro-lock Shingles
Men who build America trust
this trademark
Arrow aims at allure
Arrow brassiere
Arrow brassiere
Arrow aims at allure
Arrow Grip Mfg. Co.
Master of traction
Arrow Head Steel Products
When you substitute price
for quality, everyone
loses
Arrow headlights
For safety after dark
Safety after dark
Arrow liqueurs
Arrow means quality in any
language

Gets a hand in any land
Arrow means quality in any language
Arrow liqueurs
Arrow neckties
Pour these down your shirt front
Arrow shirts
Change your mirror from a leerer to a cheerer
Cool, calm and respected
Follow the arrow and you follow the style
Wherever you go you look better in Arrow
Arrowhead. See: Arrow Head Steel Products
Ars gratia aris
MGM Motion Pictures
Art Brown artist's supplies
America's largest art supply distributor
The original department store of artist's materials
Art Carved rings
Dream carved rings
Art Digest
The news magazine of art
Art for art's sake
MGM Motion Pictures
Art Lamp Mfg. Co.
America's most beautiful lamps
Art Metal Construction Co.
Protect the records you can't insure
Artcraft Sign Co.
Signs of long life
Artemis slips
There's art to the fit of Artemis
Arthur. See also: General Arthur cigar
Arthur Murray dance studios
Dancing is what music was created for
We change people into couples
Artificial silk at its highest point of perfection
Tubize Artificial Silk Co.
Artistic Lighting Equipment Assn.
Decorate with artistic lighting equipment

Artistry in carpets
Painter Carpet Mills, Inc., Div. Collins and Aikman
Artistry in rhythm
Stan Kenton's dance orchestra
Arvin car heater
Keeps you warm in your car
Arvin electric heaters
The biggest name in portable electric heaters
For comfort and pleasure all through the house
Arvin electric iron
The iron that's safe for any fabric
Arvin Industries, Inc.
Where great ideas are meant to happen
Arvin radio receiver
Arvin sets the pace, lead with Arvin
Arvin sets the pace, lead with Arvin
Arvin radio receiver
As a change from potatoes
Mueller's macaroni
As American as Yankee Doodle
Campbell's chicken noodle soup
As comfortable as a kitchen before a fireplace
Sloan's Liniment
As delicious as coffee can be
Hanley & Kinsella Coffee
As different as day and night
Old Overholt whiskey
As different from all other perfumes as you are from all other women
Emir perfume
As distinctive as a voice, as pleasant as a friendship
G & D vermouth
As easily as the sun shines
Blue Reprint machines
As easily washed as a China plate
Franklin Pottery
As easy as pointing your finger
Colt revolver
As easy to operate as a vacuum cleaner
Coldwell Lawn Mower Co.
As easy to use as to say
Mum deodorant

As fine as money can build
Chrysler automobile
As flattering as flickering
candlelight
Dorothy Dodd shoes
As flexible as your feet
J. P. Smith Shoe Co.
As fresh as the sea itself
Bay Food clam juice cocktail
As friendly as a letter from
home
Wine Advisory Board
As gentle as human hands
Easy Washer
As good as it looks
Bavarian Brewing Co.
As good as it tastes
American Rice Products Co.
As good as it's beautiful
Courtald's silks
As good as the best you ever
ate
Drake's cake
As intimate as firelight, as in-
finite as the stars
Steinway piano
As long as the danger line keeps
healthy, you needn't
fear pyorrhea
Squibb toothpaste
As long as you're up get me a
Grant's
Grant's Scotch whiskey
As masculine as the trade mark
Royal Flush Toiletries
As mischievous as a sidelong
glance
Adrian perfume
As modern as tomorrow
Royal Worcester Corset Co.
As national as agriculture
Farm Life
As natural as nature
Schenley Distillers Corp.
As nature made it
River brown rice
As necessary as brakes
Bosch windshield wiper
As necessary as the rain
Buhner Fertilizer Co.
As new as tomorrow
Dictaphone Corp.
As of yore
Harvard Brewing Co.
As reliable as grandfather's
clock and as portable

as the cat
Perfection oil heaters
As simple as touching the space
bar of a typewriter,
quick as the action of a
piano key
Savage Ironer
As solid as the granite hills of
Vermont
National Life Insurance Co.
of Vermont
As sturdy as they are beautiful
Rollfast bicycles
As sweet as love songs
Kerr's butterscotch
As the sign of friendly service
Mobil Oil Corp.
As they eat 'em in New England
B & M Baked Beans
As time goes by you'll know why
Lawn-Boy lawn mowers
As tonic as sunshine itself
Aetna Brewing Co.
As unique as the person who
drives one
Oldsmobile Toronado auto-
mobile
As western as the setting sun
Frontex shirts
As you travel ask us
Standard Oil Div., American
Oil Co.
ASARCO, Inc.
ASARCO is positioned for
the 80's
ASARCO is positioned for the
80's
ASARCO, Inc.
Asbestos Brake Lining Association
Brake inspection is your
protection
Asbury Mills
Smartest togs on the beach
ASEA Electric, Inc.
Power across land and sea
Ashaway Line and Twine Mfg.
Co.
First in world records
Ashcraft-Wilkinson cottonseed
meal
They moo for more
Ashland Oil and Refining Co.
The independent supplier
for independents
The industrial resources
company

The ashless ashstand
Smokador Mfg. Co.
Asian Wall Street Journal Weekly
The bridge to Asia
The news from Asia. About
Asia. Written and
edited for the reader
with an interest in Asia
We've put it all together
Asian Wall Street Journal Weekly.
See also: Wall Street
Journal
Ask Allied Chemical
Allied Chemical Corp.
Ask any owner
Buckeye Traction Ditcher
Co.
Ask anyone who knows
Ampex Corporation
Ask Barclay's first
Barclay's Bank International
Ask Dad, he knows
Sweet Caporal cigarettes
Ask for Dr. Scott's. Take no
other
Dr. Scott's Electric Tooth-
brush
Ask for K-V ... it's a known
value!
Knape and Vogt Mfg. Co.
Ask for Karpen furniture, find
the nameplate before
you buy
Karpen furniture
Ask him why he smokes a Web-
ster
Webster cigar
Ask me
New York Life Insurance
Co.
Ask our customers
Dauphin Deposit Trust Co.
Ask the man from Northern
Plains
Northern Natural Gas Co.
Ask the man who owns one
Packard automobile
Ask the pilot who flies Silvaire
Silvaire aircraft
Ask us about advertiser's co-
operation
Allentown Morning Call
Ask your dealer, he knows
Garcia y Vega cigar
Ask your doctor
All-American Premium Beer

Ask your jeweler for it
Waterbury watch
Ask your mirror about your mat-
tress
Beautyrest mattress
Ask your printer, he knows pa-
pers
Rising Paper Co.
Ask your veterinarian
Pard dog food
Associated British Railways
See it all by train
Associated Lighting Industries
Notice the lighting fixtures
Associated Oil Co.
Sustained quality
Associated Products, Inc. See:
Rival Pet Foods Div.,
Associated Products,
Inc.
Associated Salmon Packers
The king of food fish
Associated Seed Growers
Bred, not just grown
For growing satisfaction
For lovely lawns in sun or
shade
A home is known by the lawn
it keeps
Seeds of satisfaction
Seeds that grow in sales
Associated Tile Manufacturers
Never renew, yet ever new
Associates Commercial Corporation
Convert your assets into
working capital
Associates Investment Co.
Specialists in financing
Association of American Railroads
Any mountains you want
moved?
Freight trains. America's
most vital moving force
Grow, grow by the rail way
In partnership with all
America
The nation's basic transporta-
tion
Safety first, friendliness,
too
Association of North American Di-
rectory Publishers
Where buyer and seller meet
An assurance of dependable serv-
ice
Cotta transmission

Assurance of quality
   National Automotive Parts
       Association
Assurance of quality, depend-
       ability since 1917
   Moorhead Machine and Boil-
       er Co.
The asthma reliever doctors rec-
       ommend most
   Primatene Mist
Astypodine
   First thought, first aid and
       Astypodine
   No home complete without
       Astypodine
At Continental Bank it's reality
   Continental Illinois National
       Bank & Trust Co. of
       Chicago
At Crane we believe in basics
   Crane Company
At Dollar you're the greatest ...
       and we treat you that
       way!
   Dollar Rent-a-Car service
At Dun & Bradstreet our job is
       to help
   Dun & Bradstreet
At home in every room
   Glamorug floor covering
At home in more than a million
       homes
   Click Magazine
At home with your young ideas
   Bassett Furniture Indus-
       tries, Inc.
At it's pre-war best
   Three Feathers whiskey
At MAI our competitors are often
       our customers
   Management Assistance, Inc.
At Maloley's we like you!
   Maloley's grocery supermar-
       kets
At Middle South Utilities, we're
       making energy that
       makes sense
   Middle South Utilities
At the crossroads of the world
   Hotel Astor, New York City
At the first sneeze, Vick's
       Vapo-Rub
   Vick's Vapo-Rub
At the first symptom
   Listerine mouth wash
At the head of the nation

Equitable LIfe Insurance Co.
At the right of your dial
   Radio station WEW, St. Louis
At the seashore, in the country,
       near the city
   Lido Beach, N. Y.
At your call with alcohol
   Canadian Industrial Alcohol
       Co.
At your grocer's, at your finger-
       tips
   Campbell's condensed soups
At your service
   B. T. Babbitt, Inc.
Atari television repair service
   Service that's as good as
       Atari
Ateshian Turkish Cigarrets
   Ladies and gentlemen smoke
       Ateshian Turkish Cig-
       arrets
Athletes know it's best
   Olympene medicine
Athol Machine & Foundry Co.
   Strong where strength is
       needed
Atkins. See: E. C. Atkins &
   Co.
Atlanta Biltmore Hotel, Atlanta,
       Ga.
   The South's supreme hotel
   Where Southern hospitality
       flowers
Atlanta Constitution
   The South's standard news-
       paper
   The standard Southern news-
       paper
Atlanta Industrial Bureau
   Industrial headquarters of
       the South
Atlanta Journal
   The Journal covers Dixie like
       the dew
Atlantic City Steel Pier
   A vacation in itself
Atlantic Coast Line Railroad
   The aristocrat of winter
       trains
   Standard railroad of the
       South
   Thanks for using Coast Line
Atlantic Drier & Varnish Co.
   Beauty that protects
   Long life line
   Waterproofs everything

31

Atlantic Products Corp.
The portable clothes closet
Atlantic Richfield Co. See:
ARCO Atlantic Richfield
Co.
Atlas. See also: Charles Atlas
correspondence body
building course
Atlas Bradford Co.
We mass produce quality!
Atlas Chemical Industries, Inc.
See: Explosives Div.,
Atlas Chemical Indus-
tries, Inc.
Atlas Drop Forge Co.
Your life depends upon the
forgings in your car
Atlas explosives
Everything for blasting
Atlas Label Co.
Labels of character
Atlas Luminite Cement Co.
Twenty-eight day concrete
in 24 hours
Atlas Plycron tire
Ride the path of satisfaction
Ride the road of satisfaction
The round tire that rolls
3,000 miles further
Atlas Plywood Corp.
Carry the weight, save
freight
Atmore mince meat
All the old-time flavor
Atmos. The only clock in the
world powered by air
Atmos Clock Company
Atmos Clock Company
Atmos. The only clock in
the world powered by
air
Atwater Kent radio receiver
Selectivity--Distance--
Volume--and Ease of
Operation
This is a new influence in
radio
Aubrey G. Lanston & Co., Inc.
The U. S. Government
securities specialist
Auburn automobile
Let the car tell its own
story
Auburn 12 cylinder automobile
The king of the cars
Audi and Porsche automobiles

Nothing even comes close
Audi automobile
Audi: The art of engineering
Audi: The art of engineering
Audi automobile
Audio-Forum Foreign Service In-
stitute
¡Speak Spanish like a diplo-
mat!
Audiotape
It speaks for itself
Auld. See also: Old
An auld acquaintance ne'er forgot
Gavin's Scotch whiskey
Ault. See also: Alt
Ault Williamson Shoe Co.
Foot of comfort means miles
of happiness
Aunt Jane's Pickles
The perfect pickle
Aunt Jemima makes mornings
they'll remember
Aunt Jemima pancakes and
syrup
Aunt Jemima Pancake Flour
I'se in town, honey
Aunt Jemima pancakes and syrup
Aunt Jemima makes mornings
they'll remember
Aurora bathroom tissue
Two layers of softness ...
and one is purest white
Austin automobile
The dependable motor car
The Austin Company
Profit from Austin's manage-
ment consulting expertise
Austin's Dog Bread
A dog worth having is worth
right feeding
Look for Austin on every
cake
Pronounced by all who have
used it to be the best
Dog Food in the market
The Australian airline
Quantas Airline
Australia's round-the-world jet
airline
Quantas Airline
Authentically ski
Ski Industries America
The authority in the exciting
world of beauty
Max Factor and Co.
Authority of industry, national

and international
Iron Trade Review
The authority of the waterways
The Work Boat
Auto Glas goggles
The best eye protector for
motorists
Auto Owners Insurance Co.
More than you expect or
pay for
Named for those it serves
Auto-Pneumatic Action Co.
The master's fingers on
your piano
Auto-Strop razor
Auto-Strop razor---
sharpens itself
Auto-Strop razor---sharpens it-
self
Auto-Strop razor
Autocar automobile
Finger-Reach Control
Autocar truck
They cost more because
they're worth more
World's finest
Autolight Control Co.
Take the dread out of night
driving
Autolight spark plugs
The spark of genius
The automated answer to the
paper explosion
Remington Office Systems
Div., Sperry Rand
Corporation
Automatic Cycle Seat
The only perfect cycle seat
Your doctor will endorse it
Automatic Data Processing, Inc.
The computing company
Automatic defrosting
Belding-Hall refrigerator
Automatic Electric Co. tele-
phones
The telephone of tomorrow
Automatic Elec. Devices
Battery charging equipment
for every purpose
The automatic fireman
Shur-Stop automatic fire
extinguisher
The automatic fireman on the
wall
Shur-Stop automatic fire
extinguisher

The automatic gas range
Caloric Corp.
Automatic Safety Tire Valve Co.
It whistles when it's had
enough
Automatic takeup for wear
Blackmer Pump Co.
Automatic Water Heater
Instant hot water
Automatically better
Ronson cigarette lighters
Automatically yours
Chrysler Airtemp
Automation is economical
Fusion, Inc.
Automobile Blue Book
The standard road guide of
America
The automobile for women
Inter-State automobile
The automobile that wants for
nothing
Peugeot automobile
Automobile Topics
The trade authority
Automobile Trade Directory
It hangs everywhere
The automobile with a reputation
behind it
Studebaker automobile
The automotive business paper
Motor
Automotive Daily News
All the news while it is news
The automotive service shop
magazine
Motor Service
Automotive Wood Wheels Mfrs.
Note the wood wheels every-
where
Autonetics Div., North American
Rockwell Corp.
Manning the frontiers of
electronic progress
Autopoint pencil
Fit any pocket, every
pocketbook
The pencil that works
AutoStrop safety razor
Far quicker, handier than
a no-stropping razor
Strops, shaves, cleans with-
out detaching blade
Autoyre sink racks
Designed to make the
passer-BUY

AVCO Corporation
  The power of balance
  Where AVCO leads, con-
    fidence follows
Avery Label Co.
  The original self-adhesive
    pin-feed labels
Avianca
  First airline in the Americas
Avis automobile rentals
  Avis gives you the next
    best thing to a free ride
  Trying harder makes Avis
    second to none
  We try harder
Avis gives you the next best
    thing to a free ride
  Avis automobile rentals
Avoid a trip to the police court
  Warner Auto-Meter
Avoid cosmetic skin
  Lux soap
Avoid 5 o'clock shadow
  Gem razor
Avoid shaker-clog
  International Salt Co.
Avoid "tattletale gray"
  Fels Naphtha soap
Avoid teeter-totter vitality
  Horlick's Malted Milk Corp.
Avon cosmetics
  Be hostess to loveliness
  A personalized service that
    comes to your home
Awards for some, rewards for
    all
  McGraw-Hill Publications
    Div., McGraw-Hill, Inc.
Awful fresh
  MacFarlane candies
Axle Division, Eaton Manufactur-
    ing Co.
  World's largest producer of
    commercial heavy-duty
    truck drive axles
Ayds. See also: Aids
Ayds diet confection
  Taste, chew and enjoy--
    curb hunger
Ayer. See: N. W. Ayer & Son
Azar's Big Boy Family Restaur-
    ants
  Eatin' treats that can't be
    beat
Aztec Brewing Co.
  The toast of the Coast

Azteca tortillas
  Reach for the sun in the
    dairy case

-B-

B. Altman & Co.
  Shop with people of taste
B. & H. Lamp
  Best in every particular
B & M Baked Beans
  As they eat 'em in New Eng-
    land
  Down east feast
  Plenty of juice pork and
    spicy "down east" sauces
B & O is the way to go
  Baltimore & Ohio Railroad
B & O. See also: Baltimore &
    Ohio Railroad
B. B. Chemical Div., United Shoe
    Machinery Corp.
  Join with Bostik for better
    bonding
B. B. Chemical Div., United Shoe
    Machinery Corp. See
    also: United Shoe Ma-
    chinery Corp.
B. Dalton
  America's favorite bookseller
B. F. Goodrich Tire Co.
  First in rubber
  In war or peace, first in
    rubber
  The straight-talk tire people
  The tough breed of tire
  You can expect it from B.
    F. Goodrich
  You're miles ahead with B.
    F. Goodrich, first in
    rubber tires
B. Friedman Shoe Co.
  The right shoes on time
BMW automobile
  The sportman's car
  The ultimate driving machine
BMW motorcycles
  The legendary motorcycles
    of Germany
BOAC takes good care of you
  British Overseas Airway
    Corp.
BSR (USA), Ltd.
  The world's "first family"
    of changers and tape

decks
B. T. Babbitt, Inc.
At your service
B.V.D. underwear
If it hasn't this red woven
label, it isn't B.V.D.
B-Wise chewing gum
For kissable breath
Baash-Ross Div., Joy Manufac-
turing Co.
Matched tools for unmatched
performance
Baash-Ross Div., Joy Manufac-
turing Co. See also:
Joy Manufacturing Co.
Babbitt. See: B. T. Babbitt,
Inc.
Babcock. See also: Acco Bab-
cock, Inc.
Babcock carts and carriages
The finest riding carts in
the world
Babcock Model A automobile
Not a cheap car but a good
one
Babies are our business ... our
only business
Gerber baby foods
Baby Bear Products Corp.
A quality loaf for quality
folks
Baby-care is beauty-care
Ivory soap
Baby lead a "hand to mouth"
life?
Lysol disinfectant
Baby Ruth candy bar
All you can eat for a nickel
All you want for a nickel
Buy Baby Ruth by the box
"Baby talk" for a good square
meal
Biolac
Baby's milk must be safe
Challenge milk
Bacardi rum
Enjoyable always and all
ways
Love at first sip
The mixable one
The world's smoothest drink
Bache stock brokers
Trade the market without
buying stock
Bachman Chocolate Mfg. Co.
The finest chocolate in

the world
Bachrach, Inc.
Photographs of distinction
Back of your independence stands
the Penn Mutual
Penn Mutual Life Insurance
Co.
Back your trained hand with a
trained head
International Correspondence
Schools
The backbone of New York adver-
tising
New York Sunday American
Backed by a century of brewing
experience
Gerhard Lang Brewery
Backed by a century of confidence
Supple's milk
Backed by a century-old tradition
of fine craftsmanship
Amana Refrigeration, Inc.
Background of beauty
Virginia Maid Hosiery
Bacmo gloves
Bacmo gloves are better,
better buy Bacmo
A lady to her gloved finger-
tips
Bacmo gloves are better, better
buy Bacmo
Bacmo gloves
Bacsul
The active sulphur for soil
Baer. See also: Bear
Baer Bros. paint
Paint with the two bears, it
wears
The bag that works like a can
Hefty Steel Sak trash bag
The bagless vacuum cleaner
Filter Queen vacuum cleaner
Bait of champions
Fred Arbogast Co., Inc.
Bake a better cake with Swan's
Down
Swan's Down cake flour
Bake the biscuits that make the
meal
Ballard Oven-Ready Biscuits
Baked in freshness
Grocers Biscuit Co.
Baked on the hearthstone of
reputation
Dreihorn's Bread
Bakelite

The material of a thousand
uses
Baker, Frentress & Co.
Bonds that grow in security
Growing security
Baker Gun Co.
Built to endure
Baker Linen Co.
When it comes to linens,
come to Baker
Baker paint brush
The only brush worth using
is the best brush you
can buy
Baker's Breakfast Cocoa
The cocoa with more choco-
late flavor
Favorite of housewives for
150 years
A hint of many good things
to come
Is absolutely pure and is
soluble
100% pure
A quality product for every
chocolate use
Baker's Magdolite
You're always safe with
Baker's Magdolite
Bakers of America's finest bread
Langendorf United Bakeries
Bakes right because it is made
right
Made-Rite Flour
The baking aid that nature made
Falk American Potato Flour
Corp.
Balanced bird ration
Bruce's bird seed
Balanced construction means
durability
Johnson Motors Div., Out-
board Marine Co.
Balanced for perfect baking
Pillsbury's Flour
The balanced load shells
Winchester Repeating Arms
Co.
The balanced pencil
Swaberg Mfg. Co.
Balanced reading for discrim-
inating people
Circle 12 books
Balanced tailoring
Timely Clothes, Inc.
Balanced tailoring makes Timely

Clothes look better--
longer
Timely Clothes, Inc.
Baldwin. See also: J. A. Bald-
win Mfg. Co.
Baldwin National Bank & Trust
Co.
Be thrifty and be happy
Baldwin pianos
Choose your piano as the
artists do
The sound investment
Baldwin tire chain
It's the chain that stands
the strain
Bali Brassiere
Every Bali has a bow
Lovely, lilting lines
The ball-bearing shave
E. R. Squibb
Ball Brothers Co., Inc.
Your partner in packaging
progress
The ball o' candy with a heart
o' gum
Fleer's chewing gum
The ball that made baseball
A. G. Spalding & Bros.
Ballantine ale
America's largest-selling ale
The perfect glass
Ballard Oven-Ready Biscuits
Bake the biscuits that make
the meal
Ballestra. See: Ing. Mario Bal-
lestra & Co.
Bally Manufacturing Corp.
Fun is our business
Balm-O-Lem
A fountain of youth for
your skin
Baltimore. See also: Lady
Baltimore luggage
Baltimore & Ohio Railroad
All trains vestibuled from
end to end
B & O is the way to go
The friendly railroad for all
the family
A good neighbor of your
community
Linking 13 great states with
the nation
Motor coach to train side,
the New York idea of
travel convenience

Motor coach train connec-
tion, a New York travel
habit
Retire to our sleepers in-
stead of retiring to your
car
Route of the Diesel-powered
streamliners
Safest, fastest and finest
trains in America
To promote the American
way of life, depend on
the railroad
Visitrips
Baltimore News-Post
Best bet in Baltimore
Goes home and stays home
Baltimore Salesbook Co.
Every business form for
every form of business
Holding better business
with better business
forms
Modern business forms for
modern business sys-
tems
A perfect set-up for a set
up that is perfect
Baltimore Sun
Baltimoreans don't say news-
paper, they say SUNpa-
per
Everything in Baltimore re-
volves around the Sun
Baltimoreans don't say newspa-
per, they say SUNpaper
Baltimore Sun
Baltzer boats
Dependable in any weather
Ban deodorant
You and your clothes can
depend on it
Banco. See also: Bank
Banco do Brazil
Your gateway to business
in Brazil
Band-Aid
Never neglect the tiniest
cut
Band It Clamps
Band It Clamps go 'round
the world
Band It Clamps go 'round the
world
Band It Clamps
The band that jumps the blues

Jay McShann's jazz
The Band that plays the blues
Woody Herman's orchestra
The band with the little hooks
Wick Narrow Fabric Co.
The bandage that breathes
Sealtex
Bandaid flexible bandage
It moves with you so it stays
with you
Banishes ironing drudgery
Proctor electric iron
Banishes "tattletale gray"
Fels Naphtha soap
Bank. See also: Banco
The bank behind the book
Stanton Home Safe Co.
The bank for all the people
Cleveland Trust Co.
The bank for bankers and busi-
nessmen
Irving Trust Company
Bank of America
First in banking
Look to the leader
On the spot when you need
us
Think what we can do for
you
Bank of America travelers cheques
World money for world tra-
velers
Bank of Montreal
The First Canadian Bank
The Bank of New York
The bank that manages money
Good banking is good people
We're there when you need
us
A bank of personal contact
Interstate Trust Co.
Bank of Taiwan
The biggest bank knows Tai-
wan best
Bank of the Southwest
The bank with the interna-
tional point of view
Bank of the United States
A distinguished banking con-
nection
Bank on it
Dow Jones Software
The bank that makes things hap-
pen
Cleveland Trust Co.
The bank that manages money

The Bank of New York
The bank that means business
Fort Wayne National Bank
The bank that means business in
California
Crocker-Citizens National
Bank
The bank where you feel at home
Central Trust & Savings Co.
Bank with imagination
Dresdner Bank
The bank with the international
point of view
Bank of the Southwest
Bankers Accident Insurance Co.
You can bank on Bankers
The Bankers Life
Choosing the right kind of
life insurance isn't get-
ting any easier
Bankers Trust Company
A tower of strength
We've matched our strength
to your needs
The bankers who do a little more
for you
United California Bank
Bannock Food Co.
Dog food at its best
Good food for good dogs
Banquet frozen foods
Thank goodness for Banquet
cooking bag foods
Thank goodness for Banquet
frozen foods
Banquet on bacon
Armour Star bacon
Bantron smoking deterrent tablets
Helps you break the nico-
tine habit
The bar that gives you lots more
of what you buy choco-
late for
Three Musketeers candy bar
Barbarosa Beer
THE premium beer
Barbasol razor blades
No pull, no pain, no sting
Barbasol shaving cream
For modern shaving
No brush, no lather, no
rub-in
Barber Asphalt Co.
Withstands the test of time
Barber blue sea, the super
system

Barber Steamship Lines, Inc.
Barber Steamship Lines, Inc.
Barber blue sea, the super
system
Barber's Journal
The voice of the master bar-
ber
Barbers use straight, rigid
blades; so does Gem
razor
Gem razor
Barclay cigarettes
99% tar free
The pleasure is back
Barclay's American Business
Credit
We have more ways to lend
money
Barclay's Bank International
Ask Barclay's first
Bardinet Cordial
The top name in cordials is
at the bottom of the
bottle
Bared to its bones, it's still the
"beauty"
Buick automobile
Barister cigars
Judged best by the just
Barker Food Products
For the real thing in noodle
soup, ask for Barker's
The real thing in noodle soup
Barking Dog never bites
Barking Dog tobacco
Barking Dog tobacco
Barking Dog never bites
Barksdale Valves
Headquarters for hand valves
Barnes Group, Inc.
The critical parts people
Barnett Bank
Why the 1980's look brighter
in Florida than in other
states
Barney-Ahler Construction Co.
Speed with economy
Barnum & Bailey's circus
The greatest show on earth
Barrel of satisfaction
Monite Waterproof Glue
Barreled Sunlight paint
Partner of light
The Barrett Co.
Non-skid roads, rain or
shine

Southern fertilizers for the
southern farmer
Barrett Electronics Corp.
First in automated materials
handling
Barrett Portable adding machine
Printed proof on Barrett
Portable
Barrington Hall Coffee
The coffee without a regret
Barron-Anderson Co.
Fine overcoat makers since
1901
Makers of America's finest
fitting overcoats
Barron's
For those who read for
profit
Let Barron's keep you ahead
The national business and
financial weekly
To serve investors more ef-
ficiently
Today is history. Tomorrow
is Barron's
Barron's. See also: Blue Bar-
ron's orchestra
Barron's Current Corporate Re-
ports
Today is history. Tomorrow
is Barron's
Barrthea garters and suspenders
To uphold your sox, trous-
ers and dignity
Bartlay & Crown Rayon
Welcome the prodigal sun
Barton. See also: Burton
Barton and Guestier
The finest wines of France
Barton clothes washer
The washer of tomorrow
is the Barton of today
Barton Salt Co.
The salt cellar of America
Barwick. See: E. T. Barwick
Industries, Inc.
Base for soft drinks and des-
serts
Kool-Aid soft drink mix
Basic. See also: Bassick
Basic chemicals and cost-cutting
ideas
Chemical Div., PPG Indus-
tries, Inc.
The basic energy company
NICOR, Inc.

Basic for better beer
Froedtert Malt Corp.
Basic in catalyst chemistry
American Cyanamid Co.
Basic producers from mine to
finished product
Industrial Chemicals Market-
ing Div., Tennessee
Corp.
Basic products and engineering
for industry's basic work
Link-Belt Co.
Basic products for basic indus-
tries. That's what Crane
is all about
Crane Company
Basic provider of chemicals in
volume
Abbott Laboratories
Basic to America's progress
Allied Chemical Corp.
A basket of garden freshness in
every can
V-8 vegetable juice drink
Bass Moccasins
For any wear, anywhere
Bassett Furniture Industries,
Inc.
At home with your young
ideas
Bassick. See also: Basic
The Bassick Co.
How easily it rolls on Bas-
sicks
Making more kinds of cast-
ers; making casters do
more
Bastien-Blessing Co.
Quality products known
throughout the world for
engineered quality
The bat with the most on the
ball
Adirondack Bats, Inc.
Batavia Body Co.
Batavia builds better bodies
Batavia builds better bodies
Batavia Body Co.
Bates Bedspreads
Loomed to be heir-loomed
Bates knitting needles
Join the knit parade
Bates originals
Bates Shoe Co.
Bates Shoe Co.
Bates originals

Slipper-free where the foot
bends
Bathtime story with a happy end-
ing
Cannon Mills, Inc.
Battery charging equipment for
every purpose
Automatic Elec. Devices
Battery Div., Sonotone Corpora-
tion
Portable power for progress
The battery with a kick
Prest-O-Lite
The Battle Creek Health Builder
Keeps you fit!
Battle Creek Manufacturers, Inc.
The leadership line
Stay fit. Unwind tense
nerves. Have more
energy
Works with you--works for
you
Battle Creek Packaging Machines,
Inc.
Continuous flow packaging
Bauer. See also:
Brauer Bros. Shoe Co.
O. P. Bauer Confectionery
Co.
Bauer & Black
First in elastic supports
The scientific corn-ender
Bausch & Lomb Optical Co.
That eyes may see better
and farther
To greater vision through
optical science
Bavarian Brewing Co.
As good as it looks
A man's best
Bay Cities Transportation Co.
Twice a day we bridge the
bay
Bay Food clam juice cocktail
As fresh as the sea itself
Bay State Perfection hammock
A hammock that will not
pull off the buttons
Bayer aspirin
Bayer works wonders
Does not harm the heart
It happens in two seconds
The most trusted name in
aspirin
Pain is the test that Bayer
meets best

Bayer works wonders
Bayer aspirin
Be a Pepper
Dr. Pepper soft drink
Be a safety first girl with Mum
Mum deodorant
Be a winner every time
Burke, Christensen & Lewis
Securities
Be ale-wise
Old Colony Brewing Co.
Be alert, bottle Alert
Alert Beverage Co.
Be as regular as a clock
Serutan laxative
Be as soft as you can be
Johnson's baby powder
Be bright. Feel right. Take
Eno
Eno effervescent salt
Be careful lest the breath offend
May Breath
Be Chic-Chek chicks
American Chewing Products
Corp.
Be Chic-Chew chicks
American Chewing Products
Corp.
Be choosey, not whoozy
Carstairs White Seal whiskey
Be coaled now and you won't be
cold next winter
Doughtridge Fuel Co.
Be confident, comfortable, care-
free
Kotex sanitary napkins
Be considerate, serve wine
Wine Advisory Board
Be fair to your hair
Vitalbrush hair brush
Be good to your gums
Pro-Phy-Lac-Tic toothbrush
Be happy and well while traveling
Mothersill's Seasick Remedy
Be hostess to loveliness
Avon cosmetics
Be nonchalant, light a Deity
Egyptian Deity cigarettes
Be nonchalant--light a Murad
Murad cigarettes
Be our guest
The Patio Restaurant, San
Rafael, Calif.
Be pert in a skirt
Pacific worsted
Be prepared

40

Boy Scouts of America
Be profit-wise and dieselize with
    Buckeyes
    Buckeye engines
Be profit wise ... (sell only
    Buss)
    Buss fuses
Be seated by ... Bemis
    Bemis Mfg. Co.
Be slip shape and lovely
    Luxite Glory slips
Be specific, route Union Pacific
    Union Pacific Railroad
Be specific ... say "Union
    Pacific"
    Union Pacific Railroad
Be sure, insure with INA
    Insurance Co. of North
    America
Be sure our name is on the box
    Warner Bros. corsets
Be sure the name "Pope" is on
    your automobile
    Pope-Toledo automobile
Be sure to get a quote
    Allis-Chalmers Mfg. Co.
Be sure with Pure
    The Pure Oil Co.
Be SURE you save at a savings
    bank
    Savings Bank Association
Be suspicious!
    Cluett, Peabody Co., Inc.
Be sweeticular
    Imperial Candy Co.
Be the belle of the beach
    Catalina Swim Suits
Be thrifty and be happy
    Baldwin National Bank &
    Trust Co.
Be thrifty, buy quality
    Valvoline motor oil
Be true to your teeth or they'll
    be false to you
    Medisalt dentifrice
Be umbrelegant in rainy weather
    Henryson tailored umbrellas
Be wise, Aetna-ize
    Aetna Insurance Co.
Be wise, buy Wise
    Wise Rubber Products
Be wise, protect your future
    Cal-Aero Technical Insti-
    tute
Be wiser, buy Kayser
    Kayser hosiery and under-

    wear
Be your age, but look younger
    Phillips Cream
Be your own barber!!
    New Gem Safety Razor
Beach. See:
    Beech
    Hamilton Beach
Beacon Falls Rubber Co.
    The boot with the muscles
Bead Design Studio
    The world's largest manufac-
    turer and designer
Beam. See: Jim Beam whiskey
Bean 'em when they're hungry
    Heinz Oven-Baked Beans
Bear. See also: Baer
Bear Brand Yarn
    The yarn you love to use
A bear for heat
    Fraker Coal Co.
A bear for wear
    Gillette tires
Bear in mind
    Grizzly brake lining
Bear Mfg. Co.
    Re-equip/equip and profit
    with Bear
Bear Safety Device
    Thank your Bear man for
    your accident that didn't
    happen
Beardsley's codfish cakes
    Just form and fry
Bearing Co. of America
    The right bearing for every
    car
Beau
    The man's magazine
Beau Brummel of the boulevards
    Buick automobile
The Beau Ideal of a Short Smoke
    Hoffman House Magnums
Beaumont Fabrics
    Lullaby in loveliness
Beautifies before your eyes
    Hilo Varnish Corp.
Beautiful beyond belief
    Chevrolet automobile
    Hudson automobile
Beautiful beyond belief in tone
    and styling
    Bendix radio receiver
Beautiful birch for beautiful
    woodwork
    Northern Hemlock Mfrs. Assn.

A beautiful brush, lasting for
years
    Dr. Scott's Electric Flesh
Brush
A beautiful corset worn by beau-
tiful women to make
them more beautiful
    Lily of France Corset Co.
Beautiful hair
    John H. Breck, Inc.
Beautiful hair is as easy as HQZ
    HQZ hair preparations
A beautiful house for $1200
    Building Plan Association
Beautiful on the table. Care-
free in the kitchen
    Weavewood-Ware
A beautiful piano with a magnifi-
cent name
    Lester piano
A beautiful piano with a magnifi-
cent tone
    Betsy Ross spinet piano
The beautiful sheets with wear
woven in
    Pepperell sheets
A beautiful shine without a towel
    Joy dishwashing liquid
Beautiful windows at low cost
    Clopay window shades
The beauty and distinction of
custom car styling
    Kaiser automobile
Beauty and economy burned in
    Common Brick Mfrs. Assn.
of America
Beauty basis for your home
    Mohawk rugs and carpets
Beauty bath for your teeth
    Listerine toothpaste
Beauty begins with the hair
    Gabrieleen permanent wave
Beauty by the brushful
    Brooklyn Varnish Co.
Beauty designers
    Dermetics cosmetics
A beauty for double duty
    Universal washer
"Beauty Glow" cleansing
    Woodbury's Cold Cream
Beauty insurance
    Watkins Cocoanut Oil
Shampoo
Beauty is only skin deep;
    Luminiere controls
the skin

En-Ve, Inc.
The beauty lasts
    Antron carpets
The beauty laxative
    Dr. Edward's Olive Tablets
Beauty mark of fine lighting
    Champion Mfg. Co., Inc.
Beauty on a budget
    Mary Pickford Cosmetics
Beauty that endures
    Mohawk rugs and carpets
Beauty that protects
    Atlantic Drier & Varnish Co.
Beauty through whiteness
    Titanox paint
Beauty treatment for your feet
    Red Cross Shoes
Beautyrest mattress
    Ask your mirror about your
mattress
    The world's most comfortable
mattress
Beauty's master touch
    Oriental Cream
Because...
    Modess sanitary napkins
Because it might rain
    Harbor Master, Ltd., Div.
Jonathan Logan
Because it's sure to rain
    Alligator raincoats
Because it's sweet, not bitter
    Welch's marmalade
Because there is a difference
    Northwestern Mutual Life In-
surance Co.
Because you love nice things
    Van Raalte hosiery
Beck. See: Magnus Beck Brew-
ing Co.
Becker. See: A. G. Becker &
Co., Inc.
Beck's beer
    The Number One imported
German beer
Bedazzling new cosmetics for all
your shining hours
    Debutante cosmetics
Beddy bye, but no shut-eye
    Ostermoor mattress
The bedtime way to loveliness
    Woodbury's Facial Soap
Beech. See also: Hamilton
Beach
Beech Aircraft Corp.
    Accustomed to the finest ...

you'll find it in a Beech-
craft
Business travel is Beech's
business
Reliability: we count on
being counted on
The world is small when you
fly a Beechcraft
Beechalex
The ideal laxative for young
and old
Beecham's Pills
The great English medicine
The great regulator
Painless. Effectual. Worth
a guinea a box
Worth a guinea a box
Beechnut chewing tobacco
We're Beechnut nuts
Beechnut coffee
One good cup deserves
another
You can't mistake the flavor
Beechnut gum
Aids digestion
Always refreshing
It's so good for so long
Beechnut mints
The handy candy
Beechnut Packing Co.
Foods of finest flavor
Refreshing as fresh fruit
Beefeater gin
The crown jewel of England
Excellence doubly safe-
guarded
The first name for the mar-
tini
The gin of England
The imported one
Beeman's Chewing Gum
I rescued the lifeguard
Beer belongs, enjoy it
U. S. Brewers Foundation
Beer flavor at its peak
Trommer's beer
The beer for good cheer
Potosi Brewing Co.
Beer is as old as history
Budweiser beer
Beer is no better than its in-
gredients
Hammerschlag Refining Co.
Beer Nuts confection
America's favorite nuts
The beer of friendship

Jax beer
The beer that goes down smooth
as a mountain stream
Busch beer
The beer that grows its own
flavor
Edelbrew
The beer that made Milwaukee
famous
Schlitz beer
The beer that made the nineties
gay
Potosi Brewing Co.
The beer that made the old days
good
Ruppert's beer
The beer that makes friends
Lubeck beer
The beer that time ripened, time
tempered
Breidt beer
The beer that wins awards
Jacob Hornung Brewing Co.
The beer that's brewed the na-
tural way, aged the na-
tural way
Breidt beer
The beer that's extra-aged
Hyde Park beer
The beer with millions of friends
Hyde Park beer
The beer with the flavor as dif-
ferent as day from
night
Breidt beer
The beer with the 4th ingredient
Breidt beer
Before any date
Listerine mouth wash
Before you invest, investigate
Better Business Bureau
The beforehand lotion
Trushay
Beginning a second century of
leadership
Chase and Sanborn coffee
The beginning of taste
Syracuse China Corp.
Behind every happy thumb
there's a Scripto
Scripto erasable pen
Behind every Olga there really
is an Olga
Olga Co.
Behind the enduring institution,
successful customers

Farmers Deposit Bank
Behind the fame of the Jarman
    name is a finer shoe for
    you
    Jarman shoes
Behind the labels of America's
    finest products
    Continental Can Co.
Behind the panels of better built
    sets
    General Radio Corp.
The beige cigarette
    More Lights 100's cigarettes
Bekins Van and Storage Co.
    The professionals
Bel. See also:
    Bell
    Belle
Bel Air Sands hotel
    The most convenient address
    in Los Angeles
Belair cigarettes
    Lighten up with low tar
    Belair
Belcraft shirts
    Belcraft shirts, your bosom
    friend
Belcraft shirts, your bosom
    friend
    Belcraft shirts
Belding Bros.
    Silks for every purpose
    Silks of enduring quality
Belding-Hall refrigerator
    Automatic defrosting
    Built right for over forty
    years
    Defrosts itself, saves shut-
    downs
    The electric ice is self-
    defrosting
Believe your own ears
    G. E. radio receiver
Belknap automatic valve
    Always on guard
Bell. See also:
    Bel
    Belle
Bell Airacobra
    Airacobras for victory,
    future planes for
    peace
Bell Aircraft Corp.
    Pacemakers of aviation
    progress
Bell & Howell brings out the

    expert in you (automati-
    cally!)
Bell & Howell Company
Bell & Howell builds photographic
    instruments a little better
    than they really have to
    be
Bell & Howell Company
Bell & Howell Company
    Bell & Howell brings out the
    expert in you (automati-
    cally!)
    Bell & Howell builds photo-
    graphic instruments a
    little better than they
    really have to be
    Information is the business
    of today's Bell & Howell
    Leading the way into the
    80's
Bell brings the world closer
    Bell Telephone System
Bell helicopter
    The modern magic carpet
    Team it up with your cor-
    porate jet
    World standard
    Would you like to see what
    one can do for you?
Bell System telephone directory
    yellow pages
    Action people
    Advertise for action
    The company workhorse
    Find it faster in the yellow
    pages
    Let your fingers do the walk-
    ing
    Your buying guide, the
    classified
Bell Telephone System
    Bell brings the world closer
    Don't write, telephone
    Expanding your ability to
    communicate
    A friendly place to work
    From here to the ear the
    shortest distance is long
    distance
    I'm your branch office
    The knowledge business
    Long distance adds warm
    personality to cold facts
    Long distance is the next
    best thing to being there
    Long distance is the shortest

way home
Long distance takes the
CHASE out of purchase
Long distance, your fastest
highway
Long distances help unite
the nation
Phone power in action
Reach out and touch someone
Serving you
Shop early and easily
Talk things over, get things
done ... by long dis-
tance!
Telephone appointments
prevent disappointments
Use Bell to sell
Use your head to save your
heels
The voice with a smile
You gave her a ring to be
near her, now give her
a RING when away
Your everywhere everything
anytime network
Bell Telephone System. See
also: American Tele-
phone & Telegraph Co.
Bell thread
Extra strength that never
fails you
Bellaire shoe
The foot-stimulating shoe
Belle. See also:
Bel
Bell
Belle Glove Co.
Gloves that "go places"
Belle-Sharmeer stockings
Full-fashioned for flawless
fashion
Legsize stockings
Legsize stockings for leg-
wise women
Bellevue Stratford Hotel, Phila-
delphia, Pa.
One of the world's great
hotels
Bellows-Valvair Div., Interna-
tional Basic Economy
Corp.
These names assure you
the best in pneumatic,
hydraulic and electronic
components
Bell's Blended scotch whiskey

Aged for 8
Belmont Stores
Belmont Stores know what you
need
Belmont Stores know what you need
Belmont Stores
Beloit paper-making machinery
When you buy Beloit, you buy
more than a machine
Below skin level shave
Packard electric shaver
Belyea generators
Our reputation is your pro-
tection
Bemis Co., Inc.
Every day, Bemis develops a
new packaging idea to
serve you better
Bemis Mfg. Co.
Be seated by ... Bemis
Ben. See also: Big Ben West-
clox alarm clock
Ben Burk whiskey
America's social-light whiskey
Ben-Gay lotion
Feel better with Ben-Gay
Ben Hogan golf clubs
Play the best you can play
They hit good from anywhere
Ben Pearson, Inc.
The nation's big name in
archery
The benchmark in world class
computers
NEC Information Systems,
Inc.
Bendix clothes washer
Bendix does the wash with-
out you
If you can afford a washer,
you can afford a Bendix
Bendix Corporation
Built for permanence, cali-
brated for performance
First in creative engineering
However you go, you'll stop
better because of Bendix
The power of ingenuity
We speak technology
Where ideas unlock the fu-
ture
Bendix does the wash without you
Bendix clothes washer
Bendix radio receiver
Beautiful beyond belief in
tone and styling

The best in radio is better
    with a Bendix
The greatest name in air-
    craft radio
FM at its finest
Listening luxury beyond
    your highest hopes
The real voice of radio
Bends with your foot
    Red Cross Shoes
Benefax
    Vitamins you can trust
Benefit Trust Life Insurance Co.
    "Value" is a good word for
    Benefit Trust Life
Benefits all fine leather
    Leather Lather Cleaner
Beneke Corporation
    The first name in seats.
        The last word in quality
Benex brushless shave
    The brushless wonder
    Turns bristles into blotters
Benjamin Electric Mfg. Co.
    The aristocrat of electric
        ranges
    Makers of things more useful
Benjamin Moore
    For 66 years makers of the
        best in paint products
Benrus watch
    The watch that times the
        airways
Ben's. See: Uncle Ben's, Inc.
Benson & Hedges 100's De Luxe
        Ultra Lights cigarettes
    Hallmark of quality
    Only 6 mg. Yet rich
        enough to be called de
        luxe. Open a box today
Bent like a dentist's mirror to
        reach more places
    Squibb toothbrush
Benylin cough syrup
    Full prescription strength
        without a prescription
Benzer Lens
    Makes light as safe as day
Berea College Student Crafts
        Industries
    You may know us by our
        Skittle Game
Bergmann Shoe Mfg. Co.
    The life of leather
    The most powerful shoe in
        America

Bergstrom Paper Co.
    America's cities are Berg-
        strom's forests
Berkeley cigarette lighter
    Dependable all ways
Berkeley Junior Fabrics
    Exclusively yours
Berkeley razor blades
    No better blades at any
        price
Berkeley Square clothes
    When the sun goes down
Berkley neckties
    Berkley Ties the world
Berkley Ties the world
    Berkley neckties
Berkshire International Corp.
    Hosiery fashion on five
        continents
Berlitz for languages
    Berlitz School of Language
Berlitz School of Language
    Berlitz for languages
    No one can teach you another
        language faster and bet-
        ter than Berlitz
BerNARdin metal closures
    Science, guardian of quality
Bernhard. See: Arnold Bern-
        hard & Co., Inc.
Bernstein. See: M. M. Bern-
        stein
Berry. See also: Very
Berry delicious.
    Strawberry Shortcake cereal
Berth. See also: Birth
The berth of a nation
    Greenpoint Metallic Bed Co.
The Beryllium Corp.
    Developers and producers
        of extraordinary mate-
        rials
Besseler. See: Charles Besseler
        Co.
Bessemer Gas Engine Co.
    You buy the best when you
        buy the Bessemer
The best aid is first aid
    Johnson & Johnson
The best and nothing but the
        best is labeled Armour
    Armour and Co.
The best anti-freeze since mink
    Zerex anti-freeze
The best at the price
    William Rogers & Co.

46

silverware
Best baking prize is a delighted
    husband
    Pillsbury's flour
Best because it's pan-dried
    Robin Hood Rapid Oats
    cereal
The best beer by far at home,
    club or bar
    Jacob Hornung Brewing Co.
Best bet in Baltimore
    Baltimore News-Post
Best bet's Buick
    Buick automobile
Best bicycle buy
    Shelby bicycle
Best bike to sell
    Shelby bicycle
The best birch line
    Kitchen Kompact, Inc.
The best blood purifier in the
    world
    Riker's Compound Saspar-
    illa
Best buy Boling
    Boling Chair Co.
Best buy in rye
    Kasko Distillers Corp.
The best buy in the sky
    Jet American Airlines
Best buy is Bull's Eye
    Bull's Eye paint brush
Best by actual test
    Farmers Cotton Oil Co.
Best by any test
    Darleen elastic fabrics
Best by taste test
    Royal Crown Cola
Best by test
    Calumet Baking Powder
The best chimneys in the world
    Pearl Top lamp chimneys
The best comedy in America
    College Humor
Best cooks know foods fried
    in Crisco don't taste
    greasy
    Crisco shortening
The best cooks use aluminum
    Aluminum Ware Association
The best dealer in town sells
    Norge
    Norge refrigerator
The best drinking coffee in
    the world
    Lowry Coffee Co.

The best eye protector for motor-
    ists
    Auto Glas goggles
The best family soap in the world
    Dobbins' Electric Soap
The best food for dogs made.
    For all kinds of dogs
    Cheltenham Beef Fibrine Dog
    Cake
Best Foods
    Good company in your home
Best Foods mayonnaise
    America's favorite mayon-
    naise
Best for all wick type lighters
    Ronsonol lighter fuel
Best for all your baking
    Purity flour
Best for baby, best for you
    Johnson's baby powder
Best for half a century, better
    than ever today
    Admiration cigar
Best for juice and every use
    Sunkist oranges
The best for less
    Rudley's Food Stores
Best for pets
    Hieger Products Co.
Best for rest
    Rauh house slippers
Best for the camp, bears the
    Gold Medal stamp
    Gold Medal Camp Furniture
The best for the purpose
    Wiggletoe Shoes
Best for you and baby, too
    Albert soaps
Best for your canary
    Brock's bird seed
Best Form corset
    The foundation of American
    beauty
The best friend your willpower
    ever had
    Slim-Mint gum
The best glass
    American Window Glass Co.
Best glue in the joint
    Elmer's glue
The best ideas are the ideas that
    help people
    International Telephone &
    Telegraph Corp.
Best in every particular
    B. & H. Lamp

Best in new cars; best in old
cars
Sealed Power piston rings
The best in radio
American Bosch Corp.
The best in radio is better with
a Bendix
Bendix radio receiver
The best in tapes has "Able"
on the label
Arno Adhesive Tapes, Inc.
"The Best in The House" in 87
lands
Canadian Club whiskey
The best in the house is Schen-
ley
Schenley Distillers Corp.
Best in the long run
Goodrich Silvertown tire
Best in the Union, in pocket
tins
Union smoking tobacco
Best in the world
W. L. Douglas shoes
The best in the world. None
can equal it
The Unique Hair Crimper
The best Jaguar ever built
Jaguar automobile
The best known name in paper
Hammermill Paper Co.
Best-known name in sterling
Gorham Div., Textron, Inc.
Best known of automotive finishes
Duco automobile polish
The best lookin' cookin' in town
Armour and Co.
The best mixers
Silver King food mixers
The best name in all-weather
coats and rainwear
Alligator raincoats
Best nickel candy there iz-z-z
Whiz candy bar
Best of all, Edelbrew costs you
no more
Edelbrew
Best of all, it's a Cadillac
Cadillac automobile
The best of everything
Chisholm-Ryder Co.
The best of everything for the
food processor
Chisholm-Ryder Co.
The best of France to all the
world

Air France
The best of "look" to you
Fisher automobile bodies
The best of miles
Skelly Oil Co.
Best of the best
Optimo cigars
The best of the world's press
Woman's Digest
The best of two worlds
Toshiba America, Inc.
White Consolidated Indus-
tries, Inc.
The best on the market
American Cyclometer
The best papers are made from
rags
Coupon Bond paper
Best Pleat Nip-Tite
For the decorator touch
The best pump. The best buy
Reda Pump Co.
Best pumps in the oil patch
Harbison-Fischer Mfg. Co.
The best seat in the house
C. F. Church Div., Ameri-
can Standard, Inc.
Best Seed Co.
Make every plot a garden
spot
Best-selling aerosols are powered
with Freon propellants
Freon Products Div., E. I.
duPont de Nemours &
Co.
The best show window on earth
Cellophane
The best stores sell them
Feder's Pompadour Skirt
Protector
Best that science can create for
trolleying your heavy
freight
Ohio Brass Co.
The best to you each morning
Kellogg Co.
The best tobacco makes the best
smoke
Camel cigarettes
Best today, still better tomorrow
Firestone luggage
The best tonic
Brown's Iron Bitters
Pabst Blue Ribbon beer
The best typewriter for office
work where speed is

required
Hammond typewriter
The best way to better yarns
Whitten Machine Works
Best way to close an opening
Cookson Co. fire doors
Best year yet to go Ford
Ford automobile
Bethlehem spark plug
They pull you through
Bethlehem Steel Company
When you think wire rope,
think Bethlehem
Working smarter
Betsy Ross spinet piano
A beautiful piano with a
magnificent tone
Better air is our business
American Air Filter Co.,
Inc.
Better--always better
Kelvinator refrigerator
The better backbone of modern
rugs
Textilene
Better baking with less fuel
Pyrex glassware
Better banking, better service.
Better join us
Reliance State Bank
Better because brewed solely
of malt and hops
Trommer's beer
Better because it's gas ... best
because it's Caloric
Caloric Corp.
Better Bedding Alliance of Amer-
ica
Invest in rest
Better bedding by Burton
Burton bedding
Better beef and it's branded
Swift's Premium meats
Better biscuits made the better
way
Sawyer Biscuit Co.
Better block chains in the red
band bag
U. S. Chain & Forging Co.
Better built to do a better job
Launderall clothes washer
Better Business Bureau
Before you invest, in-
vestigate
Investigate before you in-
vest

We'll help you get your
money's worth
Better business is our aim
Business Advertising Agency
The better buy
Cascade detergent
Better buy Birds Eye
Birds Eye frozen vegetables
Better buy Buick
Buick automobile
A better buy, by any comparison
Safticycles, Inc.
Better buymanship
Household Finance Corp.
Better by design
Mesta Machine Co.
Better carpeting for less
Lincoln carpeting
Better cash management starts by
calling us
Commerce Bank of Kansas
City
Better castings through advanced
foundry technology
Meehanite Metal Corp.
Better coffee every time with
S & W
S & W Fine Foods
Better--cost less
Crosley radio receivers
Better hearing longer
Mini-Max hearing aid
A better hold in no time
Fasteeth denture adhesive
Better Homes & Gardens
America's biggest home
magazine
America's biggest suburban
home market
America's first service maga-
zine
For home lovers in cities,
towns and suburbs
It takes emotion to move
merchandise...
Better Homes & Gardens
is PERPETUAL EMOTION
It's the life they lead, it's
the book they read
The perfect gift, to give,
to get
Better ideas from UOP
Universal Oil Products Co.
Better light, better sight
Edison Mazda Lamps
Better little shoes are not made

Mrs. Day's Ideal Baby Shoe
Co.
Better meals by the minute
Landers household acces-
sories
Better medicines for a better
world
Parke, Davis and Co.
Better music through science
Epic phonograph records
Better, naturally
Van Camp Sea Food Co.
Better pans for better baking
Chicago Metallic Mfg. Co.
Better paper, better printing
S. D. Warren Co. Div.,
Scott Paper Co.
Better pictures with less effort
G. E. exposure meter
A better product deserves a
better label
American Press
Better products at a lower cost
through better methods
Standard Tool and Mfg. Co.
Better products for a better
world
Norge refrigerator
Better products for man's best
friend
Sergeant's pet products
Better protection with Meilink-
built safes
Meilink Steel Safe Co.
Better, quicker, cheaper
Caterpillar Tractor Co.
Better results with less effort
Independent Radio Supply
Co.
A better run for your money
Ethyl gasoline
Better shoes for less money
Samson shoes
Better sleep makes better hus-
bands
Englander mattress
Better sleep, 38% faster
Sominex sleeping pills
The better spread for our daily
bread
Interstate Cotton Oil
Better tasting, mothers say
Campbell's baby foods
Better than a mustard plaster
Musterole
Better than a pastry chef

Duncan Hines cake mix
Better than ever for less than
ever
Frigidaire Div., General
Motors Corporation
Better than mayonnaise, yet costs
less
Miracle Whip salad dressing
Better than money
First National City Bank
travelers checks
Better than the years
Haynes automobile
Better than whisky for a cold
Dr. Miles Medical Co.
The better the gas, the better
your car
Ethyl gasoline
The better the yarn the better
the fabric
Kingsport Corp. acetate
yarn
Better things for better living
... through chemistry
E. I. DuPont de Nemours &
Co.
Better tires for every farm need
U. S. Royal tires
Better trains follow better loco-
motives
Detroit Diesel Engine Div.,
General Motors Corpor-
ation
Better vision for better living
Better Vision Institute
Better vision for better looks
Better Vision Institute
Better Vision Institute
Better vision for better
living
Better vision for better
looks
A better way of living
Society for Electrical De-
velopment
A better-wearing brush for
every use
Osborn paint brush
A better wire cloth
Buffalo Wire Works Co.
A better yield in every field
York Chemical Co.
Better your home, better your
living
Drexel furniture
House Beautiful

Betters continuous production
through continuous re-
search!
J. W. Greer Co.
Betty Crocker cake mix
The cake with the snack in-
side!
Betty Lou Foods
Betty Lou means better
flavor
Betty Lou means better flavor
Betty Lou Foods
Betty Rose Clothing
The pet of the petite
Between heaven and earth there's
little we can't do
American Satellite Company
Between the Acts cigars
America's best tasting little
cigar
Between today's knowledge and
tomorrow's looms
Textile Machinery Div.,
Crompton and Knowles
Between wood and weather
Jewel Paint & Varnish Co.
Beverly-Wilshire Hotel, Los
Angeles, Calif.
This hotel is for those who
appreciate the difference
Beware Of Smoker's Teeth
Bost toothpaste
Bewley's best bakes better
Bewley's flour
Bewley's flour
Bewley's best bakes better
A sack of satisfaction
Beyond the bottom line
Deloitte, Haskins & Sells
accountants
Bi-Car chewing gum
An agreeable chewing diges-
tant
The chewing digestant
Bias Fold tapes
Turn a circle without a
wrinkle
Bicycle is the card player's
choice
Bicycle playing cards
Bicycle playing cards
Bicycle is the card play-
er's choice
Biddle automobile
Carries a message of speed,
flexibility and service

Bien Jolie
Bien Jolie creates the world's
finest corsetry
Bien Jolie creates the world's
finest corsetry
Bien Jolie
Big Ben Westclox alarm clock
Defense won't wait for the
nation that's late
First he whispers, then he
shouts
It's worth the difference to
get a Big Ben
Keeps America on time
Laughs at time
There's no better time
The big book with the orange
cover
Talking Machine World
Big Brother
It takes a man to help a boy
The big brother to the railroads
Kelly-Springfield motor
truck
Big-car quality at lowest cost
Chevrolet automobile
The Big D
Duesenberg automobile
A big deal and a big meal
Godfather's pizza restaurants
The big difference in tires is
action-traction
General tires
Big enough for any Kodak print
Engel Art Corners
Big enough to serve you--small
enough to know you
E. Kahn's Sons Co.
Big Horn Coffee
We roast it, others praise it
The big hotel that remembers the
little things
Hotel New Yorker, New
York City
The big job cleaner
Spic & Span cleaning powder
The big job matched line
Massey-Ferguson, Inc.
Big Joe Mfg. Co.
Big Joe takes a load off
your mind
Big Joe takes a load off your
mind
Big Joe Mfg. Co.
The big menthol taste from Marl-
boro Country--you get

a lot to like
    Marlboro menthol cigarettes
A big name at a little price
    Nunn-Bush Shoe Co.
Big name in batteries
    Ray-O-Vac batteries
The big name in clothes
    Styleplus Clothes
The big name in little wheels
    Cushman Motors Div., Out-
        board Marine Co.
The big news always first
    Boston Telegram
Big Red chewing gum
    Long lasting breath fresh-
        ness
Big Six Press
    Rush jobs are a special
        delight
The big sky country
    Montana Highway Commission
Big tools for a big job
    Detroit Diesel Engine Div.,
        General Motors Corpora-
        tion
Big washings on small budgets
    Maytag laundry washers
Big Yank work clothes
    What you want in work
        clothes
Bigelow-Sanford, Inc.
    People who know buy Bige-
        low
    Rugs, carpets since 1825
    A title on the door rates a
        Bigelow on the floor
The biggest bank knows Taiwan
        best
    Bank of Taiwan
Biggest, brightest, best maga-
        zine for boys in all the
        world
    American Boy
Biggest in the country
    Farm Journal
Biggest little steakhouse in the
        U.S.A.
    Ponderosa steak restaurants
The biggest mouth you feed is
        your tax bite
    Rowe Price Tax-Free In-
        come Fund, Inc.
Biggest name in fleet cars and
        trucks
    Chevrolet Motor Div., Gen-
        eral Motors Corporation

Biggest name in kitchen towels
    Excello towels
The biggest name in little com-
        puters
    Radio Shack
The biggest name in little engines
    Super-Cyclone
The biggest name in portable
        electric heaters
    Arvin electric heaters
Biggest news in infants' shoes
    Play-Poise shoes
Biggest of all in range of indus-
        trial products
    Allis-Chalmers Mfg. Co.
The biggest should do more.
        It's only right
    Hertz automobile rentals
Biggs Antique Co., Inc.
    Master craftsmen since 1890
Bijur Lubrication Co.
    The originators of constant
        chassis lubrication
The bike you'll like
    Yale bicycle
Bilco Company
    America's finest basement
        door
A billion dollar estate
    Northwestern Mutual Life
        Insurance Co.
Billions and billions served
    McDonald's fast food rest-
        aurants
Billy the Kid slacks
    The brand with loyalty to
        quality
Biltwell tires
    Built from the road up
The binder that grows with your
        business
    Stationers Loose Leaf Binder
Bingham Bros. glue
    Make your identity stick
Biolac
    "Baby talk" for a good
        square meal
Bird. See also: Byrd
Bird and Son, Inc.
    Bird takes the burden out
        of keeping up your
        home
    The classic name in the
        building field
    The one-man, one-hand
        shingle

A roof for every building
Bird Mfg. Co.
The first name in textiles
Bird takes the burden out of
keeping up your home
Bird and Son, Inc.
Birds Eye frozen vegetables
Better buy Birds Eye
Birds Eye puts the "super"
in the supper
Birds Eye puts the "super" in
the supper
Birds Eye frozen vegetables
Birmingham News
The South's greatest news-
paper
Birth. See also: Berth
The birth state of the nation
Pennsylvania
Birthday greeting cards of char-
acter
Rust Craft greeting cards
Birthplace and centre of modern
optics
Carl Zeiss, Inc.
Birthplace of the nation
Virginia Dept. of Conserva-
tion and Economic De-
velopment
Biscuit & Cracker Mfrs. Assn.
Only a good cracker is fit
to eat
Bishman Manufacturing Co.
The quality equipment line
Bishop. See also: Hazel Bishop
Cosmetics
Bishop Candy Co., Inc.
Exclusive makers of the
original old-fashioned
molasses candy in de-
lightful modern flavors
Bishopric Mfg. Co.
A complete wall unit for all
time and clime
For all time and clime
The Unit-Wall Construction
Bismarck Hotel, Chicago, Ill.
Where quality is a tradition
Bisquick, bride's best bet
Bisquick flour
Bisquick flour
Bisquick, bride's best bet
The flower of fine flour
Stop baking risk, use Bis-
quick
Bissell carpet sweeper

Empties with a thumb pres-
sure
Put your sweeping reliance
on a Bissell appliance
Bisurated Magnesia
It's a protective neutralizer
Bite size
Shredded Ralston
The biteless blend
Briggs pipe mixture
Bites deep, stays clean, like a
plow
Seiberling tires
Bixby's Jet Oil shoe polish
I live a fast life
Just spread it on
World's fastest shine
Biz bleaching powder
Discover Biz Bleach and dis-
cover a clean, white
wash
Black. See also:
Captain Black smoking tobac-
co
Block
The Black & Decker Mfg. Co.
Bubble action vacuum washer
Built to endure
For industry, shop, farm and
home
The key to better grinding
Maker of the world's finest
cordless electric tools
Weigh the loads and save the
roads
With the pistol grip and trig-
ger switch
Black & White Face Powder
Incense of flowers
Black and White Scotch whiskey
The Scotch with character
Two Scotches of exceptional
character
A black business handled white
North Memphis Coal Co.
Black-Clawson Co.
Build with machine tool ac-
curacy
Black Flag insect spray
It penetrates
It's bug tested
When mosquitoes sing the
aria from malaria
Black Label beer
Taste without waist
Black Leaf insecticide

Look for the leaf on the
package
Black Silk stove polish
A shine in every drop
Black Tower wine
The white wine in the black
bottle
Black Velvet blended Canadian
whiskey
Feel the velvet
Blackmer Pump Co.
Automatic takeup for wear
Bucket design
Ezy-Kleen strainers
The pump that is self-
adjusting for wear,
famous bucket design
Self-adjusting for wear
Blackstone cigar
The choice of successful men
The blades men swear by, not at
Durham-Duplex razor
Blair-Knox Co.
Engineering know-how ...
by Blair-Knox
Blank. See: Frederic Blank &
Co., Inc.
A blanket invitation to sleep
Seymour blanket
Blatz beer
Brewer of better beer
Brewing better beer for the
96th year
The inflation fighter
Milwaukee's first bottled beer
Milwaukee's most exquisite
beer
There is as much satisfac-
tion in the brewing of
a good beer as in the
drinking of it
Why pay more for less?
You're the winner with Blatz
quality
Bleaches out the toughest food
stains fast
Ajax cleanser
Bleaches out tough food stains.
Disinfects as it cleans
Comet cleanser
Bleachodent dentifrice
The salt dentifrice
Blekre tires
For peace of mind
The blend of a perfect day
Sportsman pipe mixture

A blend of all straight whiskies
Paul Jones whiskey
The blend of experience
Park & Tilford whiskey
Blended right
Winchester cigarettes
Blended whiskey of character
Carstairs White Seal whiskey
A blending of art and machine
Jaguar automobile
Blimp chewing gum
The largest in the world
Block. See also: Black
Block Candy Co.
Candy aristocrats
The blond beer with the body
Tecate beer
Bloomfield, N. J.
"Made in Bloomfield" is a
mark of merit
The blowout-proof tire
General tires
Blu-Cold refrigerator
A good reputation has to be
earned
Blue. See also: John Blue Co.,
Inc.
Blue Barron's orchestra
The music of yesterday and
today
Blue Bird Tea Co.
Brings happiness
Blue Bird Wanderlodge
The coach to judge others by
The ultimate motor home
Blue Bonnet Margarine
Everything's better with Blue
Bonnet on it
The Blue Book of the trade
Tea & Coffee Trade Journal
Blue brutes
Worthington Pump & Machinery
Corp.
The Blue Chip company
Connecticut Mutual Life In-
surance Co.
Blue Cross/Blue Shield
America's #1 get well card
For doctor bills
Blue Goose stands today, as al-
ways, for quality
American Fruit Growers
Assn.
Blue-Jay corn plaster
End corn pain instantly
Great aches from little toe-

54

corns grow
The quick and gentle way
to end a corn
The safe and gentle way to
end a corn
Stops pain instantly ...
ends corns completely
Blue Moon Silk Hosiery Co.
Longer wear in every pair
Blue Nun goes everywhere
Blue Nun wine
Blue Nun wine
Blue Nun goes everywhere
The blue of spotless reputation
Mrs. Stewart's Bluing
Blue Reprint machines
As easily as the sun shines
Blue Ribbon mayonnaise
Health in every jar
Blue Streak
World's foremost heavy-duty
ignition line
Blue Streak grinding wheels
Blue Streak grinding wheels,
fast and cool
Blue Streak grinding wheels,
fast and cool
Blue Streak grinding wheels
Blue Sunoco gasoline
Blue Sunoco makes molehills
out of mountains
Blue Sunoco, the Over-Drive
Motor Fuel
Gasoline, not cut price
guessoline
"Streamlined acting" motor
fuel
The wonder fuel
Blue Sunoco makes molehills out
of mountains
Blue Sunoco gasoline
Blue Sunoco, the Over-Drive
Motor Fuel
Blue Sunoco gasoline
Blue Swan undies
Fantasy in freedom
The blue tube with the life-like
tone
Arcturus Radio Tube Co.
Blue-White Bluing
Blues while you wash
Bluebird clothes washer
Brings happiness to home-
work
Bluebird phonograph records
The hottest bands, the

newest tunes, the big-
best hits
Blueprint of a perfect cocktail
G & D vermouth
Blues automatically as you wash
La France Bluing
Blues while you wash
Blue-White Bluing
Blumenthal shoes ›
Fits on the foot like a glove
on the hand
The boast of the town
Prim Miss brassieres and
girdles
Bob Evans brings you back
Bob Evans farm restaurants
Bob Evans farm restaurants
Bob Evans brings you back
Bob Evans Farms meat products
We do it right or we don't
do it
Bob Smart Shoe Co.
They neither crimp your
roll nor cramp your
style
Bobbi Motor Car
In a class by itself
Bobit barber's towels
Keep your patrons from get-
ting it in the neck
Bobrick soap dispensers
Over a million used by mil-
lions
Bock Bearing Co.
The jewels of your car
Quality built into the car
Bodine Corporation
Bodine shares the risk ...
to assure performance
The machine that pays for
itself
Bodine Electric Co.
Power behind the leading
products
Bodine shares the risk ... to
assure performance
Bodine Corporation
Body by Fisher
Fisher automobile bodies
Body by Fisher better by far
Fisher automobile bodies
The body cosmetic
Cashmere Bouquet talcum
Boeing aircraft
Capability has many faces
at Boeing

Chasing the sun, you've
gained 3 hours on the
sun that hangs high
over the Pacific
Getting people together
Tomorrow you can be any-
where
World's first family of jets
Bohack. See: H. C. Bohack
Bohn Aluminum & Brass Corp.
More than skin deep
Boise Cascade Corporation
A company worth looking at
We know where we're growing
Bokay soda
Taste test proves the qual-
ity
The bold engineering comes from
Ford
Ford Motor Company
Bolens Div., FMC Corp.
First in powered equipment
since 1918
Bolens Div., FMC Corp. See
also: FMC Corp.
Bolens tractor
The work machine
Boling Chair Co.
Best buy Boling
Chairs for all business
Bols liqueurs
Dutch name, world fame
Bon Ami cleanser
Hasn't scratched yet
I've made the world a
brighter place to live
in
Let your bathroom reflect
your good taste
The speedy cleaner that
"hasn't scratched yet"
Why struggle for a sparkle?
Bon Merito rum
The Puerto Rican mountain
rum
Boncilla Beautifier
The clasmic clay
Bond Clothes
A bright little toss-on
coat
Bond Street pipe tobacco
Change to Bond Street for
fragrant smoking
Bonded Floors Co.
Resilient floors for every
need

Bonded for life ... because
they're built that way
Ingersoll-Rand Company
Bonded pigments
Palm Bros. Decalcomania Co.
Bonded termite insulation
E. L. Bruce Co.
Bonded Tobacco Co.
Making smoking "safe" for
smokers
There's many a castle built
out of cigarette smoke
Bond's handkerchiefs
Gentlemen prefer Bond's
A "hank" for a Yank
The "hanks" are coming
It's certified quality
Yours for Victory
Bonds that grow in security
Baker, Frentress & Co.
Bonnart. See: Sam Bonnart,
Inc.
Bonwit Teller & Co.
The specialty shop of origi-
nations
Bonz dog food
The taste dogs love
Boodles London Dry Gin
Boodles, the world's costli-
est British gin
The ultra-refined British gin
Boodles, the world's costliest
British gin
Boodles London Dry Gin
Book House for Children
The child who reads is the
child who leads
A boon to woman
Q. D. corset clasp
Boost profits with the competitive
edge
Tyler Corp.
Boot and Shoe Recorder
Great national shoes weekly
National voice of the shoe
trade
The point of penetration to
the shoe market
The boot with the muscles
Beacon Falls Rubber Co.
Borden Chemical Co. See:
Smith-Douglass Div.,
Borden Chemical Co.
Borden, Inc.
Borden's just has to be
good

If it's Borden's it's got to
be good
It is better and you can
prove it
Naturally it's delicious ...
it's made by Borden's
Borden, Inc. See also: Lady
Borden ice cream
Borden Stove Co.
Quality that makes friends,
service that keeps them
Borden's chocolate malted milk
Watch your children thrive
on it
Borden's condensed milk
Keep cool with the cow,
drink milk
Milk that cuts the cost of
cooking
Pure country milk with the
cream left in/
Wherever the recipe calls
for milk
You can depend on the name
Borden's Hemo
Drink your vitamins
Hemo will help you, too
Borden's Instant Coffee
You never had coffee like
this before
Borden's just has to be good
Borden, Inc.
Border to border ... coast to
coast!
Trailer Train Co.
Bores a 300-foot hole in the
night
Niagara Searchlight Co.
Borg-Warner Acceptance Corpor-
ation
In eight major markets
Borg-Warner is a com-
pany to watch
Borg-Warner Corporation
The great engineers
Your best single source for
quality drive train re-
placement parts
Borkman radio receiver
Just as if you were there
Borland Electric automobile
Now comes the season when
comfort depends on the
car
Born 1820 ... still going
strong!

Johnnie Walker Red Label
Scotch whiskey
Born in America. Worn round
the world
Stetson hats
Born in Canada, now going great
in the 48 states
Carling's Ale
Born where a king of France was
born
Otard Cognac
Bosch. See also: American
Bosch Corp.
Bosch ignition
America's supreme ignition
system
Bosch windshield wiper
As necessary as brakes
The boss is a different man since
we changed to silence
Servel refrigerator
Boss Oil Air Stove
Built to save oil
Boss work gloves
Protecting the nation's hand-
power
Bost toothpaste
Beware Of Smoker's Teeth
Make this startling test
The smoker's friend
Use BOST and get a good
paste in the mouth
Bostitch stapler
Fasten it better and faster
with Bostitch
Fastens it better and faster
with wire
Fastens it better with wire
You're better off with
Bostitch
Boston Confectionery Co.
The life of the party
Boston electrics give people
more time for more im-
portant jobs
Boston office equipment
Boston Globe
The Globe sells Boston
Boston Herald
Where advertising pays it
stays--and grows
Boston office equipment
Boston electrics give people
more time for more
important jobs
Boston Post

A giant among newspapers
Boston Sunday Advertiser
New England's greatest Sun-
day newspaper
Boston Telegram
The big news always first
Bostonian shoes
Every pair shows the care
of the shoemaker's hand
Fit right, feel right, they're
walk-fitted
They're cool and easy as an
off-shore breeze
They're walk-fitted to fit
right, feel right
We walk and like it
You'll take a shine to bur-
nished browns
Boston's most famous hotel
Parker House
Bostrom Corp.
Innovators of research-
engineered products
Botany is my Valen-tie
Botany necktie
Botany necktie
Botany is my Valen-tie
Botany shirts
Feel the fabric and you'll
feel the difference
Botany Worsted Mills
Exciting color-drenched
woolens
The fabric is the soul of
the suit
Both sides alike
Kleerfect paper
A bottle of this should be in
every home
Mihalovitch's Hungarian
Blackberry Juice
The bottled beer with the
draught beer flavor
Globe beer
Bottled only at the springs
White Rock club soda
Bottled sunshine
Sun Spot Co. of America
Bottles of every description
Illinois Glass Co.
The bottles of unequalled
strength
American Bottle Co.
The bottom line: Taste
Merit cigarettes
Bounce fabric softener

The fabric softener that
works in the dryer
The right softener for the
right machine
Bouncin' and behavin'--that's Pert
Pert shampoo
Bound to get there
Acme Steel Co.
Bountiful almonds
Grown the natural way in
bountiful U.S.A.
Bountiful pistachio nuts
Grown the natural way in
bountiful U.S.A.
Bountiful raisins
Grown the natural way in
bountiful U.S.A.
Bounty absorbent towels
Gets spills before they get
away
The quicker picker upper
Bouquet. See: Bokay soda
Bovril
Bovril is beverage beef-
steak
Bovril puts beef in you
Bovril is beverage beefsteak
Bovril
Bovril puts beef in you
Bovril
The Bowdil Company
Always right on the job
Bower Roller Bearing Co.
Bower saves power
Bower saves power
Bower Roller Bearing Co.
Bowers spark plug
A name to remember
Bowker's fertilizers
For the land's sake use
Bowker's
Bowl where you see the Magic
Triangle
American Machine & Foundry
Co.
Bowlene cleaner
Thoughtfully designed with
a woman in mind
The box with the bow on top
Sitroux tissue
The box with the famous cutting
edge
Cut-Rite Waxed Paper
The Boy Scouts' magazine
Boys' Life
Boy Scouts of America

Be prepared
Do a good turn daily
Scouts of the world, building for tomorrow
Boyce Moto Meter
Your car deserves one
Boys' Life
The Boy Scouts' magazine
The bra that fits like magic
Genie brassiere
Brach's candies
The candy store candy
The perfect candy for smart entertaining
Brackenridge Brewing Co.
For health's sake, ask your doctor
It's smooth sailing with Brackenridge Brewing Co. beers
Brackets of steel that never break
Stewart-Warner Speedometer Corp.
Bradford. See: J. C. Bradford & Co.
Bradley & Vrooman Co.
Fresh paint is better paint
Good paint costs nothing
The skill is in the can
There's quality written all over Bradley-Vrooman unusual paint
Bradley bathing suit
The home of outdoor style
Slip into a Bradley and out-of-doors!
Bradley Two-Wheeler Carriage
Guaranteed absolutely free from horse motion
Bradshaw & Sons honey
Spun to a cream
Brain-built boxes
Milwaukee Paper Co.
Brake inspection is your protection
Asbestos Brake Lining Association
Brake linings tailored to the needs of your brake
Multibestos brake lining
The brake that brought the bike back
New Departure Coaster Brake
The brake with the mighty

grip
New Departure Coaster Brake
The branch around the corner can serve you around the world
National City Bank
Brand name of better gloves
Aris Gloves
The brand that always puts flavor first
Del Monte fruit cocktail
The brand that made tuna famous
Chicken of the Sea tuna
The brand that so successfully meets the can-opener test
Haserot Company
The brand they ask for first
Allsweet oleomargarine
The brand with loyalty to quality
Billy the Kid slacks
The brand with the grand aroma
Mail Pouch chewing tobacco
Branded with the devil but fit for the gods
Underwood's Original Deviled Ham
Brandes, Inc.
The name to know in radio
The brandy of Napoleon
Courvoisier cognac
Braniff Airways, Inc.
Specialists in international jet service to Texas or South America
Brauer. See also: Bauer & Black
Brauer Bros. Shoe Co.
She walks in beauty
Braumeister beer
Milwaukee's choice
Bray Screen Products
Brayco Light makes all things clear
Brayco Light makes all things clear
Bray Screen Products
Bread. See also: Bred
Bread is your best food, eat more of it
Fleischmann Co.
The bread spread
Miracle Whip salad dressing
BREAD to the queen's taste
Marvel Bread
The breakfast of champions

Wheaties cereal
Breakstone butter
    Famous for flavor
The Brearley Company
    World's largest producer of
        bath scales
The breath deodorant
    Clorets
Breathin' brushed pigskin
    Hush Puppies shoes
A breathless sensation
    Pioneer Mints
Brecht Candy Co.
    Make life sweeter
Breck. See: John H. Breck,
        Inc.
Bred. See also: Bread
Bred, not just grown
    Associated Seed Growers
A breed apart
    Merrill Lynch, Pierce, Fen-
        ner & Smith, Inc.
Breidt. See also:
    Bright
    Brite
Breidt beer
    Aged extra long for extra
        flavor
    The beer that time ripened,
        time tempered
    The beer that's brewed the
        natural way, aged the
        natural way
    The beer with the flavor as
        different as day from
        night
    The beer with the 4th in-
        gredient
    Breidt's for TIME, the
        part of beer you taste
        but never see
    It's TIME that turns the
        tide in Breidt's
    It's time you tasted Breidt's,
        the beer with the 4th
        ingredient
    One of America's fastest-
        growing quality brands
    Stay on the Breidt side
    Stay on the right side
Breidt's for TIME, the part of
        beer you taste but
        never see
    Breidt beer
Brentwood sportswear
    You bet it's good--it's

a Brentwood
Bretton watch bands
    First among fine watch bands
The brew for you
    American Brewing Co.
The brew of quality
    Pabst Blue Ribbon beer
The brew that brings back mem-
        ories
    Pabst Blue Ribbon beer
The brew that holds its head high
        in any company
    Senate beer
The brew with a head of its own
    Krueger beer
The brew with the small bubble
        carbonation
    Senate beer
Brewed only in Milwaukee
    Miller High Life beer
Brewed solely of malt and hops
    Trommer's beer
Brewer of better beer
    Blatz beer
Brewer's Best beer
    The new big name in beer
Brewers of old style beer
    Heilmann's beer
Brewery Corp. of America
    The taste of the nation
Brewery goodness sealed right in
    Pabst Blue Ribbon beer
Brewing better beer for the 96th
        year
    Blatz beer
The brews that satisfy
    Ruppert's beer
Breyer's ice cream
    The all-natural ice cream
Brick & Clay Board
    Dedicated to progress in the
        clay industry
Brick and Clay Record
    Leading clay journal of the
        world
Bridell cleaver
    The knack that stops the
        nick
The bridge to Asia
    Asian Wall Street Journal
        Weekly
Bridgeport Chain Co.
    Bridgeport chain will stand
        the strain
Bridgeport chain will stand the
        strain

Bridgeport Chain Co.
Bridgeport luggage
  It makes its way by the
    way it's made
Bridgestone tires
  You can feel it when you
    drive
Briggs & Stratton Corporation
  Most respected name in
    power
  Power from the world leader
Briggs pipe mixture
  The biteless blend
  The smoke with a smile
  When a feller needs a friend
Bright. See also:
  Breidt
  Brite
Bright as the sun, wears for
    years
  Hexter fabrics
Bright by day, light by night
  Pyrograph Advertising Sign
    Corp.
Bright cigarettes
  You never had it this fresh
Bright Eyes cat food
  That Bright Eyes look
Bright-keyed shades in thirsty
    textures
  Cannon Mills, Inc.
A bright little toss-on coat
  Bond Clothes
The bright new silicates for in-
    dustry
  Allegheny Industrial Chem-
    ical Co.
A bright new world of electric
    housewares
  Norelco electric housewares
Bright Star flashlight
  Gives more bright light
    longer
Brighten. See also: Brighton
Brighten up with Instant Tender
    Leaf Tea
  Instant Tender Leaf Tea
Brighten your home at little ex-
    pense
  Congoleum-Nairn floor cov-
    erings
The brighter tasting tea!
  Instant Tender Leaf Tea
The brightest name in aluminum
  Nichols Aluminum Co.
The brightest star in golf

Burke-Worthington
Brighton. See also: Brighten
Brighton Wide-Web Garters
  Your legs will thank you
Brilliant as the sun
  Lustray Shirts
Brillion Iron Works, Inc.
  Farm implements with a fu-
    ture--yours!
Brillo Cleanser
  Don't be a RUBBIT!
  From black to bright as
    quick as light
  Keeps aluminum bright
  Shines aluminum fast
Brim concentrated coffee
  Fill your cup to the rim with
    the richness of Brim
Bring out the "sleeping beauty"
    in your furniture
  O-Cedar polish
Bringing beauty to bathrooms
  Case fixtures
Bringing imagination to the busi-
    ness of energy
  Mapco, Inc.
Bringing out the music in you
  Yamaha electric organ
Bringing the marvels of science
    to your farm
  Pestroy insecticide
Bringing you life's little things
    in a big way
  Amfac Hotels (Dallas/Fort
    Worth)
Brings a touch of the tropics
  Flamingo gas heaters
Brings happiness
  Blue Bird Tea Co.
Brings happiness to homework
  Bluebird clothes washer
Brings out the goddess in you
  Diana corsetry
Brink's armored car service
  Security since 1859
Brisacher. See: Emil Brisach-
    er & Staff
Brisk as a breeze
  White Rock club soda
Brisk flavor, never flat
  Lipton's tea
A brisk magazine of Parisian
    life
  Paris Nights
The brisk tea
  Lipton's tea

61

The bristles are sealed, the
    brush will last
    Sealastic paint brush
The bristles cannot come out
    Dr. Scott's Electric Tooth-
    brush
The bristles can't come out
    Rubberset shaving brush
The Bristol Co.
    For improved production
    through measurement
    and control
Bristol Pro-Golf, Inc.
    World's finest golf clubs
    and accessories
Britannic wool hose
    First with the last word
Brite. See also:
    Breidt
    Bright
Brite floor polish
    Nothing's faster. Nothing's
    easier
Brite-Lite polish
    Don't ask for "polish," de-
    mand Brite-Lite
    Makes old things new, keeps
    new things bright
British Aerospace, Inc.
    Great aircraft don't just
    happen.... Their
    secret is versatile per-
    formance!
British European Airways
    Europe's foremost airline
British Overseas Airway Corp.
    All over the world BOAC
    takes good care of you
    BOAC takes good care of
    you
    Over the Atlantic and across
    the world
    Speedbird service
Brizard. See: Marie Brizard
    liqueurs
Broad, black and a brute for
    wear
    Cupples tires
Broadcast Redi-Meat
    A square meal from a
    square can
Broadcasts as she bakes
    Radio Cooking School of
    America
Brock clocks
    The finest clock since time

began
Brock Jewelry Co.
    Symbols of sentiment
Brock Residence Inn
    For a day, a week, a month
    or more
    Make a sweet suite deal on
    your next trip to Denver
Brock watches
    A man's treasure
Brock's bird seed
    Best for your canary
Brockway, the right way
    Brockway truck
Brockway truck
    Brockway, the right way
The broker for experienced in-
    vestors
    Source Securities Corp.
A brokerage house you can bank
    on
    Thomson McKinnon Secur-
    ities, Inc.
Bromo-Seltzer
    Bromo-Seltzer will cure that
    headache
    For FAST headache help
    Makes you feel fit faster
Bromo-Seltzer will cure that head-
    ache
    Bromo-Seltzer
A bronze as strong as nickel
    steel
    Hy-Ten-Sl bronze
Brooklawn Corduroy
    A name to remember, a fab-
    ric to remember
Brooklyn Standard Union
    Largest daily circulation in
    Brooklyn of any Brook-
    lyn newspaper
Brooklyn Varnish Co.
    Beauty by the brushful
Brooks Brothers clothing
    Established 1818
    Furnishings for men, women
    and boys
Brooks catsup
    The catsup with a kick
Brooks for hooks
    Brooks iron hooks and
    screws
Brooks iron hooks and screws
    Brooks for hooks
Brother Electronic Office Type-
    writer

Proofread your typing be-
fore it's typed
Brown. See also:
Art Brown artist's supplies
Hamilton Brown Shoe Co.
Brown & Haley
America's finest confection
Candies of distinction
Candy of distinction
A name to remember
Brown & Sharpe hardware
Choice of three generations
Standard of the mechanical
world
The Brown-Bridge Mills, Inc.
Specialists in the application
of adhesives
Brown Coal Co.
Brown treats you white
Brown Company
The ideal builder's sheath-
ing paper
Makes homes more livable
The paper people
Brown Friar whiskey
A little Brown Friar for
good cheer
No extravagant claims, just
a real good product
Only quality endures
Brown pyrometers
To measure is to economize
Brown Shoe Company
Quality at your feet
Brown Shoe Company. See
also: Risqué Shoes
Div., Brown Shoe Com-
pany
Brown Spring Oiler Co.
Not an accessory but a
necessity
Brown treats you white
Brown Coal Co.
Browning Arms Company
America's finest fishing
rods
Finest in sporting arms
Browning King men's wear
A label approved by New
Yorkers
Brown's. See also: Les
Brown's orchestra
Brown's Iron Bitters
The best tonic
Bruce. See: E. L. Bruce
Co.

Bruce's bird seed
Balanced bird ration
Brummel. See: Beau Brummel
of the boulevards
Bruning. See: Chas. Bruning
Co.
Brunswick Corp.
The No. 1 name in billiards
No. 1 name in bowling
Brunswick Corp. See also:
Keikhaefer Mercury Div.,
Brunswick Corp.
Brunswick phonograph
All phonographs in one
Brunswick phonograph records
Every artist an artist
Individuality graven into
them
Brunswick refrigerator
Food preservation without
ice
Brunswick Rubber Co.
Famous for quality
Brunswick Ultona phonograph
Now! The final achievement
Brush often with Aim
Aim toothpaste
Brush the cobwebs from your
beauty
Kent brushes
The brush with a backbone
Hummel gummed paper mois-
tener
The brush with the permanent
wave
Rubberset paint brush
Brush your breath with Dentyne
Dentyne chewing gum
Brush your hair to loveliness
Dupont plastic brush
Brush your teeth twice a day
and see your dentist
twice a year
Pebeco tooth paste
The brushless wonder
Benex brushless shave
Bryant. See also: Lane Bryant
stores
Bryant Heater Co.
Come home to comfort
Let your pup be your fur-
nace man
A single match is your
year's kindling
Brylcreem Anti-Dandruff hair
dressing

63

A little dab fights dandruff
as it grooms
Brylcreem hair dressing
Are you man enough to try
it?
A little dab will do ya
Nothing grooms hair better
than a little dab
Bubble action vacuum washer
The Black & Decker Mfg.
Co.
A buck well spent on a Spring-
maid sheet
Springmaid sheets
Bucket design
Blackmer Pump Co.
Bucket syrup
Maple at its best
Buckeye Aluminum Co.
The aluminum ware with the
smooth finish
Buckeye Cellulose Corp.
First in cellulose
Buckeye engines
Be profit-wise and dieselize
with Buckeyes
Buckeye Producing Co.
Retains all the esters
Buckeye Shirt Co.
For goodness sake wear
Buckeye Shirts
Buckeye Traction Ditcher Co.
Ask any owner
A perfect trench at one
cut
Bucyrus-Erie Company
Commitment to quality
The Budd Company
In metals, plastic and pa-
per Budd works to
make tomorrow ... to-
day
New trains, new travelers
The people movers
Ready to ride right now!
Wherever you look ... you
see Budd
Budd truck wheels
The only wheel with a cold
tapered disc
Buddie desk
The home desk for leisure
and working hours
Buddy Lee men's suits
Where style begins
Budget Rent-a-car

You get more than just a car
at Budget
The budget sets the pace
Otis Elevator Company
Budweiser beer
America has gone Budweiser
Beer is as old as history
It lives with good taste
everywhere
It's worth it ... it's Bud
The king of beers
Lives with good taste
The most popular beer in
history
The most popular beer the
world has ever known
Perfect host to a host of
friends
Something more than a beer,
a tradition
That's Bud ... that's beer!
This Bud's for you
Where there's life ... there's
Bud
Budwine beer
Makes you glad you're
thirsty
Buescher Band Instrument Co.
Made by masters, played by
artists
Buescher true-tone saxophone
Easy to play--easy to pay
Music that charms
Buescher trumpet
The trumpet you hear on
the phonograph
Buffalo Lithia Water
A solvent for stone in the
bladder
Buffalo sausage machines
Wherever you go you'll find
Buffalo
Buffalo Wire Works Co.
A better wire cloth
Bufferin is smarter
Bufferin pain reliever
Bufferin pain reliever
Bufferin is smarter
The pain stops here
Bug-free, buzz-free, bite-free
Pestolite insect repellant
Buhl Mfg. Co.
Do it with air
Buhner Fertilizer Co.
As necessary as the rain
Buick automobile

After all, life is to enjoy
Bared to its bones, it's
   still the "beauty"
Beau Brummel of the boule-
   vards
Best bet's Buick
Better buy Buick
An extra trifle buys this
   eyeful
An eyeful of fashions, a
   buy full of features
For '48 the best to date
For '49 the best of our line
Idling or full-out, its engine
   is hushed as a country
   snowfall
Livelier as well as lovelier
The standard of comparison
Styled for a party, but
   powered for a thrill
The tuned car
When better automobiles are
   built, Buick will build
   them
Wouldn't you really rather
   have a Buick?
Buick diesel-powered automobile
   Class without gas
Buick Le Sabre automobile
The more logical we made
   it, the better looking
   it got
Build a truck to do a job--
   change it only to do
   better
   International Harvester
   trucks
Build-in satisfaction ... build-in
   Frigidaire
   Frigidaire Div., General
   Motors Corporation
Build on Certain-teed, the well-
   known name
   Certain-teed roofing
Build right, with Insulite
   Insulite Div., Minnesota
   and Ontario Paper Co.
Build the Nation securely with
   the nation's building
   stone
   Indiana Limestone Quarry-
   men's Association
Build to endure
   Certain-teed roofing
Build with machine tool accuracy
   Black-Clawson Co.

Builder of business
   Service motor truck
Builder of fine inboard and out-
   board boats
   Century Boat Co.
Builder of trucks you can trust
   Studebaker trucks
Builders in and of the South
   Daniel Construction Co.,
   Inc.
Builders of better refrigerator
   bodies
   Hackney Bros. Body Co.
Builder of business
   Willmark Service System
Builders of heavy duty engines
   for over twenty years
   Waukesha Motor Co.
Builders of the tools of automation
   Reliance Electric and Engi-
   neering Co.
Builders of tomorrow's feeds ...
   today!
   Wayne feeds
The builder's selection for unfail-
   ing protection
   American Tar & Chemical Co.
Builders wise use our supplies
   Washington Lumber Co.
Building business is our business
   Tenneco, Inc.
Building Construction
   The magazine of architectural
   technology
Building for the ages
   Queenston Limestone
Building on strength
   Burroughs Corporation
Building Plan Association
   A beautiful house for $1200
Building Profit
   The magazine that saves
   building dollars doesn't
   cost you a cent
Building Supply News
   The dealer's own paper
   It is our business to help
   your business
Building the teacher into a text-
   book
   International Correspondence
   Schools
Building with Chicago and the
   nation since 1863
   First National Bank of Chi-
   cago

Builds body, brain and nerves
Ovaltine
Builds brain, nerves and body
Ovaltine
Builds for the years ahead
Maltcao chocolate
Builds robust bodies
Challenge milk
Built as though you intend to
sell your home tomorrow
Murphy in-a-door bed
Built better because it's hand-
crafted
Zenith television sets
Built by Alberthaw
Alberthaw Construction Co.
Built by locker specialists
Durabilt steel locker
Built first--to last
Reynolds Shingle Co.
Built for business
Duplex truck
Built for connoisseurs of refrig-
eration
Kelvinator refrigerator
Built for lifetime service
Icy-Hot Bottle Co.
Built for permanence
Kommon-Sense Pan Racks
Built for permanence and guar-
anteed for life
Abbott-Detroit automobile
Built for permanence, calibrated
for performance
Bendix Corporation
Built for sleep
Ostermoor mattress
Simmons Company
Built for the best
Apollo Magneto Corp.
Built for two
Ford runabout automobile
Built from the road up
Biltwell tires
Built-in quality in every shoe
Myers shoes
Built layer on layer
Miller tires
Built like a bank vault door
Master laminated padlock
Built like a fine watch
Lombardi radio receiver
Built like a safe
Yawman & Erbe steel fil-
ing cabinets
Built like a skyscraper

Shaw-Walker steel filing
cabinets
Built like a violin
Teletone radio speakers
Built like a watch
Johnson Oil Burner
Built like fine furniture
Coppes Bros. & Zook kitchen
cabinets
Built like the finest automobile
Whirlpool clothes washer
Built on bedrock
Johnson, Read & Co.
Built on reputation
Ditchburn Boats, Ltd.
Built right for over forty years
Belding-Hall refrigerator
Built stronger to last longer
Powell Muffler Co.
Built through generations
Encyclopedia Americana
Built to be the best turboprop in
the world
Saab-Fairchild 340 aircraft
Built to endure
Baker Gun Co.
The Black & Decker Mfg. Co.
The Globe-Wernicke Co.
Built to excel
Savage tires
Built to fit the trip
Miller luggage
Built to last
Armstrong tires
Built to last a business lifetime
Monroe calculators
Built to last longer
Ford Econoline van trucks
Built to last through every trip
Rennus luggage
Built to live in the water
Chrysler marine engines
Built to save oil
Boss Oil Air Stove
Built to stay alive
Good Luck Hose
Built to sustain a reputation
Handy Chair & Table Co.
Built to take it ... beautifully
Daystrom Furniture Divi-
sion, Daystrom, Inc.
Built to weather the years
Rust Sash & Door Co.
Built to win, without, within
Paige automobile
Built tough for you

Toyota automobile

Built with integrity, backed by
   service
   Sunbeam Corporation

Built with today's technology
   from the ground up
   Canadair Challenger jet
   aeroplane

Bull Dog. See also: Bulldog

Bull Dog Belting
   No drive too hard, no serv-
     ice too severe

Bull Dog Hose
   The kind that lasts longer

Bull Dog Tape
   It sticks, it holds, it lasts

Bull Durham tobacco
   The makings of a nation
   Standard of the world

Bulldog. See also: Bull Dog

Bulldog paint remover
   Eats paint and bites varnish

Bulldog Venetian blind cleaner
   It's always a shade better

Bull's Eye paint brush
   Best buy is Bull's Eye

Bulman Corporation
   Leadership built on the re-
     search and experience
     of over 48,000 store
     installations

Bulova Watch time, the gift of a
   lifetime
   Bulova watches

Bulova watches
   America runs on Bulova time
   Bulova Watch time, the gift
     of a lifetime
   When something happy hap-
     pens--it's Bulova time

Bunnell telegraph equipment
   Standard of the globe

The bump stops here
   Monroe shock absorbers

Bunko mustard
   Escape from the ordinary

Bunte Brothers cough drops
   Stop that tickle

Bur-Mil suiting
   Won't stretch in wearing
     or shrink in dry clean-
     ing

Burdett shoes
   Keep in step with youth

Burglars know no season
   Standard Accident Insur-

ance Co.

Burk. See: Ben Burk whiskey

Burke, Christensen & Lewis Securities
   Be a winner every time

Burke fishing lures
   Put a Burke where they
     lurk!

Burke-Worthington
   The brightest star in golf

Burlington carpets
   Burlington, the scatter rug
     of beauty

Burlington Northern Railroad
   The more we invest in our
     future the better we can
     serve you
   Most popular route to the
     Rockies
   The summer route you'll
     brag about

Burlington "Stay-On" horse
   blanket
   The only "Stay-on" Stable
     Blanket

Burlington Steel Co.
   Good steel, good service

Burlington, the scatter rug of
   beauty
   Burlington carpets

Burma-Shave shaving cream
   Cheer up, face

Burn your name in metal
   Arkograph Pen Co.

Burnham Mfg. Co.
   The Rolls-Royce of coaster
     wagons

Burns. See also: Robert Burns
   cigar

Burns Bros. coal
   Burns coal burns

Burns coal burns
   Burns Bros. coal

Burns coffee roaster
   Finer roasts with less gas

Burns like city gas, not a liquid
   fuel
   Pyrofax

Burroughs Corporation
   Building on strength

A burst of refreshing fruit flavor
   Starburst Fruit Chews

Bursting with juice
   Sunkist oranges

Burton. See also: Barton

Burton bedding

Better bedding by Burton
Busch beer
    The beer that goes down
       smooth as a mountain
       stream
    For a taste as smooth as
       its name
    Head for the mountains
Busch Pale Dry ale
    The prince of ales
    The prince of pales
Business Advertising Agency
    Better business is our aim
Business case that knows its
    way around the world
    Samsonite Corp.
The business jet that's backed
    by an airline
    Fan Jet Falcon aircraft
A business journal of furnishing
    and decoration
    Good Furniture Magazine
The business leaders of today
    are the I. C. S. stu-
    dents of yesterday
    International Correspondence
    Schools
The business leaders of tomorrow
    are the I. C. S. stu-
    dents of today
    International Correspondence
    Schools
The business magazine
    Fortune Magazine
The business magazine of the
    radio industry
    Radio Retailing
The business management maga-
    zine
    Dun's Review and Modern
    Industry
Business moves better with
    Wheels!
    Wheels, Inc.
A business paper for the farm
    chemical industry
    Crop Life
The business paper of the elec-
    trical industry since
    1892
    Electrical Record
A business partner you can de-
    pend on
    Minolta duplicator
The business pencil
    J. Dixon Crucible Co.

Business tools
    Diebold Safe & Lock Co.
Business travel is Beech's busi-
    ness
    Beech Aircraft Corp.
Business Week
    Sell at the decision level
Buskens shoes
    So little never bought so
    much
Buss fuses
    Be profit wise ... (sell only
    Buss)
    A trustworthy name in elec-
    trical protection
Bussman Mfg. Co.
    The handiest light in the
    world
Buster Boy suits
    Mix 'em and match 'em
But the greatest reason of all is
    that Guinness is good
    for you
    Guinness ale
Butcher Bones
    Crunchy day snack with real
    meat
Butcher's Blend dog food
    For more meaty taste
Butler-Andresen dance orchestra
    Hottest on the campus
Butler Manufacturing Co.
    That's a Butler building?
    Today's best looking build-
    ing values
Butter-Nut coffee
    Butter-Nut, the coffee de-
    licious
Butter-Nut, the coffee delicious
    Butter-Nut coffee
Butter that betters the meal
    Falfurrias Dairy Co.
Butterball turkeys
    When only the best will do
Butterick patterns
    Style leaders of the world
Butterine
    Made in the milky way
Butterworth's. See: Mrs. But-
    terworth's syrup
Butzer's bacon
    A Kansas product from
    Kansas farms
    Long, tender, golden brown
    strips
    Long, tender, golden brown

strips from Kansas
Buxton stitchless zip guard
More profit per foot
Buy. See also: By
Buy a Chevrolet, profit every
way
Chevrolet trucks
Buy a How searchlight today,
you may need it tonight
How Lamp & Mfg. Co.
Buy a rack of Rooties
Rooties soft drink
Buy Baby Ruth by the box
Baby Ruth candy bar
Buy Castle furniture for your
castle
Castle furniture
Buy china in a china store
Mutual China Co.
Buy once, buy wisely, buy Ruud
Ruud water heaters
Buy one today, you'll need it
tonight
French batteries
Buy only what you need when
you need it
Diebold Safe & Lock Co.
Buy quality, not quantity
Miessene Household Prod-
ucts
Buy spares, they stay fresh
Ray-O-Vac batteries
Buy the Big Boy
Trommer's beer
Buy them by the dozen for their
many uses
Sunkist lemons
Buy today's best truck. Own
tomorrow's best trade
Hyster Co.
Buy us like advertising ... use
us like salesmen
Home State Farm Publica-
tions
Buy word of millions
King Edward cigar
Buy your beauty needs from
beauticians
Contoure Laboratories
Buying for profit and income
Joint Security Corp.
Buying for profit and invest-
ment
Joint Security Corp.
By. See also: Buy
By design ... furniture dis-

tinguished for value
since 1904
Thomasville Furniture In-
dustries, Inc.
By the beards of three million
prophets
Schick electric shaver
By the glass, by the bottle, by
the case, buy Hyde
Park
Hyde Park beer
By the time you're 35 you've
probably got 40,000
miles on your feet. And
you can't trade them in
Dr. Scholl's bunion pads
By the world's largest maker of
dishwater detergents
Economics Laboratories, Inc.
Byers Crane
The all-purpose one-man
crane
Byrd. See also: Bird
Byrd Industries, Inc.
Developing products for
recreation through elec-
tronic research

-C-

C. A. Norgren Co.
First name in pneumatic
protection
CBS. See also: Columbia
Broadcasting System,
Inc.
CBS Evening News TV broadcast
A world of difference
CBS, The star's address
Columbia Broadcasting Sys-
tem, Inc.
C.C.A. means distinction, con-
venience, innovation,
protection, inventory
control, service
Container Corp. of America
C. D. Peacock
Jewelers since 1837
C. F. Church Div., American
Standard, Inc.
The best seat in the house
C. F. Church Div., American
Standard, Inc. See
also: American Stand-
ard, Inc.

C. F. Pease Co.
Let blue prints tell your
story
C-H magnetic gear shift
Shift your gears from the
steering wheel
Simple in operation--startling
in efficiency
C. H. Masland and Sons
The magic of Masland car-
pets
C. Howard Hunt Pen Co.
A pen is only as good as
its point
CIBA Products Co.
First in epoxies ... in the
age of ideas
CIT Financial Corporation
Our business is helping
business grow
People put their trust in
us
C-O Two Fire Equipment Co.
Carbon dioxide, kills fire,
saves lives
It's safe because it's faster
C-P Fittings Div., Essex Wire
Corp.
In products, performance,
purpose ... Essex
measures up!
C. P. Leek and Sons, Inc.
Since 1720, a family heritage
of careful boat building
CPT Corporation
CPT shows you how to get
into word processing a
step at a time
CPT takes the mystery out
of word processing
CPT shows you how to get into
word processing a step
at a time
CPT Corporation
CPT takes the mystery out of
word processing
CPT Corporation
C. S. Merton & Co.
There's a Merton cap or
hat for every sport
CSX Corporation
America's number one
transportation/natural
resources company
Train your trucks and
save

The cabinet-wood of the elect
American Walnut Mfrs. Assn.
Cable Network, Inc.
You get more with cable TV
Cabot Corp. See: Oxides Div.,
Cabot Corp.
Cadbury's, Ltd.
Old England's finest choco-
lates
Cadillac and LaSalle automobiles
The royal family of motor-
dom
Cadillac automobile
An American standard for
the world
And the world will approve
your choice
Best of all, it's a Cadillac
Combining power with luxury
Every year a leader--every
year more desirable.
That's Cadillac
A great car for today
So new! So right! So ob-
viously Cadillac!
Standard of the world
Trust Cadillac to lead the
way
Unchallenged for quality
The Cadillacs of the industry
Farnsworth television re-
ceivers
Cado computer
The unconventional business
computer
Caffeine-Free Diet 7UP soft drink
A quarter says you're gonna
love it
Caffeine-Free Diet 7UP soft
drink. See also: 7UP
soft drink
Cahners Publishing Co., Inc.
For the climate of excellence
The live ones!
The cake that tastes moist and
delicious
Duncan Hines cake
The cake with the snack inside!
Betty Crocker cake mix
Cal-Aero Technical Institute
Be wise, protect your fu-
ture
Calavo Growers of California
The aristocrat of salad
fruits
The Calculagraph Co.

The elapsed time recorder
The calculator company
Monroe calculators
Caldwell. See also: W. E.
Caldwell Co.
Caldwell boat
For those who care
Calendar of fashion
International Shoe Co.
Calgon Corporation sure has a
way with water
Calgon laundry detergent
Calgon laundry detergent
Calgon Corporation sure has
a way with water
Helps get laundry up to
30% cleaner
We need more Calgon!
California Citrus Co.
Navel oranges dripping with
health
California Computer Products,
Inc.
Leader in computer graphics
Specialists in digital tech-
nology
Standard of the plotting in-
dustry
California Growers Air Express
If time is the element, we
conquer it
To get there, try the air
California investments of greater
stability
Rogan & Co.
California Redwood Association
Resists fire and rot
Use redwood, it LASTS
California Spray-Chemical Corp.
Scientific pest control
California Walnut Growers Assn.
All they're cracked up to
be
Crackin' good walnuts
California's premier wines
Almadén Vineyards, Inc.
Call Central
Central Manufacturers Mu-
tual Insurance Co.
Call Fidelity. It's high time
Fidelity Mutual Bond Fund
Call for Philip Morris!
Philip Morris cigarettes
Call in the Orkin army
Orkin insect exterminators
Call on Central

Central National Bank & Trust
Co.
Call the Fort
Fort Howard Paper Co.
Call the man from Cozzoli
Cozzoli Machine Co.
Call the man who puts the farmer
first--your Standard Oil
Farm Man
Standard Oil Div., American
Oil Co.
Call your Investors man--today!
Investors Diversified Serv-
ices, Inc.
Call your man on the Frisco
St. Louis-San Francisco Rail-
way Co.
The calm beauty of Japan at al-
most the speed of sound
Japan Air Lines
Calo cat food
His master's choice
Caloric Corp.
The automatic gas range
Better because it's gas ...
best because it's Caloric
The gas range you want
Calox Tooth Powder
Gives your smile breath-
taking beauty
Have teeth that shine like
the stars
My life is an open look
Calumet Baking Powder
Best by test
The thriftiest of baking
powders
Calvert "Extra" whiskey
All the world loves a happy
BLENDING
Clear heads call for Calvert
Clear heads choose Calvert
Every party deserves some-
thing extra
For men of distinction
It's the real thing
The soft whiskey
Calvert "Extra" whiskey. See
also: Lord Calvert
Canadian whiskey
Calvert Litho. Co.
Outward sign of inward
quality
Camay soap
For beautiful skin all over
A lovelier skin with just

one cake

Camel. See also: Campbell's

Camel cigarettes
The best tobacco makes the best smoke
Camels agree with me
Camels ARE milder
Camels suit your T-zone to a T
Experience is the best teacher
For digestion's sake, smoke Camels
Have a Camel
I'd walk a mile for a Camel
More people are smoking Camels than ever before
More pleasure per puff, more puffs per pack
A real cigarette
They are the largest-selling cigarette in America
Your T-zone will tell you

Camel fountain pen
Fill with water, write with ink
Makes its own ink
This is the last word in fountain pen convenience

Camels agree with me
Camel cigarettes

Camels ARE milder
Camel cigarettes

Camels suit your T-zone to a T
Camel cigarettes

The camera you never leave at home
Minox Corp.

Cameron Machine Co.
A team of specialists

Cameron nylon stockings
Sheath the leg in loveliness

Cammillus Cutlery Co.
Cammillus has the edge

Cammillus has the edge
Cammillus Cutlery Co.

Campana Italian Balm
The famous skin softener
It smooths the skin
The original skin softener
Your complexion's best friend

Campbell's. See also: Camel

Campbell's baby foods
Better tasting, mothers say

Main-dish foods for baby

Campbell's chicken noodle soup
As American as Yankee Doodle

Campbell's Chunky Soup
The soup that eats like a meal

Campbell's condensed soups
All-out aid for a hungry man
Appetites don't take vacations
At your grocer's, at your fingertips
First for your feast
Glowing with health, brimming with flavor
It's making news, it's making friends
Let's ask Mother if we can have it for lunch
Like more time to tend your flowers? Campbell's soups can save you hours
A lordly touch for simple menus
An old-time soup hits an all-time high
One hot dish and no hot kitchen
Reach for Campbell's. It's right on your shelf
A soup in search of an appetite
Soup is good food
The soup most folks like best
The soup Mother gave up making
A soup that makes meal-planning easy
A taste of "June in January"
They always eat better when you remember the soup
21 kinds--12¢ per can
You are secretary of the interior

Campbell's Corn Flakes
Fresh as the morning

Campbell's tomato juice
A STOP to thirst, a STEP to health
Tomatoes, plump, firm, ruddy and ready

Campbell's tomato soup
How to TREAT guests

Campfire Girls
    WoHeLo
The campus king
    Lakeland Sportswear
Can be removed in thirty seconds
    Goodyear Auto Tire
Can Manufacturers Institute
    No other container protects
        like the can
The can opener people
    Dazey Products Co.
Can speed the nation's freight
    Timken Roller Bearing Co.
Can you afford not to be a
        member of the Club?
    Diners Club International
Canada Dry ginger ale
    America sparkles with Can-
        ada Dry
    It keeps your ginger up
    Mellow as the greeting of
        old friends
Canada Paint
    Quality in every drop
Canadair Challenger jet aero-
        plane
    The all-new business jets
    Built with today's technol-
        ogy from the ground up
    We challenge any business
        jet to match it
Canadian Club whiskey
    "The Best in The House"
        in 87 lands
    In 87 lands no other whis-
        key tastes like Canadian
        Club
Canadian Fairbanks-Morse & Co.
    In the service of industry
Canadian Fairbanks-Morse & Co.
    See also: Fairbanks-
        Morse & Co.
Canadian Industrial Alcohol Co.
    At your call with alcohol
Canadian National Railway
    Largest railway system in
        America
    The railway to everywhere
        in Canada
Canadian Pacific Air Lines
    The friendly way, C. P. A.
Canadian Pacific Railway
    Holiday all the way with
        Canadian Pacific Rail-
        way
    Spans the world

World's most complete trans-
        portation system
Canadian Pacific Steamship &
        Railroad Co.
    One management, ship and
        shore
    See this world before the
        next
    Take the sheltered route to
        Europe
    World's greatest travel sys-
        tem
Canadian Silk Products, Ltd.
    World's most beautiful stock-
        ings
Canadian Steamship Lines, Ltd.
    Niagara to the sea
    A thousand miles of travel,
        a thousand thrills of
        pleasure
Canadian Westinghouse Company
    Everything electrical for
        home and industry
Canadian Westinghouse Company.
    See also: Westinghouse
    Electric Corp.
Canaries, the only pets that sing
    The R. T. French Co.
Canby Co.
    Coffee, the perfect drink
Cancer harms elderly and tired
        employees remorselessly
    Nelots Sanatorium
Candid
    Candid Announces Nation's
        Doings In Details
Candid Announces Nation's Do-
        ings In Details
    Candid
Candies of character
    Wallace & Co.
Candies of distinction
    Brown & Haley
Candies of distinctive quality
    Tiffin Products, Inc.
Candy and Ice Cream
    The text book of the con-
        fectionery trade
Candy aristocrats
    Block Candy Co.
Candy Butcher Shops, Inc.
    The candy with a smile
Candy delicacy
    J. H. Slingerland
Candy has energy and taste
    Rebbor Candies

73

Candy makers to the American
    nation
    Curtis Candy Co.
The candy-mint alkalizer
    Alkaid
Candy of distinction
    Brown & Haley
The candy of good taste
    MacDonald's Candy Shops,
    Inc.
The candy of the South
    Nunnally Co.
The candy mint with the hole
    Life Savers candy
The candy store candy
    Brach's candies
The candy with a hole
    Wint-o-Green
The candy with a smile
    Candy Butcher Shops, Inc.
Canfield Lumber & Supply Co.
    We can help you build
    your dreams
Canfield Oil Co.
    The knock-out fuel, nox
    out nox
The canned dog food without the
    can
    Gaines-burgers
Canned food is grand food
    American Can Co.
Canners. See: Cahners
Cannon. See also: Canon
Cannon Mills, Inc.
    Bathtime story with a happy
        ending
    Bright-keyed shades in
        thirsty textures
    Cannon percale sheets give
        you up-in-the-clouds
        luxury at down-to-earth
        prices
    The first name in towels is
        the last name in sheets
    Royal family of home
        fashions
    So easy to choose, so sure
        to please
    Step into a private realm
        where cares cannot
        trespass, where moss-
        soft towels wrap you
        in colorful caress
    Whatever the towel, it's a
        top value if the label
        says Cannon

Cannon nylon stockings
    Not just nylons, but Cannon
    nylons
    They're cobwebby wonders
Cannon percale sheets give you
        up-in-the-clouds luxury
        at down-to-earth prices
    Cannon Mills, Inc.
Cannon vacuum bottle
    Liquids or solids, they keep
    hot or cold
Cannot burn or explode
    Carbona Products Co.
Canon. See also: Cannon
Canon AP-500 electronic type-
        writer
    Simply brilliant
Canon camera
    Meets tomorrow's challenge
        today
    The official camera of the
        Chicago Cubs
    So advanced it's simple
Canon electronic calculators
    The professional calculators
        that never call it quits
    Where quality is the con-
        stant factor
Canon plain paper copier
    The good stuff. And nothing
        but
    Micronics makes it simple
Canterbury Tea
    Tea in the finest tradition
Canthrox Shampoo
    Less trouble than a trip to
        the hairdresser
Cantilever shoes
    Flexible for every comfort
    A flexible shoe for your
        flexible foot
Cantrece
    Rhymes with increase
Canzoneri's. See: Tony Can-
        zoneri's Country Club,
        Marlboro, N. Y.
Cap-R-Nap sail preservative
    It's not the first cost, it's
        the upkeep
"Cap" Resina tops them all
    Resina Automatic Machinery
        Co., Inc.
The cap with the handy lever
    Kork-N-Seal Closure
The cap with the little lever
    Williams Sealing Corp.

Capability has many faces at
  Boeing
    Boeing aircraft
CaPac automobile parts
    Maximum capacity
    Performance insurance
Capehart phonograph
    The incomparable Capehart
Capewell Mfg. Co.
    A fine tool at a fair price
Capital. See also: Capitol
Capital Insulation
    Put an overcoat on that
      chilly house
Capitalist tool
    Forbes
Capitalize on your opportunities
    General Electric Credit
      Corporation
Capitol. See also: Capital
Capitol of the world
    Capitol phonograph records
Capitol phonograph records
    Capitol of the world
Caporal. See: Sweet Caporal
      cigarettes
Capper's Farmer
    The magazine farm people
      believe in
Caprolan nylon
    The most colorful nylon
Captain Black smoking tobacco
    Never a bite in a bowl
Captain Morgan Spiced Rum
    For better tasting rum
      drinks
    What a delicious difference
      Captain Morgan Spiced
      Rum makes!
The car ahead? It's Oldsmobile
    Oldsmobile automobile
The car company of France
    Renault automobile
A car for every purse and pur-
      pose
    General Motors Corporation
The car of a thousand speeds
    Owen Magnetic Motor Car
The car of no regrets
    King automobile
The car of the year in eye ap-
      peal and buy appeal
    Studebaker automobile
Car plan management and leas-
      ing specialists
    Peterson, Howell and

  Heather
The car that did what couldn't be
      done
    Mercury automobile
The car that grows with the child
    Uajustit Car
The car that has everything
    Oldsmobile automobile
The car that is complete
    Chevrolet automobile
The car that marks my limit
    Reo automobile
The car that meets war-time re-
      quirements of economy
      and fuel conservation
    Doble-Detroit steam car
The car with a longer life
    Westcott automobile
The car with the foundation
    Commonwealth automobile
A car you can believe in
    Volvo automobile
Caradco, Inc.
    Manufacturers of creative
      building products
Caradine Hat Co.
    Coolest hat under the sun
    Ventilated straw hats
Carbaloy
    The hardest metal made by
      man
Carbola Chemical Co.
    The disinfecting white paint
    Paints and disinfects, dries
      white
Carbon dioxide, kills fire, saves
      lives
    C-O Two Fire Equipment Co.
Carbona Products Co.
    Cannot burn or explode
Carbonated with its own natural
      gas
    Apollinaris carbonated water
Carbondale Machine Co.
    Lowers the cost of making
      frost
Care for your bike and you'll
      never hike
    Shelby bicycle
Care to share
    The United Way
The care we take goes into all we
      bake
    Hostess baked goods
Carefree furniture
    Viko Furniture Corp.

Carelessness is the partner of
    sabotage
    Hartford Fire Insurance Co.
Caress bath oil
    The soft you can't get from
    soap
Carey Salt Co.
    Word to the wives is suffi-
    cient
A cargo of contentment in the
    bowl of any pipe
    Half & Half smoking tobacco
Carhartt. See: Hamilton Car-
    hartt overalls
Caritol
    Easy does it, no fishy
    taste, no bad after-
    taste
Carl. See also: Karl
Carl Zeiss, Inc.
    Birthplace and centre of
    modern optics
    Symbol of excellence in
    West German optics
Carling's Ale
    Born in Canada, now going
    great in the 48 states
    Dealer's choice
    It's better, not bitter
Carlisle Chemical Works, Inc.
    Special chemicals for indus-
    try
    Specialty chemicals for in-
    dustry
Carlisle Shoe Co.
    The prettiest thing on two
    feet
Carlisle single-ply roof
    The roof that's requested
    by name
Carlton cigarettes
    Lightest smoke of all
Carnation Albers cereals
    Yours for a good morning
Carnation condensed milk
    Carnation milk from con-
    tented cows
    From contented cows
    The milk every doctor knows
Carnation milk from contented
    cows
    Carnation condensed milk
Carnes Corporation
    Leaders go to Carnes for
    the newest in air dis-
    tribution equipment

Carnu auto polish
    Your car looks like new when
    you use Carnu
Carolina Mirror Corp.
    World's largest manufacturer
    of mirrors
Carpenter Library Organ
    Something entirely new!
    The aesthetic taste
    gratified!
Carpenter-Morton paints
    It's the finish that counts
Carpenter Steel Co.
    In a word, confidence
    The logical choice in special-
    ty steels
The carpet cleaning company
    women recommend
    Stanley Steemer
Carpets of distinction
    Patcraft Mills, Inc.
Carrier Corporation
    Air conditioning's first name
    Energy ideas at work
    Make every day a good day
    More people put their con-
    fidence in Carrier air
    conditioning than in any
    other make
    Weather makers to the world
    Yesterday's vision, today's
    achievement
Carrier Corporation. See also:
    Elliott Div., Carrier
    Corporation
Carries a message of speed,
    flexibility and service
    Biddle automobile
Carroll. See: Caryl
Carry. See also: Karry
Carry the weight, save freight
    Atlas Plywood Corp.
Carryall. See: Karriall
Cars of fine feather flock to-
    gether
    Lincoln automobile
Carson. See: Tonight show,
    featuring Johnny Carson
Carstairs White Seal whiskey
    Be choosey, not whoozy
    Blended whiskey of char-
    acter
    For the man who cares
    The man who cares says
    "Carstairs White Seal"
    We're all esteemed up

Carter carburetors
  Puts the steady hum in
    motordom
Carter overalls
  Watch the wear
Carter White Lead Co.
  Carter White Lead is con-
    centrated paint
  Easy to thin, tint and spread
  Houses painted with Carter
    White Lead stay painted
  The lead with the spread
  Paint your house to stay
    painted
  The white white lead
  Whiter, finer, softer, Carter
Carter White Lead is concentrated
    paint
  Carter White Lead Co.
Carter's Compound Extract
  Will cure a cold in one night
Carter's ink
  If someone makes it--we can
    mark it
  Writes a strong, rich blue
Carter's pills
  Wake up your liver
Carven Parfums
  High fashion in fragrance
    from France
Caryl Richards, Inc.
  Everyone knows if it's Caryl
    Richards, it is just won-
    derful for your hair
Cascade detergent
  The better buy
  Cascade eliminates drops
    that spot
  For virtually spotless dishes
  Give your dishwasher the
    best
Cascade eliminates drops that
    spot
  Cascade detergent
Cascarets laxative
  They work while you sleep
  Works while you sleep
Casco cement
  Glue without goo
  Sticks most everything
Case. See also: J. I. Case
    earth moving machines
Case fixtures
  Bringing beauty to bath-
    rooms
A case of Aetna is a case of

health
  Aetna Brewing Co.
A case of good judgment
  Edelweiss beer
Cashmere Bouquet soap
  Adorns your skin with the
    fragrance men love
  The country garden soap
    for the "country com-
    plexion"
  How many kisses in a cake
    of soap?
  The lovelier soap with the
    costlier perfume
  With the fragrance men love
Cashmere Bouquet talcum
  The body cosmetic
Cashmere Swim Suits
  Like swimming in your skin
Cassini. See: Oleg Cassini,
    Inc.
Cast. See: Kast-Iron Work
    Clothes
Castle furniture
  Buy Castle furniture for
    your castle
  Come take a trip around our
    Castle
Castlecliff, Inc.
  The talked-about jewelry
Castolay soap
  Finer than the finest castile
Castrol motor oil
  The motor oil that is engi-
    neered for today's small
    cars
  Quality is the best policy
Caswell Mfg. Co.
  Portable phonographs of dis-
    tinction
Caswell-Runyan chests
  A chest for every need
  A chest for every need, a
    chest for every purse
The cat food even finicky Morris
    can't resist
  9-Lives cat food
Catalina Swim Suits
  Be the belle of the beach
The catalog house
  McDade's mail order service
Cataract clothes washer
  Cataraction, the only real
    8-figure movement
Cataraction, the only real 8-
    figure movement

77

Cataract clothes washer
Catch them yourself or buy
    Fowler's
    Fowler Sea Products Co.
Caterers to the tobacco trade
    Dillon Supply Co.
Caterpillar Tractor Co.
    Better, quicker, cheaper
    Machines that build for a
        growing America
    Wheat for your bread,
        wealth for the nation
Cat's Paw rubber heel
    The heel with nine lives
    Save from the bottom up
The catsup with a kick
    Brooks catsup
The catsup with the big tomato
    taste
    Hunt Wesson Foods, Inc.
C'Bon sunglasses
    Don't say sunglasses--say
        C'Bon!
Ceco Weatherstrip Co.
    Keep the weather out
Celanese Corp.
    Add a fiber from Celanese
        and good things get
        better
    Contemporary fibers
    Your assurance that this
        fabric has been pre-
        tested for performance
        by Celanese
Celanese Plastics Co. Div.,
    Celanese Corp.
    Celanese plastics make a
        material difference
Celanese plastics make a material
    difference
    Celanese Plastics Co. Div.,
        Celanese Corp.
Celebrate the moments of your
    life
    Irish Mocha Mint
Celestialite Glass
    The light you can look at
        without hurting your
        eyes
Cellophane
    The best show window on
        earth
    Makes paper make money
        for you
    Protection you can see
        through

Reduces friction to a fraction
Reveals what it seals
Shows what it protects
Cellu-Craft Products Co.
    Packaging materials for Amer-
        ican industry
Celo Co. of America
    Mixes in any society
    You always pay more for the
        best
Celotex Corp.
    The mark of a good roof
    There is a use for Celotex
        in every building
Cement manufacturers for nearly
    a century
    Louisville Cement Co.
Centaur. See also: Center
The centaur ... your symbol of
    quality
    Rémy Martin cognac
Centel Corporation business tele-
    phone equipment
    The future is communica-
        tions. Centel is there
        already
Centennial Flouring Mills Co.
    Count on Centennial
Center. See also: Centaur
The center for international
    business
    Exxon Corporation
The center of scenic America
    Salt Lake City, Utah
Central Breweries, Inc.
    The next one tastes as good
        as the first
Central for St. Petersburg and
    its visitors
    Central National Bank &
        Trust Co.
Central Illinois Light Co.
    When you make your move--
        make sure it's a planned
        move
Central Manufacturers Mutual In-
    surance Co.
    Call Central
    A friendly company owned
        by its policyholders
    The trend is to Mutual
Central National Bank & Trust
    Co.
    Call on Central
    Central for St. Petersburg
        and its visitors

Central Pennsylvania's greatest
daily
Harrisburg Telegraph
Central Royal Beer
Give me another Central
Royal Beer
Central Soya Co., Inc.
The foodpower people
Central Steel & Wire Company
All-American since 1909
Central Telephone & Utilities
America's fifth largest tele-
phone company (And
growing fast!)
Come grow with us
Central Trust & Savings Co.
The bank where you feel
at home
Twenty-four years of tested
service
Centrum medicine
From A to zinc
More complete than other
leading brands
Century Boat Co.
Builder of fine inboard and
outboard boats
Century Electric Co.
SERVICE, in the broadest
sense, is the difference
Service is the difference
They keep a-running
A century of confidence
Roebling mining cables
A century of universal banking
Deutsche Bank
Ceramic Industry
Devoted to the manufacture
of glass, enamel white-
ware, refractory and
allied products
Cercle. See also: Circle
Cercle D'Or wine
Here's to your health and
happiness
The cereal that tastes like
powdered doughnuts
Donutz cereal
The cereal you can serve a
dozen ways
Shredded Wheat
Certain-teed roofing
Build on Certain-teed, the
well-known name
Build to endure
The certified analysis takes

the mystery out of paint
Country Gentleman paint
Certified Extracts, Inc.
The aristocrat of flavors
Certified on checks: Lawrence
on warehouse receipts
Lawrence Warehouse Co.
Certifies the most in dry cleaning
One Hour Martinizing
Certo
For better jams and jellies
Certs
Two mints in one
Cessna Aircraft Co.
Family car of the air
More people buy Cessna twins
than any other make
More people fly Cessna air-
planes than any other
make
Where your fiscal fitness be-
gins
Chace. See:
Chase
W. M. Chace Co.
Chafe-O-Tex
The year-round pantie
Chain Store Age
A monthly business paper
for chain store execu-
tives
The chains that have grown up
with the oil fields
Rex Chainbelt, Inc.
The chair that stands by itself
Stakmore Co., Inc.
Chairs for all business
Boling Chair Co.
Challenge Cleanable Collars
Challenge Cleanable Collars
save laundry dollars
Challenge Cleanable Collars save
laundry dollars
Challenge Cleanable Collars
Challenge Machinery Co.
It's a challenge
Challenge milk
Baby's milk must be safe
Builds robust bodies
Refreshing, invigorating,
strong; the last word
in Grade A
Challenges the elements
Friedman paint
Chambers Corp.
The world's finest gas

range
Champ Hats
  HAT ease on the home front
  Style that goes to your head
Champ-Items, Inc.
  Mention Champ items on
    every call
  Pocket-paying dividend
    prices
  The problem solver people
  When you have a service
    problem think of Champ-
    Items
The champagne music of Law-
    rence Welk
  Lawrence Welk's dance or-
    chestra
The champagne of bottle beer
  Miller High Life beer
The champagne of table waters
  Perrier table water
The "Champagne Touch"
  Moore-McCormack Lines,
    Inc.
Champale
  America's original sparkling
    malt liquor
Champion Animal Food Co.
  Our business is going to the
    dogs
Champion, best for all engines
  Champion spark plugs
The champion chip
  Ruffles potato chips
Champion Mfg. Co., Inc.
  Beauty mark of fine light-
    ing
Champion of blends
  Sportsman pipe mixture
Champion of pipes
  Sportsman pipe mixture
Champion Papers, Inc.
  Consider paper
  Consider the power of pa-
    per used with imagina-
    tion
Champion radio receiver
  The heart of the set
A champion resort
  Tony Canzoneri's Country
    Club, Marlboro, N. Y.
Champion spark plugs
  Champion, best for all
    engines
  Dependable for every
    engine

Dependable spark plugs
Follow the experts, demand
    Champion
The heart of a tune-up
Nothing sparks like a
    Champion
Spark plugs are the pulse of
    your engine
To feel new power, instantly,
    install new Champions
    now and every 10,000
    miles
To rid your car of motor
    "bugs" install a set of
    Champion plugs
To save gasoline keep your
    spark plugs clean
Use the spark plugs engineers
    use
Chancellor cigars
  That Chancellor taste
Chanel, Inc.
  The most treasured name in
    perfume
Chanel No. 5 perfume
  Every woman wants Chanel
    No. 5
Chanel No. 22 perfume
  The perfume of romance
Change for the better with Alcoa
    Aluminum
  Aluminum Company of Amer-
    ica
Change the "widow's mite" to the
    "widow's might"
  Mutual Life Insurance Co.
Change to Bond Street for frag-
    rant smoking
  Bond Street pipe tobacco
Change to Reis
  Reis underwear
Change work to play three times
    a day
  Standard Electric Stove Co.
Change your mirror from a leerer
    to a cheerer
  Arrow shirts
Changes those bulges into curves
  P. N. Corsets
Changing corporate banking from
    California
  Crocker-Citizens National
    Bank
Changing the way you trade fu-
    tures
  Lind-Waldock commodity

brokers
Channel 7 for what's worth
    watching
    TV station WJZ-TV, New
    York City
Chap Stick Co.
    Specialists in skin care
Chapped hands make a man see
    red
    Hinds Honey and Almond
    Cream
Chappel Bros. dog food
    Golden cakes of energy
Charbert's Perfume
    Perfume that spins a moment
    into a memory
Charcoal mellowed drop by drop
    Jack Daniel's whiskey
Charles. See also: Chas.
Charles A. Eaton Co.
    Fine bootmakers since 1876
Charles Atlas correspondence
    body building course
    I was once a 97 pound
    weakling
Charles Beseler Co.
    Today's finest designed for
    tomorrow's needs
Charles Daly
    The custom crafted shotgun
Charles Schwab & Co., Inc.
    America's largest discount
    brokerage firm
    The #1 discount broker
    serving the Midwest
Charm that attracts others comes
    from within
    Sunkist oranges
Charm underlift brassiere
    The inner secret of outer
    beauty
Charmese foundations
    For the modern miss
Charmin bathroom tissue
    Don't squeeze the Charmin
    More squeezably soft than
    ever
    So squeezably soft
    The squeezing gets you;
    the softness keeps you
The Charter Company
    The company to watch in
    energy, insurance and
    communications
Chartreuse
    Have the genius to chill it

Chas. See also: Charles
Chas. Bruning Co.
    The most beautiful copies of
    all
Chase. See also: W. M. Chace
    Co.
Chase and Sanborn coffee
    Beginning a second century
    of leadership
    It's dated
    Look for the date on the tin
    Our coffees have a national
    reputation representing
    the finest grown
Chase and Sanborn iced coffee
    Makes hot days cool
Chase Brass & Copper Co.
    You couldn't have a sounder
    pipe dream
Chase Candy Co.
    Taste the difference
The Chase is on
    Chase Manhattan Bank
Chase Manhattan Bank
    The Chase is on
    First in loans to business
    and industry
    In the race against time, the
    Chase is on
    A major leader, worldwide,
    under all market condi-
    tions
    Professional relationship
    banking in over 100
    countries through a
    mature network of
    branches and affiliates
    We run forums for corporate
    America
    You have a friend at Chase
    Manhattan
Chases chills from cold corners
    Perfection oil heaters
Chases darkness
    American Gas Machine Co.
Chases dirt
    Old Dutch Cleanser
Chasing the sun, you've gained
    3 hours on the sun that
    hangs high over the
    Pacific
    Boeing aircraft
Chatelaine Silk Hosiery
    For sheer loveliness wear
    Chatelaine Silk Hosiery
    The hosiery of distinction

Chatham blankets
    To look well and feel well,
        sleep well
Cheap enough to throw away
    Kotex sanitary napkins
Cheaper insurance is easier to
        purchase but harder
        to collect
    Standard Accident Insurance
        Co.
Cheaper to dye than to buy
    Dyola Dyes
Cheapest and best
    New York Times
The cheapest health insurance in
        the world
    Smith Brothers cough drops
Checks first with the finest
    General Oil Burner
Checks odors instantly
    Quell household deodorant
Checks pyorrhea
    Forhan's tooth paste
Cheer detergent
    The hot, warm and cold
        water detergent
    Tough on dirt even in
        cooler water
    You can trust today's
        Cheer
Cheer up, face
    Burma-Shave shaving cream
Cheerful as its name
    Old Sunny Brook whiskey
Cheerios cereal
    We made it low in sugar
        and kids made it No. 1
The cheese most people like
    Swift's Brookfield cheese
The cheese with the paper be-
        tween the slices
    N. Dorman and Co.
Cheese: zest at its best
    American Dairy Association
The chef's flavor in home cook-
        ing
    Kitchen Bouquet
Cheltenham Beef Fibrine Dog
        Cake
    The best food for dogs
        made. For all kinds
        of dogs
Chem. See: Kem-Tone
Chemical Bank New York Trust
        Co.
    The bank that works

hardest for you
The Chemical solution:
    ChemLink for multina-
        tionals
Chemical takes you beyond
    tradition
Leader in worldwide cash
    management
Chemical Div., General Mills, Inc.
    Plus values
Chemical Div., General Mills, Inc.
    See also: General Mills,
    Inc.
Chemical Div., PPG Industries,
    Inc.
    Basic chemicals and cost-
        cutting ideas
Chemical Div., PPG Industries,
    Inc. See also: PPG
    Industries, Inc.
Chemical, rubber and plastic
        products worldwide
    Uniroyal, Inc.
The Chemical solution: ChemLink
        for multinationals
    Chemical Bank New York
        Trust Co.
Chemical takes you beyond tradi-
        tion
    Chemical Bank New York
        Trust Co.
Chemical Week
    Industry spokesman to CPI
        management
Chemicals for those who serve
        man's well being
    Pfizer Pharmaceuticals
Chemicals indispensible to indus-
        try
    Dow Chemical Co.
Chemico tire patch
    It's patch and go with
        Chemico
Chemistry working for you
    Henkel Group
Chen Yu Lipstick
    Your heart will lose its mind
Cheney Cravats
    They tie well, they wear
        well
Cheney Talking Machine Co.
    Cheney tone is nature's
        own
    The longer you play it, the
        sweeter it grows
Cheney tone is nature's own

Cheney Talking Machine
Co.
Cheramy perfume
A sheer veil of scented mist
Cherished as one of the world's
seven great fragrances
Intimate perfume
Cherristock liqueur
The aristocrat of liqueurs
Chesapeake and Ohio Railway
America's sleepheart
Now I lay me down to ...
sleep like a kitten
See the FIRST of America
first
Sleep like a kitten, arrive
fresh as a daisy
Chesapeake and Ohio Railway.
See also: Chessie System Railroads
Chesebrough-Ponds, Inc.
Consistent profitable growth
... through leadership
brands
Chess. See: Mary Chess perfume
Chessie for the 80's
Chessie System Railroads
Chessie knows the territory
Chessie System Railroads
Chessie System Railroads
Chessie for the 80's
Chessie knows the territory
Share the load and save the
expense
Chessie System Railroads. See
also: Chesapeake and
Ohio Railway
A chest for every need
Caswell-Runyan chests
A chest for every need, a chest
for every purse
Caswell-Runyan chests
Chester Suspender Co.
Marry your trousers to the
Century-Brace
Chesterfield cigarettes
Always buy Chesterfield
For real smoking pleasure
In my case it's Chesterfield
In the fresh white package
or the clean white
carton
Right combination, world's
best tobaccos properly
aged

Such popularity must be de-
served
The sum-total of smoking
pleasure
Tastes great ... yet smokes
so mild
They're milder; they taste
better
They satisfy
They satisfy and yet they're
mild
Chesterfield King cigarettes
Tastes great ... tastes mild
Chevrolet, and only Chevrolet,
is first
Chevrolet automobile
Chevrolet automobile
All that's best at lowest
cost
All that's best at lowest
price
All the way with Chevrolet
Beautiful beyond belief
Big-car quality at lowest
cost
The car that is complete
Chevrolet, and only Chevro-
let, is first
Chevrolet is taking charge
Chevy makes good things
happen
The complete car, completely
new
Drive away in comfort, drive
back in safety
Economize without any com-
promise
Eye it! Try it! Buy it!
For economical transportation
It pays to buy the leader
and get the leading buy
It's wise to choose a six!
No one can do it like Chevy
can do it
The only complete low-priced
car
Quality at low cost
Save the wheels that serve
America
Where friend meets friend
Why pay more? Why accept
less?
The world's most luxurious
low-priced automobile
You'll be ahead with Chev-
rolet

You'll go for it when you
see how it goes for you
Chevrolet is more truck ... day
in, day out
Chevrolet trucks
Chevrolet is taking charge
Chevrolet automobile
Chevrolet Monte Carlo automobile
A matter of personal pride
Monte Carlo is your car
Chevrolet Motor Div., General
Motors Corporation
Biggest name in fleet cars
and trucks
Putting you first, keeps
us first
Chevrolet trucks
Chevrolet is more truck ...
day in, day out
The lowest ton-mile cost
provided by Chevrolet
trucks
Quality trucks always cost
less
You can go a long way with
the fleet leader
The chevron--the sign of excel-
lence
Standard Oil Co. of Cali-
fornia
Chevy makes good things happen
Chevrolet automobile
Chew it after every meal
Wrigley's chewing gum
Chew Mail Pouch tobacco
Mail Pouch chewing tobacco
Chew with a purpose
Oralgene chewing gum
The chewing digestant
Bi-Car chewing gum
The chewing gum bon bon
Vi-lets
The chewing laxative
Feen-a-Mint
Chicago American
A good newspaper
Chicago and Eastern Illinois
Railroad
The service railroad of
America
Chicago Bridge and Iron Co.
Designs them ... builds
them!
Chicago, Burlington and Quincy
Railroad
Everywhere West

On time every day is the
Burlington way
Chicago Chamber of Commerce
What Chicago makes, makes
Chicago
Chicago Chemical Co.
Treat your water right and
it will treat you right
Chicago Daily News
First in Chicago
Chicago Engineering Works
HEAD work always wins on
pay day
HEAD work always wins over
HARD work on pay day
Chicago Evening Post
Chicago's best and cleanest
paper
Chicago Illustrated News
Chicago's only illustrated
tabloid newspaper
Chicago lock
Utmost security, minimum
cost
Chicago Mercantile Exchange
Man does not live by stocks
and bonds alone
The more you know the bet-
ter we look
Chicago Merchandise Mart
There's no place like this
showplace!
Chicago Metallic Mfg. Co.
Better pans for better bak-
ing
Chicago Paper Co.
The complete paper house
Chicago Printed String Co.
The gift tie of a nation
Chicago Rawhide Mfg. Co.
Quality seals build the repu-
tation of professional
mechanics
The seal mechanics see most,
use most
Chicago Roller Skate Co.
The roller skate with three
lives
Roll on rubber
Chicago School of Nursing
Why not be a nurse?
Chicago Tribune
Grow with Chicago
We give you a better look
The world's greatest news-
paper

Chicago Wheel & Mfg. Co.
  Wheels of fortune
Chicago's best and cleanest paper
  Chicago Evening Post
Chicago's only illustrated tabloid
  newspaper
  Chicago Illustrated News
Chicken of the Sea tuna
  The brand that made tuna
  famous
  Every bite a rarebit
  Makes every meal a company
  meal
  Makes fish day a red letter
  day
  Packed with the zest of the
  sea
Chief of the mouldings
  Ponderosa Mouldings, Inc.
Chief of the sixes
  Pontiac automobile
Chief of the tire tribe
  Standard Four Tire Co.
Chief of West Virginia high vola-
  tile coals
  Red Jacket Coal Sales Co.
Chiffon margarine
  So soft ... it comes in a
  tub
Chiffon Soap Flakes
  No purer soap was ever
  made
Child Life
  The children's own magazine
  Reaches the mother through
  her child
The child who reads is the child
  who leads
  Book House for Children
Children
  The magazine for parents
Children cry for it
  Fletcher's Castoria
Children like it better than milk
  Ghirardelli's hot chocolate
The children's laxative
  Fletcher's Castoria
The children's own magazine
  Child Life
Childs. See also: G. W.
  Childs cigar
The child's magazine
  John Martin's Book
Child's Restaurants
  The nation's host from
  coast to coast

Chillicothe Paper Co.
  Chillicothe papers make the
  best impressions
Chillicothe papers make the best
  impressions
  Chillicothe Paper Co.
Chilton pen
  Lasting symbol of esteem
China by Iroquois for the hosts
  of America
  Iroquois China Co.
The Chinese food that swings
  American
  La Choy Chinese food
Chinwah toilet preparations
  Distinguished by its patron-
  age
Chisholm-Ryder Co.
  The best of everything
  The best of everything for
  the food processor
Chivers & Sons marmalade
  The aristocrat of the break-
  fast table
Chix diapers
  The difference is in the
  weave
Chloraceptic throat medicine
  Fast relief for sore throat
  pain
Chlorax toothpaste
  The smooth toothpaste
Chlorine ointment, better than
  iodine
  Minox Chemical Corp.
Chock Full O' Nuts restaurants
  Untouched by human hands
The chocolate candy with the
  cookie crunch
  Twix candy bars
The chocolate candy bar that
  lasts a long time
  Tootsie Rolls candy
The chocolated laxative
  Ex-Lax laxative
The chocolates of good taste
  Van Duyn chocolates
The chocolates with the wonder-
  ful centres
  Liggett's Chocolates
Choice. See also: Lady's Choice
  deodorant
Choice of better mechanics
  Snap-On Tools Corp.
The choice of businessmen lets
  you choose with con-

fidence
  Aetna Insurance Co.
The choice of champions
  Kendall motor oil
  Western Cartridge Co.
Choice of good judges
  Three Feathers whiskey
The choice of good painters
  Merkin paint
The choice of noted music critics
  All-American radio receiver
The choice of successful men
  Blackstone cigar
The choice of the crew and the
    big boss, too
  Ohio Brass Co.
Choice of the masters
  Kilgen organ
Choice of three generations
  Brown & Sharpe hardware
The choice when you want qual-
    ity, too
  All-Steel Equipment, Inc.
The choice you make once for a
    lifetime
  Wallace Silversmiths Div.,
    The Hamilton Watch Co.
The choicest product of the
    brewer's art
  Falstaff beer
Choose your piano as the artists
    do
  Baldwin pianos
Choose your vacation from the
    entire nation
  United Air Lines, Inc.
Choosing the right kind of life
    insurance isn't getting
    any easier
  The Bankers Life
Choosy mothers choose Jif
  Jif peanut butter
Chosen by the majority
  Fordson governors
Chosen for lasting loveliness
  Orient hosiery
Christian Brothers wines
  Wines of California since
    1882
Christian Herald
  More than a magazine, an
    institution
Christian Science Monitor
  An international daily
    newspaper
Christmas greeting cards of

character
  Rust Craft greeting cards
Christmas time is Guinness time
  Guinness ale
Christy Anatomical Saddle
  Meets every requirement of
    the modern cyclist
A chronicle of current Masonic
    events
  Square and Compass
Chrysler. See also: Kreisler
  Watch Band
Chrysler Airtemp
  Automatically yours
Chrysler automobile
  As fine as money can build
  Fast-stepping stride, a mar-
    velous ride
  No priorities on color and
    charm
  San Francisco discovers a
    Golden Gait
Chrysler Corporation
  You get good things first
    from Chrysler Corp.
Chrysler Imperial automobile
  It's time for Imperial
Chrysler marine engines
  Built to live in the water
Chrysler New Yorker automobile
  Very elegant. Very exclu-
    sive. Very Fifth Avenue
Chubb Group of Insurance Com-
    panies
  Just another way of saying
    "versicherung"
Chuck Wagon dog food
  The great taste of stew that
    brings dogs running
Chuckles
  Good candy for all the family
Church. See: C. F. Church
  Div., American Stand-
  ard, Inc.
The Churchman
  The leading journal of the
    Episcopal Church
  A liberal church journal
Churned from sweet (not sour)
    cream
  Land o' Lakes butter
Cifaldi's Villa Nova restaurant,
    Indianapolis
  An eating place of distinc-
    tion
The cigar made with good judg-

ment
Tom Keene cigar
The cigar that breathes
Roi-Tan Little Cigars
The cigar that never lasts long
enough
Antonio y Cleopatra cigars
A cigarette container that lights
'em for you
Splitdorf Cigalite
Cincinnati Ball Crank Co.
More than a bumper
The style that makes 'em
look at your car
Cincinnati Electrical Products Co.
No damp amps
Cincinnati Enquirer
Goes to the home, stays in
the home
Cincinnati Post
Southern Ohio's greatest
newspaper
Cinco cigar
The holiday cigar at a week-
day price
Cine Kodak
Life is a movie; Cine Kodak
gets it all
When your picture moves,
it lives
Cine Kodak. See also: Kodak
Cinnamon spice and everything
nice, that's what these
rolls are made of
Jane Parker Rolls
CinZano vermouth
When you mix with CinZano
you mix with the best
Circle. See also: Cercle
Circle Design and Mfg. Corp.
Creates new dimensions in
automatic packaging
machinery!
Circle 12 books
Balanced reading for dis-
criminating people
Remember, for better read-
ing it's "Circle 12"
books
Circular printers of the nation
Everybody's Publishing Co.
Citi. See also:
City
city
The Citi at your front door
Citibank, New York City

The Citi never sleeps
Citibank, New York City
The Citi of tomorrow
Citibank Global Electronic
Banking
Citibank Global Electronic Banking
The Citi of tomorrow
Citibank, New York City
The Citi at your front door
The Citi never sleeps
Precise banking worldwide
When it comes to making
your savings earn more,
the Citi never sleeps
You are the main component
Citicorp. Travel the world with
us
Citicorp travelers checks
Citicorp travelers checks
Citicorp. Travel the world
with us
Cities Service Company
Energy chemicals
If it's Cities Service, it has
to be good
A natural resource company
On top of the problem, part
of the solution
Cities Service gasoline
All the way from the refin-
ery to your farm
Give your car an extra year
of youth
A citizen, wherever we serve
Georgia Railway & Power Co.
Citizens & Southern National Bank
The corporate bank that
lives in the South
Citizens Trust Co.
Distance is no barrier to our
service
Citrus Hill orange juice
A year of sunshine in every
sip
City (city). See also: Citi
A city at your door
International Harvester
trucks
City convenience ... RFD
Rapid Thermogas Co.
A City Investing Company
Home Insurance Co.
City Investing Company
City Investing fits together
for growth
City Investing fits together for

87

growth
City Investing Company
The city that does things
Norfolk, Va.
The city that knows how
San Francisco, Calif.
The civilized way of shaving
Schick electric shaver
Clabber Girl Baking Powder
Right in the mixing bowl,
light from the oven
Claim your spot. Tide gets it
clean
Tide laundry detergent
Clairex Corp.
The "light" touch in auto-
mation and control
Clairol, Inc.
The colorful shampoo
Does she ... or doesn't
she?
The girl with the beautiful
face
Hair color so natural only
her hairdresser knows
for sure
Naturally, with Clairol
Only her hairdresser knows
for sure
She has it made
Clan Crest sportswear
Fabrics used in the most
wanted women's and
children's sportswear
Clancy Publications, Inc.
We print it before it hap-
pens
Clapp's Baby Foods
The FIRST baby foods
Millions of babies have been
raised on Clapp's Baby
Foods
Strained for babies, chopped
for young children
Clarence Saunders retail grocery
stores
Sole owner of my name
Clark. See also:
J. L. Clark Mfg. Co.
James Clark Distilling
Corp.
Clark candy bar
A great name for quality
candy
Pure as the mountain air
Clark Equipment Company

Clark gets it done
Clark is material handling
Clark equipment is found
only on good motor
trucks
Clark Equipment Company. See
also: Tyler Refrigera-
tion Div., Clark Equip-
ment Company
Clark equipment is found only on
good motor trucks
Clark Equipment Company
Clark gets it done
Clark Equipment Company
Clark Harp Mfg. Co.
Easy to play, pay and carry
Clark is material handling
Clark Equipment Company
Clark Metal Grave Vault Co.
The finest tribute ... the
most trusted protection
A gift of the centuries
That they may rest in peace
Clark's Teaberry Gum
Packed with good taste
Peppermint that is pepper-
mint
The clasmic clay
Boncilla Beautifier
Class in a glass
Griesedieck Bros. Brewery
Co.
Class magazine in a class by it-
self
Harper's Bazaar
Class without gas
Buick diesel-powered auto-
mobile
A classic in wood
Kaywoodie pipe
The classic magazine of the space
age. Join us in the
future ... now!
Omni
The classic name in the building
field
Bird and Son, Inc.
Classics of optical precision
Schneider lenses
Claxton's. See also: Klaxon
Claxton's Patent Ear Cap
For remedying prominent
ears, preventing dis-
figurements in later
life
Clayton Inn, St. Louis, Mo.

That's Clayton class
Clean. See also:
   Kleen Kup
   Mr. Clean cleaning fluid
Clean across the country
   Texaco restrooms
Clean around the world
   Empire Brush Works
Clean breath hours longer
   Listerine mouth wash
Clean clear through
   Continental Distilling Corp.
The clean, convenient fuel
   Sterno
Clean floors reflect clean business
   Finnell System, Inc.
Clean hair means a healthy scalp
   Ace combs
A clean nation has ever been a strong nation
   Sapolio
A clean service for every customer
   Paper Cup & Container Institute
A clean service for every customer every time
   Paper Cup & Container Institute
A clean tooth never decays
   Pro-Phy-Lac-Tic toothbrush
Clean up with S. O. S.   It's easy
   S. O. S. Magic Scouring Pads
The clean way to kill dirty rats and mice
   d-Con Rat Killer
Cleans a million things
   Oakite
Cleans all the way through
   Era laundry detergent
Cleans as it fizzes
   Fizzadent denture cleaner
Cleans as it lubricates
   Havoline motor oil
Cleans as it polishes
   O-Cedar polish
Cleans as it shines
   O-Cedar polish
Cleans easier, works faster, won't scratch
   Sunbrite Cleanser
Cleans glass, plus a whole lot more!

Glass Plus glass cleaner
Cleans hands clean
   Gresolvent
Cleans hands cleaner
   D. Lorah cleaner
Cleans in a jiff
   Jif soap flakes
Cleans inside, outside and between the teeth
   Western toothbrush
Cleans like a white tornado!
   Ajax cleanser
Cleans, relusters and demoths upholstered furniture
   Keyspray
Cleans so well so easily, and for so little
   Mystic Foam upholstery cleaner
Cleans--softens--controls static
   Yes detergent
Cleans teeth all around
   Sealastic tooth brush
Cleans teeth the right way
   Colgate's dental cream
Cleans the oil that cleans the motor
   Fram oil filter
Cleans with a caress
   Conti olive oil castile soap
Cleans without beating and pounding
   United Electric vacuum cleaner
Cleans without scrubbing
   Tank II toilet bowl cleaner
Cleans your breath while it cleans your teeth
   Colgate's dental cream
Cleanses the pores and softens the skin
   Polar Ice Laboratories
Cleansing. See also: Klenzing
Cleansing tissue soft, toilet tissue firm
   Soft-Weve bathroom tissue
Clear and colder, says the weatherman; Snug and warmer says Johns-Manville
   Johns-Manville Corporation
Clear as a bell
   Sonora phonograph
A clear, distinctive voice in the Information Age
   United Telecommunications,

Inc.

Clear heads call for Calvert
Calvert "Extra" whiskey
Clear heads choose Calvert
Calvert "Extra" whiskey
Clear to the ear
Magnavox radio receiver
Clear to the very edge
Tillyen lenses
Clears the skin
Pompeian Massage Cream
Clears your head. Clears your
chest
Head & Chest cold medicine
Cletrac tractor
The Cletrac way makes
farming pay
The Cletrac way makes farming
pay
Cletrac tractors
Cleveland Plain Dealer
Largest morning and Sun-
day circulation in Ohio
No matter what kind or
what priced merchandise
you make, the Plain
Dealer alone will sell it
Cleveland Press
First in Cleveland
The Cleveland Range Co.
Headquarters for steam-
cookers
Cleveland-Sandusky Brewing
Corp.
The All-American ale
The All-American beer
Cleveland tractor
Greatest power on earth
Lowest cost per yard, per
hour, or per mile
So easy a child can steer
it
Cleveland Trust Co.
The bank for all the peo-
ple
The bank that makes things
happen
Cleveland Worm & Gear Co.
America's pioneers in worm
gears
Cleveland's Baking Powder
For beginners or experts
Cleveland's better food markets
Kroger supermarkets
Cleveland's favorite brew since
1862

Leisy beer
Click Magazine
At home in more than a mil-
lion homes
Climaco Corp.
Every day a COMFORTABLE
day
Climalene
It cleans so quick
It makes dishes wink and
twinkle
Cling Free washing aid
Fights odor between wash-
ings
The clinkerless grate
Argand wood-burning stoves
Clinton. See also: De Witt
Clinton Hotel, Albany,
N. Y.
Clinton Nickel Safety Pins
Used as a skirt supporter
and dress looper they
have no equal
Clipper Belt Lacer Co.
The connecting link between
power and production
Cliquot Club ginger ale
The flavor-aged ginger ale
Ginger ale with a piquant
personality
Unparch that throat
The clocks that most people want
most
Heralder clocks
Clopay window shades
Beautiful windows at low
cost
Clorets
The breath deodorant
Clorox bleach
America's favorite bleach
and household disin-
fectant
Clorox takes away dirt
detergents leave behind
First in quality, performance,
preference
A real bargain
The white line is the Clorox
line
Clorox takes away dirt deter-
gents leave behind
Clorox bleach
The close electric shave
Norelco Rototrack Shaver
The closest thing yet to a

perfect car
  Volvo 760 GLE automobile
The closet with a slant
  Naturo water closet
Clothes do help you win, dry
  clean them oftener
  American Laundry Machinery
  Co.
Clothes that enhance your public
  appearance
  Worsted-Tex clothing
Clothiers since 1888
  Norman Hilton & Co. men's
  clothing
Clover Leaf Milling Co.
  Four stars in the milky way
Clubs of character for every
  golfer
  Vulcan Golf Co.
Cluett, Peabody Co., Inc.
  Be suspicious!
The coach to judge others by
  Blue Bird Wanderlodge
Coal lights our nights and
  brightens our future
  Utah Power & Light Co.
The coal that satisfies
  Lehigh Valley Coal Sales
  Co.
Coal--the modern energy miracle
  that's as old as the
  hills
  American Coal Mining Indus-
  try
Coast soap
  No other soap picks you up
  quite like Coast--the
  eye-opener
  No tired is too tired for
  Coast
Coast to coast overnight
  American Airlines, Inc.
Coast to coast to coast
  National Airlines, Inc.
Coast to coast, we give the most
  Milner Hotels
The coat rack people
  Vogel-Peterson Co.
The coat with nine lives
  National Paint Co.
Coatings, colors and chemicals
  for industry
  Sherwin-Williams Co.
The coats for every wear,
  everywhere
  International Duplex Coat

Co.
Cobb's whiskey
  The master blend
Coca Cola Co. of Canada
  The rest-pause that re-
  freshes
Coca Cola soft drink
  Coke adds life
  Coke is it!
  Delicious and refreshing
  Drink Coca Cola
  The global high sign
  Have a Coke and smile
  It had to be good to get
  where it is
  The pause that refreshes
  Refresh yourself
  Things go better with Coke
  When you land at Atlanta
  we'll be waiting with a
  smile
  You trust its quality
Cocker. See also: Crocker
Cocker Machine and Foundry Co.
  The leader around the world
Cocoa Puffs cereal
  I'm really hung up on Cocoa
  Puffs
The cocoa with more chocolate
  flavor
  Baker's Breakfast Cocoa
The cocoa with that chocolaty
  taste
  Runkel Bros. cocoa
Cocomalt
  Adds 70% more nourishment
  to milk
  A delicious food drink
  If your child gets on your
  nerves, get on to Coco-
  malt
The cod liver oil with the plus
  value
  Scott's Emulsion
Code-a-phone telephone answer-
  ing equipment
  America's getting the mes-
  sage
Codo Manufacturing Co.
  The line with the carbon
  gripper
Coe-Stapley pump
  The pump that oils itself
Coffee. See also: Kaffee Hag
The coffee-er coffee
  Savarin coffee

91

Coffee from the magic mountains
  Folger's ground coffee
The coffee lover's decaffeinated
    coffee
  High Point coffee
Coffee--95% of the caffeine re-
    moved
  Kaffee Hag
The coffee of inspiration
  Schwabacher Bros.
Coffee rich enough to be served
    in San Francisco's fin-
    est restaurants
  Folger's Coffee Crystals
The coffee served at the
    Waldorf-Astoria
  Savarin coffee
The coffee that lets you sleep
  Kaffee Hag
The coffee that's "always good"
  Schwabacher Bros.
Coffee, the American drink
  Joint Coffee Trade Publicity
    Committee
Coffee, the perfect drink
  Canby Co.
The coffee with the flavor ad-
    vantage
  Folger's ground coffee
The coffee without a regret
  Barrington Hall Coffee
The coffee you don't have to
    make
  G. Washington Coffee
Coffield clothes washer
  Even the collars and cuffs
    are clean
The cognac brandy for every
    occasion
  Martel
Cohler. See also:
  Kohler
  Peter Cailler Kohler Swiss
    Chocolate Co.
Cohler pajamas
  Sweet dreaming from yawn
    to dawn
Coin-operated laundry store
  Launderette
Coke adds life
  Coca Cola soft drink
Coke is it!
  Coca Cola soft drink
Cold and silent as a winter
    night
  Sparton refrigerator

Cold-Free Bedtime Clothes
  Draft exempt
Cold or hot, Spam hits the spot
  Spam prepared meat
Cold Spring Brewing Co.
  Tasting is believing
Colder-than-ice refrigeration
  Iron Mountain Co.
Coldmax cold reliever
  Maximum strength cold relief
    for every cold symptom
Coldwell Lawn Mower Co.
  As easy to operate as a
    vacuum cleaner
Coleco
  The arcade game you can
    take home with you
Coleman Co., Inc.
  Cook stove and gas plant
    all in one
  Foremost name in indoor
    comfort
  Gas service for cooking, no
    matter where you live
  Greatest name in the great
    outdoors. Foremost
    name in indoor comfort
  It circulates, it radiates
  Light, heat and cook the
    Coleman way
  The light of a thousand uses
  The light of the night
  The light that always shines
    welcome
  Makes its own gas, use it
    anywhere
  A penny a night for the
    finest light
  The smooth way to rough it
  The sunshine of the night
  They finish the day for the
    sun
Colfanite finishing material
  A liquid finish that decor-
    ates as it preserves
  Things look bright with
    Colfanite
Colgate's dental cream
  Cleans teeth the right way
  Cleans your breath while
    it cleans your teeth
  It cleans your breath while
    it cleans your teeth
  Maximum fluoride protection
    in a great-tasting gel
  Now, no bad breath behind

his sparkling smile
Removes cause of tooth de-
cay
Sue sings before seven
Colgate's refill shaving stick
The only refill shaving
stick
Colgate's Ribbon Dental Cream
Comes out like a ribbon;
lies flat on the brush
Twice a day, and before
every date
Colgate's shaving cream
Softens the beard at the
base
College Humor
The best comedy in America
College is America's best friend
Council for Financial Aid
to Education
Collier's
The national weekly
Collin Armstrong, Inc.
The right angle in adver-
tising
Collins and Aikman. See:
Painter Carpet Mills,
Inc., Div. Collins and
Aikman
Collins & Wright salt shaker tops
The top that sells the bot-
tom since 1838
Collins electric blanket
Sleep electrically and enjoy
the difference
Collins Eureka Pad
Preserve your horse's feet
Collins Radio Co.
A world of experience
Colombo. See: Leopold Colom-
bo, Inc.
Colonel Sanders Kentucky fried
chicken. See: Ken-
tucky fried chicken
Colonial Bakeries
Always in good taste
Colonial Products Co.
The world's largest manu-
facturer of fine kitchen
cabinets
Colonial Salt Co.
There's a Colonial salt for
every purpose
The "color guide" tie
Wembley neckties
Color in advertising

Munro & Harford Co.
Color is nature's way of saying
flavor. Stokely is your
way of getting it
Stokely-Van Camp, Inc.
Color is the difference
American Cyanamid Co.
Color-locked
Imperial washable wallpaper
Color or white you're always
right with Martin Senour
Martin Senour Co.
The color stays on until you take
it off
Max Factor lipstick
Color, the master salesman
Franklin Process Co.
Color work at night will next day
be right
Macbeth Daylighting Co.
Colorado
Cool off in Colorado
The colorful portable computer
Sharp PC-1500 computer
The colorful shampoo
Clairol, Inc.
Colorite Plastics, Inc.
World's leading manufacturer
of plastic products for
35 diversified industries
Colors hair inside, as nature does
Inecto Hair Coloring
Colors while it cleans
Aladdin Dye Soap
The Colson Corporation
Finest quality on wheels--
since 1885
Colt revolver
As easy as pointing your
finger
Proven best by government
test
You can't forget to make a
Colt safe
Columbia
The largest Catholic maga-
zine in the world
Columbia automobile
The gem of the highway
Columbia Bar-Lock Typewriter
The music of commerce
should be played on the
best instrument
Columbia batteries
The marvel of the electrical
age

93

Columbia bicycles
  For health--business--
    pleasure
  King of the road
  Since 1877, America's first
    bicycle
Columbia Broadcasting System,
    Inc.
  CBS, The star's address
  Where what you want to
    know comes first
Columbia Broadcasting System,
    Inc. See also: CBS
Columbia Casualty Co.
  The feeling of security
  It is better to have it and
    not need it than to
    need it and not have
    it
Columbia dry and storage bat-
    teries
  It's the same old "juice"
Columbia Grafonola
  Music wherever you are
Columbia Graphophone
  The talking machine up to
    date
  When you get a talking
    machine get a Grapho-
    phone
Columbia phonograph records
  Faithfully yours on Colum-
    bia phonograph records
  Hear the great artists at
    their best
Columbia Pictures Corp.
  Gems of the screen
Columbia Protektosite Co.
  Masterpieces for the mil-
    lions
  Masterpieces in plastic
Columbia tires
  Gaining new friends through
    extra mileage
Columbia window shades
  Tone the sunlight with
    window shades just as
    you tone the electric
    light with lamp shades
  Used everywhere in beauti-
    ful homes
Columbian Steel Tank Co.
  Tanks for the world
Columbus Dispatch
  Ohio's greatest home daily
Columbus McKinnon tire chain

  Easy to put on, easy to take
    off
Columbus-Union Oil Cloth Co.
  The durable and washable
    covering
  The wipe-clean wall covering
A combination not found in any
    other car
  Reo automobile
The combination pilot light and
    switch
  Sho-Lite, Inc.
Combines fun with manly training
  Daisy air rifle
Combining power with luxury
  Cadillac automobile
Combos candy bar
  Tasty filling in every crispy
    nugget
Combustion Engineering, Inc.
  The energy systems com-
    pany
  Progress for industry
    worldwide
  World leader in energy
    technology
Come alive!
  Pepsi-Cola soft drink
Come grow with us
  Central Telephone & Util-
    ities
Come home to comfort
  Bryant Heater Co.
Come on, appetites, let's go!
  Diamond Brand walnuts
Come on, breeze, let's blow!
  Wagner electric fan
Come on, you sunners
  Jantzen bathing suits
Come take a trip around our
    Castle
  Castle furniture
Come to Kentucky! It's a
    profitable move!
  Kentucky
Come to Marlboro Country
  Marlboro cigarettes
Come to Shell for answers
  Shell Oil Company
Come to think of it, I'll have a
    Heineken
  Heineken beer
Come to where the flavor is
  Marlboro cigarettes
Come up to the Kool taste
  Kool cigarettes

Comes out like a ribbon; lies
    flat on the brush
    Colgate's Ribbon Dental
    Cream
Comet cleanser
    Bleaches out tough food
    stains. Disinfects as
    it cleans
Comet rice
    Light, white and flaky
The comfort car
    Hupmobile automobile
Comfort Coal-Lumber Co.
    A yard near you
Comfort engineered
    Koylon fabric
The "comfort first" union suit
    Imperial union suit
Comfort is what we sell
    Grossman Shoes
Comfort Magazine
    The key to happiness and
    success in over a mil-
    lion farm homes
The comfort shave
    Norelco Rototrack Shaver
The comfort shoe of tomorrow
    McLaughlin-Sweet, Inc.
Comfort without compromise
    Stay-Free maxipads
Comfort you can count on
    Stay-Free maxipads
Comfortable as old carpet slip-
    pers
    Rand Shoes
Comfortable, carefree cotton
    Cotton Producers Institute
Comfortable heat when you want
    it, where you want it,
    at a price you can af-
    ford
    Oilray Safety Heater, Inc.
Comforting America's families
    for over 50 years
    Kleenex tissue
The "coming thing" in cars--has
    come
    Nash automobile
Command records
    World leader in recorded
    sound
Commands respect on any road
    Paige automobile
Commerce Bank of Kansas City
    Better cash management
    starts by calling us

Commercial Credit Co.
    Helping people and busi-
    nesses help themselves
Commercial Photo Service Co.
    Say it with pictures
Commercial roofing systems for
    roofs that stay water-
    tight
    Tropical commercial roofing
Commercial Union Insurance Com-
    panies
    Risk control means cost con-
    trol
Commitment to quality
    Bucyrus-Erie Company
Common Brick Mfrs. Assn. of
    America
    Beauty and economy burned
    in
    For beauty with economy
    build with common brick
Common sense. See also:
    Kommon-Sense Pan Racks
Common sense about the common
    cold
    Antiphlogistine
Commonwealth automobile
    The car with the foundation
Commonwealth Edison Utilities
    Don't take tomorrow for
    granted
Commonwealth Shoe & Leather
    Co.
    Style that stays
Communications specialists since
    1920
    Trans-Lux Corporation
Community silverplate
    And the bride lived happily
    ever after
    The finest silverplate
    If it's Community it's cor-
    rect
    Leadership in design author-
    ity
    Let's make it for keeps
    This is for keeps
Comoy. See: House of Comoy
The company for people who
    travel
    American Express Company
The company for precious metals
    Handy and Harman
A company for the eighties
    Greyhound Corporation
The company of specialists

Watson Mfg. Co., Inc.
A company of uncommon enter-
prise
Dravo Corporation
The company that likes to say
YES
Personal Finance Co.
The company to watch in energy,
insurance and communi-
cations
The Charter Company
The company with the "know-
how"
Metropolitan Furniture Ad-
justers
The company with the partner-
ship philosophy
American United Life Insur-
ance Co.
The company workhorse
Bell System telephone direc-
tory yellow pages
A company worth looking at
Boise Cascade Corporation
The company you'll hear more
about
Continental Group
Compare and you'll wear
Selby Shoe Co.
Compare and you'll wear Styl-
eez
Styl-eez shoes
Compare features, compare
quality, compare per-
formance, compare
price, compare value:
you'll buy a Volkswagen
Volkswagen automobile
Compare the price
Michelob beer
Compare yields
Rowe Price Prime Reserve
Fund, Inc.
Comparison proves its superior-
ity
Hallock & Watson Radio
Corp.
Compass of industry
The Foxboro Company
The complete authority of
packaging
Modern Packaging
The complete brake lining serv-
ice
Raybestos-Manhattan, Inc.
Complete brokerage service

in the world's markets
Fenner, Beane & Co.
The complete car, completely new
Chevrolet automobile
Complete cold medicine
Cotylenol
The complete family of dog and
cat foods from the world
leader in nutrition
Friskies pet food
The complete first suds detergent
Prime Soap
Complete gas service for every
home
American Gas Machine Co.
Complete household soap
Oxydol laundry detergent
The complete line of electric
cooking equipment
Toastmaster cooking equip-
ment
The complete paper house
Chicago Paper Co.
A complete source for fine office
furniture
Desks, Inc.
A complete toothpaste
Aqua-fresh toothpaste
A complete wall unit for all time
and clime
Bishopric Mfg. Co.
The completely automatic home
laundry
Launderall clothes washer
Completes the feast
National Fruit Cake
Comptometer calculating machine
If not made by Felt & Tar-
rant it's not a Compto-
meter
Compton's Encyclopedia
The accepted educational
standard
The computer people who listen
Sperry Rand Corporation
The computing company
Automatic Data Processing,
Inc.
Comstock pie-sliced apples
Pour yourself an apple pie
Comtrex
Comtrex relieves the whole
cold
Comtrex relieves the whole cold
Comtrex
Conawanga Refining Co.

Pedigreed Pennsylvania
products
Concrete for permanence
Portland Cement Assn.
Concrete satisfaction
Gray's Harbor cement
products
Conde. See: Princesse de
Conde Chocolates
Cone-ing on the campus
Illinois Baking Corp.
The confection of the fairies
Liberty Orchards Co.
Confections that win affections
Funke Candies
Confidentially, it shrinks
Half & Half smoking tobacco
Congoleum-Nairn floor coverings
Brighten your home at little
expense
Discover Congoleum
Fine floors
The floor of enduring beauty
Gold seal is your insurance
of beauty, cleanliness
and endurance
Years of wear in every yard
Congress Cigar Co.
Mildness plus character
Conklin Pen Co.
The pen that fills itself
Right to the point
Conlon electric washers
Where efficiency is de-
manded, the Conlon is
preferred
Conmar slide fastener
The major zipper
Conmark Plastics Div., Cohn-
Hall-Marx Co.
One of the oldest names in
textiles ... for the
newest development in
synthetics
Conn musical instruments
Cultivate your musical
bump
Conn Organ Corp.
For the home that enjoys
home life
Connecticut General Life Insur-
ance Co.
Where people and ideas
create security for
millions
Connecticut Mutual Life In-

surance Co.
The Blue Chip company
It pays to insure with the
"Blue Chip" company
The connecting link between
power and production
Clipper Belt Lacer Co.
Connolly Shoe Co.
Always a step ahead in style
Connolly shoes are comfort-
able shoes
Connolly shoes are comfortable
shoes
Connolly Shoe Co.
Connor Lumber and Land Co.
Manufacturers of quality
hardwood products
since 1872
Conoco gasoline
Hottest brand going!
Conoflow Corp.
Foremost in final control
elements
Conover electric dishwasher
Why drown your soul in a
greasy dishpan?
The conquest of comfort
French S. S. Line
Conserve to serve national de-
fense
Indium Corporation of Amer-
ica
Conserving our resources and
energy. Aluminum can
and Reynolds does
Reynolds Metals Company
Consider paper
Champion Papers, Inc.
Consider the power of paper
used with imagination
Champion Papers, Inc.
Considered essential by consid-
erate men
Sportsmen grooming essen-
tials
Consistent profitable growth ...
through leadership
brands
Chesebrough-Ponds, Inc.
Consistently better
Apex Smelting Co.
Conso Products Co. Div., Con-
solidated Foods Corp.
Creators of 1,001 products
for home decorating
Consolidated Aluminum Corp.

Growth leader of the
aluminum industry
Consolidated Edison Company
Power for Progress
Consolidated Foods Corp. See:
Conso Products Co.
Div., Consolidated
Foods Corp.
Consolidated Freightways, Inc.
Leading name in truck
transportation
Consolidated Gas Fields Ltd.
The 100 largest foreign
investments in the
U. S.
Consolidated Laundry Company
Let our telephone wire be
your clothes line
Consolidated Paper Co.
Specialist in enamel papers/
printing paper
Consolidated yacht
The greatest name in yacht-
ing
Constant excellence is the key
to success
N. W. Ayer & Son
Constant excellence of product
S. D. Warren Co. Div.,
Scott Paper Co.
Constantly imitated--never
equalled
Onyx Hosiery
Construction Methods and
Equipment
Read and preferred by
construction men
Consult your physician on mat-
ters of weight control
Metrecal
Consumer certified colors
Howard Ketcham industrial
designs
Consumer certified colors and
designs
Howard Ketcham industrial
designs
Consumers Power Company
Symbol of service
Contac nasal decongestant
It's your guarantee of
quality
Proprietary pharmaceuticals
made to ethical stand-
ards
So you won't miss the good

things
Container Corp. of America
America's most comprehen-
sive packaging service
C.C.A. means distinction,
convenience, innovation,
protection, inventory
control, service
Containers of distinction
J. L. Clark Mfg. Co.
Contains no alum
Magic Baking Powder
Contains no caffeine or other
harmful stimulants
Instant Postum
Contemporary fibers
Celanese Corp.
Conti olive oil castile soap
Cleans with a caress
Continent-wide service
American Solvents & Chem-
ical Corp.
Continental Air Lines, Inc.
A most remarkable airline
Proud bird with the golden
tail
Continental automobile
Powerful as the nation
Continental Can Co.
Behind the labels of Amer-
ica's finest products
Health and freshness sealed
in cans
Continental Distilling Corp.
Clean clear through
The Scotch that circles the
globe
Continental Envelope Corp.
The house that service built
Continental Group
The company you'll hear
more about
Judge us by the agents who
represent us
Continental Illinois National Bank
& Trust Co. of Chicago
At Continental Bank it's
reality
Continental Steel Corp.
You can count on Continen-
tal to take care of you
Continental tires
Tougher than elephant hide
Continental Trailways Bus Sys-
tem
Easiest travel on earth

Continuing research for lower
cost drilling
Hycalog, Inc.
Continuous filament textured
nylon
Tyracora
Continuous flow packaging
Battle Creek Packaging
Machines, Inc.
The continuous wear contact lens
Hydrocurve II
Contoure Laboratories
Buy your beauty needs from
beauticians
Control Data Corporation
Addressing society's major
unmet needs as profit-
able business opportun-
ities
More than a computer com-
pany
Plato. Changing how the
world learns
Control with Dole
Dole Valve Co.
Controlled comfort
Spring-Air mattress
Controls temperature ... pre-
cisely
Fenwal, Inc.
Convenient to everywhere
Rittenhouse Hotel, Phila-
delphia, Pa.
Converse Rubber Co.
When you're out to beat the
world
Convert your assets into working
capital
Associates Commercial Cor-
poration
The convertible sofa with ac-
cordion action
Sofa-Niter sofa
Cook electrically and enjoy the
difference
Reddy Kilowatt
Cook stove and gas plant all in
one
Coleman Co., Inc.
Cooked the way you like it
Quaint Inn, Indianapolis,
Ind.
Cookie Jar tobacco
A honey of a tobacco
Cooking is just a SNAP on an
Estate electric range

Estate Stove Co.
Cooks in nine minutes
Mueller's macaroni
Cooks ON with the gas OFF
Dutch Oven Gas Range
Cooks tender, quicker
Mueller's macaroni
Cooks 3 things at once
Armstrong table stove
Cookson Co. fire doors
Best way to close an opening
Cool. See also: Kool
Cool as a pool
Luxite night garments
Cool, calm and respected
Arrow shirts
Cool comfort with corseted chic
Flexees foundations
Cool. Crisp. Clear
Alps Brau beer
Cool it with milk, the fresher
refresher
American Dairy Association
Cool off feet with an Ice-Mint
treat
Ice-Mint
Cool off in Colorado
Colorado
Cool shaves cited for comfort
Ingram's shaving cream
Cool shoes for hot days
Keds
Coolatronics
Applied science of Elpeco
refrigeration
Cooler on the draw
Royal Duke pipe
Coolest hat under the sun
Caradine Hat Co.
Cooley Roofing Systems
Put a roof on costs
Cools and soothes as you shave
Ingram's shaving cream
Coolwhip topping
The last spoonful is as
fresh as the first
Coon. See: W. B. Coon Co.
Cooper. See also: Frederick
Cooper Lamps, Inc.
Cooper Tire & Rubber Co.
America's fastest-growing
tire company
Cooper Tools
The difference between work
and workmanship
Cooper Underwear Co.

Every mile of yarn gives
an extra year of wear
Cooper's, Inc. See: Jockey
Menswear Div., Coop-
er's, Inc.
Coordinated fashions for bed and
bath
Field Crest Mills, Inc.
Copeland refrigeration
The perfect servant
Winter enchained in silent
service
World's greatest value in
dependable refrigeration
Year in, year out, the per-
fect servant
Copenhagen chewing tobacco
A pinch is all it takes
Copies for communication
throughout the world
American Photocopy Equip-
ment Co.
Copper. See also: Kopper
The copper people from Phelps
Dodge
Phelps Dodge Corporation
The copper topped battery
Duracell dry cell battery
Coppers Engineering Corp.
Designed for your indus-
try, engineered for
you
Coppertone sun tan lotion
Don't be a pale face
Slip into something tan.
Coppertone
Coppes Bros. & Zook kitchen
cabinets
Built like fine furniture
Corbin hardware
Good buildings deserve
good hardware
Hardware that harmonizes
It pays to make it Corbin
--throughout!
Corbin Ltd. Tailoring
A family-owned business
devoted to quality
There's a Corbin behind
every Corbin
Corby's whiskey
Fine whiskey on the mild
side
A grand old Canadian name
The Cord car creates a place
for itself no other

car has ever occupied
Cord front drive automobile
Cord front drive automobile
The Cord car creates a
place for itself no other
car has ever occupied
Cord Tire Corp.
Just what the name signifies
Cordé de Paris, Inc.
The aristocrat of fine cor-
setry
Cordova guitars
Made with the extra measure
of care
Corette slip
Eventually yours
Styled to prevent twisting
or riding
Corinthia Lipstick
Smooth as a love song, mod-
ern as jive
Cork. See also: Kork
Cork-lined houses make comfort-
able homes
Armstrong Cork Co.
A corking good drink
Korker soft drink
Corn Chex Cereal
People who don't like Chex
Cereals have never tried
Chex Cereals
Corn KIX cereal
New to look at, new to
taste
Corn Products Refining Co.
Delicious in flavor, rich in
nutrition
The corn with stand ability
Pfister Associated Growers
The corn with husk ability
Pfister Associated Growers
The corn with yield ability
Pfister Associated Growers
Corning means research in glass
Corning Ware
Corning Ware
Corning means research in
glass
50 years of brighter tasting
meals
Corno Mills
The feed that is all feed
Coro jewelry
America's best-dressed
women wear Coro jewelry
Corona typewriter

The first portable
The personal writing
machine
Coronado clothes
Very coolly yours
Coronado Hotel, St. Louis, Mo.
In keeping with a fine old
tradition
Coronet toys
Playtime pals for the nation's
kiddies
Coronet vibrator
Put your best face forward,
every day
The corporate bank that lives
in the South
Citizens & Southern Na-
tional Bank
Correct in every weigh
Counselor Bath Room Scale
The correct toothpaste
Orphos toothpaste
The correct writing paper
Eaton Paper Corp.
Correcting your mistakes now
costs less at Sears
Sears Roebuck & Co. elec-
tric typewriters
Correctol
The modern gentle laxative
Corroon & Black insurance
brokers
Put Corroon & Black at the
helm
Put Corroon & Black on the
job
Putting insurance risks into
perspective
Corrugated packaging special-
ists
Hoerner Boxes, Inc.
Corrugated Paper Mills
Headquarters for corru-
gated products in New
England
The Corselette
The ultimate in fine cor-
setry
Corvair/Monza automobile
The great highway per-
formers
Cory
The greatest name in
coffee-brewing
equipment
Cosray skin freshener

Your skin, wake it up be-
fore you make it up
The costliest perfume in the
world
Joy de Jean Patou
Costs less by the biscuit
Mrs. Tucker's Shortening
Costs less per month of service
Vesta Accumulator Co.
Costs less when used
Dr. Price's vanilla
Costs more but does more
Zenith radio receiver
Costs more by the gallon, less
by the winter
Prestone anti-freeze
Costs more, worth more
Occident flour
Costs nothing unless we grow
hair
Van Ess Liquid Scalp Mas-
sage
The costume jewelry of the home
Mersman Tables
Cotta transmission
An assurance of dependable
service
Cotton
The manufacturing and con-
struction journal of the
textile industry
Cotton Producers Institute
Comfortable, carefree cotton
The fiber you can trust
Cotton, you can feel how good
it looks
National Cotton Council
Cottonelle bathroom tissue
It's cotton-soft
Coty cosmetics
A heart to heart fragrance
His duty to serve, hers to
inspire
It lulls the skin
Tomorrow's skin care--today
Coty 24 hour lipstick
Stays on till you take it off
Cotylenol
Complete cold medicine
A cough is a social blunder
Smith Brothers cough drops
Could it be the real thing?
Marvella pearls
Council for Financial Aid to
Education
College is America's best

friend
Council Meats
    All the taste without the
      waste
    Fresh from sunshine and
      pure air
Counselor Bath Room Scale
    Correct in every weigh
Count on Centennial
    Centennial Flouring Mills
      Co.
Count on steel from National
    National Steel Corp.
The counter sign of quality
    Koch Butcher's Supply Co.
Country charm quality
    Dean Foods Co.
Country Doctor pipe mixture
    That's putting it MILDLY
Country fresh
    June Dairy Products Co.
The country garden soap for
      the "country com-
      plexion"
    Cashmere Bouquet soap
Country Gardens canned vege-
      tables
    A treasure for eating
      pleasure
Country Gentleman
    The modern farm paper
Country Gentleman paint
    The certified analysis
      takes the mystery out
      of paint
Country Life Insurance Co.
    Salesman extraordinary to
      your biggest consumers
County. See: Kounty Kist
    Peas
Coupon Bond paper
    The best papers are made
      from rags
The coupon to bigger success
    Funk & Wagnalls Company
The courage to change. The
      strength to grow
    International Harvester Co.
Courtald's rayon
    The greatest name in rayon
Courtald's silks
    As good as it's beautiful
Courtesy, efficiency, service
    Manufacturers Trust Co.
Courtley toiletries
    The last word in gifts for

men
Courvoisier cognac
    The brandy of Napoleon
Coventry. See: Sarah Coventry,
    Inc.
Cover the earth
    Sherwin-Williams Co.
Coveralls. See: Koveralls
Covering a continent
    American News Co.
Covers a world of sports
    Slazengers, Inc.
Covers all filtration problems
    Purolator filter
Covers the country intensively
    American Press Association
Covers the whole range
    Sander loud speaker
Covers with one coat
    Red Devil enamel
Cowden work clothing
    If it's Cowden, it fits
    Work clothing that conquers
      hard wear
Cowles Detergent Co.
    Good washing wins good
      will
Cozy. See also: Kozy
Cozy comfort for chilly days
    American Gas Machine Co.
Cozzoli Machine Co.
    Call the man from Cozzoli
Cracker Jack confection
    From America's popcorn
      people
    The more you eat, the
      more you want
The cracker that makes a thou-
      sand other things taste
      better
    Ritz crackers
Crackin' good walnuts
    California Walnut Growers
      Assn.
Cradled silence
    Doe oil burner
Craftsmen built the Kurtsmann
    Kurtsmann piano
Craftsmen of fine solid wood
      furniture
    Davis Cabinet Company
Crandall Type-Writer
    Unequalled for speed, ac-
      curacy and durability
Crane and Company, Inc.
    Fine papers

Letters on Crane's papers
command attention and
win respect
Crane beauty in the open.
Crane quality in all
hidden fittings
Crane Company
Crane Company
At Crane we believe in
basics
Basic products for basic
industries. That's what
Crane is all about
Crane beauty in the open.
Crane quality in all
hidden fittings
For every piping system
The name is Crane
Technology. Fundamental
to Crane's growth
Crane's papers
The mark that is a message
in itself
Crave catfood
Protein-rich foods cats
crave
Cream. See also: Creme
The cream of coffees
Albert Ehlers, Inc.
Cream of olive oil soaps
Cream Oil Soap
Cream of Rice
Fortified to whole grain
levels
Tastes so good and so good
for you
Cream of Wheat
The great American family
cereal
Top of the morning
Cream Oil Soap
Cream of olive oil soaps
The cream shampoo for true
hair loveliness
Lustre-Cream shampoo
Creamer's Bakery, Inc.
Freshest thing in town
Creamona cream substitute
Creamy aroma--creamy
taste
Cream's rival
Sego evaporated milk
Creamy aroma--creamy taste
Creamona cream substitute
Create happy hours
Selznick Pictures Corp.

Created to carry your belongings
in perfection throughout
your lifetime
Halliburton travel cases
Creates essentials of beauty
Schiaparelli beauty creams
Creates new dimensions in auto-
matic packaging machin-
ery!
Circle Design and Mfg.
Corp.
Creating a new world with elec-
tronics
Hughes Aircraft Co.
Creating better ways to hold
things together
National Screw and Mfg.
Co.
Creating new advances in flight
Lockheed Aircraft Corpora-
tion
Creating useful products and
services for you
Texas Instruments, Inc.
Creating world-famed fishing
tackle since 1893
South Bend Tackle Co., Div.
Gladding Corp.
Creative aerosol valve engineer-
ing
Newman-Green, Inc.
Creative ideas in glass
American Saint Gobain Corp.
Creative insurance services.
We've got what it takes
Frank B. Hall & Co. insur-
ance brokers
Creator of advanced writing in-
struments
Microprint, Inc.
Creators of chemicals for modern
agriculture
Geigy Chemical Corp.
Creators of dependability
Geartronics Corp.
Creators of direct mail literature
D. H. Ahrend Co.
Creators of distinctive luggage
Unique luggage
Creators of farm wealth
Hart-Parr Co.
Creators of fashions in oilcloth
Weiss & Klau Co.
Creators of 1,001 products for
home decorating
Conso Products Co. Div.,

Consolidated Foods Corp.
Creators of the world famous
Stratolounger
Futorian Manufacturing
Corp.
Creme. See also: Cream
The creme cold wave
Toni Home Permanent
Cremora ... creamy aroma, rich
taste
Cremora non-dairy cream
Cremora non-dairy cream
Cremora ... creamy aroma,
rich taste
Creole Pralines
The South's most famous
confection
Crescent Belt Fasteners
For continuous production
Creslan acrylic fiber
Luxury acrylic fiber
Cress Corn and Bunion Salves
Just rub in
The crest of American engineer-
ing
Duesenberg automobile
The crest of quality wine since
1889
Cresta Blanca wine
Crest toothpaste
A lot fewer cavities
Working for the day kids
won't know what a
cavity feels like
With Crest your kids could
have even fewer cavities
than you did
Cresta Blanca wine
The crest of quality wine
since 1889
From the finest of the
vines
The wine that tastes as
good as it looks
Crex Carpet Co.
It's your protection and
our guarantee
The criminal within
Eno effervescent salt
Crisby Frisian Fur Co.
Let us tan your hide
Crisco shortening
Best cooks know foods
fried in Crisco don't
taste greasy
In everything you fry or

bake
It's digestible
Makes fried foods taste de-
licious--not greasy
Tastes great. Not greasy
Zero weather, summer heat,
always creamy fresh
and sweet
The crisp, dry cold of a frosty
night
Iroquois Electric Refrigera-
tion Co.
The crispy chocolate bar so good
you'll roar
Kit Kat candy bar
Criss Cross. See: Kriss Kross
Blades
The critical parts people
Barnes Group, Inc.
Crocker. See also:
Cocker
Betty Crocker cake mix
H. S. Crocker Co., Inc.
Crocker-Citizens National Bank
The bank that means busi-
ness in California
Changing corporate banking
from California
Crocker Hamilton Papers, Inc.
Your printer's performance
starts with fine papers
The Cromar Co.
Originators of prefinished
hardwood flooring
Crompton and Knowles. See:
Textile Machinery Div.,
Crompton and Knowles
Crop Life
A business paper for the
farm chemical industry
Crosby Square Shoes
A step to distinction
Crosley radio-phonograph
Whether you look or listen,
it's perfect both ways
Crosley radio receivers
Better--cost less
A radio in every room, a
radio for every purpose
The wandering minstrel of
today
Crosman Arms Co.
The gun that knows no
closed season
Power without powder
Cross. See also: A. T. Cross

Co.
The Cross Company
    First in automation
Crosse & Blackwell pickles
    The pick of pickles
Croton watch
    On your wrist, off your
        mind
    Runs accurately without
        winding
    The world's most "care-
        free" watch
Crouse-Hinds Company
    Our business is electrifying
        ideas
Crown & Headlight overalls
    Give a look INSIDE to get
        value outside (and in)
Crown Brand corn syrup
    The famous energy food
Crown Central Petroleum Corp.
    Quality you can trust
Crown Cork & Seal Co., Inc.
    Your packaging deserves
        Crown quality
Crown Dominion gasoline
    Not a knock in a tankful
Crown Iron Works Co.
    First in fencing
The crown jewel of England
    Beefeater Gin
The crown jewels of ignition
    Filko Ignition
The crown jewels of ignition and
        carburetion
    Filko Ignition
Crown Overall Mfg. Co.
    The million dollar overall
Crown slide fastener
    The zipper of tomorrow
Crown Tested Rayon Fabrics
    The first name in rayon,
        the last word in qual-
        ity
The crowning achievement of
        vintner skill
    Grand Estate wines
The crowning touch of quality
    Red Cedar Shingle and
        Handsplit Shake Bureau
Croydon. See: Kroydon
The cruiser of tomorrow
    Richardson Ranger boat
Cruising everywhere under the
        sun
    American President Lines

Crum & Forster Insurance Com-
        panies
    The policy makers
Crunchy day snack with real
        meat
    Butcher Bones
Crunchycheweynuttysweet
    Raisin Grape Nuts
The crystal clear gin in the
        crystal clear bottle
    American Distilling Corp.
Crystal Dairy Products
    Nature's best food at its
        best
Crystal Tips ice machine
    Make the seasons come to
        you
Crystal washing machine
    To lighten the burden of
        womankind
A cube makes a cup
    Steero bouillon cubes
Cubs cereal
    America's new breakfast
        banquet of shredded
        whole wheat
    For a livelier life
Cudahy Packing Co.
    The taste tells
Cuddles doll
    A reliable doll
Culligan, Inc.
    Hey! Culligan man!
    The world-wide water con-
        ditioning people
Cultivate your musical bump
    Conn musical instruments
Cultured Boston people use
        Electric Lustre Starch
    Electric Lustre Starch
Cummins Engine Co., Inc.
    Cummins means diesel
Cummins means diesel
    Cummins Engine Co., Inc.
Cunard Steamship Lines
    Sail with the British tradi-
        tion wherever you go
Cunningham automobile
    The Cunningham Car
The Cunningham Car
    Cunningham automobile
Cunningham radio tube
    It bridges the vastness of
        space
    Radio's motive power since
        1915

The cup of southern hospitality
  Duncan Coffee Co.
The cup that cheers
  Reichardt Cocoa & Chocolate Co.
Cupid foundation
  Your closest friend
Cupples tires
  Broad, black and a brute for wear
  A fighting heart of honest rubber
  Tough as a rhino
Curad bandages
  They still don't ouch me
Curity diapers
  Wash easier, dry faster, absorb more, wear longer
Curtis. See also: Helene Curtis Industries, Inc.
Curtis Candy Co.
  Candy makers to the American nation
Curtis Homes
  Curtis puts the own back in home ownership
Curtis Hotel, Minneapolis, Minn.
  Largest in the northwest
Curtis Mathes television sets
  The most expensive television sets in America. And worth it
Curtis 1000
  1000 different products to make business work
Curtis Pneumatic Machinery Co.
  Free from oil
Curtis puts the own back in home ownership
  Curtis Homes
A curve-for-curve copy of the bottom of your foot
  Matrix Shoes
Curvfit razor
  The woman's razor
Cusette foundations
  Fitting the purse as well as the figure
Cushion every step
  Weyenberg Shoe Mfg. Co.
Cushman. See also: H. T. Cushman Mfg. Corp.
Cushman Motors Div., Outboard Marine Co.
  The big name in little

wheels
Custom-built quality at production line prices
  Fruehauf Corporation
A custom-built support for foot troubles
  New Method Foot Foundation
The custom crafted shotgun
  Charles Daly
Custom engineered conveying systems for every industry since 1919
  Jervis B. Webb Company
Custom made luggage
  Lark luggage
Custom, of course
  Lew Smith Beads
Custom tailored throughout
  Stratford Clothes
The customer is always No. 1
  National Car Rental System, Inc.
Customer satisfaction--our No. 1 job
  Detroit Steel Corporation
A cut above the commonplace
  Danish Blue Cheese
A cut above the rest
  Allen Edmonds shoes
Cut coal bills 1/2 to 2/3-- guaranteed with the Underfeed
  Underfeed furnace and boiler stoker
Cut-Rite Waxed Paper
  The box with the famous cutting edge
  It costs little, saves much
Cut to fit the mouth
  James Bros. salt water taffy
Cut your tire upkeep with a Diamond
  Diamond tires
Cutex nail polish
  Cutex nails are loveliest
  Paris approves the colors; America perfects the wear
Cutex nails are loveliest
  Cutex nail polish
The cuticle vanishes
  Softol cuticle remover
Cuticura ointment
  The great skin cure
Cuticura resolvent

The new blood purifyer
Cuticura soap
    An exquisite skin beautifier
       and toilet requisite
Cutler desks
    They express success
Cutler-Hammer, Inc.
    Engineered for value
    Industrial efficiency de-
       pends on electrical con-
       trol
    Pioneer manufacturers of
       electrical control appar-
       atus
    Pressroom efficiency depends
       on electrical control
    Starts--stops--regulates--
       controls
    What's new? Ask Cutler
Cutlery. See: Hoffritz for
    Cutlery
Cuts costs, creates sales
    Molybdenum metal
Cuts dishpan time in half
    Washington Powder
Cuts down delivery costs
    Steinmetz Elec. Motor Car
       Corp.
Cuts grease quicker
    S. O. S. detergent
Cuts the cost of clean hands
    Soapitor Co., Inc.
The cutter that does not clog
    Paper Machine Co.
Cutting costs is our business
    Addressograph-Multigraph
       Corp.
Cutty Sark Scotch whiskey
    Even the colour of the
       label separates Cutty
       Sark from the rest
    A gentleman's drink
    The Scotch with a following
       of leaders
Cutty 12 Scotch whiskey
    The 12-year-old Scotch
       well worth looking for
Cuyamaca Water Co.
    You taste its freshness
Cyanamid serves the man who
    makes a business of
    agriculture
    American Cyanamid Co.
Cycle Trades of America
    Ride a bicycle
Cyclone Catch-All Basket

The safe bonfire
Cyclotherm Steam Generators
    It's your best buy
Czechoslovak Glass Products Co.
    Glassware of distinction

-D-

d-Con Rat Killer
    No rat becomes immune to
       d-Con Rat Killer
    The clean way to kill dirty
       rats and mice
D. H. Ahrend Co.
    Creators of direct mail lit-
       erature
DHL Worldwide Courier
    Once it leaves your hands
       it never leaves our
       network
    You couldn't express it
       better
DH125 airplane
    This one means business
DKI. See: Dart & Kraft
D. Lorah cleaner
    Cleans hands cleaner
DX. See: Sunray DX Oil
    Company
Da-Lite Screen Co., Inc.
    Perfection in projection
       since 1909
A dab makes you dainty as a
    deb
    Zip hair remover
Dacro Metal Coverall Caps
    The safest package of milk
       you can buy
Dacron fabric
    America lives in Dacron
Dad played marbles, too
    Akro Agate Co.
Daddy of them all
    Waterman's Ideal Fountain
       Pen
Daggett & Ramsdell cold cream
    The kind that keeps
    The perfect cold cream
Dailey's jams
    Eat Dailey's with your
       daily bread
Daily Forward
    Gateway to the Jewish
       market
Daily Metal Trade

The news of the day in
the newsiest way
Daily News Record
The dry goods daily
The dainty deodorant
Eversweet deodorant
Dainty Flour
Its purity shows in every-
thing you bake
Pure, always pure
The Dairy Farmer
America's largest dairy
magazine
The dairy paper of the New
York City milk shed
Dairymen's League News
Dairy Queen confectionery
restaurants
We treat you right
Dairymen's League Cooperative
Assn.
Inspected, protected
Dairymen's League News
The dairy paper of the
New York City milk
shed
Daisy. See also: Dazey
Daisy air rifle
Combines fun with manly
training
Daisy/Heddon Div., Victor
Comptometer Corp.
World's largest producer
of non-powder guns
and ammo
Dallas is the door to Texas
Dallas Morning News
Dallas, Texas
Dallas Morning News
Dallas is the door to Texas
Dallas, Texas
Dallas is the door to Texas
Dallas Times-Herald
The South's fastest-growing
newspaper
Dalsimer shoes
'Tis a feat to fit feet
Dalton. See also: B. Dalton
Dalton lathe
The small lathe for the
big job
Daly. See: Charles Daly
Damart Thermolactyl underwear
The proof is in the wear-
ing!
There is no warmer un-

derwear made!
Dan River sheets
Service beyond the contract
Sleep beautifully on Dan
River sheets
Dana Corp. See: Spicer Div.,
Dana Corp.
The danciest band in the land
Orrin Tucker's orchestra
Dancing is what music was cre-
ated for
Arthur Murray dance
studios
Dancing to the music of the
Victrola is the favorite
pastime
Victrola talking machine
Danderine
Grows thick, heavy hair
Dandy candy
Yankee Toffee
Danersk Furniture
A new bed that is almost
sinfully comfortable
Danger Perfume
It cuts through competition
like a rapier
Daniel Construction Co., Inc.
Builders in and of the
South
Daniel Orifice Fitting Co.
Products made to measure
Daniel Webster whiskey
Made right, aged right,
priced right
Daniel's. See: Jack Daniel's
whiskey
Danish Blue Cheese
A cut above the common-
place
Darbrook silks
Darbrook silks of character
and quality
If it's Darbrook it's durable
Darbrook silks of character and
quality
Darbrook silks
D'Arcy Advertising Co.
Advertising is the power of
an idea multiplied
Dare. See also: Virginia Dare
wines
Dare you move your pictures?
Sunworthy Wallpapers
Daring brassiere
The strapless bra that

stays up
Dark eyes gin
Look into a new pair of
eyes
Dark eyes vodka
Look into a new pair of
eyes
Darleen elastic fabrics
Best by any test
Darling Metal Fixtures
Worth their WAIT in gold
Dart & Kraft
Keep your eye on DKI
A new face across the mar-
ket place
Dart Industries, Inc. See:
Syroco Div., Dart In-
dustries, Inc.
The dash that makes the dish
A-1 Sauce
Data General Corporation
The first computer designed
solely for the purpose
of being a first com-
puter
We engineered the anxiety
out of computers
Data processing is our only
business
National Cash Register Co.
Datamec Corp.
Leadership in low cost/
high reliability mag-
netic tape handling
Datapoint Corporation
Systems that work together
now
Dated Mayonnaise, Inc.
If it's dated, you know
it's fresh
You know it's fresh, it's
dated
Dates depend on daintiness
Mum deodorant
Datsun automobile
The difference is value
We are driven
Dauphin Deposit Trust Co.
Ask our customers
Davencrepe hosiery
Davencrepes with the in-
visible extra silks
Davencrepes with the invisible
extra silks
Davencrepe hosiery
Davenport Hosiery Mills

Wear longer
Davey Tree Expert Co.
Father of tree surgery
The oldest and largest tree
saving service in the
world
Our wounded friends, the
trees
David. See also: Mogen David
wine
David Lupton's Sons
Pioneer makers of modern
steel windows
Davidow Suits, Inc.
The label to ask for
Davidson radio receiver
Every one a good one
Davis'. See: Perry Davis' Pain
Killer
Davis Bros. fish foods
The home of Deep Sea Dave
Davis Cabinet Company
Craftsmen of fine solid wood
furniture
Davis-Howland Oil Corp.
Headquarters for lubricants
and lubri-counsel
Davis Manufacturing, Inc.
The world's most distinctive
digging machines are
Davis
Davis tennis rackets
Often imitated, never dupli-
cated
Dawn dishwashing liquid
Handle more grease for your
money
Keeps grease away from
dishes
Takes grease out of your
way
Dawson's Ale
Naturally better
Day. See also: Da-Lite Screen
Co., Inc.
Day-Fan Electric Co.
The radio used by the
broadcasting stations
Daydreams perfume
For memories that linger
Daylight, the ideal
Macbeth Daylighting Co.
Daylight's only rival
Silverglo lamps
Day's. See: Mrs. Day's Ideal
Baby Shoe Co.

Daystrom Furniture Division,
Daystrom, Inc.
Built to take it ...
beautifully
The daytime fragrance
Lentheric perfume
Daytime is selling time
Morning Newspaper Pub-
lishers Assn.
Dayton Engineering Laboratories
Wherever it must be the
best
Dayton Wire Wheel Co.
For the man who drives or
the man who flies
Daytona Beach Journal
First in the Halifax country
Dazey. See also: Daisy
Dazey Products Co.
The can opener people
Your kitchen companion
since 1899
Dead moths eat no holes
Moth-Tox insecticide
Deadly on bugs; gentle on
plants
No-Pest insect spray
Deagan Chimes
The memorial sublime
A deal with Diel means a good
deal
Diel Watch Case Co.
Dealer's choice
Carling's Ale
The dealer's own paper
Building Supply News
Dean Foods Co.
Country charm quality
Dean Witter is 4 times better
than the average
Dean Witter Reynolds in-
vestments
Dean Witter Reynolds invest-
ments
Dean Witter is 4 times
better than the average
One investment firm you'll
be glad to hear from
Dean's Mentholated Cough
Drops
Get the drop on that
cough
They cure the tickle
Dear. See: Deere
Death wailed through the
hideous night

Eveready flashlights and
batteries
Deb. See: Lorrie Deb Corpora-
tion
De Beers Consolidated Mines,
Ltd.
A diamond is forever
World's leading supplier of
diamonds for industry
Debu-Form girdles
Keeps you in form
Debutante cosmetics
Bedazzling new cosmetics
for all your shining
hours
Debutante Originals
Sophisticute dresses
Decca phonograph records
The all-star record
Listen to America
Decorate with artistic lighting
equipment
Artistic Lighting Equipment
Assn.
Dedicated to excellence
American Motors Corp.
Dedicated to people on the move
U. S. Van Lines, Inc.
Dedicated to progress in the clay
industry
Brick & Clay Board
Dedicated to serving the families
of the West and Hawaii
... no one else
Sunset
Dedicated to the pursuit of ex-
cellence
Rohr Corp.
Deep Downy softness--a notice-
able improvement
Downy laundry washing aid
Deep inside trust Prestone
Prestone anti-freeze
Deere & Co.
John Deere on the move
Lets you take weekends
easy the year around!
Nothing runs like a Deere
Deerfoot Farm Sliced Bacon
Popular for flavor, taste,
price
Deering Coal & Wood Co.
The anthracite that serves
you right
Defense won't wait for the nation
that's late

Big Ben Westclox alarm
    clock
Defies weather and wear
    Sun Varnish Co.
Definitely Glenoit for happy per-
    sons
    Glenoit Mills, Inc.
Definitive modern furniture
    Founders Furniture, Inc.
De Forest-Crosley radio receivers
    World-wide reception
Defrosts itself, saves shut-downs
    Belding-Hall refrigerator
Deity. See: Egyptian Deity
    cigarettes
De Laval Separator Co.
    The distinguished service
        separator
De Luxe sanitary belt
    It fits the form because
        it's formed to fit
Del Monte Canned Food
    How to make light work of
        heavy metals
Del Monte Coffee
    Just as you'd expect, right
        EVERY way
    Seven good coffees in one
Del Monte fruit cocktail
    The brand that always puts
        flavor first
Del Monte fruits
    Flavor first
    Short on work, long on
        flavor
Del Monte pineapple
    Have a dish of sunshine
        and have the laugh on
        winter
    Hungry for sunshine?
        Have it sliced
    It pays to be particular
    Pure, natural, unsweetened
    Sliced sunshine, straight
        from the tropics
Del Monte prune juice
    The prune juice with the
        fruit juice appeal
Del Monte prunes
    Prunes give you so much
        for so little
Delco appliances
    Does the job better
Delco Heat
    A stitch in time service
Delco shock absorbers

If it's Delco it's designed
    for the job
Delco storage batteries
    For starting power, for
        lasting power
    Forget the thermometer,
        remember the guarantee
    Simply say Delco
    Wherever wheels turn or
        propellers spin
Deliberate witchery
    Menace perfume
Delicious and refreshing
    Coca Cola soft drink
The delicious cheddar cheese
        food
    Pabst-ette
Delicious, deLIGHTful, demand
    it
    Piel's beer
A delicious food drink
    Cocomalt
A delicious health confection
    Post's Bran Chocolates
A delicious holiday tradition
    Dinner Bell restaurants
Delicious in flavor, rich in
        nutrition
    Corn Products Refining Co.
The delicious whole wheat
        cereal
    Wheatena cereal
Deliciously home-y
    Kirgan's Arcadian Farms
The deliciously perfumed hair
        lacquer
    Nestle Hairlac
A delightful dream ... a deli-
        cious reality
    Lowney's Chocolate Bonbons
Delightfully see-worthy
    Jordan swim suits
Delineator
    Founder of better homes in
        America
Delivers the goods
    Pioneer Box Co.
Dellinger, Inc.
    Think original, think
        Dellinger
    Where every carpet is
        custom made
Deloitte, Haskins & Sells ac-
        countants
    Beyond the bottom line
De Lorean automobile

The vanishing breed
Delrich Margarine
 After all, "The taste tells"
 A new American favorite
Delta Air Lines, Inc.
 The airline run by profes-
  sionals
 The airline with the big
  jets
 Delta is ready when you
  are
Delta Cocktail Onions
 Has that knack for meal
  or snack
Delta is ready when you are
 Delta Air Lines, Inc.
Deltah pearls
 World's finest reproductions
DeLuxe Golden State Limited,
  Southern Pacific Co.
 Saves a business day
DeLuxe Golden State Limited,
  Southern Pacific Co.
 See also: Southern
  Pacific Co.
A demonstration is a revelation
 Savage Arms Div., Emhart
  Corp.
Demuth. See: Wm. Demuth &
  Co.
Denham's shoes
 Found at last. Perfection
  in shoes
De Nicotea cigarette holder
 It filters the smoke
Dennison diapers liners
 For the seat of your diaper
  troubles
Dennison Mfg. Co.
 No. 1 source of gummed
  papers
Denny's restaurants
 You'll like our prices and
  you'll love our food
Densylon carpets
 The remarkable new carpet
  that's flooring the
  country!
The dental concept of the fu-
  ture
 Omnicare Dental Services
Dental Hi-gene Products, Inc.
 Guard your mouth
Dentally different
 Orphos toothpaste
The dentifrice that made fine

 teeth fashionable
 Dr. Lyons tooth powder
Dentrol dental adhesive
 For a comfortable hold
Dent's Toothache Gum
 Stops toothache instantly
Dentyne chewing gum
 Brush your breath with
  Dentyne
 Flavor to spare and share
 Helps keep teeth white
 Mary's no longer contrary
Dentyne toothpaste
 Keeps the teeth white
Denver & Rio Grande Western
  Railroad
 The scenic line of the world
Denver Hanna coke
 Tons of comfort
The deodorant bar that leaves
  no sticky film
 Zest soap
A deodorant in every Kotex nap-
  kin at no extra cost
 Kotex sanitary napkins
Depend on Farnsworth for fidel-
  ity
 Farnsworth radio receiver
Depend on Potlatch for every-
  thing in quality lumber
 Potlatch Forests, Inc.
Depend on Purina Cat Chow
 Purina Cat Chow
Depend protective undergarment
 The name says it all
The dependability people
 Maytag Company
Dependable all ways
 Berkeley cigarette lighter
The dependable automatics
 Maytag laundry washers
Dependable for every engine
 Champion spark plugs
The dependable hosiery
 Mojud hosiery
Dependable in any weather
 Baltzer boats
Dependable long life
 Ken-Rad radio tubes
The dependable motor car
 Austin automobile
Dependable power, absolute
  safety
 Troy Engine & Machine Co.
Dependable power units
 Domestic Engine & Pump

112

Co.
Dependable power units for
contractors
Domestic Engine & Pump
Co.
A dependable railway
Great Northern Railway
Dependable spark plugs
Champion spark plugs
Dependable time
Sessions clocks
Depression spells opportunity
for the real investor
Sloat & Scanlon
Derby sealer
First in simplicity, first in
value
Derby steak sauce
First aid for clever cooks
Dermassage
P. S. And it's especially
great as a hand lotion
Super-moisturizes dry skin
zones instantly!
Dermetics cosmetics
Beauty designers
Derryvale Irish linen
If it's Derryvale, it's Irish
linen
Des Moines Capital
Nothing to serve but the
public interest
Des Moines Evening Tribune
Iowa's greatest evening
paper
Design/plus
Steelcase, Inc.
Design simplicity and depend-
ability
Adel Precision Products
Corp.
Designed by women for women
Hotpoint Div., General
Electric Company
Designed for giving
Schrafft's chocolates
Designed for going places in
style, in comfort
Pediforme shoes
Designed for touring comfort
Owen Magnetic Motor Car
Designed for your industry,
engineered for you
Coppers Engineering Corp.
Designed for your pleasure
today, tomorrow and

always
Seagram's Distillers Corp.
Designed to be lived in
Irwill sweaters
Designed to guard the integrity
of the contents
Dodge cork closures
Designed to make the passer--
BUY
Autoyre sink racks
Designs for the world's best
dressed
Mr. John
Designs that dreams are made of
M./B. Designs, Inc.
Designs them ... builds them!
Chicago Bridge and Iron
Co.
Desks, Inc.
A complete source for fine
office furniture
De Soto automobile
Fun is where you drive it
Graduate to a De Soto
The great American family
car
Lets you drive without
shifting
Look and ride, then decide
Sets the style
Tell 'em Groucho sent you!
Tomorrow's style today
Detecto
The personal bathroom scale
Determined to serve you best
Eastern Air Lines, Inc.
Detroit Aluminum & Brass Corp.
America's leading bearing
specialists since 1925
Detroit Diesel Engine Div., Gen-
eral Motors Corporation
Better trains follow better
locomotives
Big tools for a big job
Diesel brawn without the
bulk
One proven design through-
out the line builds
greater value into
every engine
Detroit Diesel Div., General
Motors Corporation.
See also: General
Motors Corporation
Detroit Edison utility
Keeping the power in your

hands
Detroit Electric automobile
Society's town car
Detroit Free Press
Starts the day in Detroit
Detroit Life Insurance Co.
First in life, first in death
Detroit News
Always in the lead
Detroit's home newspaper
The home newspaper
Detroit Steel Corporation
Customer satisfaction--our
No. 1 job
Detroit Times
The home newspaper
The newspaper of the buy-
ing population
Detroit's home newspaper
Detroit News
Dettra Flag Co.
We flag the nation
Deutsche Bank
A century of universal
banking
Time is money--24 hours a
day
Developers and producers of
extraordinary materials
The Beryllium Corp.
Developing products for recrea-
tion through electronic
research
Byrd Industries, Inc.
Develops a beautiful line
Jordan swim suits
Deviled Ham. See: Underwood's
Original Deviled Ham
Deviled Spam
The Spam that's ready to
spread
Deviled Spam. See also: Spam
prepared meat
Devilicious!
Underwood's deviled meats
Devoe & Reynolds paint
Fewer gallons, wears longer
The oldest, most complete
and highest quality
line in America
Devoted to the best interests
of South Florida
Palm Beach Times
Devoted to the manufacture of
glass, enamel white-
ware, refractory and

allied products
Ceramic Industry
De Wald radio receivers
A famous name in radio
since 1921
If you want something bet-
ter, demand De Wald
Dewar's Blended Scotch Whiskey
The good things in life stay
that way. Dewar's
never varies
The medal Scotch of the
world
One of the good things in
life that never varies
Dewar's White Label Whiskey
Upon reflection, the best
De Witt Clinton Hotel, Albany,
N. Y.
They all speak well of it
Dexter cigar
Famous for quality
The dial of pleasure
North electric radio receiver
Dial soap
Aren't you glad you use
Dial? Don't you wish
everybody did?
Diamond Brand walnuts
Come on, appetites, let's
go!
Does he love you for your
meals, too?
Diamond Chain Co.
Purposeful growth in power
transmission
Diamond Crystal Salt
Flows freely, dissolves
readily, develops food
flavor
If it isn't Diamond Crystal,
it isn't shaker
It's mild because it's pure
Makes good food taste bet-
ter
The salt that's all salt
Diamond Dyes
Fashion's greatest allies
Diamond International Corpora-
tion
Diamond International is
expanding because you
are
When you grow, we grow
Diamond International is expand-
ing because you are

114

Diamond International Corporation
A diamond is forever
De Beers Consolidated Mines, Ltd.
Diamond roller chain
Today's anti-friction path for power
Diamond Shamrock Corporation
The resourceful company
Diamond T truck
The nation's freight car
Diamond tires
Cut your tire upkeep with a Diamond
Diana corsetry
Brings out the goddess in you
Fast becoming the greatest name in corsetry
Diaparene baby powder
If babies were born trained, they wouldn't need Diaparene baby powder
Dick Jurgens' dance orchestra
Here's that band again!
Dickson. See: Dixon
Dictaphone Corp.
As new as tomorrow
Dictate to the Dictaphone
Doubles your ability to get things done
It's a whole new way to dictate
It's said and done
The shortest route to the mail chute
The trend to Dictaphone swings on
Dictate to the Dictaphone
Dictaphone Corp.
Did you Nugget your shoes this morning?
Nugget shoe polish
Die casting is the process ... zinc, the metal
St. Joseph Lead Co.
Diebold Safe & Lock Co.
Business tools
Buy only what you need when you need it
In case of fire push the button and run
Motion economizer
Office tools
Push the button and run

Record systems that talk facts fast
Space economizer
Talk facts fast
Twilight zone
Diel Watch Case Co.
A deal with Diel means a good deal
Dierks Forests, Inc.
Where quality is a tradition
Diesel brawn without the bulk
Detroit Diesel Engine Div., General Motors Corporation
Diesel Motors Corp.
We help to light and power the world
The diesel truck that pays for itself
Iveco diesel trucks
Diet Center
The natural way to lose weight
Diet-Rite Cola soft drink
America's most modern cola
America's No. 1 low-calorie cola
Dietec
It's strong, caffein-free and safe
Dietrich & Gambrill
Practical feeds for practical feeders
Dietz lanterns
Safe as sunshine
The difference between "party clean" and "partly clean"
Hoover vacuum cleaner
The difference between work and workmanship
Cooper Tools
The difference is in the weave
Chix diapers
The difference is quality
Epiphone, Inc.
The difference is value
Datsun automobile
The difference makes the difference
Anne Alt brassiere
Different and better
Folger's ground coffee
The different antacid
Gelusil
Different because they're dif-

ferent
Pal razor blades
Different, delicious, digestible
Doughnut Corp. of America
Dig for all the world
Hayward buckets
Digby slacks
You can't knock the crease
out
Digestible as milk itself
Velveeta cheese slices
Digital Equipment Corporation
More personal. More com-
puter
We change the way the
world thinks
We're changing the way
people feel about work
Dignifying the pipe
One-Up tobacco case
Dillard Paper Co.
If it's paper
Dillinger. See: Dellinger
Dillon Supply Co.
Caterers to the tobacco
trade
Dill's Best pipe tobacco
It's a mighty fine pipe
tobacco
The dime that covers the world
Newsweek
Dimetane allergy tablets
Give your allergy the bene-
fit of the Dimetane Dif-
ference
Diners Club credit card
Finally, a credit card de-
signed for the people
who use it most
Suddenly, it's the obvious
choice
Diners Club International
Can you afford not to be
a member of the Club?
Even when all roads seem
blocked, Diner's Club
can help you get there
We mean business
Dinner Bell restaurants
A delicious holiday tradi-
tion
Dioxygen Face Cream
Don't put it off, put it on
The dipstick tells the story
Fram oil filter
Dirilyte Flatware

Lovely, logical, alluring
Discount stock brokerage: an
idea whose time has
come
Haas Securities Corporation
Discover award-winning taste
Inglenook Wines
Discover Biz Bleach and discover
a clean, white wash
Biz bleaching powder
Discover Congoleum
Congoleum-Nairn floor cov-
erings
Discover extra coolness
Kool cigarettes
Discover the cleaner feeling of
Zest
Zest soap
Discover the difference
Snapper lawn mower
Southern Comfort liquor
Discover the dry difference
Leisure Lawn gardening
service
Discover the new in New York
State
New York State Dept. of
Commerce
Discover us
St. Joe Minerals Corporation
Discover Viceroy satisfaction
Viceroy cigarettes
Discover what sound is all about
James B. Lansing Sound,
Inc.
The discovery company
Union Carbide Corp.
The disinfecting white paint
Carbola Chemical Co.
Dispels dressing discords
Harmony Brand snap fasten-
ers
Display World
The international authority
on visual merchandising
Disston saws
The saw most carpenters
use
Distance is no barrier to our
service
Citizens Trust Co.
Distance without distortion
Perryman radio receiver
Distilled by the celebrated Old
English process
American Distilling Corp.

Distilled from selected grains
American Distilling Corp.
The distilled motor oil
Sun Oil Company
Distillers & Brewers Corp. of
America
The sign of good taste
Distinctive as your own finger-
print
Rust-Oleum Corp.
Distinctive designs in leather
accessories
Prince Gardner Co.
Distinctive floor coverings since
1917
Ernest Treganowan
A distinguished banking connec-
tion
Bank of the United States
Distinguished by its patronage
Chinwah toilet preparations
Distinguished from every view-
point
Hart Schaffner & Marx
men's clothing
Distinguished furniture for dis-
tinguished offices
Stow and Davis Furniture
Co.
The distinguished service line
W. H. Page Boiler Co.
The distinguished service sep-
arator
De Laval Separator Co.
Ditch the itch with Absorbine,
Jr.
Absorbine, Jr.
Ditchburn Boats, Ltd.
Built on reputation
Ditto duplicating machine
The quickest way to dup-
licate
Diurex pills
The gentle diuretic
The diversified energy company
Reading & Bates
Diversified energy for Mid-
America
Peoples Gas Company
Diversified financial services
growing together
Industrial National Cor-
poration
Divides the road in half
Saf-De-Lite headlights
Diving or driving, you've got

to beat heat
Veedol motor oil
Dixie paper cups
Nowadays they eat and drink
from Dixies
Dixon. See: J. Dixon Crucible
Co.
Do. See also: Du
Do a good turn daily
Boy Scouts of America
Do as your dentist does
Dr. Lyons tooth powder
Do away with shaker-clog
International Salt Co.
Do business with a leader
Rose & Company discount
brokers
Do it all at Nationwise
Nationwise Auto Parts
Do it tomorrow's way ... with
gas
American Gas Association,
Inc.
Do it with air
Buhl Mfg. Co.
Do not ask for toilet paper, ask
for ScotTissue
ScotTissue
Do something for you
Style-Mart suit
Do you wear pants?
Plymouth Rock Pants Co.
Do your smile a favor
Ipana toothpaste
Doan's Pills
Help you get the better of
simple backache pain
Dobbins' Electric Soap
The best family soap in the
world
Doble-Detroit steam car
The car that meets war-
time requirements of
economy and fuel con-
servation
Needs only kerosene for
fuel
Dr. Edward's Olive Tablets
The beauty laxative
Dr. Grabo pipes
Faithfully maintaining qual-
ity at no advance in
price
Ripe 'n' ready for smokin'
steady
Dr. Hand's teething lotion

Just rub it on the gums
The doctor in candy form
Partola
Dr. Lyons tooth powder
The dentifrice that made
fine teeth fashionable
Do as your dentist does
Dr. Miles Medical Co.
Better than whisky for a
cold
Dr. Owen's Body Battery
For man and woman
Dr. Pepper made a Pepper out
of me
Dr. Pepper soft drink
Dr. Pepper soft drink
Be a Pepper
Dr. Pepper made a Pepper
out of me
Good for life
Once you try it you'll love
the difference
Dr. Price's vanilla
Costs less when used
Dr. Scholl's arch supporters
Get relief for your tired,
aching feet
Watch your feet
Dr. Scholl's bunion pads
By the time you're 35
you've probably got
40,000 miles on your
feet. And you can't
trade them in
Feel their cushioning soft-
ness
Give new shoes old shoe
ease
Dr. Scott's Electric Flesh Brush
A beautiful brush, lasting
for years
Dr. Scott's Electric Foot Salve
Something new
Dr. Scott's Electric Toothbrush
Ask for Dr. Scott's. Take
no other
The bristles cannot come
out
See that name is on the
box and brush
Dr. West's Miracle Tuft Tooth-
brush
It reaches the surface of
every tooth
Water-proofed against sogginess

The doctor's prescription
Father John's Medicine
Doctors prove Palmolive's beauty
results
Palmolive soap
Doctors recommend Reast's patent
Invigorator corsets
Invigorator corsets
Dodd. See: Dorothy Dodd shoes
Dodge automobile
America's driving machines
A good name
Dodge builds tough trucks
Dodge Div., Chrysler Cor-
poration
Dodge cork closures
Designed to guard the in-
tegrity of the contents
Dodge Div., Chrysler Corpora-
tion
All-fluid drive belongs to
Dodge, the results be-
long to you
Dodge builds tough trucks
Faster on the getaway, bet-
ter on the hills
Dodge 400 automobile
America's personal driving
machine
Dodge Manufacturing Corp.
The product with the pluses
Dodge trucks
Fit for the job; last longer
Dodger soft drink
The 5-minute vacation
Doe oil burner
Cradled silence
Doelger beer
Millions remember Doelger,
a glass tells why
Does a lot for you
Scovill Mfg. Co.
Does both jobs: cleans teeth,
saves gums
Forhan's tooth paste
Does four jobs at once
Shell motor oil
Does he love you for your
meals, too?
Diamond Brand walnuts
Does Niagara make a noise?
Young & Rubicam advertis-
ing agency
Does not boil away
Prestone anti-freeze
Does not harm the heart

Bayer aspirin
Does she ... or doesn't she?
    Clairol, Inc.
Does something for you
    Style-Mart suit
Does the job better
    Delco appliances
Does the washing where the
        water is
    Home Devices Corp.
Does 20 years experience count
        for anything?
    Woodbury's Facial Soap
Does your hair sing when you
        rinse it?
    Modart Fluff Shampoo
Doesn't scratch
    Old Dutch Cleanser
Doesn't stun 'em, kills 'em
    The Fly-Foon Co.
Doesn't your dog deserve ALPO?
    ALPO beef flavored dog
        food
Dog Food at its best
    Bannock Food Co.
Dog food of champions
    Ken-L-Biskit
A dog worth having is worth
        right feeding
    Austin's Dog Bread
Doggone good tools
    Duro Metal Products Co.
Dogs GO for Gro-Pup
    Gro-Pup dog food
Dogs love Praise
    Praise dog food
Doing one diesel of a job
    Mercedes-Benz trucks
Doing one thing well
    Norman Hilton & Co. men's
        clothing
Dole Pineapple
    The season's eatings bring
        season's greetings
Dole Refrigeration Co.
    Maximum refrigeration ef-
        ficiency
Dole Valve Co.
    Control with Dole
Dollar for dollar, your best
        buy
    Tru-Val shirts
Dollar Rent-a-car service
    At Dollar you're the great-
        est ... and we treat
        you that way!

The new standard in world-
        wide car rental
Dollar Steamship Lines
    Sunshine belt to the Orient
Dollar wise group insurance
    Pan-American Life Insurance
        Co.
DOM B and B
    The drier liqueur
DOM Benedictine
    La grande liqueur francaise
Domestic Engine & Pump Co.
    Dependable power units
    Dependable power units for
        contractors
Domestic Engineering
    The plumbing and heating
        weekly
The dominant newspaper of the
        Great Northwest
    Minneapolis Tribune
Dominate Philadelphia
    Philadelphia Bulletin
Dominion Seed House
    Seeds that satisfy
Dominion shoes
    How much of your overhead
        is underfoot?
Domino. See also: Fats Domino
        and his music
Domino sugar
    Sweeten it with Domino
    When it's Domino sugar,
        you're sure it's pure!
Don Juan Lipstick
    Looks better hours longer
Don Lee Broadcasting System
    We lend you their ears
Don Q Rum
    It's the golden touch that
        means so much
Don X carbonated beverage
    That South American thrill
Donald Duck orange juice
    We know what we CAN
        'cause we can what we
        grow
Donmoor Donbrook
    America's best-liked junior
        wear
Donnatol medicine
    Wide range of therapeutic
        usefulness
Don't ask for "polish," demand
        Brite-Lite
    Brite-Lite polish

119

Don't be a dead-eye Dick
American Chain Co.
Don't be a lemon squeezer, use
Hoffman Tom Collins
Mixer
Hoffman Tom Collins Mixer
Don't be a pale face
Coppertone sun tan lotion
Don't be a ragged individual
Hart Schaffner & Marx
men's clothing
Don't be a RUBBIT!
Brillo Cleanser
Don't be a stranger to Granger
Granger tobacco
Don't be a year behind-er
Ford six cylinder automobile
Don't be satisfied with less than
Lennox
Lennox Industries, Inc.
Don't be vague ... ask for Haig
and Haig
Haig and Haig Scotch whis-
key
Don't buy motors, buy Motor-
Gard
Motor-Gard motor protector
Don't economize on light--
economize on lighting
bills
Welsbach Junior gas mantle
Don't envy a good complexion;
use Pompeian and have
one
Pompeian massage cream
Don't envy beauty, use Pompeian
Pompeian massage cream
Don't feed your canary a diet
of dust
The R. T. French Co.
Don't forget that Koveralls keep
kids klean
Koveralls
Don't get bit, get Flit
Flit insecticide
Don't get mad, get Mystic
Mystic adhesive products
Don't just fertilize ... Spencer-
ize
Spencer Chemical Div.,
Gulf Oil Corporation
Don't live in a "bug house"
Magic Mist bug spray
Don't make "glaring" mistakes
Polaroid Sun Glasses
Don't miss the magic of Rit

Rit dyes
Don't play games with your pim-
ples
Oxy 10 Skin Salve
Don't put a cold in your pocket
Kleenex tissue
Don't put it off, put it on
Dioxygen Face Cream
Kuehnle-Wilson paint
Don't put your assets on ice
SteinRoe Cash Reserves,
Inc.
Don't say "paper," say "Star"
St. Louis Star
Don't say underwear, say Mun-
singwear
Munsingwear underwear
Don't take less than the best,
don't take less than a
Lee
H. D. Lee Co., Inc.
Don't write, telegraph
Western Union Corporation
Don't write, telephone
Bell Telephone System
Don't say beer, say Falstaff
Falstaff beer
Don't say it can't be done ...
talk to Olin
Olin Mathieson Chemical
Corp.
Don't say sunglasses--say
C'Bon!
C'Bon sunglasses
Don't sell our discount short
Rose & Company discount
brokers
Don't squeeze the Charmin
Charmin bathroom tissue
Don't stand still for the 80's
Shakey's, Incorporated
Don't stir without Noilly Prat
Noilly Prat vermouth
Don't take needless chances
Lysol Disinfectant
Don't take tomorrow for granted
Commonwealth Edison Util-
ities
Don't tobacco spit and smoke
your life away!
No-To-Bac
Don't wait 'til it storms
Trico windshield wiper
blades
Don't wait to inherit Spode
Spode, Inc.

Don't wait to order a shrimp
  cocktail--open one
  Sau-Sea shrimp cocktail
Don't write, Voice-O-Graph
  Voice-O-Graph voice re-
  corder
Don't you feel good about 7UP?
  7UP soft drink
Donutz cereal
  The cereal that tastes like
  powdered doughnuts
Door. See also: Dorr
The door that stands the famous
  soaking test
  Wheeler, Osgood Co.
Doree Products Co.
  The modern method of
  beauty care
Doris Miller clothes
  For that good-looking feel-
  ing
Dorman. See also: N. Dorman
  and Co.
Dorman Products, Inc.
  The quality line that's easy
  to find
Dormeyer food mixers
  The new first name in
  mixers
Dorothy Dodd shoes
  As flattering as flickering
  candlelight
Dorothy Gray cosmetics
  Enchanting ladies choose
  Dorothy Gray
Dorothy Gray suntan oil
  Promotes a tan while it pro-
  tects your skin
  Refresh, revive that sleepy
  skin
  Screens out burn and makes
  you brown
Dorr. See also: Door
Dorr-Miller Differential Co.
  Every pound of power pulls
Dorr-Oliver, Inc.
  World-wide engineering,
  manufacturing and
  construction
Dort automobile
  Quality goes clear through
Dot fasteners
  It's a snap with Dot
  Make it a snappy new year
Dots
  Dots for periodical pains

Dots for periodical pains
  Dots
Double action
  Easy Spindrier washer
Double action, single cost
  Sunbrite Cleanser
Double action; washes more
  clothes faster
  Easy Spindrier washer
Double doom to flies and mos-
  quitoes
  Fly-Ded insect spray
The double duty searchlight
  Wakefield searchlight
Double Rotary Sprinkler
  Next best to rain
Double-tumble action
  Launderall clothes washer
Double-value cigar that guaran-
  tees more satisfaction
  La Fendrich cigar
Double wear in every pair
  U. S. Gloves
Double welt means double wear
  Shaft-Pierce Shoe Co.
Double-X Floor Cleaner
  Makes varnish vanish
Double your pleasure with Dou-
  blemint Gum
  Wrigley's Doublemint Gum
Doubles your ability to get things
  done
  Dictaphone Corp.
Doubles your ability to handle
  your car
  Ross Steering Gear
Doubles your face value
  Dreskin cosmetics
Doughboy does it better ... for
  a wide range of indus-
  tries
  Doughboy Industries, Inc.
Doughboy Industries, Inc.
  Doughboy does it better
  ... for a wide range
  of industries
  Doughboy packages it bet-
  ter ... for a wide
  range of industries
Doughboy packages it better
  ... for a wide range
  of industries
  Doughboy Industries, Inc.
Doughnut Corp. of America
  Different, delicious, digest-
  ible

Doughnuts. See: Donutz
   cereal
Doughtridge Fuel Co.
   Be coaled now and you
      won't be cold next
      winter
   One good ton deserves
      another
Douglas. See:
   McDonnell-Douglas Corpora-
      tion
   W. L. Douglas Shoes
Dove creams your skin while
   you wash
   Dove deodorant soap
Dove deodorant soap
   Dove creams your skin
      while you wash
   For softer, smooth skin
      switch to Dove
Dove Skin undies
   Above all, under all
   It's Dove Skin for loveli-
      ness
Dover Farms topping
   The topping that's too
      good to stop with one
      plop
Dow aromatics
   Indispensable to the crea-
      tive perfumer
Dow Chemical Co.
   Chemicals indispensible to
      industry
Dow Corning Corporation
   Where experience guides
      exploration
Dow Jones and Co.
   Instant news service
Dow Jones News Retrieval
   Take control of your in-
      vestments
Dow Jones Software
   Bank on it
Dow Theory Forecasts, Inc.
   A world of profits awaits
      the well informed
Dower Lumber Co.
   Everything to build any-
      thing
Down east feast
   B & M Baked Beans
Down, Gilmore, down!
   Gilmore Oil Co.
Downtown St. Louis at your
   doorstep

Lennox Hotel, St. Louis,
   Mo.
Mayfair Hotel, St. Louis,
   Mo.
Downtowner Corporation
   Sign of happy travel
Downy laundry washing aid
   April-fresh Downy
   Deep Downy softness--a
      noticeable improvement
Dox motor remedy
   When she knocks, use Dox
Doxidan can do it
   Doxidan laxative
Doxidan laxative
   Doxidan can do it
Dozier & Gay Paint Co.
   Make the home look cheerful
Draft exempt
   Cold-Free Bedtime Clothes
Drafted for beauty
   Rap-I-Dol beauty aids
Drake Hotel, Chicago, Ill.
   Where tradition works won-
      ders
Drake's cake
   As good as the best you
      ever ate
Drano drain cleaner
   Drano, the all-purpose
      drain cleaner
   Stop playing lady-in-waiting
      to lazy drains
Drano, the all-purpose drain
   cleaner
   Drano drain cleaner
Drapes of wrath
   Glo-Sheen Drapes
Dravo combines experience and
   innovation to solve its
      customers' problems
   Dravo Corporation
Dravo Corporation
   A company of uncommon
      enterprise
   Dravo combines experience
      and innovation to solve
      its customers' problems
Dream carved rings
   Art Carved rings
A dream of luxury and ease
   Foster's Ideal spring beds
      and accident-proof
      cribs
Dream your dreams at the wish-
   ing well

The Patio restaurant, San
    Rafael, Calif.
Dreft soap flakes
    Acclaimed by millions from
        coast to coast
    Helps stockings wear longer
Dreihorn's Bread
    Baked on the hearthstone
        of reputation
Drene shampoo
    For all types of hair
    It's Spring and she has
        shiny hair; no wonder
        love is in the air
    Let your hair shine like
        the stars
    Makes midsummer "knights"
        dream
    What gives a girl most
        "flair?" Lovely,
        gleaming lustrous hair
    With hair-conditioning ac-
        tion
Dresdner Bank
    Bank with imagination
    Where you see obstacles,
        we may see paths
Dreskin cosmetics
    Doubles your face value
Dress it up with Durkee's
        Dressing
    Durkee's Salad Dressing
Drew Furniture Co.
    Quality shows through
Drexel, Burnham, Lambert Se-
        curities
    Follow your head, not the
        herd
    Your bottom line is our top
        concern
Drexel furniture
    Better your home, better
        your living
    The most trusted name in
        furniture
Dreyfus Tax Exempt Money
        Market Fund
    For the higher tax bracket
        investor
The drier liqueur
    DOM B and B
Dries before your eyes
    Hilo Varnish Corp.
Dries hard overnight
    U. S. Deck Paint
Drilling

So long as the rig is on the
    location
Drink a bunch of quick energy
    Welch grape juice
Drink a glass of "summertime"
    sometime every day
    V-8 vegetable juice drink
Drink a salad
    Vegemato cocktail
Drink Coca Cola
    Coca Cola soft drink
The drink for you
    Honey Dew soft drink
Drink it and sleep
    Sanka Brand decaffeinated
        coffee
Drink moderately, insist on
        quality
    James Clark Distilling Corp.
The drink of friendship
    Jax beer
Drink RC--for quick, fresh
        energy
    RC Cola soft drink
The drink that made Milwaukee
        famous
    Schlitz beer
The drink that tastes like real
        fruit
    Peachy soft drink
Drink V-8 every day for vege-
        tables the tasty way
    V-8 vegetable juice drink
The drink with quick food-
        energy
    Pepsi-Cola soft drink
Drink your vitamins
    Borden's Hemo
Drinking and driving do not mix
    Seagram's Distillers Corp.
Drinks never taste thin with
        Gordon's Gin
    Gordon's Distilled London
        Dry Gin
Dristan
    Relieves twelve cold symp-
        toms
Drive a jeep
    Jeep automobile
Drive America's safest car
    Hudson automobile
Drive away in comfort, drive
        back in safety
    Chevrolet automobile
Drive down your driving costs
    Studebaker automobile

Dromedary gingerbread mix
  It's Washington's mother's
    recipe
The drop-forging people
  J. H. Williams & Co.
Drop that cough
  Smith Brothers cough drops
Drug Products Co.
  In the service of medicine
    for over three decades
Drum makers to the profession
  Ludwig & Ludwig
Drum standard of the world
  Ludwig & Ludwig
Dry cleaning gets clothes
    cleaner
  Sanitone Cleaners
The dry, constant cold of the
    mountain top
  General Refrigeration Co.
The dry goods daily
  Daily News Record
Dry Goods Merchants Trade
    Journal
  A national magazine for
    dry goods and depart-
    ment stores
Dryad
  New kind of cream deo-
    dorant
Du. See also: Do
Du-Ons underwear
  Like wearing a shadow
  Next to nothing at all
Dual duty
  Timken Roller Bearing Co.
Dual's the finest ... the record
    proves it since 1900
  United Audio Products,
    Inc.
DuBarry cosmetics
  The most elegant name in
    cosmetics
Dubilier Condenser & Radio
    Corp.
  It's the working voltage
Dublife collars
  Make old shirts like new
DuBois Chemical Div., W. R.
    Grace & Co.
  Use-engineered for clean-
    ing, protecting and
    processing
DuBois Chemical Div., W. R.
    Grace & Co. See also:
    W. R. Grace & Co.

Dubonnet wine
  It's smart to say "I'll take
    Dubonnet!" Chill it
    ... pour it ... enjoy
Dubuque Ham
  From the tall corn country
Duchin's. See: Eddie Duchin's
    dance orchestra
Duck. See: Donald Duck orange
    juice
Duco automobile polish
  Best known of automotive
    finishes
  Polish Duco with Duco polish
Duesenberg automobile
  The Big D
  The crest of American engi-
    neering
  She drives a Duesenberg
Duff Gordon sherry
  Imported from Spain, of
    course. True sherry
    is
Duff Mfg. Co.
  The aristocrat of auto jacks
  It's light on Duff jacks
Duff's ginger bread mix
  America's most famous line
    of baking mixes
  Just add water, that's all
Duke electric clocks
  New models for the new
    deal
Dumari fabrics
  Makes fashion a fine art
Dumont television receivers
  The first with the finest in
    television
  Get the most out of televi-
    sion with a Dumont Tele-
    set
Dun. See also:
  Dunn
  Dunne
Dun & Bradstreet
  At Dun & Bradstreet, our
    job is to help
  The essential business
  An essential link in the
    sales and profit chain
Dun & Bradstreet credit serv-
    ices
  It's not just a phone. It's
    Dun's dial
Dunbar Furniture Corp.
  Tomorrow is a friend of

Dunbar

Duncan Coffee Co.
The cup of southern hos-
pitality
For goodness sake buy Ad-
miration coffee

Duncan Hines cake
The cake that tastes moist
and delicious

Duncan Hines cake mix
Better than a pastry chef
Moist as homemade

Duncan Hines packaged foods
Always an adventure in
good eating

Dundee towels
The name to remember when
buying towels
Thick thirsty thrifty Dundee
towels

Dunhill cigarettes
Why not smoke the finest?

The Dunhill difference
Dunhill National Personnel
System

Dunhill National Personnel System
The Dunhill difference
Dunhill's got the reach to
find the person you
can't find
We make your hiring job
easier

Dunhill's got the reach to find
the person you can't
find
Dunhill National Personnel
System

Dunlany Foods, Inc.
The finest name in frozen
foods

Dunlop hats
Dunlop hats cover the
population

Dunlop hats cover the population
Dunlop hats

Dunlop Tire & Rubber Corp.
Around the world on Dun-
lops
For the long run
Known 'round the world
for quality in sporting
goods and tires

Dunn. See also:
Dun

Dunne

Dunn-Pen
The pen with the red-headed
filling pump
A regular camel for ink

Dunne. See also:
Dun
Dunn

Dunne skates
Out-speed and out-last all
others

Dun's Review and Modern Industry
The business management
magazine

Duo-Fastener Corp.
In fast to hold fast

Duo-Therm Oil Burner
Heats the room, not the
chimney
Sizzling is silly

Duplex truck
Built for business

Dupont. See also: E. I. DuPont
de Nemours & Co.

Dupont combs
Lovely hair deserves fine
care

Dupont cooling system cleanser
No rust for the wary

Dupont plastic brush
Brush your hair to loveliness

Dur-O-Wal masonry
The original masonry wall
reinforcement with the
truss design

Dura Corporation
Speed. Simplicity. Ver-
satility

Dura-Gilt polish
Polishes all metals

Dura-Gloss is like liquid jewelry
Dura-Gloss lotion

Dura-Gloss lotion
Dura-Gloss is like liquid
jewelry
Keep Dura-Gloss always on
hand
Keep 'em pretty

Dura-Sheen Signs
Permanence for economy

Durabilt steel locker
Built by locker specialists
No better built than Dura-
bilt

Remember the name, it
   signifies locker satis-
   faction
The durable and washable
   covering
   Columbus-Union Oil Cloth
   Co.
Duracell dry cell battery
   The copper topped battery
   It really lasts!
Duraflake Company
   Duraflake makes only par-
   ticleboard and only the
   best
Duraflake makes only particle-
   board and only the
   best
   Duraflake Company
Duraglass bottles
   Guardian of your family's
   health
Durant automobile
   Just a real good car
Durant Star automobile
   Low cost transportation
   Tomorrow's car today
Duration nasal spray
   Get your mind off your
   nose for up to twelve
   hours
Durex Razor Blades
   Saves shaving seconds and
   second shavings
Durez plastics
   Plastics that fit the job
Durez resins
   Resins that fit the job
Durham. See also: Bull Dur-
   ham tobacco
Durham corn starch
   Have you tried it?
Durham-Duplex razor
   The blades men swear by,
   not at
   A real razor, made safe
   Shave with a smile
Durkee's Salad Dressing
   Dress it up with Durkee's
   Dressing
Durkee's Seasoned Salt
   Taste the difference
Duro Metal Products Co.
   Doggone good tools
Dutch Boy White Lead
   Good paint's other name
   I'm a home defender from

'way back
Lead soaps mean fine paint
   (L. S. M. F. P.)
More years to the gallon
Treat your home like an old
   friend
The weather-weight champ
Dutch, dependable and develop-
   ing worldwide
   Amsterdam-Rotterdam Bank
Dutch Masters cigar
   Always a good companion
Dutch name, world fame
   Bols liqueurs
Dutch Oven Gas Range
   Cooks ON with the gas
   OFF
Dutenhofer. See: Stanley Dut-
   enhofer Shoe Co.
Duz does everything
   Duz washing powder
Duz washing powder
   All along the line, Duz does
   everything
   Duz does everything
   Fast for dishes, yet kind
   to your hands
   The finest Duz there ever
   was
Dwight Edwards Coffee
   Matched flavor
   Rich coffee always tastes
   better
Dyed for lasting loveliness
   Hollander Furs
Dyeing with Rit is fast, fun, al-
   most foolproof!
   Rit dyes
A dynamic force with paper
   Kimberly-Clark Corp.
Dynamo is dynamite
   Dynamo laundry detergent
Dynamo laundry detergent
   Dynamo is dynamite
   Penetrates deep for a dyna-
   mite clean
Dyneto-Entz automobile starter
   Simple--Sturdy--Accessible.
   Absolutely prevents
   stalling
Dyola Dyes
   Cheaper to dye than to buy

E. C. Atkins & Co.
  The name back of saw value
E. Edelmann and Co.
  Precisioneered by Edelmann
E. F. Houghton and Co.
  Industry's partner in pro-
    duction
E. F. Hutton & Co., Inc.
  Service to investors
  When E. F. Hutton talks,
    people listen
E. F. Hutton Life Insurance Co.
  Hutton Life. A new way of
    life
E. F. Johnson Co.
  Manufacturers of world's
    most widely used per-
    sonal communications
    transmitters
E. F. MacDonald Co.
  Since 1922, leader in moti-
    vating people
E. H. Titchener Co.
  Working wonders with wire
E. I. DuPont de Nemours &
    Co. See also: Freon
    Products Div., E. I.
    DuPont de Nemours &
    Co.
E. I. DuPont de Nemours & Co.
  Better things for better
    living ... through
    chemistry
  Laughs at time
  Maker of better things for
    better living
  Your investment success is
    our success
E. Kahn's Sons Co.
  Big enough to serve you--
    small enough to know
    you
E. L. Anderson whiskey
  The famous old E. L. And-
    erson Pure Whiskey
  The Little Brown Jug
E. L. Bruce Co.
  Bonded termite insulation
  Leader in prefinished
    hardwoods
E. R. Squibb
  The ball-bearing shave
  Guards the danger line
  It tastes better

Keep fighting, keep work-
    ing, keep singing,
    America
Keep singing, keep working,
    America
Keep singing, keep working,
    keep fighting, America
Keep working, keep singing,
    America
Priceless ingredient of every
    product is the honor
    and integrity of its
    maker
ESB, Inc.
  World leader in packaged
    power
ESPN television broadcasting
    system
  The total sports network
E-Systems
  The problem solvers
E. T. Barwick Industries, Inc.
  World's largest maker of
    tufted carpets and
    rugs
E-Z. See also:
  Easy
  Ezy
E-Z garters
  The one that won't bind
E-Z Polish
  The woman who uses it,
    knows
E-Z underwear
  For any child of any age
Each grain salutes you
  Uncle Ben's, Inc.
Each week the facts add up to
    success
  Sports Illustrated
Eagle clothes
  Eagle means style
  High-sign of style
  What Eagle shows, goes
Eagle computer
  Eagle makes it easier
Eagle makes it easier
  Eagle computer
Eagle means style
  Eagle clothes
Eagle Pencil Co.
  The nation's largest-selling
    drawing pencils and
    leads
  34% stronger points
  The yellow pencil with the

red band
Eagle Radio Co.
    All that is best in radio
Eagle whiskey
    The kind of blends
Earhart. See: Amelia Earhart
    luggage
Early American Toiletries
    Flower-fragrant bath salts
        to make your bath as
        refreshing as perfumed
        rain
Early Times bourbon whiskey
    Always smoother because
        it's slow-distilled
    The true old-style Kentucky
        bourbon
    You'll have better times
        with Early Times
Earn today's high money market
    yields. Tax free
    Fidelity Tax-exempt Money
        Market Trust
Earn while you learn
    International Correspondence
        Schools
Ease your feet ankle-deep into
    Massagic comfort
    Massagic Air Cushion shoes
Easier and quicker than sewing
    LePage's glue
Easier steering, less road shock
    Ross Steering Gear
The easiest and cheapest way to
    heat your home
    Electrol, Inc.
The easiest belt a man ever felt
    Pioneer Suspender Co.
The easiest kind because skele-
    ton lined
    Florsheim Shoe Co.
The easiest line to sell
    Wise shears
The easiest name for a man to
    remember
    Wilson Bros. shirts
The easiest shoe for women
    Utz & Dunn Co.
Easiest travel on earth
    Continental Trailways Bus
        System
The easiest way out
    National Pneumatic Co.
Easily distinguished by the
    yellow back
    Ross Mfg. Co.

Easily identified by the yellow
    back
    Ross Mfg. Co.
Easter greeting cards of charac-
    ter
    Rust Craft greeting cards
Eastern Air-Freight
    Air speed at truck rates
Eastern Air Lines, Inc.
    America's favorite way to
        fly
    Determined to serve you
        best
    See how much better an
        airline can be
    We have to earn our wings
        every day
    The wings of man
Eastern Air Lines, Inc. package
    delivery
    Here today. There today
Eastern beer flavor, local beer
    prices
    Tecate beer
Eastern Express, Inc.
    The motor carrier with more
        go-how
Eastern Mfg. Co.
    The rag-content loft-dried
        paper at the reasonable
        price
Eastern Specialties Co., Inc.
    The roll specialists
Eastham. See: P. W. Eastham
    & Co.
Eastman & Krauss Razor Co.
    It is absolutely impossible
        to cut your face
Eastman Chemical Products, Inc.
    Interested personal service
        --always--when you
        buy from Eastman
Eastman Chemical Products, Inc.
    See also: Plastic Sheet-
        ing Div., Eastman
        Chemical Products, Inc.
Eastman Kodak. See:
    Cine Kodak
    Kodak cameras
Easy. See also:
    E-Z
    Ezy
Easy as opening a book
    Van Camp's pork and beans
Easy at every point
    Hunt Hygienic Saddles

Easy, delicious ... versatile,
    nutritious...
    Rice Council
Easy does it
    Enders shaver
Easy does it, no fishy taste,
    no bad after-taste
    Caritol
The easy food. Easy to buy,
    easy to cook, easy to
    digest
    Quaker White Oats
Easy listening stirs with Seven
    and Seven
    Seagram's Seven Crown
    whiskey
Easy-off Oven Cleaner
    Makes oven cleaning easier
Easy on the sugar, the arm,
    the eye
    Swan's Down cake flour
Easy on your clothes, easier
    still on your pocket-
    book, that's White
    King Soap
    White King Soap
The easy ones
    Kodak cameras
Easy Spindrier washer
    Double action
    Double action; washes more
    clothes faster
Easy to buy, easy to fly
    Stinson aircraft
Easy to buy when new, easy to
    sell when old
    Ford automobile
Easy to play
    Gulbransen piano
Easy to play--easy to pay
    Buescher true-tone saxo-
    phone
Easy to play, pay and carry
    Clark Harp Mfg. Co.
Easy to put on, easy to take
    off
    Columbus McKinnon tire
    chain
Easy to spread, good to taste,
    economical to use
    June Dairy Products Co.
Easy to spread, hard to beat
    National Mortar & Supply
    Co.
Easy to take, quick to make
    Rookie Cookies

Easy to thin, tint and spread
    Carter White Lead Co.
Easy to use
    Listerine toothpaste
    Pompeian Massage Cream
Easy to use, just shake in your
    shoes
    Allen's Foot-Ease
Easy Washer
    As gentle as human hands
    Washes more clothes faster
The easy way to turn
    L. & L. Travel Agency
Eat a 100% breakfast
    Maltex
Eat bread ... more bread
    Fleischmann Co.
Eat candy for energy
    National Confectioners' As-
    sociation
Eat Dailey's with your daily
    bread
    Dailey's jams
Eat it all the year
    Quaker Oats
Eat Johnston Cookies, the taste
    that thrills
    E. A. Johnston Co.
Eat less saturated fat
    American Heart Association
Eat more apples, take less medi-
    cine
    Virginia Horticultural Soci-
    ety
Eat more Jolly Time popcorn
    Jolly Time popcorn
Eatin'. See also: Eaton
Eatin' treats that can't be beat
    Azar's Big Boy Family
    Restaurants
An eating place of distinction
    Cifaldi's Villa Nova restaur-
    ant, Indianapolis
Eaton. See also:
    Charles A. Eaton Co.
    Eatin'
Eaton Manufacturing Co. See:
    Axle Division, Eaton
    Manufacturing Co.
Eaton Paper Corp.
    Always correct
    Any mail for me?
    The correct writing paper
    Famous for generations
    Fine letter papers
    If you can't fight, you can

write
Letters are victory weapons
There is no ration on let-
ters
To get a letter, write a
letter
Write often, write cheer-
fully, WRITE!
Eaton Yale and Towne, Inc.
Applying advanced technol-
ogy to bring you excit-
ing new products
Eats by the clock, pays for it
in time
Pepto-Bismol
Eats dirt
Gellett's lye
Eats everything in the pipe
Sunshine drain pipe cleaner
Eats paint and bites varnish
Bulldog paint remover
Eberhard Faber, Inc.
Insures a new kind of
faultless, effortless
writing
Look to Eberhard Faber
for the finest ... first!
Paint with pencils
Puts its quality in writing
Select the right pencil for
your use
Ebling beer
Aged in natural rock caves
Quality at its best
Echo. See also: Ekco
Echo chain saw
The one that lasts
Echo grass trimmer
The one that lasts
Eckhardt radio receiver
The musical instrument of
radio
A radio that you can play
Eckrich sausages and processed
meats
Good meat from the Heart-
land
Eclipse starter
The mechanical hand that
cranks your car
Economics Laboratories, Inc.
By the world's largest
maker of dishwasher
detergents
Economize without any com-
promise

Chevrolet automobile
The economy gasoline
Tydol gasoline
The economy oil for Fords
Forzol lubricating oil
Ecusta Paper Corp.
The world's finest cigarette
paper
Eddie Duchin's dance orchestra
The magic fingers of radio
Eddy paper
Every Eddy paper takes a
good impression, makes
a good impression
Edelbrew
The beer that grows its own
flavor
Best of all, Edelbrew costs
you no more
Edelman. See: E. Edelman &
Co.
Edelweiss beer
A case of good judgment
The Eden cleans by gentle means
Eden clothes washer
Eden clothes washer
The Eden cleans by gentle
means
Edge Moor Iron Co.
For increased fuel economy
Edge shaving preparation
Nothing shaves closer than
Edge
Edgeworth Tobacco
America's finest pipe tobacco
Ediphone Dictograph
Get your man, no waiting,
no walking
Preference for Ediphone
persists
Think once, write once, at
once
World-wide voice writing
Edison Electric Institute
Live better electrically
Edison Mazda Lamps
Better light, better sight
Edison phonograph
The phonograph with a
soul
The voice at her finger
tips
Edison-Splitdorf Corp.
In electricity it's Edison
from start to finish
Edison-Splitdorf spark plugs

Performance as great as
the name
Edited by yachtsmen for yachts-
men
Yachting
Edited for the woman who must
keep au courant with
the smart world
Harper's Bazaar
Editorial excellence in action
Pit and Quarry
An education by mail
International Correspondence
Schools
Educator shoe
Lets the feet grow as they
should
Room for 5 toes!
The shoe that's standard-
ized
Educator Thinsies
Whole wheat, deliciously
different because
hammered
Edward. See also: King Ed-
ward cigar
Edward Freeman
The last word in fine
leather luggage
Edward Sleep Tire Sales
When you re-tire, go to
Sleep
Edwards. See: Dwight Ed-
wards Coffee
Edward's. See: Dr. Edward's
Olive Tablets
Edwin G. Smith and Co., Inc.
Smitty builds walls for
keeps
Edwin Guth Co.
More light where most
needed
Edwin Jackson, Inc.
Fireplace specialists for
four generations
Egyptian Deity cigarettes
Be nonchalant, light a
Deity
The utmost in cigarettes
Egyptian Lacquer Mfg. Co.
Everlastingly beautiful
The maker who is proud
of what he makes
uses Egyptian Lacquer
Ehlers. See: Albert Ehlers,
Inc.

Eichler beer
Foaming with flavor
New York's finest
Eight companies running hard
Trans Union Corp.
The eight with eighty less parts
Apperson automobile
Ekco. See also: Echo
Ekco Containers, Inc.
Plus packaging
El Dueno cigar
Every El Dueno cigar is
smooth sailing
El Paso, Texas
Where sunshine spends the
winter
Elaine brassiere
For that certain "lift"
Elam Mills, Inc.
The heart's in it
The elapsed time recorder
The Calculagraph Co.
Elastic Stop Nut Corp.
Lock fast to make things
last
The red nylon ring of re-
liability
Elbert Hubbard's Scrap Book
I'd like to know _that_ man!
Elcar automobile
A well-built car
Elco motor boat
The home afloat
The ideal pleasure boat
Elder steam iron
Irons while it steams
Electric. See also: Lectric
Electric battery
The long-life battery for
your car
Electric Hoist Mfrs. Assn.
The strong arm of industry
The electric hoist that operates
in the minimum
American Engineering Co.
The electric ice is self-
defrosting
Belding-Hall refrigerator
Electric Lustre Starch
Cultured Boston people use
Electric Lustre Starch
The electric range with the
safety top
Presteline
Electric refrigeration, a way to
better living

Society for Electrical Development

Electrical Record
The business paper of the
electrical industry since
1892

Electrical refrigeration, a way
to better living
Society for Electrical Development

Electrical World
The weekly journal of the
electrical industry

ElectrICE refrigerator
The simplified electric refrigerator

Electricity gives you matchless
cooking
Los Angeles Bureau of
Power and Light

Electricity gives you matchless
water heating
Los Angeles Bureau of Power and Light

Electro-Copyist
Electro-Copyist, a photo-
copying machine for
every office

Electro-Copyist, a photo-
copying machine for
every office
Electro-Copyist

Electro-Kold Corp.
The simplest electric re-
frigerator

Electro-Tint Engraving Co.
Pioneer process plate
makers

Electro-Voice, Inc.
Setting new standards in
sound

Electrol, Inc.
The easiest and cheapest
way to heat your home

Electrolux Refrigerator
Matchless quality ... superior service ... en-
during excellence
The refrigerator you hear
about but never HEAR
Silent as a Christmas
candle
We went, we saw, we lis-
tened to ... silence

Electromaster range
Leadership born of quality

Electronic Data Systems
Our business is the intelligent use of computers

Electronics
The industry's marketplace

Electronics Corp. of America.
See: Photoswitch Div.,
Electronics Corp. of
America

The elegant 8 year old
Walker's Deluxe bourbon
whiskey

Elegant. Yet so practical
The Wilton Company

Elevators. Quality leather footwear that will make you
almost 2" taller
Richlee elevator shoes

11 kinds--better than most people
make
Heublein cocktails

Elgin Softener, Inc.
Only Elgin gives you Engineering

Elgin watches
America's most distinguished
timepiece
Guard your time
Made in America by Amer-
ican craftsmen
Mark of American leadership
since 1865
Timed to the stars
The watch word of elegance
and efficiency

Eli Lilly and Co.
Prescription medicines
around the world

Eliminate sewing on shank buttons
Pinettes

Eliminates troublesome shaker-
clog
International Salt Co.

Elizabeth Arden cosmetics
The woman of tomorrow
guards today's beauty

Elizabeth Arden suntan oil
Stay pretty in the sun

Eljer Plumbingware Div.,
Wallace-Murray Corp.
Master crafted
Since 1904 fine plumbing
fixtures

Elkay Sturdibilt metal products
The mark of a distinctive

kitchen

Elks Magazine
   The largest magazine for
      men
Elliott Mfg. Co., Inc.
   Wherever fruit grows, our
      machinery goes
Elliott Paint & Varnish
   One coat covers all surfaces
Elliott Div., Carrier Corporation
   Keep your eye on Elliott
Elliott Div., Carrier Corporation.
   See also: Carrier
      Corporation
Elmer Candy Co.
   Goodness knows they're
      good
Elmer's glue
   Best glue in the joint
El Producto cigar
   For real enjoyment
El Rado Depilatory
   The womanly way to remove
      hair
Elto Outboard Motor
   Starts with a quarter turn
Elwell-Parker Electric Co.
   Pioneer in the development
      and construction of
      electric industrial
      trucks
Embassy cigarettes
   It's king-size smoking at
      its best, yet priced no
      higher than the rest
An emblem of security, a pledge
      of service
   Hanover Fire Insurance
      Co.
The emblem of worth in radio
   Kodel radio receiver
Emeralite Desk Lamp
   Kind to the eyes
The emerging giant in financial
      opportunities
   Hereth, Orr & Jones, Inc.
Emerson radio receiver
   World's largest maker of
      small radios
Emery Air Freight Co.
   The air force in freight
Emhart Corp. See:
   Kwikset Div., Emhart
      Corp.
   Savage Arms Div., Em-
      hart Corp.

Emil Brisacher & Staff
   Repetition makes reputation
Emir perfume
   As different from all other
      perfumes as you are
      from all other women
Emkay, Inc.
   A pioneer in the leasing
      field
Empire Brush Works
   Clean around the world
Empire Furniture Corp.
   Where pride of craftsman-
      ship comes first
Empire levels
   Used by skilled craftsmen
      everywhere
Empire memorials, the perfect
      tribute
   Empire Monument Co.
Empire Monument Co.
   Empire memorials, the per-
      fect tribute
Empire Scientific Corp.
   World's most perfect high
      fidelity components
Employers Group Insurance
   The man with the plan
Employers Liability Assurance
      Corp.
   Wise men seek wise counsel
Employers Mutual Insurance Co.
      of Wisconsin
   Good people to do business
      with
   Make insurance understand-
      able
Empties with a thumb pressure
   Bissell carpet sweeper
Emraude perfume
   For the woman who dares to
      be different
En-Ve, Inc.
   Beauty is only skin deep;
      Luminiere controls the
      skin
Enchanting ladies choose Dorothy
      Gray
   Dorothy Gray cosmetics
Enchantment that endures
   Paine Furniture Co.
Enco Div., Humble Oil and Refin-
      ing Co.
   America's leading energy
      company
   First in resources/first in

capability
Happy motoring!
Put a tiger in your tank
Enco Div., Humble Oil and Re-
fining Co. See also:
Humble Oil and Refining
Co.
Encyclopaedia Britannica
A million dollar library for
$25
Encyclopedia Americana
Built through generations
End corn pain instantly
Blue-Jay corn plaster
The end of burdensome tire ex-
pense
Motz cushion tires
The end of the road for athlete's
foot
Micatin Spray
End the day with a smile
Royal typewriter
Ender-Kress leather goods
The mark of America's
smartest leather goods
Enders shaver
Easy does it
Ends that painted look
Tangee lipstick
Enduring as the mountains
Western Life Insurance Co.
Enduring loveliness
Iron Clad hosiery
Enduring masterpieces
Kiel Furniture Co.
Endust
It makes a dust magnet of
your dust mop or cloth
Energene
Keep it clean with Energene
Energy chemicals
Cities Service Company
The energy control company
Robertshaw Controls Com-
pany
Energy for a strong America
Exxon Corporation
Energy ideas at work
Carrier Corporation
The energy people are environ-
mental people too!
Public Service Electric &
Gas Co.
The energy systems company
Combustion Engineering,
Inc.

Enfield. See: Royal Enfield
bicycle
Engel Art Corners
Big enough for any Kodak
print
Small enough to mount on a
stamp
Engine life preserver
Quaker State Oil Refining
Corp.
Engineered brake service
Russell brake lining
Engineered for accuracy
Rensie watches
Engineered for longer life
Minneapolis-Moline, Inc.
Engineered for the ultimate in
precision
Kwik-Way Brake Service
Centers
Engineered for value
Cutler-Hammer, Inc.
Engineered like no other car
in the world
Mercedes-Benz automobile
Engineered sets
Russell brake lining
Engineered to the job
Rollway Bearing Co.
Engineered transportation
Fruehauf Corporation
Engineering consultants on the
South
J. E. Sirrine & Co.
Engineering for boys
Meccano construction toy
The engineering journal of the
industry
Oil Field Engineering
Engineering know-how ... by
Blair-Knox
Blair-Knox Co.
The engineering magazine
Industrial Management
Engineers to the woodworking
industry
Wisconsin Knife Works, Inc.
Englander mattress
America's most luxurious
mattress
Better sleep makes better
husbands
The finest name in sleep
Production for sleep and
rest
Enjay Chemical Co. Div., Humble

Oil and Refining Co.
Anticipating tomorrow's
needs today
Newest look in laminates
Enjay Chemical Co. Div., Humble
Oil & Refining Co.
See also: Humble Oil
and Refining Co.
Enjoy a sip of California Sun-
shine
Alta Vineyards Co.
Enjoy our quality in moderation
Seagram's V. O. whiskey
Enjoy perfect health by using
Oxydonor
Oxydonor cure-all medicine
Enjoy the rest of your life
Koolfoam pillows
Enjoy their smoothness and give
your throat a rest
Spud menthol cigarettes
Enjoy your coffee and enjoy
yourself
Sanka Brand decaffeinated
coffee
Enjoyable always and all ways
Bacardi rum
Enka Crepeset yarn
The yarn with the "crepe"
built in
Enna Jettick shoes
America's smartest walking
shoes
Fashion with comfort
They fit better because
they are better fitted
Eno effervescent salt
Be bright. Feel right.
Take Eno
The criminal within
First thing in the morning
Just put it in and drink--
it stirs itself
The world-famed efferves-
cent salt
The enriched flavor cigarette
Merit cigarettes
Enterprise Flour
Makes baking taste better
Rich in strength
Strength is the foundation
of all good baking
Enterprise meat chopper
The meat chopper for the
people
Enterprise raisin and grape

seeder
Saves time, labor, patience
Enterprising capital
General Electric Credit Cor-
poration
Entertaining New York and New
Jersey 24 hours a day
Radio station WNEW
The envelope is the first impres-
sion
Standard Envelope Mfg. Co.
Envy. See: En-Ve, Inc.
Epic phonograph records
Better music through sci-
ence
Epiphone, Inc.
The difference is quality
Equal low-calorie sweetener
Equal. The taste of sugar,
without sugar's calories
Welcome to the Sweet Life!
Equal. The taste of sugar,
without sugar's calories
Equal low-calorie sweetener
Equipment for every electrical
need
Western Electric Co.
An Equitable Life annuity puts
gold in your purse
when there's silver in
your hair
Equitable Life Insurance Co.
Equitable Life Assurance Society
of the United States
Living insurance
Look ahead with living in-
surance
Equitable Life Insurance Co.
At the head of the nation
An Equitable Life annuity
puts gold in your purse
when there's silver in
your hair
Incoming checks for oncom-
ing years
Equitable Paper Bag
Reflects good taste
Equivalent in light power to 80
sperm candles
Incandescent Metallic petro-
leum lamp
Era laundry detergent
Cleans all the way through
Eradicates dandruff--promotes
hair growth
Rexall "93" Hair Tonic

Erie Railroad
    The heavy duty railroad
        Serving the heart of in-
            dustrial America
Erlanger Brewery
    Thirst come, thirst served
Ernest Holmes Co.
    Outselling all others ... by
        far
Ernest Treganowan
    Distinctive floor coverings
        since 1917
Erving. See also: Irving
Erving Paper Mills
    For serving ... it's Erving
Escape from the ordinary
    Bunko mustard
    Norm Thompson mail order
        service
    Oldsmobile automobile
Espotabs laxative
    Everything will come out
        all right
    Just a good laxative
    Laxate with Espotabs
    The time-tested laxative
Esquire boot polish
    For a "looking glass" shine
Esquire lanolin shoe cleaner
    Keeps white shoes cleaner
        longer
Esquire raincoat
    The perfect raincoat that
        millions of mothers
        have been seeking
Esquire sock
    The smartest thing on two
        feet
The essential business
    Dun & Bradstreet
An essential link in the sales
        and profit chain
    Dun & Bradstreet
Essex automobile
    A thirty minute ride will
        win you
Essex Wire Corp. See: C-P
        Fittings Div., Essex
        Wire Corp.
Essley shirt
    Neatness lasts from break-
        fast to bedtime
Esso farm products
    You can DEPEND on Esso
        farm products
Esso gasoline

For happy motoring
    The sign of extra service
Esso Retread Tires
    Keep the home tires turning
Established 1818
    Brooks Brothers clothing
Established 1826
    Heywood-Wakefield Rattan
        Furniture
Estate Stove Co.
    Cooking is just a SNAP on
        an Estate electric range
    Heats every room, upstairs
        and down
    It's a woman-wise range
    The ranges that bake with
        fresh air
    There is only one Heatrola,
        Estate builds it
    You can't pay for a Heatro-
        la, it pays for itself
Esterbrook Steel Pen Co.
    Quality first ... from Amer-
        ica's first penmaker
    The right point for the way
        you write
    We've got your number
Estey organ
    Unrivaled in tone. Elegant
        in finish. Reasonable
        in price
Esther. See: Lady Esther face
    powder
Ethyl gasoline
    A better run for your money
    The better the gas, the
        better your car
    Knock out that "knock"
    Next time get Ethyl
Etiquet
    The safe-and-sure deodor-
        ant
Euclid Crane & Hoist Co.
    In advance of progress
    Raise profits
Euclid Road Machinery Co.
    Moves the earth
Eureka vacuum cleaner
    Gets the dirt you can't see
    Gets the dirt, not the car-
        pet
    It gets the dirt
    Yours for leisure
Eureka Williams Co.
    The very best in floor
        care products

Europe's foremost airline
  British European Airways
Europe's most helpful airline
  Sabena Belgian World Air-
    ways
Evans. See also:
  Bob Evans farm restaurants
  Bob Evans Farms meat
    products
Evans Products Co.
  The action line
Evans slippers
  Your guide to the best in
    men's slippers
Evans Transportation Equipment
    Div., Evans Products
    Co.
  The "Kid Glove Treatment"
Even a child can tell the differ-
    ence
  Reichardt Cocoa & Chocolate
    Co.
Even beginners can now put up
    "Jewels in Jars"
  Karo Syrup
Even finicky eaters love the
    meaty taste
  Mealtime dry dog food
Even the collars and cuffs are
    clean
  Coffield clothes washer
Even the colour of the label
    separates Cutty Sark
    from the rest
  Cutty Sark Scotch whiskey
Even when all roads seem
    blocked, Diners Club
    can help you get there
  Diners Club International
Even when weather says NO,
    these famous trains
    say GO
  New York Central System
Even your best friends will not
    tell you when you have
    halitosis
  Listerine mouth wash
Evenflo nursing nipple
  America's most popular
    nurser
  It breathes as it feeds
Eventually, why not now?
  Washburn Crosby flour
Eventually yours
  Corette slip
Ever Green Garden Spray

Protects your garden, and
    you
Ever Ready. See also: Eveready
Ever Ready calendars
  That reminds me
Everbest Tomato Preserves
  Made from rosy, baby toma-
    toes, ginger root and
    golden twists of lemon
    peel, it's spicy sweet
Everlastingly beautiful
  Egyptian Lacquer Mfg. Co.
Eveready. See also: Ever
    Ready
Eveready flashlights and batteries
  Death wailed through the
    hideous night
  The light that says "There
    it is"
  Power to spare
  They last longer
  A thousand things may hap-
    pen in the dark
Eveready Nurser
  The second best nurser in
    the world
Eveready radio batteries
  See the difference
  They last longer
  When radio called, Eveready
    was ready
Everess sparkling water
  Makes drinks taste better,
    cost less
  The new sparkling water
  Yes, he's used to the best
Evergreen. See: Ever Green
Everite Pump
  Water by fire
Everlast sporting goods
  The world over, it's Ever-
    last
Eversharp mechanical pencil
  Always sharp, never
    sharpened
  Give Eversharp and you
    give the finest
  Write! Write with Ever-
    sharp!
Eversharp pen
  Writes dry with permanent
    ink
Everstick invisible rubber
  Light and comfortable.
    Easy to put on and take

The rubbers of a gentle-
man
Eversweet deodorant
The dainty deodorant
Everwear trunks
Travel begins with Everwear
Every Acason is a good truck
Acason truck
Every artist an artist
Brunswick phonograph
records
Every Bali has a bow
Bali Brassiere
Every bite a delight
Grennan Cake Co.
Every bite a rarebit
Chicken of the sea tuna
Every bottle guaranteed
Modene Hair Remover
Every business form for every
form of business
Baltimore Salesbook Co.
Every cup's a cup of joy
American Coffee Co.
Every day a COMFORTABLE
day
Climaco Corp.
Every day, Bemis develops a
new packaging idea to
serve you better
Bemis Co., Inc.
Every day in some way
Sunsweet prunes
Every day is a gift day
National Gift and Art Assn.
Every driver an escort
Yellow taxicabs
Every drop delicious
Nash Coffee Co.
Every Eddy paper takes a good
impression, makes a
good impression
Eddy paper
Every El Dueno cigar is smooth
sailing
El Dueno cigar
Every family should have it
Whitman's Instantaneous
Chocolate
Every granule licks dirt 8 ways
Noctil
Every inch has style, every
foot has comfort
Wohl Shoes
Every line a leader
Fairbanks-Morse & Co.

Every man should wear at least
three straw hats
National Association of Straw
Hat Mfrs.
Every mile of yarn gives an extra
year of wear
Cooper Underwear Co.
Every mortgage irrevocably in-
sured
National Union Mortgage Co.
Every one a good one
Davidson radio receiver
Every packet dated; you know
they're fresh
Ferry-Morse seeds
Every pair is full of wear
Kinder-Garten shoes
Every pair made to wear
Gutta Percha rubbers
Every pair shows the care of the
shoemaker's hand
Bostonian shoes
Every party deserves something
extra
Calvert "Extra" whiskey
Every pen pre-tested for instant
touch and go
Venus pen
Every piece a sweet surprise
Milady chocolates
Every pound of power pulls
Dorr-Miller Differential Co.
Every road is a Maxwell road
Maxwell automobile
Every room a separate building
Thorpe Fire Proof Door Co.
Every single time you clean,
disinfect with Lysol
Lysol Disinfectant
Every taste a treat
Pittsburgh Brewing Co.
Every type of adhesive for every
industrial use
National adhesives
Every woman needs a little Vanity
Vanity foundation
Every woman wants Chanel No.
5
Chanel No. 5 perfume
Every year a better Ford, this
year a bigger Ford
Ford automobile
Every year a leader--every year
more desirable. That's
Cadillac
Cadillac automobile

Every year, more Royal type-
    writers are bought in
    America than any other
    brand
Royal typewriter
Everybody appreciates the finest
    Radi-Oven
Everybody deserves a chance
    to make it on their own.
    Everybody
National Urban League
Everybody knows Myers
    F. E. Myers and Bro., Inc.
Everybody loves Admiration
    Admiration cigar
Everybody thinks it's silk
    Lingette
Everybody wants one
    Royal typewriter
Everybody's chewing it
    Val chewing gum
Everybody's Daily
    America's largest Polish
    newspaper
Everybody's Publishing Co.
    Circular printers of the
    nation
Everyday good ... glass with
    flair
    Anchor Hocking Glass Co.
Everyday greeting cards of
    character
    Rust Craft greeting cards
Everyone knows if it's Caryl
    Richards, it is just
    wonderful for your
    hair
    Caryl Richards, Inc.
Everyone needs a little Comfort
    Southern Comfort liquor
Everyone needs the Sun
    Sun Insurance Co.
Everything between the formula
    and the sale
    Illinois Glass Co.
Everything electrical for home
    and industry
    Canadian Westhinghouse
    Company
Everything electrical for the
    theater
    Major Equipment Co.
Everything for blasting
    Atlas explosives
Everything for every mill and
    elevator

Strong-Scott Mfg. Co.
Everything for fire prevention
    and fire protection
    American La France Fire
    Engine
Everything for lithography
    Excelsior transfer paper
Everything for the fireplace since
    1827
    Wm. H. Jackson Co.
Everything for the radio man
    Midwest Radio Co.
Everything hinges on Hager
    Hager Hinge Co.
Everything in Baltimore revolves
    around the Sun
    Baltimore Sun
Everything is under control
    Vogue foundations
Everything its name promises
    Moisturewear makeup
Everything to build anything
    Dower Lumber Co.
Everything to wear
    Genesco, Inc.
Everything to write home about
    Four Seasons Hotel, Toron-
    to, Ont.
Everything we sell, we make
    J. L. Mott Iron Works
Everything will come out all
    right
    Espotabs laxative
Everything you always wanted
    in a beer. And less
    Miller High Life beer
Everything you ever wanted in
    a coat
    Alpagora
Everything you ever wanted in
    an automatic home
    laundry
    Launderall clothes washer
Everything you need in a motor
    oil
    Valvoline motor oil
Everything you want a bank to
    be
    Toledo Trust Co.
Everything's better with Blue
    Bonnet on it
    Blue Bonnet Margarine
Everything's getting smaller but
    performance
    Toshiba desktop copier
Travel with Everwear;

Everwear travels every-
where
Trunks may come and
trunks may go, but
Everwear goes on for-
ever
Everywhere on everything
Glidden paints
Everywhere West
Chicago, Burlington and
Quincy Railroad
Evinrude Motors Div., Outboard
Marine Co.
Evinruding is rowboat
motoring
First in outboards
Evinruding is rowboat motoring
Evinrude Motors Div., Out-
board Marine Co.
Ex-Lax laxative
Acts well, tastes swell
America's largest selling
laxative
The chocolated laxative
The family friend
Join the regulars
Keep regular
Keep regular with Ex-Lax
The original chocolate laxa-
tive
The overnight wonder
When nature forgets, re-
member EX-LAX
Exacting standards only
Sommers Brass Co., Inc.
Exactly resembles Morocco
leather
Pantasote upholstering
material
Excedrin pain reliever
The extra-strength pain
reliever
Helps you relax so you
can sleep
Of all leading brands,
nothing you can buy
gives you more relief.
Absolutely nothing
Excellence doubly safeguarded
Beefeater gin
Excellence in electronics
Raytheon Co.
Excello shirts
Expensive shirts ought to
look it
Excello towels

Biggest name in kitchen
towels
Excelsior Baking Co.
You'll like our krust
Excelsior transfer paper
Everything for lithography
The exception to the law of dim-
inishing returns
Volkswagen automobile
Excitement afoot
Geuting Shoes
Exciting color-drenched woolens
Botany Worsted Mills
Exclusive makers of the original
old-fashioned molasses
candy in delightful mod-
ern flavors
Bishop Candy Co., Inc.
Exclusively yours
Berkeley Junior Fabrics
Executive America's top cigar
Webster cigar
The executive decision
Stouffer hotels
Executive training for business
leadership
Woodbury College
Exide storage batteries
Stampede of power
When it's an Exide you
start
Expanded coverage for
E-X-P-A-N-D-I-N-G
Mid-America
Radio station KCMO
Expanding your ability to com-
municate
Bell Telephone System
Expandra
The fabric with reflex ac-
tion
Expello
Kills moth worms
Sudden death to moths
Expensive shirts ought to look
it
Excello shirts
Experience is the best teacher
Camel cigarettes
Experience is the best teacher,
quality the soundest
lesson
Florsheim Shoe Co.
Experience the difference quality
makes
Hart Schaffner & Marx

men's clothing
The experienced cruise line
  Furness, Withy & Co.,
    Ltd.
Expert's choice ... since 1880
  Ithaca Gun Co., Inc.
Experts know these lamps
  Sylvania Electric Products,
    Inc.
Experts pronounce it beer
  Krueger beer
Explore our objectives
  Penn Square Mutual Fund
Exploring, producing, refining,
    transporting, market-
    ing energy
  Mapco, Inc.
Explosives Div., Atlas Chemical
    Industries, Inc.
  It's what's inside that
    counts
The Expositor
  The minister's trade journal
    since 1899
Exquisite as America's beauties
  Rensie watches
Exquisite, but not expensive
  April Showers talcum powder
Exquisite Form Brassiere
  Wear the bra that gives
    you bravada
An exquisite skin beautifier and
    toilet requisite
  Cuticura soap
Extension Magazine
  The world's greatest Catho-
    lic monthly
The external tonic
  Mifflin Alkohol Massage
The extra action in Tide means
    dirt can't hide
  Tide laundry detergent
The extra care airline
  United Air Lines, Inc.
An extra collar for a dollar
  League Collars
Extra! Extra! News that's
    hot; Spam 'n' pancakes
    hit the spot
  Spam prepared meat
Extra gentle. Soothes, smooths
    as it removes hair fast!
  Nudit cream hair remover
Extra health at no extra cost
  Florida Citrus Commission
An extra measure of quality

Hewlett-Packard Co.
The extra miles are free
  Lion Oil Refining Co.
An extra quart of lubrication in
    every gallon
  Quaker State Oil Refining
    Corp.
Extra-rich fruit flavor
  Jell-o gelatin dessert
The extra-strength pain reliever
  Excedrin pain reliever
Extra strength that never fails
    you
  Bell thread
The EXTRA-sweet corn syrup
  Sweetose syrup
An extra trifle buys this eyeful
  Buick automobile
The extra years of service cost
    no more
  Flintkote paint
The extraordinary fiber
  Trevira
Exxon Corporation
  The center for international
    business
  Energy for a strong Amer-
    ica
  We're more than 100,000
    people working on en-
    ergy
Exxon Office Systems Co.
  People committed to making
    technology work
  Start with us. Stay with
    us
Eye. See also: Birds Eye
    frozen vegetables
Eye-ease at the snap of the
    switch
  Silverglo lamps
An eye for comfort
  Wilsonite sun glasses
Eye it! Try it! Buy it!
  Chevrolet automobile
An eye for your gas tank
  Ford gas gauge
The eye make-up in good taste
  Maybelline
An eye to the future, an ear to
    the ground
  General Motors Corporation
An eyeful of fashions, a buy
    full of features
  Buick automobile
The eyes have it

141

Transit Advertisers, Inc.
Eyes of the night
Ilco headlight
Eyes right
Wilsonite sun glasses
Ezy. See also:
Easy
E-Z
Ezy-Kleen strainers
Blackmer Pump Co.

-F-

F. A. Hoppe, Inc.
For more than 25 years
the authority on gun
cleaning
F. E. Myers & Bro., Inc.
Everybody knows Myers
Myers the finest name in
pumps
Take off your hat to the
Myers
FM at its finest
Bendix radio receiver
FMC Corp.
Putting ideas to work ...
in machinery, chemi-
cals, defense, fibers
and films
FMC Corp. See also:
Bolens Div., FMC Corp.
Oil Center Tool Div., FMC
Corp.
F. Mayer Shoe Co.
For the active woman of
today
FOSTI. See: Fuel Oil Supply
& Terminating, Inc.
F. S. Royster Guano Co.
Field-tested fertilizers
Have stood the test
F. W. Woolworth Co.
Nothing over fifteen cents
Faber. See: Eberhard Faber,
Inc.
The fabric is the soul of the
suit
Botany Worsted Mills
The fabric of tomorrow on the
looms of today
Velon
Fabric shrinkage held to mere
1%
Sanforized cloth

The fabric softener that works
in the dryer
Bounce fabric softener
The fabric with reflex action
Expandra
Fabrics of integrity
Lorraine worsteds
Fabrics used in the most wanted
women's and children's
sportswear
Clan Crest sportswear
Fabrics with the character of
quality
Greenwood Mills, Inc.
Face the facts about your figure
Maidenform corsets
Fact
The money management
magazine
Factor. See:
Max Factor and Co.
Max Factor lipstick
Factory
The magazine for all manu-
facturing
The magazine of manage-
ment
Factory Mutual Insurance Co.
Industry-owned to conserve
property and profits
Factory to rider saves you
money
Mead Cycle Co.
Facts show it, owners know it
Plymouth automobile
Fada Radio, Ltd.
The grand piano of the
radio world
Faerie. See also:
Fairy
Ferry
Faerie undergarments
With that hand-made look
Fafner Bearing Co.
Makers of high grade ball-
bearings, the most
complete line of types
and sizes in America
Fagged? Drink a bunch of
quick energy
Welch grape juice
Fair. See: Fehr beer
Fairbanks-Morse & Co.
Every line a leader
Fairbanks-Morse & Co. See

142

also: Canadian Fair-
banks-Morse & Co.
Fairbanks-Morse Home Water
Systems
For only $70 you can stop
this drudgery!
Fairbanks-Morse scales
A name worth remembering
A time-honored name in scales
Fairchild-Wood Viasphone Corp.
Look and listen
Fairfax and Martex towels
Twin names in quality
towels
Fairmont Coal Bureau
Service to industry
Fairy. See also:
Faerie
Ferry
Fairy Foot shoe
The preferred corrective
shoe
Faithful to the last
Nunn-Bush Shoe Co.
Faithfully maintaining quality at
no advance in price
Dr. Grabow pipes
Faithfully yours on Columbia
phonograph records
Columbia phonograph
records
The faithfulness of an old friend
North East Electric Co.
Falcon Jet Corporation
The leaders fly the Falcon
The legend that started an
airline
We build them better than
we have to. We have
to
Falcon Sportswear
In action and relax-ion
Falfurrias Dairy Co.
Butter that betters the
meal
Falk--a good name in industry
Falk couplings
Falk American Potato Flour
Corp.
The baking aid that nature
made
Falk couplings
Falk--a good name in in-
dustry
It always pays to consult
Falk

The spring damps out the
shock
Fall asleep faster
Unisom
Falstaff beer
America's premium quality
beer
The choicest product of the
brewer's art
Don't say beer, say Falstaff
Good as ever
Those who really know drink
Falstaff
Unmistakably ... America's
premium quality beer
Fame perfume
Anything can happen when
you wear Fame
Famed for flavor
Purity Oats Co.
Famed from toast to toast
Toastmaster toaster
A familiar name of national fame
Printing Machinery Co.
Families that move the most call
the world's largest
mover
Allied Van Lines, Inc.
The family barber
Sta-Neet hair cutting set
Family car of the air
Cessna Aircraft Co.
Family Circle
A magazine only a home-
maker could love
The family friend
Ex-Lax laxative
The family liniment
Sloan's Liniment
A family of companies building
for the future
National Gypsum Company
A family-owned business de-
voted to quality
Corbin Ltd. Tailoring
The family plate for seventy
years
International Silver Co.
The family that prays together,
stays together
Family Theater, Inc.
Family Theater, Inc.
The family that prays to-
gether, stays together
A famous brand in glass
Latchford Glass Co.

A famous camera from camera-
  famous West Germany
  Minox Corp.
The famous energy food
  Crown Brand corn syrup
The famous family of Gorton's
  sea foods
  Gorton-Pew Fisheries, Inc.
Famous for biscuits
  E. A. Johnston Co.
Famous for candy flavors
  Fenn Bros., Inc.
Famous for five generations
  Oil City Brewing Co.
Famous for flavor
  Breakstone butter
  New State Coffee
Famous for food
  Hotel Indiana, Fort Wayne,
  Ind.
Famous for generations
  Eaton Paper Corp.
Famous for its flavor
  Flavor flour
Famous for its perfect head
  Guinness ale
Famous for power mowers for
  over 50 years
  Toro power mowers
Famous for products that really
  work
  Glamorene Products Corp.
Famous for quality
  Brunswick Rubber Co.
  Dexter cigar
Famous for quality the world
  over
  Philco radio receiver
Famous for their razor-sharp
  edges
  Remington cutlery
A famous name in automobile
  history
  Warner radiator cleaner
Famous name in pain relief
  Sloan's Liniment
A famous name in radio
  Johnson indicator lights
A famous name in radio since
  1921
  De Wald radio receivers
The famous old E. L. Ander-
  son Pure Whiskey
  E. L. Anderson whiskey
The famous pencil with green
  and yellow plastips

J. Dixon Crucible Co.
Famous Recipe Chicken
  How do you get famous in
  the chicken business?
  The way we make it is mak-
  ing us famous
The famous rubbing liniment
  Minard's Liniment
Famous shoes for women
  Queen Quality shoes
Famous since 1847
  Smith Brothers cough drops
The famous skin softener
  Campana Italian Balm
Famous. Smooth. Mellow
  Old Crow whiskey
The famous Southern Praline
  Southern Candy Co.
Famously good
  Skookum Packers Assn.
The fan-jet airline
  Northwest Airlines, Inc.
Fan Jet Falcon aircraft
  The business jet that's
  backed by an airline
Fancy Feast Gourmet catfood
  One moist and delicious
  meal in every can
Fant Milling Co.
  Stands the oven test
Fantasy in freedom
  Blue Swan undies
Far quicker, handier than a no-
  stropping razor
  AutoStrop safety razor
Far sighted planners choose
  Herman Nelson
  Herman Nelson air filters
Faradon radio receiver
  Fit out with Faradon
Fargo-Hallowell Shoe Co.
  From first step to fourteen
  years
  Made stronger to wear
  longer
The farm-fresh spread betters
  any bread
  Pillsbury's Flour
Farm implements with a future--
  yours!
  Brillion Iron Works, Inc.
Farm Journal
  Biggest in the country
  First in the farm field
  Getting results in rural
  America is Farm

Journal's business
The magazine farm families
depend on
Farm Life
As national as agriculture
The farm paper of service
Michigan Business Farmer
The farm paper with a mission
American Farming
Farm Store Merchandising
Sell the man who talks to
the farmer just before
the sale
The farm weekly of largest cir-
culation and most influ-
ence
Progressive Farmer
The Farmer
The northwest's only weekly
farm paper
Farmers believes life insurance
is a celebration of life
Farmers New World Life In-
surance Company
Farmers Cotton Oil Co.
Best by actual test
Suits your land
We make a brand to suit
your land
Farmers Deposit Bank
Behind the enduring insti-
tution, successful
customers
Farmers New World Life Insur-
ance Company
Farmers believes life insur-
ance is a celebration
of life
The farmer's service station
Successful Farming
The Farmer's Wife
A magazine for farm women
Only one magazine edited
for rural women ex-
clusively
Farnsworth radio receiver
It costs no more to enjoy
Farnsworth fidelity
Depend on Farnsworth for
fidelity
Farnsworth television receivers
The Cadillacs of the industry
Farrel-Birmingham Co.
The gear with a backbone
Farrell-Cheek Steel Co.
First name in cast steel!

Farrell Lines, Inc.
African business is our
business
We never stop widening our
horizons
Fascinating brilliancy
Glenn's Sulphur Soap
Fashion begins with your fabric
Peter Pan
Fashion Eze shoes
Styled to comfort
Fashion forecasters
International Shoe Co.
Fashion in action
Wrangler's ranch togs
Fashion loomed to last
Magee Carpet Co.
Fashion luggage
Lady Baltimore luggage
Fashion over-the-shoe
U. S. Gaytees rubbers
The fashion shoe
Mademoiselle shoe
Fashion with comfort
Enna Jettick shoes
Fashionable Dress
The magazine for milady
Fashioned by Master craftsmen
Nunn-Bush Shoe Co.
Fashioned each season to fit
each season's fashions
Royal Worcester Corset Co.
Fashioned for those who enjoy
extra-ordinary quality
Gerber Legendary Blades
Fashion's favored footwear
Washington Shoe Mfg. Co.
Fashion's greatest allies
Diamond Dyes
Fast becoming the greatest name
in corsetry
Diana corsetry
Fast colors without slow boiling
Rit dyes
Fast for dishes, yet kind to
your hands
Duz washing powder
Fast relief for sore throat pain
Chloraceptic throat medicine
Fast running
Whippet Bond paper
Fast-stepping stride, a marvelous
ride
Chrysler automobile
Fasteeth denture adhesive
A better hold in no time

Fasten it better and faster
with Bostitch
Bostitch stapler
Fastens it better and faster with
wire
Bostitch stapler
Fastens it better with wire
Bostitch stapler
Faster on the getaway, better
on the hills
Dodge Div., Chrysler Cor-
poration
Faster starts with Monarch
Monarch automobile batteries
The fastest growing battery
business in America
Prest-O-Lite
The fastest-growing newspaper
and fastest-growing
city in Texas
Houston Post-Dispatch
The fat of the lime is Urshelime
Urshelime
Fated to be dated
June Arden Dress
Father & Son shoes
A million Americans can't
be wrong
Father John's Medicine
The doctor's prescription
Father of tree surgery
Davey Tree Expert Co.
Fatima cigarettes
Just enough Turkish
A sensible cigarette
What a whale of a difference
just a few cents make
Fats Domino and his music
The million dollar magic of
Fats Domino
Faucets without a fault
Mueller Co.
Faultless casters
Move the Faultless way
Faultless laundry starch
Faultless starch lightens
laundry labor
A touch of Faultless adds
that faultless touch
Faultless Nightwear Corp.
Faultless since 1881--the
nightwear of a nation
The NIGHTwear of a na-
tion
Faultless since 1881--the night-
wear of a nation

Faultless Nightwear Corp.
Faultless starch lightens laundry
labor
Faultless laundry starch
Faust Chili Powder
Faust Chili Powder is a
"different" seasoning
Faust Chili Powder is a "differ-
ent" seasoning
Faust Chili Powder
Faust Shoe Co.
Little shoes for little devils
Favor furniture polish
Touchable shine
Favored footwear of Her Majesty,
"Queen for a Day"
Queen Quality shoes
A favorite dessert for over 40
years
Jell-O gelatin dessert
The favorite home-sewing notion
of the nation
Slide Fasteners, Inc.
Favorite "meating" for particular
people
A & P Super Market
Favorite of housewives for 150
years
Baker's Breakfast Cocoa
Favorite of the nation's bakers
National Bakery Div., Pack-
age Machinery Co.
Favorite shells satisfy good
shooters
Federal Cartridge Corp.
A favorite wherever buddies
bunk
Almond Candies
Fay. See: Leslie Fay, Inc.
A feast for the least
Van Camp's pork and beans
Feather touch control
Acme Life Products Co.
Feature rich
Aiwa tape recorders
The featured brand throughout
the land
Sanpeck fabric
Fedders. See also: Feder's
Fedders Corp.
World's largest selling air
conditioners
Federal Advertising Agency
In Federation there is power
The interrupting idea
Put it up to men who know

your market
Federal Bond & Mortgage Co.
  Safety and conservation,
    our aim and policy
Federal Cartridge Corp.
  Favorite shells satisfy good
    shooters
Federal Express Corporation
  When it absolutely, posi-
    tively has to be there
    overnight
  Why wait when you don't
    have to?
Federal Mill
  Good flours make good
    bakers better
  Good flours make good
    cooks better
Federal-Mogul Corp.
  First for fast service
Federal Radio Corp.
  Rivaled only by reality
Federal School
  America's foremost school
    of commercial art
Federal tires
  Good for a long, safe ride
  Skip the rest and drive
    the best
Feder's. See also: Fedders
Feder's Pompadour Skirt Pro-
    tector
  The best stores sell them
The feed that is all feed
  Corno Mills
The feeder's silent partner
  Tuxedo Feeds
Feeds that never vary
  Larrowe Milling Co.
Feel better with Ben-Gay
  Ben-Gay lotion
Feel fine, go alkaline
  Saratoga Vichy Spring Co.
Feel it heal
  Noxema skin cream
The feel of silk, the strength
    of linen
  Utica sheets
Feel the air cushion
  Weyenberg Shoe Mfg. Co.
Feel the fabric and you'll feel
    the difference
  Botany shirts
Feel the Velvet
  Black Velvet blended Cana-
    dian whiskey

Feel their cushioning softness
  Dr. Scholl's bunion pads
The feeling of security
  Columbia Casualty Co.
Feeling safe. Feeling secure.
    It's a Mutual feeling
  Liberty Mutual Insurance
    Company
Feels better, too
  Pfister Associated Growers
Feels slickery
  N'ice cough lozenges
Feen-a-Mint
  The chewing laxative
  The laxative chewing gum
  Three minutes of chewing
    makes the difference
Fehr beer
  It's always Fehr weather
Feist. See: Leo Feist, Inc.,
    music publishers
FEL-PRO sets the standards for
    the gasketing industry
  Felt Products Mfg. Co.,
    Inc.
Felin's fresh sausage
  Serve the meats your butch-
    er eats
Fellows Gear Shaper Co.
  The precision line
Fellowship Forum
  The national weekly news-
    paper devoted to the
    fraternal interpretation
    of the world's current
    events
Fels Naphtha soap
  Avoid "tattletale gray"
  Banishes "tattletale gray"
Felt Products Mfg. Co., Inc.
  FEL-PRO sets the standards
    for the gasketing indus-
    try
Felton, Sibley & Co.
  No other paint stays
    brighter under the sun
The feminine way to beautiful
    skin
  Nudit cream hair remover
Fenn Bros., Inc.
  Famous for candy flavors
Fenner, Beane & Co.
  Complete brokerage service
    in the world's markets
Fenwal, Inc.
  Controls temperature ...

precisely
Ferguson. See also: H. Fer-
guson Farm Equipment
Ferguson radio receiver
The gold standard of radio
receivers
Ferguson Tractor
That makes the difference
Fernstrom Storage and Van Co.
The people who care about
people who move
Ferranti transformer
The nearly perfect trans-
former
Ferry. See also:
Faerie
Fairy
Ferry-Morse seeds
Every packet dated; you
know they're fresh
Seeds you can trust
The fertilizer, energy and
metals company
The Williams Companies
Fess oil burner
It costs less to run a Fess
Festive evenings often start
with Red
Johnnie Walker Red Label
Scotch whiskey
Fewer gallons, wears longer
Devoe & Reynolds paint
Fiat automobile
Motor cars in the great
European tradition
Nothing moves you like a
Fiat Sportscar
Fiber. See also: Fibre
Fiber Glass Div., PPG Indus-
tries, Inc.
Makes products better,
safer, stronger, lighter
Fiber Glass Div., PPG Indus-
tries, Inc. See also:
PPG Industries, Inc.
The fiber that carpets the
country
Antron carpets
The fiber you can trust
Cotton Producers Institute
Fiberfab MG Replica
You don't know what it is
to love a car until you
build one
The fiberglass for finer fabrics
PPG Industries, Inc.

Fibre. See also: Fiber
Fibre-sorted soles
A. C. Laurence Leather Co.
Ficks Reed Co.
The most famous name in
rattan furniture
Fidelity Bond & Mortgage Co.
Fidelity means keeping faith
Fidelity Group
High tax-free yield with no
sales charge. That
makes us a star
Over $9 billion of assets
under management
Fidelity Magellan Fund
Magellan: top performance.
Consistently
Fidelity means keeping faith
Fidelity Bond & Mortgage
Co.
Fidelity Mutual Bond Fund
Call Fidelity. It's high
time
Fidelity/Source Discount Brok-
erage
All you have to lose is high
commissions
Fidelity Tax-exempt Money Mar-
ket Trust
Earn today's high money
market yields. Tax
free
Fidelity U. S. Government Re-
serves
Today's high yields. Plus
U. S. Government se-
curity
Field & Flint Co.
The shoe that's different
Field & Stream
America's magazine for the
outdoorsman
America's number one sports-
man's magazine
Field Crest Mills, Inc.
Coordinated fashions for bed
and bath
Field Crest Mills, Inc. See
also: Karastan Rug
Mills Div., Field Crest
Mills, Inc.
Field-tested fertilizers
F. S. Royster Guano Co.
5th Ave. Candy Bar
Tastes like a million, mil-
lions love its taste

51 writes dry with wet ink
  Parker 51 pen
Fifty per cent more wear
  H. D. Lee Co., Inc.
57 varieties
  Heinz food products
50 years of brighter tasting
    meals
  Corning Ware
Fifty years of fine baking
  National Biscuit Co.
Fight headache pain and win
  Anacin pain reliever
Fight motor oil breakdown
  STP oil additive
Fight pain and win with Anacin
  Anacin pain reliever
A fighting heart of honest rub-
    ber
  Cupples tires
Fights bad breath, doesn't give
    medicine breath
  Scope breath deodorant
Fights colds and sore throats
  Listerine mouth wash
Fights odor between washings
  Cling Free washing aid
Fights the enemies of your
    mouth
  Gleem toothpaste
Fights wetness and odor
  Arrid anti-perspirant
A file for every purpose
  Nicholson File Co.
Fileworthy
  St. Louis Post-Dispatch
Filko. See also: Philco
Filko Ignition
  The crown jewels of igni-
    tion
  The crown jewels of igni-
    tion and carburetion
Fill up before you freeze up
  Thermo anti-freeze
Fill with water, write with ink
  Camel fountain pen
Fill your cup to the rim with
    the richness of Brim
  Brim concentrated coffee
Fills a universal need
  Universal Cooler Corp.
Film Daily
  First in film news
Film finished painter
  Woodbury's face powder
The film of protection

Veedol motor oil
Filmo movie camera
  For superb personal movies
The filter for the taste that's
    right!
  Viceroy cigarettes
Filter Queen vacuum cleaner
  The bagless vacuum cleaner
Filters sun, speeds tan
  Sutra lotion
Filters the smoke from bowl to
    tip
  Forecaster pipe
Fin. See: Phin, Inc.
Final Net hair spray
  Final Net holds up longer
    than you do
Final Net holds up longer than
    you do
  Final Net hair spray
Final Touch
  For a soft, whiter wash
The final touch to a tasty dish
  Liberty Cherry & Fruit Co.
Finally, a copier that gives you
    an original
  Ricoh Copiers
Finally, a credit card designed
    for the people who use
    it most
  Diners Club credit card
Finally, Businessware
  Honeywell, Inc.
Finally, you can get a good se-
    lection of great-looking
    clothes that fit
  King-Size men's clothing
The Finance Company of America
  Over 60 years of financing
    for commerce and indus-
    try
Financial. See also: CIT Finan-
    cial Corporation
The financial printer
  Pandick Press, Inc.
The financial service. Worldwide
  Manufacturers Hanover
    Bank
Financial Times
  Where politics and economics
    converge ... the Finan-
    cial Times excells
Financial World
  America's investment weekly
The financing people from Gen-
    eral Motors

149

General Motors Acceptance
Corporation
Find it faster in the yellow
pages
Bell System telephone di-
rectory yellow pages
Find this button and you've
found the belt
Modern Belt Co.
Find your place in the sun
San Francisco peninsula
Fine bootmakers since 1876
Charles A. Eaton Co.
Fine cabinetmakers since 1886
Karges Furniture Co.
A fine car made finer
Pontiac automobile
Fine chemicals
Allied Chemical Corp.
Fine coffee liqueur ... from
sunny Mexico
Kahluá coffee liqueur
Fine combed, fine count percale
sheets
Utica sheets
Fine dinnerware
Vernonware
Fine fabrics made in America
since 1813
J. P. Stevens and Co.,
Inc.
Fine fashion jewelry
Sarah Coventry, Inc.
Fine flooring
Ruberoid Company
Fine floors
Congoleum-Nairn floor cov-
erings
Fine food products
Geo. A. Hormel and Co.
Fine for the breath
Wrigley's P. K. chewing
gum
Fine furniture
George J. Kempler Co.
Henredon furniture Indus-
tries, Inc.
Fine labeling identifies finer
products
New Jersey Machine Corp.
Fine letter papers
Eaton Paper Corp.
A fine new value and a fine
old name
Pontiac automobile
The fine old innkeeping tradi-

tion in a modern setting
Holiday Inns of America, Inc.
Fine overcoat makers since 1901
Barron-Anderson Co.
Fine papers
Crane and Company, Inc.
Fine photography for 40 years
Minolta Corporation
Fine soaps--naturally
Americore Soaps
Fine tobacco is what counts in a
cigarette
Lucky Strike cigarettes
A fine tool at a fair price
Capewell Mfg. Co.
Fine watchmakers since 1791
Jean R. Graef, Inc.
Fine whiskey on the mild side
Corby's whiskey
Finely designed as the ultimate
kind
Ohio Brass Co.
Finer filter. Finer flavor
Winston cigarettes
Finer flavor from the Land O'
Corn
Rath sausages
Finer fuels for the age of flight
Shell Oil Company
Finer roasts with less gas
Burns coffee roaster
Finer seamless stockings
Oleg Cassini, Inc.
Finer taste and after-taste
Spud menthol cigarettes
Finer than ever before
Hamilton Watch Co.
Finer than many face powders
Mavis talcum powder
Finer than the finest
Pittsburgh Brewing Co.
Finer than the finest castile
Castolay soap
A finer typewriter at a fair
price
Oliver typewriter
The finest aluminum
Mirro Aluminum Co.
Finest American wines since 1835
Virginia Dare wines
Finest anti-knock non-premium
gasoline ever offered
at no extra cost
Union Oil Company
The finest beer we ever brewed
Schaefer beer

The finest bread in America
Langendorf United Bakeries
Finest china since 1735
Richard Ginori china
The finest chocolate in the world
Bachman Chocolate Mfg. Co.
The finest clock since time began
Brock clocks
The finest Duz there ever was
Duz washing powder
The finest dye that money can
buy
Rit dyes
The finest food preparer for the
home
Kitchen Aid food mixer
The finest handmade and exotic
Western boots for men
and women
Jonathan Western boots
The finest human hands can
achieve
Langrock Clothing Co.
The finest ice making unit ever
made
Henry Vogt Machine Co.
The finest in expanded vinyl
fabric
Royal Naugahyde
Finest in flooring since 1898
Harris Hardwood Co.
Finest in sporting arms
Browning Arms Company
The finest in the field
Rawlings Corp.
The finest in vinyl upholstery
Royal Naugahyde
The finest name in fabrics
Goodall Worsted Co.
The finest name in frozen foods
Dunlany Foods, Inc.
The finest name in locks and
hardware
Yale and Towne locks
The finest name in sleep
Englander mattress
The finest of natural cheeses--
naturally from Kraft
Kraft Foods Div., Kraftco
Corp.
Finest of the famous "Silver
Streaks"
Pontiac automobile
The finest oil that man produces,
suited for a thousand
uses

3-in-1 oil
The finest pads have purple
bindings
The Universal Pad and
Tablet Corp.
Finest personalized values since
1919
The American Stationery
Company, Inc.
The finest protection available
for your family, your
property and your
business
Fireman's Fund American
Insurance
Finest quality on wheels--since
1885
The Colson Corporation
The finest reproducing phono-
graph
Steger & Sons Piano Co.
The finest riding carts in the
world
Babcock carts and carriages
The finest silverplate
Community silverplate
The finest tribute ... the most
trusted protection
Clark Metal Grave Vault
Co.
Finest way to make a pick-up
supper super
Stokely-Van Camp, Inc.
The finest wines of France
Barton and Guestier
Finger-Reach Control
Autocar automobile
Fingers of steel
Red Devil Pliers
A finished picture in a minute
Nodark Camera
The finishing touch you can't
afford to forget
Seaforth deodorant
Finnell System, Inc.
Clean floors reflect clean
business
It waxes, it polishes, it
sands, it scrubs
Fir. See also: Furs
Fir Door Institute
Nature makes Douglas fir
durable
Fire Association Group
Symbol of security since
1817

Fire Equipment Mfrs. Inst.
    Fortify for fire fighting
The fire extinguisher anyone
        can use
    Stop-Fire extinguisher
Fire insurance is as old as the
        Sun
    Sun Insurance Co.
Fire need have no terrors
    Harris Portable Fire Es-
        capes
Fire up with Firebird
    Firebird gasoline
Firebird gasoline
    Fire up with Firebird
    Worth changing brands to
        get
Fireman's Fund American Insur-
        ance
    Always worth par when
        misfortune strikes
    The finest protection avail-
        able for your family,
        your property and your
        business
    Inventor and scientist make
        dreams come true; the
        insurance man keeps
        nightmares from hap-
        pening
    Strength, permanence and
        stability
    Your hometown agent
    Your premium's worth
Fireplace specialists for four
        generations
    Edwin Jackson, Inc.
The fireproof sheathing
    U. S. Gypsum Co.
The fireproof wallboard
    U. S. Gypsum Co.
Firestone luggage
    Best today, still better
        tomorrow
Firestone Mechanically Fastened
        Pneumatic Tires
    Quality. Security. Sim-
        plicity
Firestone Tire and Rubber Co.
    The name that's known is
        Firestone--all over the
        world
    Pioneer and pacemaker in
        essential fields of in-
        dustry
    Your symbol of quality

and service
Firestone tires
    The greatest tire name in
        racing
    High-performance tire power
    It's one tough tire to stop
    Most miles per dollar
    Outcleans, outpulls, outlasts
Firox insulation
    Firox saves the firebox
Firox saves the firebox
    Firox insulation
First aid for all the family
    Sodiphene antiseptic
First aid for clever cooks
    Derby steak sauce
First aid for thirst
    Lime Cola
First airline in the Americas
    Avianca
First always, finest all ways
    Florsheim Shoe Co.
The first American watch
    Waltham watches
First among fine watch bands
    Bretton watch bands
First among fine whiskies
    Three Feathers whiskey
First and finest in copper and
        brass. Fully integrated
        in aluminum
    Revere Copper and Brass,
        Inc.
First and foremost in microfilm-
        ing since 1928
    Recordak Corp.
First and foremost line of clean-
        ing products
    Gunk Laboratories, Inc.
The first and greatest name in
        electronics
    General Electric Company
The first and last word in fa-
        mous pens
    Waterman's Ideal Fountain
        Pen
The FIRST baby foods
    Clapp's Baby Foods
First Boston Bank
    Thinking capital
First, by choice
    Sunbeam Ironmaster electric
        iron
First by far with a postwar car
    Studebaker automobile
First, by merit

Milwaukee Journal
The First Canadian Bank
  Bank of Montreal
First choice for aprons
  Lawrence Leather Co.
First choice in fishing tackle
    hardware
  Allan Mfg. Co.
First choice in food, lodging and
    service naitonwide!
  Holiday Inns of America,
    Inc.
The first choice of experience
  Quaker State Oil Refining
    Corp.
First class on Asia's first airline
  Philippine Airlines
The first computer
  Sperry Rand Corporation
The first computer designed
    solely for the purpose
    of being a first com-
    puter
  Data General Corporation
The first cost is the last ex-
    pense
  New Jersey Zinc Co.
The first different smoking
    tobacco in a generation
  Half & Half smoking tobacco
First--every year
  Goodyear Auto Tire
First family in drapery hardware
    since 1903
  Newell Manufacturing Co.
The first family of fireworks
  Grucci fireworks
First for fast service
  Federal-Mogul Corp.
First for flavor
  Pittsburgh Brewing Co.
First for the South
  New Orleans Time-Picayune
First for your feast
  Campbell's condensed soups
First, from the very first
  Ray Oil Burner Co.
The first great perfume born in
    America
  Norell
The first hands to touch it are
    yours
  Kraft Foods Div., Kraftco
    Corp.
First he whispers, then he
    shouts

Big Ben Westclox alarm
    clock
First in airfreight with airfreight
    first
  Flying Tiger Line, Inc.
First in all-metal personal planes
  Silvaire aircraft
First in aluminum
  Aluminum Company of Amer-
    ica
First in automated materials
    handling
  Barrett Electronics Corp.
First in automation
  The Cross Company
First in banking
  Bank of America
First in canned dog food
  Ken-L-Ration
First in carbonless papers
  National Cash Register Co.
First in cellulose
  Buckeye Cellulose Corp.
First in Chicago
  Chicago Daily News
First in Cleveland
  Cleveland Press
First in creative engineering
  Bendix Corporation
First in dependability
  Johnson Motors Div., Out-
    board Marine Co.
First in elastic supports
  Bauer & Black
First in engineered plastics
  Hareg Industries, Inc.
First in epoxies ... in the age
    of ideas
  CIBA Products Co.
First in fabric forming equipment
  Textile Machinery Div.,
    Crompton and Knowles
First in fabrics for industry
  Industrial Fabrics Div.,
    West Point-Pepperell,
    Inc.
First in fashion
  Patcraft Mills, Inc.
First in fencing
  Crown Iron Works Co.
First in film news
  Film Daily
First in foods
  American Dairy Association
First in grassland farming
  New Holland Div., Sperry

153

Rand Corporation
First in home service
Watkins Products, Inc.
First in insulations
Johns-Manville Corporation
First in Latin America
Pan American World Airways,
Inc.
First in life, first in death
Detroit Life Insurance Co.
First in loans to business and
industry
Chase Manhattan Bank
First in marine propulsion
Keikhaefer Mercury Div.,
Brunswick Corp.
First in outboards
Evinrude Motors Div., Out-
board Marine Co.
First in powered equipment since
1918
Bolens Div., FMC Corp.
First in quality
Schenley Distillers Corp.
First in quality!
Nunn-Bush Shoe Co.
First in quality conveyers and
driers for the plastics
industry
Whitlock Associates, Inc.
First in quality, performance,
preference
Clorox bleach
First in resources/first in capa-
bility
Enco Div., Humble Oil and
Refining Co.
First in rubber
B. F. Goodrich Tire Co.
Goodrich Silvertown tire
First in simplicity, first in value
Derby sealer
First in the farm field
Farm Journal
First in the field
Moving Picture World
First in the Halifax country
Daytona Beach Journal
First in urethane chemistry
Mobay Chemical Co.
First in wear, first in peace
Pequot sheets
First in world records
Ashaway Line and Twine
Mfg. Co.
First Index Investment Trust

You've read about it. Now
you can invest in it
First magazine for women
McCall's
The first name for the martini
Beefeater Gin
The first name in American sta-
tionery
Puritan Stationery Co.
The first name in business sys-
tems
Remington Office Systems
Div., Sperry Rand
Corporation
First name in cast steel!
Farrell-Cheek Steel Co.
The first name in cognac since
1724
Rémy Martin cognac
The first name in custom bedding
Hein and Kopkins, Inc.
First name in filing
Oxford Filing Supply Co.
The first name in first aid
Johnson & Johnson
The first name in ham, the last
word in flavor
Armour's Star Ham
First name in herbicide research
Amchem Products, Inc.
First name in paper punches
Mutual Products Co., Inc.
First name in pneumatic protec-
tion
C. A. Norgren Co.
First name in power transmission
equipment
Lovejoy Flexible Coupling
Co.
The first name in rayon, the
last word in quality
Crown Tested Rayon Fabrics
First name in refractories
A. P. Green Fire Brick Co.
The first name in seats. The
last word in quality
Beneke Corporation
The first name in textile machinery
Platts Bros., Ltd.
The first name in textiles
Bird Mfg. Co.
First name in time, last word in
watch styling
Omega watch
First name in tire valves for
original equipment and

replacement
A. Schrader's Son
The first name in towels is the
last name in sheets
Cannon Mills, Inc.
First National Bank of Boston
We tackle the tough ones
We've done it. We can do
it for you
First National Bank of Chicago
Building with Chicago and
the nation since 1863
The productivity bankers
First National City Bank
Partners in progress around
the world
First National City Bank travel-
ers checks
Better than money
The first national newspaper
network
Metropolitan Newspapers
The first new no-filter cigarette
in years
York cigarettes
First of all, for flavor
Paul Jones whiskey
First of the Northern Transcon-
tinentals
Northern Pacific Railway
First on famous waters
Johnson Reels, Inc.
First on the Atlantic
Pan American World Air-
ways, Inc.
First on the finish
Regatta yacht paints
First on the Pacific
Pan American World Air-
ways, Inc.
First over the bars
Hunter whiskey
First Penn Banking and Trust
Co.
First Pennsylvania means
business
First Pennsylvania means busi-
ness
First Penn Banking and
Trust Co.
The first portable
Corona typewriter
The first really different maga-
zine in a generation
Interlude
First 'round the world

Pan American World Airways,
Inc.
The first safety tooth brush
Rubberset tooth brush
The first sip sooths it
Veno's cough medicine
The first sip tells
Fletcher Coffee & Spice Co.
The first taste tells you, it's
good to the last drop
Maxwell House Master Blend
Coffee
The first taste will tell you why!
Fleischmann's whiskey
First thing in the morning
Eno effervescent salt
First thing on arising
Sunkist lemons
First thought, first aid and
Astypodine
Astypodine
The first thought in burns
Unguentine ointment
The first thought in the morning
Folger's ground coffee
First to last, the truth: news,
editorials, advertise-
ments
New York Herald-Tribune
First to serve the farmer
International Harvester Co.
First Trust & Deposit Co.
See the First Trust first
First with better ways to build
Gold Bond building materials
First with the features women
want most
Hotpoint Div., General Elec-
tric Company
First with the finest
Arkatex Ceramic Corp.
The first with the finest in tele-
vision
Dumont television receivers
First with the finest in wallcov-
erings ... always!
Timbertone Decorative Co.,
Inc.
First with the last word
Britannic wool hose
Firth Sterling, Inc.
Pioneer in powder and
molten metallurgy
Fischer. See also: Fisher
Fischer Lime & Cement Co.
The TOP in roofing values

155

Fish "Heddon" and fish better
  Heddon fishing tackle
Fish Net & Twine Co.
  Serving the fishermen's
    needs for over 100
    years
  Weavers of the world's
    finest netting
Fishback and Moore, Inc.
  Who we serve proves how
    we serve
Fisher. See also: Fischer
Fisher automobile bodies
  The best of "look" to you
  Body by Fisher
  Body by Fisher better by
    far
  Look to the body!
  The SEE story of the year
Fisher Flouring Mills
  If you can boil water, you
    can cook ZOOM
  It's blended to better your
    best in baking
  Use the wheat and spare
    the meat
Fisher Governor Co.
  If it flows through pipe,
    chances are it's con-
    trolled by Fisher
Fisher-Price Toys, Inc.
  Our work is child's play
  World's largest creator of
    pre-school toys
Fishing tackle for every kind of
    fishing
  South Bend Tackle Co.,
    Div. Gladding Corp.
Fisk tires
  Makers of the safety stripe
    tread
  Time to Re-tire? (Buy Fisk)
  To skid or not to skid
Fist grip clips
  Thomas Laughlin Co.
Fit all hands and all purses
  Simmons gloves
Fit & Trim dog food
  Fitness food that tastes
    good
  If you think they won't
    love it, think again
Fit any pocket, every pocket-
    book
  Autopoint pencil
Fit as a fiddle

Society Girl foundations
Fit for a golden spoon
  Lady Borden ice cream
Fit for a queen
  Queen slide fastener
Fit for every foot
  Kinney shoes
Fit for the job; last longer
  Dodge trucks
The fit-from-any-angle, patented
    pantie girdle
  Sport-Tights
Fit out with Faradon
  Faradon radio receiver
Fit right, feel right, they're
    walk-fitted
  Bostonian shoes
Fit to be tried
  Musebeck Shoe Co.
Fitch. See also: Francis Emory
    Fitch, Inc.
Fitch Shampoo
  It washes your dandruff
    away
Fitness food that tastes good
  Fit & Trim dog food
Fits and matches the car you're
    driving
  Motorola car radio
Fits any ice box
  Isko Company iceless re-
    frigeration
Fits in the right places
  Freeman Shoe Corp.
Fits on the foot like a glove on
    the hand
  Blumenthal shoes
Fits the foot in action or repose
  United States Shoe Co.
Fits to precision
  Pre-cize girdle
Fitted flame burners
  Roberts & Mander Corp.
Fitting the purse as well as the
    figure
  Cusette foundations
A "fitting" tribute to the feminine
    figure
  Primrose foundations
Fittings. See: C-P Fittings
    Div., Essex Wire Corp.
Fitzjohn motor bus
  If it's made by Fitzjohn,
    it's made to save you
    money
A $5 razor with 1000 new edges

Super razor
The 5-minute vacation
　Dodger soft drink
Five Roses Flour
　You'll bake it better with
　　Five Roses
Fix-All Liquid Cement
　Mends everything but a
　　broken heart
　A million and one uses
Fizzadent denture cleaner
　Cleans as it fizzes
Flag Pet Food Corp.
　His master's choice
　Their tails will wag if you
　　feed them Flag
Flag Products, Inc.
　Show your colors; live with
　　the symbol of liberty
The flagship of the financial
　world
　Shearson/American Express
A flair for elegance
　Sylvania Electric Products,
　　Inc.
Flak insecticide
　It's a killer
Flame-Glo Lipstick
　Keep kissable with Flame-
　　Glo Lipstick
The flame that freezes
　Servel refrigerator
Flamingo gas heaters
　Brings a touch of the
　　tropics
Flare brake fluid
　It's too late when your
　　brakes fail
Flash
　When all soaps fail, Flash
　　cleans
Flat folded stationery
　American Register Co.
Flatt. See: R. A. Flatt Tire
　　Co.
Flattering as moonlight
　Iron Clad hosiery
Flatters where it matters
　Adola brassiere
Flav-R-Pac canned goods
　To serve something fancy
　　start with something
　　fancy
The flavor-aged ginger ale
　Cliquot Club ginger ale
Flavor baked in, labor baked

out
　Heinz Oven-Baked Beans
The flavor can't be matched be-
　　cause only Nescafe knows
　　the secret
　Nescafe instant coffee
"Flavor-fillip" for your meals
　Libby's pineapple juice
Flavor first
　Del Monte fruits
Flavor Flour
　Famous for its flavor
Flavor-frock for foods
　Heinz ketchup
The flavor is sealed in the flavor
　　bud
　Shirriff's Lushus jelly
The flavor lasts
　Wrigley's chewing gum
The flavor lingers longer
　Leaf chewing gum
Flavor-mellowed in wood for
　　years
　Verner's ginger ale
Flavor sealed in the brown bottle
　Orange Crush soft drink
The flavor secret of the finest
　　cocktails
　Martini & Rossi Vermouth
The flavor sensation that sold
　　the nation on coffee
　　made in the cup
　Nescafe instant coffee
Flavor so delicious only your
　　figure knows they're low
　　calorie
　Wish Bone salad dressings
The flavor-tested coffee
　Haserot Company
Flavor to spare and share
　Dentyne chewing gum
The flavor touch they like so
　　much
　Parkay Margarine
A flavor you can't forget
　Nu-Grape soft drink
The flavor's all yours
　Philip Morris cigarettes
Flavory, firm, tender
　Foulds macaroni
The flawless Barre Granite
　Rock of Ages Corp.
Flax-li-num Insulating Co.
　The mark of a well-built
　　house
　Select building insulation

and sound control material

Fleecy White Laundry Bleach
Makes washday a heyday
A peach of a bleach

Fleer's chewing gum
The ball o' candy with a
heart o' gum
The sucker with a heart o'
gum

The fleet that's NEVER in
Ford motor trucks

Fleets chap stick
Keeps lips fit

Fleetwood radio products
True to our aim

Fleischer yarns
Knit goods are only as good
as the yarn of which
they are made

Fleischmann Co.
Bread is your best food,
eat more of it
Eat bread ... more bread

Fleischmann's gin
America's first gin

Fleischmann's margarine
America's largest selling
corn oil margarines

Fleischmann's whiskey
The first taste will tell you
why!
No wonder Fleischmann's
Preferred is PREFERRED

Fleischmann's Yeast
Fleischmann's Yeast for
health
Fleischmann's Yeast is a
natural corrective food
Health
It's ironized
Life begins at forty
Yeast builds resistance

Fleischmann's Yeast for health
Fleischmann's Yeast

Fleischmann's Yeast is a natural
corrective food
Fleischmann's Yeast

Fletcher Coffee & Spice Co.
The first sip tells

Fletcher Works, Inc.
It's truly a whale of a
washer

Fletcher's Castoria
Children cry for it
The children's laxative

Fleurette Frocks
There's something about
them you'll like

Flex-O-Film, Inc.
Pioneers in plastics

Flexees foundations
Cool comfort with corseted
chic

Flexible for every comfort
Cantilever shoes

A flexible shoe for your flexible
foot
Cantilever shoes

Flexible Steel Lacing Co.
Just a hammer to apply it

Flexible where you want it, rigid
where you need it
United States Shoe Co.

Flintkote paint
The extra years of service
cost no more

Flit insecticide
Don't get bit, get Flit
Flit spray does not stain
One whiff and they're stiff
Quick, Henry, the Flit

Flit spray does not stain
Flit insecticide

Flo-Glaze paint
Leaves no brush marks

Flo-Sweet
The trademarked sugar that
F-L-O-W-S

The Flo-Thru Bag
Lipton tea bags

Floods o' suds for dishes and
duds
Supersuds

The floor finishing authorities
S. C. Johnson & Son

Floor of beauty, economy and
durability
Sana-bestos Tiles

The floor of enduring beauty
Congoleum-Nairn floor coverings

Floor truck specialists since 1891
Nutting Truck Co.

Floor with maple, beech or birch
Maple Flooring Mfrs. Assn.

Floor without flaws
General Floorcraft, Inc.

Florence Heaters
Heat plus beauty
More heat, less care

Florence Stoves

The stove with focused
heat
Floress Lipstick
Lips radiant as glowing
embers
Florida Citrus Commission
Extra health at no extra
cost
The real thing from Florida
Florida Citrus Exchange
Tune the meal and tone the
system
Florida Farmer
Florida's oldest farm paper
Florida Power Corporation
The power to please!
Florida's fastest-growing news-
paper
Miami Tribune
Florida's great home daily
Tampa Daily Times
Florida's most important news-
paper
Miami Herald
Florida's oldest farm paper
Florida Farmer
Florists Telegraph Delivery
Assn.
Say it with flowers, by
wire
Florsheim Shoe Co.
The easiest kind because
skeleton lined
Experience is the best
teacher, quality the
soundest lesson
First always, finest all ways
Florsheims afoot means com-
fort ahead
Florsheims, of course!
For any wear and every-
where
For men who measure value
in terms of quality
alone
For the man who cares
The kind of support that's
kind to your arches
A lively life for lazy arches
Look at your shoes, others
do
Makers of fine shoes for men
and women
Men wear them everywhere
The most walked about shoe
in America

New life to weak arches,
long life to healthy ones
A new lower price, a new
higher value
Not how many, but how good
Start the day with style,
end it with a smile
Stormy leather
Stormy leather; when it
rains, it scores
A style for any taste, a fit
for any foot
There's no substitute for
experience
When quality counts most,
most men count on Flor-
sheim quality
When you pay for quality,
why not get the finest?
Florsheim Shoe Co. See also:
Royal Imperial Flor-
sheim shoes
Florsheims afoot mean comfort
ahead
Florsheim Shoe Co.
Florsheims, of course!
Florsheim Shoe Co.
Flotex Foundry Shakeout
Shakes the flask, not the
building
Flour. See also: Flower
The flour of a thousand uses
Jenny Wren Co.
The flour of the nation
American Ace
Flow. See: Flo
Flower. See also: Flour
Flower-fragrant bath salts to
make your bath as re-
freshing as perfumed
rain
Early American Toiletries
The flower of fine flour
Bisquick flour
A flowering beauty, yet she's a
wallflower
Odorono deodorant
Flows fast, stays tough
Pennzoil motor oil
Flows freely, dissolves readily,
develops food flavor
Diamond Crystal Salt
Fluid handling is Stewart-
Warner's business
Stewart-Warner Corporation
Fly anywhere in Europe via

Air France
Air France
Fly-Ded insect spray
Double doom to flies and
mosquitoes
The Fly-Foon Co.
Doesn't stun 'em, kills 'em
Fly in the best of circles
Airbus Industrie of North
America
Fly the friendly skies of United
United Air Lines, Inc.
Fly-Tox insecticide
There is only one Fly-Tox
Flying saucers are just looking
for a cup of richer,
stronger Martinson's
Martinson's coffee
Flying Tiger Line, Inc.
Air-freight specialists
First in airfreight with air-
freight first
It's on time or it's on us
Now there's one all-cargo
airline with scheduled
service around the
world
Foaming with flavor
Eichler beer
Foamite-Childs Corp.
All fires are not alike, nor
are all fire extinguish-
ers
You can't ride home on an
insurance policy
The folding furniture with the
permanent look
Stakmore Co., Inc.
Foley Mfg. Co.
Kitchen tested utensils
Stars for your kitchen
Folger's Coffee Crystals
Coffee rich enough to be
served in San Fran-
cisco's finest restaurants
Folger's ground coffee
America's No. 1 mountain
grown coffee
Coffee from the magic
mountains
The coffee with the flavor
advantage
Different and better
The first thought in the
morning
Folger's is good cooking

Its high quality makes it
economical
Mountain grown
A mountain of flavor in every
spoonful
Remember the name, Fol-
ger's; you'll not forget
the taste
Vigorous flavor
You can't drink Folger's
coffee without smiling--
try it and see
Folger's is good cooking
Folger's ground coffee
Folks favor Fromm's flavor
Fromm Bros. meat products
Follmer umbrellas
They reign in the rain
We shelter the world from
sun and rain
Follow the arrow and you follow
the style
Arrow shirts
Follow the experts, demand
Champion
Champion spark plugs
Follow the Journal and you follow
the oil industry
Oil and Gas Journal
Follow the leader
Honda motorized tricycles
Follow through--with your help
to prevent birth defects
March of Dimes
Follow your head, not the herd
Drexel, Burnham, Lambert
Securities
Fond of things Italiano? Try a
sip of Galiano
Galiano wine
Food of the gods
Hoffman honey
Food preservation without ice
Brunswick refrigerator
Food purveyors to the nation
Swift and Co.
Food shot from guns
Quaker Puffed Rice
Quaker Puffed Wheat
The food that builds bonnie
babies
Glaxo
The Food-Tonic
Sanatogen
The foodpower people
Central Soya Co., Inc.

Foods of fine flavor
Greenspan Bros.
Foods of finest flavor
Beechnut Packing Co.
Foot Bath Crystal
Make your feet happy by
keeping them healthy
Foot-fresh around the clock
Massagic Air Cushion shoes
Foot-Joy shoes
Since 1857 ... the standard
of excellence in men's
footwear
A foot nearer perfection
Kinney shoes
Foot of comfort means miles of
happiness
Ault Williamson Shoe Co.
Foot Saver shoes
Shaped to fit like your
stockings
The foot-stimulating shoe
Bellaire shoe
Footwear for all occasions
Latterman Shoe Mfg. Co.
Footwear of distinction
M. M. Bernstein
For. See also: Four
For a better shave
Stanley Shave Cream
For a better tomorrow
Hires' Improved Root Beer
For a better tomorrow for every-
body
National Association of
Manufacturers
For a big choice there's only
one choice
Sony Corp. of America
For a big difference in your
profits ... the line
with the big difference
Meilink Steel Safe Co.
For a change, try Sohio
Sohio gasoline
For a come-closer smile
Pepsodent tooth paste
For a comfortable hold
Dentrol dental adhesive
For a cooling shave
Ingram's shaving cream
For a day, a week, a month
or more
Brock Residence Inn
For a figure to remember
RumBRA

For a good look at the times of
your life
Kodak photographic paper
For a good night's sleep
Nytol
For a good turn faster, turn to
Monarch
Monarch turning machines
For a lifetime of hunting
Savage Arms Div., Emhart
Corp.
For a lifetime of proud possession
Omega Watch
For a livelier life
Cubs cereal
For a "looking glass" shine
Esquire boot polish
For a man who plans beyond to-
morrow
Seagram's Distillers Corp.
For a more attractive bathroom
Northern bathroom tissue
For a narrow point of view
Tiecrafters
For a royal shave
King Razor Co.
For a smooth, fast professional
finish
Krylon spray paint
For a soft, whiter wash
Final Touch
For a sure tomorrow--insure
enough today
American Hardware Mutual
Insurance Co.
For a taste as smooth as its
name
Busch beer
For a taste that's Springtime
fresh
Salem cigarettes
For all industry
Snap-On Tools Corp.
For all kinds of insurance in a
single plan, call your
Travelers man
The Travelers Insurance
Cos.
For all kinds of itching
Lanacane skin lotion
For all the family
Loma Linda Food Co.
For all time and clime
Bishopric Mfg. Co.
For all types of hair
Drene shampoo

For almost any product,
aluminum makes it
better and Kaiser
Aluminum makes alumi-
num work best
Kaiser Aluminum and Chem-
ical Corp.

For any air conditioning
Trane Co.

For any child of any age
E-Z underwear

For any wear and everywhere
Florsheim Shoe Co.

For any wear, anywhere
Bass Moccasins

For beautiful skin all over
Camay soap

For beauty exercise
Wrigley's chewing gum

For beauty to have and to hold
Petalpoint Motif brassiere

For beauty with economy build
with common brick
Common Brick Mfrs. Assn.
of America

For beginners or experts
Cleveland's Baking Powder

For better and faster baking
Pyrex glassware

For better and faster cooking
Pyrex glassware

For better eyesight
American Optical Co.

For better jams and jellies
Certo

For better living
G. E. refrigerator

For better reception
Raytheon radio tubes

For better results always use
the best paper
Nekoosa-Edwards Paper
Co.

For better tasting rum drinks
Captain Morgan Spiced
Rum

For boys from six to sixty
Springfoot socks

For bracing up digestion,
nerves and appetite
Quaker Oats

For businessmen who know
their diesels
Iveco diesel trucks

For busy businessmen
Forbes

For clean hits and clean barrels
Remington shells

For clean lubrication
American Grease Stick Co.

For cleaning ease
Hamilton Beach vacuum
cleaner

For comfort and pleasure all
through the house
Arvin electric heaters

For commercial cooking ... gas
is good business
American Gas Association,
Inc.

For continuous production
Crescent Belt Fasteners

For digestion's sake, smoke
Camels
Camel cigarettes

For doctor bills
Blue Cross/Blue Shield

For double care, both scalp and
hair
Vaseline Hair Tonic

For "dream hands" cream your
hands
Paquins hand cream

For economical transportation
Chevrolet automobile

For emergencies, carry a Lifetime towline
Lifetime Corp.

For entertaining royalty or royally
Richardson's Mints

For ever-changing fashion, the
never-changing beauty
of Marvella pearls
Marvella pearls

For every business need
Nekoosa-Edwards Paper Co.

For every financial need
Wachovia Bank & Trust Co.

For every floor in the house
Armstrong linoleum

For every machine of every degree of wear there is
a Sinclair oil to suit
its speed and seal its
power
Sinclair Oil Co.

For every occasion of social
correspondence
White & Wyckoff Mfg. Co.

For every piping system
Crane Company

For every purpose
  Nicholson File Co.
For every room in the home
  The Globe-Wernicke Co.
For every room in the house
  Armstrong linoleum
  Michigan Seating Co.
For every service
  Goulds pumps
For every walk in life
  Melville Shoe Corp.
  Monarch socks
For everything green that grows
  Loma Plant Food
For everything "under the sun"
  Willsonite sun glasses
For exacting service
  Whitey Research Tool Co.
For FAST headache help
  Bromo-Seltzer
For fast, reliable trades, just
  dial the letters
  L.A.S.A.L.L.E.
  La Salle Securities, Inc.
For favorable "first impressions"
  Armstrong Cork Co.
For feminine hygiene use Lysol
  always
  Lysol disinfectant
For firmer gums
  Forhan's tooth paste
For '48 the best to date
  Buick automobile
For '49 the best of our line
  Buick automobile
For 40 years the standard of
  West Virginia
  Red Jacket Coal Sales Co.
For fresher bread tomorrow,
  buy Taystee Bread
  today
  Taystee Bread
For gifts of love
  N. Pfeffer
For gifts that last consult your
  jeweler
  National Jewelers Publicity
  Association
For good advice ... and good
  products ... depend
  on your Mobil dealer
  Mobil Oil Corp.
For good and FITTING reasons
  Kayser hosiery and under-
  wear
For good business stationery

Uncle Sam Bond
For good eating at sensible cost
  Great Atlantic & Pacific Tea
  Stores
For good food and good food
  ideas
  Kraft Foods Div., Kraftco
  Corp.
For good Marx-manship
  Marx identification tags
For GOODness sake
  June Dairy Products Co.
For goodness sake buy Admira-
  tion Coffee
  Duncan Coffee Co.
For goodness sake, eat Reagan
  bread
  Reagan bread
For goodness sake wear Buckeye
  Shirts
  Buckeye Shirt Co.
For gracious living
  Northern Furniture Co.
For growing satisfaction
  Associated Seed Growers
For halitosis use Listerine
  Listerine mouth wash
For handsome hair, come sun,
  wind, water
  Vitalis hair tonic
For happy motoring
  Esso gasoline
For health--business--pleasure
  Columbia bicycles
For health's sake, ask your doc-
  tor
  Brackenridge Brewing Co.
For heating and cooling ... gas
  is good business
  American Gas Association,
  Inc.
For high moments in distinguished
  living
  Lelong perfume
For home lovers in cities, towns
  and suburbs
  Better Homes & Gardens
For husky throats
  Zymole Trokeys
For imagination in communication,
  look to 3M business
  product centers
  Minnesota Mining & Manu-
  facturing Co.
For improved production through
  measurement and control

The Bristol Co.
For increased fuel economy
Edge Moor Iron Co.
For industry, shop, farm and
home
The Black & Decker Mfg.
Co.
For internal cleanliness
Nujol laxative
For irritated eyes it's just what
the doctor ordered
Murine eye drops
For keener refreshment
Pabst Blue Ribbon beer
For kissable breath
B-Wise chewing gum
For lazy people
Listerine toothpaste
For lifetime service
General Electric Company
For longer-lasting beauty,
stucco paint
Rocktite
For looks, luxury and low cost
LaSalle automobile
For lovely lawns in sun or
shade
Associated Seed Growers
For low cost hauling
International Harvester
trucks
For making good things to eat
Southern Cotton Oil Co.
For making shipments "bound to
get there"
Acme Steel Co.
For man and woman
Dr. Owen's Body Battery
For many converting purposes
Nekoosa-Edwards Paper
Co.
For matching lips and fingertips
Revlon lipstick and nail
enamel
For material help in material
handling it's Robins
Robins conveyor belt
For maximum production with
minimum maintenance
Industrial Process Engi-
neering
For memories that linger
Daydreams perfume
For men of action
Ranger shoes
For men of distinction

Calvert "Extra" whiskey
For men who care what they wear
Pioneer Suspender Co.
For men who know fine whiskies
Kentucky Tavern whiskey
For men who measure value in
terms of quality alone
Florsheim Shoe Co.
For modern bathrooms
Rubberized Products Co.
For modern industry
New Departure-Hyatt Bear-
ings Div., General
Motors Corporation
For modern shaving
Barbasol shaving cream
For more meaty taste
Butcher's Blend dog food
For more relief than creams or
ointments alone
Tucks hemorrhoid remedy
For more than a century makers
of fine furniture in
traditional and modern
idiom
John Widdicomb Co.
For more than 25 years the au-
thority on gun cleaning
F. A. Hoppe, Inc.
For more than 25 years the na-
tional magazine of the
furniture trade
Furniture Record
For my pipe
Granger tobacco
For normal foot growth
Pro-tek-tiv shoes
For now-and-forever-after love-
liness
Woodbury's Facial Soap
For oil marketing
National Petroleum News
For on-the-spot relief
Oragel CSM canker sore
medicine
For 130 years we've been making
things people need--
including profits
Pennwalt Corporation
For only $70 you can stop this
drudgery!
Fairbanks-Morse Home Water
Systems
For out-of-doors writing
Waterman's Ideal Fountain
Pen

For particular people
    Salada tea
For peace of mind
    Blekre tires
For pen-tied or pen-clever
    people
    Wits End stationery
For penetrating relief get Hall's
    Vapor Action
    Hall's cough drops
For people who love coffee but
    not caffeine
    Sanka Brand decaffeinated
    coffee
For people who travel ... and
    expect to again and
    again
    Starflite Luggage
For perfection of the Swiss
    watchmaking art
    Marvin watch
For Pleasant Moments
    P. M. Whiskey
For pleasure and energy, too
    Welch grape juice
For prescriptions: let us be
    the one
    Hook's drug stores
For professional cocktails at
    home
    Heublein cocktails
For protection today and progress
    tomorrow
    Lockheed Aircraft Corpora-
    tion
For proved beauty results
    Palmolive soap
For PURE enjoyment
    Welch's grape juice
    Welch's marmalade
For quality and dependability,
    shouldn't you have a
    Quasar?
    Quasar television sets
For quality paper products you
    can't beat Marathon
    Marathon Div., American
    Can Co.
For quality western lumber
    products, look to T,
    W and J
    Tarter, Webster and John-
    son Div., American
    Forest Products Corp.
For quality you can depend
    on--depend on Skelgas

    Skelgas gasoline
For real enjoyment
    El Producto cigar
For real smoking pleasure
    Chesterfield cigarettes
For relief of sensitive teeth
    Promise tooth paste
For remedying prominent ears,
    preventing disfigurements
    in after life
    Claxton's Patent Ear Cap
For safety after dark
    Arrow headlights
For serving ... it's Erving
    Erving Paper Mills
For 75 years, America's link with
    the Orient
    American President Lines
For sheer loveliness wear Chate-
    laine Silk Hosiery
    Chatelaine Silk Hosiery
For short stops and long service
    Thermoid brake lining
For silken-sheen hair easier to
    arrange
    Kreml shampoo
For silken-sheen hair easy to ar-
    range
    Kreml shampoo
For 66 years makers of the best
    in paint products
    Benjamin Moore
For smooth shaves
    Twinplex razor
For smoother ice cream
    Junket powder
For softer, smooth skin switch to
    Dove
    Dove deodorant soap
For solid comfort
    LHS pipes
For special industrial require-
    ments
    Nekoosa-Edwards Paper Co.
For sports it's Sportmart
    Sportmart athlete's shoes
For springy-soft hair
    Admiration soapless shampoo
For starting power, for lasting
    power
    Delco storage batteries
For strength, toughness and
    durability
    Vanadium Corp. of America
For strength where the stress
    comes

International Nickel Co.
For superb personal movies
Filmo movie camera
For sure allure
Life brassiere
For that certain "lift"
Elaine brassiere
For that "come hither" look
Angelus lipstick
For that good-looking feeling
Doris Miller clothes
For that priceless young look
Formaid brassiere
For that smart sun-tan look
Max Factor and Co.
For that young, young look
Tussy cosmetics
For the active woman of today
F. Mayer Shoe Co.
For the best combination of
filter and good taste
Kent satisfies best
Kent cigarettes
For the best in rest
Southern Comfort Mattress
For the best night's rest you
ever had, sleep on a
Hodgman Air Bed
Hodgman Air Bed
For the best of everything in-
cluding the price let's
go Krogering
Kroger supermarkets
For the betterment of newspaper
advertising
Gagnier Stereotype Foundry
For the climate of excellence
Cahners Publishing Co.,
Inc.
For the decorator touch
Best Pleat Nip-Tite
For the elegant petite
Lilli-Ann Corp.
For the finest in air circulation
Vornadofan
For the full figure
Youthline foundation
For the girl who knows value
by heart
Loveable brassiere
For the great moments
Great Western champagne
For the gums
Forhan's tooth paste
For the heads of the family
Lustre-Cream shampoo

For the higher tax bracket in-
vestor
Dreyfus Tax Exempt Money
Market Fund
For the holidays and all year
long
André champagne
For the home that enjoys home
life
Conn Organ Corp.
For the illustrated side, a coated
paper, for the letter
side, a bond paper
Standard Paper Mfg. Co.
For the king of old-fashioneds
King whiskey
For the lady of your heart
Sierra Candy Co.
For the land's sake use Bowker's
Bowker's fertilizers
For the land's sake use Shur-
Gro
Shur-Gro fertilizer
For the lift of your lifetime
Life brassiere
For the long run
Dunlop Tire & Rubber Corp.
For the long term
Lonestar Industries, Inc.
For the man on the move
McGregor-Doniger, Inc.
For the man who cares
Carstairs White Seal whiskey
Florsheim Shoe Co.
For the man who drives or the
man who flies
Dayton Wire Wheel Co.
For the man who reaches higher
Hawk lotion
For the men in charge of change
Fortune Magazine
For the modern miss
Charmese foundations
For the nation's factories and the
nation's farms
International Harvester Co.
For the nicest youngsters you
know
Mason Clothes
For the one man in 7 who shaves
every day
Glider Brushless Shave
For the private world of the bath
House of Wrisley, Inc.
For the real thing in noodle
soup, ask for Barker's

Barker Food Products

For the REST of your life
Streit Slumber Chair

For the safety of your smile
Pepsodent tooth paste

For the seafood lover in you
Red Lobster seafood rest-
aurants

For the seat of your diaper
troubles
Dennison diapers liners

For the shave that never fails
Rock Flint Co.

For the smart young woman
Mademoiselle

For the smile of beauty
Ipana toothpaste

For the smile of health
Sal Hepatica

For the softest adorable hands
Jergens Lotion

For the sparkle of youth
Miss Saylor's Chocolates

For the taste that's right
Viceroy cigarettes

For the tummy
Tums

For the typical American size
Leslie Fay, Inc.

For the woman who can afford
the best. Even though
it costs less
Hazel Bishop cosmetics

For the woman who dares to be
different
Emraude perfume

For those frisky years
Spree Togs for children

For those letters you owe
White & Wyckoff Mfg. Co.

For those who can hear the difference
Pickering and Co., Inc.

For those who care
Caldwell boat

For those who go first class
Horn luggage

For those who read for profit
Barron's

For those who really like to eat
Smithfield Meat

For those who think young
Pepsi-Cola soft drink

For those who want every puff
to taste as fresh as
the first puff!

Montclair cigarettes

For those who want the finest
Willys-Knight automobile

For tired, tender feet
Orthopedic Shoes

For twenty-five years, first in
professional hair care
Rayette-Faberge, Inc.

For use once by one user
ScotTissue

For virtually spotless dishes
Cascade detergent

For waxing satisfaction
Minerva Wax Paper Co.

For what's worth watching
TV station WJZ-TV, New
York City

For women whose eyes are older
than they are
John Robert Powers Products
Co.

For you and your car
Hires Auto Parts

For you and your town
Kansas City Kansan

For you--every banking service
Times Square Trust Co.

For young men and men who stay
young
Society Brand Clothes

For young men and men with
young ideas
General Cigar Co.

For your family and business--
your auto, home and
everything you own
Aetna Insurance Co.

For your taste in toast
Toastmaster toaster

For your eyes
Murine eye drops

For your paper needs
Schlosser Paper Co.

For your pressing needs
Hydraulic Press Mfg. Co.

For youthful figures of all ages
Lasticraft foundations

Forbes
Capitalist tool
For busy businessmen
Let Forbes make their ship
come in
Reach the affluent in
Forbes

The "forbidden" fragrance
Tabu perfume

Ford accelerators
  It rolls as you step on the
    gas
Ford Authorized Leasing System
  America's largest leasing
    system
Ford automobile
  Across the continent in
    comfort
  Best year yet to go Ford
  Easy to buy when new,
    easy to sell when old
  Every year a better Ford,
    this year a bigger Ford
  Ford has it. Now
  Ford's out front
  Ford's out front in every-
    thing
  Fresh and relaxed to the
    journey's end
  Have you driven a Ford
    lately?
  Look out, world; here
    comes Ford!
  Spend the difference
  There's a Ford in America's
    future
  There's a Ford in your fu-
    ture
  Today's high peak in motor
    car value
  Watch the buyers go Ford
  Watch the Fords go by
  We'd rather point to char-
    acter than chromium
  Wheelbarrow economy but
    Pullman pleasure
  A wower for power
Ford built means better built
  Ford Motor Company
Ford Econoline van trucks
  Built to last longer
Ford gas gauge
  An eye for your gas tank
Ford has a better idea
  Ford Motor Company
Ford has it. Now
  Ford automobile
Ford LTD automobile
  The total car
Ford means business in big
    trucks ... and our
    prices prove it
  Ford motor trucks
Ford Model T automobile
  The universal car

Ford Motor Company
  The bold engineering comes
    from Ford
  Ford built means better
    built
  Ford has a better idea
  It's the going thing
  Quality is Job 1
  Test drive total performance
    '65
  Total performance
Ford Motor Company. See also:
    Industrial Engine Dept.,
    Ford Div., Ford Motor
    Company
Ford Motor Company Research
    Laboratories
  Probing deeper to serve
    you better
Ford motor trucks
  America's truck. Built
    Ford-tough
  The fleet that's NEVER in
  Ford means business in big
    trucks ... and our
    prices prove it
  Ford trucks last longer
  Service with a style
Ford Mustang automobile
  America's favorite fun car
Ford runabout automobile
  Built for two
Ford six cylinder automobile
  Don't be a year behind-er
Ford Thunderbird automobile
  Unique in all the world
Ford Tractor Div., Ford Motor
    Company
  World's first mass produced
    tractor
Ford Tri-Motor airplane
  Where Ford planes fly
Ford trucks last longer
  Ford motor trucks
Ford's out front
  Ford automobile
Ford's out front in everything
  Ford automobile
Fordson governors
  Chosen by the majority
  Master hand at the throttle
Forecaster pipe
  Filters the smoke from bowl
    to tip
Foremost brand in outdoor living
  American Thermos Products

Co.
Foremost foundations
     With the wire part for the
          part of beauty
The foremost in drums
     Slingerland Drum Co.
Foremost in final control ele-
          ments
     Conoflow Corp.
Foremost name in indoor comfort
     Coleman Co., Inc.
Forest Products Div., Owens-
     Illinois, Inc.
     Important name in the box
          business
Forever yours
     Kodak cameras
Forget the moth; save the cloth
     Larvex
Forget the thermometer, remem-
          ber the guarantee
     Delco storage batteries
Forgings that stand the test
     Akron-Selle Co.
Forhan's tooth paste
     Does both jobs: cleans
          teeth, saves gums
     Checks pyorrhea
     For firmer gums
     For the gums
     Four out of five get it be-
          fore they are forty
     More than a tooth paste--it
          checks pyorrhea
     The original tooth paste for
          gums and teeth
     Pyorrhea attacks 4 out of 5
     Use it as a dentifrice
     Win the smile of perfection
          through Forhan's pro-
          tection
     Your teeth are only as
          healthy as your gums
Formaid brassiere
     For that priceless young
          look
Formfit Brassiere
     Tailored to fit
Formfit Underwear
     In conversation it's wit;
          in foundations it's fit
     What's your "eye-cue?"
Formica Corp.
     The surprise of Formica
          products
Formulabs, Inc.

World-wide suppliers of the
          finest ball pen inks
Fort Howard Paper Co.
     America's most used prod-
          ucts away from home
     Call the Fort
     From rags to riches
Fort Wayne National Bank
     The bank that means busi-
          ness
     Proud of our past and com-
          mitted to your future
     That's my bank
     We have a daily interest in
          you
Fortified to whole grain levels
     Cream of Rice
Fortify for fire fighting
     Fire Equipment Mfrs. Inst.
     Pyrene fire extinguisher
Fortune Magazine
     The business magazine
     For the men in charge of
          change
     Fortune means business
     The magazine of business
          leaders around the world
     The magazine of business
          leadership
Fortune means business
     Fortune Magazine
Fortune shoes
     Step into a Fortune, your
          key to a wealth of
          satisfaction
     A wealth of value in For-
          tune shoes
     Your feet are worth For-
          tunes
     You're in style when you
          step into a Fortune
Forty-eight hours of glorious
          travel
     New York-Miami route, Ad-
          miral Line
Forum
     America's quality magazine
          of discussion
Forzol lubricating oil
     The economy oil for Fords
Fosset brush
     Guaranteed use in anything
Foster's Ideal spring beds and
          accident-proof cribs
     A dream of luxury and
          ease

Fostoria Screw Co.
    Made to blue print
Foulds macaroni
    Flavory, firm, tender
Found at last. Perfection in
    shoes
    Denham's shoes
Foundation blocks of profitable
    printing
    Printing Machinery Co.
Foundation for Commercial Banks
    Full service bank
    The place where you keep
        your checking account
The foundation of American
    beauty
    Best Form corset
Founded by merchants for mer-
        chants
    Merchants National Bank
Founder of better homes in
        America
    Delineator
Founders Furniture, Inc.
    Definitive modern furniture
Founders of the tractor industry
    Hart-Parr Co.
Foundettes foundations
    Paint-box colors in tissue-
        light Foundettes
    There's a future in YOUR
        figure in Foundettes
The Foundry
    Wherever metals are cast
        you'll find The Foundry
The fountain head of modern
    tube development is
    RCA
    RCA Corp.
The fountain of youth
    Horlick's Malted Milk Corp.
A fountain of youth for your
    skin
    Balm-O-Lem
Four. See also: For
Four great routes of transcon-
    tinental travel
    Southern Pacific Co.
4-H Club
    Make the best better
Four hours fresher
    Remar bread
Four out of five get it before
    they are forty
    Forhan's tooth paste
Four Roses whiskey

America's finest whiskey
    regardless of age or
    price
America's most famous bou-
    quet
Same great whiskey today
    as before the war
What more could a man ask?
Four Seasons Hotel, Toronto,
    Ont.
    Everything to write home
        about
Four stars in the milky way
    Clover Leaf Milling Co.
Fourth Estate
    A newspaper for the makers
        of newspapers
The fourth necessity
    Metropolitan Life Insurance
    Co.
Fowler Sea Products Co.
    Catch them yourself or buy
        Fowler's
Fownes gloves
    If it's Fownes, that's all
        you need to know about
        a glove
Fox Automotive Products Corp.
    Fox necessaries for Fords
Fox necessaries for Fords
    Fox Automotive Products
        Corp.
Fox River Hose
    Warm toes in Fox River Hose
The Foxboro Company
    Compass of industry
    Specialists in process and
        energy control
    Synthetic or natural, we can
        help fashion the pro-
        cessing system you need
Foy Paint Co.
    Neighbor tells neighbor
The fragrance of youth
    April Showers perfume
Fraker Coal Co.
    A bear for heat
Fram oil filter
    Cleans the oil that cleans
        the motor
    The dipstick tells the story
    The modern oil filter
France. See:
    Franz Butter-Nut Bread
    Lily of France Corset Co.
Francette corsets

Puts your best figure
forward
Francis Emory Fitch, Inc.
Printing with a plus
Francisco Auto Heater
Fresh, warm air every min-
ute
Warms you and your motor
Frank Adam Electric Co.
The sign of a better job
Frank B. Hall & Co. insurance
brokers
Creative insurance services.
We've got what it takes
Growth essential in a cor-
porate protector
We make you safe. You
make us famous
Frank Miller's Harness Dressing
Unequalled for use in liv-
ery, express and private
stables
Frank Siddalls Soap
Only think! One soap for
all uses!
Frank trumpet
You can bank on a Frank
Frankel Manufacturing Co.
The world leaders in dupli-
cating supplies since
1906
Frankfort Distilleries
The American whiskey for
the American taste
Franklin automobile
The airplane feel of the
Franklin opens the road
to new motoring thrills
No tire trouble. No cool-
ing trouble. Always
comfortable
Franklin Life Insurance Co.
The friendly
Franklin Linotype Co.
Nothing to sell but service
Franklin Pottery
As easily washed as a
China plate
Vitrified pottery is ever-
lasting
Franklin Process Co.
Color, the master salesman
Franz Butter-Nut Bread
Rich as butter, sweet as
a nut
Fraser and Johnston Co.

Since 1928--industry leader-
ship in heating and air
conditioning
Fred Arbogast Co., Inc.
Bait of champions
Fred S. James & Co., Inc.
Risk management is essen-
tial to sound financial
management
Frederic Blank & Co., Inc.
Oldest in permanent type
wall coverings
Frederick Advertising & Display
Co.
We'll make you believe in
signs
Frederick Cooper Lamps, Inc.
Lamps of elegance
Frederick, Maryland
You can do better in Fred-
erick
Frederick Nelson Dry Goods
Quality costs no more
Free-coasting files
Shaw-Walker steel filing
cabinets
The free enterprise system is
working. FOSTI is an
example
Fuel Oil Supply & Terminal-
ing, Inc.
Free from oil
Curtis Pneumatic Machinery
Co.
Free from "rings" and "shadows"
No-Sha-Do hosiery
Free 'n' Soft fabric softener
The once a month fabric
softener
Free running
Regal salt
The free-running ring with the
safety center unit
Wausau Motor Parts Co.
Freed-Eisemann Radio Corp.
Mastery in radio
The radio in America's fin-
est homes
The thoroughbred radio
Freedent gum
It won't stick to most dental
work
Freedom follows a furrow
Allis-Chalmers Mfg. Co.
Freeman. See also:
Edward Freeman

171

Miller Freeman Publications
Freeman Shoe Corp.
Fits in the right places
Sole-satisfying comfort
Worn with pride by millions
Freight by air
Slick Airways
Freight trains. America's most
vital moving force
Association of American
Railroads
French. See also: The R. T.
French Co.
French batteries
Buy one today, you'll need
it tonight
Radio's best batteries
The French face powder made in
America
Jardin de Rose
French National Railroads
The railway is the right
way
French S. S. Line
The conquest of comfort
Pride without prejudice
French's mustard
It's creamed
Millions prefer it
Freon Products Div., E. I.
duPont de Nemours &
Co.
Best-selling aerosols are
powered with Freon
propellants
Freon Products Div., E. I.
DuPont de Nemours &
Co. See also: E. I.
DuPont de Nemours &
Co.
Fresh air by Odac
Odac Mfg. Co.
Fresh and clean as a whistle
Irish Spring soap
Fresh and relaxed at the jour-
ney's end
Ford automobile
Fresh as a daisy
June Dairy Products Co.
Fresh as dewy dawn
Pacific Egg Producers
Fresh as the morning
Campbell's Corn Flakes
Fresh because vacuum-packed
Hanley & Kinsella Coffee
Fresh corn off the cob

Niblets canned corn
Fresh feeds are best
Syn-Kro Mills
Fresh from sunshine and pure
air
Council Meats
Fresh from the gardens
Salada tea
Fresh from the mill to you
Livingstone's Oats
Fresh ideas in meat ... from
Hormel
Geo. A. Hormel and Co.
Fresh ideas to meet basic world
needs
Allis-Chalmers Mfg. Co.
Fresh paint is better paint
Bradley & Vrooman Co.
Fresh Start laundry detergent
Get a Fresh Start every day
Fresh to the last slice
Stuhmer's Pumpernickel
Fresh-up with 7UP
7UP soft drink
A fresh vegetable garden in
every can
Veg-All Larsen Co.
Fresh, warm air every minute
Francisco Auto Heater
Freshest thing in town
Creamer's Bakery, Inc.
Freshlike canned vegetables
The most like fresh
Freshness is the first food law
of nature
Syn-Kro Mills
Friden Div., Singer Co.
Make no mistake about
figurework; call Friden
Make no mistake about pa-
perwork automation.
Call Friden
Friedman. See also: B. Fried-
man Shoe Co.
Friedman paint
Challenges the elements
The friend-making work shirt
McCawley & Co., Inc.
The friend of fine fabrics
Linit laundry starch
A friend of the family
Air Canada
The friend of the family for fifty
years
Jewel Amusement Park
Friend of the family for over

fifty years
Jewel Grady supermarkets
The friend of your fine fabrics
Linit laundry starch
The friendly
Franklin Life Insurance Co.
The friendly beer for friendly
people
Ruppert's beer
A friendly company owned by
its policyholders
Central Manufacturers Mutual Insurance Co.
The friendly drink from good
neighbors
Pan-American Coffee Bureau
Friendly, familiar, foreign and
near
Ontario, Canada, Dept. of
Tourism and Information
The friendly hands people
State Farm Insurance Co.
The friendly hotel
Hotel Wentworth, New York
City
Friendly land of infinite variety
South Dakota Dept. of
Highways
A friendly place to work
Bell Telephone System
The friendly railroad for all the
family
Baltimore & Ohio Railroad
The friendly smoke
Royalist cigar
Friendly to the feet
Jarman shoes
The friendly way, C. P. A.
Canadian Pacific Air Lines
The friendly world of Hilton
Hilton Hotels Corp.
The friendship beers
Jax beer
Frigidaire Div. , General Motors
Corporation
Better than ever for less
than ever
Build-in satisfaction ...
build-in Frigidaire
Jet action washers
More beauty outside, more
features within
You're twice as sure with
Frigidaire
Frigidaire Div., General Motors
Corporation. See also:

General Motors Corporation
Frigidaire Electric Refrigeration
Make your ice box a Frigidaire
Frisian. See: Crisby Frisian
Fur Co.
Friskies pet food
The complete family of dog
and cat foods from the
world leader in nutrition
From world leaders in nutrition
Fritos corn chips
America's favorite corn chip
Froedtert Malt Corp.
Basic for better beer
Frog in Your Throat
Greatest cough and voice
lozenge on earth
Stops that tickle!
Frolic Perfume
A head-spinning, heartwinning perfume
Heart-winning, headspinning
One drop for beauty, two
drops for a beau, three
drops for romance, it's
Frolic, you know
From A to zinc
Centrum medicine
From America's popcorn people
Cracker Jack confection
From bees to combs to you
Hoffman honey
From black to bright as quick as
light
Brillo Cleanser
From contented cows
Carnation condensed milk
From design to distribution
Tudor Press, Inc.
From famous orchards of the
great West
Pinnacle Orchards
From first step to fourteen years
Fargo-Hallowell Shoe Co.
From fleece to fabric
United States Worsted
Corp.
From flower to bee to you
Airline honey
From generation to generation
Heirloom Sterling Silver
Wagner aluminum ware
From here to the ear the short-

est distance is long
distance
Bell Telephone System
From juice-heavy beauties
Webster's Tomato Juice
From maker to wearer
Regal shoes
From mill to millions
Hamilton Carhartt overalls
Real Silk Hosiery
From mine to consumer
American Brass Co.
From mine to market
La Belle Iron Works
From natural gas and oil ...
heat, power petrochem-
icals that mean ever
wider service to man
Tenneco, Inc.
From Oregon mountain meadows
Jane Amherst Food Prod-
ucts
From out of the west
Samson tires
From pit to penthouse
Otis Elevator Company
From rags to riches
Fort Howard Paper Co.
From raw cotton through finished
product
Morgan dish cloths
From Sharp minds come Sharp
products
Sharp Electronics Corp.
From the client's point of view
Alexander & Alexander in-
surance brokers
From the finest of the vines
Cresta Blanca wine
From the heart of California
Roma wines
From the heart of the grain
country
American Distilling Corp.
From the land of sky blue
waters
Hamm's beer
From the largest cellars in the
world
Moët champagne
From the salt of the earth
Hooker chemicals
From the seed of the sunflower
Sunlite Sunflower Cooking
Oil
From the skin of Gorton's cod-

fish
Gorton glue
From the space age laboratories
of Olympic
Olympic Radio and Television
Div., Lear Siegler, Inc.
From the speedway comes their
stamina, from the sky-
way their style
Packard automobile
From the sunny Rogue River
Valley
Knight Packing Co.
From the tall corn country
Dubuque Ham
From the tiniest to the mightiest
General Electric Company
From the tractor people who make
the big ones
Allis-Chalmers Mfg. Co.
From the world's most renowned
cosmetic research labor-
atories
Revlon, Inc.
From top to floor there's space
galore
Norge refrigerator
From western mountain meadows
Jane Amherst Food Products
From wire bar to finished copper
wire
Rome Wire Co.
From world leaders in nutrition
Friskies pet food
From yarn to you, it's Textron
all the way
Textron
Fromm Bros. meat products
Folks favor Fromm's flavor
Frontex shirts
As western as the setting
sun
Frostilla
Skin's greatest guardian
Frozen Foods Magazine
The magazine that grew up
with the industry
Frozen with the wiggle in its
tail
New England Fish Co.
Fruehauf Corporation
Custom-built quality at
production line prices
Engineered transportation
Fruehauf's rolling!
It can pull more than it can

174

carry
The only truck bodies built
  like a trailer
Total transportation
Fruehauf's rolling!
  Fruehauf Corporation
The fruit and cereal lover's
  cereal
  Post's Raisin Bran
Fruit Bowl Drink
  A winner wherever it's sold
Fruit Dispatch Co.
  Feel a bite of health
The fruit of connoisseurs
  Pinnacle Orchards
Fruiterers of distinction
  Smilen Bros.
The fuel of the future
  Shell gasoline
Fuel Oil Supply & Terminaling,
  Inc.
  Accentuate the positive
  The free enterprise system
    is working. FOSTI is
    an example
The fuel that satisfies
  Scranton & Reading Coal
    Co.
The fuel without a fault
  Semet-Solvay Co. coke
Fuji Electric Co., Ltd.
  Put quality first and every-
    thing follows
Full circle packaging
  Alton Box Board Co.
Full-fashioned for flawless fash-
  ion
  Belle-Sharmeer stockings
A full meal in two biscuits
  Shredded Wheat
Full measure of time
  Kelbert watch
Full of sunshine and good health
  Sunsweet prunes
A full package of light
  Sylvania Electric Products,
    Inc.
Full powered
  Pomiac gasoline
Full prescription strength with-
  out a prescription
  Benylin cough syrup
Full. Rich. Delightful. Taste
  the pleasure
  Golden Lights cigarettes
Full service bank

Foundation for Commercial
  Banks
The full service bookstores
  Kroch's & Brentano's
The full-sized pads filled with
  freshness
  Stay-Free maxipads
Full tights for bathing
  Jersey bathing suits
Fuller. See also: H. B. Fuller
  Co.
Fuller brushes
  Head to foot, cellar to attic
  Simplify the business of
    homekeeping
Fullerton-Kearney funeral flag
  The only flag that fits all
    cars
Fulton Cotton Mills Div., Allied
  Products Corp.
  America's leading producer
    of quality canvas prod-
    ucts
Fulton truck
  The repeat order truck
Fun is our business
  Bally Manufacturing Corp.
Fun is where you drive it
  De Soto automobile
Functional papers
  Thilmany Pulp and Paper
    Co.
Functions when the engine
  breathes
  Webber Supercharger
Funk & Wagnalls Company
  The coupon to bigger suc-
    cess
Funke Candies
  Confections that win affec-
    tions
Fur. See:
  Fir
  Furs
Furnace freedom
  Penn Electric Switch Co.
Furnace heat for every home
  Monitor Stove Co.
Furness, Withy & Co., Ltd.
  The experienced cruise line
Furnishings for men, women and
  boys
  Brooks Brothers clothing
Furniture of timeless beauty
  Romweber Industries
Furniture Record

For more than 25 years
the national magazine
of the furniture world
A magazine of better
merchandising for home
finishing merchants
Furniture that's fun to live
with
H. T. Cushman Mfg. Corp.
Furs. See also: Fir
Furs that reflect youth
Zimmerman-Scher Co.
Fusion, Inc.
Automation is economical
Futorian Manufacturing Corp.
Creaters of the world
famous Stratolounger
The future belongs to those
who prepare for it
Prudential Insurance Co.
of America
Future business insurance
Juvenile Group Foundation
The future is building now at
Garrett
The Garrett Corporation
The future is calling
RCA Telephone Systems
The future is communications.
Centel is there already
Centel Corporation business
telephone equipment

-G-

GAB Business Services, Inc.
A pioneer in claim services
G. and C. Merriam Co.
The leading name in dic-
tionaries since 1847
Since 1847 the trusted and
authoritative name in
dictionaries
There's a world of differ-
ence in Webster dic-
tionaries
To be sure you're right
... insist on Merriam-
Webster
The trusted and authori-
tative name in diction-
aries
G & D vermouth
As distinctive as a voice,
as pleasant as a

friendship
Blueprint of a perfect cock-
tail
G-B means Great Beer
Grace Bros. beer
G. D. Searle and Co.
Research in the service of
medicine
G. E. See also: General Elec-
tric
G. E. exposure meter
Better pictures with less
effort
G. E. radio receiver
Believe your own ears
The radio with the big plus
value
Wake up to music
G. E. refrigerator
For better living
A gift she'll open every day
A million in service ten
years or longer
Tops in preference because
it's tops in performance
You'll always be glad you
bought a G. E.
GK Technologies
We'll give you the full pic-
ture
G. W. Childs cigar
Generously good
G. Washington Coffee
The coffee you don't have
to make
Made in the cup at the
table
Gabriel, only Gabriel, is a snub-
ber
Gabriel Snubber Mfg. Co.
Gabriel Snubber Mfg. Co.
Gabriel, only Gabriel, is a
snubber
Gabrieleen permanent wave
Beauty begins with the hair
Gaby anti-chap lotion
When your lips take a
"weather-beating"
Gagnier Stereotype Foundry
For the betterment of news-
paper advertising
Gaines-burgers
The canned dog food without
the can
Nourishes every inch of
your dog

176

Gaining new friends through
    extra mileage
    Columbia tires
Gala absorbent towels
    When others run out we
    keep going
Galiano wine
    Fond of things Italiano?
    Try a sip of Galiano
The Galion Iron Works and Mfg.
    Co.
    Miles ahead
Gallagher & Burton whiskey
    A luxury blend for the
    "carriage trade"
Galveston News
    Texas' oldest newspaper
Gander Publishing Co.
    Take a gander
Gannett newspapers and broad-
    casting systems
    A world of different voices
    where freedom speaks
The Garcia Corp.
    Service guaranteed for
    life!
Garcia y Vega cigar
    Ask your dealer, he knows
Gardco paint
    Light in the darkest corner
Garden State Racing Assn.
    Racing planned for pleasure
Gardner. See also: Prince
    Gardner Co.
Gardner automobile
    Over 50 years of building
    well
    Rising higher and higher
    in public esteem
Gardner-Denver Co.
    See what air can do for
    you
    See what air-conditioning
    is doing now
Garfield Manufacturing Co.
    The registered symbol of
    quality since 1908
Garford motor truck
    Users know
Garland stoves and ranges
    If it is a Garland, that is
    all you need to know
    about a stove or range
Garlock Packing Service
    Mechanical packing service
    The standard packing of

    the world
Garrard phonograph record
    changer
    World's finest
    World's finest automatic
    record changer
The Garrett Corporation
    The aerospace company with
    its feet on the ground
    The future is building now
    at Garrett
    Garrett is experience
Garrett is experience
    The Garrett Corporation
Gary Safe Co.
    The safe investment
Gas-au-lec automobile
    Marks a new era in auto-
    mobile construction
    The simple car
The Gas-Electric Car
    Woods automobile
Gas makes the big difference
    American Gas Association,
    Inc.
The gas range with the lifetime
    burner guarantee
    Magic Chef gas range
The gas range you want
    Caloric Corp.
Gas service for cooking, no mat-
    ter where you live
    Coleman Co., Inc.
Gas Station Topics
    The national filling station
    magazine
Gas, the comfort fuel
    Philadelphia Gas Works Co.
Gas: The future belongs to the
    efficient
    American Gas Association,
    Inc.
Gasoline, not cut price guessoline
    Blue Sunoco gasoline
Gates Learjet Corporation
    Proven performance systems
    We outperform our competi-
    tion to help you outper-
    form yours
    The world's most efficient
    business jet. Now
    building our second
    1000
Gates Rubber Co.
    No. 1 in V-belts and hose
    World's largest maker of fan

belts
World's largest maker of
    V-belts
Gateway to and from the booming
    West
    Union Pacific Railroad
Gateway to and from your world
    markets
    Union Pacific Railroad
Gateway to the Jewish market
    <u>Daily Forward</u>
Gateway to the world of fabrics
    Westgate fabrics
Gavin's Scotch whiskey
    An auld acquaintance ne'er
    forgot
Gay. See also: Ben-Gay lotion
Gay and spirited as young
    laughter
    Skylark fragrance
Gay as May
    Textron Summer Blouses
Gay Diversion Perfume
    Prelude to adventure
The gay-hearted fragrance
    Yardley's Old English soap
Gayla Curlers
    Stop tearing your hair
Gear craftsmen for over a quar-
    ter century
    Van Dorn & Dutton Co.
The gear with a backbone
    Farrel-Birmingham Co.
Geared to the road
    Miller tires
Geartronics Corp.
    Creators of dependability
Gehl Bros. Mfg. Co.
    Where quality is a family
    tradition
Geier. See: P. A. Geier Co.
Geigy Chemical Corp.
    Creators of chemicals for
    modern agriculture
Gellett's lye
    Eats dirt
Gelusil
    The different antacid
Gem blades never irritate the
    face
    Gem razor
Gem, Inc.
    The trusted name in house-
    hold products since
    1917
The gem of the highway

Columbia automobile
Gem paper clips
    Millions daily
Gem razor
    All one piece; twist, it
    opens; twist, it closes
    Avoid 5 o'clock shadow
    Barbers use straight, rigid
    blades; so does Gem
    razor
    Gem blades never irritate
    the face
    Save with safety; shave
    with safety
    Smoother faces
    You pay less for Gem blades
    because you need so
    few
Gem razor. See also: New Gem
    Safety Razor
Gems of the screen
    Columbia Pictures Corp.
Genco razors
    Must make good or we will
General Arthur cigar
    Kick if you don't get the
    General Arthur cigar
General Box Company
    One service from forests to
    finished product
General Cigar Co.
    For young men and men with
    young ideas
    Millions are saying "tasting
    better than ever"
    The sophistocrat of cigars
    With pleasure, sir!
General Dynamics Communications
    Company
    We'll make your business
    telephones pay dividends
General Electric. See also:
    G. E.
General Electric Christmas tree
    lights
    A new touch of beauty for
    the wired home
General Electric Company
    The first and greatest name
    in electronics
    For lifetime service
    From the tiniest to the
    mightiest
    The house of magic
    Initials of a friend
    The leading research or-

ganization of the world
The mark of research serv-
ice
Motorized power, fitted to
every need
The problem solvers
Progress is our most im-
portant product
We bring good things to life
Where the brightest ideas
come to light
General Electric Company. See
also: Hotpoint Div.,
General Electric Com-
pany
General Electric Credit Corpora-
tion
Capitalize on your oppor-
tunities
Enterprising capital
General Electric furnace
Get your furnace off your
mind
General Electric Mazda Lamp
His only rival
The light to live with
Made to stay brighter longer
Mark of economical light
A necessary refinement in
lighting
Not the name of a thing but
the mark of a service
Stay brighter longer
They stay brighter longer
This mark means good light
at low cost
General Electric toaster
Toast to your taste, every
time
General Electric vacuum cleaner
All that the name implies
General Floorcraft, Inc.
Floor without flaws
General Foods Corporation
Like Grandma's, only more
so
People who talk about good
food talk about General
Foods
General Mills, Inc.
New foods, new ideas for
a better world
General Mills, Inc. See also:
Chemical Div., General
Mills, Inc.
General Motors Acceptance Cor-

poration
The financing people from
General Motors
The leasing people from
General Motors
General Motors Corporation
A car for every purse and
purpose
An eye on the future, an
ear to the ground
General Motors means Good
Measure
Mark of excellence
Merchant in mileage
More and better things for
more people
People building transporta-
tion to serve people
People profit when a busi-
ness prospers
A public-minded institution
To increase value is to en-
rich life
We're the best GM ever
Your money goes farther in
a General Motors car
General Motors Corporation.
See also:
A. C. Spark Plug Div.,
General Motors Corpora-
tion
Chevrolet Motor Div., Gen-
eral Motors Corporation
Detroit Diesel Engine Div.,
General Motors Corpora-
tion
Frigidaire Div., General
Motors Corporation
New Departure-Hyatt Bear-
ings Div., General
Motors Corporation
Saginaw Steering Gear Div.,
General Motors Corpora-
tion
General Motors Corporation,
Truck Division
Just miles
Outpulls, outperforms, out-
saves
Truck of value
Trucks are what we're all
about
General Motors means Good
Measure
General Motors Corporation
General Nutrition Centers

America's best nutrition
values are at GNC
General Oil Burner
Checks first with the finest
General Radio Corp.
Behind the panels of better
built sets
General Refrigeration Co.
The dry, constant cold of
the mountain top
General Telephone & Electronics
Corp.
Let's give the customer a
choice
More light per barrel
Sharing greatly in Amer-
ica's growth
We're a total communications
company
General Time Corp. See:
Westclox Div., General
Time Corp.
General Tire & Rubber Co.
The sign of tomorrow ...
today
Top quality for 50 years
Where research and develop-
ment make exciting
ideas
General tires
The big difference in tires
is action-traction
The blowout-proof tire
Goes a long way to make
friends
It's the second 10,000 miles
that makes the big hit
The least of the difference
is the difference in
price
Made in America since 1915
The shortest word for long-
est mileage
You're miles ahead with
General
General Transformer Co.
Let's create markets
A generation of worldwide ac-
ceptance
Torginol of America, Inc.
Generously good
G. W. Childs cigar
Genesco, Inc.
Everything to wear
Genesee Cream Ale
Tailored to taste

Genetron aerosol
Putting the "push" in Amer-
ica's finest aerosols
Genie brassiere
The bra that fits like magic
It fits like magic
Genie garage door opener
Genie keeps you in the
driver's seat
Genie keeps you in the driver's
seat
Genie garage door opener
Genstar Corporation
Our success is unheard of
Gentle as a lamb
Train & McIntyre Scotch
whiskey
Gentle dental care
Teel mouth wash
The gentle diuretic
Diurex pills
A gentleman's drink
Cutty Sark Scotch whiskey
Gentlemen, be treated
P. O. N. beer
A gentleman's whiskey since
1865
Paul Jones whiskey
The gentlemen of the moving in-
dustry
North American Van Lines,
Inc.
Gentlemen prefer Bond's
Bond's handkerchiefs
Gentlemen's fine shoes
Nettleton shoes
The gentler cream deodorant
Yodora
Gently as a whisper
Sargent door checks
Genuine Pfister hybrids
Pfister Associated Growers
Geon vinyls
The material difference in
building
Geo. A. Hormel and Co.
Fine foods products
Fresh ideas in meat ...
from Hormel
George J. Kempler Co.
Fine furniture
Georgia-Pacific Corp.
The growth company
Georgia Railway & Power Co.
A citizen, wherever we
serve

Georgiana frocks
A national buyword
Styled for a figure, not for
an age
Gerber baby foods
Babies are our business ...
our only business
Gerber Legendary Blades
Fashioned for those who
enjoy extra-ordinary
quality
Gerhard Lang Brewery
Backed by a century of
brewing experience
Geritol iron and vitamin supple-
ment
America's #1 iron and vita-
min supplement
Geritol. It's still going
strong
Geritol. It's still going strong
Geritol iron and vitamin
supplement
Get a Fresh Start every day
Fresh Start laundry deter-
gent
Get a jump on athlete's foot
with Tinactin
Tinactin
Get a lot more done in a lot
less time
Lanier Business Products,
Inc.
Get a piece of the rock
Prudential Insurance Co. of
America
Get a tan in one day
QT suntan lotion
Get all your vitamins in food
Ovaltine
Get better yields from your
fields with Armour
Armour and Co.
Get brighter windows quicker
with Windex
Windex glass cleaner
Get brighter windows with
Windex
Windex glass cleaner
Get going great--with Graco
Gray Co., Inc.
Get it done right
Milex Car Care
Get it in glass
Glass Container's Manufac-
turers Institute

Get macho close
Schick Super II razor blades
Get more, get Kelvinator
Kelvinator refrigerator
Get more go from every gallon
Oldsmobile automobile
Get more out of it
Red Man chewing tobacco
Get more out of life with coffee
Pan-American Coffee Bureau
Get more with Thor
Thor clothes washer
Get more worth from air with
Worthington
Worthington Pump & Machin-
ery Corp.
Get needed
Taylor Business Institute
Get on the ball with Sun Ball
juices
Sun Ball fruit juices
Get relief for your tired, aching
feet
Dr. Scholl's arch supporters
Get that golden glow with Rhein-
gold
Rheingold beer
Get the Anacin difference
Anacin pain reliever
Get the best in screw worm
killers
Globe Remedy
Get the best in the world
World Fire and Marine In-
surance Co.
Get the best things first, get
Kelvinator
Kelvinator refrigerator
Get the drop on that cough
Dean's Mentholated Cough
Drops
Get the most out of television
with a Dumont Teleset
Dumont television receivers
Get the plus of a Packard
Packard automobile
Get time from a timepiece, but
if you want a watch get
a Hamilton
Hamilton Watch Co.
Get your furnace off your mind
General Electric furnace
Get your hands on a Toyota ...
you'll never let go
Toyota automobile
Get your man, no waiting, no

walking
Ediphone Dictograph
Get your mind off your nose
for up to twelve hours
Duration nasal spray
Get Zest. Feel your best
Zest soap
Gets a hand in any land
Arrow liqueurs
Gets a lot more done in a lot
less time
Lainier Business Products,
Inc.
Gets all the dirt by air alone
P. A. Geier Co.
Gets at the core of every clean-
ing chore
Softwash Cleaner
Gets dirt you can't see
Eureka vacuum cleaner
Gets great pictures
Graflex, Inc.
Gets spills before they get away
Bounty absorbent towels
Gets the dirt, not the carpet
Eureka vacuum cleaner
Gets there first
Air Express
Gets windows brighter quicker
Windex glass cleaner
Gets your whole wash clean!
Wisk laundry detergent
Getting people together
Boeing aircraft
Getting results in rural America
is Farm Journal's busi-
ness
Farm Journal
Getting the most from winding
Universal Winding Co.
Geuting Shoes
Excitement afoot
Gevaert Film
The negative for positive
results
Ghirardelli's hot chocolate
Children like it better than
milk
A giant among newspapers
Boston Post
The giant of the South
Southern Agriculturist
Gibbs boat
The world's outstanding
small boat
Gibson's goes down easily

Gibson's whiskey
Gibson's whiskey
Gibson's goes down easily
Giddings & Lewis Machine Tool
Co.
Unexcelled accuracy
Giese Bros. Coal Co.
Stays dustless until the
last shovelful
The gift candy of America
Huyler's, Inc.
A gift of the centuries
Clark Metal Grave Vault Co.
A gift she'll open every day
G. E. refrigerator
The gift that continues to give
Underwood typewriter
The gift that endears and en-
dures
Lektro Shaver
The gift that keeps on giving
Victrola talking machine
The gift that lives and grows
Add-A-Pearl Co.
The gift that really remembers
Kodak cameras
The gift tie of a nation
Chicago Printed String Co.
A gift to remember
Princesse de Conde Choco-
lates
A gift with a lift
Paris Garters
Gifts and art gladden the heart
National Gift and Art Assn.
Gifts long remembered
Hotpoint Div., General
Electric Company
Gilbarco, Inc.
Leader in the field. Choice
of the leaders
Gilbert. See also: A. C. Gil-
bert Co.
Gilbert & Barker oil burner
Most heat per dollar
Gilbert Paper Co.
A good business letter is
always better ... writ-
ten on a Gilbert paper
Red and blue make white
Gilbert radium dial clock
Makes night time plain as
day
Time in sight, day or night
Gilbert Shoe Co.
Keep good feet healthy

Gilbert Vitalator
Hair relief without grief
Gilbey's vodka
Smart, smooth, sensibly
priced
Gillette Blue Blades
Slides over the face like
skies over snow
Gillette safety razor
Look sharp! Feel sharp!
Be sharp!
More shaving comfort for
your money
No stropping, no honing
The quality razor of the
world
Gillette tires
A bear/for wear
Gillson furnaces
Makes many warm friends
Gilmore Oil Co.
Down, Gilmore, down!
It's fortified, just try it
I've tried 'em all
The most highly-filtered
motor oil in America
Roar with Gilmore
Roar with silence
The gin of England
Beefeater Gin
Ginger ale with piquant personal-
ity
Cliquot Club ginger ale
Ginger ale with the long-life
bubble
Pabst ginger ale
Gingiss Formalwear
Outfitters for the rugged
indoorsman
Ginori. See: Richard Ginori
china
Girard cigar
Never gets on your nerves
Girdles of grace
Real-form girdles
The girl with the beautiful face
Clairol, Inc.
Gisholt Machine Co.
Machines for total productiv-
ity
Give a canary for companionship
The R. T. French Co.
Give a look INSIDE to get value
outside (and in)
Crown & Headlight overalls
Give Eversharp and you give

the finest
Eversharp mechanical pencil
Give her a Hoover and you give
her the best
Hoover vacuum cleaner
Give him Schick's appeal
Schick electric shaver
Give his neck a break
Van Heusen shirts
Give light and the people will
find their own way
Scripps-Howard newspapers
Give long-lasting light, bullet-
fast
Winchester flashlight
Give me a Dew!
Mountain Dew soft drink
Give me another Central Royal
Beer
Central Royal Beer
Give memory insurance
Standard Diary Co.
Give new shoes old shoe ease
Dr. Scholl's bunion pads
Give Red Bands your hard job
Howell Electric Motors Co.
Give so more will live
Heart Fund
Give them ALL a good time
Telechron Electric Clock
Give them life and make it worth
living
United Jewish Appeal
Give to conquer cancer
American Cancer Society
Give Whitman's Chocolates, it's
the thoughtful thing to
do
Whitman's Sampler candy
Give your allergy the benefit of
the Dimetane Difference
Dimetane allergy tablets
Give your car an extra year of
youth
Cities Service gasoline
Give your child a career for
Christmas
Royal portable typewriter
Give your dishwasher the best
Cascade detergent
Give your feet young ideas
Weyenberg Shoe Mfg. Co.
Give your guest what he wishes
National Distillers
Gives cream and butter flavor
Pet milk

Gives more bright light longer
Bright Star flashlight
Gives your engine an extra
margin of safety
Pennzoil motor oil
Gives your smile breath-taking
beauty
Calox Tooth Powder
Giving industry a lift since
1878
Shephard Niles Crane and
Hoist Corp.
Glad garbage bags
It's what you don't smell
that counts
Gladding Corp. See: South
Bend Tackle Co. Div.,
Gladding Corp.
Glamorene Products Corp.
Famous for products that
really work
Glamorug floor covering
At home in every room
Glamour for every figure
Kabo corset
Glamour for teen-age and queen
age
Kabo brassiere
Glas-Col Apparatus Co.
Specialists in solving un-
usual heating problems
A glass arm conveys the light
Sho-Lite, Inc.
Glass Container's Manufacturers
Institute
Get it in glass
A glass of Guinness is a cheer-
ful sight
Guinness ale
Glass Plus glass cleaner
Cleans glass, plus a whole
lot more!
Glass sealed, the perfect cof-
fee, the perfect pack-
age
Iris coffee
Glassware of distinction
Czechoslovak Glass Prod-
ucts Co.
Glaxo
The food that builds bon-
nie babies
Gleam. See: Gleem toothpaste
Gleaming armor for your floors
Old English No Rubbing
Wax

Gleaming silver on your gown,
but no shine on your
nose
Woodbury's face powder
Gleem toothpaste
Fights the enemies of your
mouth
The Glen Falls Group
Where you are always num-
ber one
The Glenlivet Scotch whiskey
How dare the Glenlivet be
so expensive?
The taste beyond 12-year-
old Scotch
12-year-old unblended
Scotch. About $20 the
bottle
Unchanged since 1824
Glenmore whiskey
Pour Glenmore, you get
more
Glenn's Sulphur Soap
Fascinating brilliancy
Glenoit Mills, Inc.
Definitely Glenoit for happy
persons
Glenwood Range Co.
Glenwood ranges make cook-
ing easier
When it's time to change,
get a Glenwood range
Glenwood ranges make cooking
easier
Glenwood Range Co.
Glessner cold cream
Kissable hands
Glidden paints
Everywhere on everything
The pacemaker in paints
When you make a very good
paint it shows
Glider Brushless Shave
For the one man in 7 who
shaves every day
Gliss. See: Silent Gliss, Inc.
Glo-Sheen Drapes
Drapes of wrath
Glo Soapy Scouring Pads
Scours the pan, not your
hands
The global high sign
Coca Cola soft drink
Globe beer
The bottled beer with the
draught beer flavor

It's flavoripe
Globe Hoist Company
   A world of engineering
      experience
Globe Laboratories
   Takes TOIL out of toilet
      cleaning
Globe radiator shutters
   Laugh at zero
Globe Remedy
   Get the best in screw worm
      killers
The Globe sells Boston
   Boston Globe
Globe Steel Products Corp.
   Only when the finest is
      good enough
The Globe-Wernicke Co.
   Built to endure
   For every room in the
      house
   The touch of tomorrow in
      office living
Glorifies every dish it touches
   Heinz ketchup
Glorifying the world's fare
   Heinz ketchup
Glover's Imperial Mange Medicine
   Less hair in the comb,
      more hair on the head
Gloves that "go places"
   Belle Glove Co.
Glow. See: Glo
Glowing with health, brimming
   with flavor
   Campbell's condensed soups
Glue without goo
   Casco cement
Glyco-Thymoline
   The alkaline antiseptic
Go as a travel adventurer
   Travel Adventures
Go by air-conditioned train
   North Coast Limited
Go first class ... go Phillips 66
   Phillips 66 gasoline
Go international ... with all the
   comforts of Hilton
   Hilton Hotels Corp.
Go Naked to make money
   Naked unfinished furni-
      ture
Go to high school in bedroom
   slippers
   International Correspondence
   Schools

Go with the pick of the pros
   Skil Corp.
Go with the spirit--the spirit of
   '76
   Union Oil Company
Goblin soap
   Works wonders
God of two faces
   American Banker's Associa-
      tion
Godfather's pizza restaurants
   A big deal and a big meal
Godfrey rollers
   They're better because
      they're seamless
Goding shoe
   The last fits, the fit lasts
Goebel beer
   Nationally famous for good
      taste
   RIGHT from the cyprus casks
      of Goebel
Goes a long way to make friends
   General tires
Goes farther safer
   Pennzoil motor oil
Goes home and stays home
   Baltimore News-Post
Goes to the home, stays in the
   home
   Cincinnati Enquirer
Going, going, gone!
   Herpicide hair tonic
Gold. See also: R. J. Gold
   chewing tobacco
Gold Bond building materials
   First with better ways to
      build
   Gold Bond material methods
      make the difference in
      modern building
   One of many fine products
      that come from 40 years
      of thinking new
Gold Bond material methods
   make the difference in
   modern building
   Gold Bond building mate-
      rials
Gold Center wheat cereal
   Anatomic energy
The Gold Coins of Mexico
   Now there's an even better
      way to own gold
   Once you know the story
      behind them you'll know

why so many Americans
are purchasing them
Gold Dust Soap Powder
Have you a little fairy in
your home?
It's sudsy
Let the Gold Dust Twins
do your work
Makes hard water soft
Gold Label cigars
World leader in luxury
cigars
Gold Medal Camp Furniture
Best for the camp, bears
the Gold Medal stamp
Gold Medal Flour
Good for everything you
bake and everything
you bake with it is
good
The gold medal Kentucky bour-
bon since 1872
I. W. Harper bourbon
whiskey
The gold medal whiskey
I. W. Harper bourbon
whiskey
Gold Pack Canner
Makes canning a pleasure
Gold seal is your insurance of
beauty, cleanliness and
endurance
Congoleum-Nairn floor cov-
erings
Gold Seal radio tube
The perfect tube
Gold Seal wines
Made in the "champagne
district of America"
The gold standard
Wix Corp.
The gold standard of radio re-
ceivers
Ferguson radio receiver
The gold standard of value
Reo automobile
Gold Stripe stockings
The long stocking that fits
every leg
On a pedestal
Golden Age Macaroni
Meat from wheat
Golden cakes of energy
Chappel Bros. dog food
Golden Dipt breading
Seals flavor in and

grease out
Golden Fleece tissue
The aristocrat of tissues
Golden Graham breakfast cereal
Have a Golden day!
Golden Harvest wheat paste
Spreads like backyard news
Golden Knight watchband
The watchband that was
taken from history is
now making history
Golden Lights cigarettes
Full. Rich. Delightful.
Taste the pleasure
Golden nugget jet service
Alaska Airlines, Inc.
Golden nugget jets
Alaska Airlines, Inc.
The golden opportunity for the
80's
Loews hotels
Golden Ram golf ball
Just enough better to win
Golden Rule garments
Hamilton Carhartt overalls
The golden touch of Lipton
Lipton food additives
Golden Virginia tobacco
Once tried, always satisfied
Golden Wedding whiskey
Has had no peers for fifty
years
The whiskey you feel good
about
Goldenrod Ice Cream Co.
Quality is not accidental
Golfcraft for the finest Golf-
craft, Inc.
Golfcraft, Inc.
Golfcraft, Inc.
Golfcraft for the finest
The name to look for
Golfer's Magazine
The world's greatest travel
publication
Good as ever
Falstaff beer
Good banking is good people
The Bank of New York
A good broom sweeps cleaner
and lasts longer
American Broom & Brush Co.
Good buildings deserve good
hardware
Corbin hardware
A good business letter is always

better ... written on a
Gilbert paper
Gilbert Paper Co.
Good candy for all the family
Chuckles
The good coffee folks
P. W. Eastham & Co.
Good coffee that makes good
sense. Anywhere
Sanka Brand decaffeinated
coffee
Good company in your home
Best Foods
A good cook deserves a Grand
Gas Range
Grand Gas Range
Good dogs deserve good food
Tally Ho
Good flours make good bakers
better
Federal Mill
Good flours make good cooks
better
Federal Mill
Good food for good dogs
Bannock Food Co.
Good food for pleased guests
John Sexton Co.
Good food is good health
National Restaurant Associ-
ation
The good food service
Prophet Co.
Good food tastes better with
Star Ale
Star Ale
The good food wrap
Reynolds aluminum foil wrap
Good for a long, safe ride
Federal tires
Good for everything you bake
and everything you bake
with it is good
Gold Medal Flour
Good for good business
Linen Supply Assn. of
America
Good for its face value
Vantine shaving cream
Good for life
Dr. Pepper soft drink
Good for tender gums
Ipana toothpaste
Good for you and good to you
Ry-Krisp
The good for your cat catfood

Purina Cat Chow
Good Furniture Magazine
A business journal of fur-
nishing and decoration
A good habit
Waxtex wax paper
The good hands people
State Farm Insurance Co.
Good Hardware
The national magazine of
the hardware trade
A good job for you
U. S. Army Recruiting
Service
The good kind to keep handy--
because they stay soft
Kraft Foods Div., Kraftco
Corp.
Good looking--long wearing
Holeproof Hosiery
Good Looks Merchandising
The magazine of the toiletries
trade
A good low-priced car
Saxon automobile
Good Luck Hose
Built to stay alive
Good meat from the Heartland
Eckrich sausages and pro-
cessed meats
The good mechanic's choice
U. S. Electrical Tool Co.
Good morning! Have you used
Pears' Soap?
Pears' Soap
A good name
Dodge automobile
The good neighbor is you. Be-
long
American Red Cross
A good neighbor of your com-
munity
Baltimore & Ohio Railroad
A good newspaper
Chicago American
Good nutrition doesn't have to
be whole wheat
Wonder white bread
Good paint costs nothing
Bradley & Vrooman Co.
Good paint's other name
Dutch Boy White Lead
Good papers for good business
W. C. Hamilton & Sons
Good people
Olsten Temporary Services

187

Good people make good things
  Philip Morris cigarettes
Good people to do business with
  Employers Mutual Insurance
    Co. of Wisconsin
A good reputation has to be
  earned
  Blu-Cold refrigerator
Good soap is good business
  Proctor & Gamble Co.
A good society is good business
  McGraw-Hill Publications
    Div., McGraw-Hill, Inc.
Good steel, good service
  Burlington Steel Co.
The good stuff. And nothing
  but
  Canon plain paper copier
Good taste--compliments of
  nature
  Grape-Nuts cereal
  Grape-Nuts flakes
Good taste for 100 years
  Pabst Blue Ribbon beer
Good taste in a remedy
  Alka-Seltzer
Good things from the garden
  Green Giant Co.
The good things in life stay
    that way. Dewar's
    never varies
  Dewar's Blended Scotch
  Whiskey
The good things of milk and
  malt
  Horlick's Malted Milk Corp.
Good things to eat come from
  1 Mustard Street
  The R. T. French Co.
Good times stir with Seven and
  Coke
  Seagram's Seven Crown
  whiskey
Good to be in, good to be seen
  in
  Pontiac automobile
Good to eat and good for you
  Ry-Krisp
Good to the core
  Pacific Northwest Fruits,
  Inc.
Good to the last drop
  Maxwell House Master
  Blend Coffee
Good to the last luscious left-
  over

Swift's Premium meats
Good to your finger tips
  Strathmore nail polish
Good vibrations!
  Sunkist Fresh Fruit Drinks
Good washing wins good will
  Cowles Detergent Co.
Good workmen know the differ-
  ence
  Manning Abrasive Co.
Goodall Worsted Co.
  The finest name in fabrics
  The national summer suit
Goodness knows they're good
  Elmer Candy Co.
Goodrich. See also: B. F.
  Goodrich Tire Co.
Goodrich-Gulf Chemicals, Inc.
  Leading innovators in poly-
    mer chemistry
  The one to watch for new
    developments
Goodrich Silvertown tire
  America's first cord tire
  Best in the long run
  First in rubber
Goods well displayed are half
  sold
  Olsen & O'Brien
Goodwill Industries, Inc.
  Not charity, but a chance
  Our business works so peo-
    ple can
Goody Root Beer
  Thirst come, thirst served
Goodyear Auto Tire
  Can be removed in thirty
    seconds
  First--every year
  I couldn't get a better
    Christmas gift to save
    my life
  More people ride on Good-
    year tires than on any
    other kind
  No tools but the hands
  Now less money buys more
    miles
  Test-and-farm proved
  You don't stay first unless
    you're best
Goodyear radial tires
  When you need radials
    come up to Goodyear
Goodyear Safety Tubes
  Makes a blow-out harmless

Goodyear shoe soles
Greatest name in rubber
Goodyear Tire & Rubber Co.
Out front. Pulling away
Out front. World wide
Gordon. See also:
Duff Gordon sherry
Gorton
Gordon hosiery
The label to take home
Gordon's Distilled London Dry
Gin
Drinks never taste thin
with Gordon's Gin
The heart of a good cock-
tail
It's a bit more expensive,
but for a flawless, cool
Tom Collins, the world
comes to Gordon's
It's crystal-clear
Gorham Div., Textron, Inc.
America's leading silver-
smiths since 1831
Best-known name in sterling
Majoring in marriage
When the name says Gor-
ham, the gift says
everything
Gorton. See also: Gordon
Gorton glue
From the skin of Gorton's
codfish
Gorton-Pew Fisheries, Inc.
The famous family of Gor-
ton's sea foods
Steady as she goes
Gorton's Codfish Cakes
Nothing to do but fry
Gospel Pencil Co.
Tag them for good
Gossard girdles
The Gossard line of beauty
The lady with a line
Line of beauty
Nicest next to you
The Gossard line of beauty
Gossard girdles
Gotham silk hosiery
Silk stockings that wear
Gotham watch
Time for a lifetime
Time for a lifetime and
longer
Gottschalk-Humphrey
An agency is known by

the clients it keeps
Gould-National Batteries, Inc.
Longest life by owners'
records
More power from more re-
search
Off when it's on and on
when it's off
Goulds pumps
For every service
The gourmet breath mint
Läkerol
Goya Guitars, Inc.
The world's finest
Grabow. See: Dr. Grabow
pipes
Grabowsky Power Wagons
Mechanically correct
Grace. See also: W. R. Grace
& Co.
Grace Bros. Beer
G-B means Great Beer
Grace the face and stay in place
Kirstein glasses
A grade for each type of motor
Socony Vacuum Oil Co.
Graduate to a De Soto
De Soto automobile
Graduate to Kaywoodie
Kaywoodie pipe
Grady. See: Jewel Grady super-
markets
Graef. See: Jean R. Graef,
Inc.
Graflex, Inc.
Gets great pictures
With the Graflex the payoff
is in the picture
Graham-Paige automobile
The most imitated car on the
road
Grammes & Sons, Inc.
Packaged metal engineering
Granada Royale Hometels
Welcome to the Suite life
Granco Steel Products Co.
Imagination in steel for the
needs of today's archi-
tecture
Grand Award Canadian whiskey
The only 12-year-old Cana-
dian whiskey
Grand Estate wines
The crowning achievement
of vintner skill
Grand Gas Range

A good cook deserves a
Grand Gas Range
Grand Hotel, High Mount, N. Y.
A "grand" hotel in every
sense
A "grand" hotel in every sense
Grand Hotel, High Mount,
N. Y.
A grand investment
Webster's International
Dictionary
Grand Maison de Blanc
The trousseau house of
America
Grand Marnier Liqueur
There may still be places
on earth where Grand
Marnier isn't offered
after dinner
A grand old Canadian name
Corby's whiskey
The grand old drink of the
South
Southern Comfort liquor
The grand piano of the radio
world
Fada Radio, Ltd.
A "Grand" product is a "qual-
ity" product
Grand shellac
Grand Rapids Hardware Co.
No sash hardware installs
faster than Grand
Rapids hardware
Grand Rapids Refrigerator Co.
Like a clean China dish
Grand shellac
A "Grand" product is a
"quality" product
A grand slam favorite
American Chewing Products
Corp.
Grand Slam golf clubs
They take every trick
Grandalf Data, Inc.
Grandalf Data. Rapidly
growing communications
wizard
Grandalf Data. Rapidly grow-
ing communications
wizard
Grandalf Data, Inc.
Grange Mutual Insurance
Your partner in protec-
tion
Granger tobacco

Don't be a stranger to
Granger
For my pipe
Granite Mfrs. Assn.
Lasting until everlasting
Granola Snack
Light and crunchy
Grant. See also: W. T. Grant
Co.
Grant Oil Tool Co.
Used where performance
counts
Grantly sun glasses
Styled for the stars
Grant's Scotch whiskey
As long as you're up get
me a Grant's
We'll wait
Grape-Nuts cereal
Good taste--compliments of
nature
In this food is nourishment
you need, in the form
your body can digest
There's a reason
There's a reason for Grape-
Nuts
You can't do a man-size
job on a bird-size
breakfast
Grape-Nuts cereal and Grape-
Nuts Flakes
One delicious flavor in two
delicious forms
Grape-Nuts Flakes
Good taste--compliments of
nature
Here's a thrill for breakfast
Thrill for breakfast
Grapefruit drink that gives you
GO
Squirt soft drink
The grass people
C. M. Scott and Co.
Graton & Knight Co.
The hand that builds cer-
tainty at the point of
seal
The orange line, one quality
control from hide to
loom
Research belting's double
plus
Gravely Motor Plow and Culti-
vator
A midget in size, a giant

in power

Graves Timing Device Co.
Stop cheating yourself

The gravy aid every body's talking about
Gravy Master

Gravy it up with Gravy Train
Gravy Train dog food

Gravy Master
The gravy aid everybody's talking about
Makes your cookin' good-lookin'
Masters gravy making
Sign of good cooking

Gravy Train dog food
Gravy it up with Gravy Train
Makes its own gravy

Gray. See also:
Dorothy Gray cosmetics
Dorothy Gray suntan oil
Grey

Gray & Davis home lighting
Lights the home, lightens the work

Gray & Dudley stoves and ranges
Worthy of the name

Gray Co., Inc.
Get going great--with Graco
The pumportation people

Gray's Harbor cement products
Concrete satisfaction

Grease just vanishes from pots, pans, dishes
Rinso

Great aches from little toe-corns grow
Blue-Jay corn plaster

Great aircrafts don't just happen.... Their secret is versatile performance!
British Aerospace, Inc.

The great American dog food
Purina Dog Chow

The great American family car
De Soto automobile

The great American family cereal
Cream of Wheat

Great American Insurance Cos.
Protecting the nation--through hometown

agents

Great Atlantic & Pacific Tea Stores
For good eating at sensible cost

A great car for today
Cadillac automobile

The great cough remedy for children as well as adults
Hale's Honey of Horehound and Tar

The great engineers
Borg-Warner Corporation

The great English medicine
Beecham's Pills

Great grapes, what a flavor
Welch's grape jelly and grapelade

The great highway performers
Corvair/Monza automobile

A great hotel doesn't have to be expensive
Harley Hotel, New York City

Great Lakes Carbon Corp.
World leader in filtration

Great meat makes great jumbo franks
Kahn's sausages

Great movies are just the beginning
Home Box Office cable television

A great name for quality candy
Clark candy bar

The great name in American ceramics
Haeger Potteries, Inc.

A great name in aviation
Pacific Northern Airlines

A great name in oil
Sinclair Oil Corp.

Great name in science
Pfanstiehl Chemical Co.

A great name in tackle
Pflueger fishing tackle

Great national shoes weekly
Boot and Shoe Recorder

The great newspaper of the great Southwest
Los Angeles Examiner

Great Northern Railway
A dependable railway
Route of the incomparable empire builder

See America first
The great penetrative liniment
  Omega Oil
Great people to fly with
  Pakistan International Air-
  lines
Great people to ship with
  Pakistan International Air-
  lines
The great regulator
  Beecham's Pills
Great shoes for little Americans
  Little Yankee shoes
The great skin cure
  Cuticura ointment
A great state in which to live
  and work
  Rhode Island
The great taste of stew that
  brings dogs running
  Chuck Wagon dog food
Great taste, one calorie
  Tab soft drink
Great taste that only happens
  here
  Velamints candy
A great team in steam
  Worthington Pump &
  Machinery Corp.
Great thrill in radio by the
  pioneers of short-wave
  radio
  Stewart-Warner radio re-
  ceiver
A great way to fly
  Singapore Airlines
A great way to get back in touch
  with those two things
  at the ends of your
  arms
  MG Kitcar
Great-West Life Assurance Co.
  Six and a half billion dol-
  lars of protection for
  our policyholders
Great Western champagne
  For the great moments
  Great Western for great
  moments
Great Western Cordage Co.
  Merits your confidence
Great Western for great mo-
  ments
  Great Western champagne
The great wheatsworth taste
  Nabisco, Inc.

Greatest breeze with the least
  current consumption
  Western Electric fans
Greatest concentration in the
  world's richest farm
  region
  Successful Farming
Greatest cough and voice lozenge
  on earth
  Frog in Your Throat
The greatest hotel value in
  America
  Ambassador Hotel, Los
  Angeles, Calif.
The greatest invention of the
  age
  Whitman's Instantaneous
  Chocolate
The greatest invention since the
  face
  Vestpok Dry Shaver
The greatest line in glassware!
  Anchor Hocking Glass Co.
The greatest music the world
  has known
  RCA Corp.
The greatest name in aircraft
  radio
  Bendix radio receiver
The greatest name in bourbon
  Old Crow whiskey
The greatest name in building
  United States Gypsum Co.
The greatest name in coffee-
  brewing equipment
  Cory
Greatest name in color
  Technicolor Corp.
The greatest name in door chimes
  Nu-Tone Chimes, Inc.
The greatest name in golf
  MacGregor golf equipment
The greatest name in health in-
  surance
  Mutual of Omaha Insurance
  Co.
Greatest name in housekeeping
  O-Cedar products
The greatest name in outboard
  boats
  Thompson Bros. Boat Mfg.
  Co.
The greatest name in rayon
  Courtald's rayon
Greatest name in rubber
  Goodyear shoe soles

Greatest name in shoe polish
  Griffin shoe polish
The greatest name in socks
  Interwoven socks
Greatest name in the great out-
    doors. Foremost name
    in indoor comfort
  Coleman Co., Inc.
The greatest name in vodka
  Smirnoff vodka
The greatest name in wine
  Roma wines
The greatest name in yachting
  Consolidated yacht
Greatest power on earth
  Cleveland tractor
The greatest recent advance in
    building and heating
    economy
  Thermolath
The greatest show on earth
  Barnum & Bailey's circus
The greatest spectacle in racing
  Indianapolis annual 500
    mile automobile race
The greatest taste in chocolate
  Nestle's Milk Chocolate Bar
The greatest tire name in racing
  Firestone tires
Greatest weld that you've beheld
  Ohio Brass Co.
Grecian Formula hair dressing
  With Grecian Formula you'll
    play longer
Green. See also: A. P. Green
    Fire Brick Co.
The green cleans in-between ...
    the white polishes
    bright
  Pro-Phy-Lac-Tic toothbrush
Green Giant Co.
  Good things from the gar-
    den
Green Giant Peas
  Picked at the fleeting mo-
    ment of perfect flavor
  Soft and sweet like big
    drops of honey
  They give you the sweetest
    and most tender mo-
    ments of their lives, the
    fleeting moment of per-
    fect flavor
Greene Bros. Inc.
  Jewelry for the home
Greenfield Tap & Die Corp.

"Show-How" is know-how in
    action
Greenpoint Metallic Bed Co.
  The berth of a nation
Greenspan Bros.
  Foods of fine flavor
Greenwald. See: Louis Green-
    wald
Greenwood Mills, Inc.
  Fabrics with the character
    of quality
Greer. See:
  J. W. Greer Co.
  Jimmie Grier's dance or-
    chestra
Greeting Card Association
  Replace fear with cheer.
    Send Christmas cards
    this year
  Scatter sunshine with greet-
    ing cards
Greeting cards of character
  Rust Craft greeting cards
Grenay. See: Sparkling Grenay
Grennan Cake Co.
  Every bite a delight
Gresolvent
  Cleans hands clean
Grewen gloves
  A thoroughbred air in every
    pair
Grey. See also: Gray
Grey Advertising Agency
  Thematic advertising
Grey Poupon Mustard
  It even has wine in it
Grey-Rock Div., Raybestos-
    Manhattan, Inc.
  Three steps to safety
  You can't buy a better
    brake lining to save
    your life!
Grey-Rock Div., Raybestos-
    Manhattan, Inc. See
    also: Raybestos-
    Manhattan, Inc.
Greyhound Corporation
  A company for the eighties
  Keep a date with summer
    this winter
  Leave the driving to us
  Leave the moving to us
  The omnibus company
  Roll south into summer this
    winter
  We do the planning, you

have the fun
We're as basic to America
  as a summer vacation
We're as basic to America
  as the 4th of July
We're as basic to America
  as the Sunday funnies
Greystone Fruit Wines
  Orchard flavor in every
  sip
  The profit line in wine
The Greystone, New York City
  A residential hotel of re-
  finement
Grier's. See: Jimmie Grier's
  dance orchestra
Griesedieck Bros. Brewery Co.
  Class in a glass
Griffin Hosiery Mills
  You are reading through
  its invisible sheerness
Griffith shoe polish
  Greatest name in shoe
  polish
Grime does not pay
  A. C. Spark Plugs
Grinnell Corp.
  Total capability in fire pro-
  tection
  When the fire starts, the
  water starts
  Wherever piping is involved
The gripes of wrath
  Pepto-Bismol
Gripper fasteners
  The laundry-proof snap
  fastener that ends
  button-bother
Grisby-Grunow refrigerators
  Mighty monarch of the
  Arctic
Griswold cooking utensils
  The line that's fine at
  cooking time
Grizzly brake lining
  Bear in mind
Gro-Pup dog food
  Dogs GO for Gro-Pup
Groceries
  A national publication for
  the wholesale grocer
Grocers Biscuit Co.
  Baked in freshness
Grossman shoes
  Comfort is what we sell
Ground Gripper shoes

The most comfortable shoe
  in the world
  Shoes for all the family
Grover's. See: J. J. Grover's
  Sons Co.
Grow, grow by the rail way
  Association of American
  Railroads
Grow what you eat
  S. L. Allen & Co.
Grow with Chicago
  Chicago Tribune
The growers brand
  Ocean Spray cranberry juice
Growing in more ways than one
  Union Camp Corporation
Growing old gracefully
  Nujol laxative
Growing security
  Baker, Frentress & Co.
Growing with solar energy
  Ametek solar panels
The growing world of Libbey-
  Owens-Ford
  Libbey-Owens-Ford Co.
Grown the natural way in bounti-
  ful U.S.A.
  Bountiful almonds
  Bountiful pistachio nuts
  Bountiful raisins
Grown to be America's favorite
  Lay's potato chips
Grows bountiful, beautiful hair
  Hall's Hair Renewer
Grows more beautiful with use
  Wallace Silversmiths Div.,
  The Hamilton Watch Co.
Grows thick, heavy hair
  Danderine
Growth by design
  I. C. Industries
The growth company
  Georgia-Pacific Corp.
Growth essential in a corporate
  protector
  Frank B. Hall & Co. insur-
  ance brokers
The growth fund
  National Investors Corp.
Growth leader of the aluminum
  industry
  Consolidated Aluminum Corp.
Grucci fireworks
  The first family of fireworks
Gruen Verithin Watch
  Only half as thick as the

194

ordinary watch, yet
guaranteed accurate and
even more durable
Gruen watch
The precision watch, America's choice
A thousand tender words
in one
Grumman Corporation
Grumman is helping Americans use energy from
the sun, the wind and
the sea
An idea whose time has
come
Another idea whose time
has come
The technology for the job
at hand
Grumman is helping Americans
use energy from the
sun, the wind and the
sea
Grumman Corporation
Guarantee Liquid Measure Co.
Always accurate
Guaranteed absolutely free from
horse motion
Bradley Two-Wheeler Carriage
Guaranteed by the name
Westinghouse Electric Corp.
Guaranteed for the life of the
motor
Richmond Piston Rings
Guaranteed heating
U. S. Radiator Corp.
Guaranteed, the hardest working workwear
H. D. Lee Co., Inc.
Guaranteed use in anything
Fosset brush
A guaranty of purity and reliability
Merck, Sharp and Dohme
Div., Merck & Co.,
Inc.
Guard your mouth
Dental Hi-gene Products,
Inc.
Guard your time
Elgin watches
The Guardian Life Insurance
Co. of America
Guardian of American
families for 80 years

Guardian will enrich and
safeguard your retirement years
Here dwells security
Will bring peace of mind to
you and your family
Your Guardian for life
Guardian Light Co.
Guardian lighting
Guardian lighting
Guardian Light Co.
Guardian of American families for
80 years
The Guardian Life Insurance Co. of America
Guardian of highway safety
Robox emergency auto control
The guardian of your grove
Owl Fumigating Corp.
Guardian of the nation's health
Smith water heaters
Guardian of your family's health
Duraglass bottles
Guardian will enrich and safeguard your retirement
years
The Guardian Life Insurance
Co. of America
Guardians of good grooming
Owens hair brushes
Guards the danger line
E. R. Squibb
The guest coffee
Yuban
Guest-room luxury for every bed
in your house
Pepperell sheets
A Guinness a day is good for
you
Guinness ale
Guinness ale
But the greatest reason of
all is that Guinness is
good for you
Christmas time is Guinness
time
Famous for its perfect head
A glass of Guinness is a
cheerful sight
A Guinness a day is good
for you
Guinness and oysters are
good for you
A Guiness at one is good
for you

A Guinness at two is good
for you
Guinness for appetite
Guinness is good for you
Have a glass of Guinness
when you're tired
It strikes one; it's Guin-
ness time
It's good to get home to a
Guinness
Lunch time is Guinness time
Nothing takes the place of
Guinness
Strength ... in a glass by
itself
Ten to one ... it's Guin-
ness time
Who can resist a Guinness?
You feel you've had some-
thing when you've had
a Guinness
Guinness and oysters are good
for you
Guinness ale
A Guinness at one is good for
you
Guiness ale
A Guinness at two is good for
you
Guinness ale
Guinness for appetite
Guinness ale
Guinness is good for you
Guinness ale
Guittard Chocolate Co.
You can have your cake
and drink it, too
Gulbransen piano
Easy to play
With all the grace and
beauty of its name
Gulden's mustard
Tested goodness
Gulf and Western Industries,
Inc.
The 21st century company
Gulf Coast Lumberman
The livest lumber journal
on earth
Gulf Engineering Co.
Service, not promises
Gulf makes things run better
Gulf Oil Corporation
Gulf Oil Corporation
Gulf makes things run
better

The world's finest motor oil
World's finest petrochemical
products
Gulf Oil Corporaiton. See also:
Spencer Chemical Div.,
Gulf Oil Corporation
Gulf Publishing Co.
World's largest specialized
publisher
Gulflube motor oil
A premium motor oil at
regular price
Gulfstream American executive
jet airplanes
There has never been a
bad time to make a
good investment
Gulfstream Commander 980 air-
craft
The performance-minded
fuel saver
Gum-rub dentifrice
A massage for the gums
The gum with the fascinating
artificial flavor
Wrigley's chewing gum
Gumdingers are new, from Brach
Gumdingers candies
Gumdingers candies
Gumdingers are new, from
Brach
A gun for every American shoot-
ing need
Marlin Firearms Co.
The gun that knows no closed
season
Grosman Arms Co.
Gund toys
It must be good to be a
Gund
Gunk Laboratories, Inc.
First and foremost line of
cleaning products
Gunther Brewing Co.
Timed to perfection
Gus Arnheim's dance orchestra
It's Arnheim time!
Guth. See: Edwin Guth Co.
Gutta Percha rubbers
Every pair made to wear
Guy Lombardo's Royal Canadians
orchestra
The sweetest music this
side of heaven
Gyproc wallboard
Why build to burn?

Gypsum. See: U. S. Gypsum
Co.

-H-

H & D delivers the goods
Hinde & Dauch Paper Co.
H & D shipping boxes move
merchandise
Hinde & Dauche Paper Co.
H & D shipping boxes protect
in transit
HInde & Dauch Paper Co.
H. B. Fuller Co.
Holds the world together
Leader in adhesive tech-
nology
HBO & Company
The hospital computer com-
pany
H. C. Bohack
The stores of friendly serv-
ice
H. D. Lee Co., Inc.
Don't take less than the
best, don't take less
than a Lee
Fifty per cent more wear
Guaranteed the hardest
working workwear
Official tailors to the West
There's a Lee for every
job
H. Ferguson Farm Equipment
The sign of a new prosper-
ity in agriculture
H. G. Parks, Inc. sausage
packers
More pork sausages, Mom
H. H. Robertson Co.
World-wide building service
H. J. Scheirich Co.
The most beautiful kitchens
of them all
H. K. Porter Co., Inc.
Who changed it?
The H. O. N. Co.
More and more the complete
source for your store
HPM Div., Kohlring Co.
The performance line
HP 125. The personal office
computer
Hewlett-Packard computers
H. P. Smith Paper Co.

Pioneers in polycoatings
H. P. Snyder Mfg. Co.
It speaks for itself
HQZ hair preparations
Beautiful hair is as easy
as HQZ
H. S. Crocker Co., Inc.
Pioneers in automated
lithography
H. S. Whiting Co.
Put your lighting up to
Whiting
H. T. Cushman Mfg. Corp.
Furniture that's fun to live
with
H. W. Merriam
Scientifically correct shoes
for juveniles
Sturdy to the last
Haas & Howell
Service beyond the con-
tract
Haas Securities Corporation
Discount stock brokerage:
an idea whose time has
come
The only discount broker
to offer complete dis-
count commodity service
Habirshaw Electric Cable Co.
Proven by the test of time
Hackney Bros. Body Co.
Builders of better refriger-
ator bodies
Had your iron today?
Sun-Maid raisins
Had your Wheaties today?
Wheaties cereal
Hadley watch band
Your wrist watch deserves
the best
Haeger Potteries, Inc.
The great name in American
ceramics
Haffenreffer Ale
The tang of good old ale
Hagen. See: Walter Hagen
Golf Equipment Co.
Hager Hinge Co.
Everything hinges on Hager
Hagerty. See: W. J. Hagerty
and Sons, Ltd., Inc.
Haig & Haig Scotch whiskey
Don't be vague, ask for
Haig and Haig
It had to be better to enjoy

197

such universal preference
for 320 years
The world knows no better
Scotch
Hair. See also:
Hear
Here
Hair color so natural only her
hairdresser knows for
sure
Clairol, Inc.
The hair net that sits true
Sitroux hair net
Hair relief without the grief
Gilbert Vitalator
Hair today and gone tomorrow
Herpicide hair tonic
Hairlainers hairpins
They won't fall out
The hairs on your head are
numbered
Kreml shampoo
Hal Kemp's dance orchestra
The international favorites
Hal Sharp's Golden Bears dance
orchestra
And that's Hal at the
piano!
Hale. See also: Alfred Hale
Rubber Co.
Hale and hearty
Kasko Distillers Corp.
Hale's Honey of Horehound and
Tar
The great cough remedy
for children as well as
adults
Half & Half smoking tobacco
A cargo of contentment in
the bowl of any pipe
Confidentially, it shrinks
The first different smok-
ing tobacco in a gen-
eration
Half the fun of having feet
Red Cross Shoes
Half the sugar of most sugar-
coated cereals
Quaker Halfsies cereal
Hall. See:
Barrington Hall Coffee
Belding Hall Electric Corp.
Frank B. Hall & Co. in-
surance brokers
Hampton Hall, Ltd.
L. W. Hall Co.

Halliburton travel cases
Created to carry your be-
longings in perfection
throughout your life-
time
The Hallicrafters Co.
Quality through craftsman-
ship
Hallmark greeting cards
If you care enough to send
the very best
When you care enough to
send the very best
The hallmark of a system, the
symbol of accuracy
Remington Office Systems
Div., Sperry Rand Cor-
poration
Hallmark of quality
Benson & Hedges 100's De
Luxe Ultra Lights
cigarettes
Hallock & Watson Radio Corp.
Comparison proves its
superiority
Hall's. See also: Hauls
Hall's cough drops
For penetrating relief get
Hall's Vapor Action
Hall's Hair Renewer
Grows bountiful, beautiful
hair
Halo shampoo
Reveals the hidden beauty
of your hair
Soaping dulls hair, Halo
glorifies it
Halves the cost and doubles the
satisfaction
Tru-Taste Mayonnaise
The ham what am
Armour's Star Ham
Hamburger Helper
Hamburger Helper helped
her hamburgers help
her
Hamburger Helper helped her
hamburgers help her
Hamburger Helper
Hamilton. See also: W. C.
Hamilton & Sons
Hamilton Beach food mixer
The lift you've longed for
Hamilton Beach vacuum cleaner
For cleaning ease
Hamilton Brown Shoe Co.

American gentleman shoes
designed for the
American man
American lady shoes de-
signed for the Amer-
ican woman
Hamilton Carhartt overalls
From mill to millions
Golden Rule garments
Hamilton coke
Knocks one-third off your
fuel costs
Hamilton Cosco, Inc.
Useful products for family
living
Hamilton Watch Co.
America marches forward
on TIME
Finer than ever before
Get time from a timepiece,
but if you want a
watch get a Hamilton
If you want more than
time, get a Hamilton
If you want to give more
than time, give a
Hamilton
Particular people prefer
Hamilton
The railroad timekeeper
of America
The watch of railroad ac-
curacy
Hamilton Watch Co. See also:
Wallace Silversmiths
Div., The Hamilton
Watch Co.
Hammer Blow Tool Co.
Never lets go
Hammer the hammer
Iver Johnson Arms &
Cycle Works
The hammer with a backbone
American Hammer Corp.
Hammermill Paper Co.
The best known name in
paper
Hammermill paper makes
copies, not trouble
Look for the watermark
Our word of honor to the
public
The utility business paper
Hammermill paper makes copies,
not trouble
Hammermill Paper Co.

Hammerschlag refining Co.
Beer is no better than its
ingredients
A hammock that will not pull off
the buttons
Bay State Perfection ham-
mock
Hammond. See also: W. A.
Hammond Drierite Co.
Hammond Cedar Co.
Smooth as a kitten's ear
Hammond Iron Works
The sun never sets on Ham-
mond tanks
The Hammond is the largest-
selling organ in the
world
Hammond organ
Hammond organ
The Hammond is the largest-
selling organ in the
world
Music's most glorious voice
No other instrument so rich-
ly rewards the efforts
of the beginner
The one and only
Hammond typewriter
The best typewriter for of-
fice work where speed
is required
Many typewriters in one
Hamm's beer
From the land of sky blue
waters
Preferred ... for mellow
moments
Hampden Brewing Co.
You get more out of Hamp-
den
Hampden face powder
Soft as a butterfly wing
Hampden Specialty Products Co.
Solid comfort seating
Hampton Hall, Ltd.
The new school of thought
in old school ties
Hancock. See: John Hancock
Variable Life Insurance
Co.
The hand crafted world of Allen-
Edmonds. Step into it
Allen-Edmonds shoes
Hand in hand with fashion
Whiting & Davis mesh bags
Hand made to fit you

Kenneth Smith
Hand-ee. See also: Handy
Hand-ee, the tool of 1001 uses
Hand-ee Tool
Hand-ee Tool
    Hand-ee, the tool of 1001
      uses
    Jack of all trades and
      master of plenty
The hand of a master crafts-
    man is behind this
    trusted trademark
    W. L. Douglas shoes
The hand that builds certainty
    at the point of seal
    Graton & Knight Co.
The handcrafted T.V.
    Zenith television sets
The handiest light in the world
    Bussman Mfg. Co.
The handiest thing in the house
    Vaseline
Handle more grease for your
    money
    Dawn dishwashing liquid
Handles your car like an in-
    visible giant
    Ross Steering Gear
Hand's. See: Dr. Hand's
    teething lotion
Handsome and doubly useful
    Simplicity davenport sofa
    bed
Handsome, stylish, reliable
    Manhattan watch
The handsomest car in the
    world
    American Mercedes auto-
    mobile
Handy. See also: Hand-ee
Handy and Harman
    The company for precious
    metals
The handy candy
    Beechnut mints
Handy Chair & Table Co.
    Built to sustain a reputa-
    tion
The handy light on a reel
    Appleton Electric Co.
Handy Mandy
    The pad that's kind to
    your hands
Hanes. See also: Haynes
Hanes Corporation
    Hanes knows how to

please him
Hanes knows how to please him
    Hanes Corporation
Hanes makes you feel good all
    under
    Hanes underwear
Hanes underwear
    The anti-freeze underwear
    for men and boys
    Hanes makes you feel good
    all under
    The label of quality knitting
    in sportswear and under-
    wear
    Unaware of underwear
A "hank" for a Yank
    Bond's handkerchiefs
The "hanks" are coming
    Bond's handerchiefs
Hanley & Kinsella Coffee
    As delicious as coffee can
    be
    Fresh because vacuum-
    packed
    Vacuum-packed to preserve
    the flavor
    Where only the best will do
    You'll like it, too
Hanley & Kinsella Spices
    Sifted through silk
Hanover Fire Insurance Co.
    An emblem of security, a
    pledge of service
Hanseatic. See: T. S. Han-
    seatic German Atlantic
    Line
Hanson. See: Henry L. Han-
    son Co.
Happiness in every box
    United Retail Candy Stores
Happy Days chewing tobacco
    A pinch is all it takes
Happy Home Foods
    In season, all seasons
The happy medium
    Judge
Happy motoring!
    Enco Div., Humble Oil and
    Refining Co.
Har-tru tennis courts
    Serving with distinction
Harbison-Fischer Mfg. Co.
    Best pumps in the oil patch
Harbor Master, Ltd., Div.
    Jonathan Logan
    Because it might rain

Harbor Plywood Corp.
　　The outdoor plywood
　　Panels of permanence
Hard soft coal
　　Lumaghi Coal Co.
Hard to mill but easy to bake
　　Made-Rite Flour
Hardeman hats
　　I look my best in a Harde-
　　　man
The hardest hardwoods grow in
　　the north
　　Northern Hard Maple Mfrs.
The hardest metal made by man
　　Carbaloy
Hardware Age
　　The most influential hard-
　　　ware paper
　　Sells hard wherever hard-
　　　ware sells
Hardware is the jewelry of the
　　home
　　McKinney Mfg. Co.
Hardware Mutual Casualty Co.
　　The policy back of the
　　　policy
Hardware that harmonizes
　　Corbin hardware
Hareg Industries, Inc.
　　First in engineered plastics
Harlan Insurance Co.
　　An idea whose time has
　　　come!
Harley-Davidson motorcycle
　　More than a machine
　　The motorcycle that is not
　　　uncomfortable
　　The silent grey fellow
Harley Hotel, New York City
　　A great hotel doesn't have
　　　to be expensive
　　We're going to be your
　　　favorite hotel
Harmon Kardon, Inc.
　　The leader in solid-state
　　　high-fidelity components
　　We want you to hear more
　　　music
Harmony Brand snap fasteners
　　Dispels dressing discords
Harmony vitamins
　　Keep your health in tune
　　Vitamins for the millions
Harnischfeger Corp.
　　The right hoist for every
　　　application

Harp-maker to the world since
　　1889
　　Lyon & Healy
Harper. See also: I. W. Harper
　　bourbon whiskey
Harper simmer burner
　　Holds the line for gas
Harper's Bazaar
　　Class magazine in a class by
　　　itself
　　Edited for the woman who
　　　must keep au courant with
　　　the smart world
　　The taste that sets the trend
Harris Corporation
　　Harris technology works
　　　worldwide
Harris Publications
　　Widen your circle of influence
Harrisburg couplings
　　Recognized as a standard
Harris Hardwood Co.
　　Finest in flooring since 1898
Harris Portable Fire Escapes
　　Fire need have no terrors
Harris technology works worldwide
　　Harris Corporation
Harrisburg Telegraph
　　Central Pennsylvania's great-
　　　est daily
Harrison cooled, the mark of
　　radiator satisfaction
　　Harrison radiators
Harrison radiators
　　Harrison cooled, the mark
　　　of radiator satisfaction
　　It's the long hard pull that
　　　proves the radiator
　　Temperature made to order
Hart. See also: Heart
Hart-Parr Co.
　　Creators of farm wealth
　　Founders of the tractor in-
　　　dustry
Hart Schaffner & business
　　Hart Schaffner & Marx men's
　　　clothing
Hart Schaffner & Marx men's
　　clothing
　　Distinguished from every
　　　viewpoint
　　Don't be a ragged individual
　　Experience the difference
　　　quality makes
　　Hart Schaffner & business
　　Hart Schaffner & success

Largest makers in the world
of fine clothing for men
Styled for tomorrow to enjoy
today
Hart Schaffner & success
Hart Schaffner & Marx men's
clothing
Harter Corporation
Specialists in seating--and
seating only--since 1927
Hartford Fire Insurance Co.
Carelessness is the partner
of sabotage
The seal of certainty upon
an insurance policy
Hartford Insurance Group
Let us protect your world
Your Hartford agent does
more than he really has
to
Hartford shock absorber
Makes every road a boule-
vard
Hartford Steam Boiler Inspection
and Insurance Co.
Inspection is our middle
name
Insurers of energy systems
Hartman radio receiver
The single six
Hartmann Trunk Co.
Look for the Hartmann Red
on the trunk you buy
Hartshorn. See: Stewart Hart-
shorn Co.
Harvard Brewing Co.
As of yore
Harvard Mfg. Co.
The one bed frame people
ask for by name
Harvel watches
America's distinguished
timepiece
One of America's fine
watches
The right choice for the
right time
The watch for busy men
The watch that times the
stars
Harvey. See: P. J. Harvey
Shoe Co.
Harvey's Bristol Cream Sherry
It's downright sociable
Has 'em all beat
International Coffee Co.

Has had no peers for fifty years
Golden Wedding whiskey
Has stood the test for years
Hoffman House cigar
Has that knack for meal or snack
Delta Cocktail Onions
Has that rich beefy flavor
Armour's Extract of Beef
Has the "edge" five ways
Pal razor blades
Has the quiet refinement of an
exclusive club
Mayfair House, New York
City
Haserot Company
The brand that so success-
fully meets the can-
opener test
The flavor-tested coffee
It's flavor-tested
Its rare bouquet sealed in
to stay
Quality leaves no regrets
Sure to deight your appetite
Haskell, Inc.
The accepted name for value
Hasn't scratched yet
Bon Ami cleanser
Haspel seersucker
The smartest cool suit, the
coolest smart suit
Hasselblad cameras
When you shoot for perfec-
tion
Hastings piston rings
Tough, but oh so gentle
The hat corner of the world
Knox hats
HAT ease on the home front
Champ Hats
A hat for every face
Sam Bonnart, Inc.
The hat that goes with good
clothes
Mallory hats
Hathaway shirts
"Never wear a white shirt
before sundown," says
Hathaway
Hats made so fine that all others
must be compared to
them
Knox hats
Hatter to gentlemen for over half
a century
Wolthausen hats

Hauls. See also: Hall's
Hauls more freight and handles
　　more passengers than
　　any other railroad in
　　the world
　　Pennsylvania Railroad
Hauser-Stander Tank Co.
　　We win with quality
Have a Camel
　　Camel cigarettes
Have a Coke and a smile
　　Coca Cola soft drink
Have a dish of sunshine and
　　have the laugh on
　　winter
　　Del Monte pineapple
Have a glass of Guinness when
　　you're tired
　　Guinness ale
Have a Golden day!
　　Golden Graham breakfast
　　cereal
Have a Pepsi day
　　Pepsi-Cola soft drink
Have a slice of Sunshine
　　Sunshine Bread
Have fun, be gay on the Santa
　　Fe
　　Santa Fe System Lines
Have one built for you
　　Oldsmobile automobile
Have stood the test
　　F. S. Royster Guano Co.
Have teeth that shine like the
　　stars
　　Calox Tooth Powder
Have the genius to chill it
　　Chartreuse
Have you a little fairy in your
　　home?
　　Gold Dust Soap Powder
Have you "Acid Mouth," the
　　forerunner of tooth
　　destruction?
　　Pebeco tooth paste
Have you driven a Ford lately?
　　Ford automobile
Have you tried a Lucky lately?
　　Lucky Strike cigarettes
Have you tried it?
　　Durham corn starch
Have you tried one lately?
　　Robert Burns cigar
Haven't you waited long enough?
　　Volvo automobile
Havoline motor oil

Cleans as it lubricates
Hot, but not bothered
It makes a difference
Keeps your engine clean
Hawes Floor Wax
　　Preferred in fine homes for
　　many years
Hawk lotion
　　For the man who reaches
　　higher
Hawk Model Co.
　　Most trusted name in model-
　　ing
Hawkeye Clock Co.
　　Tells time, saves time
　　Watchful of the time
Hawkeye Refrigerator Basket
　　It keeps contents ice cold
Hay. See: Hey
Hayes-Hamilton, Inc.
　　Sponsored group travel
Hayes Pump & Planter Co.
　　Plants like human hands
Haynes. See also:
　　Hanes
　　Wm. S. Haynes Co.
Haynes automobile
　　America's first car
　　Better than the years
　　The Haynes goes everywhere
The Haynes goes everywhere
　　Haynes automobile
Haynes Stellite Co.
　　No steel, but it's master
Hayward buckets
　　Dig for all the world
Hazard Wire Rope
　　Your safety is our business
Hazel-Atlas Glass Co.
　　A smile in every glass
Hazel Bishop cosmetics
　　For the woman who can af-
　　ford the best. Even
　　though it costs less
HE builds a house, SHE makes
　　a home
　　McCall's
He has "hayfield" hair
　　Kreml shampoo
He won't be happy till he gets it
　　Wright's coal tar soap
He won't change from shoes to
　　slippers because he's
　　enjoying Massagic com-
　　fort
　　Massagic Air Cushion shoes

Head & Chest cold medicine
    Clears your head. Clears
        your chest
Head and Shoulders shampoo
    It's so easy
    Show off your hair, not the
        itching dandruff
Head for the mountains
    Busch beer
Head of the bourbon family
    Old Grand-Dad whiskey
Head Ski Co.
    And who makes great skies?
    Head, of course
A head-spinning, heart-winning
    perfume
    Frolic Perfume
Head to foot, cellar to attic
    Fuller brushes
HEAD work always wins on pay
    day
    Chicago Engineering Works
HEAD work always wins over
    HARD work on pay day
    Chicago Engineering Works
The headlight that floodlights
    the road
    Ilco headlight
Headquarters for corrugated
    products in New Eng-
    land
    Corrugated Paper Mills
Headquarters for hand valves
    Barksdale Valves
Headquarters for lubricants and
    lubri-counsel
    Davis-Howland Oil Corp.
Headquarters for nitrogen
    chemicals
    American Cyanamid Co.
Headquarters for steam-cookers
    The Cleveland Range Co.
Health
    Fleischmann's Yeast
Health and freshness sealed in
    cans
    Continental Can Co.
Health and growth for boys and
    girls
    Ralston Purina Co.
The health builder keeps you
    fit
    Sanitarium Equipment Co.
Health in every jar
    Blue Ribbon mayonnaise
Health insurance for the whole

family
    Shredded Wheat
The health soap
    Lifebuoy Soap
Health ... your happiness, our
    business
    Mountain Valley Water
Healthful and good
    Kaffee Hag
The healthy home is the happy
    home
    International Incinerator
Hear. See also:
    Hair
    Here
Hear more, carry less
    Ontario single pack hearing
    aid
Hear the great artists at their
    best
    Columbia phonograph records
Hearst's Magazine
    A magazine with a mission
Heart. See also: Hart
The heart and soul of a master-
    piece
    Rolls-Royce automobile
Heart Fund
    Give so more will live
The heart of a good cocktail
    Gordon's Distilled London
    Dry Gin
The heart of a tune-up
    Champion spark plugs
The heart of reliable radio power
    Raytheon radio tubes
The heart of the grain plus the
    art of the grain
    Arkadelphia Milling Co.
The heart of the market
    Pennsylvania Power and Light
    Co.
"Heart of the root" briar
    Rembrandt pipe
The heart of the set
    Champion radio receiver
The heart of your radio
    RCA Radiotron Co.
Heart Throb Dresses
    U must try me on
A heart to heart fragrance
    Coty cosmetics
Heart-winning, head-spinning
    Frolic Perfume
The heart's desire for every
    youngster

Reliable dolls
Hearts in harmony until she
smiles
Ipana toothpaste
The heart's in it
Elam Mills, Inc.
Heat alone is not comfort
Holland Furnace Co.
Heat, eat, enjoy
Van Camp's pork and beans
Heat how and when you want it
Home Appliance Corp.
Heat like the rays of the sun
American Gas Machine Co.
Heat plus beauty
Florence Heaters
Heat-proof lining for walls and
roof
Armstrong Cork Co.
The heating sensation of the
century
Richardson & Boynton Co.
Heats every room, upstairs and
down
Estate Stove Co.
Heats the room, not the chim-
ney
Duo-Therm Oil Burner
The heaven-sent nougat
National Nougat Co.
Heavenly aroma that hangs like
a fragrant halo 'round
your coffee pot
Wakefield Coffee
The heavy duty railroad
Erie Railroad
Heck Transfer & Storage Co.
Moved by Heck
Hecker H-O Co., Inc.
The saving flour, it goes
farther
Heddon fishing tackle
Fish "Heddon" and fish
better
Make your own luck with
Heddon
The river-runt does the
stunt
The rod with the fighting
heart
Heeeeeere's Johnny!
Tonight show, featuring
Johnny Carson
The heel that won't peel
Mears shoe heel
The heel with nine lives

Cat's Paw rubber heel
Heelproof, marproof and water-
proof
Pratt & Lambert varnish
Heery Associates, Inc.
A new and better way
Hefty Steel Sak trash bag
The bag that works like a
can
Tough enough to overstuff
Heidt. See also: Horace Heidt
and his Musical Knights
orchestra
The Heidt of entertainment
Horace Heidt and his Musi-
cal Knights orchestra
Heigh-ho, everybody!
Rudy Vallee's Connecticut
Yankees dance orchestra
Heilmann's beer
Brewers of old style beer
Pure brewed in God's coun-
try slowly and naturally
Hein and Kopkins, Inc.
The first name in custom
bedding
Heineken beer
Come to think of it, I'll
have a Heineken
Heine's Blend smoking tobacco
A pipe's best friend is
fragrant Heine's Blend
Heinold Commodities, Inc.
He's sure. He's bold. He's
Heinold
Heinz. See also:
Hinds
Hines
Heinz chicken-noodle soup
With oodles of noodles and
chicken, too
Heinz food products
57 varieties
The taste is best
Heinz ketchup
America's thickest, best-
tasting ketchup
Flavor-frock for foods
Glorifies every dish it
touches
Glorifying the world's fare
Make good foods taste better
The season's best and the
best of seasoning
Still the shortest route to
your man's heart

Heinz makes YOUR soup YOUR
way
Heinz soup
Heinz Oven-Baked Beans
Bean 'em when they're
hungry
Flavor baked in, labor
baked out
Heinz soup
Heinz makes YOUR soup
YOUR way
Heinz spaghetti
Yours, in haste
Heinz tomato soup
It tastes home-made
Heinz vinegar
Mellowed in wood to full
strength
The heirloom of the future
Rome kitchen ware
Heirloom quality pianos since
1896
Kohler and Campbell, Inc.
Heirloom Sterling Silver
From generation to genera-
tion
Helen Keller Centennial Fund
And you thought there was
no such thing as mira-
cles
Helene brassiere
It's time to Re-form
Helene Curtis Industries, Inc.
When a Studio Girl enters
your home a new kind
of beauty brightens
your life
Where beautiful young ideas
begin
Heller. See: Walter E. Heller
& Co.
Hellmann's mayonnaise
America's favorite mayon-
naise
Made in the home-made way
More than a salad dressing,
a food
This is no place for "second
best"
Hello, everybody!
Kate Smith radio greeting
Hello, everybody! Lopez speak-
ing!
Vincent Lopez' dance
orchestra
Helmar cigarettes

Queen of distinctive cigar-
ettes
Help build personality
Stadium clothes
Help make him all the dog he's
meant to be
Ken-L-Biskit
Help others help themselves
Salvation Army
Help others. Help yourself
U. S. Coast Guard
Help the blind to help themselves
Industrial Home for the
Blind
Help you get the better of simple
backache pain
Doan's Pills
Help your beauty bloom this
spring
Ivory soap
Help yourself financially without
financial help
Illinois National Bank
Help yourself to health
Kellogg Co.
Helping a nation to avoid severe
colds
Vick's Vapo-Rub
Helping America make intelligent
insurance decisions
since 1887
American Mutual Insurance
Companies
Helping people and businesses
help themselves
Commercial Credit Co.
Helping people communicate
Addressograph-Multigraph
Corp.
Helping your product speak for
itself
Markem Machine Co.
Helps build strong bodies 12 ways!
Wonder bread
Helps get laundry up to 30%
cleaner
Calgon laundry detergent
Helps hands look young
Ivory dishwashing liquid
Helps keep a little baby a lot
dryer
Pampers diapers
Helps keep teeth white
Dentyne chewing gum
Helps keep you going
Milky Way candy bar

Helps no-wax floors keep shin-
ing bright
Mr. Clean cleaning fluid
Helps stockings wear longer
Dreft soap flakes
Helps stop the greasies
Agree hair conditioner
Helps you break the nicotine
habit
Bantron smoking deterrent
tablets
Helps you do things right
The Stanley Works
Helps you relax so you can
sleep
Excedrin pain reliever
Hemo. See also: Borden's Hemo
Hemo will help you, too
Borden's Hemo
Henkel Group
Chemistry working for you
Hennessy cognac
Richer. And, of course,
costlier
Henredon Furniture Industries,
Inc.
Fine furniture
There's quality about a
home with Henredon
Henry L. Hanson Co.
You expect the best from
Hanson ... and you
get it
Henry Sutliff Tobacco Co.
Now every man can enjoy
his pipe
She likes the fragrance
Henry Vogt Machine Co.
The finest ice making unit
ever made
Henryson tailored umbrellas
Be umbrelegant in rainy
weather
Hen's only rival
103 Degree Incubator Co.
Her Easter token
Whitman's Sampler candy
Her Majesty slip
It's sharp to be sure
Heralder clocks
The clocks that most peo-
ple want most
Herbox Bouillon Cubes
Turn a little meat into a
big treat
Hercules bed springs

Real restful rest on steel
feathers
Hercules Powder Co.
Perhaps we can help you
Hercules tanks and heaters
They last longer
Hercules umbrellas
Strong as its name
Herculon
The home furnishings fiber
Here. See also:
Hair
Hear
Here and there it's sterling
Holmes & Edwards silverplate
Here dwells security
The Guardian Life Insurance
Co. of America
Here today. There today
Eastern Air Lines, Inc.
package delivery
Here's a thrill for breakfast
Grape-Nuts Flakes
Here's Horace for Philip Morris
Horace Heidt and his Musi-
cal Knights orchestra
Here's riding at its level best
Oldsmobile automobile
Here's that band again!
Dick Jurgens' dance or-
chestra
Here's the diet you can live with!
Rotation Diet Center
Here's to your health and happi-
ness
Cercle D'Or wine
Hereth, Orr & Jones, Inc.
The emerging giant in finan-
cial opportunities
A heritage of quality, craftsman-
ship, service
Virginia Mirror Company
A heritage to remember
Philadelphia whiskey
The heritage whiskey
Philadelphia whiskey
Herman Nelson air filters
Far sighted planners choose
Herman Nelson
Herman's. See: Woody Herman's
orchestra
Herpicide hair tonic
Going, going, gone!
Hair today and gone tomor-
row
If hair's your pride use

Herpicide
  Too late for Herpicide
Herrick refrigerator
  The aristocrat of refriger-
    ators
Herschell-Spillman Motor Co.
  The motor's the thing
  The pick of the field
Hershey locks
  Refined protection for motor
    cars
Hertz automobile rentals
  Anywhere in the wide world
  The biggest should do more.
    It's only right
  Hertz puts you in the driv-
    er's seat faster than
    anybody else
  Let Hertz put you in the
    driver's seat
  #1 for everyone
  Where winners rent
  The world's fastest way to
    rent a car
Hertz credit card
  The superstar in rent-a-
    car
Hertz puts you in the driver's
    seat faster than any-
    body else
  Hertz automobile rentals
He's a man after my own hands
  Hinds Honey and Almond
    Cream
He's stone deaf until you say
    RITZ
  Ritz crackers
He's sure. He's bold. He's
    Heinold
  Heinold Commodities, Inc.
Hesston Corp.
  World champions of worth!
Heublein's cocktails
  Are your cocktails such
    great shakes?
  11 kinds--better than most
    people make
  For professional cocktails
    at home
  12 kinds--better than most
    people make
Hewlett-Packard Co.
  An extra measure of quality
  Quality, reliability, serv-
    ice, support and avail-
    able softwear

Where performance must be
    measured by results
Hewlett-Packard computers
  HP 125. The personal of-
    fice computer
Hews. See also: Hughes
Hews & Potter belts
  Soft as a kitten's ear
Hexter fabrics
  Bright as the sun, wears
    for years
Hey! Culligan man!
  Culligan, Inc.
Hey! Give me a tall one
  The Tall-One Co.
Hey man! ... say Heyman
  Heyman Mfg. Co.
Hey, Mom, this marmalade is
    different
  Welch's marmalade
Heyman Mfg. Co.
  Hey man! ... say Heyman
Heywood-Wakefield Rattan Furni-
    ture
  Established 1826
Hi. See also:
  High
  Hy
Hi-chair to hi-school
  Nazareth underwear
Hi Dri paper towels
  Value ... it runs in the
    family!
Hi-Ten-S1 bronze
  A bronze as strong as nickel
    steel
Hickock Buckles
  Very individually yours
Hickory Farms of Ohio
  We'll give you a taste of
    old-time country good-
    ness
Hieger Products Co.
  Best for pets
Higgins drawing ink
  Permanent as the pyramids
High. See also:
  Hi
  Hy
High above all and snow-white
  Nekoosa-Edwards Paper Co.
High as the Alps in quality
  Peter Cailler Kohler Swiss
    Chocolate Co.
High atop Nob Hill
  Hotel Mark Hopkins, San

Francisco
High fashion in fragrance from
France
Carven Parfums
High fidelity phone cartridges
... world standard
wherever sound quality
is paramount
Shure Brothers, Inc.
High-grade. See also: Hygrade
A high-grade car at a moderate
price
OhiO automobile
High-performance tire power
Firestone tires
High Point coffee
The coffee lover's decaf-
feinated coffee
High pressure lubrication
Alemite automobile lubrica-
tion system
The high quality household oil
3-in-1 oil
High-sign of style
Eagle clothes
High tax-free yield with no sales
charge. That makes us
a star
Fidelity Group
Highest continuous record in of-
ficial scoring tests
Adohr Creamery Co.
Highest quality for health
Knox Gelatine, Inc.
The highest standard of quality
Lanson champagne
Highland Scotch Mist
It's smart to buy right
Highway Cruisers, Inc.
America's finest campers
Hillsdale Nurseries
It's not a home until it's
planted
Hilo Varnish Corp.
Beautifies before your eyes
Dries before your eyes
Hilti, Inc.
We promote excellence
Hilton. See also: Norman
Hilton & Co. men's
clothing
Hilton Hotels Corp.
America's business address
The friendly world of Hil-
ton
Go international ... with

all the comforts of Hilton
There's no place like Hilton
Hinde & Dauch Paper Co.
H & D delivers the goods
H & D shipping boxes move
merchandise
H & D shipping boxes pro-
tect in transit
Packed to attract
Hinds. See also:
Heinz
Hines
Hinds for hands and wherever
skin needs softening
Hinds Honey and Almond
Cream
Hinds Honey and Almond Cream
Chapped hands make a man
see red
He's a man after my own
hands
Hinds for hands and wher-
ever skin needs soften-
ing
Hines. See:
Duncan Hines cake
Duncan Hines cake mix
Duncan Hines packaged
foods
Heinz
Hinds
A hint of many good things to
come
Baker's Breakfast Cocoa
Hiram Walker bourbon whiskey
Wherever you go, there it
is!
Hiram Walker Ten High whiskey
A new high in whiskey
smoothness
Hiram Walker's cordials
A rainbow of distinctive
flavors
Hires Auto Parts
For you and your car
Hires' Improved Root Beer
An aristocratic beverage at
a democratic price
For a better tomorrow
Hires to you for a better
tomorrow
Is a toast to good health
Just right at night
The most delicious and
wholesome Temperance
Drink in the world

Those who think are proud
to drink--Hires
The toast to good taste
With real root juices
Hires to you for a better tomor-
row
Hires' Improved Root Beer
His duty to serve, hers to in-
spire
Coty cosmetics
His master's choice
Calo cat food
Flag Pet Food Corp.
His master's voice
RCA Corp.
Victor phonograph records
Victrola talking machine
His only rival
General Electric Mazda Lamp
History tells which line excels
Ohio Brass Co.
Hit it with a hammer
Pratt & Lambert varnish
A "Hit" with two hammers in
bicycle bell construction
Mossberg Tire Bell
Hits the mark
Staley stock feed
Hits the spot
Pepsi-Cola soft drink
Hits where you aim
United States Cartridge Co.
Hoard's Dairyman
The national dairy farm
magazine
The Hobart Mfg. Co.
Quality all the way
Hobby Stationers
Make writing your hobby,
use Hobby for writing
Hodgman Air Bed
For the best night's rest
you ever had, sleep on
a Hodgman Air Bed
Hoenshel Fruit Cake
Knows no season
Hoerner Boxes, Inc.
Corrugated packaging spe-
cialists
Hoffman. See also: U. S.
Hoffman Machinery
Corp.
Hoffman Beverage Co.
The winter brew for brew
drinkers
Hoffman club soda

Imprisoned carbonation
makes the sparkle last
Makes any liquor taste like
a better liquor
Stays alive
Hoffman honey
Food of the gods
From bees to combs to you
The honey what am honey
Hoffman House cigar
Absolutely unequaled
Has stood the test for years
Hoffman House Magnums
The Beau Ideal of a Short
Smoke
Hoffman Pale Dry ginger ale
More dry, less sweet
Hoffman rye mixer
What soda is to Scotch, Hoff-
man rye mixer is to rye
Hoffman Tom Collins Mixer
Don't be a lemon squeezer,
use Hoffman Tom Collins
Mixer
Hoffman valves
More heat from less coal
Hoffritz for Cutlery
A store a woman should look
into
Hogan. See: Ben Hogan golf
clubs
Hoke gauges
Laboratory accuracy at a
toolroom price
Hold the bustline and you hold
youth
La Resista corset
Holding better business with
better business forms
Baltimore Salesbook Co.
Holds the line for gas
Harper simmer burner
Holds the world together
H. B. Fuller Co.
Holds up even better under water
Top Job cleaning liquid
Holds your foot like a gentle
hand
Selby Shoe Co.
Holeproof Hosiery
Good looking--long wearing
Number One in the fit
parade
Holiday all the way with Canadian
Pacific Railway
Canadian Pacific Railway

The holiday cigar at a week-
day price
Cinco cigar
Holiday Inn gives you a guaran-
tee ... not excuses
Holiday Inns of America,
Inc.
Holiday Inns of America, Inc.
The fine old innkeeping
tradition in a modern
setting
First choice in food, lodg-
ing and service nation-
wide!
Holiday Inn gives you a
guarantee ... not ex-
cuses
The nation's innkeeper
Holiday tobacco
Aromatic in the pack,
aromatic in the pipe
Holidays are Kodak days
Kodak cameras
Holland-American Line
The people who invented
a nicer way to cruise
Sail a happy ship
Holland Furnace Co.
Heat alone is not comfort
Make warm friends
Holland House cocktail mixes
The original and the
largest-selling in the
world
Hollander Furs
Dyed for lasting loveliness
Holley Carburetor Co.
Quality parts for auto
makers and owners
Hollow Bldg. Tile Assn.
The most economical form
of permanent construc-
tion
Hollycourt pipes
Hollycourt. 77.7% drier
than other pipes
Try Hollycourt. Why? The
bowl stays dry
Hollycourt. 77.7% drier than
other pipes
Hollycourt pipes
Holmes. See also:
Ernest Holmes Co.
Homes
Holmes & Edwards silverplate
Here and there it's sterling

Protected where the wear
comes
Solid silver where it wears
Holophane directs light scientifi-
cally
Holophane Glass Co.
Holophane Glass Co.
Holophane directs light sci-
entifically
The home afloat
Elco motor boat
Home Appliance Corp.
Heat how and when you
want it
A home away from home
Park Central Hotel, New
York City
Home Box Office cable television
Great movies are just the
beginning
Home builders to the nation
Aladdin prefabricated houses
Home-care-know-how ... at your
doorstep!
Amway Corporation
The home craft magazine
People's Popular Monthly
The home desk for leisure and
working hours
Buddie desk
Home Devices Corp.
Does the washing where the
water is
The home furnishings fiber
Herculon
Home Insurance Co.
A City Investing Company
Home key agents give you
that "something extra"
A home is known by the lawn
it keeps
Associated Seed Growers
Home key agents give you that
"something extra"
Home Insurance Co.
Home Life Insurance Co.
A policy for every purse
and purpose
The home newspaper
Detroit News
Detroit Times
The home of Deep Sea Dave
Davis Bros. fish foods
The home of hospitality
Kenilworth Inn, Asheville,
N. C.

The home of human security
Provident Life and Accident
Insurance Co.
The home of outdoor style
Bradley bathing suit
The home paper of the industrial
worker and the farmer
Industrial News
Home State Farm. See also:
State Farm
Home State Farm Publications
Buy us like advertising ...
use us like salesmen
The home with a smile is the
home with a Hoover
Hoover vacuum cleaner
Homes. See also: Holmes
Homes of character
Lewis Mfg. Co.
Homes of the better sort
Schneider-Mittelzwei
The homes teamwork builds
Inland Homes Corp.
A homey hotel for home folks
The Westminster, New York
City
Honda automobile
We make it simple
Honda motorcycle
You meet the nicest people
on a Honda
World's biggest seller!
Honda motorized tricycles
Follow the leader
Honest wear in every pair
Marston & Brooks shoes
Honey Dew soft drink
The drink for you
Honey Nut Cheerios breakfast
cereal
Love that taste!
A honey of a tobacco
Cookie Jar tobacco
Honey Scotch Candy
More than sweetness
Something more than sweet-
ness
When you think of sweet-
ness
The honey what am honey
Hoffman honey
The Honeymoon Line
International Railway Co.
Honeytones by Inecto Hair
Coloring
Inecto Hair Coloring

Honeywell, Inc.
Finally, Businessware
It's a good business to run
a fine-tuned building
The other computer company
Hood. See also:
Robin Hood Flour
Robin Hood Rapid Oats
cereal
Hood River Apple Growers Assn.
Red apples for red cheeks
Hood rubbers
Quality always maintained
A sure sign they're good
Hood tire
If it's a Hood it's good
Hooker chemicals
From the salt of the earth
Hook's drug stores
All you need in a drug
store ... more
For prescriptions: let us
be the one
Hooray for Raisinets!
Raisinets candy
Hoosier Mfg. Co.
The kitchen cabinet that
saves miles of steps
The silent servant with a
hundred hands
Hoosier tents
America's finest camping
tents
Hoover Bearing Div., Hoover
Ball & Bearing Co.
Hoover leads in quiet bear-
ings that last longer
Hoover leads in quiet bearings
that last longer
Hoover Bearing Div.,
Hoover Ball & Bearing
Co.
Hoover Sales Corp.
Stockings of matchless
beauty
Hoover vacuum cleaner
All the dirt, all the grit,
Hoover gets it, every
bit
The difference between
"party clean" and
"partly clean"
Give her a Hoover and
you give her the best
The home with a smile is
the home with a Hoover

It beats--as it sweeps--
as it cleans
Hopp Plastics Div., Hopp Press,
Inc.
Pioneers in plastics
Hoppe. See: F. A. Hoppe,
Inc.
Horace Heidt and his Musical
Knights orchestra
The Heidt of entertainment
Here's Horace for Philip
Morris
Horace Heidt for Alemite
Horace Heidt for Alemite
Horace Heidt and his Musi-
cal Knights orchestra
Horizons widen through Shell
research
Shell Oil Company
Horlick's Malted Milk Corp.
Avoid teeter-totter vitality
The fountain of youth
The good things of milk
and malt
Keep your vitality up.
Drink Horlick's
When your energy takes a
dive, drink Horlick's
and revive
Hormel. See also: Geo A.
Hormel and Co.
Hormel Bacon Bits salad dressing
Real bacon. No fakin'
Horn & Hardart automat restaur-
ants
The public appreciates qual-
ity
The Horn Harmonious
Aermore exhaust horn
Horn luggage
For those who go first
class
Take your travel lightly
The horn that lasts
North East Electric Co.
The horn with the "Why"
Jewett superspeaker radio
loudspeaker
Hornung. See: Jacob Hornung
Brewing Co.
Horrocks-Ibbotson Co.
World's most complete fish-
ing tackle line
Horton Pilsener
It's better than it used to
be and it used to be

the best
Takes the simmer out of
summer
Hosiers, Ltd.
Style and wear in every
pair
Hosiery fashion on five continents
Berkshire International
Corp.
The hosiery of distinction
Chatelaine Silk Hosiery
The hospital company
Humana, Inc.
The hospital computer company
HBO & Company
Hospital Corporation of America
In health care, America is
still number one!
People caring for people
The hospitality state
Mississippi
Host of the highways
Howard Johnson Co.
The host to the Coast
Jimmie Grier's dance orches-
tra
Hostess baked goods
The care we take goes into
all we bake
Hot biscuits in a jiffy
Abilene Flour Mills
Hot, but not bothered
Havoline motor oil
"Hot-Line" claims service
Imperial Auto Insurance
The hot, warm and cold water
detergent
Cheer detergent
Hot water at the turn of a faucet
Humphrey Co.
A hot weather hot cereal
Zoom cereal
Hotel Astor, New York City
At the crossroads of the
world
Hotel Delmonico, New York City
Register socially
Hotel Fort Shelby, Detroit
Aglow with friendliness
Hotel Indiana, Fort Wayne, Ind.
Famous for food
Hotel Lincoln, New York City
House of hospitality
Hotel Mark Hopkins, San Fran-
cisco
High atop Nob Hill

Hotel New Yorker, New York
City
The big hotel that remem-
bers the little things
Where the best costs less
An hotel of discrimination
Mayfair House, New York
City
Hotel Plaza, New York City
The Plaza pleases
A hotel so luxurious no other
name would do
Ritz-Carlton Hotel, Wash-
ington, D. C.
Hotel Statler, New York City
and elsewhere
Nothing old-fashioned but
the hospitality
Where the guest is always
right
Hotel Touraine, Buffalo, N. Y.
Where good cheer abides
Hotel Wentworth, New York City
The friendly hotel
Hotkaps
Individual hothouse for
plants
Hotpoint Div., General Electric
Company
Absence makes the meat grow
tender
Designed by women for
women
First with the features wom-
en want most
Gifts long remembered
Servants for the home
There's a Hotpoint electric
range for every purse
and purpose
Hotpoint Div., General Electric
Company. See also:
General Electric Company
The hottest bands, the newest
tunes, the biggest hits
Bluebird phonograph records
Hottest brand going!
Conoco gasoline
Hottest name in golf
Kroydon Golf Corp.
Hottest on the campus
Butler-Andresen dance or-
chestra
Houbigant
Sheer makeup for sheer
beauty

Houdaille Industries. See: Man-
zel Div., Houdaille In-
dustries
Houde Engineering Corp.
They keep the springs like
new
Houdry means progress ...
through catalysis
Houdry Process & Chemical Co.
Houdry Process & Chemical Co.
Houdry means progress ...
through catalysis
Houghton. See:
E. F. Houghton and Co.
Hutton
Hour. See also: One Hour
Martinizing
Hour Magazine television program
You can't afford to miss a
minute
House. See also: Houze
House and Home
Management publication of
the housing industry
House Beautiful
Better your home, better
your living
Where quality makes sense
The house of a million nuts
MacFarlane candies
The house of adhesives
Testor Cement Co.
House of Comoy
The oldest name in pipes
The house of experience
Mirror Aluminum Co.
The house of flavor
McCormick and Co., Inc.
House of hospitality
Hotel Lincoln, New York
City
The house of magic
General Electric Company
House of Tre-Jur perfumes
There's a difference worth
knowing
House of Wrigley, Inc.
For the private world of the
bath
The house that pays millions for
quality
Mishawaka Woolen Mfg. Co.
The house that service built
Continental Envelope Corp.
A houseful of housewares
Lewis & Conger

Household Finance Corp.
  Better buymanship
  Money management
  Your doctor of family fi-
    nances
A household friend
  Mortite cement
A household help for every home
    need
  Landers household acces-
    sories
Houses painted with Carter White
    Lead stay painted
  Carter White Lead Co.
Houston Lighting and Power Co.
  Service first
Houston Post-Dispatch
  The fastest-growing news-
    paper and fastest-growing
    city in Texas
Houze. See also: House
Houze Glass Corp.
  Pioneers in colored glass
    technology
How. See also: Howe
How can just 1 calorie taste so
    good!
  Tab soft drink
How dare the Glenlivet be so
    expensive?
  The Glenlivet Scotch whiskey
How do you get famous in the
    chicken business?
  Famous Recipe Chicken
How do you spell "relief"?
  Rolaids pain reliever
How easily it rolls on Bassicks
  The Bassick Co.
How Lamp & Mfg. Co.
  Buy a How searchlight to-
    day, you may need it
    tonight
How man was meant to fly
  Thai Airlines
How many kisses in a cake of
    soap?
  Cashmere Bouquet soap
How much of your overhead is
    underfoot?
  Dominion shoes
How sweet it is!
  Pillsbury's cake mix
How to get a Pike's pique
  Montague Fishing Rod
How to get further with father
  Seaforth deodorant

How to give a budget supper a
    banquet air
  Stokely-Van Camp, Inc.
How to make a bright child
    brighter
  Royal portable typewriter
How to make a man's face glow
    on a dark morning
  Pillsbury's pancake flour
How to make light work of heavy
    meals
  Del Monte Canned Food
How to put the lovelight in her
    eyes
  Whitman's Chocolates
How to ring a wedding belle
  Kreml shampoo
How to TREAT guests
  Campbell's tomato soup
How young will you be at 50?
  Sun-Maid raisins
Howard Industries, Inc.
  Powered by Howard
Howard Johnson Co.
  Host of the highways
  Landmark for hungry Amer-
    icans
Howard Ketcham industrial de-
    signs
  Consumer certified colors
  Consumer certified colors
    and designs
Howard Paper Co.
  The nation's business paper
Howdy-licious!
  Howdy soft drink
Howdy soft drink
  Howdy-licious!
Howe. See also: How
Howe Folding Furniture, Inc.
  If it folds ... ask Howe
Howell Electric Motors Co.
  Give Red Bands your hard
    job
However you go, you'll stop bet-
    ter because of Bendix
  Bendix Corporation
Hoytt Construction Co.
  According to Hoytt
Hubbard's. See: Elbert Hub-
    bard's Scrap Book
Huddlespun sweater
  A sweater is better if it's
    a Huddlespun
Hudnut. See:
  Richard Hudnut Sportsman

Richard Hudnut toilet
specialties
Hudson automobile
Beautiful beyond belief
Drive America's safest car
Master of the highway
Strength, safety, style and
speed
The Super-Six
Hudson Brakes
I just broke a date with a
smash-up
Hudson Hosiery
Whisper sheer
Hudson National, Inc.
World's leading direct-by-
mail vitamin and drug
company
The hug you love
Luxite girdles
Huggies diapers
They help keep babies dry
Hughes. See also: Hews
Hughes Aircraft Co.
Creating a new world with
electronics
Hughes Electric Ranges
Making a nation of better
cooks
Hughes Helicopters, Inc.
And an unbeatable flyaway
price
Hughes Tool Co.
Standard of the industry
Hughson Chemical Co. Div.,
Lord Corp.
Watch Hughson ... for
progress through crea-
tive research
Human & Oppenheim hair nets
Made stronger, lasts longer
A human interest newspaper
New York Evening Graphic
Humana, Inc.
The hospital company
Where private enterprise is
making possible a better
kind of hospital
Humble Oil and Refining Co.
Service insurance for your
machinery
Humble Oil and Refining Co.
See also:
Enco Div., Humble Oil and
Refining Co.
Enjay Chemical Co. Div.,

Humble Oil and Refining
Co.
Hummel gummed paper moistener
The brush with a backbone
A million yards of good will
The modern way to moisten
Proper moistening is essen-
tial to good sealing
Hump hairpin
Keeps the hair in place
See that hump
Humphrey Co.
Hot water at the turn of a
faucet
Instant hot water service
Keeps you in hot water
Hungry for sunshine? Have it
sliced
Del Monte pineapple
Hunt. See also: C. Howard
Hunt Pen Co.
Hunt for the best
Hunt Wesson Foods, Inc.
Hunt--for the best
Hunt's Tomato Sauce
Hunt Hygienic Saddles
Easy at every point
Hunt phonograph sound boxes
Win their way by their play
Hunt Wesson Foods, Inc.
The catsup with the big
tomato taste
Hunt for the best
Hunter Div., Robbins & Myers,
Inc.
It's matchless
Hunter Div., Robbins & Myers,
Inc. See also: Robbins
& Myers electric fan
Hunter Mills
Only the Hunter Mills be-
tween the wheat field
and your bakery
Hunter whiskey
An American gentleman's
whiskey since 1860
First over the bars
Making friends through the
years
Huntingdon Industries, Inc.
New concepts in corrugated
packaging machinery
Huntington Banks
The Huntington. Precisely
the bank your business
needs

Huntington Clothiers
  Traditional clothing for less
The Huntington. Precisely the
    bank your business
    needs
  Huntington Banks
Hunt's Tomato Sauce
  Hunt--for the best
  Into big shiny kettles go
    the prettiest tomatoes
    that ever blushed red
    in the California sun-
    shine
Hupmobile automobile
  The comfort car
  Hupp has always built a
    good car
  Step up with Hupp
Hupp has always built a good
    car
  Hupmobile automobile
Hurricane dryer
  Ideal drying every day
Hurricane paper
  Hurricane wrapped for your
    protection
Hurricane wrapped for your pro-
    tection
  Hurricane paper
Hurts only dirt
  Kitchen Klenzer
Hush deodorant
  HUSH takes the odor out of
    perspiration
  Stay sweet with Hush
HUSH takes the odor out of per-
    spiration
  ׳ Hush deodorant
Hush Puppies shoes
  Breathin' brushed pigskin
  So comfortable anything
    goes
Huttom Photo Stamp Co.
  Make the world brighter,
    send a smile
Hutton. See also:
  E. F. Hutton & Co., Inc.
  E. F. Hutton Life Insur-
    ance Co.
  Houghton
Hutton Life. A new way of life
  E. F. Hutton Life Insur-
    ance Co.
Huyler's, Inc.
  The gift candy of America
Hy. See also:

Hi
High
Hy-Ten-Sl bronze
  A bronze as strong as
    nickel steel
Hyatt hotels.
  All things considered, Hyatt
    hotels continue to be a
    touch above the rest
Hyatt quiet
  New Departure-Hyatt Bear-
    ings Div., General
    Motors Corporation
Hycalog, Inc.
  Continuing research for
    lower cost drilling
Hyde Park beer
  The beer that's extra-aged
  The beer with millions of
    friends
  By the glass, by the bottle,
    by the case, Buy Hyde
    Park
  Seldom equalled, never ex-
    celled
Hydraulic Press Mfg. Co.
  For your pressing needs
Hydro-Line Mfg. Co.
  Works best under pressure
Hydro-United tires
  The most beautiful tire in
    America
Hydrocrat plumbing fixture
  The successor to the sink
Hydrocurve II
  The continuous wear con-
    tact lens
Hydromatic Transmission
  Only Hydromatic is com-
    pletely automatic
Hygeia Nursing Bottle Co.
  The safe nursing bottle
Hygienic Productions
  Moral pictures most mothers
    approve
  Morally straight, physically
    strong, mentally awake
Hygrade. See also: High-grade
Hygrade Food Products Co.
  Hygrade in name. Hygrade
    in fact
  Twice as good because it's
    pork and beef
Hygrade in name. Hygrade in
    fact
  Hygrade Food Products Co.

217

Hyomei Antiseptic Skin Soap
  A perfect skin and toilet
    soap, made without
    fats, grease or danger-
    ous alkali
Hypnosis without Narcosis
  Tucker Pharmacal Co.
Hysol Div., Dexter Corp.
  Progressive products thru
    chemical research
Hyster Co.
  Buy today's best truck.
    Own tomorrow's best
    trade

-I-

I am valet to millions
  Swank jewelry
IBM. See also: International
  Business Machines
  Corp.
IBM computer systems
  Lease for le$$
IBM personal computer
  A tool for modern times
IBM Series III copier/duplicator
  No other copier can copy
    this
I. C. Industries
  Growth by design
I can't believe I ate that whole
    thing!
  Alka Seltzer
I can't make all the candy in
    the world, so I just
    make the best of it
  Snyder's confections
I could have had a V-8!
  V-8 vegetable juice drink
I couldn't get a better Christ-
    mas gift to save my life
  Goodyear Auto Tire
I did it myself
  Rinsenvac rug cleaner
I envy men the pleasant puffing
    of their pipes
  Tuxedo tobacco
I got rid of kitchen jitters
  Red Cross towels
I have a new man for a husband
  Shredded Wheat
I just broke a date with a
    smash-up
  Hudson Brakes

ILG Electric Ventilating Co.
  Air change, not just air
    movement
  Vitalized ventilation
I live a fast life
  Bixby's Jet Oil shoe polish
I look my best in a Hardeman
  Hardeman hats
I make it easy. You make it
    delicious
  Tio Sancho Mexican food
    flavorings
I rescued the lifeguard
  Beeman's Chewing Gum
ITT Grinnell Corporation
  The source you can build on
I tank I go home, I have a Philco
    there
  Philco radio receiver
I. W. Harper bourbon whiskey
  The gold medal Kentucky
    bourbon since 1872
  The gold medal whiskey
  It's always a pleasure
I was a lemon in the garden of
    love
  Listerine mouthwash
I was a Mellin's Food baby
  Mellin's Food
I was once a 97-pound weakling
  Charles Atlas correspondence
    body building course
I-X-L Co., Inc.
  The kitchen people with dif-
    ferent ideas
Iberia Air Lines of Spain
  The way to get there
  Where only the plane gets
    more attention than you
iBEX desk-top business computers
  King of the mountain in
    microcomputers
Ice by wire
  Servel refrigerator
Ice cream for health
  National Association of Ice
    Cream Manufacturers
Ice cream parlor taste at super-
    market prices
  Sealtest ice cream
Ice cubes instantly, tray to
    glass
  Inland Mfg. Co.
Ice is cheaper, better, safer
  Ice Publicity Association
Ice Maid refrigeration

A new queen reigns where
    ice was king
Ice-Mint
    Cool off feet with an Ice-
    Mint treat
Ice Publicity Association
    Ice is cheaper, better,
    safer
Ice that never melts
    Sanat Refrigerating Co.
Iceland Products, Inc.
    Specialists in frozen food
    packaging
Icelandic Airlines
    The pioneer of low fares to
    Europe
Icy-Hot Bottle Co.
    Built for lifetime service
I'd like to know that man!
    Elbert Hubbard's Scrap
    Book
I'd rather Rax
    Rax sandwich restaurants
I'd walk a mile for a Camel
    Camel cigarettes
Idaho Potato Growers, Inc.
    Look-alikes aren't cook-
    alikes
Idea creators, not just illus-
    trators
    Martin Ullman Studios
Idea leader in storage systems
    Acme Steel Co.
Idea leader in strapping
    Acme Steel Co.
An idea whose time has come
    Grumman Corporation
    Harlan Insurance Co.
The ideal builder's sheathing
    paper
    Brown Company
The ideal camp stove
    Kampkook
The ideal complete plant food
    Olds & Whipple
Ideal dog food
    Reach for Ideal
    The seven course meal
Ideal drying every day
    Hurricane dryer
Ideal for any meal
    Stuhmer's Pumpernickel
The ideal laxative for young
    and old
    Beechalex
Ideal Leather Case Co.

We evolved the styles that
    the world admires
Ideal lighter fluid
    Never fails
The ideal pleasure boat
    Elco motor boat
The ideal second home for Amer-
    ican business
    Puerto Rico
Ideal Sight Restorer
    Save your eyes
Ideal Vacuum Cleaner
    It eats up the dirt
Ideas, Inc.
    Think of it first
Ideas to build on
    Johns-Manville Corporation
Idling or full-out, its engine is
    hushed as a country
    snowfall
    Buick automobile
If all lawn mowers look the same
    to you maybe you're
    not looking close enough
    Toro power mowers
If anyone tells you Michelin qual-
    ity is too expensive
    they're putting you on
    Michelin tires
If babies were born trained, they
    wouldn't need Diaparene
    baby powder
    Diaparene baby powder
If every smoker knew what
    Philip Morris smokers
    know, they'd all change
    to Philip Morris
    Philip Morris cigarettes
If hair's your pride use Herpi-
    cide
    Herpicide hair tonic
If it calls for concrete, it calls
    for Ransome
    Ransome concrete
If it doesn't sell itself don't keep
    it
    Maytag laundry washers
If it flows through pipe, chances
    are it's controlled by
    Fisher
    Fisher Governor Co.
If it folds ... ask Howe
    Howe Folding Furniture,
    Inc.
If it has anything to do with
    money, anywhere in

the world, we can help
Security Pacific Bank
If it hasn't this red woven label,
    it isn't B.V.D.
B.V.D. underwear
If it is a Garland, that is all you
    need to know about a
    stove or range
Garland stoves and ranges
If it isn't an Eastman it isn't a
    Kodak
Kodak cameras
If it isn't Diamond Crystal, it
    isn't shaker
Diamond Crystal Salt
If it isn't P. M., it isn't an
    evening
P. M. whiskey
If it's a bag ... we make it!
KOBI Polyethylene Bag
    Mfg. Co., Inc.
If it's a candy wrapper, we
    make it
L. A. Liebs Co.
If it's a Hood it's good
Hood tire
If it's a Paramount picture, it's
    the best show in town
Paramount Pictures Corp.
If it's a question of cleaning/
    conditioning ... ask
    Oakite
Oakite
If it's a Regens, it lights
Regens cigarette lighter
If it's a Steger it's the most
    valuable piano in the
    world
Steger & Sons Piano Co.
If it's AA-grade malted milk,
    it's White Cross
White Cross malted milk
If it's an envelope, we make it
Northwest Envelope Co.
If it's Borden's it's got to be
    good
Borden, Inc.
If it's chairs ... it's Miele!
Ralph A. Miele, Inc.
If it's chicken you're wishin'--
    look for Lynden
Lynden chicken fricasse
If it's Cities Service, it has to
    be good
Cities Service Company
If it's Community it's correct

Community silverplate
If it's conveyed, processed or
    mined, it's a job for
    Jeffrey
The Jeffrey Mfg. Co.
If it's Cowden, it fits
Cowden work clothing
If it's Darbrook it's durable
Darbrook silks
If it's dated, you know it's fresh
Dated Mayonnaise, Inc.
If it's Delco it's designed for the
    job
Delco shock absorbers
If it's Derryvale, it's Irish linen
Derryvale Irish linen
If it's done with heat, you can
    do it better with gas
American Gas Association,
    Inc.
If it's dust-proof it's a Mendel
Mendel-Drucker trunks
If it's Fownes, that's all you
    need to know about a
    glove
Fownes gloves
If it's in the air Thermiodyne
    will get it
Thermiodyne radio receivers
If it's lovely to wear it's worth
    Ivory Flakes care
Ivory Flakes
If it's made by Fitzjohn, it's
    made to save you money
Fitzjohn motor bus
If it's Madewell it's made well
Madewell underwear
If it's marked AO, it suits you
    so
AO polaroid day lens
If it's marked AO, it's smartly
    styled, optically cor-
    rect
AO polaroid day lens
If it's new, Saks has it
Saks Shoe Corp.
If it's paper
Dillard Paper Co.
If it's Remington it's right
Remington shells
If it's safe in water, it's safe
    in Lux
Lux soap
If it's Speakman, it's quality
Speakman plumbing fix-
    tures

If it's Speakman, it's unsur-
passed
Speakman plumbing fixtures
If it's Thompson's, it's double
malted
Thompson's Double Malted
Milk
If it's Truhn, it's washable
Truhn silk
If it's worth painting it's worth
a Wooster brush
Wooster paint brush
If Miele doesn't have it ... no
one has!
Ralph A. Miele, Inc.
If not made by Felt & Tarrant,
it's not a Comptometer
Comptometer calculating
machine
If Purina chows won't make your
hens lay, they are
roosters
Purina poultry feed
If she does an about face when
you want her to present
arms, try Life Savers
Life Savers candy
If someone makes it--we can
mark it
Carter's ink
If speed is what you need, get
Swingline
Swingline stapler
If the glass is empty it must be
Tang
Tang orange drink
If the Snider folks put it up,
it tastes like home
Snider's tomato products
If there is a way to get it done,
Quaker will do it
Quaker Rubber Corp.
If this gold seal is on it--
there's better meat in
it
Wilson & Co., Inc.
If time is the element, we con-
quer it
California Growers Air Ex-
press
If washday lasts an hour, I've
loafed
Maytag laundry washers
If you can afford a washer,
you can afford a Ben-
dix

Bendix clothes washer
If you can boil water, you can
cook ZOOM
Fisher Flouring Mills
If you can't fight, you can write
Eaton Paper Corp.
If you can't stop, don't start
American Brake-Block Brake
Lining
If you care enough to send the
very best
Hallmark greeting cards
If you could see inside oranges,
you'd buy Sunkist every
time
Sunkist oranges
If you do more, you want more
Myadec vitamin supplement
If you have an instinct for qual-
ity ...
Amelia Earhart luggage
If you like chocolate, you'll like
Mavis
Mavis chocolate drink
If you like peanuts, you'll like
Skippy
Skippy peanut butter
If you look like a lobster, you'll
act like a crab
Skol suntan oil
If you prize it ... Krylon-ize it
Krylon spray paint
If you really care about picture
and sound, you have no
choice
Pioneer Laser Disc
If you see rust, you'll know it's
not aluminum
Reynolds Metals Company
If you think clothes don't make
a difference, try walk-
ing down the street
without any
Wolf Tailoring
If you think the best sipping
brandy is cognac, you
haven't sipped America's
XO
XO Rare Reserve brandy
If you think they won't love it,
think again
Fit & Trim dog food
If you want a treat instead of a
treatment, smoke Old
Golds
Old Gold cigarettes

If you want better service
Otis Elevator Company
If you want more than time, get
a Hamilton
Hamilton Watch Co.
If you want something better,
demand De Wald
De Wald radio receivers
If you want the right truck, buy
Toyota
Toyota trucks
If you want to be loved, be
loveable
Mum deodorant
If you want to give more than
time, give a Hamilton
Hamilton Watch Co.
If you'd walk without a care do
your sleeping on Spring-
Air
Spring-Air mattress
If your child gets on your
nerves, get on to Coco-
malt
Cocomalt
If your trucks are eating you
alive, lease a Ryder
Ryder Truck Rental, Inc.
If you're not using Vano,
you're working too
hard
Vano
If you've got the time Miller's
got the beer
Miller High Life beer
Ignition starts with P and D
P and D Mfg. Co.
Ilco headlight
Eyes of the night
The headlight that flood-
lights the road
I'll cling to the powder that
clings to me
Roger & Gallet face powder
Illinois Baking Corp.
Cone-ing on the campus
Keep that "youthful" look
with Safe-T cones
Let's go Cone-ing
M-m-m-m, we go for Safe-T
cones
Safe-T Cone, the official
Coneing cone
Illinois Central Railroad
Road of travel luxury
Illinois Glass Co.

Bottles of every description
Everything between the
formula and the sale
Look for the Diamond I on
every bottle you buy
Illinois-Iowa Power Co.
The most for your money in
fuel
Illinois National Bank
Help yourself financially
without financial help
Illinois Refrigerator Co.
Saves food, chills water
Illinois Shade Div., Slick Indus-
trial Co.
Quality-made by Illinois
Shade
Illinois State Register
Always Springfield's great-
est newspaper
The illustrated voice
Magnavox television receiver
An illustrated weekly of current
life
Outlook
I'm a home defender from 'way
back
Dutch Boy White Lead
I'm always stopping at the Ritz
Ritz crackers
I'm holding out for Kasko
Kasko dog food
I'm in a class by myself
International Correspondence
Schools
I'm particular
Pall Mall cigarettes
I'm really hung up on Cocoa
Puffs
Cocoa Puffs cereal
I'm sick of playing solitaire, I
want to wear one
Mum deodorant
I'm well. You well?
Sterizol Co.
I'm your branch office
Bell Telephone System
Imagination in steel for the
needs of today's archi-
tecture
Granco Steel Products Co.
Imperial Auto Insurance
"Hot-Line" claims service
Imperial Candy Co.
Be sweeticular
Imperial-Eastman Corp.

222

To "test with the best"
Imperial Furniture Co.
The world's greatest table
makers
The imperial line of road machin-
ery
Sawyer-Massey Co.
Imperial Margarine
Makes you feel like a king
More buttery taste
There's only one Imperial
Imperial union suit
The "comfort first" union
suit
Imperial washable wallpaper
Color-locked
Imperial whiskey
The incomparable
It's good to know
It's "velveted"
Knowledgeable people buy
Imperial
Important name in the box busi-
ness
Forest Products Div., Owens-
Illinois, Inc.
Important occasion dresses
Lorrie Deb Corporation
Important to important people
Advertising Age
Imported from Spain, of course.
True sherry is
Duff Gordon sherry
The imported one
Beefeater gin
Importers and makers of fine
furniture
Leopold Colombo, Inc.
The impossible is now possible
Turtle Wax automobile
polish
Imprisoned carbonation makes
the sparkle last
Hoffman club soda
Improves with use
Knight internal combustion
engine
In a class by itself
Bobbi Motor Car
In a word, confidence
Carpenter Steel Co.
In a word ... it's Selig
Selig Manufacturing Co.,
Inc.
In action and relax-ion
Falcon Sportswear

In advance of progress
Euclid Crane & Hoist Co.
In all canned goods, look to
Libby's for performance
Libby, McNeill and Libby
In business for your safety
American Chain and Cable
Co.
In cars under $1000 the Allen
is without peer
Allen automobile
In case of fire push the button
and run
Diebold Safe & Lock Co.
In conversation it's wit; in
foundations it's fit
Formfit Underwear
In cool step, to the minute
Mansfield shoes
In design and performance, al-
ways a year ahead
Prodex Div., Koehring Co.
In eight major markets Borg-
Warner is a company to
watch
Borg-Warner Acceptance
Corporation
In 87 lands no other whiskey
tastes like Canadian
Club
Canadian Club whiskey
In electricity it's Edison from
start to finish
Edison-Splitdorf Corp.
In every home
Sperry Flour Co.
In everything you fry or bake
Crisco shortening
In fast to hold fast
Duo-Fastener Corp.
In Federation there is power
Federal Advertising Agency
In harmony with home and air
Magnavox radio receiver
In health care, America is still
number one!
Hospital Corporation of
America
In home, health, farm and in-
dustry, science in ac-
tion for you
American Cyanamid Co.
In industry world-wide
Swift and Co.
In keeping with a fine old tradi-
tion

Coronado Hotel, St. Louis,
Mo.
In Los Angeles, why settle for
less?
Ambassador Hotel, Los
Angeles, Calif.
In Manhattan, a breath of fresh
air on Central Park
Marriott's Essex House
In metals, plastics and paper
Budd works to make
tomorrow ... today
The Budd Company
In my case, it's Chesterfield
Chesterfield cigarettes
In name and reputation, this
truck is International
International Harvester
trucks
In other words, results
International Business
Machines Corp.
In partnership with all America
Association of American
Railroads
In Philadelphia nearly everybody
reads the Bulletin
Philadelphia Bulletin
In plastics, it's Spencer ... for
action
Spencer Chemical Div.,
Gulf Oil Corporation
In products, performance, pur-
pose ... Essex measures
up!
C-P Fittings Div., Essex
Wire Corp.
In pursuit of happiness, Revere
adds to your pleasure
Revere movie camera
In rhyme with time
Kingston watch
In San Francisco, it's the
Palace
Palace Hotel
In season, all seasons
Happy Home Foods
In seasoning, it's Stange
Stange seasonings
In silver it's sterling, in cor-
setry it's "Wonder-
form"
Wonderform corsets
In-Sink-Erator Manufacturing
Co.
Originator and perfecter

of the garbage disposer
In stainless, too, you can take
the pulse of progress at
Republic
Republic Steel Corp.
In step with fashion
Lampe Shoe Co.
In the air or outer space Douglas
gets things done
McDonnell-Douglas Corpora-
tion
In the best of regulated families
Phillips' Milk of Magnesia
In the fresh white package or the
clean white carton
Chesterfield cigarettes
In the garden today, on your
table tomorrow
Smilen Bros.
In the race against time, the
Chase is on
Chase Manhattan Bank
In the service of industry
Canadian Fairbanks-Morse &
Co.
In the service of medicine for
over three decades
Drug Products Co.
In the twinkling of an eye
Trans-Canada Telephone
System
In this food is nourishment you
need, in the form your
body can digest
Grape-Nuts cereal
In touch with tomorrow
Toshiba America, Inc.
In tune with a tune
Ladd ocarina
In tune with fashion and keyed
to fit
Lori-Lou girdles
In Viviani's the value is in, not
on the package
Viviani's beauty products
In war or peace, first in rubber
B. F. Goodrich Tire Co.
Incandescent Metallic petroleum
lamp
Equivalent in light power to
80 sperm candles
Incense of flowers
Black & White Face Powder
An inch of Pinch, please
Pinch Scotch whiskey
Inco Nickel

Your unseen friend
Incoming checks for oncoming
    years
    Equitable LIfe Insurance
    Co.
The incomparable
    Imperial whiskey
The incomparable Capehart
    Capehart phonograph
Independent Insurance Agent
    Serves you first
An independent newspaper
    Los Angeles Evening Herald
Independent Radio Supply Co.
    Better results with less ef-
    fort
The independent supplier for
    independents
    Ashland Oil and Refining
    Co.
Index and Option Market
    Markets for today's investor
    When the market moves, you
    should too
The Index with a name you can
    trade on
    New York Futures Exchange
India produces the finest tea in
    the world
    India Tea Bureau
India Tea Bureau
    India produces the finest
    tea in the world
    There's more to it
India tire
    The tire with the gum-weld
    cushions
Indian Archery Corp.
    Named for the original
    American professionals
Indian Hill ginger ale
    Mixes well with any friend
Indiana & Michigan Electric Com-
    pany
    We give it our best
Indiana Dept. of Commerce
    Where free enterprise is
    still growing
Indiana Limestone Quarrymen's
    Association
    The aristocrat of building
    materials
    Build the Nation securely
    with the nation's
    building stone
    The nation's building stone

Indiana National Bank
    Pioneers in banking
Indiana Steel & Wire Co.
    Netting that stands alone
Indiana Truck Corp.
    Proved by proofs
Indiana Vocational Technical Col-
    lege
    Learn a living at Ivy Tech
Indianapolis annual 500 mile auto-
    mobile race
    The greatest spectacle in
    racing
Indianapolis Star
    Always first, always fair
Indianapolis Tent & Awning Co.
    We fool the sun
Indiscreet Perfume
    The shortest distance be-
    tween two hearts
Indispensable to the creative
    perfumer
    Dow aromatics
Indium Corporation of America
    Conserve to serve national
    defense
Individual hothouse for plants
    Hotkaps
Individuality graven into them
    Brunswick phonograph
    records
Individuals have poured this
    smooth mellow whiskey
    since 1608
    Old Bushmill's Irish Whiskey
Indoor weather as you want it,
    with a weatherator
    Premier Warm Air Heater
Industrial Chemicals Marketing
    Div., Tennessee Corp.
    Basic producers from mine
    to finished product
Industrial Distributors, Ltd.
    The right hand of produc-
    tion
Industrial efficiency depends on
    electrical control
    Cutler-Hammer, Inc.
Industrial Engine Dept., Ford
    Div., Ford Motor Com-
    pany
    Your job is well powered
    when it's Ford powered
Industrial Engine Dept., Ford
    Div., Ford Motor Com-
    pany. See also: Ford

225

Motor Company
Industrial Equipment News
    Industry's original product
    information reporting
    service
    Useful facts in advertising
Industrial Fabrics Div., West
    Point-Pepperell, Inc.
    First in fabrics for industry
Industrial headquarters of the
    south
    Atlanta Industrial Bureau
Industrial Home for the Blind
    Help the blind to help
    themselves
Industrial Laboratories
    The magazine of research
    and development
Industrial Management
    The engineering magazine
Industrial Marketing
    Selling and advertising to
    business and industry
Industrial Marketing Div., Jas.
    H. Matthews and Co.
    Marketing methods since 1850
Industrial National Corporation
    Diversified financial serv-
    ices growing together
Industrial News
    The home paper of the in-
    dustrial worker and
    the farmer
Industrial Process Engineering
    For maximum production
    with minimum mainten-
    ance
The industrial resources company
    Ashland Oil and Refining
    Co.
Industries. See: I. C. Indus-
    tries
Industrious Maine, New Eng-
    land's big stake in the
    future
    Maine
Industry, concentration, self-
    reliance
    International Correspondence
    Schools
Industry is on the move to Iowa
    Iowa Development Commis-
    sion
Industry-owned to conserve
    property and profits
    Factory Mutual Insurance

Co.
Industry spokesman to CPI man-
    agement
    Chemical Week
Industry's friendliest climate
    Public Service of Indiana,
    Inc.
Industry's helping hand
    Rex Chainbelt, Inc.
Industry's leading insurance
    brokers
    Marsh & McLennan, Inc.
The industry's marketplace
    Electronics
Industry's original product in-
    formation reporting
    service
    Industrial Equipment News
Industry's partner in production
    E. F. Houghton and Co.
Inecto Hair Coloring
    Colors hair inside, as nature
    does
    Honeytones by Inecto Hair
    Coloring
Inexpensive. And built to stay
    that way
    Subaru automobile
Inexpensive, comfortable, hygienic
    and safe
    Kotex sanitary napkins
The inflation fighter
    Blatz beer
Information is the business of
    today's Bell & Howell
    Bell & Howell Company
Information that leads to action
    McGraw-Hill, Inc.
Informing and entertaining the
    American family
    Taft Broadcasting Company
Ing. Mario Ballestra & Co.
    World's most experienced
    detergent engineers
Ingenious electronics in step
    with the times
    Synchronics electronic
    equipment
Ingersoll dollar watch
    Ingersoll, the watchword of
    the nation
    The watch that made the
    dollar famous
Ingersoll flashlight
    There's an Ingersoll for
    everyone

Ingersoll-Rand Company
Bonded for life ... because
they're built that way
Ingersoll-Rand power tools,
the ones professionals
reach for
We build our machines better
than they have to be
We build our products to
weather the worst of
conditions
Where innovative engineer-
ing, essential equipment
and energy add up to
growth
Ingersoll-Rand power tools, the
ones professionals reach
for
Ingersoll-Rand Company
Ingersoll, the watchword of the
nation
Ingersoll dollar watch
Inglenook Wines
Discover award-winning
taste
Ingram's Mlkweed Cream
There is beauty in every
jar
Ingram's rouge
Just to show a proper glow
Ingram's shaving cream
Cool shaves cited for com-
fort
Cools and soothes as you
shave
For a cooling shave
A little goes a longer way
Marines beat tough scrapes
with cool shaves
The world's coolest shave
Initials of a friend
General Electric Company
The ink that never fades
Sanford Mfg. Co.
Inkograph
The pen that writes like a
pencil
Inland Florida's greatest news-
paper
Orlando Morning Sentinel
Inland Homes Corp.
The homes teamwork builds
Inland Mfg. Co.
Ice cubes instantly, tray
to glass
Inland Printer

Leading business and tech-
nical journal of the world
in printing and allied
industries
The inner secret of outer beauty
Charm underlift brassiere
Innovation plus performance
Salomon Brothers, Inc.
Innovations that squeeze the
waste out of distribution
Southern Railway Co.
The innovators
Torrington Co.
Innovators in the design and
manufacture of quality
labeling equipment
Phin, Inc.
Innovators of research-engineered
products
Bostrom Corp.
Inryco, Inc.
Inryco is everywhere in
construction
Inryco is everywhere in con-
struction
Inryco, Inc.
The inside track to profits
Socony Vacuum Oil Co.
Inspected, protected
Dairymen's League Cooper-
ative Assn.
Inspection is our middle name
Hartford Steam Boiler In-
spection and Insurance
Co.
The inspiration coffee
Schwabacher Bros.
Install confidence ... install
Thermoid
Thermoid brake lining
Install it, forget it
Kodel radio receiver
Installed in minutes, lasts for
years
Oak Ridge Antenna
Instant elevatoring
Otis Elevator Company
Instant hot water
Automatic Water Heater
Premier Water Heater
Instant hot water service
Humphrey Co.
Instant. In writing. Inexpen-
sive
Western Union Telex Net-
work

227

Instant news service
    Dow Jones and Co.
Instant Postum
    Contains no caffeine or other
        harmful stimulants
    The natural lift
    One of America's great meal-
        time drinks
Instant Tender Leaf Tea
    Brighten up with Instant
        Tender Leaf Tea
    The brighter tasting tea!
Instantly known when blown
    Royal Crystal fuse plug
An institution of service
    Reading Industrial Loom
An institution that sticks to its
        last
    Traung Label & Lithograph
        Co.
Institutions
    Magazine of mass feeding,
        mass housing
The instrument of the immortals
    Steinway piano
Instruments of quality by one
        family for 100 years
    Story and Clark Piano Co.
Instruments worthy of the mas-
        ters since 1857
    W. W. Kimball Co.
Insulite Div., Minnesota and On-
        tario Paper Co.
    Build right, with Insulite
    Sells easy ... sells fast ...
        makes resales
Insurance Co. of North America
    Be sure, insure with INA
    Protect what you have
Insure clerical efficiency and
        profit protection, use
        multiple copy forms
    Malady & MacLauchlan
Insure in the Travelers
    The Travelers Insurance
        Cos.
Insure today to save tomorrow
    Rain & Hail Insurance
        Bureau
Insure your profits, use Stimp-
        son products
    Stimpson Computing Scale
        Co.
The insured pipe
    Wm. Demuth & Co.
Insured Savings and Loan As-

sociations
    Where your dollar works
        harder ... grows bigger!
Insures a new kind of faultless,
        effortless writing
    Eberhard Faber, Inc.
Insurers of energy systems
    Hartford Steam Boiler In-
        spection and Insurance
        Co.
Intense heat
    Jackson-Sheridan Fuel Co.
Inter-State automobile
    The automobile for women
Interested personal service--
        always--when you buy
        from Eastman
    Eastman Chemical Products,
        Inc.
Interlake bathroom tissue
    Pure, soft, absorbent
Interlude
    The first really different
        magazine in a generation
The internal lubricant
    Nujol laxative
The international authority on
        visual merchandising
    Display World
The international banking services
        you expect, from a single
        integrated source
    Lloyd's Bank International
International Basic Economy Corp.
    See: Bellows-Valvair
    Div., International Basic
        Economy Corp.
International Business Machines
        Corp.
    In other words, results
    System/360, the computer
        with a future
    Think
    The way we put it all to-
        gether is what sets us
        apart
    World peace through world
        trade
International Business Machines
        Corp. See also:
    IBM
    Office Products Div., Inter-
        national Business Ma-
        chines Corp.
International Coffee Co.
    Has 'em all beat

228

International Correspondence
    Schools
    Back your trained hand with
    a trained head
    Building the teacher into a
    textbook
    The business leaders of to-
    day are the I. C. S.
    students of yesterday
    The business leaders of to-
    morrow are the I. C. S.
    students of today
    Earn while you learn
    An education by mail
    Go to high school in bed-
    room slippers
    I'm in a class by myself
    Industry, concentration,
    self-reliance
    To earn more, learn more
    Universal university
    University of the night
    We teach wherever the mails
    reach
    Wherever the mails reach,
    there we teach
    Your mind is burglar-proof
An international daily newspaper
    Christian Science Monitor
International Duplex Coat Co.
    The coats for every wear,
    everywhere
International Express Mail Service
    Packages delivered around
    the world in three days
    or less
    The international favorites
    Hal Kemp's dance orchestra
International Gold Bullion Ex-
    change
    The wise investor knows
    when to invest
International Harvester Co.
    Any price is too high if it
    can be reduced
    The courage to change.
    The strength to grow
    First to serve the farmer
    For the nation's factories
    and the nation's farms
    The leading truck builder
    in America
    The people who bring you
    the machines that work
    We're not giving in. We're
    going on

International Harvester trucks
    Build a truck to do a job--
    change it only to do
    better
    A city at your door
    For low cost hauling
    For name and reputation,
    this truck is Interna-
    tional
    Internationals will see you
    through
    Light duty, but ALL truck
    No. 1 heavy-duty sales
    leader
The international health care
    services company
    American Medical Interna-
    tional
International Herald Tribune
    The only global daily news-
    paper
International Incinerator
    The healthy home is the
    happy home
International knows how
    International Piston Ring
    Co.
International Magazine
    To talk little, to hear much
International Management
    The magazine of world busi-
    ness
The international newsmagazine
    Newsweek
International Nickel Co.
    For strength where the
    stress comes
    Nickel ... its contribution
    is quality
The international one
    Toshiba America, Inc.
International Paper Co.
    An international value
International Piston Ring Co.
    International knows how
International Railway Co.
    The Honeymoon Line
International Salt Co.
    Avoid shaker-clog
    Do away with shaker-clog
    Eliminate troublesome shaker-
    clog
    It's in the bag
    No more shaker-clog
    A salt for every purpose
International Shoe Co.

Calendar of fashion
Fashion forecasters
Quality at modest cost
International Silver Co.
The family plate for seventy
years
Silver with a past, a present
and a future
Wrought from solid silver
International Telephone & Tele-
graph Corp.
The best ideas are the ideas
that help people
Worldwide electronics tele-
communications
An international value
International Paper Co.
Internationally known mark of
quality
Manhattan Industries, Inc.
Internationals will see you through
International Harvester
trucks
Internorth
The right mix at the right
time
The interrupting idea
Federal Advertising Agency
Interstate Cotton Oil
The better spread for our
daily bread
Interstate Motor Freight System
More than a truck line--a
transportation system
Interstate Trust Co.
A bank of personal contact
Intertype Corp.
Made it's way by the way
it's made
Interwoven socks
The greatest name in socks
Intimate as her diary, personal
as a back-fence chat
Woman's Home Companion
The intimate hotel on Chicago's
Gold Coast
Ambassador West hotel,
Chicago, Ill.
Intimate perfume
Cherished as one of the
world's seven great
fragrances
Into big shiny kettles go the
prettiest tomatoes that
ever blushed red in
the California sunshine

Hunt's Tomato Sauce
Invented by a doctor--now used
by millions of women
Tampax, Inc.
The invention of a medical expert
Safety Poise Cycle Seat
Inventor and scientist make
dreams come true; the
insurance man keeps
nightmares from happen-
ing
Fireman's Fund American In-
surance
Invest in a quality name
Scudder Cash Investment
Trust
Invest in memory insurance
Standard Diary Co.
Invest in Nelson's triple-culled
chix
Nelson's Hatchery
Invest in rest
Better Bedding Alliance of
America
Invest in the car that stands up
best
Plymouth automobile
Investigate before you invest
Better Business Bureau
An investment in good appearance
Kuppenheimer clothes
Investment services under the
same name for 55 years
Wertheim & Co.
Investor-Owned Electric Light
and Power Companies
People you can depend on
to power America's
progress
You've got good things go-
ing for you with service
by Investor-Owned Elec-
tric Light and Power
Companies
Investors Diversified Services,
Inc.
Call your Investors man--
today!
We help people manage
money
Invigorator corsets
Doctors recommend Reast's
patent Invigorator cor-
sets
Ion-Guard Security paint
Paint thieves into a corner

Permanently identifies your
property
Iona Mfg. Co.
Quality you can trust.
Value you can recognize
Iowa Development Commission
Industry is on the move to
Iowa
Iowa's greatest evening paper
Des Moines Evening Tribune
Ipana toothpaste
Do your smile a favor
For the smile of beauty
Good for tender gums
Hearts in harmony until she
smiles
Ipana toothpaste for your
smile of beauty
Men look, men linger, until
she smiles
Wake up lazy gums with
Ipana and massage
Your smile of beauty
Ipana toothpaste for your smile
of beauty
Ipana toothpaste
Iris coffee
Glass sealed, the perfect
coffee, the perfect
package
Irish & Scottish Linen Damask
Guild
Linen damask, impressively
correct
Irish Mist liqueur
The legendary spirit
Irish Mocha Mint
Celebrate the moments of
your life
Irish Spring soap
Fresh and clean as a whistle
Iron Age
The world's greatest indus-
trial paper
Iron city beer
Makes every bite a banquet
Iron Clad Hosiery
Enduring loveliness
Flattering as moonlight
Iron Fireman
The machine that made coal
an automatic fuel
Pays for itself by what it
saves
The standard of value in
automatic coal firing

equipment
Iron horse quality
Matthews Co.
Iron Mountain Co.
Colder-than-ice refrigeration
The iron that's safe for any fabric
Arvin electric iron
Iron Trade Review
Authority of industry, na-
tional and international
Irons while it steams
Elder steam iron
Iroquois China Co.
China by Iroquois for the
hosts of America
Iroquois Electric Refrigeration Co.
The crisp, dry cold of a
frosty night
Irresistible Lipstick
Puts the YOU in irresistible
YOUth
Irving. See also: Erving
Irving Air Chute Co.
Safety on the road. Secur-
ity in space
Irving Trust Company
The bank for bankers and
businessmen
Unique. Worldwide
Irving Varnish & Insulator Co.
The liner makes the closure
Irwill sweaters
Designed to be lived in
Is a toast to good health
Hires' Improved Root Beer
Is absolutely pure and is soluble
Baker's Breakfast Cocoa
Is as safe to eat as bread and
butter
Mackintosh's Toffee
Is THAT all Pontiac costs?
Pontiac automobile
Is the Telegram on your list?
New York World-Telegram
Is your refrigerator a Success?
Success refrigerator
I'se in town, honey
Aunt Jemima Pancake Flour
Iselin. See: William Iselin and
Co., Inc.
Isko Company iceless refrigeration
Fits any ice box
Islon
The luxury of velvet with
the worry left out
Isn't your skin worth it?

Apri Apricot facial scrub
Isuzu trucks
Tougher than the world's
toughest roads
It always pays to consult Falk
Falk couplings
It bears close inspection
Long-Bell Lumber Co.
It beats--as it sweeps--as it
cleans
Hoover vacuum cleaner
It beats the Dutch
Phillips cocoa
It bends with the heat
W. M. Chace Co.
It breathes as it feeds
Evenflo nursing nipple
It bridges the vastness of space
Cunningham radio tube
It budgets the oil
Williams Oil-O-Matic Heating
Corp.
It can help you look younger,
too
Oil of Olay beauty liquid
It can pull more than it can
carry
Fruehauf Corporation
It can't under-measure, it can't
over-charge
Wayne Pump Co.
It circulates, it radiates
Coleman Co., Inc.
It clamps everywhere
Adjusto-Lite
It cleans so quick
Climalene
It cleans the air, then cleans
itself
National Air Filter
It cleans your breath while it
cleans your teeth
Colgate's dental cream
It cleanses, preserves, and
beautifies the teeth so
perfectly
Rubifoam dentifrice
It costs less to pay more
Lucas paints
It costs less to run a Fess
Fess oil burner
It costs little, saves much
Cut-Rite Waxed Paper
It costs more because it lasts
longer
Olds & Whipple

It costs no more to buy a Kelly
Kelly-Springfield Tire Co.
It costs no more to enjoy Farns-
worth fidelity
Farnsworth radio receiver
It costs no more to reach the
first million first
National Geographic
It covers, it beautifies, it lasts,
it protects, it's econom-
ical
Lucas paints
It cuts through competition like
a rapier
Danger Perfume
It does the work
Aetna Explosives Co.
It doesn't leave my kitchen unless
it's delicious
Mrs. Paul's fish fillets
It eats up the dirt
Ideal Vacuum Cleaner
It eliminates the noise that an-
noys
Speakman plumbing fixtures
It even has wine in it
Grey Poupon Mustard
It filters the smoke
De Nicotea cigarette holder
It fits like magic
Genie brassiere
It fits the form because it's
formed to fit
De Luxe sanitary belt
It floats
Ivory soap
It gets the dirt
Eureka vacuum cleaner
It gets there right in Wirebounds
Wirebound Box Manufactur-
er's Association
It had to be better to enjoy such
universal preference for
320 years
Haig & Haig Scotch whiskey
It had to be good to get where
it is
Coca Cola soft drink
It had to have quality, the steel
is Lukens
Lukens Steel Co.
It hangs everywhere
Automobile Trade Directory
It happens in two seconds
Bayer aspirin
It has no pernicious odor

Koverslak varnish
It helps treasurers budget their
time
Sheaffer Eaton
It is. See also: 'Tis
It is a mark of intelligent house-
keeping to possess a
Simplex Ironer
Simplex Ironer
It is absolutely impossible to cut
your face
Eastman & Krauss Razor
Co.
It is accurate and it stays ac-
curate
National Meter Co.
It is better and you can prove
it
Borden, Inc.
It is better to buy Lincoln lubri-
cating equipment than
to wish you had
Lincoln lubricating equip-
ment
It is better to have it and not
need it than to need it
and not have it
Columbia Casualty Co.
It is our business to help your
business
Building Supply News
It is profitable to produce in
Massachusetts
Massachusetts
It is sterling, more cannot be
said
Sterling Silversmiths of
America
It is the body itself
Knight-ware sinks
It isn't child labor, it's child's
play
Thor clothes iron
It keeps contents ice cold
Hawkeye Refrigerator Basket
It keeps your ginger up
Canada Dry ginger ale
It lasts longer because it runs
cooler
Seiberling tires
It leaves you breathless
Smirnoff vodka
It lives with good taste every-
where
Budweiser beer
It looks like you just put it on

when you didn't just put
it on
Revlon lipstick
It lox the sox
Pittsburgh Garter Co.
It lulls the skin
Coty cosmetics
It magnifies your performance
Turner microphone
It makes a difference
Havoline motor oil
It makes a dust magnet of your
dust mop or cloth
Endust
It makes dishes wink and twinkle
Climalene
It makes graduation day a golden
occasion
Krugerrand coin jewelry
It makes its way by the way it's
made
Bridgeport luggage
It moves with you so it stays
with you
Bandaid flexible bandage
It must be good to be a Gund
Gund toys
It only tastes expensive
Maxwell House Master Blend
Coffee
It pays to be in the news
Architectural and Engineer-
ing News
It pays to be particular
Del Monte pineapple
It pays to be particular about
your oil
Wolf's Head Motor Oil
It pays to buy the leader and
get the leading buy
Chevrolet automobile
It pays to insure with the "Blue
Chip" company
Connecticut Mutual Life In-
surance Co.
It pays to join hands with Oppen-
heimer
Oppenheimer Investor Serv-
ices, Inc.
It pays to keep clean
American Linen Companies
It pays to know when to relax
Metropolitan Life Insurance
Co.
It pays to make it Corbin
throughout!

Corbin hardware
It pays to spend for the best
    in the end
    Ohio Brass Co.
It pays to use good tools
    Vaughan & Bushnell Mfg.
    Co.
It pays you to buy at Schwa-
    bacher-Frey
    Schwabacher-Frey stationery
    store
It penetrates
    Black Flag insect spray
It pleases everybody!
    Overland automobile
It puts the sunshine in your
    hair
    Pine Tree Shampoo
It reaches the surface of every
    tooth
    Dr. West's Miracle Tuft
    Toothbrush
It really lasts!
    Duracell dry cell battery
It remembers so YOU can for-
    get
    James automatic clock
It rests the back
    The Perfect chair
It rolls as you step on the gas
    Ford accelerators
It sho sticks
    Wortendyke gummed tape
It slices, it cooks, it keeps
    Kraft Foods Div., Kraftco
    Corp.
It smells so clean
    Teele Soap
It smooths the skin
    Campana Italian Balm
It snuggles in your fingers
    J. Dixon Crucible Co.
It speaks for itself
    Audiotape
    H. P. Snyder Mfg. Co.
    Transformer Corp. of
    America
It splits in two
    Tak-hom-a-biscuit
It staples, it tacks, it pins
    Swingline stapler
It started me smoking cigars
    Robert Burns cigar
It stays on the salad
    Wright's French Dressing

It sticks, it holds, it lasts
    Bull Dog Tape
It stops that howl
    McDonald radio howl arrester
It S-T-R-E-T-C-H-E-S and
    springs back
    Speidel Corp. watch bands
It strikes one; it's Guinness time
    Guinness ale
It takes a man to help a boy
    Big Brother
It takes a smart company to make
    computer technology
    simple
    Management Assistance, Inc.
It takes a tough man to make a
    tender chicken
    Perdue Farms, Inc.
It takes art to make a company
    great
    Philip Morris cigarettes
It takes emotion to move mer-
    chandise ... Better
    Homes & Gardens is
    PERPETUAL EMOTION
    Better Homes & Gardens
It takes energy to control the
    future
    Research-Cottrell
It takes less to give more flavor
    Lipton's tea
It takes more than a flame and
    a casting to make a good
    fast-fired circulation
    heater
    The Moore Corp.
It takes more than advertising
    to make a good product
    Owens-Illinois Glass Co.
It takes more than brains to go
    to college
    U. S. Army Recruiting
    Service
It takes on added beauty in the
    shoe
    Surpass Leather Co.
It takes so little
    White King Soap
It takes so little for every
    household use
    White King Soap
It takes the best to make the
    best
    Worcester Salt Co.
It tastes better

E. R. Squibb
It tastes expensive ... and is
    Maker's Mark whiskey
It tastes good to the last crumb
    Stuhmer's Pumpernickel
It tastes home-made
    Heinz tomato soup
It tastes so good you forget the
    fibre
    New Fruit and Fibre cereal
It tumbles the clothes as it cir-
    culates them
    Whirlpool clothes washer
It ventilates
    Perfolastic girdle
It was. See also: 'Twas
It was inevitable
    Silver Spray soft drink
It washes your dandruff away
    Fitch Shampoo
It waxes, it polishes, it sands,
    it scrubs
    Finnell System, Inc.
It wears--and wears--and wears
    Zapon leather cloth
It whistles when it's had enough
    Automatic Safety Tire Valve
    Co.
It will tell your eyes before your
    eyes tell you
    Tampa Elec. Co. sight
    meter
It won't. See also: 'Twont
It won't stick to most dental
    work
    Freedent gum
It works
    U. S. B. Electric Bicycle
    Lamp
    Wall Street Journal
It works beneath your skin
    where softness really
    begins
    Monchel bath soap
It writes. It adds. It sub-
    tracts
    Remington typewriter
It zips me through my cleaning
    Old Dutch Cleanser
Italian Line
    More fun per ton than any
    other line
    Unwind your way to Europe
Itek Corp.
    An American leader in
    advanced systems of

    photo-optics for informa-
    tion processing
Ithaca Gun Co., Inc.
    Expert's choice ... since
    1880
It's a bit more expensive, but
    for a flawless, cool Tom
    Collins, the world comes
    to Gordon's
    Gordon's Distilled London
    Dry Gin
It's a challenge
    Challenge Machinery Co.
It's a good feeling to buckle up
    for safety
    Toyota automobile
It's a great automobile
    Marmon automobile
    Nordyke automobile
It's a killer
    Flak insecticide
It's a life insurance policy for
    your engine
    Valvoline motor oil
It's a lucky day for your car
    when you change to
    Quaker State motor oil
    Quaker State Oil Refining
    Corp.
It's a mark of distinction to own
    a Parker pen
    Parker Pen Co.
It's a matter of good taste
    Royal Gelatin
It's a matter of life and breath
    American Lung Association
It's a mighty fine pipe tobacco
    Dill's Best pipe tobacco
It's a protective neutralizer
    Bisurated Magnesia
It's a real fuse, built for real
    service
    Trico Fuse Mfg. Co.
It's a short street without a
    Plymouth
    Plymouth automobile
It's a snap with Dot
    Dot fasteners
It's a snap with Superflash
    Superflash photolamp
It's a whole new way to dictate
    Dictaphone Corp.
It's a winner
    PlastiCraft motor boat
It's air washed
    Southern Rice Sales Co.

It's all color in all colors
American Cyanamid Co.
It's all in fun
Skylark fragrance
It's all in the finish
American Cyanamid Co.
It's all in the moisturizing
Mmm! What a tan! tanning
lotion
It's all in the wheel
Red Devil Glass Cutter
Smith glass cutter
It's all quality because it's all
barley
Puritan Malt
It's all worth, if Walworth
Walworth valves
It's all you need to know for
Christmas
Zale's diamond store
It's always a pleasure
I. W. Harper bourbon
whiskey
It's always a shade better
Bulldog Venetian blind
cleaner
It's always coal weather
Stearns Coal & Lumber Co.
It's always Fehr weather
Fehr beer
It's an eager-to-go, low, long,
lovely melody in metal
Studebaker automobile
It's an "open and shut" case
K & M Kontrol motor valve
Swingline stapler
It's Arnheim time!
Gus Arnheim's dance or-
chestra
It's as cool as it's tall, and it's
good for you
The Tall-One Co.
It's as good as the best and
better than the rest
Queen's Health salt
It's beer as beer should taste
Rheingold beer
It's better because it's made of
Koroseal
Koroseal fabric
It's better, not bitter
Carling's Ale
It's better than it used to be
and it used to be the
best
Horton Pilsener

It's better with butter
American Dairy Association
Its blend is our secret, its frag-
rance your delight
Old Briar pipe tobacco
It's blended, it's splendid
Pabst Blue Ribbon beer
It's blended to better your best
in baking
Fisher Flouring Mills
It's bug tested
Black Flag insect spray
It's built to sell when it's built
of wood
National Lumber Manufactur-
ers Association
It's butter rich
Snacks candy
It's certified quality
Bond's handkerchiefs
It's cheaper to buy good pads
than new hose
Quix foot pads
It's clean, pure, healthful if it's
Wrigley's
Wrigley's chewing gum
It's cotton-soft
Cottonelle bathroom tissue
It's creamed
French's mustard
It's crystal-clear
Gordon's Distilled London
Dry Gin
It's "curtains" for dirt when
your curtains are Koro-
seal
Koroseal fabric
It's dated
Chase and Sanborn coffee
It's different, naturally
Tendermint Gum
It's digestible
Crisco shortening
It's Dove Skin for loveliness
Dove Skin undies
It's downright sociable
Harvey's Bristol Cream
Sherry
It's easy to vacuum clean with-
out electricity
Vacuette non electric vacuum
cleaner
Its favor has grown through
flavor alone
McCormick and Co., Inc.
It's finger lickin' good

Kentucky Fried Chicken
It's flavor-tested
Haserot Company
Its flavor wins favor
Tetley's Tea
It's flavoripe
Globe beer
It's fortified, just try it
Gilmore Oil Co.
It's fun to own a gift by Rival
Rival Mfg. Co.
It's gonna be a great day
Kellogg's raisin bran
It's good because it's fresh
Tuxedo tobacco
It's good business to begin with
good water
Permutit water treatment
It's good business to do business
with Mallory
P. R. Mallory and Co., Inc.
It's good business to run a fine-
tuned building
Honeywell, Inc.
It's good for your teeth
Kolynos dental cream
Its good taste always stands out
Old Overholt whiskey
It's good to get home to a Guin-
ness
Guinness ale
It's good to have a great bank
behind you
Manufacturers Hanover
Bank
It's good to know
Imperial whiskey
It's got a smooth punch
Lincoln Inn Distilling Co.
It's hard to beat Skippy
Skippy peanut butter
It's heavier
Molle shaving cream
Its high quality makes it eco-
nomical
Folger's ground coffee
It's in her home where he plans
his
Sonora phonograph
It's in the bag
International Salt Co.
It's ironized
Fleischmann's Yeast
It's joy in a jar
Smithfield Meat Spread
It's just ham unless it's Swift's

Swift's ham
It's king-size smoking at its
best, yet priced no
higher than the rest
Embassy cigarettes
It's Kodak for color
Kodak cameras
It's life insurance for your engine
Valvoline motor oil
It's light on Duff jacks
Duff Mfg. Co.
It's made of New Castle, more
need not be said
New Castle Leather Co.
It's making news, it's making
friends
Campbell's condensed soups
It's matchless
Hunter Div., Robbins & My-
ers, Inc.
It's meat and drink to you
Oxo
It's mild and mellow
Revelation pipe tobacco
It's mild because it's pure
Diamond Crystal Salt
It's Miller time
Miller High Life beer
It's moisturized
Raleigh cigarettes
It's more than what you earn.
It's what you keep that
counts
John Nuveen & Co., Inc.
It's More you
More Lights 100's cigarettes
It's mother who guards the
family's health
Shredded Wheat
Its name indicates its character
The Lincoln National Life
Insurance Co.
It's nature's freshness--indoors
Lennox Industries, Inc.
It's no accident that America's
trucks set the standards
for safety
Armstrong tires
It's no secret ... Schilling flavor
makes all the difference
in the world!
Schilling Div., McCormick
and Co., Inc.
It's not a home until it's planted
Hillsdale Nurseries
It's not easy, being Number 1

Jay's potato chips
It's not Jockey brand if it
doesn't have the Jockey
boy
Jockey Menswear Div.,
Cooper's, Inc.
It's not just a phone. It's Dun's
dial
Dun & Bradstreet credit
services
It's not just for winning races
Valvoline motor oil
It's not the first cost, it's the
upkeep
Cap-R-Nap sail preservative
It's off because it's out
Zip hair remover
It's on time or it's on us
Flying Tiger Line, Inc.
It's one Hulluva chain saw
Pioneer chain saw
It's one of the three great beers
Krueger beer
It's one tough tire to stop
Firestone tires
It's "packed with satisfaction"
when you use R/M
Raybestos-Manhattan, Inc.
It's patch and go with Chemico
Chemico tire patch
It's perfect for scores of chores
Widget cutting tool
Its purity shows in everything
you bake
Dainty Flour
It's quick wetting
Williams' Shaving Cream
Its rare bouquet sealed in to
stay
Haserot Company
It's really sweet
Sweetose syrup
It's safe because it's faster
C-O Two Fire Equipment
Co.
It's said and done
Dictaphone Corp.
It's sharp to be sure
Her Majesty slip
It's smart to buy right
Highland Scotch Mist
It's smart to choose the finest
sterling
Reed & Barton sterling
silver
It's smart to choose what

Hollywood chews
Mint Cocktail Gum
It's smart to say "I'll take Du-
bonnet!" Chill it ...
pour it ... enjoy
Dubonnet wine
It's smart to say Seagram's V. O.
Seagram's V. O. whiskey
It's smooth sailing with Bracken-
ridge Brewing Co. beers
Brackenridge Brewing Co.
It's smooth sailing with Old
Anchor Beer
Old Anchor Beer
It's so easy
Head and Shoulders shampoo
It's so good for so long
Beechnut gum
It's Spring and she has shiny
hair; no wonder love
is in the air
Drene shampoo
It's standard
Socony Vacuum Oil Co.
It's still smart to be healthy
Quality Ice Cream
It's straight whiskey
Kentucky Tavern whiskey
It's strong, caffein-free and
safe
Dietec
It's sudsy
Gold Dust Soap Powder
It's sugar for your mouth
Advanced Formula Sugar
Twin
It's terribly smart in a cherry
tart
Angostura Bitters
It's the blend that betters the
beer
Pabst Blue Ribbon beer
It's the buttermilk that does it
Teco Pancake Flour
It's the chain that stands the
strain
Baldwin tire chain
It's the contact that counts
Alden radio sockets
It's the contacts that count
Amerio Contact Plate
Freezers, Inc.
It's the finish that counts
Carpenter-Morton paints
It's the flavor
Teacher's Highland Cream

Scotch whiskey
It's the going thing
    Ford Motor Company
It's the golden touch that means
    so much
    Don Q Rum
It's the life they lead, it's the
    book they read
    Better Homes & Gardens
It's the little daily dose that
    does it
    Krushen Salts
It's the long hard pull that
    proves the radiator
    Harrison radiators
It's the lowest calorie bread you
    can buy
    Perfection bread
It's the real thing
    Calvert "Extra" whiskey
It's the same old "juice"
    Columbia dry and storage
    batteries
It's the second 10,000 miles that
    makes the big hit
    General tires
It's the specification-finished
    surface that does it
    American Silversheet
It's the thoughtful thing to do
    Whitman's Chocolates
It's the tobacco that counts
    Lucky Strike cigarettes
    Player cigarettes
It's the twisted teeth that lock
    Shakeproof Lock Washer
    Co.
It's the very finest because it's
    Rubee
    Rubee Furniture Mfg. Corp.
It's the woman-wise range
    Estate Stove Co.
It's the working voltage
    Dubilier Condenser & Radio
    Corp.
It's the yarn that counts
    American Yarn & Process
    Co.
It's time for Imperial
    Chrysler Imperial auto-
    mobile
It's TIME that turns the tide
    in Breidt's
    Breidt beer
It's time to Re-form
    Helene brassiere

It's time you tasted Breidt's, the
    beer with the 4th in-
    gredient
    Breidt beer
It's toasted
    Lucky Strike cigarettes
It's too late when your brakes
    fail
    Flare brake fluid
It's tops for kitchen tops
    Weiss & Klau Co.
It's truly a whale of a washer
    Fletcher Works, Inc.
It's two ways light
    Trommer's beer
It's uncanny
    Knorr soups
It's "velveted"
    Imperial whiskey
It's Washington's mother's recipe
    Dromedary gingerbread mix
It's what you don't smell that
    counts
    Glad garbage bags
It's what you put in to make the
    flavor come out
    Angostura Bitters
It's what's inside that counts
    Explosives Div., Atlas
    Chemical Industries,
    Inc.
It's Wilson today in sports
    equipment
    Wilson Sporting Goods Co.
It's wise to conveyorize
    Rapids-Standard Co., Inc.
It's wonderful, it's Welch's
    Welch grape juice
Its wood-smoky fragrance warms
    up appetites
    Armour Star Bacon
It's worth it ... it's Bud
    Budweiser beer
It's worth the difference
    Munsingwear underwear
It's worth the difference to get
    a Big Ben
    Big Ben Westclox alarm
    clock
It's your best buy
    Cyclotherm Steam Generators
It's your guarantee of quality
    Contac nasal decongestant
It's your protection and our
    guarantee
    Crex Carpet Co.

Iu International
Iu's P-I-E is the first
choice for the long haul
Iu's P-I-E is the first choice for
the long haul
Iu International
Ivaline Motor Oil
The one right oil for Ford
cars
The sooner the better
I've made the world a brighter
place to live in
Bon Ami cleanser
I've tried 'em all
Gilmore Oil Co.
Iveco Diesel Transport Manu-
facturer
Iveco. A world of diesel
research and technol-
ogy
Iveco. A world of trans-
port
Iveco. A world of diesel re-
search and technol-
ogy
Iveco Diesel Transport
Manufacturer
Iveco. A world of transport
Iveco Diesel Transport
Manufacturer
Iveco diesel trucks
The diesel truck that pays
for itself
For businessmen who know
their diesels
Iver-Johnson Arms & Cycle
Works
Hammer the hammer
Iver-Johnson shotguns
The arms that protect Amer-
ican farms
Ives Manufacturing Co.
Ives toys make happy boys
Makes happy boys
Ives toys make happy boys
Ives Manufacturing Co.
Ivory dishwashing liquid
Helps hands look young
No wonder more women
rely on Ivory Liquid
to help them keep their
hands soft, young-
looking!
Ivory Flakes
If it's lovely to wear it's
worth Ivory Flakes

care
Ivory is kind to everything it
touches
Ivory soap
Ivory-mild for safety; granulated
for speed
Ivory Snow
Ivory Snow
Ivory-mild for safety; gran-
ulated for speed
Kindness to hands, speed in
the dishpan
Ivory soap
Baby-care is beauty-care
Help your beauty bloom
this spring
Ivory is kind to everything
it touches
It floats
Kind to everything it touches
More doctors advise Ivory
than any other soap
99 44/100% pure
No soap can get you cleaner
Now better than ever for
everything
"Velvet-Suds"
Ivory tips protect your lips
Marlboro cigarettes

-J-

J. See also: Jay
J. A. Baldwin Mfg. Co.
World's finest
J & B Rare Scotch whiskey
Pennies more in cost ...
worlds apart in qual-
ity
Rare taste. Ask for it by
name
J. C. Bradford & Co.
We do business as if we
had only one customer.
You
J. C. Penney and Co.
Always first quality
A nationwide institution
J. C. Penney Auto Center
We won't steer you wrong
J. C. Pitman and Sons, Inc.
World's first and largest
manufacturer of deep
fat frying equipment
J. Dixon Crucible Co.

The business pencil
The famous pencil with the
green and yellow plas-
tips
It snuggles in your fingers
The master drawing pencil
Smooth as silk, strong as
steel
J. E. Sirrine & Co.
Engineering consultants on
the South
J. H. Slingerland
Candy delicacy
Marshmallow treat
J. H. Williams & Co.
The drop-forging people
Small in size, great other-
wise
The wrench people
J. I. Case earth moving machines
Partners in providing
We've made a deep impres-
sion
J. J. Grover's Sons Co.
Soft shoes for tender feet
J. L. Clark Mfg. Co.
Containers of distinction
J. L. Mott Iron Works
Everything we sell, we
make
J. P. Smith Shoe Co.
As flexible as your feet
You can't wear out their
looks
J. P. Stevens and Co., Inc.
Fine fabrics made in
America since 1813
Just everyday things for
the home made beauti-
ful by Stevens
JS&A Group, Inc.
Products that think
J. W. Greer Co.
Betters continuous produc-
tion through continu-
ous research!
J. Walter Thompson Co.
Advertising with a basic
idea
More for the money
Stability based on progress
Jabsco Pump Co.
The pump with the flexible
impeller
The pump with the rubber
impeller

Jack. See also: Jax
Jack Daniel's whiskey
Charcoal mellowed drop by
drop
The Jack for Jill
Weed Chain-Jack
Jack of all trades and master of
plenty
Hand-ee Tool
Jack Tar Togs
Rub 'em, tub 'em, scrub
'em, they come up
smiling
The jack that saves your back
American Chain Co.
Rees jack
The Jackrabbit
Apperson automobile
Jackson. See also:
Edwin Jackson, Inc.
Wm. H. Jackson Co.
Jackson China Co.
Know the best by this mark
Jackson 4-wheel drive trucks
No hill too steep, no sand
too deep
Jackson-Sheridan Fuel Co.
Intense heat
Jacob Hornung Brewing Co.
The beer that wins awards
The best beer by far at
home, club or bar
Jacquard. See: AM Jacquard
Systems
Jaguar automobile
A blending of art and
machine
The best Jaguar ever built
More than just a beautiful
car
A jam is easy to fix, but you
seldom have to
Kodak photocopiers
Jamaica's legendary liqueur
Tia Maria liqueur
James. See also: Fred S.
James & Co., Inc.
James automatic clock
It remembers so YOU can
forget
James B. Lansing Sound, Inc.
Discover what sound is all
about
World renowned for perfec-
tion in sound
James Bros. salt water taffy

Cut to fit the mouth
James Clark Distilling Corp.
    Drink moderately, insist
        on quality
Jas. H. Matthews and Co.
    See: Industrial Market-
        ing Div., Jas. H.
        Matthews and Co.
James Lees and Sons Co.
    Those heavenly carpets by
        Lees
James Means' $3 shoe
    Absolutely without a rival
James Montgomery Flagg. See:
    World War I recruiting
        poster drawn by James
        Montgomery Flagg
Jameson. World's largest selling
        Irish whiskey
    Jameson Irish whiskey
Jameson Irish whiskey
    Jameson. World's largest
        selling Irish whiskey
    Not a drop is sold till it's
        seven years old
Jamestown Panel Co.
    They last forever
Jan suntan oil
    Tan with Jan
Jane Amherst Food Products
    From Oregon mountain
        meadows
    From western mountain
        meadows
Jane Parker Fruit Cake
    'Twas the bite before
        Christmas
Jane Parker Rolls
    Cinnamon spice and every-
        thing nice, that's what
        these rolls are made of
Jane's. See: Aunt Jane's
        Pickles
Janitrol Div., Midland-Ross
        Corp.
    Janitrol gives you more to
        work with
Janitrol gives you more to work
        with
    Janitrol Div., Midland-
        Ross Corp.
Jantzen bathing suits
    Come on, you sunners
    Just wear a smile and a
        Jantzen
    To trim you, slim you, to

give you more swing,
        more zing, for Spring
Jantzen, Inc.
    Sportswear for sportsmen
Japan Air Lines
    The calm beauty of Japan at
        almost the speed of
        sound
Jarcons Bros. scales
    Watches your weight
Jardin de Rose
    The French face powder
        made in America
Jarman shoes
    Behind the fame of the Jar-
        man name is a finer
        shoe for you
    Friendly to the fact
    Try on a pair of Jarmans
        today, let the shoe
        horn be the judge
    Until Friendly Fives were
        made, good shoes were
        expensive
    Wear tested for your com-
        fort
Jartran Truck Rental
    The professional moving
        system for the amateur
        mover
Jax. See also: Jack
Jax beer
    The beer of friendship
    The drink of friendship
    The friendship beers
Jay. See also: J
Jay McShann's jazz band
    The band that jumps the
        blues
Jaynell radio speaker
    The speaker that speaks for
        itself
Jay's potato chips
    It's not easy, being Number
        1
    A pip of a chip
    Sing out for Jay's, a pip
        of a chip
Jean R. Graef, Inc.
    Fine watchmakers since
        1791
Jeep automobile
    Drive a jeep
    The "unstoppables"
    Why drive a car?
    Work horse of the world

The Jeffrey Mfg. Co.
  If it's conveyed, processed
    or mined, it's a job for
    Jeffrey
Jell-O gelatin dessert
  America's most famous des-
    sert
  Extra-rich fruit flavor
  A favorite dessert for over
    40 years
  Six delicious flavors--
    strawberry, raspberry,
    cherry, orange, lemon
    and lime
  Tastes twice as good as
    ever before
Jemima. See:
  Aunt Jemima Pancake Flour
  Aunt Jemima pancakes and
    syrup
Jenkins Bros.
  Most trusted trademark in
    the valve world
Jenkins valves
  Made for lifetime service
Jenn-Air Corp.
  America's finest cooking
    centers
  So beautifully practical
Jenny Wren Co.
  The flour of a thousand
    uses
  Jenny Wren Ready-Mixed
    Flour, it simplifies
    baking
Jenny Wren Ready-Mixed Flour,
  it simplifies baking
  Jenny Wren Co.
Jergens. See also: Dick Jur-
    gens' dance orchestra
Jergens Face Powder
  More manpower to you,
    sweet siren you
Jergens Lotion
  For the softest adorable
    hands
  "Kiss me" skin
  The losing hand in the
    game of love is a
    chapped one
  The skin you love to touch
  Touch his heart with
    smooth, soft hands
Jeris hair tonic
  To grow healthy hair, keep
    your scalp clean

Jersey bathing suits
  Full tights for bathing
Jersey City has everything for
    industry
  Jersey City, N. J.
Jersey City, N. J.
  Jersey City has everything
    for industry
Jersey Maid Ice Cream Co.
  You'll fall in love with Jer-
    sey Maid
Jersild Knitting Co.
  Knitted sportswear from
    Wisconsin's sportsland
Jervis B. Webb Company
  Custom engineered convey-
    ing systems for every
    industry since 1919
Jest Alkalizer
  Laugh it off with a "Jest"
Jet action washers
  Frigidaire Div., General
    Motors Corporation
Jet American Airlines
  The best buy in the sky
  Sorry, all you other air-
    lines. We just beat
    you to it. Again
Jet Oil. See: Bixby's Jet Oil
    shoe polish
Jet that bug
  Airosol insecticide
The jet that justifies itself
  North American Rockwell
    Corp.
The jet with the extra engine
  Western Air Lines, Inc.
Jettick. See: Enna Jettick
    shoes
Jewel Amusement Park
  The friend of the family for
    fifty years
Jewel Grady supermarkets
  Friend of the family for
    over fifty years
The jewel of patent leather
  Lawrence Leather Co.
The jewel of perfumes
  Ybry perfume
Jewel Paint & Varnish Co.
  Between wood and weather
  Right on the floor
  There's a Jewel for every
    use
Jewel Tea Co., Inc.
  Always fresh

243

The jeweler's quality watch
Vantage Products, Inc.
Jewelers since 1837
C. D. Peacock
Jewell Heat Regulator
Keeps heat just right both
day and night
Jewelry for the home
Greene Bros., Inc.
Jewelry for years to come
Speidel Corp. watch bands
Jewelry Industry Council
Something from the jewel-
er's is always something
special
Jewelry of tradition for the con-
temporary man
Swank jewelry
Jewels of Pen-dom
Parker 51 Pen
The jewels of your car
Bock Bearing Co.
Jewett New Era water cooler
The only cooler for milk,
lemonade, mead and all
summer drinks
Jewett superspeaker radio loud-
speaker
The horn with the "Why"
There is no substitute for
the best
The Jewish market at its best
Workmen's Circle Call
Jif peanut butter
Choosy mothers choose Jif
Jif soap flakes
Cleans in a jiff
Suds in a jiffy
Jim Beam whiskey
The world's finest bourbon
since 1795
Jimmie Grier's dance orchestra
The host to the Coast
Jobbers Overall Co.
Strong for wear
Strong for work
Jockey Menswear Div., Cooper's,
Inc.
It's not Jockey brand if it
doesn't have the Jockey
boy
There is only one Jockey
Joe. See:
Big Joe Mfg. Co.
Lazy Joe Casuals Shoes
Johansen Bros. Shoe Co.

More than mere economy,
more than sheer economy
John. See also: Mr. John
John A. Lane
Advertising that makes sense
makes dollars
John Blue Co., Inc.
Since 1886 ... scientifically
designed for practical
use
John Deere on the move
Deere & Co.
John H. Breck, Inc.
Beautiful hair
John Hancock Variable Life In-
surance Co.
We help you here and now.
Not just hereafter
John Lees frames and mouldings
John Lees keeps you in
trim
John Lees keeps you in trim
John Lees frames and
mouldings
John Martin's Book
The child's magazine
John Nuveen & Co., Inc.
It's more than what you
earn. It's what you
keep that counts
The national municipal bond
specialist
Nobody knows municipal
bonds like Nuveen
John Robert Powers Products
Co.
For women whose eyes are
older than they are
John Royle and Sons
Pioneered the continuous
extrusion process in
1880
John Sexton Co.
Good food for pleased guests
Quality foods
John Silver's. See: Long John
Silver's seafood restaur-
ants
John Widdicomb Co.
For more than a century
makers of fine furniture
in traditional and mod-
ern idiom
Johnnie Walker Black Label
Scotch whiskey
No matter how you give

Johnnie Walker Black,
it's impressive
Johnnie Walker Red Label Scotch
whiskey
Born 1820 ... still going
strong!
Festive evenings often start
with Red
Just smooth, very smooth
The right Scotch when all
is said and done
Johnny Carson. See: Tonight
show, featuring Johnny
Carson
John's. See also: Father
John's Medicine
Johns-Manville Corporation
Clear and colder, says the
weatherman; Snug and
warmer says Johns-Man-
ville
First in insulations
Ideas to build on
One of the many quality
home improvement prod-
ucts made by J. M.
Serves in conservation
There is one best in every-
thing
When you think of asbestos,
think of Johns-Manville
Johns-Manville Corporation. See
also: Manville Corp.
Johnson. See also:
E. A. Johnston Co.
E. F. Johnson Co.
Howard Johnson Co.
Iver-Johnson Arms & Cycle
Works
Johnston's Chocolates
Nestor Johnson ice skates
S. C. Johnson & Son
Johnson & Higgins
J and H sets the standard
in world-wide insurance
brokerage service
The private insurance brok-
er. We answer only to
you
Johnson & Johnson
The best aid is first aid
The first name in first aid
Next to safety, first aid
Quality is paramount to
price
Johnson & Murphy shoe

The shoe with a memory
Johnson Controls, Inc.
Managing energy, comfort
and protection
The total controls company
Johnson indicator lights
A famous name in radio
Johnson Iron Horse gas engine
Portable pony power
Johnson Motors Div., Outboard
Marine Co.
Another carefree Johnson
Balanced construction means
durability
First in dependability
Johnson Oil Burner
Built like a watch
Johnson, Read & Co.
Built on bedrock
Johnson Reels, Inc.
First on famous waters
Johnson sea-horse motor
World-wide favorite
Johnson sea-worthy boats
Precision-built, water-tight
Johnson tire lock
On every spare a Johnson
Lock to keep it there
Johnson Vacu-Draft heater
Modernized heating
Johnson's baby lotion
New! Hospitals prove it's
better
Johnson's baby powder
Be as soft as you can be
Best for baby, best for you
Johnson's Pie Co. Div., Ward
Foods, Inc.
Not just good ... but won-
derful
Johnson's self-shining shoe polish
The shine won't crack off
Johnson's wax
Let's begin with the finish
Self-polishing wax
Wax makes housework click
like clockwork
Johnston. See:
E. A. Johnston Co.
Johnson
Johnston's
Johnston's Chocolates
The appreciated chocolates
Join the knit parade
Bates knitting needles
Join the regulars

245

Ex-Lax laxative
Join the "regulars" with Kellogg's All-Bran
Kellogg's All-Bran
Join with Bostik for better bonding
    B. B. Chemical Div., United Shoe Machinery Corp.
Joint Coffee Trade Publicity Committee
    Coffee, the American drink
Joint Security Corp.
    Buying for profit and income
    Buying for profit and investment
"The Joker's Wild" television quiz program
    No TV game comes close to this one!
Jolly cabs
    Wherever you go, go Jolly
Jolly Time popcorn
    Eat more Jolly Time popcorn
Jonathan Logan. See: Harbor Master, Ltd., Div. Jonathan Logan
Jonathan Western boots
    The finest handmade and exotic Western boots for men and women
Jones. See also: Paul Jones whiskey
Jones Dairy Farm
    Most little pigs go to market but the best little pigs go to Jones
    Real farm sausage from a real Wisconsin farm
Jones, he pays the freight
    Jones scales
Jones scales
    Jones, he pays the freight
Jordan automobile
    The Suburban Seven
Jordan swim suits
    Delightfully see-worthy
    Develops a beautiful line
Jordan-Williams shoes
    Styled for comfort
The Journal covers Dixie like the dew
    Atlanta Journal
A journal for all who write
    Writer's Monthly

The journal of diagnosis and treatment
    Modern Medicine
Joy de Jean Patou
    The costliest perfume in the world
Joy dishwashing liquid
    A beautiful shine without a towel
    A lemon-fresh clean that shines
    Your everyday dishes don't look everyday
Joy Manufacturing Co.
    Machines at work around the world
    When all is said and done, service makes the difference
Joy Manufacturing Co. See also: Baash-Ross Div., Joy Manufacturing Co.
Juan. See: Don Juan Lipstick
Judge
    The happy medium
Judge for yourself
    London whiskey
    Murad cigarettes
Judge it by its users
    New Castle Leather Co.
Judge us by the agents who represent us
    Continental Group
Judged best by the just
    Barister cigars
Julian & Hokenge Co.
    Smart shoes for beautiful feet
Julian Messner, Inc.
    Messner biographies lead all the rest
Julius Wile Sons and Co., Inc.
    Let this seal be your guide to quality
Jumping Jacks
    Soft shoes for hard wear
June Arden Dress
    Fated to be dated
June Dairy Products Co.
    Always churned from sweet cream
    Country fresh
    Easy to spread, good to taste, economical to use
    For GOODness sake

Fresh as a daisy
No rind, no waste
Salted just right
Junior Achievement, Inc.
    A little pride will go a long,
      long way
    Teaching kids business is
      our business
Junket powder
    For smoother ice cream
    Makes milk into delicious
      desserts
Jurgens'. See:
    Dick Jurgens' dance orches-
      tra
    Jergens
Just a good laxative
    Espotabs laxative
Just a hammer to apply it
    Flexible Steel Lacing Co.
Just a little works up a good,
      rich lather
    Liqua 4 Skin Cleansing
      System
Just a minute, please
    Abilene Flour Mills
Just a real good car
    Durant automobile
Just a "shade" better
    Thorpe awnings
Just a smile, all the while
    Allen's Foot-Ease
Just add water, that's all
    Duff's ginger bread mix
Just another way of saying
      "versicherung"
    Chubb Group of Insurance
      Companies
Just as if you were there
    Borkman radio receiver
Just as you'd expect, right
      EVERY way
    Del Monte Coffee
Just enough!
    Montclair cigarettes
Just enough better to win
    Golden Ram golf ball
Just enough Turkish
    Fatima cigarettes
Just everyday things for the
      home made beautiful by
      Stevens
    J. P. Stevens and Co.,
      Inc.
Just for the sun of it
    T. S. Hanseatic German

Atlantic Line
Just form and fry
    Beardsley's codfish cakes
Just miles
    General Motors Corporation,
      Truck Division
Just plug in then tune in
    Standard batteryless radio
      receivers
Just pour it in and drink--it
      stirs itself
    Eno effervescent salt
Just right at night
    Hires' Improved Root Beer
Just rub in
    Cress Corn and Bunion
      Salves
Just rub it on
    Vick's Vapo-Rub
Just rub it on, inhale the vapors
    Vick's Vapo-Rub
Just rub it on the gums
    Dr. Hand's teething lotion
Just slightly ahead of our time
    Panasonic microcassette
      recorder
    Panasonic video systems
Just smooth, very smooth
    Johnnie Walker Red Label
      Scotch whiskey
Just spread it on
    Bixby's Jet Oil shoe polish
Just that much better
    Seagram's Distillers Corp.
Just the kiss of the hops
    Schlitz beer
Just the thing
    Q-tips cotton swabs
Just to show a proper glow
    Ingram's Rouge
Just wear a smile and a Jantzen
    Jantzen bathing suits
Just wet the pad and rub
    Magic scouring pad
Just what the name signifies
    Cord Tire Corp.
Justice for genius
    American Society of Com-
      posers, Authors and
      Publishers
Justly famous
    Red Jacket Coal Sales Co.
Justrite is just right for your
      pets
    Justrite pet food
Justrite pet food

Justrite is just right for
    your pets
Juvenile Group Foundation
    Future business insurance
    Tomorrow's citizens
Juvenile Shoe Corp.
    The quality is higher than
        the price

-K-

K & M Kontrol motor valve
    It's an "open and shut"
        case
KC Baking Powder
    The power behind the dough
K-D Manufacturing Co.
    Make hard jobs easy
KMPC, the station of the stars
    Radio station KMPC, Bever-
        ly Hills, Calif.
K mart Stores
    Let K take care of you
    The saving place
K. Mikimoto, Inc.
    The originator of cultured
        pearls
Kabo brassiere
    Glamour for teen-age and
        queen age
Kabo corset
    Glamour for every figure
    Live mode corset
Kaffee. See also: Coffee
Kaffee Hag
    Coffee--95% of the caffeine
        removed
    The coffee that lets you
        sleep
    Healthful and good
    Saves your nerves
Kahlúa coffee liqueur
    Fine coffee liqueur ... from
        sunny Mexico
Kahn Tailoring Co.
    The kind of clothes gentle-
        men wear
Kahn's. See also: E. Kahn's
    Sons Co.
Kahn's department store
    The always busy store
Kahn's sausages
    Great meat makes great
        jumbo franks
Kaiser Aluminum and Chemical

Corp.
    For almost any product,
        aluminum makes it better
        and Kaiser Aluminum
        makes aluminum work
        best
Kaiser automobile
    The beauty and distinction
        of custom car styling
Kalak Water Co.
    Puts pep in your step
    There is no substitute
        for Kalak
Kalamazoo, direct to you
    Kalamazoo Stove Co.
Kalamazoo Stove Co.
    Kalamazoo, direct to you
Kampkook
    The ideal camp stove
Kansas City Kansan
    For you and your town
Kansas City Post
    Published in the heart of
        America: most prosper-
        ous district of the world
    The truth without courting
        favor or fearing con-
        demnation
Kansas City Power and Light
    Company
    Tomorrow's energy since
        1882
Kansas City Star
    The Star is Kansas City
        and Kansas City is the
        Star
Kansas City's finest hotel at
    Kansas City's finest
        address
    Alameda Plaza Hotel, Kansas
        City, Mo.
A Kansas product from Kansas
    farms
    Butzer's bacon
Kaplan Wheel Co.
    One bolt turns the trick
Karastan Rug Mills Div., Field
    Crest Mills, Inc.
    America's finest power-
        loomed rug
    The wonder rug of America
Karastan Rug Mills Div., Field
    Crest Mills, Inc.
    See also: Field Crest
    Mills, Inc.
Karat gold jewelry

Nothing feels like giving
real gold
Kardon. See: Harmon Kardon,
Inc.
Karges Furniture Co.
Fine cabinetmakers since
1886
Karl. See also: Carl
Karl Seeger
Known the world over as
the world's best
Karo Syrup
Even beginners can now
put up "Jewels in Jars"
Karpen furniture
Ask for Karpen furniture,
find the nameplate be-
fore you buy
Karriall trailers
Vacation where you please
Karry. See also: Carry
Karry-Lite luggage
Takes the "lug" out of lug-
gage
Kasko Distillers Corp.
Best buy in rye
Hale and hearty
Kasko dog food
I'm holding out for Kasko
Kasko feeds
Keep all farm stock well fed
Kast-Iron Work Clothes
Work clothes that fit and
look like dress clothes
Kate Smith radio greeting
Hello, everybody!
Katz. See: Samuel Katz
Kaufman Hats, Inc.
World's largest retailer of
hats
Kawai piano
The master builder
Kay Musical Instrument Co.
More music for the money
Kaye's. See: Sammy Kaye's
dance orchestra
Kayser hosiery and underwear
Be wiser, buy Kayser
For good and FITTING
reasons
Wear Kayser, you owe it
to your friends
Kayser night gowns
Lush loops of lovely lace
Kaywoodie defies the thermome-
ter

Kaywoodie pipe
The Kaywoodie flavor
Kaywoodie pipe
Kaywoodie pipe
A classic in wood
Graduate to Kaywoodie
Kaywoodie defies the ther-
mometer
The Kaywoodie flavor
The last word in pipes
A man is known by his Kay-
woodie
One of the good things in
life
The pipe that everybody
knows
Six good companions
Sweeter as the years go by
You can't get a drink from
a drinkless Kaywoodie
Keds
Cool shoes for hot days
The shoe of champions
Washable shoes
Keekin cans
Tin keeps it better
Keene. See also: Tom Keene
cigar
Keene Corporation
We're finding new growth
in some of America's
newer growth fields
We've just begun to grow
Keener Rubber, Inc.
The name indicates the
quality
Keep a cupboard full of cans
National Steel Corp.
Keep a date with summer this
winter
Greyhound Corporation
Keep all farm stock well fed
Kasko feeds
Keep on saving as you drive
Texaco, Inc.
Keep cold away with Magnavox
Magnavox heaters
Keep cool with the cow, drink
milk
Borden's condensed milk
Keep Dura-Gloss always on hand
Dura-Gloss lotion
Keep 'em cozy with Mortite
Mortite window weatherstrip
Keep 'em pretty
Dura-Gloss lotion

Keep fighting, keep working,
keep singing, America
E. R. Squibb
Keep going with Pep
Kellogg's Pep-Bran Flakes
Keep good feet healthy
Gilbert Shoe Co.
Keep hair-conditioned
The Nawa Company
Keep healthy, be examined regu-
larly
Metropolitan Life Insurance
Co.
Keep heat where it belongs
Mason Fibre Co.
Keep in step with Paris
Paris shoes
Keep in step with youth
Burdett shoes
Keep in touch with Prospect
Prospect foundations
Keep it clean with Energene
Energene
Keep it handy
Sloan's Liniment
Keep it under your hat
Lan-O-Tone hair cream
Lan-O-Tone shampoo
Keep kissable with Flame-Glo
Lipstick
Flame-Glo Lipstick
Keep-Kool suit
The national summer suit
for men
Keep mechanics good tempered
Velchek Tool Co.
Keep on saving as you drive
Texaco, Inc.
Keep on the ball with Sun Ball
juices
Sun Ball fruit juices
Keep regular
Ex-Lax laxative
Keep regular as clockwork with
Nujol
Nujol laxative
Keep regular this healthful way
Sunkist lemons
Keep regular with Ex-Lax
Ex-Lax laxative
Keep singing, keep working,
America
E. R. Squibb
Keep singing, keep working,
keep fighting, America
E. R. Squibb

Keep smiling with Kellys
Kelly-Springfield Tire Co.
Keep that schoolgirl complexion
Palmolive soap
Keep that "youthful" look with
Safe-T cones
Illinois Baking Corp.
Keep the car on the go
Reflex Ignition Co.
Keep the foot well
Arch Preserver Shoe
Keep the home fires burning, but
not the toast
Toastmaster toaster
Keep the home tires turning
Esso Retread Tires
Vulcanizers Material Co.
Keep the weather out
Ceco Weatherstrip Co.
Keep time off your face
Luxuria Face Cream
Keep working, keep singing,
America
E. R. Squibb
Keep young feet young
Simplex shoes
Keep your bob at its best
Marcus-Lesoine bobbie pin
Keep your boy out of danger!
American Boy
Keep your cans on wheels
Nutting Truck Co.
Keep your car beautiful always
Raynorshyne
Keep your eye on DKI
Dart & Kraft
Keep your eye on Elliott
Elliott Div., Carrier Cor-
poration
Keep your eye on Maidenform
Maidenform brassieres
Keep your eye on Troster
Troster Singer Stevens
Rothchild Corp. stock
brokers
Keep your feet dry
Miner rubbers
Keep your feet young
Simplex shoes
Keep your floors beautiful always
Raynorshyne
Keep your foot fresh
Massagic Air Cushion shoes
Keep your furniture beautiful
always
Raynorshyne

Keep your hands youthful
Ammonite
Keep your health in tune
Harmony vitamins
Keep your leather goods beautiful always
Raynorshyne
Keep your motor young
Motor Rhythm lubricating oil
Keep your patrons from getting it in the neck
Bobit barber's towels
Keep your shoes beautiful always
Raynorshyne
Keep your vitality up. Drink Horlick's
Horlick's Malted Milk Corp.
Keepers of the light
Soft Lite Lens Co.
Keeping radio in its place
Windsor loudspeaker console
Keeping the power in your hands
Detroit Edison utility
Keeping tradition alive
Meldan Co., Inc.
Keeps aluminum bright
Brillo Cleanser
Keeps America on time
Big Ben Westclox alarm clock
Keeps breath pure and sweet 1 to 2 hours longer
Pepsodent antiseptic
Keeps car new
Simoniz
Keeps cars younger longer
MacMillan Lubricating Oil
Keeps children's feet as nature made them
Shaft-Pierce Shoe Co.
Keeps cows contented from sunrise to sunset
Usol Fly Spray
Keeps food out, dentures in
Poli-grip denture cream
Keeps food pure and sweet
White Frost refrigerators
Keeps grease away from dishes
Dawn dishwashing liquid
Keeps hair better groomed without looking greasy
Kreml shampoo
Keeps heat just right both day and night
Jewell Heat Regulator

Keeps hot all night
M. H. P. Aluminum Hot Water Bottle
Keeps lips fit
Fleets chap stick
Keeps litter odors top secret
Top Secret pet disinfectant
Keeps mites out of hen houses for one year
Usol Mite Killer
Keeps plates and bridges odor-free
Polident denture cleaner
Keeps shirts smooth and trousers snug
Snugtex
Keeps step with the weather
Northern oil burner
Keeps the cops away
Kopp's lens
Keeps the foot well
Arch Preserver Shoe
Keeps the gums healthy
Pyorrhocide Powder
Keeps the hair in place
Hump hairpin
Stacomb hair dressing
Keeps the mouth glands young
Pebeco toothpaste
Keeps the shape
Pellon Corp.
Keeps the teeth white
Dentyne toothpaste
Keeps things to eat good to eat
Sunshine Ice Co.
Keeps white shoes cleaner longer
Esquire lanolin shoe cleaner
Keeps you fit!
The Battle Creek Health Builder
Keeps you hummin'
Wrigley's Spearmint Gum
Keeps you in form
Debu-Form girdles
Keeps you in hot water
Humphrey Co.
Keeps you nice to be near
Mum deodorant
Keeps YOU sparkling, too
White Rock club soda
Keeps you sweet as an angel
Neet deodorant
Keeps you vibrantly healthy
Vip medicine
Keeps you warm in your car
Arvin car heater

Keeps your engine clean
  Havoline motor oil
Keeps your entire system under
    your fingertips
  Metameter
Keeps your face fit
  Aqua Velva skin bracer
Keeps your hair healthy and
    handsome
  Vitalis hair tonic
Keeps your motor clean as a
    whistle
  Sinclair Oil Corp.
Keepsake Diamond Rings
  Lovely to look at, lovely to
    own
Keikhaefer Mercury Div., Bruns-
    wick Corp.
  First in marine propulsion
Keikhaefer Mercury Div., Bruns-
    wick Corp. See also:
    Brunswick Corp.
Keith Furnace Co.
  Always save money in the
    end
Keith Highlanders
  The proudest name in shoes
Kelbert watch
  Full measure of time
Keller. See: Helen Keller
    Centennial Fund
Kellermann. See: Annette
    Kellermann health
    studios
Kellogg Co.
  America's best-liked cereal
    assortment
  America's grandest cereal
    assortment
  The best to you each
    morning
  Help yourself to health
  Parade of the immortals
Kellogg's All-Bran
  Health without hazard
  Join the "regulars" with
    Kellogg's All-Bran
  The plus food for minus
    meals
  To keep happy, keep well
  Zest for breakfast, best
    for health
Kellogg's Krumbles
  The only whole-wheat food
    with a delicious flavor
  Whatever you do, eat

    Krumbles
  Whole wheat--ready to eat!
Kellogg's Pep-Bran Flakes
  Keep going with Pep
  The Peppy Bran Food
Kellogg's raisin bran
  It's gonna be a great day
Kellogg's Shredded Mini-Wheat
    cereal
  Shredded wheat that's fun
    to eat
Kellogg's Shredded Mini-Wheat
    cereal. See also:
    Shredded Wheat
Kellogg's Sugar Pops cereal
  Sugar Pops are tops
Kellogg's toasted corn flakes
  The original
  The original corn flakes
  The sweetheart of the corn
  Won its favor through its
    flavor
Kelly can do
  Kelly temporary office help
    services
Kelly cigar
  Measure yourself for a
    Kelly
The "Kelly girl" people
  Kelly temporary office help
    services
Kelly helps America work
  Kelly temporary office help
    services
Kelly-Springfield motor truck
  The big brother to the rail-
    roads
Kelly-Springfield Tire Co.
  It costs no more to buy a
    Kelly
  Keep smiling with Kellys
  New dimensions in driving
    on the safer Kelly road
  Proved and improved for 55
    years
  Tires with nine lives
  We're out to change Amer-
    ica's tires
Kelly temporary office help
    services
  Kelly can do
  The "Kelly girl" people
  Kelly helps America work
  100% guaranteed temporary
    office help
  One source, one standard

252

--nationwide

Kelsey-Hayes Co.
World's largest producer
of automotive wheels,
hubs and drums

Kelvination, cold that keeps
Kelvinator refrigerator

Kelvinator air conditioning
Air conditioning for profit

Kelvinator range
Set it and forget it

Kelvinator refrigerator
Better--always better
Built for connoisseurs of
refrigeration
Get more, get Kelvinator
Get the best things first,
get Kelvinator
Kelvination, cold that keeps
The oldest domestic refrig-
eration
The record is trouble-free
Set it and forget it
There is no substitute for
experience
To be opened at Christmas
and every day there-
after

Kem-Tone
The modern miracle wall
finish

Kemper Insurance Co.
You can count on Kemper
care under the Kemper
flag

Kempler. See: George J.
Kempler Co.

Kemp's. See also: Hal Kemp's
dance orchestra

Kemp's tomato sauce
Never thin or watery

Ken-L-Biskit
Dog food of champions
Help make him all the dog
he's meant to be

Ken-L-Ration
First in canned dog food

Ken-Rad radio tubes
Dependable long life

Kendall motor oil
The choice of champions
Protect your investment
with Kendall confidence
Road proven by millions of
motorists
Unsurpassed to help motors

last
Unsurpassed to help your car
last

Kenilworth Inn, Asheville, N. C.
The home of hospitality

Kennedy radio receiver
The royalty of radio

Kennel. See:
Ken-L-Biskit
Ken-L-Ration

Kenneth Smith
Hand made to fit you

Kenney Needle Shower
A Millionaire's Luxury

Kent. See also: Percy Kent
bags

Kent brushes
Brush the cobwebs from
your beauty

Kent cigarettes
For the best combination of
filter and good taste
Kent satisfies best
The low tar that won't
leave you hungry for
taste
The one cigarette for
everyone who smokes!
Satisfies best

Kenton's. See: Stan Kenton's
dance orchestra

Kentucky
Come to Kentucky! It's a
profitable move!
Kentucky & Co.: The state
that's run like a busi-
ness
Where big things are hap-
pening

Kentucky & Co.: The state
that's run like a busi-
ness
Kentucky

Kentucky Fried Chicken
It's finger lickin' good
We do chicken right

Kentucky Rock Asphalt Co.
Kyrok, the perfect pave-
ment

Kentucky Tavern whiskey
For men who know fine
whiskies
It's straight whisky
The whiskey of the gour-
met

Kenwood Blankets

253

Sleep under a Kenwood for
the rest of your life
Kenwood Electronics, Inc.
The sound approach to
quality
Kepner Leather Co.
The leather that sells more
shoes
A Kermath always runs
Kermath trucks
Kermath trucks
A Kermath always runs
Kero-Sun portable heaters
We bring comfort to inner
space
Kerr Fruit Jar co.
Smile while you can, and
can while you smile
Kerr's butterscotch
As sweet as love songs
A sweet among sweets
Kessler's blended whiskey
Smooth as silk but not high
hat
Ketcham. See: Howard Ketcham
industrial designs
The key magazine of industry
Manufacturers News
The key to better grinding
The Black & Decker Mfg.
Co.
The key to happiness and suc-
cess in over a million
farm homes
Comfort Magazine
Keyboard of the nation
Kimball piano
Keyed to family harmony
7UP soft drink
Keyspray
Cleans, relusters and de-
moths upholstered furn-
iture
Removes the film of dirt
and smudge
Keystone Emery Mills
Relieves the daily grind
Unexcelled for grinding and
polishing
The keystone of your vacation
Pennsylvania
Keystone Steel & Wire Co.
Wire for industry
Kick. See also: Kix
Kick if you don't get the Gen-
eral Arthur cigar

General Arthur cigar
Kid. See also: Billy the Kid
slacks
Kid flatters the foot
Tanners Council of America
The "Kid Glove Treatment"
Evans Transportation Equip-
ment Div., Evans Prod-
ucts Co.
Kid tested ... Mother approved
Kix cereal
Kidder, Peabody & Co., Inc.
Kidder, Peabody thinks
twice
Kidder, Peabody thinks twice
Kidder, Peabody & Co., Inc.
Kidder Press Co.
Three point presses
Kiddie-Kar
Made in America for Ameri-
can boys and girls
Kiddies' feet are safe in Kinney's
hands
Kinney shoes
Kiel Furniture Co.
Enduring masterpieces
Kilgen organ
Choice of the masters
Kill lawn weeds without killing
grass
Weedone weed killer
Kills ants in the nest
Antrol
Kills fire, saves life
Pyrene fire extinguisher
Kills garden bugs dead. Natu-
rally
Raid tomato and vegetable
fogger
Kills moth worms
Expello
Kills pain
Sloan's Liniment
Kills them off and keeps them
off
Pulvex Flea Powder
Kimball. See also:
Kimble glass
Miles Kimball mail order
service
W. W. Kimball Co.
Kimball piano
Keyboard of the nation
Kimberly-Clark Corp.
A dynamic force with paper
Kimberly-Clark Corp. See

The better the yarn the
better the fabric
Kingston watch
In rhyme with time
Kinnear Corp.
Saving ways in doorways
since 1895
Kinney shoes
Fit for every foot
A foot nearer perfection
Kiddies' feet are safe in
Kinney's hands
Kino Petrol hair tonic
What we have we hold
Kinsey whiskey
The unhurried whiskey for
unhurried moments
Kirchner Moore & Company
You'll like our style
Kirgan's Arcadian Farms
Deliciously home-y
Kirstein glasses
Grace the face and stay in
place
Kirsten photo-electric cell
The wake tells the story
Kirsten Pipe Co.
America's most distinguished
cigarette holder
Look through and see
Thrill of a pipetime
"Kiss me" skin
Jergens Lotion
Kissable hands
Glessner cold cream
Kit Kat candy bar
The crispy chocolate bar
so good you'll roar
The kit that hands you money
Ad-Novelty Sales Co.
Kitchen Aid food mixer
The finest food preparer
for the home
Kitchen Bouquet
The chef's flavor in home
cooking
The kitchen cabinet that saves
miles of steps
Hoosier Mfg. Co.
Kitchen fresh
Kraft Foods Div., Kraftco
Corp.
Kitchen Klenzer
Hurts only dirt
Kitchen Kompact, Inc.
The best birch line

The kitchen people with different
ideas
I-X-L Co., Inc.
Kitchen tested utensils
Foley Mfg. Co.
KIX. See: Corn KIX cereal
Kix. See also: Kick
Kix cereal
Kid tested ... Mother ap-
proved
Klaxon. See also: Claxton's
Klaxon auto horn
Klaxon gets action
Klaxon gets action
Klaxon auto horn
Kleen. See also: Clean
Kleen Kup
The push-out bottom
Kleenex is softer
Kleenex tissue
Kleenex tissue
Comforting America's fam-
ilies for over 50 years
Don't put a cold in your
pocket
Kleenex is softer
The only tissue that pops
up
The sanitary cold cream re-
mover
She gave me bride ideas
Your best buy in tissue
Kleerex
The wonder-healing salve
Kleerfect paper
Both sides alike
Kind to your eyes
Kleinert Rubber Co.
Maker of fine rubber goods
for over fifty years
Oh, Kleinert's? OK!
Standard in rubber goods
for nearly half a cen-
tury
Klenzing. See also: Cleansing
Klenzing Emulsion
Adds magic to soap
Knabe piano
Acknowledged the world's
best piano
The knack that stops the nick
Bridell cleaver
Knape and Vogt Mfg. Co.
Ask for K-V ... it's a
known value!
Knapp and Tubbs, Inc.

America's oldest and
largest showroom dis-
tributor of fine decor-
ative furniture
Knickerbocker Grill, New York
City
The public be dined
Knight internal combustion engine
Improves with use
Knight Packing Co.
From the sunny Rogue River
Valley
Knight wallet
The thin man in leather
Knight-ware sinks
It is the body itself
Knit goods are only as good as
the yarn of which they
are made
Fleischer yarns
Knit to fit
Thom McAn socks
Knitted sportswear from Wiscon-
sin's sportsland
Jersild Knitting Co.
Knob. See: Nob Hill Coffee
The knock-out fuel, nox out
nox
Canfield Oil Co.
Knock out that "knock"
Ethyl gasoline
Knockdown bleachers
They rise to the occasion
Knocks. See also: Knox
Knocks one-third off your fuel
costs
Hamilton coke
Knorr soups
It's uncanny
The knowledge we put in your
head guides the skill
we put in your hands
Michigan State Automobile
School
Know the best by this mark
Jackson China Co.
Know them by the jet black
tread
Pennsylvania Tires
Knowing what it's worth can be
worth a lot
American Appraisal
The knowledge business
Bell Telephone System
Knowledgeable people buy
Imperial

Imperial whiskey
Known by the company it keeps
Seagram's V. O. whiskey
Known by the customers we keep
Sunray DX Oil Company
Known for extra care
United Air Lines, Inc.
Known for tone
Stradivara phonograph
Known for values
W. T. Grant Co.
Known in millions of homes
Nutone, Inc.
Known 'round the world for
quality in sporting
goods and tires
Dunlop Tire & Rubber Corp.
Known the world over as the
world's best
Karl Seeger
Knows no season
Hoenshel Fruit Cake
Knows the Pacific
Matson Navigation Co.
Knox. See also: Knocks
Knox Gelatine, Inc.
Highest quality for health
Start with--stay with Knox
Whenever a recipe calls for
gelatine, think of Knox
Knox hats
The hat corner of the world
Hats made so fine that all
others must be com-
pared to them
Knox Waterless Limousine
No water cooled car can
do this
KOBI Polyethylene Bag Mfg.
Co., Inc.
If it's a bag ... we make
it!
Koch Butcher's Supply Co.
The counter sign of quality
Kodak. See also: Cine Kodak
Kodak as you go
Kodak cameras
Kodak cameras
America's storyteller
The easy ones
Forever yours
The gift that really remem-
bers
Holidays are Kodak days
If it isn't an Eastman it
isn't a Kodak

It's Kodak for color
Kodak as you go
Kodak service: good training, good tools, good
 people
Kodak service pays off in
 performance
Make more of your time this
 year
A man with a family snap-
 shot in his pocket is
 never far from home
The more you learn about
 photography, the more
 you count on Kodak
New advances in office
 copying keep coming
 from Kodak
Only Eastman makes Kodak
 cameras
Only Eastman makes Kodak
 film, the film in the
 familiar yellow box
Only Eastman makes the
 Kodak
Only Eastman makes the
 Kodak camera
Serving human progress
 through photography
The snapshots you'll want
 tomorrow, you must
 take today
There is no Kodak but the
 Eastman Kodak
There's a picture ahead
Visit him in snapshots
Visit your man in the
 service with snapshots
You press the button, we
 do the rest
Kodak Carousel projectors
 The pro in Projectors
Kodak copiers keep uptime up
 Kodak photocopiers
Kodak Ektalith
 Puts you ahead in offset
 duplicating
Kodak photocopiers
 A jam is easy to fix, but
 you seldom have to
 Kodak copiers keep uptime
 up
 A 100-year start on tomor-
 row
Kodak photographic paper
 For a good look at the

times of your life
 Photos never forget
Kodak service: good training,
 good tools, good people
 Kodak cameras
Kodak service pays off in per-
 formance
 Kodak cameras
Kodel radio receiver
 The emblem of worth in
 radio
 Install it, forget it
Kodiak chewing tobacco
 A new adventure in smoke-
 less tobacco
Koehler Motors Corp.
 The line of least resistance
Koehring Co. See: Prodex
 Div., Koehring Co.
Koh-I-Noor Pencil Co.
 The perfect pencil
Kohler. See also:
 Cohler pajamas
 Peter Cailler Kohler Swiss
 Chocolate Co.
Kohler and Campbell, Inc.
 Heirloom quality pianos
 since 1896
Koehler truck
 The land tug boat
Kokan. See: Nippon Kokan
Kolynos dental cream
 The antiseptic dental cream
 It's good for your teeth
 Teeth whiten 3 shades in 3
 days
Kommon-Sense Pan Racks
 Built for permanence
Kommon-Sense Pan Racks. See
 also: Common sense
 about the common cold
Krushen Salts
 It's the little daily dose
 that does it
Kool. See also: Cool
Kool-Aid soft drink mix
 Base for soft drinks and
 desserts
 The one for kids
Kool cigarettes
 Come up to the Kool taste
 Discover extra coolness
 The password is Kools
 There's only one way to
 play it
Koolfoam pillows

258

Enjoy the rest of your life
Kopp Glass, Inc.
　　Unusual reliability and serv-
　　　ice ... the usual at
　　　Kopp Glass
Kopper. See also: Copper
Kopper Gas & Coke Co.
　　Laugh at winter
Koppers Co., Inc.
　　Check with Koppers
　　Modern fuel for modern
　　　heating
　　We're careful of your com-
　　　fort
Kopp's lens
　　Keeps the cops away
Kork. See also: Cork
Kork-N-Seal Closure
　　The cap with the handy
　　　lever
Korker soft drink
　　A corking good drink
Koroseal fabric
　　It's better because it's
　　　made of Koroseal
　　It's "curtains" for dirt
　　　when your curtains
　　　are Koroseal
Koroseal raincoat
　　A miracle in the rain
Kotex sanitary napkins
　　Be confident, comfortable,
　　　carefree
　　Cheap enough to throw
　　　away
　　A deodorant in every Kotex
　　　napkin at no extra
　　　cost
　　Inexpensive, comfortable,
　　　hygienic and safe
　　Not a shadow of a doubt
Kounty Kist Peas
　　Sweet as a kiss, honest as
　　　Mother Earth
Koveralls
　　Don't forget that Koveralls
　　　keep kids klean
Koverslak varnish
　　It has no pernicious odor
Koylon fabric
　　Comfort engineered
Koylon mattress
　　The modern mattress
Kozy. See also: Cozy
Kozy Komfort slippers
　　Slippers of merit

Kraft Foods Div., Kraftco Corp.
　　All fresh-fruit good!
　　The finest of natural
　　　cheeses--naturally from
　　　Kraft
　　The first hands to touch it
　　　are yours
　　For good food and good food
　　　ideas
　　The good kind to keep
　　　handy--because they
　　　stay soft
　　It slices, it cooks, it keeps
　　The kind you cook up fresh
　　　--and quick
　　Kitchen fresh
　　Pasteurized for purity
　　The quick kind you cook
　　　up fresh
Kreisler Watch Band
　　Neatest trick up your
　　　sleeve
Kreisler Watch Band. See also:
　　Chrysler
Kreml shampoo
　　For silken-sheen hair easier
　　　to arrange
　　For silken-sheen hair easy
　　　to arrange
　　The hairs on your head are
　　　numbered
　　He has "hayfield" hair
　　How to ring a wedding belle
　　Keeps hair better groomed
　　　without looking greasy
　　Relieves itching of dry scalp
Kreolite floors
　　Outlast the factory
　　The paving that's saving
Kresky oil burners
　　Nearest thing to trouble-
　　　proof
Kriss Kross Blades
　　Like the cool side of a pil-
　　　low on a hot night
Kroch's & Brentano's
　　The full service bookstores
Kroehler Mfg. Co.
　　One name in furniture every-
　　　body knows
　　A world of furniture made
　　　in a way that makes a
　　　world of difference
　　The world's largest makers
　　　of furniture
Kroger. See also: Krueger

Kroger supermarkets
Cleveland's better food
markets
For the best of everything
including the price let's
go Krogering
Let's go Krogering
Kroydon Golf Corp.
Hottest name in golf
Krucraft Leather Co.
Works of art in leather
Krueger. See also: Kroger
Krueger beer
The beer with a head of its
own
Experts pronounce it beer
It's one of the three great
beers
Naturally a better brew
Taste how rootie it is
Krueger Metal Products Co.
Another fine creation by
Krueger
Krugerrand coin jewelry
It makes graduation day a
golden occasion
Krugerrand gold coins
The world's best way to
own gold
The world's most popular
gold coin
Krupp. A tradition of progress
Krupp International, Inc.
Krupp International, Inc.
Krupp. A tradition of
progress
Kruschen salts
That Kruschen feeling
Krylon spray paint
For a smooth, fast, profes-
sional finish
If you prize it ... Krylon-
ize it
No runs--no drips--no
errors
Kryptar Corp.
All-purpose film
Kuehnle-Wilson paint
Don't put it off, put it on
Kuppenheimer clothes
An investment in good ap-
pearance
Kurtsmann piano
Craftsmen built the Kurts-
mann
Kwik. See also:

Quick
Quik
Kwik-Way Brake Service Centers
Engineered for the ultimate
in precision
Kwikset Div., Emhart Corp.
America's largest selling
residential locksets
Kyanize paints
The life of the surface
Simply brush it on
Kyrok, the perfect pavement
Kentucky Rock Asphalt Co.

-L-

L. A. Liebs Co.
If it's a candy wrapper, we
make it
L & H Stern Co.
The pipe of distinction
Smoke all you like, like all
you smoke
L. & L. Travel Agency
The easy way to turn
LHS pipes
For solid comfort
L.S.M.F.P. See: Lead soaps
mean fine paint
(L.S.M.F.P.)
LS/MFT. See: Lucky Strike
means fine tobacco
(LS/MFT)
L. W. Hall Co.
Splendid nursery stock of
all kinds
LaBarge Mirrors, Inc.
The look of quality
La Belle Iron Works
From mine to market
La Choy Chinese food
The Chinese food that
swings Americans
La Choy chow mein
The more you buy, the
more you save!
La Fendrich cigar
Double-value cigar that
guarantees more satis-
faction
La France Bluing
Blues automatically as you
wash
La France Hosiery
The stocking beautiful

260

La grande liqueur francaise
DOM Benedictine
La Mode foundations
There's magic in La Mode
La Primadora cigars
Product of Cuban soil and
Cuban sun
La Resista corset
Hold the bustline and you
hold youth
La Salle Coke Co.
Warmth without waste
La Salle Extension University
The world's largest business
training institute
La Salle Securities, Inc.
For fast, reliable trades,
just dial the letters
L.A.S.A.L.L.E.
La Salle St. Press, Inc.
No. 1 in financial printing
since 1775
La Trique brassiere
Perfect fit not only in the
cup, but all around the
torso
La Vor jelly
Seven cents a glass
A label approved by New Yorkers
Browning King men's wear
The label of quality knitting in
sportswear and under-
wear
Hanes underwear
The label to ask for
Davidow Suits, Inc.
The label to take home
Gordon hosiery
Labels of character
Atlas Label Co.
Laboratory accuracy at a tool-
room price
Hoke gauges
Lace papers of character
Milwaukee Lace Paper Co.
Laclede Steel Co.
Producers of quality steel
for industry and con-
struction
The lacquer finish that stays
new
Zapon lacquer finish
Ladd ocarina
In tune with a tune
Ladies and gentlemen smoke
Ateshain Turkish

Cigarrets
Ateshian Turkish Cigarrets
Ladies Home Journal
The magazine women believe
in
Never underestimate the
power of a woman
Ladish Drop Forge Co.
Where quality counts most
Wherever quality counts
most
Wherever reliability counts
most
Lady Baltimore luggage
America's greatest luggage
value
Fashion luggage
Lady Borden ice cream
Fit for a golden spoon
Lady Borden ice cream. See
also: Borden, Inc.
Lady Esther face powder
The wrong shade of powder
can turn the right man
away
Lady Remington electric shaver
The perfect gift for her
A lady to her gloved finger tips
Bacmo gloves
The lady with a line
Gossard girdles
Lady's Choice deodorant
Make your choice Lady's
Choice
Lake Central Airlines, Inc.
We pamper passengers
throughout mid-central
U. S. A.
Lakeland Sportswear
The campus king
Protects you handsomely
Läkerol
The gourmet breath mint
There are breath mints and
there's Läkerol
Lamar Life Insurance Co.
The tower of strength in
Dixie
Lambert radio invites you to rest
Lambert radio receiver
Lambert radio receiver
Lambert radio invites you to
rest
Laminex doors
Will not shrink, swell or
warp

The lamp that chases gloom
and glare
Silverglo lamps
The lamp with the 1500-hour
guarantee
Solex lamp
Lampe Shoe Co.
In step with fashion
Lamps for see-ability
Westinghouse Electric Corp.
Lamps of elegance
Frederick Cooper Lamps,
Inc.
Lan-O-Tone hair cream
Keep it under your hat
Lan-O-Tone shampoo
Keep it under your hat
Lancaster tires
One of America's best
Land o' Lakes butter
Churned from sweet (not
sour) cream
Lane. See: John A. Lane
Lana Oil Soap
Your skin knows and shows
the difference
Lanacane skin lotion
For all kinds of itching
The land of elbow room and el-
bow grease
Omaha Public Power Dis-
trict
Land of enchantment
New Mexico Dept. of De-
velopment
The land that was made for
vacations
Wisconsin Vacation and
Travel Service
The land tug boat
Koehler truck
Landers household accessories
Better meals by the minute
A household help for every
home need
Landmark for hungry Americans
Howard Johnson Co.
Lane Bryant stores
Stout women dress fashion-
ably--look slender
Lang. See: Gerhard Lang
Brewery
Langenberg Hat Co.
The right hat for real men
Langendorf, bakers of America's
finest bread

Langendorf United Bakeries
Langendorf Bread, thoro-baked
Langendorf United Bakeries
Langendorf cakes, like homemade
Langendorf United Bakeries
Langendorf United Bakeries
America's finest bread
Bakers of America's finest
bread
The finest bread in America
Langendorf, bakers of Amer-
ica's finest bread
Langendorf Bread, thoro-
baked
Langendorf cakes, like
homemade
Langrock Clothing Co.
The finest human hands can
achieve
Languid splendour set to frag-
rance
Lentheric perfume
Lanier Business Products, Inc.
Get a lot more done in a lot
less time
We've matched our strengths
to your needs
Lanier "thought processing"
recorders
Move ahead at the speed of
sound
Lanier typewriter
The no-problem typewriter.
It does more than just
type
We make your good people
even better
Lansing. See: James B. Lans-
ing Sound, Inc.
Lanson champagne
The highest standard of
quality
Lanston. See: Aubrey G.
Lanston & Co., Inc.
The lantern with the blue porce-
lain top
American Gas Machine Co.
The largest Catholic magazine
in the world
Columbia
Largest circulation of any paper
in America
National Enquirer
Largest daily circulation in Brook-
lyn of any Brooklyn
newspaper

Brooklyn Standard Union
The largest evening circulation
in America
New York Evening Journal
The largest immediate delivery
fur house
Samuel Katz
Largest in the northwest
Curtis Hotel, Minneapolis,
Minn.
The largest in the world
Blimp Chewing Gum
Largest in the world because we
serve the people best
United Cigar Stores
The largest magazine for men
Elks Magazine
Largest makers in the world of
fine clothing for men
Hart Schaffner & Marx men's
clothing
Largest manufacturer of shotguns
in the world
Savage Arms Div., Emhart
Corp.
The largest monogram house in
the world
Monocraft
Largest morning and Sunday cir-
culation in Ohio
Cleveland Plain Dealer
Largest morning and Sunday cir-
culation west of St.
Louis
Los Angeles Examiner
The largest multiple life organi-
zation in the world
The Travelers Insurance
Cos.
Largest paid net circulation in
the textile field
Textile World
The largest plate makers in the
world
Rapid Electrotypes
Largest railway system in Amer-
ica
Canadian National Railway
Largest selling pain reliever
Anacin
The largest-selling transformer
in the world
All-American Radio Corp.
Largest vehicle manufacturers
in the world
Studebaker automobile

Lark luggage
Custom made luggage
Larkwood hosiery
You'll love the look of your
leg in Larkwood
Larro, the safe ration for dairy
cows
Larrowe Milling Co.
Larrowe Milling Co.
Feeds that never vary
Larro, the safe ration for
dairy cows
Larvex
Forget the moth; save the
cloth
Treat the cloth and starve
the moth
LaSalle and Cadillac automobiles
The royal family of motor-
dom
LaSalle automobile
For looks, luxury and low
cost
Lasso fertilizer
You can see the difference
at harvest
Lassus Bros. retail gasoline
stations
Your hometown oil company
We care about you
The last fits, the fit lasts
Goding shoe
Stacy Adams shoe
Last longer, crank faster, don't
let you down
Willard battery
The last of the great shirtmakers
Sero Shirtmakers
The last spoonful is as fresh as
the first
Coolwhip topping
The last word in auto wax
Puritan Soap Co.
The last word in fine leather
luggage
Edward Freeman
The last word in gifts for men
Courtley toiletries
The last word in pipes
Kaywoodie pipe
The last word in sea food
Oyster Growers & Dealers
Assn.
Lastex
The miracle yarn
The miracle yarn that makes

things fit
Lastex swim suit
   Shows good form in the
      stretch
Lasticraft foundations
   For youthful figures of all
      ages
Lasting impressions begin with
      Oxford papers
   Oxford Paper Co.
Lasting loveliness
   Sapphire hosiery
Lasting symbol of esteem
   Chilton pen
A lasting tribute of modern
      interment
   Sozonian metal vaults
Lasting until everlasting
   Granite Mfrs. Assn.
Latchford Glass Co.
   A famous brand in glass
The latest words in communica-
      tions: Rockwell-Collins
   Rockwell-Collins Communica-
      tions Systems
Latrobe Steel Company
   The specialty steel company
Latterman Shoe Mfg. Co.
   Footwear for all occasions
Laucks paints
   Start with the finish
Laugh at winter
   Kopper Gas & Coke Co.
Laugh at zero
   Globe radiator shutters
Laugh it off with a "Jest"
   Jest Alkalizer
Laughlin. See: Thomas Laugh-
      lin Co.
Laughs at time
   Big Ben Westclox alarm
      clock
   E. I. DuPont de Nemours
      & Co.
Laughter
   A magazine of good, clean
      humor
Launderall clothes washer
   Better built to do a better
      job
   The completely automatic
      home laundry
   Double-tumble action
   Everything you ever wanted
      in an automatic home
      laundry

Launderette
   Coin-operated laundry store
Laundry Age
   Supreme in the laundry in-
      dustry
The laundry-proof snap fastener
      that ends button-bother
   Gripper fasteners
Laundryette Mfg. Co.
   Washes and dries without a
      wringer
Laura Secord Candy
   Wholesome sweets for chil-
      dren
Laurence. See:
   A. C. Laurence Leather Co.
   Lawrence
Lava soap
   We'll Lava ya clean
   World's worst beauty soap.
      World's best hand soap
Lavena beauty preparation
   The sensational new oatmeal
      skin beauty treatment
      that softens, whitens
      and protects the com-
      plexion
Laventhol & Horwath, Certified
      Public Accountants
   Our partners work with you.
      That's why they work
      with us
Lavoris mouthwash
   More dentists use Lavoris
      than any other mouth-
      wash. Shouldn't you?
Lawn-Boy lawn mowers
   As time goes by you'll know
      why
   The mower with the 2-cycle
      advantage
   Quick to start. Quiet on
      the go
The lawn people
   O. M. Scott and Co.
Lawrence. See also:
   Laurence
   Vollman Lawrence Co.
Lawrence Leather Co.
   First choice for aprons
   The jewel of patent leather
   Proofs of leadership
   That's why, where quality
      counts, calfskin spins
      the yarn
Lawrence Warehouse Co.

Certified on checks:
Lawrence on warehouse
receipts
Lawrence Welk's dance orchestra
The champagne music of
Lawrence Welk
Laxate with Espotabs
Espotabs laxative
The laxative chewing gum
Feen-a-Mint
Lay's potato chips
Grown to be America's
favorite
Lazy Joe Casuals Shoes
Smooth 'n' easy-going
The lazy way to a lovely lawn
Vigoro Plant Food
Lea & Perrin's Sauce
The added touch that means
so much
Naturally good--over two
years in the making
The original Worcestershire
Lead Industries Assn., Inc.
Look ahead with lead
Rely on lead
You're money ahead when
you paint with white
lead
Lead soaps mean fine paint
(L.S.M.F.P.)
Dutch Boy White Lead
Lead the Ship 'n Shore life
Ship 'n Shore, Inc.
The lead with the spread
Carter White Lead Co.
Leadclad fences make good
neighbors
Leadclad Wire Co.
A Leadclad roof is lightning
proof
Wheeling Metal & Mfg. Co.
Leadclad Wire Co.
Leadclad fences make good
neighbors
The leader around the world
Cocker Machine and Foundry
Co.
The leader by design
Airstream motor coach
Leader in adhesive technology
H. B. Fuller Co.
Leader in business insurance
New York Life Insurance
Co.
Leader in computer graphics

California Computer Prod-
ucts, Inc.
A leader in dental research
Squibb Beech-Nut, Inc.
Leader in prefinished hardwoods
E. L. Bruce Co.
The leader in solid-state high-
fidelity components
Harmon Kardon, Inc.
Leader in the field. Choice of
the leaders
Gilbarco, Inc.
Leader in the manufacture of
custom built-in refrig-
eration
Revco, Inc.
The leader in vibration/shock/
noise control
Lord Manufacturing Co.
Leader in worldwide cash manage-
ment
Chemical Bank New York
Trust Co.
Leaders by design
Precision Valve Corp.
The leaders fly the Falcon
Falcon Jet Corporation
Leaders go to Carnes for the
newest in air distribu-
tion equipment
Carnes Corporation
Leaders in lawn research
C. M. Scott and Co.
Leaders in thermal engineering
design
Struthers Thermo-Flood
Corp.
Leadership born of quality
Electromaster range
Leadership built on the research
and experience of over
48,000 store installations
Bulman Corporation
Leadership in design authority
Community silverplate
Leadership in low cost/high
reliability magnetic tape
handling
Datamec Corp.
The leadership line
Battle Creek Manufacturers,
Inc.
Leadership through accomplish-
ment
Therm-O-Disc, Inc.
Leadership through creative

engineering
McCulloch Corp.
Leadership through design
Mercury Record Corp.
Leadership through quality
The Steril-Sil Co.
The leading alternative to the
phone company
SPC Communications
Leading business and technical
journal of the world in
printing and allied in-
dustries
Inland Printer
Leading clay journal of the world
Brick and Clay Record
Leading direct sellers of fine
fashion jewelry
Sarah Coventry, Inc.
Leading innovators in polymer
chemistry
Goodrich-Gulf Chemicals,
Inc.
The leading journal of the Epis-
copal Church
The Churchman
Leading maker of watches of the
highest character for
almost a century
Longines-Wittnauer Watch
Co.
The leading name in dictionaries
since 1847
G. and C. Merriam Co.
Leading name in truck trans-
portation
Consolidated Freightways,
Inc.
The leading paper!
New York Tribune
The leading research organization
of the world
General Electric Company
The leading syrup
Mrs. Butterworth's syrup
Leading the do-it-yourself
industry
The Stanley Works
Leading the way into the '80's
Bell & Howell Company
The leading truck builder in
America
International Harvester Co.
Leads in automatic log com-
putation
Schlumberger, Ltd.

Leads the industry in quality
and dependability
Universal Metal Products
Div., UMC Industries,
Inc.
Leads the way
Red Devil Pliers
Leads the world for value
Royal vacuum cleaner
Leads the world in motor car
value
Nash automobile
Leaf chewing gum
The flavor lingers longer
Leaf tobaccos that satisfy
Louis Greenwald
League Collars
An extra collar for a dollar
Lear plane radio
The name men fly by
The wire that remembers
Learn a living at Ivy Tech
Indiana Vocational Techni-
cal College
Learn about little women from us
Schwartz Bros. Dress Co.
Learn the economy of quality in
Solitaire Coffee
Solitaire Coffee
Lease for le$$
IBM computer systems
The leasing people from General
Motors
General Motors Acceptance
Corporation
The least of the difference is the
difference in price
General tires
The leather for fine shoes
Standard Kid Mfg. Co.
The leather is there in every
pair
Peters Shoe Co.
Leather Lather Cleaner
Benefits all fine leather
The leather that sells more shoes
Kepner Leather Co.
Leave the driving to us
Greyhound Corporation
Leave the moving to us
Greyhound Corporation
Leaves no brush marks
Flo-Glaze paint
Leaves that clean taste in your
mouth
Amberdent tooth paste

Lectric. See also: Electric
Lectric Shave lotion
    Makes electric shaving easier
Lee. See also:
    Buddy Lee men's suits
    Don Lee Broadcasting Sys-
        tem
    H. D. Lee Co., Inc.
    Sara Lee coffee cake
Lee L. Woodward Sons, Inc.
    Style authority in wrought
        iron
Lee Machinery Corp.
    There should be a Lee in
        your future
Lee tires
    Safe driving is a frame of
        mind
    Smile at miles
Leeds and Northrup Co.
    Pioneers in precision
Leek. See: C. P. Leek and
        Sons, Inc.
Lees. See:
    James Lees and Sons Co.
    John Lees frames and mold-
        ings
Lee's Magnesia
    Tonight at bedtime
The legend that started an air-
        line
    Falcon Jet Corporation
The legendary motorcycles of
        Germany
    BMW motorcycles
The legendary spirit
    Irish Mist liqueur
L'eggs pantyhose
    Nothing beats a great pair
        of L'eggs
Legs are young in Quaker stock-
        ings
    Quaker stockings
Legs look young in Quaker
        stockings
    Quaker stockings
Legsize stockings
    Belle-Sharmeer stockings
Legsize stockings for leg-wise
        women
    Belle-Sharmeer stockings
Lehigh Portland Cement Co.
    More Lehigh cement used
        than any other
Lehigh Valley Coal Sales Co.
    The coal that satisfies

Lehigh Valley Railroad
    The route of the Black
        Diamond
Lehn & Fink
    Our sign is our bond
Leisure Lawn gardening service
    Discover the dry difference
Leisy beer
    Cleveland's favorite brew
        since 1862
    Ohio's favorite brew since
        1862
Lektro Shaver
    The gift that endears and
        endures
Leland-built
    Lincoln automobile
Lelong perfume
    For high moments in distin-
        guished living
Lemar lamps
    The line of beauty
A lemon-fresh clean that shines
    Joy dishwashing liquid
Lemon in water, first thing on
        arising
    Sunkist lemons
Lengthens your days
    Arco paint
Lennox Hotel, St. Louis, Mo.
    Downtown St. Louis at
        your doorstep
    Live in the atmosphere of
        an exclusive club
    There is no better place to
        eat
Lennox Industries, Inc.
    Don't be satisfied with less
        than Lennox
    It's nature's freshness--
        indoors
    Round the calendar comfort
Lentheric perfume
    The daytime fragrance
    Languid splendour set to
        fragrance
Leo Feist, Inc., music publish-
        ers
    You can't go wrong with
        any "Feist" song
Leopold Colombo, Inc.
    Importers and makers of
        fine furniture
LePage's glue
    Easier and quicker than
        sewing

The universal mender
Les Brown and his band of re-
known
Les Brown's orchestra
Les Brown's orchestra
Les Brown and his band of
reknown
Leschen & Sons Rope Co.
The wire rope with the
service record
Leslie Fay, Inc.
For the typical American
size
Less Bread
The lowest calorie bread
you can buy
Less hair in the comb, more
hair on the head
Glover's Imperial Mange
Medicine
Less than a cent's worth will
flavor a cake
Shirriff's vanilla
Less trouble than a trip to the
hairdresser
Canthrox Shampoo
Lester piano
A beautiful piano with a
magnificent name
Let Barron's keep you ahead
Barron's
Let blue prints tell your story
C. F. Pease Co.
Let Forbes make their ship come
in
Forbes
Let Hertz put you in the driv-
er's seat
Hertz automobile rentals
Let K take care of you
K mart Stores
Let Lyon guard your goods
Lyon Van Lines, Inc.
Let Munsingwear cover you with
satisfaction
Munsingwear underwear
Let our telephone wire be your
clothes line
Consolidated Laundry Com-
pany
Let the car tell its own story
Auburn automobile
Let the furnace man go ...
forever
May Oil Burner Corp.
Let the Gold Dust Twins do

your work
Gold Dust Soap Powder
Let the "kitchen maid" be your
kitchen aid
Wassmuth-Endicott kitchen
cabinet
Let the user judge
Wollensack Optical Co.
Let this seal be your guide to
quality
Julius Wile Sons and Co.
Let time tell your story
Publicity Clock Co.
Let Tung-Sol light the way
Tung-Sol lamp
Let us. See also: Let's
Let us help put Armour Idea
chemicals to work for
you
Armour and Co.
Let us protect your world
Hartford Insurance Group
Let us take the risks
The AIG Companies
Let us tan your hide
Crisby Frisian Fur Co.
Let White build it of concrete
White Construction Co., Inc.
Let your bathroom reflect your
good taste
Bon Ami cleanser
Let your fingers do the walking
Bell System telephone direc-
tory yellow pages
Let your motor be the judge, it
knows
Nicholas Oil Co.
Let your taste decide--take the
Pepsi challenge!
Pepsi-Cola soft drink
Let yourself go ... Plymouth
Plymouth automobile
Let's. See also: Let us
Let's ask Mother if we can have
it for lunch
Campbell's condensed soups
Let's begin with the finish
Johnson's wax
Let's create markets
General Transformer Co.
Let's find better ways ... we'll
follow through
Strapping Div., Signode
Corp.
Let's give the customer a choice
General Telephone &

Electronics Corp.
Let's go Cone-ing
Illinois Baking Corp.
Let's go dancin' with Anson!
Anson Weeks' dance orches-
tra
Let's go Krogering
Kroger supermarkets
Let's make it for keeps
Community silverplate
Let's talk about facts and figures
AM Jacquard Systems
Let's talk Maxitorq
Maxitorq machinery
Lets the feet grow as they
should
Educator shoe
Let's win the Games again
Miller High Life beer
Lets you drive without shifting
De Soto automobile
Lets you take weekends easy the
year around!
Deere & Co.
Lets your hair shine like the
stars
Drene shampoo
Lets your pup be your furnace
man
Bryant Heater Co.
Letters are victory weapons
Eaton Paper Corp.
Letters on Crane's papers com-
mand attention and win
respect
Crane and Company, Inc.
Leverage gives control
Ross Steering Gear
Levi jeans
Quality never goes out of
style
Levine. See: Sainthill Levine
uniforms
Lew Smith Beads
Custom, of course
Lewis. See also:
Louis
William Lewis and Son
Lewis & Conger
A houseful of housewares
Lewis Mfg. Co.
Homes of character
Lewis-Shepard Co.
World's largest exclusive
manufacturer of elec-
trical industrial trucks

Lexington automobile
The Minuteman Six
Lexitron Corp. word processors
Where modern WP began.
Where modern WP is
going
Libbey-Owens-Ford Co.
The growing world of
Libbey-Owens-Ford
The quality mark to look for
This is the open world of
LOF glass
You can enjoy eight months
of June
Libby, McNeill and Libby
In all canned goods, look
to Libby's for perform-
ance
Look to Libby's for perfec-
tion
The most experienced food
processor in the world
Where food grows finest,
there Libby packs the
best
Libby's pineapple juice
"Flavor-fillip" for your
meals
A liberal church journal
The Churchman
Liberty carillon
The voice of the cathedrals
Liberty Cherry & Fruit Co.
The final touch to a tasty
dish
Liberty Magazine
America's best read weekly
A weekly for the whole
family
Liberty Mutual Insurance Com-
pany
Feeling safe. Feeling se-
cure. It's a Mutual
feeling
Protection in depth
We work to keep you safe
Your friend in the home,
on the highway, where
you work
Your friend on the highway
Liberty Orchards Co.
The confection of the
fairies
Lido Beach, N. Y.
At the seashore, in the
country, near the city

Liebman Breweries
We'll rest our case on a
case
Liebs. See: L. A. Liebs Co.
Life
America's most potent editor-
ial force
Obey that impulse and sub-
scribe regularly to Life
Through pictures to inform
While there is Life there is
hope
World trade UNITES nations
Life and growth for baby chicks
Purina poultry feed
Life at sea is like nothing on
earth
P and O Lines
Life begins at breakfast with
McLaughlin's Coffee
McLaughlin's Coffee
Life begins at forty
Fleischmann's Yeast
Life brassiere
For sure allure
For the lift of your lifetime
Stand out in a crowd, be
figure proud
Sure allure for the more
mature
Life Insurance Company of
Georgia
The old reliable since 1891
Life International
Where telling the world
means selling the world
Life is a family affair
U. S. Life Corporation
Life is a movie; Cine Kodak gets
it all
Cine Kodak
Life is swell when you keep well
Post's Bran Flakes
Life looks brighter
Univis glasses
The life of leather
Bergmann Shoe Mfg. Co.
The life of paint
Spencer-Kellogg linseed oil
The life of the pantry
Royledge Shelving
The life of the party
Boston Confectionery Co.
The life of the surface
Kyanize paints
A life preserver for foods

Alaska Refrigerator Co.
Life Savers candy
The candy mint with the
hole
If she does an about face
when you want her to
present arms, try Life
Savers
The sweetest story ever
sold
What fine fresh fruit flavor
for five cents!
When taste desires cooling
flavor try refreshing
Lime Life Saver
You bet your Life Savers
Life Stride shoes
The young point of view in
shoes
Lifebuoy Shaving Cream
The shave is better when
the lather stays wetter
Lifebuoy Soap
The health soap
Stops B. O.
The lifeline of your equipment
Aeroquip Corp.
The lifelong paint
Murphy paint
Lifelong security through pro-
grammed protection
Monarch Life Insurance Co.
Lifetime Corp.
For emergencies, carry a
Lifetime towline
Lifetime towline, a friend
in need
A lifetime of safety-first service
Trico Fuse Mfg. Co.
Lifetime office equipment
Shaw-Walker steel filing
cabinets
Lifetime towline, a friend in need
Lifetime Corp.
Lift DUST out of inDUSTry
W. W. Sly Mfg. Co.
A lift for the lunch box
Pillsbury's flour
The lift that never lets you down
Perma-Lift brassiere
The lift you've longed for
Hamilton Beach food mixer
Lifting America from under the
paper weight
NBI Office Automation Sys-
tem

270

Liggett's Chocolates
  The chocolates with the
    wonderful centres
Light after you drink it
  Trommer's beer
Light and comfortable. Easy to
    put on and take off
  Everstick invisible rubber
Light and crunchy
  Granola Snack
Light as a breeze, soft as a
    cloud
  Rand dress shields
Light as foam, yet holds oceans
    of powder
  Rho-Jan plastic compacts
Light as wood and twice as good
  American Pulley Co.
Light as you drink it
  Trommer's beer
Light beer of Broadway fame
  Trommer's beer
Light duty, but ALL truck
  International Harvester
    trucks
Light, heat and cook the Cole-
    man way
  Coleman Co., Inc.
Light in the darkest corner
  Gardco paint
The light moisturizing bath oil
    for dry skin
  Tender Touch
The light of a thousand uses
  Coleman Co., Inc.
The light of the night
  Coleman Co., Inc.
Light or dry, in step with the
    times
  Maraca rum
The light that always shines
    welcome
  Coleman Co., Inc.
The light that lightens labor
  Silverglo lamps
The light that never fails
  Metropolitan Life Insurance
    Co.
  Rapid Mfg. Co.
The light that says "There it
    is"
  Eveready flashlights and
    batteries
Light the modern way
  Owens-Illinois Glass Co.
The light to live with

General Electric Mazda Lamp
The "light" touch in automation
    and control
  Clairex Corp.
Light, white and flaky
  Comet rice
The light you can look at without
    hurting your eyes
  Celestialite Glass
Light your house with Westing-
    house
  Westinghouse Electric Corp.
Lighten up with low tar Belair
  Belair cigarettes
The lighter side of business
  Ronson cigarette lighters
The lighter that made the world
    lighter-conscious
  Zippo Manufacturing Co.
The lighter that works
  Zippo Manufacturing Co.
The lightest, loudest, simplest,
    cheapest of them all
  Mossberg Tire Bell
Lightest smoke of all
  Carlton cigarettes
Lighting from concealed sources
  National X-Ray Reflector
    Co.
Lighting over a million homes to-
    night
  Aladdin Mfg. Co.
Lightolier, Inc.
  After sunset, Lightoliers
  America's first name in
    lighting
Lights the home, lightens the
    work
  Gray & Davis home lighting
Like a clean China dish
  Grand Rapids Refrigerator
    Co.
Like a garden in your pantry
  UCO Quality Foods
Like a good neighbor, State
    Farm is there
  State Farm Insurance Co.
Like Grandma's, only more so
  General Foods Corporation
Like more time to tend your
    flowers? Campbell's
    soups can save you
    hours
  Campbell's condensed soups
Like pearl temples behind the
    ears

No-Ease spectacles
Like sending your family to college
    Webster's International Dictionary
Like sleeping on a cloud
    Sealy Mattress Co.
Like soft drink
    You don't need caffeine, and neither does your cola
Like strolling on a cloud
    Sportster Moccasins
Like swimming in your skin
    Cashmere Swim Suits
Like the cool side of a pillow on a hot night
    Kriss Kross Blades
Like walking on air
    Weyenberg Shoe Mfg. Co.
Like wearing a shadow
    Du-Ons underwear
Like wine, a company's future value will depend on how well it ages
    Rowe Price Growth Stock Fund
Lilli. See also:
    Lilly
    Lily
Lilli-Ann Corp.
    For the elegant petite
Lilly. See:
    Eli Lilly and Co.
    Lilli
    Lily
Lilt: A professional touch
    Lilt hair set rollup sponges
Lilt hair set rollup sponges
    Lilt: A professional touch
Lily. See also:
    Lilli
    Lilly
Lily of France Corset Co.
    A beautiful corset worn by beautiful women to make them more beautiful
Lily-Tulip Cup Corp.
    Serve the drink, save the bottle
    Your lips are the first and last to touch a Lily cup
    Yours are the only lips to touch a Lily cup

Lilyette brassiere
    Naturally yours
Lime Cola
    America's finest cola drink
    First aid for thirst
    Not twice as much but twice as good
    A pick-up for a let-down
LimiTorque Corp.
    When so much depends on a valve ... so many depend on LimiTorque
Lincoln. See also: Mary Lincoln Candies, Inc.
Lincoln automobile
    Cars of fine feather flock together
    Leland-built
    Nothing could be finer
Lincoln carpeting
    Better carpeting for less
Lincoln Continental automobile
    America's most distinguished motorcar
Lincoln Electric Co.
    Link up with Lincoln
Lincoln Inn Distilling Co.
    It's got a smooth punch
Lincoln lubricating equipment
    It is better to buy Lincoln lubricating equipment than to wish you had
Lincoln luggage
    America looks to Lincoln for leadership in luggage
The Lincoln National Life Insurance Co.
    Its name indicates its character
Lincoln Zephyr automobile
    The style leader
Lind-Waldock commodity brokers
    Changing the way you trade futures
Lindsay Ripe Olive Co.
    The world's largest and finest
Lindy Pen Co., Inc.
    Originators of the world-famous Utility ball pen
The line and design for creative window planning
    Malta Manufacturing Co.
Line of beauty
    Gossard girdles
The line of beauty

Lemar lamps
The line of least resistance
  Koehler Motors Corp.
The line that moves
  Murray Corp.
The line that's fine at cooking
    time
  Griswold cooking utensils
The line with the carbon gripper
  Codo Manufacturing Co.
Linen damask, impressively cor-
    rect
  Irish & Scottish Linen
    Damask Guild
Linen Supply Assn. of America
  Good for good business
Linenized for softness
  Northern bathroom tissue
The liner makes the closure
  Irving Varnish & Insulator
    Co.
Lingette
  Everyone thinks it's silk
The lining most car makers
    specify
  Multibestos brake lining
The lining that gives you the
    brakes
  Thermoid brake lining
Linit laundry starch
  Adds the finishing touch
  The friend of fine fabrics
  The friend of your fine
    fabrics
  Makes cotton look and feel
    like linen
  The perfect laundry starch
Link-Belt Co.
  Basic products and engi-
    neering for industry's
    basic work
Link up with Lincoln
  Lincoln Electric Co.
Linking 13 great states with the
    nation
  Baltimore & Ohio Railroad
Linkman. See: M. Linkman &
    Co.
Linton Mfg. Co.
  All ways look to Linton
    for leadership!
Lion. See also:
  Lyon
  Lyons
Lion Oil Refining Co.
  The extra miles are free

Lionel electric trains
  The trains that railroad men
    buy for their boys
Lionel Toy Corporation
  Sane toys for healthy kids
Lipe delivers in the clutch
  Lipe-Rollway Corp.
Lipe-Rollway Corp.
  Lipe delivers in the clutch
  Pioneers in pneumatic bar
    feeding
Lips radiant as glowing embers
  Floress Lipstick
The lipstick without the dye
  Ar-ex Products, Inc.
Lipton food additives
  The golden touch of Lipton
Lipton tea bags
  The Flo-Thru Bag
Lipton's tea
  Brisk flavor, never flat
  The brisk tea
  It takes less to give more
    flavor
  World's largest selling tea
Liqua 4 Skin Cleansing System
  Just a little works up a
    good, rich lather
  Shower yourself with skin
    care
  You'll feel softer and silkier
    after only one use
Liquid dynamite under control
  Sinclair gasoline
A liquid finish that decorates as
    it preserves
  Colfanite finishing material
The Liquidometer Corp.
  Always on the level
  Safeguards liquid assets
Liquids or solids, they keep hot
    or cold
  Cannon vacuum bottle
Listen and you'll buy Westing-
    house
  Westinghouse radio receiver
Listen to America
  Decca phonograph records
Listening luxury beyond your
    highest hopes
  Bendix radio receiver
Listerine Luster-Foam
  Told on the petals of a rose
Listerine mouth wash
  At the first symptom
  Before any date

Clean breath hours longer
Even your best friends will
   not tell you you have
   halitosis
Fights colds and sore throats
For halitosis use Listerine
I was a lemon in the garden
   of love
Often a bridesmaid but never
   a bride
The safe antiseptic
The safe antiseptic with the
   pleasant taste
The tested treatment
Twice a day
Twice a day and before
   every date
Listerine shaving cream
   104 shaves in the big tube
   The tube that lasts and
   l-a-s-t-s
   You've got a treat ahead of
   you
Listerine toothpaste
   Beauty bath for your teeth
   Easy to use
   For lazy people
   162 brushings in the 40¢
   tube
   Prescription for your teeth
   What are your teeth saying
   about you today?
Lithographers National Associa-
   tion
   Advertising that follows
   through to sales
The little barber in a box
   American Safety Razor
   Corp.
A little Brown Friar for good
   cheer
   Brown Friar whiskey
The Little Brown Jug
   E. L. Anderson whiskey
Little cigars that win
   Admiration cigar
A little dab fights dandruff as
   it grooms
   Brylcreem Anti-Dandruff
   hair dressing
A little dab will do ya
   Brylcreem hair dressing
A little extra glass means a lot
   of extra charm
   Pittsburgh Plate Glass Co.
The little extra that makes it

better
   Royson auto signals
A little goes a longer way
   Ingram's shaving cream
The little nurse for little ills
   Mentholatum
The little piano with the big tone
   Miessner piano
A little pride will go a long, long
   way
   Junior Achievement, Inc.
Little shoes for little devils
   Faust Shoe Co.
Little things mean a lot
   White Cloud bathroom tissue
A little varnish makes a lot of
   difference
   O'Brien Varnish Co.
Little Yankee shoes
   Great shoes for little Amer-
   icans
Little's Onion Flakes
   Weep no more, my ladies
Litton microwave ovens
   Nobody knows more about
   microwave cooking
Live and die with Assurance
   Maryland Assurance Corpor-
   ation
Live better electrically
   Edison Electric Institute
Live electrically and enjoy the
   difference
   Reddy Kilowatt
Live in the atmosphere of an ex-
   clusive club
   Lennox Hotel, St. Louis,
   Mo.
   Mayfair Hotel, St. Louis,
   Mo.
   Mayfair House, New York
   City
Live-Lure
   World's liveliest bait
Live mode corset
   Kabo corset
Live modern for less with gas
   American Gas Association,
   Inc.
The live ones!
   Cahners Publishing Co.,
   Inc.
A live picture tabloid newspaper
   for all the family
   New York Daily Mirror
Livelier as well as lovelier

274

Buick automobile
A lively life for lazy arches
Florsheim Shoe Co.
Lives with good taste
Budweiser beer
The livest lumber journal on
earth
Gulf Coast Lumberman
Living insurance
Equitable Life Assurance
Society of the United
States
Livingstone's Oats
Fresh from the mill to you
Lloyd's Bank International
The international banking
services you expect,
from a single integrated
source
A load for every purpose and a
shell for every purse
United States Cartridge
Co.
Localized for you
Texaco, Inc.
Lock fast to make things last
Elastic Stop Nut Corp.
Lockheed Aircraft Corporation
Creating new advances in
flight
For protection today and
progress tomorrow
Lockheed knows how
Look to Lockheed for lead-
ership
Years ahead in the science
of flight
Lockheed knows how
Lockheed Aircraft Corpora-
tion
Locks recommended by the
world's leading lock
experts
Yale and Towne locks
Loco-Builder electric trains
Twice as much fun
Loews hotels
The golden opportunity for
the 80's
Log Cabin Syrup
Makes home sweet home
The way to a man's heart
Logan. See also: Harbor
Master, Ltd., Div.,
Jonathan Logan
Logan County Coal Corp.

Standard of perfection
The logical choice in specialty
steels
Carpenter Steel Co.
Loma Linda Food Co.
For all the family
A nation's health is a na-
tion's strength
Loma Plant Food
For everything green that
grows
The perfect plant food
Lombardi radio receiver
Built like a fine watch
Lombardo's. See: Guy Lom-
bardo's Royal Canadians
orchestra
London House brushes
London House fine English
brushes for good
grooming
London House fine English
brushes for good
grooming
London House brushes
London whiskey
Judge for yourself
Lonestar Industries, Inc.
For the long term
No. 1 in cement
Serving America's great
builders
Long ago distanced all competitors
Packer's Tar Soap
Long-Bell Lumber Co.
It bears close inspection
Long-Bell, the mark on
quality lumber
The post everlasting
A quality name in forest
products
Long-Bell, the mark on quality
lumber
Long-Bell Lumber Co.
Long distance adds warm per-
sonality to cold facts
Bell Telephone System
Long distance is the next best
thing to being there
Bell Telephone System
Long distance is the shortest
way home
Bell Telephone System
Long distance takes the CHASE
out of purchase
Bell Telephone System

Long distance, your fastest
highway
Bell Telephone System
Long distances help unite the
nation
Bell Telephone System
A long-established name in cups
Puritan paper cups
Long John Silver's seafood rest-
aurants
Put a smile on your taste
Shrimply delicious
Long lasting breath freshness
Big Red chewing gum
The long-life battery for your
car
Electric battery
Long life line
Atlantic Drier & Varnish
Co.
The long life radio tube
Tung-Sol radio tube
The long line of construction
machinery
Allis-Chalmers Mfg. Co.
A long, low, lovely "melody in
metal"
Studebaker automobile
Long Mileage Hosiery
Phoenix hosiery
The long stocking that fits every
leg
Gold Stripe stockings
Long, tender, golden brown
strips
Butzer's bacon
Long, tender, golden brown
strips from Kansas
Butzer's bacon
Long the ring leader! Now the
line leader
Sealed Power piston rings
Longchamps Restaurants, New
York City
There is no compromise
with quality at Long-
champs
Longer between fill-ups. Longer
between cars
Volvo diesel automobile
"Longer-life" line for heavy duty
service
Thermoid brake lining
Longer wear in every pair
Blue Moon Silk Hosiery
Co.

The longer you play it, the
sweeter it grows
Cheney Talking Machine Co.
Longest life by owners' records
Gould-National Batteries,
Inc.
Longines-Wittnauer Watch Co.
Leading maker of watches
of the highest character
for almost a century
Since 1867 maker of watches
of the highest character
The world's most honored
hands wear the world's
most honored watch
The world's most honored
watch
Look ahead, look South
Southern Railway Co.
Look ahead with lead
Lead Industries Assn., Inc.
Look ahead with living insurance
Equitable Life Assurance
Society of the United
States
Look-alikes aren't cook-alikes
Idaho Potato Growers, Inc.
Look and listen
Fairchild-Wood Visaphone
Corp.
Look and ride, then decide
De Soto automobile
Look at your shoes, others do
Florsheim Shoe Co.
Look for Austin on every cake
Austin's Dog Bread
Look for more from Morton
Morton Chemical Co. Div.,
Morton International,
Inc.
Look for the cured-in Red "W"
Webster Rubber Co.
Look for the date on the tin
Chase and Sanborn coffee
Look for the Diamond I on every
bottle you buy
Illinois Glass Co.
Look for the dog
Victrola talking machine
Look for the Hartmann Red on
the trunk you buy
Hartmann Trunk Co.
Look for the label with the Big
Red "1"
One-A-Day vitamins

Look for the leaf on the
package
Black Leaf insecticide
Look for the Mission when you
buy a pipe
Monterey pipe
Look for the name in the selvage
Skinner garment linings
Look for the red ball
Mishawaka Rubber Co., Inc.
Look for the red wheel
Loraine stove
Look for the spinning wheel
label
Magee Carpet Co.
Look for the Tinnerman "T", the
mark of total reliability
Tinnerman Products, Inc.
Look for the watermark
Hammermill Paper Co.
Look for this famous name in the
oval
Philadelphia Brand cream
cheese
Look for this Sunshine biscuit
rack
Sunshine biscuits
Look for Tillamook on the rind
Tillamook Cheese
Look into a new pair of eyes
Dark eyes gin
Dark eyes vodka
Look Magazine
America's family magazine
The magazine of the Ameri-
can market
The look of quality
LaBarge Mirrors, Inc.
Look of the month
Tampax, Inc.
Look out, world; here comes
Ford!
Ford automobile
Look Risqué from the ankles
down
Risqué Shoes Div., Brown
Shoe Company
Look sharp! Feel sharp! Be
sharp!
Gillette safety razor
Look smart, feel fresh
Porto-Red shoes
Look smarter, wear better
Shane Uniform Co.
Look through and see
Kirsten Pipe Co.

Look to Eastman to look your
best!
Plastic Sheeting Div., East-
man Chemical Products,
Inc.
Look to Eberhard Faber for the
finest ... first!
Eberhard Faber, Inc.
Look to Libby's for perfection
Libby, McNeill and Libby
Look to Lockheed for leadership
Lockheed Aircraft Corpora-
tion
Look to MFG for the shape of
things to come
Molded Fiber Glass Companies,
Inc.
Look to Olds for the new
Oldsmobile automobile
Look to Paris to look your best
Paris Garters
Look to the body!
Fisher automobile bodies
Look to the fabric first
Pacific fabrics
Look to the fabric first, buy
Pacific
Pacific fabrics
Look to the leader
Bank of America
Look to the leader for good safe
planes you can afford
to buy and fly
Piper Aircraft Corporation
Look to 3M for imagination in
image-making
Minnesota Mining & Manufac-
turing Co.
Look what Plymouth's up to now
Plymouth automobile
Looks better hours longer
Don Juan Lipstick
Looks clean, is clean, stays
clean
Red Jacket Coal Sales Co.
Looks good from any angle
Naturalizer shoes
Looks like a Strohlight night
Stroh's beer
Looks like stone, works like wood
Zenitherm Co.
Looks out for you
Sentry Insurance Co.
Loomed by American labor to
beautify American
homes

Magee Carpet Co.
Loomed to be heir-loomed
Bates Bedspreads
Lopez'. See: Vincent Lopez'
dance orchestra
Lopsided diet may ruin your
canary's song
The R. T. French Co.
Lorah. See: D. Lorah cleaner
Lorain. See also: Lorraine
Lorain stove
Look for the red wheel
Unless it has a red wheel
it is not a Lorain
Lord & Thomas
True salesmanship in print
Lord Calvert Canadian whiskey
Lord of the Canadians
Lord Calvert Canadian whiskey.
See also: Calvert
"Extra" whiskey
Lord Corp. See: Hughson
Chemical Div., Lord
Corp.
Lord Manufacturing Co.
The leader in vibration/
shock/noise control
Lord of the Canadians
Lord Calvert Canadian
whiskey
Lord Oxford cigarette lighter
The up-draft lighter
A lordly touch for simple menus
Campbell's condensed soups
Lori-Lou girdles
In tune with fashion and
keyed to fit
Lorraine. See also: Lorain
Lorraine worsteds
Fabrics of integrity
Lorrie Deb Corporation
Important occasion dresses
Los Angeles Bureau of Power
and Light
Electricity gives you match-
less cooking
Electricity gives you match-
less water heating
Matchless electric water
heating
Matchless in more ways than
one
Los Angeles, Calif.
Where nature helps indus-
try most
Los Angeles Evening Herald

An independent newspaper
Los Angeles Examiner
The great newspaper of the
great southwest
Largest morning and Sunday
circulation west of St.
Louis
Los Angeles Times
World's largest newspaper
The losing hand in the game of
love is a chapped one
Jergens Lotion
A lot fewer cavities
Crest toothpaste
Lots of Flatt tires running
around
R. A. Flatt Tire Co.
Lou. See:
Betty Lou Foods
Lew
The Louden Machinery Co.
Since 1867 ... the first
name in materials
handling
Sunny Monday clothes dryer
Louis. See also: Lewis
The Louis Allis Co.
More than horse power
Pace setting engineered
systems to control mate-
rials in motion
Louis Greenwald
Leaf tobaccos that satisfy
Louis Rich preserved meats
Louis Rich stacks up leaner
Louis Rich stacks up leaner
Louis Rich preserved meats
Louisiana Dept. of Commerce and
Industry
Means profits for business
The Louisiana-Mississippi farm
paper
Modern Farming
Louisville and Nashville Railroad
Rely on us
Louisville Cement Co.
Cement manufacturers for
nearly a century
Louver Mfg. Co., Inc.
World's largest manufacturer
of ventilating louvers
Love at first bite
Suchard chocolate bars
Love at first sip
Bacardi rum
Love does not live by calendars

Whitman's Chocolates
Love does not live by calendars
alone
Whitman's Chocolates
Love lives on little things
Whitman's Chocolates
A love of a glove
Acme Glove Corp.
Love that taste!
Honey Nut Cheerios break-
fast cereal
Loveable brassiere
For the girl who knows
value by heart
You'll be lovely, too, in a
Loveable brassiere
Lovejoy Flexible Coupling Co.
First name in power trans-
mission equipment
Lovejoy shock absorbers
Take the rough spots out
of the road
Lovelier skin in 14 days
Palmolive soap
A lovelier skin with just one
cake
Camay soap
The lovelier soap with the cost-
lier perfume
Cashmere Bouquet soap
Loveliest of leathers
New Castle Leather Co.
The loveliest pearls made by
man
Varvella artificial pearls
Lovell All-Clamp Roller Skate
We challenge the world to
produce its equal
Lovely hair deserves fine care
Dupont combs
Lovely, lilting lines
Bali Brassiere
Lovely, logical, alluring
Dirilyte Flatware
A lovely skin comes from within
Nujol laxative
Lovely to look at, lovely to own
Keepsake Diamond Rings
Lovely to look at, pleasant to
use
Tek toothbrush
Loving Care hair color
Makes your husband feel
younger, too ... just
to look at you!
Low cost transportation

Durant Star automobile
Low rate--low cost
Provident Mutual Life Insur-
ance Co. of Philadelphia
Low-swung, new-look, soft-
sprung, new-ride
Studebaker automobile
The low tar that won't leave you
hungry for taste
Kent cigarettes
Lowenberg golf bags
One of the everlasting kind
Löwenbräu beer
Tonight let it be Löwenbräu
Lowerator Div., American Machine
and Foundry Co.
There is no equal
Lowerator Div., American Machine
& Foundry Co. See
also: American Machine
& Foundry Co.
Lowers the cost of making frost
Carbondale Machine Co.
The lowest calorie bread you can
buy
Less Bread
Lowest cost, per yard, per hour,
or per mile
Cleveland tractor
The lowest in tar of all brands
Now cigarettes
The lowest ton-mile cost pro-
vided by Chevrolet
trucks
Chevrolet trucks
Lowney's Chocolate Bonbons
A delightful dream ... a
delicious reality
Lowry Coffee Co.
The best drinking coffee in
the world
Lowry Hotel, St. Paul, Minn.
The luxury hotel of the
northwest
Lubeck beer
The beer that makes friends
Lubricants of quality
Manufacturers Oil & Grease
Co.
Lubrication is a major factor in
cost control
Texaco, Inc.
Lucas paints
It costs less to pay more
It covers, it beautifies, it
lasts, it protects, it's

economical
    Purposely made for every
    purpose
Luce Packing Co.
    Where quality counts
Luckies are gentle on my throat
    Lucky Strike cigarettes
Lucky for boots
    Paire Bros. shoe laces
The lucky ones go Anchor Line
    Anchor Line
Lucky Strike cigarettes
    Fine tobacco is what counts
        in a cigarette
    Have you tried a Lucky
        lately?
    It's the tobacco that counts
    It's toasted
    Luckies are gentle on my
        throat
    Lucky Strike green has
        gone to war
    Lucky Strike means fine
        tobacco (LS/MFT)
    Lucky Strikes again. The
        moment is right for it
    Nature in the raw is seldom
        mild
    Reach for a Lucky instead
        of a sweet
    So round, so firm, so fully
        packed, so free and
        easy on the draw
    With men who know tobacco
        best, it's Luckies 2 to 1
Lucky Strike green has gone to
    war
    Lucky Strike cigarettes
Lucky Strike means fine tobacco
    (LS/MFT)
    Lucky Strike cigarettes
Lucky Strikes again. The
    moment is right for it
    Lucky Strike cigarettes
Ludlum Steel Co.
    The steels with Indian
        names
Ludwig & Ludwig
    Drum makers to the profes-
        sion
    Drum standard of the world
    Ludwig beats the world
        over
    The most famous name on
        drums
Ludwig beats the world over

Ludwig & Ludwig
The Lufkin Rule Co.
    Measure up with the best
    White is right
    You're right with Lufkin
Luggage and Leather Goods
    More effective because it's
        more sell-ective
Luggage of distinction
    Tufraw luggage
The luggage that knows its way
        around the world
    Samsonite Corp.
The luggage that sets the pace
        for luxury
    Samsonite Corp.
Luggage you will love to travel
        with
    Rauchbach-Goldsmith lug-
        gage
Lukens Steel Co.
    It had to have quality, the
        steel is Lukens
    The specialist in plate
        steels
Lullaby in loveliness
    Beaumont Fabrics
Luma, the radium luminous com-
        pound
    Radium Dial Co.
Lumaghi Coal Co.
    Hard soft coal
Luminal paint
    The paint for all interiors
Lunch time is Guinness time
    Guinness ale
The Lunkheimer Co.
    The one great name in
        valves
Lunt silverware
    Sterling of lasting good
        taste
Lupton's. See: David Lupton's
    Sons
Lush loops of lovely lace
    Kayser night gowns
Lustray shirts
    Brilliant as the sun
Lustre-Cream shampoo
    The cream shampoo for
        true hair loveliness
    For the heads of the family
    Sparkling hair that thrills
        men
Luvs diapers
    Your baby's comfort begins

with Luvs
Lux every day keeps old hands
    away
    Lux soap
Lux girls are lovelier
    Lux soap
Lux life means long life for un-
    dies
    Lux soap flakes
Lux soap
    Avoid cosmetic skin
    If it's safe in water, it's
        safe in Lux
    Lux every day keeps old
        hands away
    Lux girls are lovelier
    Won't shrink woolens
Lux soap flakes
    Lux life means long life
        for undies
Luxite girdles
    The hug you love
Luxite Glory slips
    Be slip shape and lovely
Luxite night garments
    Cool as a pool
Luxuria Face Cream
    Keep time off your face
Luxury acrylic fiber
    Creslan acrylic fiber
Luxury and comfort with utmost
    safety
    United States Lines, Inc.
A luxury blend at a thrifty
    price
    Nob Hill Coffee
A luxury blend for the "car-
    riage trade"
    Gallagher & Burton whiskey
Luxury for less
    Ramada Inns, Inc.
The luxury hotel of the north-
    west
    Lowry Hotel, St. Paul,
        Minn.
Luxury in quality, not in price
    Welch's tomato juice
A luxury millions enjoy
    Maxwell House Master
        Blend Coffee
The luxury of velvet with the
    worry left out
    Islon
The luxury soap of the world
    Yardley's Old English
        soap

Luzier, Inc.
    Personalized cosmetic serv-
        ices
Lydia E. Pinkham's Vegetable
    Compound
    A medicine for a woman.
    Invented by a woman.
    Prepared by a woman
Lyman Gun Sight Corp.
    They better your aim
Lynch. See: Merrill Lynch,
    Pierce, Fenner & Smith,
    Inc.
Lynchburg Hardware and Central
    Store
    All goods worth price
        charged
Lynden chicken fricassee
    If it's chicken you're wishin'
        --look for Lynden
    You get half a chicken in a
        can
Lyon. See also: Lion
Lyon & Healy
    Harp-maker to the world
        since 1889
    You can't fool the micro-
        phone
Lyon Van Lines, Inc.
    Let Lyon guard your goods
Lyon Whitewall Tires
    The smartest thing on
        wheels
Lyons. See: Dr. Lyons tooth
    powder
Lyradion radio receivers
    The perfection of natural
        tone in radio
Lysol disinfectant
    Baby lead a "hand to
        mouth" life?
    Don't take needless chances
    Every time you clean, dis-
        infect with Lysol
    For feminine hygiene use
        Lysol always
    The whole bowl cleaner

-M-

MAI. See: Management As-
    sistance, Inc.
M.A.N. Truck and Bus Corp.
    We redesign the conven-
        tional to create the

exceptional

M&F Case Co.
  We run rings around the
    competition

M & M milk chocolate
  The rich milk chocolate
    melts in your mouth,
    not in your hand

M./B. Designs, Inc.
  Designs that dreams are
    made of

M.C.I.
  The nation's long distance
    telephone company

MG Kitcar
  A great way to get back in
    touch with those two
    things at the ends of
    your arms

MGM Motion Pictures
  Ars gratia aris
  Art for art's sake
  More stars than there are
    in heaven

M. H. P. Aluminum Hot Water
    Bottle
  Keeps hot all night

M. Linkman & Co.
  Pathfinders in pipedom
  The pipe that's broken in

M. M. Bernstein
  Footwear of distinction

M. Mittman Co.
  America's largest manufac-
    turer of custom day
    beds and sofa beds

MPA Magazines
  Your world of ideas and
    products

MPB, Inc.
  Missile quality ball bearings

Maag gears
  Strongest at the base where
    strength is needed

Mac-It endurance, your best
    insurance
  Mac-It screws

Mac-It screws
  Mac-It endurance, your
    best insurance

McAn. See:
  Thom McAn shoes
  Thom McAn socks

Macbeth Daylighting Co.
  Color work at night will
    next day be right

Daylight, the ideal

McCall's
  First magazine for women
  HE builds a house, SHE
    makes a home
  Three magazines in one

McCallum Hosiery Co.
  You just know she wears
    them

Macanudo cigar
  The ultimate cigar

Maccar truck
  The truck of continuous
    service

McCawley & Co., Inc.
  The friend-making work
    shirt

Machinery specialists to the
    tobacco industry
  American Machine & Foundry
    Co.

McClure's
  The magazine of romance

McCord Corp.
  McCord is go ... go with it

McCord is go ... go with it
  McCord Corp.

McCormick and Co., Inc.
  The house of flavor
  Its favor has grown through
    flavor alone
  Smoother than velvet
  Standard of quality the
    whole world over

McCormick and Co., Inc. See
    also: Schilling Div.,
    McCormick and Co.,
    Inc.

McCray Refrigerator Corp.
  Refrigerators for all pur-
    poses

McCulloch Corp.
  Leadership through creative
    engineering

McDade's mail order service
  The catalog house

McDermott International, Inc.
  No matter how the world
    solves its energy prob-
    lems, McDermott is in-
    volved
  Where the world comes for
    energy solutions

MacDonald. See: E. F. Mac-
    Donald Co.

McDonald radio howl arrester

282

It stops that howl
MacDonald's Candy Shops, Inc.
The candy of good taste
McDonald's fast food restaurants
Billions and billions served
More than 40 billions sold
Taste the thrill of Atari at
McDonald's
You deserve a break today
McDonnell-Douglas Corporation
In the air or outer space
Douglas gets things done
More people fly more places
by Douglas
New wings for a new world
McDonnell-Douglas Finance Cor-
poration
The yes people
MacFarlane candies
Awful fresh
The house of a million nuts
One taste is worth a thou-
sand words
The scotchman who KILT
high prices, awful fresh
MacFarlane
Taste B4U buy
You can't eat the box
McGinnis restaurants
The roast beef king
McGraw-Hill, Inc.
Information that leads to
action
Serving man's need for
knowledge ... in many
ways
McGraw-Hill Publications Div.,
McGraw-Hill, Inc.
Awards for some, rewards
for all
A good society is good
business
Market directed
McGraw tires
That we may ride in com-
fort
McGregor-Doniger, Inc.
For the man on the move
MacGregor golf equipment
The greatest name in golf
McGruff Crime Prevention Coali-
tion
Take a bite out of crime
A machine for every purpose
Remington typewriter
The machine that made coal

an automatic fuel
Iron Fireman
The machine that makes produc-
tion
Wilcox & Gibbs sewing ma-
chine
The machine that pays for itself
Bodine Corporation
The machine to count on
Ohner adding machine
The machine you will eventually
buy
Underwood typewriter
Machines at work around the
world
Joy Manufacturing Co.
Machines for total productivity
Gisholt Machine Co.
Machines should work. People
should think
Office Products Div., Inter-
national Business Ma-
chines Corp.
Machines that build for a growing
America
Caterpillar Tractor Co.
Machines that make data move
Teletype Corp.
Machines that understand people
Sony Corp. of America
Mack trucks
Always the leader
The money truck
Performance counts
Since 1900, America's hard-
est working truck
Trucks for every purpose
What America needs is less
bull and more Bulldog
McKinney Mfg. Co.
Hardware is the jewelry of
the home
Mackintosh's Toffee
Is as safe to eat as bread
and butter
MacLaren radio receiver
The ultimate in radio re-
ception
McLaughlin-Sweet, Inc.
The comfort shoe of tomor-
row
McLaughlin's Coffee
Life begins at breakfast
with McLaughlin's Coffee
MacMillan Lubricating Oil
Keeps cars younger longer

McNally. See also: Rand
McNally and Co.
McNally Pittsburgh Mfg. Corp.
Manufacturers of equipment
to make coal a better
fuel
McQuay-Norris Mfg. Co.
Take the slant out of hills
McShann's. See: Jay Mc-
Shann's jazz band
Macy's department store
No one is in debt to Macy's
Made. See also: Maid
Made a little better than seems
necessary
Rhinelander Refrigerator
Co.
Made by masters, played by
artists
Buescher Band Instrument
Co.
Made by our family for yours
Sohmer piano
Made by the makers of fine
furniture
Tennessee Furniture Corp.
Made by the makers of the Ham-
mond organ
Solovox piano attachment
Made by the mile, sold by the
foot
Sectional Steel Buildings
Made by tiny Arcadians
Arcade toys
Made for lifetime service
Jenkins valves
Made for the professional!
Permatex Co., Inc.
Made from a rare old recipe
Shirriff's marmalade
Made from REAL oranges
Nesbitt's orange drink
Made from rosy, baby tomatoes,
ginger root and golden
twists of lemon peel,
it's spicy sweet
Everbest Tomato Preserves
Made in America by American
craftsmen
Elgin watches
Made in America for American
boys and girls
Kiddie-Kar
Made in America since 1915
General tires
"Made in Bloomfield" is a mark

of merit
Bloomfield, N. J.
Made in California for enjoyment
throughout the world
Roma wines
Made in the bakery of a thousand
windows
Sunshine biscuits
Made in the "champagne district
of America"
Gold Seal wines
Made in the cup at the table
G. Washington Coffee
Made in the home-made way
Hellmann's mayonnaise
Made in the milky way
Butterine
Made it's way by the way it's
made
Intertype Corp.
Made like a gun
Royal Enfield bicycle
Made like, tastes like fine im-
ported beer
Trommer's beer
Made of the metal that cooks
best
Wear-Ever aluminum
Made on honor, sold on merit
Narragansett malt beverage
Made right, aged right, priced
right
Daniel Webster whiskey
Made-Rite Flour
Bakes right because it is
made right
Hard to mill but easy to
bake
Made soft to work hard
Tempo antacid
Made strong to work hard
ScotTissue
Made stronger, last longer
Pequot sheets
Made stronger, lasts longer
Human & Oppenheim hair
nets
Made stronger to wear longer
Fargo-Hallowell Shoe Co.
Made to blue print
Fostoria Screw Co.
Made to last
Rollfast bicycles
Made-to-measure fit in ready-to-
wear shoes
W. B. Coon Co.

Made to order for America's
business farmer and
his wife
Successful Farming
Made to stand the gaff
Nogar Clothing Mfg. Co.
Made to stay brighter longer
General Electric Mazda
Lamp
Made with home care
Otto Stahl meat products
Made with the extra measure of
care
Cordova guitars
Made without rubber
Armstrong S.S. Gentlemen's
Garters
Mademoiselle
For the smart young woman
The magazine for smart
young women
Mademoiselle shoe
The fashion shoe
Madewell underwear
If it's Madewell, it's made
well
Maduff & Sons, Inc. commodities
trading advisors
We've already done your
homework
The magazine farm families de-
pend on
Farm Journal
The magazine farm people believe
in
Capper's Farmer
A magazine for all Americans
American Legion Monthly
The magazine for all manufactur-
ing
Factory
A magazine for farm women
The Farmer's Wife
The magazine for milady
Fashionable Dress
The magazine for parents
Children
The magazine for professional
builders
NAHB Journal of Home-
building
The magazine for smart young
women
Mademoiselle
A magazine for southern
merchants

Merchants Journal and Com-
merce
The magazine for women who ex-
pect to be taken serious-
ly
Working Woman
The magazine of a re-made world
Redbook
The magazine of architectural
technology
Building Construction
A magazine of better merchandis-
ing for home finishing
merchants
Furniture Record
The magazine of broadcast adver-
tising
Sponsor
The magazine of business
System
The magazine of business leaders
around the world
Fortune Magazine
The magazine of business leader-
ship
Fortune Magazine
A magazine of good, clean humor
Laughter
The magazine of management
Factory
Magazine of mass feeding, mass
housing
Institutions
The magazine of methods, per-
sonnel and equipment
Administrative Management
The magazine of opportunities
Money Making
The magazine of research and
development
Industrial Laboratories
The magazine of romance
McClure's
The magazine of service
The Rotarian
The magazine of the American
market
Look Magazine
The magazine of the fifth estate
Photoplay
The magazine of the hour
Radio Age
Magazine of the paper industry
Paper Trade Journal
The magazine of the radio trade
Radio Merchandising

The magazine of the toiletries
    trade
    Good Looks Merchandising
Magazine of today and tomorrow
    American Magazine
The magazine of Western living
    Sunset
The magazine of world business
    International Management
A magazine only a homemaker
    could love
    Family Circle
The magazine that brings the
    outdoors in
    Outdoor Recreation
The magazine that grew up with
    the industry
    Frozen Foods Magazine
The magazine that moves the
    men who move the
    merchandise
    Progressive Farmer
The magazine that saves building
    dollars doesn't cost you
    a cent
    Building Profit
The magazine to watch
    Panorama
A magazine with a mission
    Hearst's Magazine
The magazine with America's
    largest primary audi-
    ence
    TV Guide
The magazine women believe in
    Ladies Home Journal
Magazines of clean fiction
    All Fiction Field
Magee Carpet Co.
    Fashion loomed to last
    Look for the spinning wheel
    label
    Loomed by American labor
    to beautify American
    homes
    Magee rugs and carpets
    make a house a home
    The mill of 2000 dinner
    pails
    Woven with a warp of
    honesty and a woof
    of skill
Magee rugs and carpets make
    a house a home
    Magee Carpet Co.
Magellan: top performance.

Consistently
    Fidelity Magellan Fund
Magic Baking Powder
    Contains no alum
Magic Chef gas range
    The gas range with the life-
    time burner guarantee
    You can cook it better with
    Magic Chef
The magic fingers of radio
    Eddie Duchin's dance or-
    chestra
Magic-Keller Soap Works
    Seems to work like magic
Magic Mist bug spray
    Don't live in a "bug house"
The magic of Masland carpets
    C. H. Masland and Sons
Magic scouring pad
    Just wet the pad and rub
Magic sewmanship
    Van Heusen shirts
The magic suds
    Swerl
The magic wand of a good cook
    Ohio Thermometer Co.
Magic word in junior sportswear
    Petti sportswear
Magill-Weinsheimer window enve-
    lope
    No "peeping Tom" can
    decipher the contents
Magirus diesel trucks
    Trucks that can handle
    America's problems be-
    cause they're built to
    handle the world's
Magnavox heaters
    Keep cold away with Mag-
    navox
Magnavox radio receiver
    Air unlox to Magnavox
    Alone in tone
    Clear to the ear
    In harmony with home and
    air
    The radiant name in radio
    Radio-ize your phonograph
    The reproducer supreme
    The reproducer with the
    movable coil
    The symbol of quality in
    radio since 1915
Magnavox radio tube
    The tube to buy to satisfy
Magnavox television receiver

The illustrated voice
The magnificent
The magnificent
Magnavox television receiver
Magnolia Products, Inc.
The seat of the in house
Magnus Beck Brewing Co.
Naturally smooth
Mahogany Assn., Inc.
The master wood of the
ages
Maid. See also: Made
Maid-Easy Cleansing Products
Corp.
Wizard of the wash
Maidenform brassieres
Keep your eye on Maiden-
form
There is a Maidenform for
every type of figure
This is the dream you can
be--with Maidenform
Maidenform corsets
Face the facts about your
figure
Mail Pouch chewing tobacco
The brand with the grand
aroma
Chew Mail Pouch tobacco
Treat yourself to the best
Main-dish foods for baby
Campbell's baby foods
The main line airway
United Air Lines, Inc.
Main Street of the Northwest
Northern Pacific Railway
Maine
Industrious Maine, New
England's big stake in
the future
Maine Development Commission
The potato is man's great-
est food
Majestic coal window
The mark of a modern home
Majestic radio receiver
Mighty monarch of the air
Majestic Range
The range with a reputation
Major Equipment Co.
Everything electrical for
the theater
A major lender, worldwide un-
der all market condi-
tions
Chase Manhattan Bank

The major zipper
Conmar slide fastener
Majorica
The world's most precious
simulated pearls
Majoring in marriage
Gorham Div., Textron, Inc.
Make a date with Model
Model tobacco
Make a date with Muriel
Muriel cigar
Make a sweet suite deal on your
next trip to Denver
Brock Residence Inn
Make Alta your home port
Alta Vineyards Co.
Make an heirloom
Woodcraft tools
Make every day a good day
Carrier Corporation
Make every plot a garden spot
Best Seed Co.
Make good foods taste better
Heinz ketchup
Make hard jobs easy
K-D Manufacturing Co.
Make insurance understandable
Employers Mutual Insurance
Co. of Wisconsin
Make it a habit, take "her" a
bar
Mary Lincoln Candies, Inc.
Make it a snappy new year
Dot fasteners
Make it Amoco all the way
Amoco Chemicals Corp.
Make it yourself on a Singer
Singer sewing machine
Make life sweeter
Brecht Candy Co.
Make men of boys
Structo toys
Make mine Ruppert
Ruppert's beer
Make more of your time this
year
Kodak cameras
Make no mistake about figure-
work; call Friden
Friden Div., Singer Co.
Make no mistake about paper-
work automation. Call
Friden
Friden Div., Singer Co.
Make old shirts like new
Dublife collars

Make Sunsweet your daily good
health habit
Sunsweet prunes
Make sure. Make it Minute
Maid
Minute Maid Orange Juice
Make the best better
4-H Club
Make the capital choice
Port Authority of the City
of St. Paul
Make the children happy
Yankiboy Play Clothes
Make the greeting sweeter
Quaker Maid Candies
Make the home look cheerful
Dozier & Gay Paint Co.
Make the jump to Toyota
Toyota automobile
Make the seasons come to you
Crystal Tips ice machine
Make the world brighter, send
a smile
Huttom Photo Stamp Co.
Make this startling test
Bost toothpaste
Make thy mark
Marx identification tags
Make tomorrow pay, Standardize
today
Standard Life Insurance Co.
Make warm friends
Holland Furnace Co.
Make writing your hobby, use
Hobby for writing
Hobby Stationers
Make you want to walk
Nature-Tread shoe
Make your choice Lady's Choice
Lady's Choice deodorant
Make your feet happy by keeping
them healthy
Foot Bath Crystal
Make your ice box a Frigidaire
Frigidaire Electric Refriger-
ation
Make your identity stick
Bingham Bros. glue
Make your own luck with Heddon
Heddon fishing tackle
Make your trucks help sell your
business
Nason Paint Co.
Make your windows avenues of
health
Vita Glass Corp.

Maker of America's number 1 cat
food
Quaker Oats Company
Maker of fine rubber goods for
over fifty years
Kleinert Rubber Co.
Maker of the world's finest cord-
less electric tools
The Black & Decker Mfg.
Co.
Maker of the world's most wanted
pens
Parker Pen Co.
The maker who is proud of what
he makes uses Egyptian
Lacquer
Egyptian Lacquer Mfg. Co.
Maker's Mark whiskey
It tastes expensive ... and
is
The maker's name proclaims its
quality
Pabst Blue Ribbon beer
Makers of America's finest fitting
overcoats
Barron-Anderson Co.
Makers of America's most useful
vehicles
Willys-Overland automobile
Makers of better things for better
living
E. I. DuPont de Nemours &
Co.
Makers of fine shoes for men and
women
Florsheim Shoe Co.
Makers of high grade ball-
bearings, the most
complete line of types
and sizes in America
Fafner Bearing Co.
Makers of medicines prescribed
by physicians
Parke, Davis and Co.
Makers of the safety stripe
tread
Fisk tires
Makers of the world's only elec-
tronic blanket
Simmons Company
Makers of things more useful
Benjamin Electric Mfg. Co.
Makes a blow-out harmless
Goodyear Safety Tubes
Makes a joint that's tight, plus
alignment that's right

Ohio Brass Co.
Makes any good shoe better
  United Shoe Machinery Corp.
Makes any liquor taste like a
    better liquor
  Hoffman club soda
Makes baking taste better
  Enterprise Flour
Makes better breakfasts
  Shirriff's marmalade
Makes canning a pleasure
  Gold Pack Canner
Makes cats playful!
  Premium Catnip
Makes cotton look and feel like
    linen
  Linit laundry starch
Makes drinks taste better, cost
    less
  Everess sparkling water
Makes electric shaving easier
  Lectric Shave lotion
Makes every acre do its best
  Armour's Fertilizer
Makes every bite a banquet
  Iron City beer
Makes every meal a company
    meal
  Chicken of the Sea tuna
Makes every meal an event
  Premier Salad Dressing
Makes every road a boulevard
  Hartford shock absorber
Makes eyes sparkle and mouths
    water
  Mazola vegetable oil
Makes fashion a fine art
  Dumari fabrics
Makes fine, better cakes
  Swan's Down cake flour
Makes fish day a red letter day
  Chicken of the Sea tuna
Makes fried foods taste delicious
    --not greasy
  Crisco shortening
Makes good beds better
  Wittliff Furniture Brace Co.
Makes good food taste better
  Diamond Crystal Salt
Makes good tea a certainty
  Tetley's Tea
Makes happy boys
  Ives Manufacturing Co.
Makes hard water soft
  Gold Dust Soap Powder
Makes him love every hair of

your head
  Rayve Shampoo
Makes home sweet home
  Log Cabin Syrup
Makes homes more livable
  Brown Company
Makes hot days cool
  Chase and Sanborn iced cof-
    fee
Makes its mark around the world
  Waterman's Ideal Fountain
    Pen
Makes its own gas, use it any-
    where
  Coleman Co., Inc.
Makes its own gravy
  Gravy Train dog food
Makes its own ink
  Camel fountain pen
Makes kids husky
  National Oats Co.
  Three Minute Cereals
Makes many warm friends
  Gillson furnaces
Makes midsummer "knights"
    dream
  Drene shampoo
Makes milk into delicious desserts
  Junket powder
Makes more loaves of better
    bread
  Robin Hood Flour
Makes night as safe as day
  Benzer Lens
Makes night time plain as day
  Gilbert radium dial clock
Makes old paint brushes new
  Savabrush cleaner
Makes old things new, keeps new
    things bright
  Brite-Lite polish
Makes oven cleaning easier
  Easy-off Oven Cleaner
Makes pancakes mother's way
  Armour Grain Co.
Makes paper make money for you
  Cellophane
Makes products better, safer,
    stronger, lighter
  Fiber Glass Div., PPG In-
    dustries, Inc.
Makes the skin like velvet
  Mystic Cream
Makes tires last longer
  Schrader products
Makes tires look new and last

longer
Tirenew rubber tire preser-
    vative
Makes today's hash as tasty as
    yesterday's roast
    A-1 Sauce
Makes varnish vanish
    Double-X Floor Cleaner
Makes washday a heyday
    Fleecy White Laundry Bleach
Makes water wetter
    PN-700 washing powder
Makes writing easier
    White & Wyckoff Mfg. Co.
Makes you feel fit faster
    Bromo-Seltzer
Makes you feel like a king
    Imperial Margarine
Makes you feel sunny inside
    Mars candy bar
Makes you glad you're thirsty
    Budwine beer
Makes your cookin' good-lookin'
    Gravy Master
Makes your hair look its best
    Watkins Cocoanut Oil
    Shampoo
Makes your house a White House
    O'Brien Varnish Co.
Makes your husband feel young-
    er, too ... just to
    look at you!
    Loving Care hair color
Making a nation of better cooks
    Hughes Electric Ranges
Making advanced technology
    work
    Northrop Corporation
Making friends through the
    years
    Hunter whiskey
Making houses into homes
    Rheem Mfg. Co.
Making machines do more so man
    can do more
    Sperry Rand Corporation
Making more kinds of casters;
    making casters do
    more
    The Bassick Co.
Making music possible for every-
    one
    Oscar Schmidt International,
    Inc.
Making petroleum do more
    things for more people

ARCO Atlantic Richfield Co.
Making smoking "safe" for smok-
    ers
    Bonded Tobacco Co.
Making strong the things that
    make America strong
    Russell, Bursdall Bolts
Making the world safe for baby
    Trimble Nurseryland Furni-
    ture, Inc.
Making the world sweeter
    Tootsie Rolls candy
Making things happen in Mid-
    America
    AmeriTrust Bank, Cleveland,
    Ohio
Making things happy with petro-
    leum energy
    ARCO Atlantic Richfield
    Co.
Making today's medicines with
    integrity ... seeking
    tomorrow's with per-
    sistence
    A. H. Robins Co.
Making your world a little easier
    Whirlpool Corporation
The makings of a nation
    Bull Durham tobacco
Malady & MacLauchlan
    Insure clerical efficiency
    and profit protection,
    use multiple copy forms
    Multiple copy forms for
    profit preservation
Maley's slot machines
    The queen of all slot ma-
    chines
Malleable Iron Range Co.
    The stay-satisfactory range
The mallet with the oval handle
    Warren Handle Works Co.
Mallory. See also: P. R. Mal-
    lory and Co., Inc.
Mallory controls
    You expect more and get
    more from Mallory
Mallory hats
    All that you like in a hat
    The hat that goes with
    good clothes
Maloley's grocery supermarkets
    At Maloley's we like you!
The malt beverage that looks
    and tastes like a
    champagne

Sparkling Grenay
Malta Manufacturing Co.
The line and design for
creative window plan-
ning
Maltcao chocolate
Builds for the years ahead
Maltex
Eat a 100% breakfast
Man alive! Two for five
Standard Cigar Co.
Man does not live by stocks and
bonds alone
Chicago Mercantile Exchange
The man from A. G. Becker is
always worth listening
to
A. G. Becker & Co., Inc.
A man is known by his Kay-
woodie
Kaywoodie pipe
Man-O-West trousers
There are no dudes in our
duds
Man, that's corn
Pfister Associated Growers
Man to man, Roi Tan, a cigar
you'll like
Roi-Tan Little Cigars
A man who can't remember his
last hailstorm is likely
to get one he will never
forget
Rain & Hail Insurance
Bureau
The man who cares says: "Car-
stairs White Seal"
Carstairs White Seal whiskey
The man who put the EE's in
FEET
Allen's Foot-Ease
A man with a family snapshot in
his pocket is never far
from home
Kodak cameras
The man with the plan
Employers Group Insurance
A man worth knowing
Aetna Insurance Co.
Management Assistance, Inc.
At MAI our competitors
are often our customers
It takes a smart company
to make computer tech-
nology simple
Our business is helping

other businesses grow
Management publication of the
housing industry
House and Home
Management Science America, Inc.
The softwear company
Managing energy, comfort and
protection
Johnson Controls, Inc.
Managing energy is our business
Peoples Energy Corporation
Manatool Div., Perry-Fay Co.
Progressive products for
fluid control
Manges. See: Simon Manges
and Son, Inc.
Manhattan brake lining
Sets a new braking standard
Manhattan Industries, Inc.
Internationally known mark
of quality
Manhattan Soap Sales Corp.
Use the Sweetheart Skin
Diet
Manhattan Vericool shirts
When it's hot it's Vericool
Manhattan watch
Handsome, stylish, reliable
The manicure everyone knows
Peggy Sage
Mannesmann builds for the future
Mannesmann-Export Corp.
Mannesmann-Export Corp.
Mannesmann builds for the
future
Manning Abrasive Co.
Good workmen know the
difference
Manning the frontiers of elec-
tronic progress
Autonetics Div., North
American Rockwell Corp.
Mannings Coffee
More flavor per cup
Manpower, Inc.
The very best in temporary
help
World leader in temporary
help
A man's best
Bavarian Brewing Co.
A man's first choice
Weyenberg Shoe Mfg. Co.
The man's magazine
Beau
The man's spice so many women

love
Old Spice lotion
The man's styleful shoe on a real
    chassis
    Wright Arch Preserver
        shoes
A man's treasure
    Brock watches
Mansfield shoes
    In cool step, to the minute
Mansfield wheat flour
    Strong as leather
Manuel Feldman Co., Inc.
    Wholesale floor coverings of
        distinction
Manufacturer's Hanover Bank
    America's premier banker's
        bank
    The financial service.
        Worldwide
    It's good to have a great
        bank behind you
Manufacturers Liability Insurance
    Co.
    We aim to humanize the sci-
        ence of insurance
Manufacturers News
    The key magazine of indus-
        try
Manufacturers of creative build-
    ing products
    Caradco, Inc.
Manufacturers of equipment to
    make coal a better fuel
    McNally Pittsburgh Mfg.
        Corp.
Manufacturers of quality drapery
    hardware since 1903
    Silent Gliss, Inc.
Manufacturers of quality hard-
    wood products since
    1872
    Connor Lumber and Land
        Co.
Manufacturers of world's most
    widely used personal
    communications trans-
    mitters
    E. F. Johnson Co.
Manufacturers Oil & Grease Co.
    Lubricants of quality
Manufacturers Trust Co.
    Courtesy, efficiency,
        service
    Unit banking speeds busi-
        ness

The manufacturing and construc-
    tion journal of the tex-
    tile industry
    Cotton
Manville Corp.
    Manville's assets are a con-
        spicious strength
Manville Corp. See also: Johns-
    Manville Corporation
Manville's assets are a conspicious
    strength
    Manville Corp.
Many are picked. Few are frozen
    Tree Top frozen apple juice
Many typewriters in one
    Hammond typewriter
Manzel Div., Houdaille Industries
    No one is in a better posi-
        tion to solve your lub-
        rication problems
Manzelle brassiere
    Rest assured
Mapco, Inc.
    Bringing imagination to the
        business of energy
    Exploring, producing, re-
        fining, transporting,
        marketing energy
Maple at its best
    Bucket syrup
Maple Flooring Mfrs. Assn.
    Floor with maple, beech or
        birch
Mar-VEL-ous for dishes, stock-
    ings, lingerie, woolens
    Vel
Maraca rum
    Light or dry, in step with
        the times
Marathon Div., American Can Co.
    For quality paper products
        you can't beat Marathon
    Your paper problems are in
        good hands with Mara-
        thon
Marathon Div., American Can
    Co. See also: Ameri-
    can Can Co.
March of Dimes
    Follow through--with your
        help to prevent birth
        defects
    To protect the unborn and
        the newborn
Marchant. See also: Merchant
Marchant calculating machine

Master of mathematics
Marcus. See also: Markus
Marcus-Lesonine bobbie pin
    Keep your bob at its best
Marfak motor oil
    That cushiony feeling lasts
      longer with Marfak
Maria. See: Tia Maria liqueur
Marie Brizard liqueurs
    Yes, I know ... Marie
      Brizard
Marine Midland Bank
    Tell it to the Marine
Marine Review
    A national publication de-
      voted to ship operation
      and shipbuilding
Marines beat tough scrapes with
    cool shaves
    Ingram's shaving cream
Marion Power Shovel Co.
    Progress begins with dig-
      ging
Marion Tool Works
    Tools you can sell with
      confidence
Maritz, Inc.
    Motivating men to sell your
      product is our business
Mark every grave
    Memorial Craftsmen of Amer-
      ica
Mark it for market ... the Weber
    way
    Weber Marking Systems,
      Inc.
The mark of a distinctive kitchen
    Elkay Sturdibilt metal prod-
      ucts
The mark of a good case
    Puffer-Hubbard cabinet
The mark of excellence
    Par-X Vegetables
Mark of good plate glass
    Pittsburgh Plate Glass Co.
The mark of a good roof
    Celotex Corp.
The mark of a modern home
    Majestic coal window
The mark of a well-built house
    Flax-li-num Insulating Co.
Mark of American leadership
    since 1865
    Elgin watches
The mark of America's smartest
    leather goods

Ender-Kress leather goods
The mark of distinction
    Sanpeck fabric
Mark of economical light
    General Electric Mazda
      Lamp
Mark of excellence
    General Motors Corporation
    Oneida, Ltd.
The mark of good insulators
    Victor Insulators
The mark of quality
    Schick Electric, Inc.
The mark of quality in tobacco
    products
    Viceroy cigarettes
Mark of quality throughout the
    world
    Admiral television sets
The mark of research service
    General Electric Company
The mark of the world's most
    famous hat
    Stetson hats
The mark of total reliability
    Speed Nuts
The mark that is a message in
    itself
    Crane's papers
Markem Machine Co.
    Helping your product speak
      for itself
Market-directed
    McGraw-Hill Publications
      Div., McGraw-Hill, Inc.
Marketing methods since 1850
    Industrial Marketing Div.,
      Jas. H. Matthews and
      Co.
Markets for today's investor
    Index and Option Market
Marks. See also: Marx
Marks a new era in automobile
    construction
    Gas-au-lec automobile
Markus. See also: Marcus
Markus-Campbell Co.
    Personalized home study
      training
Marlboro cigarettes
    Come to Marlboro Country
    Come to where the flavor
      is
    Ivory tips protect your
      lips
    Mild as May

The perfect cigarette
Marlboro menthol cigarettes
The big menthol taste from
Marlboro Country--you
get a lot to like
Marlboro shirts
Most admired, most desired
for cool comfort
Marlin Firearms Co.
A gun for every American
shooting need
Symbol of accuracy since
1870
Marlin razor blades
Shave and save with Marlin
blades
Marmola
Pleasant way to reduce
Marmon automobile
Ace of the eights
America's first truly fine
small car
Merit And Reliability Made
Our Name
Square deals revolve on
Marmon wheels
A streak of good luck
Visitors welcome, customers
pleased
Where sales and service
meet
You select, we protect
Marriott hotels
This is living ... this is
Marriott
When Marriott does it, they
do it right
Marriott's Essex House
In Manhattan, a breath of
fresh air on Central
Park
Marry your trousers to the
Century-Brace
Chester Suspender Co.
Mars candy bar
Makes you feel sunny in-
side
You get big, crunchy nuts
in a Mars Bar
Marsh & McLennan, Inc.
Industry's leading insurance
brokers
On the job wherever a cli-
ent's interest is at
stake
When it comes to insur-

ance, come to the leader
Marsh Gauges
The standard of accuracy
Marshall mattress
Rest assured
Marshmallow treat
J. H. Slingerland
Marston & Brooks shoes
Honest wear in every pair
Martel
The cognac brandy for
every occasion
Martex and Fairfax towels
Twin names in quality towels
Martin. See: Remy Martin
cognac
Martin L. Roman
Use the mails to increase
your sales
Martin outboard motors
The new standard of per-
formance
Martin Reel Co.
Precision fishing reels since
1883
Martin Senour Co.
Color or white you're always
right with Martin Senour
Master of color finishes
since 1858
Master of color since 1858
Voice of quality
Martin Ullman Studios
Idea creators, not just il-
lustrators
Martini & Rossi Vermouth
The flavor secret of the
finest cocktails
Martinizing. See: One Hour
Martinizing
Martin's. See: John Martin's
Book
Martinson's coffee
Flying saucers are just
looking for a cup of
richer, stronger Mar-
tinson's
Marvel Bread
BREAD to the queen's taste
The marvel of the electrical age
Columbia batteries
Marvella pearls
Could it be the real thing?
For ever-changing fashion,
the never-changing
beauty of Marvella

294

pearls
A marvelous new perfume
    Raquel, Inc.
Marvelube lubricant
    New freedom from lubrica-
        tion worries
Marvin watch
    For perfection of the Swiss
        watchmaking art
Marx. See also: Marks
Marx identification tags
    For good Marx-manship
    Make thy mark
Mary Chess perfume
    Surround your life with
        fragrance
Mary Lincoln Candies, Inc.
    Make it a habit, take "her"
        a bar
    Old-fashioned goodness in
        every piece
Mary Pickford Cosmetics
    Beauty on a budget
Maryland Assurance Corporation
    Live and die with Assurance
Maryland's Masterpiece
    National Premium Beer
Mary's no longer contrary
    Dentyne chewing gum
Masland. See also: C. H.
        Masland and Sons
The Masland Duraleather Co.
    Where beauty is material
Mason. See also: Nason
Mason Clothes
    For the nicest youngsters
        you know
Mason Fibre Co.
    Keep heat where it belongs
Mason tires
    Means more mileage
Masonite Corp.
    Shows the way!
Massachusetts
    It is profitable to produce
        in Massachusetts
    Work in the state that works
        for you
A massage for the gums
    Gum-rub dentifrice
Massagic Air Cushion shoes
    Absorb shocks and jars
    Ease your feet ankle-deep
        into Massagic comfort
    Foot-fresh around the clock
    He won't change from shoes

to slippers because he's
    enjoying Massagic com-
        fort
Keep your foot fresh
Yield with every step
Massey-Ferguson, Inc.
    The big job matched line
The massive men's market in
        print
    True
Masson. See: Paul Masson
        wines
The master blend
    Cobb's whiskey
The master builder
    Kawai piano
The master car builders of Japan
    Mitsubishi automobile
Master crafted
    Eljer Plumbingware Div.,
        Wallace-Murray Corp.
Master craftsmanship in steel
    Van Dorn Iron Works Co.
Master craftsmen since 1890
    Biggs Antique Co., Inc.
Master designers of modern
        centrifugal pumps
    Morris Machine Works
The master drawing pencil
    J. Dixon Crucible Co.
The master hair coloring
    Rap-I-Dol hair coloring
Master hand at the throttle
    Fordson governors
Master laminated padlock
    Built like a bank vault door
Master Lock Co.
    World's leading padlock
        manufacturers
Master of mathematics
    Marchant calculating machine
Master of road and load
    Russel Motor Axle Co.
Master of the highway
    Hudson automobile
Master jeweler
    Monet Jewelers
Master Lock Company
    World's strongest padlocks
Master Mix feed
    Serving the businessman in
        the blue denim suit
Master navigators through time
        and space
    A. C. Spark Plug Div.,
        General Motors Corpor-

ation
Master of color finishes since
1858
Martin Senour Co.
Master of color since 1858
Martin Senour Co.
Master of the load on any road
Master trucks
Master of traction
Arrow Grip Mfg. Co.
Master trucks
Master of the load on any
road
The master wood of the ages
Mahogany Assn., Inc.
Mastercraft seat cover
Nothing could be finer
Masterpieces for the millions
Columbia Protektosite Co.
Masterpieces in plastic
Columbia Protektosite Co.
The master's fingers on your
piano
Auto-Pneumatic Action Co.
Masters gravy making
Gravy Master
Masterworkers in machinery for
printing and converting
Mecca Machinery Co.
Mastery in linens
Moygashel linens
Mastery in radio
Freed-Eisemann Radio Corp.
Mastery of precision optics
Varo Optical, Inc.
Matched flavor
Dwight Edwards Coffee
Matched tools for unmatched
performance
Baash-Ross Div., Joy
Manufacturing Co.
Matchless cooking
Norge electric range
Matchless electric water heating
Los Angeles Bureau of
Power and Light
Matchless in more ways than
one
Los Angeles Bureau of
Power and Light
Matchless in outdoor excellence
Mercury outboard motor
Matchless quality ... superior
service ... enduring
excellence
Electrolux Refrigerator

The matchless tone of the
"Golden Throat"
Victrola talking machine
Matchless valves for exacting
service
Whitey Research Tool Co.
The material difference in build-
ing
Geon vinyls
The material handling systems
house
Acco Babcock, Inc.
The material of a thousand uses
Bakelite
Mathes. See: Curtis Mathes
television sets
Mathews. See also: Matthews
Mathews Conveyor Co.
Mathews conveyor systems
increase plant profits
Modern conveying means
Mathews
Mathews conveyor systems in-
crease plant profits
Mathews Conveyor Co.
Mathews Industries, Inc.
Metal, the fifth medium
Mathieson. See: Olin Mathieson
Chemical Corp.
Matrix shoes
A curve-for-curve copy of
the bottom of your foot
Your footprints in leather
Your footprints in leather
Matson Navigation Co.
Knows the Pacific
The ships that serve Hawaii,
South Seas and Australia
Unforgettable Hawaii, no
land so hard to bid
adieu
The vacation way to Hawaii
A matter of personal pride
Chevrolet Monte Carlo auto-
mobile
A matter of pride, pleasure and
good, plain sense
Skinner garment linings
Matthews. See also:
Industrial Marketing Div.,
Jas. H. Matthews and
Co.
Mathews
Matthews boat
Wherever you cruise you'll
find a Matthews

Matthews Co.
    Iron horse quality
The mattress that feels so good
    Spring-Air mattress
Mavis chocolate drink
    If you like chocolate, you'll
        like Mavis
Mavis talcum powder
    Finer than many face pow-
        ders
Max Factor and Co.
    The authority in the excit-
        ing world of beauty
    For that smart sun-tan look
Max Factor lipstick
    The color stays on until
        you take it off
Maxfer Truck
    This is the answer to the
        high cost of horse
        delivery
    The whale for work
Maximum capacity
    CaPac automobile parts
Maximum fluoride protection in
    a great-tasting gel
    Colgate's dental cream
Maximum refrigeration efficiency
    Dole Refrigeration Co.
Maximum strength cold relief for
        every cold symptom
    Coldmax cold reliever
Maxitorq machinery
    Let's talk Maxitorq
Maxwell automobile
    Every road is a Maxwell
        road
    More miles per gallon--
        more miles on tires
    Pay as you ride!
Maxwell House Master Blend
        Coffee
    America's largest selling
        high grade coffee
    The first taste tells you,
        it's good to the last
        drop
    Good to the last drop
    It only tastes expensive
    A luxury millions enjoy
    Maxwell House, too, is
        part of the American
        scene
    The Old South's treasure
        now all America's
        pleasure

One of the Old South's fin-
        est traditions
    Part of the American scene
    When life needs a lift
    Maxwell House, too, is part of
        the American scene
    Maxwell House Master Blend
        Coffee
May Breath
    Be careful lest the breath
        offend
May Oil Burner Corp.
    Let the furnace man go ...
        forever
Maybelline
    The eye make-up in good
        taste
    The most prized eye cos-
        metics in the world
Mayer. See:
    F. Mayer Shoe Co.
    Oscar Mayer wieners
Mayfair Hotel, St. Louis, Mo.
    Downtown St. Louis at your
        doorstep
    Live in the atmosphere of
        an exclusive club
    There is no better place to
        eat
Mayfair House, New York City
    Has the quiet refinement
        of an exclusive club
    An hotel of discrimination
    Live in the atmosphere of
        an exclusive club
    There is no better place to
        eat
Mayflower Moving Agency
    Our name means moving
Maytag Company
    The dependability people
Maytag laundry washers
    Big washings on small bud-
        gets
    The dependable automatic
    If it doesn't sell itself
        don't keep it
    If washday lasts an hour,
        I've loafed
    Millions of women have their
        hearts set on a new
        Maytag
    You're money ahead with a
        Maytag
Mazda automobile
    The more you look, the

more you like
Mazola makes good eating sense
  Mazola margarine
Mazola margarine
  Mazola makes good eating
    sense
  The name you can trust in
    margarine
Mazola vegetable oil
  Makes eyes sparkle and
    mouths water
  The salad and cooking oil
The Mead Corp.
  Paper makers of America
Mead Cycle Co.
  Factory to rider saves you
    money
Meakin & Ridgeway
  The world's most beautiful
    china
A meal in a glass
  Toddy
Meals without meat are incom-
    plete
  Theobald Industries
Mealtime dry dog food
  Even finicky eaters love the
    meaty taste
Mean more power to you
  Nordberg engines
The meanest chore is a chore
    no more
  Saniflush Toilet Bowl
    Cleaner
Means'. See: James Means' $3
    shoe
Means better underwear
  Amho underwear
Means more mileage
  Mason tires
Means profits for business
  Louisiana Dept. of Com-
    merce and Industry
Means safety made certain
  Raybestos-Manhattan, Inc.
Mears shoe heel
  The heel that won't peel
The measure of perfection
  William Penn whiskey
Measure of quality
  Uncle Ben's, Inc.
Measure up with the best
  The Lufkin Rule Co.
Measure yourself for a Kelly
  Kelly cigar
Measured heat

Williams Oil-O-Matic Heating
    Corp.
The meat chopper for the people
  Enterprise meat chopper
Meat from wheat
  Golden Age Macaroni
The meat makes the meal
  Swift's Premium meats
The meats that wear the Armour
    Star are the meats the
    butcher brings home
  Armour & Co.
Mecca Machinery Co.
  Masterworkers in machinery
    for printing and con-
    verting
Mecca Ointment
  Soothing, healing, pain-
    relieving
Meccano construction toy
  Engineering for boys
The mechanical hand that cranks
    your car
  Eclipse starter
Mechanical packing service
  Garlock Packing Service
Mechanically correct
  Grabowsky Power Wagons
Mechling. See: A. L. Mechling
    Barge Lines, Inc.
The medal scotch of the world
  Dewar's Blended Scotch
    Whiskey
Medicamenta vera
  Parke, Davis and Co.
A medicine for a woman. In-
    vented by a woman.
    Prepared by a woman
  Lydia E. Pinkham's Vege-
    table Compound
Medisalt dentifrice
  Be true to your teeth or
    they'll be false to you
Meehanite Metal Corp.
  Better castings through
    advanced foundry
    technology
Meets every requirement of the
    modern cyclist
  Christy Anatomical Saddle
Meets today's requirements, sets
    tomorrow's standard
  Raritan truck tires
Meets tomorrow's challenge today
  Canon camera
Mehron cosmetics

The kind you will always
want
Meigs Glasses
You can't be optimistic with
misty optics
Meilink Steel Safe Co.
Better protection with
Meilink-built safes
For a big difference in your
profits ... the line with
the big difference
Meiselbach Mfg. Co., Inc.
Veteran reel for veteran
fishermen
Melachrino cigarettes
The one cigarette sold the
world over
Melbroke ties
Soft as kitten's ears
Meldan Co., Inc.
Keeping tradition alive
Mellin's Food
I was a Mellin's Food baby
Mellin's Food is a true
Liebig's Food
We are advertised by our
loving friends
Mellin's Food is a true Liebig's
Food
Mellin's Food
Mellon National Bank
All your banking under one
roof
One of the banks that de-
fine banking
Mellow as moonlight
Vogan Candy Co.
Mellow as old Bourbon
Old Bushmill's Irish Whis-
key
Mellow as the greeting of old
friends
Canada Dry ginger ale
Mellowed in wood to full strength
Heinz vinegar
Melts dirt away
Old English Powdered
Cleaner
Melville Shoe Corp.
For every walk in life
The shoe everybody knows,
and almost everybody
wears
They walk with you
Mem toiletries
Tailor-made toiletries

Tailored men's toiletries
Memorial Craftsmen of America
Mark every grave
The memorial sublime
Deagan Chimes
Memphis Commercial Appeal
The South's greatest news-
paper
Men go wild about splendid teeth
Sozodont toothpaste
Men like the quiet type
Servel refrigerator
Men look, men linger, until she
smiles
Ipana toothpaste
Men ... perfect fit ... by mail!
We guarantee it!
Wright Arch Preserver
shoes
The men. The cigarette. No-
body does it better
Winston cigarettes
Men wear them everywhere
Florsheim Shoe Co.
Men who build America trust
this trade mark
Arro-lock Shingles
Men who know back OSCO
OSCO motors
Men who know valves know
Powell
The Wm. Powell Co.
The men who make it make the
difference
Steel and Tube Div., Tim-
ken Roller Bearing Co.
Menace perfume
Deliberate witchery
Mendel-Drucker trunks
America's best traveling
companion
If it's dust-proof it's a
Mendel
Mends everything but a broken
heart
Fix-All Liquid Cement
Mennen for men in service
Mennen's talcum powder
Mennen's baby oil
The antiseptic baby oil
Mennen's shave cream
Wilts whiskers
Mennen's talcum powder
Mennen for men in service
Nothing too good for men
in service

Nothing too good for our
boys
There's nothing too good
for men in service
Menthol-cooled
Spud menthol cigarettes
Mentholatum
The little nurse for little
ills
Mention Champ items on every
call
Champ-Items, Inc.
Meow Mix catfood
Tastes so good cats ask
for it by name
Mercantile Bank, St. Louis, Mo.
We're with you
Mercedes-Benz automobile
Engineered like no other
car in the world
Mercedes-Benz automobile. See
also: American Mer-
cedes automobile
Mercedes-Benz trucks
Doing one diesel of a job
Mercedes-Benz trucks save
you plenty now. And
more later
Mercedes-Benz trucks save you
plenty now. And
more later
Mercedes-Benz trucks
Merchant. See also: Marchant
Merchant in mileage
General Motors Corporation
The merchant-minded mill with
variety and reliability
Riegel Paper Corp.
Merchants Journal and Commerce
A magazine for southern
merchants
Merchants National Bank
Founded by merchants for
merchants
Merck, Sharp and Dohme Div.,
Merck and Co., Inc.
A guaranty of purity and
reliability
Where today's theory is
tomorrow's remedy
Mercury automobile
The car that did what
couldn't be done
More of everything you
want with Mercury
60,000 owners drove it

to success
Mercury Comet automobile
The world's 100,000 mile
durability champion
Mercury Marquis automobile
The substance shows
Mercury outboard motor
Matchless in outdoor excel-
lence
Mercury Record Corp.
Leadership through design
Meredith moves merchandise
Meredith Publishing Co.
Meredith Publishing Co.
Meredith moves merchandise
Merit And Reliability Made Our
Name
Marmon automobile
Merit cigarettes
The bottom line: Taste
The enriched flavor cigar-
ettes
Merit continues as proven
taste alternative to
higher tar smoking
Merit taste stands alone
Merit continues as proven taste
alternative to higher
tar smoking
Merit cigarettes
Merit taste stands alone
Merit cigarettes
Merits your confidence
Great Western Cordage Co.
Merkin paint
The choice of good painters
Merriam. See:
G. and C. Merriam Co.
H. W. Merriam
Merrichild Sleepers
Snug as a mother's hug
Merrill Lynch, Pierce, Fenner
& Smith, Inc.
A breed apart
We're bullish on America
Merrily we bowl along
American Magazine
Merry crispness
Proctor toaster
Mersman Tables
The costume jewelry of the
home
Tables are the costume
jewelry of the home
Merton. See: C. S. Merton
& Co.

A message of purity
Angelus Marshmallows
Messinger Bearings, Inc.
Smoothing industry's path-
way for nearly half a
century
Messner. See also: Julian
Messner, Inc.
Messner biographies lead all the
rest
Julian Messner, Inc.
Mesta Machine Co.
Better by design
Metal Hydrides, Inc.
Pioneers in hydride chemis-
try
Metal lath to reinforce and
preserve
National Council for Better
Plastering
Metal Package Corp.
A worthy product deserves
a fitting package
Metal Sponge Sales Co.
The modern dish cloth
Metal, the fifth medium
Mathews Industries, Inc.
Metallurgy is our business
Vanadium-Alloys Steel Co.
Metalworking News
Thundering power in the
eye of the market
Metameter
Keeps your entire system
under your fingertips
Methods that keynote the future
of business
Remington Office Systems
Div., Sperry Rand
Corporation
Metrecal
Consult your physician on
matters of weight con-
trol
Metropolitan Furniture Adjusters
The company with the
"know-how"
Metropolitan Life Insurance Co.
The fourth necessity
It pays to know when to
relax
Keep healthy, be examined
regularly
The light that never fails
More choose Metropolitan.
Millions more than any

other company
There's no obligation ...
except to those you love
Metropolitan Newspapers
The first national newspaper
network
Mexicana Airlines
We give you more
Meyer. See also: Mayer
Meyer Bros. Drug Co.
We cover the earth with
drugs of worth
Meyers. See: Myers
Miami, Fla.
America's business gateway
to the world
Where the summer spends
the winter
The wonder city of America
Miami Herald
Florida's most important
newspaper
Miami Tribune
Florida's fastest-growing
newspaper
Micatin Spray
The end of the road for
athlete's foot
Michelin tires
If anyone tells you Michelin
quality is too expensive
they're putting you on
We put America on radials
Michelob beer
Compare the price
Michelob light ... compare
the taste
One step ahead
Put a little weekend in
your week
Some things speak for them-
selves
Michelob light ... compare the
taste
Michelob beer
Michigan
Michigan, state of happiness
for everyone
Michigan Bell Telephone Co.
Our ambition: ideal tele-
phone service for
Michigan
Michigan Business Farmer
The farm paper of service
Michigan Seating Co.
For every room in the

house
With a heart of steel
Michigan State Automobile
School
The knowledge we put in
your head guides the
skill we put in your
hands
Michigan, state of happiness for
everyone
Michigan
Michigan's greatest advertising
medium
Radio station WJR
Mickleberry's Sausage
Our wurst is the best
Micronics makes it simple
Canon plain paper copier
Micropore adhesive tape
The tape that won't hurt
coming off
Microprint, Inc.
Creator of advanced writ-
ing instruments
Midas muffler and brake shops
Trust the Midas Touch
Midcon Corporation
Pipelines. Energy. And
the experience to go
from there
Middle South Utilities
At Middle South Utilities
we're making energy
that makes sense
Middleby-Marshall Oven Co.
World's largest commercial
oven manufacturer since
1888
A midget in size, a giant in
power
Gravely Motor Plow and
Cultivator
Midland-Ross Corp. See:
Janitrol Div., Midland-
Ross Corp.
Midol
What a difference Midol
makes
Whenever you need it
Midol has the strength
Midway Airlines
You won't find a better
value than Midway
Airlines
Midwest Radio Co.
Everything for the radio

man
Miele. See: Ralph A. Miele.
Inc.
Miessene Household Products
Buy quality, not quantity
Miessner piano
The little piano with the
big tone
Mifflin Alkohol Massage
The external tonic
The national rub down
Migell fabrics
Selvage will tell if made by
Migell
Mighty Dog dog food
The pure beef brand
Mighty good shoes for boys
Teeple Shoe Co.
A mighty good thought
Perfection bread
Mighty monarch of the air
Majestic radio receiver
Mighty monarch of the Arctic
Grisby-Grunow refrigerators
Mihalovitch's Hungarian Black-
berry Juice
A bottle of this should be
in every home
Mikimoto. See: K. Mikimoto,
Inc.
Milady chocolates
Every piece a sweet sur-
prise
Mild as May
Marlboro cigarettes
The mild chewing plug in a
pouch
R. J. Gold chewing tobacco
The milder, better-tasting
cigarette
Regent cigarettes
Mildness plus character
Congress Cigar Co.
Mileage hogs
Victor tires
Miles. See also: Dr. Miles
Medical Co.
Miles ahead
The Galion Iron Works and
Mfg. Co.
Miles Kimball mail order service
The armchair shopper's
favorite for 48 years
Miles of smiles
American Motors Corp.
Miles of travel comfort

Missouri-Kansas-Texas
Railroad
Miles tires
More miles with Miles
Milex Car Care
Get it done right
Military Brand Camembert
Cheese
The pride of the pantry
Milk at its best
Pet milk
The milk every doctor knows
Carnation condensed milk
Milk that cuts the cost of cook-
ing
Borden's condensed milk
Milky Way candy bar
Helps keep you going
When you crave good candy
The mill of 2000 dinner pails
Magee Carpet Co.
Mill-packed for your protection
Milwaukee Lace Paper Co.
Miller. See also: Doris Miller
clothes
Miller Freeman Publications
Serving industry construc-
tively since 1902
Miller High Life beer
America's quality beer
Brewed only in Milwaukee
The champagne of bottle
beer
Everything you always
wanted in a beer.
And less
If you've got the time
Miller's got the beer
It's Miller time
Let's win the Games again
Miller luggage
Built to fit the trip
Miller tires
Built layer on layer
Geared to the road
Uniform mileage
Miller's. See: Frank Miller's
Harness Dressing
Miller Falls Co.
Toolmaker to the master
mechanic
A million Americans can't be
wrong
Father & Son Shoes
A million and one uses
Fix-All Liquid Cement

Million dollar beauty in the lowest
priced field
Nash automobile
A million dollar library for $25
Encyclopaedia Britannica
The million dollar magic of Fats
Domino
Fats Domino and his music
The million dollar overall
Crown Overall Mfg. Co.
A million in service ten years or
longer
G. E. refrigerator
A million yards of good will
Hummel gummed paper mois-
tener
A Millionaire's Luxury
Kenney Needle Shower
Millions are saying "tasting better
than ever"
General Cigar Co.
Millions daily
Gem paper clips
Million's favor that Brookfield
flavor
Swift's Brookfield sausage
Millions of babies have been
raised on Clapp's Baby
Foods
Clapp's Baby Foods
Millions of Spud smokers can't
be wrong
Spud menthol cigarettes
Millions of women have their
hearts set on a new
Maytag
Maytag laundry washers
Millions prefer it
French's mustard
Millions remember Doelger, a
glass tells why
Doelger beer
Millis Advertising Co.
Teaching the millions to buy
Millprint, Inc.
Packaging headquarters to
American industry
Where the newest in packag-
ing is happening today
Milner Hotels
Coast to coast, we give the
most
Milo Hose
Will not kink
Milwaukee Journal
First, by merit

Milwaukee Lace Paper Co.
  Lace papers of character
  Mill-packed for your pro-
    tection
Milwaukee Paper Co.
  Brain-built boxes
Milwaukee River HIlton hotel
  We make you feel at home
    in Milwaukee
Milwaukee Road
  America's resourceful rail-
    road
  The railroad of "Creative
    Crews"
Milwaukee Tank Works
  The pump of compulsory
    accuracy
Milwaukee, Wis.
  America's best-managed
    city
Milwaukee won't run out of gas
  Wisconsin Gas Company
Milwaukee's choice
  Braumeister beer
Milwaukee's first bottled beer
  Blatz beer
Milwaukee's most exquisite beer
  Blatz beer
Min-A-Grow Corp. pet food
  Pep for your pup
Minard's Liniment
  The famous rubbing lini-
    ment
  The king of pain
A mind is a terrible thing to
    waste
  United Negro College Fund
Miner rubbers
  Keep your feet dry
The mineral salt laxative
  Sal Hepatica
Minerva Wax Paper Co.
  For waxing satisfaction
Ming Tea
  The most expensive tea
    grown
  Officially certified as the
    finest tea grown
The mini-brutes
  Opel-Kadette automobile
Mini-Max hearing aid
  Better hearing longer
The minister's trade journal
    since 1899
  The Expositor
Minit. See also: Minute

Minit-Rub
  The modern rub-in
Minneapolis Hilton Inn
  We make you feel at home
    in the Twin Cities
Minneapolis-Moline, Inc.
  Engineered for longer life
Minneapolis Tribune
  The dominant newspaper of
    the Great Northwest
Minnesota
  Minnesota brainpower builds
    profits
Minnesota and Ontario Paper Co.
  See: Insulite Div.,
    Minnesota and Ontario
    Paper Co.
Minnesota brainpower builds
    profits
  Minnesota
Minnesota Mining & Manufacturing
    Co.
  For imagination in communi-
    cation, look to 3M
    business product centers
  Look to 3M for imagination
    in image-making
  One of the oldest names in
    the business
  Talk with the microfilm
    systems people
  3M hears you...
Minnesota Mining & Manufacturing
    Co. See also: Revere-
    Wollensack Div., Minne-
    sota Mining & Manufac-
    turing Co.
Minolta Corporation
  Fine photography for 40
    years
Minolta duplicator
  A business partner you can
    depend on
Minox Chemical Corp.
  Chlorine ointment, better
    than iodine
Minox Corp.
  The camera you never leave
    at home
  A famous camera from
    camera-famous West
    Germany
Mint Cocktail Gum
  It's smart to choose what
    Hollywood chews
The mint within your reach

Strong, Cobb & Co.
Minton, Inc.
  The world's most beautiful
    china
Minute. See also: Minit
Minute Maid Orange Juice
  Make sure. Make it Minute
    Maid
  Tastes like you squeezed
    it
The Minuteman Six
  Lexington automobile
Mira-Pak, Inc.
  Pacemakers in flexible
    package-makers
A miracle in the rain
  Koroseal raincoat
Miracle Whip salad dressing
  Better than mayonnaise,
    yet costs less
  The bread spread
The miracle yarn
  Lastex
The miracle yarn that makes
    things fit
  Lastex
Mirawal Co.
  Quality products for quality
    living
Mirro Aluminum Co.
  The finest aluminum
  The house of experience
  Reflects good housekeeping
Mishawaka Rubber Co., Inc.
  Look for the red ball
Mishawaka Woolen Mfg. Co.
  The house that pays mil-
    lions for quality
Miss Saylor's Chocolates
  America's finest chocolates
  For the sparkle of youth
Missile quality ball bearings
  MPB, Inc.
Missing the boat? Own an
    Owens
  Owens Yacht Co.
Mississippi
  The hospitality state
Missoula Shopping News
  Save your money, time and
    shoes; read Missoula
    Shopping News
Missouri
  Missouri is right ... in
    the center
  Missouri is right ... in the

center
  Missouri
Missouri-Kansas-Texas Railroad
  Miles of travel comfort
  Pioneer railroad of the south-
    west
Missouri Pacific Railroad
  The outstanding scenic way
    west
Mr. Clean cleaning fluid
  Helps no-wax floors keep
    shining bright
  The shine of approval
Mr. John
  Designs for the world's best
    dressed
Mistere cold cream
  Soft as a mist
Mistol rub
  Rub your cold away
Mrs. Butterworth's syrup
  The leading syrup
Mrs. Day's Ideal Baby Shoe Co.
  Better little shoes are not
    made
  Not made to a price, but a
    perfect product
Mrs. Paul's fish fillets
  It doesn't leave my kitchen
    unless it's delicious
Mrs. Stewart's Bluing
  The blue of spotless reputa-
    tion
  Sold by the carload, used
    by the drop
Mrs. Tucker's Shortening
  Costs less by the biscuit
Mitsubishi Aircraft International,
    Inc.
  Quality takes wing
Mitsubishi automobile
  The master car builders of
    Japan
Mittman. See: M. Mittman Co.
Mix 'em and match 'em
  Buster Boy suits
Mix fun and history in Virginia
  Virginia Dept. of Conserva-
    tion and Economic De-
    velopment
The mixable one
  Bacardi rum
Mixes in any society
  Celo Co. of America
Mixes well with any friend
  Indian Hill ginger ale

305

Mmm! What a tan! tanning
 lotion
 It's all in the moisturizing
MMMM--Murine
 Murine eye drops
M-m-m-m, we go for Safe-T
 cones
 Illinois Baking Corp.
Mobay Chemical Co.
 First in urethane chemistry
Mobil Oil Corp.
 As the sign of friendly
 service
 For good advice ... and
 good products ... de-
 pend on your Mobil
 dealer
 There's a good future with
 Mobil
Mobil Tires
 More miles, more smiles
Mobilgas
 Protect horsepower; that's
 horse sense
 That Red Horse outpaces
 them all
 You get power, pick-up and
 pep
Modart Fluff Shampoo
 Does your hair sing when
 you rinse it?
Model it with Modelit
 Modelit construction toy
Model tobacco
 Make a date with Model
 Smells better in the pouch;
 smokes better in the
 pipe
Modelit construction toy
 Model it with Modelit
Modene Hair Remover
 Every bottle guaranteed
The modern aid to appetite con-
 trol
 Slim-Mint gum
The modern bed of coals
 Tampa electric range
Modern Belt Co.
 Find this button and
 you've found the belt
Modern business forms for
 modern business
 systems
 Baltimore Salesbook Co.
Modern conveying means
 Mathews

Mathews Conveyor Co.
The modern dish cloth
 Metal Sponge Sales Co.
The modern farm paper
 Country Gentleman
Modern Farming
 The Louisiana-Mississippi
 farm paper
Modern fuel for modern heating
 Koppers Co., Inc.
The modern genii of the lamp
 Silverglo lamps
The modern gentle laxative
 Correctol
Modern heat with oldtime fireside
 cheer
 Allen parlor furnace
The modern light conditioning
 bulb
 Wabash Appliance Corp.
Modern Machine
 Put your money where the
 market is
The modern magic carpet
 Bell helicopter
Modern masters of time
 Seiko Time Corp.
The modern mattress
 Koylon mattress
Modern Medicine
 The journal of diagnosis
 and treatment
The modern method of beauty
 care
 Doree Products Co.
The modern miracle wall finish
 Kem-Tone
The modern oil filter
 Fram oil filter
Modern Packaging
 The complete authority of
 packaging
The modern plumbers' trade
 magnet
 Republic Brass Co.
Modern Priscilla
 The trade paper of the
 home
The modern rub-in
 Minit-Rub
Modern silver with the beauty
 of old masterpieces
 Watson sterling silver
The modern toothbrush
 Tek toothbrush
The modern way to grow

National Rain Bird Sales and
    Engineering Corp.
The modern way to moisten
    Hummel gummed paper mois-
    tener
Modern, yet proved by centuries
    of use
    Stainwax
Modernized heating
    Johnson Vacu-Draft heater
Modess sanitary napkins
    Because...
    Try the new "free-stride"
    Walk with comfort
Moët champagne
    From the largest cellars in
    the world
Mogen David wine
    America's spunky spritzer
Mohawk Rubber Co.
    Standard of the industry
Mohawk rugs and carpets
    Beauty basis for your home
    Beauty that endures
    Theme-inspired beauty for
    budget brides
Moist as homemade
    Duncan Hines cake mix
Moisturewear makeup
    Everything its name prom-
    ises
Mojud hosiery
    The dependable hosiery
    So sheer, so sleek, so
    smooth fitting
    That's all you need to know
    about stockings
Molded Fiber Glass Companies,
    Inc.
    Look to MFG for the shape
    of things to come
Molle shaving cream
    It's heavier
    You need a heavier cream
    to shave a tender skin
Molybdenum metal
    Cuts costs, creates sales
Monarch automobile batteries
    Faster starts with Monarch
    Power that stays
Monarch Cleaner
    Monarch cleans a house and
    all that's in it
    There's not a cleaner like
    it
Monarch cleans a house and

all that's in it
    Monarch Cleaner
Monarch Life Insurance Co.
    Lifelong security through
    programmed protection
Monarch Metal Weatherstrip Co.
    Monarch out-strips them all
Monarch of the Dailies
    San Francisco Examiner
Monarch out-strips them all
    Monarch Metal Weatherstrip
    Co.
Monarch socks
    For every walk in life
Monarch turning machines
    For a good turn faster, turn
    to Monarch
Monchel bath soap
    It works within your skin
    where softness really
    begins
    Where softness begins
Monet Jewelers
    Master jeweler
Monex International, Ltd.
    Monex. The investment
    house of precious
    metals
Monex. The investment house
    of precious metals
    Monex International, Ltd.
Money Making
    The magazine of opportun-
    ities
Money management
    Household Finance Corp.
The money management magazine
    Fact
Money-saver--butter flavor
    Ohio Butterine Co.
The money truck
    Mack trucks
Monite Waterproof Glue
    Barrel of satisfaction
    Sticks to its job
    Stronger than wood, endur-
    ing as the rock
Monitor radio-phonograph
    The most distinguished
    family of home appli-
    ances
Monitor Stove Co.
    Furnace heat for every
    home
Monmouth Hosiery Mills
    They're wear-conditioned

Wear-conditioned stockings
Monocraft
The largest monogram house
in the world
Monogram Models, Inc.
The name for quality hobby
kits
Monroe Auto Equipment Co.
World leader on highway
and speedway
Monroe calculators
Built to last a business
lifetime
The calculator company
A Monroe for every figure
job
Systems for business
A Monroe for every figure job
Monroe calculators
Monroe shock absorbers
America rides Monroe
The bump stops here
Monsanto Company
Another example of how
Monsanto moves on
many fronts to serve
you
Mother Nature is lucky her
products don't need
labels
Serving industry which
serves mankind
Without chemicals, life it-
self would be impos-
sible
Monsanto Company. See also:
Textile Div., Monsanto
Company
Montag, Inc., Div., Westab,
Inc.
Writing papers that create
an impression
Montag, Inc., Div., Westab,
Inc. See also: Westab,
Inc.
Montague Fishing Rod
How to get Pike's pique
Montana Farmer
Your home state farm
paper
Montana Highway Commission
The big sky country
Montauk Paint Mfg. Co.
A right kind for every
purpose
Montclair cigarettes

For those who want every
puff to taste as fresh
as the first puff!
Just enough!
Monte Carlo is your car
Chevrolet Monte Carlo auto-
mobile
Monterey pipe
Look for the Mission when
you buy a pipe
Montgomery Ward & Co.
The oldest mail order house
is today the most pro-
gressive
A monthly business paper for
chain store executives
Chain Store Age
A monthly magazine devoted to
more profitable painting
American Painter and Decor-
ator
A monthly review of romance
novels
Romance Readers' Guide
Monumental Life Insurance Co.
Protection in a new light
MONY. See also:
Money
Mutual of New York
MONY men care for people
Mutual of New York
Moody Bible Institute of Chicago
Radio School of the Bible
The West Point of Christian
service
Moog Industries, Inc.
Moog means more under car
business
Moog means more under car
business
Moog Industries, Inc.
Moon automobile
The price of a Moon is an
appeal to your reason
Moore. See also: Benjamin
Moore
Moore Business Forms, Inc.
The right business form
for every form of busi-
ness
The Moore Corp.
It takes more than a flame
and a casting to make
a good fast-fired cir-
culation heater
Moore for your money

Moore's, since 1857
Moore for your money
    The Moore Corp.
Moore-McCormack Lines, Inc.
    The "Champagne Touch"
Moore Pins
    Pin-up favorites since 1900
Moore Shoe Co.
    To sell more shoes, buy
      Moore shoes
Moorhead Machine and Boiler Co.
    Assurance of quality, de-
      pendability since 1917
Moore's Hi-Lo Broiler
    Takes the burns out of
      broiling
Moore's, since 1857
    The Moore Corp.
Moral pictures most mothers ap-
    prove
    Hygienic Productions
Morally straight, physically
    strong, mentally awake
    Hygienic Productions
More acres of corn, more corn
    per acre
    Pfister Associated Growers
More airplane for the dollar
    Piper Aircraft Corporation
More and better things for more
    people
    General Motors Corporation
More and more the complete
    source for your store
    The H. O. N. Co.
More beauty outside, more fea-
    tures within
    Frigidaire Div., General
      Motors Corporation
More buttery taste
    Imperial Margarine
More by the pair, less by the
    year
    Stetson Shoe Co.
More choose Metropolitan. Mil-
    lions more than any
    other company
    Metropolitan Life Insurance
    Co.
More complete than the other
    leading brands
    Centrum medicine
More corn, less cob; it's bred
    that way
    Pfister Associated Growers
More dentists use Lavoris than

any other mouthwash.
    Shouldn't you?
    Lavoris mouthwash
More doctors advise Ivory than
    any other soap
    Ivory soap
More doors fold on Fold-Aside
    than any other kind!
    Acme Appliance Mfg. Co.
More dry, less sweet
    Hoffman Pale Dry ginger ale
More effective because it's more
    sell-ective
    Leather and Leather Goods
More flavor per cup
    Mannings Coffee
More ... for less
    TV Guide
More for the money
    J. Walter Thompson Co.
More fun per ton than any other
    line
    Italian Line
More gallons per horse power
    Northern Pump Co.
More goes into it
    Time
More goods for more people at
    lower cost
    National Machine Tool Build-
      ers Assn.
More graceful stairsteps in magic
    Air Steps
    Air Step shoe
More growth, more balance and
    more ahead
    Scott & Fetzer Company
More heat from less coal
    Hoffman valves
More heat, less care
    Florence Heaters
More heat per dollar
    Red Jacket Coal Sales Co.
More home to the house
    Aeroshade Co.
More ideas from the Armstrong
    world of interior design
    Armstrong Cork Co.
More important than soap and
    water
    Nujol laxative
More Lehigh cement used than
    any other
    Lehigh Portland Cement Co.
More light per barrel
    General Telephone & Elec-

tronics Corp.
More light where most needed
Edwin Guth Co.
More Light's 100's cigarettes
The beige cigarette
It's More you
The more living you do, the
more you need Samson-
ite
Samsonite Corp.
The more logical we made it, the
better looking it got
Buick Le Sabre automobile
More manpower to you, sweet
siren you
Jergens Face Powder
More mental impressions from
each printing impres-
sion
Standard Paper Mfg. Co.
More menthol refreshment than
any other low "tar" cig-
arette
Arctic Lights cigarettes
More miles, more smiles
Mobil Tires
More miles per gal
Rhythm Step shoes
More miles per gallon--more
miles on tires
Maxwell automobile
More miles with Miles
Miles tires
More milker for less money
Rite-Way Milker
More MMM MM after every
crunch
Planters cheese balls
More music for the money
Kay Musical Instrument
Co.
More of everything you want
with Mercury
Mercury automobile
More people are smoking Camels
than ever before
Camel cigarettes
More people buy Cessna twins
than any other make
Cessna Aircraft Co.
More people fly Cessna airplanes
than any other make
Cessna Aircraft Co.
More people fly more places by
Douglas
McDonnell-Douglas Corpor-

ation
More people have bought Pipers
than any other plane in
the world
Piper Aircraft Corporation
More people put their confidence
in Carrier air condition-
ing than in any other
make
Carrier Corporation
More people ride on Goodyear
tires than on any other
kind
Goodyear Auto Tire
More people want more aluminum
for more uses than ever
before
Aluminum Company of Amer-
ica
More personal. More computer
Digital Equipment Corpora-
tion
More pillow-y than willow-y
Ry-Krisp
More pleasure per mile
American Bosch automobile
radio receiver
More pleasure per puff, more
puffs per pack
Camel cigarettes
More pork sausages, Mom
H. G. Parks, Inc. sausage
packers
More power from more research
Gould-National Batteries,
Inc.
More practical than ever
Old Spice shaving mug re-
fill
More profit per foot
Buxton stitchless zip guard
The more protection you need,
the more protection you
get
Right Guard anti-perspirant
More savings with Symons
Symons Mfg. Co.
More shaving comfort for your
money
Gillette safety razor
More shelled corn per ear, per
acre, per farm, 8 out
of 10 times
Pfister Associated Growers
More squeezably soft than ever
Charmin bathroom tissue

More stars than there are in
heaven
MGM Motion Pictures
More steam with less coal
Stanwood Corporation
More than a bumper
Cincinnati Ball Crank Co.
More than a cedar chest, a
piece of fine furniture
Tennessee Furniture Corp.
More than a computer company
Control Data Corporation
More than a machine
Harley-Davidson motorcycle
More than a magazine, an insti-
tution
Christian Herald
More than a salad dressing, a
food
Hellmann's mayonnaise
More than a tooth paste--it
checks pyorrhea
Forhan's tooth paste
More than a truck line--a trans-
portation system
Interstate Motor Freight
System
More than 40 billions sold
McDonald's fast food res-
taurant
More than horse power
The Louis Allis Co.
More than just a beautiful car
Jaguar automobile
More than just a name. It's our
way of doing business
True Value hardware stores
More than just beautiful shoes
Rhythm Step shoes
More than mere economy, more
than sheer economy
Johansen Bros. Shoe Co.
More than 125 stores in the West
Western Auto Supply Co.
More than skin deep
Bohn Aluminum & Brass
Corp.
More than sweetness
Honey Scotch Candy
More than you expect or pay
for
Auto Owners Insurance
Co.
More than you'd expect!
NLT Marketing Services
More trucks in use than any

other
Republic truck
The more we invest in our future
the better we can serve
you
Burlington Northern Rail-
road
More years to the gallon
Dutch Boy White Lead
The more you buy, the more you
save!
La Choy chow mein
The more you eat, the more you
want
Cracker Jack confection
The more you know about com-
modities the more
you'll like RW
Rouse Woodcock Commodities
Brokers
The more you know the better
we look
Chicago Mercantile Exchange
The more you learn about photog-
raphy, the more you
count on Kodak
Kodak cameras
The more you look, the more you
like
Mazda automobile
Morgan. See also: Captain Mor-
gan Spiced Rum
Morgan Bank of Canada
Morgan Bank of Canada: an
important link in a
worldwide network
Morgan Bank of Canada: an im-
portant link in a world-
wide network
Morgan Bank of Canada
Morgan dish cloths
From raw cotton through
finished product
Morgan varnish
The varnish invulnerable
Morgan's. See: Russ Morgan's
dance orchestra
Morin Wet Wash Laundry
We soak the clothes, not
the public
Morning Newspaper Publishers
Assn.
Daytime is selling time
Morning uplift
Otis Elevator Company
Morning upsetting exercises

Schick injector razor
Morning's first thought
    Royal Blend Coffee
Morris. <u>See also</u>: Philip Morris
    cigarettes
Morris Machine Works
    Master designers of modern
        centrifugal pumps
Morris Plan
    No man's debts should live
        after him
    The smart way to plan
Morrison tractor
    Your way of life depends
        upon your day of work
Mortite cement
    A household friend
Mortite window weatherstrip
    America's best-selling win-
        dow weatherstrip for
        over 40 years
    Keep 'em cozy with Mortite
Morton Chemical Co. Div., Mor-
    ton International, Inc.
    Look for more from Morton
Morton's chicken giblets
    Reach, heat and eat
Morton's salt
    The original iodized salt
    The salt of the earth
    When it rains it pours
Mosinee Paper Mills Co.
    Value-engineered papers
        from the mills of
        Mosinee
Mosler Safe Co.
    Quality is standard equip-
        ment
Mossberg. <u>See also</u>: C. F.
    Mossberg and Sons,
    Inc.
Mossberg for accuracy
    C. F. Mossberg and Sons,
    Inc.
Mossberg Tire Bell
    A "Hit" with two hammers
        in bicycle bell con-
        struction
    The lightest, loudest,
        simplest, cheapest of
        them all
Most-a-pound-a-piece
    Pinnacle Orchards
Most admired, most desired for
    cool comfort
    Marlboro shirts

The most asked-for brand of all
    Allsweet oleomargarine
The most beautiful car in Amer-
    ica
    Paige automobile
The most beautiful copies of all
    Chas. Bruning Co.
The most beautiful curtains in
    America
    Robertson Factories, Inc.
The most beautiful kitchens of
    them all
    H. J. Scheirich Co.
The most beautiful thing on
    wheels
    Pontiac automobile
The most beautiful tire in Amer-
    ica
    Hydro-United tire
The most colorful coverage of
    the week
    <u>Time</u>
The most colorful nylon
    Caprolan nylon
The most comfortable hat made
    Resistol self-conforming
    hats
The most comfortable shoe in
    the world
    Ground Gripper shoe
The most complete line of elec-
    tronic ovens
    Raytheon Co.
The most complete line of fire-
    arms in the world
    Savage Arms Div., Emhart
    Corp.
The most convenient address in
    Los Angeles
    Bel Air Sands hotel
The most delicious and wholesome
    Temperance Drink in
    the world
    Hires' Improved Root Beer
The most dependable joint known
    Rivet-Grip Steel Co.
The most distinguished family of
    home appliances
    Monitor radio-phonograph
The most economical form of per-
    manent construction
    Hollow Bldg. Tile Assn.
Most economical in upkeep
    Royal Tourist automobile
The most elegant name in cos-
    metics

DuBarry cosmetics
The most expensive tea grown
  Ming Tea
The most expensive television
  sets in America. And
  worth it
  Curtis Mathes television
  sets
The most experienced food
  processor in the world
  Libby, McNeill and Libby
The most famous name in rattan
  furniture
  Ficks Reed Co.
The most famous name on drums
  Ludwig & Ludwig
The most for your money in fuel
  Illinois-Iowa Power Co.
Most heat per dollar
  Gilbert & Barker oil burner
The most highly-filtered motor
  oil in America
  Gilmore Oil Co.
The most imitated car on the
  road
  Graham-Paige automobile
The most important magazine to
  the world's most impor-
  tant people
  Time
The most in dry cleaning
  One Hour Martinizing
The most influential hardware
  paper
  Hardware Age
The most intelligent car ever
  built
  Saab automobile
The most like fresh
  Freshlike canned vege-
  tables
Most little pigs go to market
  but the best little pigs
  go to Jones
  Jones Dairy Farm
Most miles per dollar
  Firestone tires
Most modern of lightweight
  typewriters
  Royal typewriter
The most particular house-
  keeper in town dusts
  with paper
  Munising paper
The most personal computer
  Apple computers

The most popular beer in history
  Budweiser beer
The most popular beer the world
  has ever known
  Budweiser beer
Most popular route to the Rockies
  Burlington Northern Rail-
  road
Most powerful of all signals
  Strombos Air Whistle
The most powerful shoe in Amer-
  ica
  Bergmann Shoe Mfg. Co.
The most powerful uric acid sol-
  vent known
  Piperazine W-a-t-e-r
The most prized eye cosmetics in
  the world
  Maybelline
The most profitable of all acces-
  sories
  American Chain Co.
The most progressive name in
  steel
  Nippon Kokan
Most radio per dollar
  King-Buffalo radio receiver
A most remarkable airline
  Continental Air Lines, Inc.
Most respected name in power
  Briggs & Stratton Corpora-
  tion
The most salable shoe in America
  Red Cross Shoes
The most salable shoe in America
  today
  Red Cross Shoes
The most talked-about food in
  America
  Pabst-ette
The most treasured name in per-
  fume
  Chanel, Inc.
The most trusted name in aspirin
  Bayer aspirin
The most trusted name in elec-
  tronics
  RCA Corp.
The most trusted name in furni-
  ture
  Drexel furniture
Most trusted name in modeling
  Hawk Model Co.
The most trusted name in pet
  food
  Purina Cat Chow

Purina Dog Chow
The most trusted name in sound
  RCA Corp.
The most trusted name in tele-
  vision
  RCA Corp.
Most trusted trademark in the
  valve world
  Jenkins Bros.
The most trustworthy tires built
  Oldfield tires
The most useful magazine in
  metalworking
  American Machinist
The most valuable piano in the
  world
  Steger & Sons Piano Co.
The most walked about shoe in
  America
  Florsheim Shoe Co.
The most widely used electric
  hoist in America
  Shephard Niles Crane and
  Hoist Corp.
Moth-Tox insecticide
  Dead moths eat no holes
Mother Nature is lucky her
  products don't need
  labels
  Monsanto Company
Mother Parker's Tea
  A personal blend
Mother's first thought for every
  milk need
  White House evaporated
  milk
Mothersill's Seasick Remedy
  Be happy and well while
  traveling
  The world over
Motion economizer
  Diebold Safe & Lock Co.
Motion pictures are the nation's
  relaxation
  Royal Pictures
Motivating men to sell your
  product is our busi-
  ness
  Maritz, Inc.
Motor
  The automotive business
  paper
The motor carrier with more
  go-how
  Eastern Express, Inc.
Motor cars in the great Euro-

pean tradition
  Fiat automobile
Motor coach to train side, the
  New York idea of travel
  convenience
  Baltimore & Ohio Railroad
Motor coach train connection, a
  New York travel habit
  Baltimore & Ohio Railroad
Motor drive is more than power
  Reliance Electric and Engi-
  neering Co.
Motor-Gard motor protector
  Don't buy motors, buy
  Motor-Gard
Motor Land
  The Pacific Coast magazine
  of motoring
The motor oil that is engineered
  for today's small cars
  Castrol motor oil
Motor Rhythm lubricating oil
  Keep your motor young
Motor Service
  The automotive service shop
  magazine
  The service shop authority
Motor Trips
  The simplified travel guide
The motorcycle that is not un-
  comfortable
  Harley-Davidson motorcycle
Motorists wise Simoniz
  Simoniz
Motorists wise Simoniz; house-
  wives do likewise
  Simoniz
Motorized power, fitted to every
  need
  General Electric Company
Motorola. A world leader in
  electronics
  Motorola, Inc.
Motorola car radio
  Fits and matches the car
  you're driving
Motorola, Inc.
  Motorola. A world leader
  in electronics
  New leader in the lively
  art of electronics
  Quality and productivity
  through employee par-
  ticipation in manage-
  ment
  Tomorrow's cellular system

today
A tradition of leadership in
advanced state of the
art technologies
Motorola radio receiver
The proof is in the listen-
ing
Motors cry for it
Sohio motor oil
The motor's the thing
Herschell-Spillman Motor
Co.
Motorstoker Corp.
Nothing to shovel, nothing
to explode
Mott. See: J. L. Mott Iron
Works
Mott's Apple Juice
The sign of better taste
Motz cushion tires
The end of burdensome tire
expense
Moulded to your foot
Aid-A-Walker shoes
Moulding the future through
chemistry
American Cyanamid Co.
Mount Zircon Spring Water Co.
The water of health
Mountain Dew soft drink
Give me a Dew!
Mountain grown
Folger's ground coffee
A mountain of flavor in every
spoonful
Folger's ground coffee
Mountain Valley Water
Health ... your happiness,
our business
Mountain water makes the dif-
ference
Old Export beer
Move ahead at the speed of
sound
Lanier "thought processing"
recorders
Move the Faultless way
Faultless casters
Moved by Heck
Heck Transfer & Storage
Co.
Moves the earth
Euclid Road Machinery Co.
The movie time candy
Raisinets candy
Movies make many merry mo-

ments
Royal Pictures
Movies mean many merry moments
Royal Pictures
Moving ahead fast ... to keep you
competitive
National Castings Co.
Moving Picture World
First in the field
Moving up
U. S. Van Lines, Inc.
Moving with care ... everywhere
United Van Lines, Inc.
The mower with the 2-cycle ad-
vantage
Lawn-Boy lawn mowers
Moygashel linens
Mastery in linens
Mu-Rad. See also: Murad
Mu-Rad radio receivers
Turn your switch and get
Cuba or Seattle
Mueller Co.
Faucets without a fault
Mueller's macaroni
As a change from potatoes
Cooks in nine minutes
Cooks tender, quicker
Short lengths, easy to eat
With the better taste
Muffets
The rounded shredded
wheat
There's a meal in every
Muffet
Mulsified Cocoanut Oil Shampoo
Splendid for children--fine
for men
Multi-Call Co.
Multiplied insulation
Multi-Vest Securities, Inc.
Tax free bonds. Ask the
man who owns them
Multibestos brake lining
Brake linings tailored to
the needs of your brake
The lining most car makers
specify
On the skill of a mechanic
may depend your life
Stop and start on Multi-
bestos
Tailored to the needs of the
brake
Multinational Insurance Brokers
Secure, fore and aft

Multiple copies without carbons
    National Cash Register
        Co.
Multiple copy forms for profit
        preservation
    Malady & MacLauchlan
Multiplied insulation
    Multi-Cell Co.
Multistamp Co.
    Pays for itself in the money
        it saves
Mum deodorant
    As easy to use as to say
    Be a safety first girl with
        Mum
    Dates depend on daintiness
    If you want to be loved, be
        loveable
    I'm sick of playing solitaire,
        I want to wear one
    Keeps you nice to be near
    Mum helps to make a miss
        a hit
    Mum is the word
    Takes the odor out of per-
        spiration
Mum helps to make a miss a hit
Mum is the word
    Mum deodorant
Mumm's champagne
    The word for champagne
Munising paper
    The most particular house-
        keeper in town dusts
        with paper
Munro & Harford Co.
    Color in advertising
Munsingwear--beyond compare
    Munsingwear underwear
Munsingwear underwear
    Action underwear for active
        men
    Don't say underwear, say
        Mungsingwear
    It's worth the difference
    Let Munsingwear cover you
        with satisfaction
    Munsingwear--beyond com-
        pare
    Not too loose, not too tight,
        fits just right
Murad. See also: Mu-Rad
Murad cigarettes
    Be nonchalant--light a
        Murad

Judge for yourself
Muriel cigar
    Make a date with Muriel
    That pleasing cigar
    You ought to meet Muriel
Murine eye drops
    For irritated eyes it's just
        what the doctor or-
        dered
    For your eyes
    MMMM--Murine
    Soothes. Cleanses. Re-
        freshes
Murphy & Saval
    Spring step shoes
Murphy in-a-door bed
    Built as though you intend
        to sell your home tomor-
        row
    One purpose rooms make
        houses too big
    There is only one in-a-
        door bed--the Murphy
Murphy paint
    The lifelong paint
Murphy's Oil Soap
    People have trusted Murphy's
        for 75 years
Murray. See also: Arthur Mur-
        ray dance studios
Murray Corp.
    The line that moves
Musebeck Shoe Co.
    Fit to be tried
    They're tops for the bot-
        toms
    Your feet are your fortune
Musette piano
    A piano is the soul of the
        home
The music America loves best
    RCA Corp.
Music in the Morgan manner
    Russ Morgan's dance or-
        chestra
The music of commerce should
        be played on the best
        instrument
    Columbia Bar-Lock Type-
        writer
The music of yesterday and to-
        day
    Blue Barron's orchestra
Music that charms
    Buescher true-tone saxo-
        phone

316

Music to your mouth
   Nestle's Crunch candy bar
Music wherever you are
   Columbia Grafonola
The music you want
   RCA Corp.
The music you want when you
   want it
   RCA Corp.
Musical fun for everyone
   Wurlitzer phonograph
A musical instrument of quality
   Philco radio receiver
The musical instrument of radio
   Eckhardt radio receiver
Music's most glorious voice
   Hammond organ
Muskegon Piston Ring Co.
   Since 1921 ... the engine
   builders source!
Must clear your skin
   Sixteen skin lotion
A "must" for every wardrobe
   Sportleigh's briefer coat
Must make good or we will
   Genco razors
Musterole
   Better than a mustard
   plaster
Mutual Benefit Life Insurance
   Company
   Another volunteer
Mutual China Co.
   Buy china in a china store
Mutual Life Insurance Co.
   Change the "widow's mite"
   to the "widow's might"
   Our second century of
   service
Mutual of New York
   MONY men care for people
   You don't have to be rich
   to have MONY
Mutual of Omaha Insurance Co.
   The greatest name in health
   insurance
   People you can count on
Mutual Products Co., Inc.
   First name in paper punches
Mutual truck
   America's greatest truck
Mutual Union Auto Insurance
   Co.
   Safety with saving
My beer is the dry beer
   Rheingold Beer

My life is an open look
   Calox Tooth Powder
My right hand in the home
   American Steel Wool Mfg.
   Co.
Myadec vitamin supplement
   If you do more, you want
   more
Myers. See also: F. E. Myers
   & Bro., Inc.
Myers means merit
   Myers shoes
Myers shoes
   Built-in quality in every
   shoe
   Myers means merit
Myers the finest name in pumps
   F. E. Myers and Bro.,
   Inc.
Mystery. See: Mistere cold
   cream
Mystic Cream
   Makes the skin like velvet
Mystic Foam upholstery cleaner
   Cleans so well so easily,
   and for so little
Mystik adhesive products
   Anything that sticks
   Don't get mad, get Mystik
   The tape that tackles every-
   thing

-N-

NAHB Journal of Homebuilding
   The magazine for profes-
   sional builders
NAR: Confidence based on suc-
   cess
   North American Royalties,
   Inc.
NAR: Meeting needs vital to
   the nation's economy
   North American Royalties,
   Inc.
NBC is the magic key to in-
   creased profits
   National Broadcasting Co.
NBI Office Automation System
   Lifting America from under
   the paper weight
N. Dorman and Co.
   The cheese with the paper
   between the slices
NEC Information Systems, Inc.

317

The benchmark in world
    class computers
Your NEC computer grows
    with you
NL Industries, Inc.
    Petroleum services and
        equipment worldwide
    We help discover oil
    We might not be known on
        the street, but we're
        famous in the field
NLT Marketing Services
    More than you'd expect!
N. Pfeffer
    For gifts of love
NR tonight, tomorrow all right
    Nature's Remedy laxative
NVF Co.
    Products you can depend
        on ... day in ... day
        out
N. W. Ayer & Son
    Constant excellence is the
        key to success
Nabisco, Inc.
    The great wheatsworth taste
    People think of us when
        they're in the market
The nail enamel your manicurist
    recommends
    Revlon nail enamel
Naked unfinished furniture
    Go Naked to make money
Nala Press
    Printing and typography
        are related
The name again ... Nationwide
    Life
    Nationwide Life Insurance
        Co.
The name back of saw value
    E. C. Atkins & Co.
The name for fine rattan furni-
        ture
    Whitecraft, Inc.
The name for quality
    Planters salted peanuts
The name for quality athletic
        goods
    Nocona Athletic Goods Co.
The name for quality hobby
        kits
    Monogram Models, Inc.
The name indicates the quality
    Keener Rubber, Inc.
The name insures the quality

Velie automobile
The name is Crane
    Crane Company
The name known in millions of
        American homes
    Nutone, Inc.
The name men fly by
    Lear plane radio
The name of the game is living.
        Explore a new home
        today
    National Association of Home
        Builders
The name on any orange drink
        is like "sterling"
        stamped on silver
    Nesbitt's orange drink
The name quality made famous
    Zoom 8 camera
The name really means something
    Niles Tools Works Co.
The name says it all
    Depend protective under-
        garment
The name that means everything
        in electricity
    Westinghouse Electric Corp.
The name that means everything
        in luggage
    Rauchbach-Goldsmith lug-
        gage
The name that means quality
    Trade wind ventilating hood
The name that means temperature
        control
    Robertshaw Controls Com-
        pany
The name that protects your
        name
    Watts Regulator Co.
The name that's known is Fire-
        stone--all over the
        world
    Firestone Tire and Rubber
        Co.
The name to know in radio
    Brandes, Inc.
The name to look for
    Golfcraft, Inc.
A name to remember
    Almond Roca candy
    Bowers spark plug
    Brown & Haley
    Pen Metal Co., Inc.
A name to remember, a fabric
        to remember

Brooklawn Corduroy
The name to remember in flutes
Armstrong flutes
The name to remember in rain-
wear
Weatherbee raincoat
The name to remember when
buying towels
Dundee towels
A name worth remembering
Fairbanks-Morse scales
A name you can trust
Squibb Beech-Nut, Inc.
Squibb toothpaste
The name you can trust in
margarine
Mazola margarine
The name you know in lamps
Westinghouse Electric
Corp.
Named for the original American
professionals
Indian Archery Corp.
Named for those it serves
Auto Owners Insurance
Co.
Napa power storage battery
Without it you don't have
the power
Narco rayon
The tag always gets 'em
Narragansett malt beverage
Made on honor, sold on
merit
Nash automobile
Another Nash
The "coming thing" in cars
--has come
Leads the world in motor
car value
Million dollar beauty in the
lowest priced field
One of America's most dis-
tinguished motor cars
You'll be ahead with Nash
Nash Coffee Co.
Every drop delicious
Nashua blankets and sheets
They can rest assured
Wake up refreshed
Nason. See also: Mason
Nason Paint Co.
Make your trucks help sell
your business
Paint for profit instead of
expense

Nata-Pax
Always fresh, wet-proof
panties
National adhesives
Every type of adhesive for
every industrial use
National Air Filter
It cleans the air, then
cleans itself
National Airlines, Inc.
Coast to coast to coast
National Aluminate Corp.
The scientific system of
water treatment for all
National Association of Home
Builders
The name of the game is
living. Explore a new
home today
National Association of Ice Cream
Manufacturers
Ice cream for health
National Association of Manufac-
turers
For a better tomorrow for
everybody
National Association of Marble
Dealers
There is no substitute for
marble
National Association of Printing
Ink Makers
Your best salesman, print-
ing ink
National Association of Realtors
Working for America's
property owners
National Association of Retail
Druggists
Your druggist is more than
a merchant
National Association of Straw Hat
Mfrs.
Every man should wear at
least three straw hats
National Autofinders
America's No. 1 used car
company
National Automatic Gas Light
Your gas bills cut in two
National Automotive Parts As-
sociation
Assurance of quality
National Bakery Div., Package
Machinery Co.
Favorite of the nation's

bakers
National Bank of Tulsa
    The oil bank of America
National Better Business Bureau.
    See: Better Business
    Bureau
National bicycle
    A National rider never
    changes his mount
National Biscuit Co.
    Fifty years of fine baking
    Uneeda Biscuit
National Blank Book Co.
    The retailer's line
The national breakfast
    Shredded Wheat
The national broadcast authority
    Radio Digest
National Broadcasting Co.
    NBC is the magic key to
    increased profits
    Now's the time to talk it
    over
    Parade of Stars
    Tell the millions in their
    own homes
National Broadcasting Co. Blue
    Network
    Sales through the air with
    the greatest of ease
National Broadcasting Co. Red
    Network
    The network most people
    listen to most
The national business and finan-
    cial weekly
    Barron's
A national buyword
    Georgiana frocks
National Car Rental System, Inc.
    The customer is always No.
    1
    You deserve National atten-
    tion
National Cash Register Co.
    Data processing is our only
    business
    First in carbonless papers
    Multiple copies without
    carbons
    98 years experience in
    business systems
    Wherever money is handled
    or records are kept
National Castings Co.
    Moving ahead fast ... to

keep you competitive
National City Bank
    The branch around the
    corner can serve you
    around the world
National Commercial Disposers
    Pioneers of disposers dedi-
    cated to quality
National Committee for Prevention
    of Child Abuse
    Abused children are helpless.
    Unless you help
National Confectioners' Associa-
    tion
    Eat candy for energy
National Cotton Council
    Cotton, you can feel how
    good it looks
    100% cotton. The fiber you
    can trust
National Council for Better Plas-
    tering
    Metal lath to reinforce and
    preserve
The national dairy farm magazine
    Hoard's Dairyman
National Distillers
    Give your guest what he
    wishes
    One taste will tell you why
    Your guide to good liquors
    Your guide to good living
The national drink
    Welch's grape juice
National Enquirer
    Largest circulation of any
    paper in America
National Fiberstock Envelope Co.
    They last longer
The national filling station maga-
    zine
    Gas Station Topics
National Food Brokers Assn.
    Sales specialists in every
    market area
National Fruit Cake
    Completes the feast
National Fuel Company
    National Fuel heats Denver
National Fuel heats Denver
    National Fuel Company
National Geographic
    It costs no more to reach
    the first million first
    Public policy advertising
National Gift and Art Assn.

Every day is a gift day
Gifts and art gladden the
heart
The national guide to motion
pictures
Photoplay
National Gypsum Company
A family of companies build-
ing for the future
National headquarters for uniform
caps
Superior Uniform Cap Co.
National Huntington's Disease
Association
You have the power to end
H. D.
The national inspirational monthly
for men and women who
sell
Specialty Salesman Magazine
National Investors Corp.
The growth fund
National Jewelers Publicity As-
sociation
For gifts that last consult
your jeweler
The national joy smoke
Prince Albert pipe and
cigarette tobacco
National LP-Gas Market Develop-
ment Council
Of America's great sources
of energy, only Na-
tional serves you in so
many ways
National Life Insurance Co. of
Vermont
As solid as the granite
hills of Vermont
Protecting the American
home
National Lumber Manufacturers
Association
It's built to sell when it's
built of wood
National Machine Tool Builders
Assn.
More goods for more people
at lower cost
A national magazine for dry
goods and department
stores
Dry Goods Merchants Trade
Journal
National magazine for mothers
of infants

American Baby
The national magazine of sports
and recreation
Sportlife
The national magazine of the
grocery trade
The Progressive Grocer
The national magazine of the
hardware trade
Good Hardware
The national magazine with local
influence
American Weekly
National Meter Co.
It is accurate and it stays
accurate
National Microtech, Inc.
Apollo satellite TV systems
bring the world to you
National Mortar & Supply Co.
Easy to spread, hard to
beat
National Motor Bearing Co.
Seal in oil, seal out trouble
The national municipal bond
specialist
John Nuveen & Co., Inc.
The national newspaper of mar-
keting
Advertising Age
National Nougat Co.
The heaven-sent nougat
National Oak Lumbermen's Assn.
Wood that weathers every
storm
Wood that you always pre-
fer
Wood that you would and
should use
National Oats Co.
Makes kids husky
National Oil Fuel Institute, Inc.
You can depend on it
National Paint Co.
The coat with nine lives
Save two ways
National Patent Council, Inc.
Patents make jobs
National Paving Brick Mfrs.
The pavement that outlasts
the bonds
National Petroleum News
For oil marketing
National Premium Co.
The easiest way out
National Premium Beer

Maryland's Masterpiece
National Presto Industries, Inc.
  The pressure cooker people
National Printing Co.
  Risky to pay less, needless
    to pay more
A national publication devoted to
    ship operation and ship-
    building
  Marine Review
A national publication for the
    wholesale grocer
  Groceries
National Radio Institute
  Originators of radio home-
    study training
National Rain Bird Sales and
    Engineering Corp.
  The modern way to grow
National Refrigerating Co.
  Silent refrigeration at low
    cost
  The silent servant
National Reserve Life Insurance
    Co.
  A refuge in time of storm
A national resources company
  Pennzoil Company
National Restaurant Association
  Good food is good health
  Travel follows good food
    routes
A National rider never changes
    his mount
  National bicycle
The national rub down
  Mifflin Alkohol Massage
National Safety Council
  One of two might be you
  Reckless drivers are seldom
    wreckless long
  Shorter days mean longer
    odds--against you
National Screw and Mfg. Co.
  Creating better ways to
    hold things together
National Slate Association
  Slate--consider its uses
National Steel Corp.
  Count on steel from Na-
    tional
  Keep a cupboard full of
    cans
National sterling silver
  There is no finer solid
    silver than National

The national summer suit
  Goodall Worsted Co.
The national summer suit for men
  Keep-Kool suit
National Surety Co.
  Your peace of mind is worth
    the premium
The national system with local
    authority
  National Truck Leasing Sys-
    tem
National Transitads, Inc.
  To sell millions, tell millions
National Truck Leasing System
  The national system with
    local authority
  Our leases are as individual
    as you are
National Underwriter
  A weekly newspaper of in-
    surance
National Union Mortgage Co.
  Every mortgage irrevocably
    insured
National Urban League
  Everybody deserves a chance
    to make it on their own.
    Everybody
National voice of the shoe trade
  Boot and Shoe Recorder
The national weekly
  Collier's
The national weekly newspaper
    devoted to the fraternal
    interpretation of the
    world's current events
  Fellowship Forum
The national weekly of programs
    and personalities
  Radio Guide
National Westminster
  The Action Bank
National Wildlife Federation
  Save a place for wild life
National X-Ray Reflector Co.
  Lighting from concealed
    sources
Nationally famous for good taste
  Goebel beer
A nationally known name
  Nedick's restaurants
Nationally recognized as the
    "straw pioneer"
  Simon Bros. straw handbags
The nation's basic transporta-
    tion

322

Association of American
Railroads
The nation's big name in archery
Ben Pearson, Inc.
The nation's breakfast food
Amerikorn cereal
The nation's building stone
Indiana Limestone Quarry-
men's Association
Nation's Business
What's happening in busi-
ness--to business
The nation's business paper
Howard Paper Co.
The nation's freight car
Diamond T truck
The nation's going-est railroad
Norfolk and Western Rail-
way
A nation's health is a nation's
strength
Loma Linda Food Co.
The nation's host from coast to
coast
Child's Restaurants
The nation's innkeeper
Holiday Inns of America,
Inc.
The nation's largest airline
United Air Lines, Inc.
The nation's largest-selling
drawing pencils and
leads
Eagle Pencil Co.
The nation's long distance tele-
phone company
M.C.I.
The nation's printing papers
St. Regis Paper Company
The nation's station
Radio station WLW
A nationwide institution
J. C. Penney and Co.
Nationwide Life Insurance Co.
The name again ... Nation-
wide Life
Nationwide, worldwide depend
on ...
Trans World Airlines, Inc.
Nationwise Auto Parts
Do it all at Nationwise
The natural beautifier
Peach Bloom Mineral Corp.
The natural beauty spray
Alberto VO-5 beauty spray
Natural Bridge Shoemakers

Smarter shoes for natural
walking
The natural lift
Instant Postum
Natural Light beer
Ahh, the beer with the
taste for food!
A natural resource company
Cities Service Company
The natural way to lose weight
Diet Center
Naturalizer shoes
Looks good from any angle
The shoe with the beautiful
fit
Naturally a better brew
Krueger beer
Naturally aged--over two years
in the making
Lea & Perrin's Sauce
Naturally better
Dawson's Ale
Naturally finer
Washburn's beans
Naturally it's delicious ... it's
made by Borden's
Borden, Inc.
Naturally smoked. Delicately
seasoned
Swift's Premium frankfurter
sausage
Naturally smooth
Magnus Beck Brewing Co.
Naturally superior
Reading anthracite
Naturally, with Clairol
Clairol, Inc.
Naturally yours
Lilyette brassiere
Nature. See also: Mother Nature
Nature in the raw is seldom mild
Lucky Strike cigarettes
Nature made aluminum friendly to
food
Wear-Ever aluminum
Nature made it, TWA flies it,
the sunny Santa Fe
Trail
Transcontinental & Western
Airline
Nature makes Douglas fir durable
Fir Door Institute
Nature-Tread shoe
Makes you want to walk
Nature's best food at its best
Crystal Dairy Products

Nature's chosen apple land
Wenatachee District Co-op
Assn.
Nature's health water
Navaho Mineral Water
Nature's method of wood preser-
vation
Osmose Wood Preserving
Co.
Nature's paradise, man's oppor-
tunity
Washington State
Nature's Remedy laxative
NR tonight, tomorrow all
right
Nature's Rival corset
Nothing rivals Nature's
Rival
Nature's sweet restorer
Simmons Company
Naturo water closet
The closet with a slant
Nautical Preparatory School
Prepares for college or
business while touring
the world
Navaho Mineral Water
Nature's health water
Navel oranges dripping with
health
California Citrus Co.
The navy needs you! Don't
READ American history
--MAKE IT!
U. S. Navy Recruiting
Service
The Nawa Company
Keep hair-conditioned
Nazareth underwear
Hi-chair to hi-school
Nearest thing to trouble-proof
Kresky oil burners
Nearly a quarter-century of
leadership
Stevens-Duryea automobile
The nearly perfect transformer
Ferranti transformer
Neat. See: Neet deodorant
Neatest trick up your sleeve
Kreisler Watch Band
Neatness lasts from breakfast to
bedtime
Essley shirt
Nebraska Farmer
Nebraska's farm paper
Nebraska's farm paper

Nebraska Farmer
A necessary refinement in light-
ing
General Electric Mazda
Lamp
The necessary two million
True Story
Nedick's restaurants
A nationally known name
Now it's a pleasure to be
thirsty
A needle for every need
Walco phonograph needles
Needlecraft Magazine
Salt of the earth, the sub-
scribers to Needlecraft,
over one million of them
Needs no chaser
Spot Bottle whiskey
Needs only kerosene for fuel
Doble-Detroit steam car
Neenah Paper Co.
Note the tear and wear as
well as the test
Neet deodorant
Keeps you sweet as an
angel
The negative for positive results
Gevaert Film
Nehi for a nickle
Nehi soft drink
Nehi soft drink
Nehi for a nickle
Relax and enjoy
Taste champ of the colas
Taste test winner
Tops in taste
Neighbor tells neighbor
Foy Paint Co.
Nekoosa-Edwards Paper Co.
For better results always
use the best paper
For every business need
For many converting pur-
poses
For special industrial re-
quirements
High above all and snow-
white
Nelots Sanatorium
Cancer harms elderly and
tired employees re-
morselessly
Nelson. See also:
Frederick Nelson Dry Goods
Herman Nelson air filters

Nelson Knitting Co.
  The sock America wears to
    work
Nelson's Hatchery
  Invest in Nelson's triple-
    culled chix
Neo-Syn Pills
  Swift as the swallow, relief
  Swift relief follows the
    swallow
  Take it easy
  Take two, pain's through
Neolite shoe soles
  Sole idea
  Sole of fashion
Neosho Nurseries
  Yours for growing satis-
    faction
Nepco locker paper
  Sure protection for frozen
    foods
Neptolac quick drying enamel
  Resists heat and moisture
Nesbitt's orange drink
  Made from REAL oranges
  The name on any orange
    drink is like "sterling"
    stamped on silver
Nescafe instant coffee
  Answer to a modern's
    prayer
  The flavor can't be matched
    because only Nescafe
    knows the secret
  The flavor sensation that
    sold the nation on cof-
    fee made in the cup
  Roaster-fresh coffee made
    in the cup
Nesco utensils
  The sterling of cooking
    ware
Nestea
  There's nothing like it under
    the sun
Nestle Color Tint
  Approved by professional
    hair colorists
Nestle Hairlac
  The deliciously perfumed
    hair lacquer
Nestle's Crunch candy bar
  Music to your mouth
Nestle's Milk Chocolate Bar
  The greatest taste in
    chocolate

  Richest in cream
Nestor Johnson ice skates
  Wings of steel
Netting that stands alone
  Indiana Steel & Wire Co.
Nettleton shoes
  Gentlemen's fine shoes
  Put your money on Nettle-
    ton shoes, they win in
    a walk
  There are no finer shoes
The network most people listen
    to most
  National Broadcasting Co.
    Red Network
Nevamar plastic
  Tops everything for lasting
    beauty
Never a bite in a bowl
  Captain Black smoking to-
    bacco
Never a dull moment
  Reflecto Letters, Inc.
  Wiss shears
Never an upset stomach
  Pepto-Bismol
Never before utensils like these
  Reynolds lifetime aluminum
Never fails
  Ideal lighter fluid
Never fasten or unfasten it
  Speidel Corp. watch bands
Never gets on your nerves
  Girard cigar
Never let a cold get a start
  Vick's Vapo-Rub
Never let your hair down
  Scoldy Lox bobby pins
Never lets go
  Hammer Blow Tool Co.
Never neglect a break in the
    skin
  Newskin Co.
Never neglect the tiniest cut
  Band-Aid
Never renew, yet ever new
  Associated Tile Manufactur-
    ers
Never say dye, say Rit
  Rit dyes
Never thin or watery
  Kemp's tomato juice
Never underestimate the power
    of a woman
  Ladies Home Journal
Never upset an upset stomach

Pepto-Bismol
"Never wear a white shirt before
    sundown," says Hath-
    away
    Hathaway shirts
New. See also: Nu
New advances in office copying
    keep coming from Kodak
    Kodak cameras
A new adventure in smokeless
    tobacco
    Kodiak chewing tobacco
A new American favorite
    Delrich Margarine
The new American marmalade
    Sunkist marmalade
A new and better way
    Heery Associates, Inc.
New angle on brushing teeth
    Squibb toothbrush
A new bed that is almost sinfully
    comfortable
    Danersk Furniture
The new big name in beer
    Brewer's Best beer
The new blood purifyer
    Cuticura resolvent
New Castle Leather Co.
    It's made of New Castle,
        more need not be said
    Judge it by its users
    Loveliest of leathers
New concepts in corrugated
    packaging machinery
    Huntingdon Industries,
        Inc.
A new-day car for new-day
    needs
    Paige automobile
The new-day dentifrice
    Pepsodent toothpaste
New Departure Bicycle Bells
    They have a tone that's
        all their own
New Departure Coaster Brake
    The brake that brought the
        bike back
    The brake with the mighty
        grip
New Departure-Hyatt Bearings
    Div., General Motors
        Corporation
    For modern industry
    Hyatt quiet
    Nothing rolls like a ball
New Departure-Hyatt Bearings

    Div., General Motors
        Corporation. See also:
        General Motors Corpora-
        tion
New dimensions in driving on the
    safer Kelly road
    Kelly-Springfield Tire Co.
New driving feel that's slick as
    silk
    Plymouth automobile
New England Coke Co.
    Your neighbors know New
        England Coke
New England Fish Co.
    Frozen with the wiggle in
        its tail
    Packed with the wiggle in
        its tail
New England mince meat
    The kind mother used to
        make
New England's greatest Sunday
    newspaper
    Boston Sunday Advertiser
New Era Check Protector
    You see what you write as
        you write it
The new era toothbrush
    Pepsodent Decoater tooth
        brush
The new fabric paint
    Paintex Products Corp.
A new face across the market
    place
    Dart & Kraft
The new first name in mixers
    Dormeyer food mixers
A new flush mounted unit cooler
    Unitron
New foods, new ideas for a bet-
    ter world
    General Mills, Inc.
A new frame if the wind breaks
    it
    Storm Hero umbrella
New freedom from lubrication
    worries
    Marvelube lubricant
New fresh taste. Only 5 mg.
    Vantage Ultra Lights
        menthol cigarettes
New Fruit and Fibre cereal
    It tastes so good you forget
        the fibre
New Gem Safety Razor
    Be your own barber!!

New Gem Safety Razor. See
    also: Gem razor
New Haven Clock & Watch Co.
    Right time since 1817
A new high in auto test equip-
    ment ... a new high
    for you!
    Sun Electric Corp.
A new high in whiskey smooth-
    ness
    Hiram Walker Ten High
    whiskey
New Holland Div., Sperry Rand
    Corporation
    First in grassland farming
    Practical in design. De-
    pendable in action
    Specialists in farmstead
    mechanization
New Holland Div., Sperry Rand
    Corporation. See also:
    Sperry Rand Corpora-
    tion
New! Hospitals prove it's better
    Johnson's baby lotion
New Idea Farm Equipment Co.
    Where bold new ideas pay
    off for profit-minded
    farmers
New ideas for happier home-
    making
    The West Bend Co.
New ideas in automation control
    Photoswitch Div., Elec-
    tronics Corp. of Amer-
    ica
New Jersey Machine Corp.
    Fine labeling identifies
    finer products
New Jersey Public Service Elec-
    tric and Gas Co.
    Taxpaying servant of a
    great state
New Jersey Zinc Co.
    The first cost is the last
    expense
    Once in a lifetime
    Paint saves the surface,
    zinc saves the paint
    White paint that stays
    white
    The world's standard for
    zinc products
New kind of cream deodorant
    Dryad
New leader in the lively art

    of electronics
    Motorola, Inc.
New life to weak arches, long
    life to healthy ones
    Florsheim Shoe Co.
A new lower price, a new higher
    value
    Florsheim Shoe Co.
New Method Foot Foundation
    A custom-built support for
    foot troubles
New Mexico Dept. of Development
    Land of enchantment
New Mill Kluski Egg Noodles
    One taste is all it takes
New models for the new deal
    Duke electric clocks
New Orleans' most famous sauce
    Remoulade
New Orleans Times-Picayune
    First for the South
New Prell puts the ooooo in
    shampoo
    Prell shampoo
A new queen reigns where ice
    was king
    Ice Maid refrigeration
The new school of thought in
    old school ties
    Hampton Hall, Ltd.
New ScotTissue is stronger than
    ever
    ScotTissue
New-Skin Liquid Court Plaster
    Paint it with New-Skin and
    forget it
The new slick way to chase dirt
    Quick-Way Household Paste
    Cleaner
The new smokeless coal from
    Old Virginia
    Red Jacket Coal Sales Co.
The new sparkling water
    Everess sparkling water
The new standard in world-
    wide car rental
    Dollar Rent-a-car service
The new standard of performance
    Martin outboard motors
New State Coffee
    Famous for flavor
New steels are born at Armco
    Armco Steel Corp.
A new talc with a new odor
    Pompeian talcum powder
New taste enjoyment, new

smoking convenience ...
anywhere, anytime
Roi-Tan Little Cigars

The new tender touch tissues
Yes Tissues

New to look at, new to taste
Corn KIX cereal

A new touch of beauty for the
wired home
General Electric Christmas
tree lights

New trains, new travelers
The Budd Company

New Vibro-Shave stops the old
drudgery of scraping
it off
Vibro-Shave electric razor

The new way to do prestige advertising
Strathmore Paper Co.

New wings for a new world
McDonnell-Douglas Corporation

New York Central System
Even when weather says
NO, these famous trains
say GO
Road to the future
The scenic route
Water level route, you
can sleep
The world's standard of
quality

New York Commercial
The paper that blazes trade
trails

New York Daily Mirror
A live picture tabloid newspaper for all the family

New York Evening Graphic
A human interest newspaper

New York Evening Journal
The largest evening circulation in America

New York Futures Exchange
The Index with a name you
can trade on

New York Herald-Tribune
First to last, the truth:
news, editorials, ad-
vertisements

The New York Life agent in
your community is a
good man to know
New York Life Insurance
Co.

New York Life Insurance Co.
Ask me
Leader in business insur-
ance
The New York Life agent in
your community is a
good man to know
Safety is always the first
consideration, nothing
else is so important
Through every "storm" since
1845

New York-Miami route, Admiral
Line
Forty-eight hours of glori-
ous travel

New York Shipbuilding Corp.
Where outstanding performance is standard

New York State Dept. of Com-
merce
Discover the new in New
York State

New York Stock Exchange Members
Own your share of American
business
Promoting high standards in
the public interest

New York Sunday American
The backbone of New York
advertising
Sell it in the all-day home
newspaper

New York Times
All the news that's fit to
print
Cheapest and best
A newspaper for the people

New York Title & Mortgage Co.
Secure as the bedrock of
New York

New York Tribune
The leading paper!
Sells for three cents and is
worth it!

New York World
The three-cent quality
medium of America's
greatest market

New York World-Telegram
Is the Telegram on your
list?

New Yorker
Where were you last week?

New York's finest

328

Eichler beer
Newark Evening News
    Always reaches home
A Newark institution
    Yellow taxicabs
Newell Manufacturing Co.
    First family in drapery
        hardware since 1903
Newest look in laminates
    Enjay Chemical Co. Div.,
        Humble Oil and Refining
        Co.
Newman-Green, Inc.
    Creative aerosol valve engi-
        neering
Newport cigarettes
    After all, if smoking isn't
        a pleasure, why bother?
    Alive with pleasure!
    Smokes fresher--and tastes
        better than any other
        menthol cigarette
    Tastes better than any other
        menthol cigarette!
News and management monthly
    of the graphic arts
    Printing Magazine
The news from Asia. About
    Asia. Written and
    edited for the reader
    with an interest in Asia
    Asian Wall Street Journal
    Weekly
The news magazine of art
    Art Digest
News of consequence for people
    of consequence
    U. S. News and World Re-
    port
The news of the day in the
    newsiest way
    Daily Metal Trade
The news unbiased and unbossed
    Ohio State JOurnal
Newskin Co.
    Never neglect a break in
    the skin
A newspaper for the makers of
    newspapers
    Fourth Estate
A newspaper for the people
    New York Times
The newspaper of the buying
    population
    Detroit Times
Newsweek

The dime that covers the
    world
The international newsmaga-
    zine
    Newsweek knows
The newsweekly that separ-
    ates fact from opinion
Nobody gives you opinion
    like Newsweek
We don't fit the mold. We
    break it
Newsweek knows
    Newsweek
The newsweekly that separates
    fact from opinion
    Newsweek
Next best to rain
    Double Rotary Sprinkler
Next day service
    U. S. Postal Service Express
    Mail
Next
    While other magazines are
    looking at today this
    one is looking at tomor-
    row
The next one tastes as good as
    the first
    Central Breweries, Inc.
Next time get Ethyl
    Ethyl gasoline
Next to mine I like your face
    Star Razor Blades
Next to my heart
    Renee brassiere
Next to nothing at all
    Du-Ons underwear
Next to safety, first aid
    Johnson & Johnson
Niagara Cyclo Massage
    A trusted name ... proved
    by medical research and
    the experience of mil-
    lions
Niagara Searchlight Co.
    Bores a 300-foot hole in the
    night
Niagara to the sea
    Canadian Steamship Lines,
    Ltd.
Niblets canned corn
    Fresh corn off the cob
    Sunny magic for simple
    meals
N'ice cough lozenges
    Feels slickery

Put your throat on N'ice
    Nice work, and you CAN get it
        Schick electric shaver
Nicest next to you
    Gossard girdles
Nicholas Oil Co.
    Let your motor be the
        judge, it knows
Nichols Aluminum Co.
    The brightest name in
        aluminum
Nicholson File Co.
    A file for every purpose
    For every purpose
Nickel drink worth a dime
    Pepsi-Cola soft drink
Nickel ... it's contribution is
        quality
    International Nickel Co.
The nickel lunch
    Planters salted peanuts
Nickel Plate Railroad
    The railroad that runs by
        the customer's clock
NICOR, Inc.
    The basic energy company
Niedecken Showers
    Niedecken Showers give
        refreshing hours
    Niedecken Showers give refresh-
        ing hours
    Niedecken Showers
Night or day it safens the way
    Preflex auto mirror
The NIGHTwear of a nation
    Faultless Nightwear Corp.
Nil deodorant
    NIL that odor
    To kill that odor just NIL
        that odor
NIL that odor
    Nil deodorant
Niles Tools Works Co.
    The name really means
        something
Nimrod Ward Mfg. Co.
    America's largest builder of
        camping trailers
    America's largest selling
        camping trailer
9-Lives cat food
    The cat food even finicky
        Morris can't resist
    The nutritious foods cats
        really like
    Real juices for real taste

98% kill-power
    Whiz insect killer
98 years experience in business
        systems
    National Cash Register Co.
Ninety golden brown biscuits
        from each package
    Abilene Flour Mills
99 44/100% pure
    Ivory Soap
99% tar free
    Barclay cigarettes
97% caffeine-free
    Sanka Brand decaffeinated
        coffee
Nip it with Sip-It
    Sip-It cough remedy
Nippon Kokan
    The most progressive name
        in steel
Nixdorf computer
    Step up your business with
        Nixdorf
No belts, no pins, no pads, no
        odor
    Tampax, Inc.
No better blades at any price
    Berkeley razor blades
No better built than Durabilt
    Durabilt steel locker
No brush marks
    Red Devil enamel
No brush, no lather, no rub-in
    Barbasol shaving cream
No buttons down the front
    Oneita Elastic Ribbed Union
        Suits
No caffeine. Never had it.
        Never will
    7UP soft drink
No claim is ever made about
        Samson tires that can-
        not be proven
    Samson tires
No cleaner bag or container to
        empty
    Air-Way Sanitary System
No colic. No sickness. No
        trouble
    King Silver Nipple
No damp amps
    Cincinnati Electrical Prod-
        ucts Co.
No drive too hard, no service
        too severe
    Bull Dog Belting

No-Ease spectacles
  Like pearl temples behind
    the ears
No estate too small for our ad-
    ministration
  Royal Trust Co.
No extravagant claims, just a
    real good product
  Brown Friar whiskey
No finer-tasting cigar at any
    price
  Seidenberg cigar
No hill too steep, no sand too
    deep
  Jackson 4-wheel drive
    trucks
No home complete without Astypo-
    dine
  Astypodine
No home's complete without a
    telechime
  Telechime
No ifs, ands or additives
  Adolph's meat tenderizer
No irritation--does not shrink
  Pearce Hygienic Fleeced
    Underwear
No leakage risk with Flextite
    disc
  Ohio Brass Co.
No long waits, no short weights
  North Memphis Coal Co.
No man's debts should live after
    him
  Morris Plan
No matter how diluted, it is
    never skimmed milk
  Pet milk
No matter how the world solves
    its energy problems,
    McDermott is involved
  McDermott International,
    Inc.
No matter how you give Johnnie
    Walker Black, it's im-
    pressive
  Johnnie Walker Black Label
    Scotch whiskey
No matter what kind or what
    priced merchandise
    you make, the Plain
    Dealer alone will sell
    it
  Cleveland Plain Dealer
No metal can touch you
  Paris garters

No more cooking by guess
  Westinghouse electric oven
No more shaker-clog
  International Salt Co.
No name in corsetry is better
    known
  Rengo Belt
No one can do it like Chevy can
    do it
  Chevrolet automobile
No one can teach you another
    language faster and
    better than Berlitz
  Berlitz School of Language
No one is in a better position to
    solve your lubrication
    problems
  Manzel Div., Houdaille In-
    dustries
No one is in debt to Macy's
  Macy's department store
No other container protects like
    the can
  Can Manufacturers Institute
No other copier can copy this
  IBM Series III copier/
    duplicator
No other paint stays brighter
    under the sun
  Felton, Sibley & Co.
No other has round-end bristle
  Pro-Phy-Lac-Tic toothbrush
No other instrument so richly
    rewards the efforts of
    the beginner
  Hammond organ
No other pen writes like Water-
    man's
  Waterman's Ideal Fountain
    Pen
No other soap picks you up
    quite like Coast--the
    eye-opener
  Coast soap
No other tobacco is like it
  Prince Albert pipe and
    cigarette tobacco
No over-soaped feeling
  Swan Soap
No parboiling, it's ovenized
  Swift's ham
No "peeping Tom" can decipher
    the contents
  Magill-Weinsheimer window
    envelope
No-Pest insect spray

Deadly on bugs; gentle
on plants
No-Pest kills fleas and
keeps killing them for
weeks
No-Pest kills fleas and keeps
killing them for weeks
No-Pest insect spray
No priorities on color and charm
Chrysler automobile
The no-problem typewriter. It
does more than just
type
Lanier typewriter
No pull, no pain, no sting
Barbasol razor blades
No purer soap was ever made
Chiffon Soap Flakes
No rat becomes immune to d-Con
Rat Killer
d-Con Rat Killer
No rind, no waste
June Dairy Products Co.
No runs--no drips--no errors
Krylon spray paint
No rest for the wary
Dupont cooling system
cleanser
No-Salt salt substitute
Shake the salt habit
No sash hardware installs faster
than Grand Rapids
hardware
Grand Rapids Hardware
Co.
No Scotch improves the flavour
of water like Teacher's
Teacher's Highland Cream
Scotch whiskey
No-Sha-Do hosiery
Free from "rings" and
"shadows"
No soap but Palmolive
Palmolive soap
No soap can get you cleaner
Ivory soap
No speed too high, no pulley
too small
Perfection Belting
No springs. Honest weight
Toledo Scale Co.
No steel, but it's master
Haynes Stellite Co.
No-stick cooking with no-
scour clean-up
Teflon

No straps to stretch, fray or rot
American Chain Co.
No stropping, no honing
Gillette safety razor
No tire trouble. No cooling
trouble. Always com-
fortable
Franklin automobile
No tired is too tired for Coast
Coast soap
No-To-Bac
Don't tobacco spit and
smoke your life away!
No tools but the hands
Goodyear Auto Tire
No TV game comes close to this
one!
"The Joker's Wild" television
quiz program
No watching, no burning, no
turning
Toastmaster toaster
No watching, no turning, no
burning
Waters-Center toaster
No water cooled car can so this
Knox Waterless Limousine
No water needed
Phillips' Milk of Magnesia
tablets
No wonder Fleischmann's Pre-
ferred is PREFERRED
Fleischmann's whiskey
No wonder more women rely on
Ivory Liquid to help
them keep their hands
soft, young-looking!
Ivory dishwashing liquid
Nob Hill Coffee
A luxury blend at a thrifty
price
A noble Scotch
Train & McIntyre Scotch
whiskey
The noblest of all cabinet woods
American Walnut Mfrs.
Assn.
Nobody doesn't like Sara Lee
Sara Lee coffee cake
Nobody ever had enough time
Telechron Electric Clock
Nobody gives you opinion like
Newsweek
Newsweek
Nobody knows chicken like the
folks at Weaver

Weaver fried chicken
Nobody knows more about micro-
wave cooking
Litton microwave ovens
Nobody knows municipal bonds
like Nuveen
John Nuveen & Co., Inc.
Nobody offers you more than
Quasar
Quasar television sets
Nobody serves our republic like
Republic Airlines
Republic Airlines
Nocona Athletic Goods Co.
The name for quality
athletic goods
Noctil
Every granule licks dirt 8
ways
Nodark Camera
A finished picture in a
minute
Nogar Clothing Mfg. Co.
Made to stand the gaff
Noilly Prat vermouth
Don't stir without Noilly
Prat
Noise Abatement Comm.
Rely on your brakes in-
stead of your horn
The noiseless oil burner
Silent Automatic Corp.
Noiseless typewriter
When it writes, it whispers
Non-skid roads, rain or shine
The Barrett Co.
Nopco Chemical Co.
A skilled hand in chemistry
... at work for you
Norand data systems
We put data systems where
the action is
Norcold, Inc.
Refrigeration is our busi-
ness ... our only
business
Norcross greeting cards
America's best loved greet-
ing cards
Nordberg engines
Mean more power to you
Nordic Enterprises, Inc.
See: Rapala Div.,
Nordic Enterprises,
Inc.
Nordyke automobile

It's a great automobile
Norelco electric housewares
A bright new world of elec-
tric housewares
Norelco Rototrack Shaver
The close electric shave
The comfort shave
Tough on your beard, not
on your face
You can't get any closer
Norell
The first great perfume
born in America
Norfolk and Western Railway
The nation's going-est rail-
road
Norfolk Paint & Varnish Co.
We make it, we guarantee
it
Norfolk, Va.
The city that does things
Norge electric range
Matchless cooking
See Norge before you buy
Norge refrigerator
The best dealer in town
sells Norge
Better products for a better
world
From top to floor there's
space galore
A roller rolls and there's
ice
See Norge before you buy
Why be a servant to your
refrigerator?
Working for today, planning
for tomorrow
Years from now you'll be
glad it's Norge
Norgren. See: C. A. Norgren
Co.
Norm Thompson mail order serv-
ice
Escape from the ordinary
Norman Hilton & Co. men's
clothing
Clothiers since 1888
Doing one thing well
Norris, Inc.
Variety box of exquisite
gift candies
North American Aviation, Inc.
The airplanes that mean
business
North American Aviation

is at work in the fields
of the future
North American Aviation is at
work in the fields of
the future
North American Aviation,
Inc.
North American Rockwell and the
future are made for
you
North American Rockwell
Corp.
North American Rockwell Corp.
The jet that justifies itself
North American Rockwell and
the future are made for
you
North American Royalties, Inc.
NAR: Confidence based on
success
NAR: Meeting needs vital
to the nation's economy
North American Van Lines, Inc.
The gentlemen of the mov-
ing industry
North Carolina Dept. of Conser-
vation
Where good government is
a habit
North Coast Limited
Go by air-conditioned train
North East Electric Co.
The faithfulness of an old
friend
The horn that lasts
A real magnetic horn
The responsiveness of a
well trained servant
The urge to instant action
North electric radio receiver
The dial of pleasure
North Memphis Coal Co.
A black business handled
white
No long waits, no short
weights
North Western. See also:
Northwestern
North Western Expanded Metal
Co.
Steel strengthened plas-
tering
Northcool suits
The tropical suit that
"breathes" fresh air
Northeast. See: North East

Electric Co.
Northern bathroom tissue
For a more attractive bath-
room
Linenized for softness
Softness is Northern
Softness you can feel and
see
Northern Electric Co.
World's oldest and largest
manufacturer of electric
blankets
Northern Furniture Co.
For gracious living
Northern Hard Maple Mfrs.
The hardest hardwoods grow
in the north
Northern Hemlock Mfrs. Assn.
Beautiful birch for beautiful
woodwork
Northern Insurance Co.
Security is the keynote to-
day, and every day
Northern Natural Gas Co.
Ask the man from Northern
Plains
Northern oil burner
Keeps step with the weather
Northern Pacific Railway
First of the Northern Trans-
continentals
Main Street of the Northwest
Route of the Vista-Dome
North Coast limited
This is the way to run a
railroad
Northern Pump Co.
More gallons per horse
power
Northern Texas Traction Co.
Speed with safety
You don't have to park
your street car
Northill anchor
Standard of reliability since
1935
Northland Ski Mfg. Co.
World's largest ski maker
World's most experienced
ski maker
Northrop Corporation
Making advanced technology
work
Northwest Airlines, Inc.
The fan-jet airline
Serving America's billionarea

Northwest Envelope Co.
If it's an envelope, we make it
Northwest Industries, Inc.
Subtract all our acquisitions and the numbers still look good
You can't run 11 successful companies with just one man
Northwest Orient Airlines
The roomier ride
The wide-cabin airline
The world is going our way
Northwest Paper Co.
Always makes good printing better
Northwestern. See also: North Western
Northwestern Mutual Life Insurance Co.
Because there is a difference
A billion dollar estate
The quiet company
A tough act to follow
The northwest's only weekly farm paper
The Farmer
Norwalk Vault
The seal that endures is the seal that insures
Norwood tires
Service that saves
Not a cheap car but a good one
Babcock Model A automobile
Not a cough in a carload
Old Gold cigarettes
Not a drop is sold till it's seven years old
Jameson Irish whiskey
Not a knock in a tankful
Crown Dominion gasoline
Not a shadow of a doubt
Kotex sanitary napkins
Not a toy but a machine
Planetary Pencil Pointer
Not an accessory but a necessity
Brown Spring Oiler Co.
Not charity, but a chance
Goodwill Industries, Inc.
Not how many, but how good
Florsheim Shoe Co.
Not just a gallon of oil, but a gallon of oil

service
Paragon Oil Co.
Not just good ... but wonderful
Johnson's Pie Co. Div., Ward Foods, Inc.
Not just nylons, but Cannon nylons
Cannon nylon stockings
Not made to a price, but a perfect product
Mrs. Day's Ideal Baby Shoe Co.
Not one American car lasts as long as Reo, not one
Reo automobile
Not only light but deliciously light
Planters peanut oil
Not the biggest--but the best
Seven Seas slacks
Not the name of a thing but the mark of a service
General Electric Mazda Lamp
Not the price per pair but the cost per mile
Stacy Adams shoe
Not too loose, not too tight, fits just right
Munsingwear underwear
Not twice as much but twice as good
Lime Cola
Note the tear and wear as well as the test
Neenah Paper Co.
Nothing acts like Analax
Analax
Note the wood wheels everywhere
Automotive Wood Wheels Mfrs.
Nothing beats a great pair of L'eggs
L'eggs pantyhose
Nothing better has come to light
Solar Electric Corp.
Nothing but nylon makes you feel so female
Textile Div., Monsanto Company
Nothing but Spandex makes you look so female
Spandex
Nothing could be finer
Lincoln automobile
Mastercraft seat cover

Nothing else is a Volkswagen
    Volkswagen automobile
Nothing else is like it
    Plate Glass Mfrs. of Amer-
        ica
Nothing else is made like it
    Philadelphia Brand cream
        cheese
Nothing else like it
    Prudential Insurance Co.
        of America
Nothing else quite measures up
    Walker's Deluxe bourbon
        whiskey
Nothing equals stainless steel
    United States Steel Corp.
Nothing even comes close
    Audi and Porsche automo-
        biles
Nothing feels like giving real
        gold
    Karat gold jewelry
Nothing grooms hair better than
        a little dab
    Brylcreem hair dressing
Nothing is better in floor trucks
    Nutting Truck Co.
Nothing like the flavor
    Wrigley's chewing gum
Nothing moves you like a Fiat
        Sportscar
    Fiat automobile
Nothing old-fashioned but the
        hospitality
    Hotel Statler, New York
        City and elsewhere
Nothing over fifteen cents
    F. W. Woolworth Co.
Nothing rivals Nature's Rival
    Nature's Rival corset
Nothing rolls like a ball
    New Departure-Hyatt Bear-
        ings Div., General
        Motors Corporation
Nothing runs like a Deere!
    Deere & Co.
Nothing shaves closer than Edge
    Edge shaving preparation
Nothing sparks like a Champion
    Champion spark plugs
Nothing takes the place of
        Guinness
    Guinness ale
Nothing takes the place of
        leather
    American Leather Prod-

ucts, Inc.
Nothing talks like actual per-
        formance
    American La France Fire
        Engine
Nothing tastes as good as Ritz,
        but RITZ
    Ritz crackers
Nothing to do but fry
    Gorton's Codfish Cakes
Nothing to sell but service
    Franklin Linotype Co.
Nothing to serve but the public
        interest
    Des Moines Capital
Nothing to shovel, nothing to
        explode
    Motorstoker Corp.
Nothing too good for men in
        service
    Mennen's talcum powder
Nothing too good for our boys
    Mennen's talcum powder
Nothing washes like soap, and
        there is no soap like
        White King
    White King Soap
Nothing's faster. Nothing's
        easier
    Brite floor polish
Notice the lighting fixtures
    Associated Lighting Indus-
        tries
Nottingham desks
    America's handsomest desks
Nourishes every inch of your
        dog
    Gaines-burgers
Novelty Shoe Co.
    True to its name
Now better than ever for every-
        thing
    Ivory soap
Now cigarettes
    The lowest in tar of all
        brands
Now clean the tartar zone
    Tek toothbrush
Now comes the season when
        comfort depends on the
        car
    Borland Electric automobile
Now every man can enjoy his
        pipe
    Henry Sutliff Tobacco Co.
Now everybody can have

Xerocopies
Xerox Corporation
Now I lay me down to ... sleep
    like a kitten
    Chesapeake and Ohio Rail-
      way
Now it's a pleasure to be thirsty
    Nedick's restaurants
Now less money buys more miles
    Goodyear Auto Tire
Now, more WEAR than EVER
    Wear-Ever aluminum
Now, no bad breath behind his
    sparkling smile
    Colgate's dental cream
Now over 21 million jars used
    yearly
    Vick's Vapo-Rub
Now! Tastes better than ever
    Purina Cat Chow
Now that's the best tasting
    pickle I ever heard
    Vlasic pickles
Now! The final achievement
    Brunswick Ultona phono-
      graph
Now there's an even better way
    to own gold
    The Gold Coins of Mexico
Now there's one all-cargo air-
    line with scheduled
    service around the
    world
    Flying Tiger Line, Inc.
Now we're building our best in
    the U. S. A.
    Volvo trucks
Now you have a friend in the
    diamond business
    Shane Co. direct diamond
    importers
Now you'll like bran
    Postum Cereal Co., Inc.
Nowadays Purex quality makes
    even more sense
    Purex cleaning materials
Nowadays they eat and drink
    from Dixies
    Dixie paper cups
Now's the time to get away to
    it all!
    Southwest Sun Country
    Assn.
Now's the time to talk it over
    National Broadcasting
      Co.

Noxema skin cream
    Feel it heal
Nu. See also: New
Nu Finish automobile polish
    The once a year automobile
    polish
Nu-Grape soft drink
    A flavor you can't forget
Nu-Made Mayonnaise
    Nu-Made tastes home-made
Nu-Made tastes home-made
    Nu-Made Mayonnaise
Nu-Tone Chimes, Inc.
    The greatest name in door
    chimes
Nu Vision
    We put the "care" back in
    "eye care"
Nuclear power cuts oil imports
    Public Service Electric &
    Gas Co.
Nudit cream hair remover
    Extra gentle. Soothes,
    smooths as it removes
    hair fast!
    The feminine way to beauti-
    ful skin
Nugget shoe polish
    Did you Nugget your shoes
    this morning?
Nujol laxative
    For internal cleanliness
    Growing old gracefully
    The internal lubricant
    Keep regular as clockwork
    with Nujol
    A lovely skin comes from
    within
    More important than soap
    and water
    Regular as clockwork
Numatics, Inc.
    The air valve people
The No. 1 buy in the design
    field
    Product Engineering
The #1 discount broker serving
    the Midwest
    Charles Schwab & Co., Inc.
#1 for everyone
    Hertz automobile rentals
No. 1 heavy-duty sales leader
    International Harvester
    trucks
The Number One imported Ger-
    man beer

Beck's beer
Number 1 in acceptance
    Airtex Products, Inc.
No. 1 in cement
    Lonestar Industries, Inc.
No. 1 in financial printing since
    1775
    La Salle St. Press, Inc.
No. 1 in V-belts and hose
    Gates Rubber Co.
The No. 1 men's service maga-
    zine
    Argosy
The No. 1 name in billiards
    Brunswick Corp.
No. 1 name in bowling
    Brunswick Corp.
Number One on the fit parade
    Holeproof Hosiery
No. 1 recommended for athlete's
    foot
    Tinactin
The No. 1 sleep aid in America
    Unisom
No. 1 source of gummed papers
    Dennison Mfg. Co.
Nunn-Bush Shoe Co.
    Ankle-fashioned shoes
    A big name at a little price
    Faithful to the last
    Fashioned by master crafts-
        men
    First in quality!
    Quality beyond the call of
        duty
Nunnally Co.
    The candy of the South
Nunziola accordion
    The world's most respected
        accordion
Nupercainal
    Tomorrow's medicines from
        today's research
Nutone, Inc.
    Known in millions of homes
    The name known in millions
        of American homes
Nutone Security System
    The professional in home
        security
Nutrition at its best
    Thrive catfood
The nutritious foods cats really
    like
    9-Lives cat food
Nutting Truck Co.

Floor truck specialists since
    1891
    Keep your cans on wheels
    Nothing is better in floor
        trucks
    The trailer that leads
Nuveen. See: John Nuveen &
    Co., Inc.
Nytol
    For a good night's sleep
    A sleep-aid for the eighties

-O-

O. See also: Oh
O-B has won where mining is
    done
    Ohio Brass Co.
O-B is bought where service
        is sought
    Ohio Brass Co.
O-B on a Bull Dog clamp proves
        the safest quality stamp
    Ohio Brass Co.
O. C. Pecan Fudge
    Too good for words
O-Cedar polish
    Bring out the "sleeping
        beauty" in your furni-
        ture
    Cleans as it polishes
    Cleans as it shines
O-Cedar products
    Greatest name in house-
        keeping
O. F. Mossberg and Sons, Inc.
    Mossberg for accuracy
O-I takes many shapes to serve
        you
    Owens-Illinois Glass Co.
O I C valves
    Sets the pace in valves
O. K. Storage & Transfer Co.
    The world moves, so do we
O. M. Scott and Co.
    Leaders in lawn research
    The grass people
    The lawn people
O. P. Bauer Confectionery Co.
    Sweet magic
O. P. Skaggs Food Stores
    A surety of purity
O, what a feeling!
    Toyota automobile
Oak Ridge Antenna

Installed in minutes, lasts
for years
Oakite
Cleans a million things
If it's a question of clean-
ing/conditioning ...
ask Oakite
Oakland automobile
Winning and holding good
will
Oakland Tribune
One of the west's great
newspapers
Obey that impulse and subscribe
regularly to Life
Life
O'Brien Varnish Co.
A little varnish makes a lot
of difference
Makes your house a White
House
Obviously it must be Western
Union
Western Union Corporation
Occident flour
Costs more, worth more
Occidental Petroleum Corporation
Twenty-five years of record
growth and progress
have led us to this
moment--the threshold of
a new era
Ocean fresh
Sea-Seald Cod Liver Oil
Ocean Spray cranberry juice
The growers brand
Take good care of your-
self; have an Ocean
Spray
Ochee beverages make friends
on taste
Ochee Spring Water Co.
Ochee Spring Water Co.
Ochee beverages make
friends on taste
Oculens sun glasses
Seeing is believing
Odac Mfg. Co.
Fresh air by Odac
Odorono deodorant
A flowering beauty, yet
she's a wallflower
She's sure--are you?
24 hour protection
Of all leading brands, nothing
you can buy gives

you more relief. Abso-
lutely nothing
Exedrin pain reliever
Of America's great sources of en-
ergy, only National
serves you in so many
ways
National LP-Gas Market
Development Council
Of paramount importance to the
housewife
Arcraft Brooms
Of topmost choice
Old Taylor whiskey
The off-airport car rental centers
Thrifty Rent-a-car System,
Inc.
Off when it's on and on when
it's off
Gould-National Batteries,
Inc.
The office automation computer
company
Wang Laboratories, Inc.
Office help--temporary or per-
manent
American Girl Service
Office Products Div., Interna-
tional Business Machines
Corp.
Machines should work.
People should think
Office Products Div., Interna-
tional Business Machines
Corp. See also:
IBM
International Business Ma-
chines Corp.
Office supplies to business-like
buyers
Schwabacher-Frey stationery
store
Office tools
Diebold Safe & Lock Co.
The official camera of the Chi-
cago Cubs
Canon camera
Official tailors to the West
H. D. Lee Co., Inc.
Officially certified as the finest
tea grown
Ming Tea
Often a bridesmaid but never a
bride
Listerine mouth wash
Often imitated, never duplicated

Davis tennis rackets
Pilsner Beer
Oh. See also: O
Oh, Kleinert's? OK!
Kleinert Rubber Co.
Oh, my aching back! Ah, my
Absorbine, Jr!
Absorbine, Jr.
OhiO automobile
A high-grade car at a
moderate price
Ohio Brass Co.
Best that science can cre-
ate for trolleying your
heavy freight
The choice of the crew and
the big boss, too
Finely designed as the
ultimate kind
Greatest weld that you've
beheld
History tells which line ex-
cells
It pays to spend for the
best in the end
Makes a joint that's tight
plus alignment that's
right
No leakage risk with Flex-
tite disc
O-B has won where mining
is done
O-B is bought where serv-
ice is sought
O-B on a Bull Dog clamp
proves the safest qual-
ity stamp
Relieve the strains of coupling trains
Rightly put together to
fight both time and
weather
Service in years sells Mara-
thon gears
Signal safety with O-B
bonds
A world-wide reputation
for high-tension insul-
ation
Ohio Butterine Co.
Money-saver--butter flavor
Ohio Edison Power
This is the center of in-
dustrial America
Ohio Fuel Supply Co.
We seek to serve

Ohio State Journal
The news unbiased and un-
bossed
Ohio Thermometer Co.
The magic wand of a good
cook
Ohio's favorite brew since 1862
Leisy beer
Ohio's greatest home daily
Columbus Dispatch
Ohner adding machine
The machine to count on
Oil and Gas Journal
Follow the Journal and you
follow the oil industry
The oil bank of America
National Bank of Tulsa
Oil Center Tool Div., FMC Corp.
Where progress is a daily
practice
Oil Center Tool Div., FMC Corp.
See also: FMC Corp.
Oil City Brewing Co.
Famous for five generations
Oil Field Engineering
The engineering journal of
the industry
The oil of endurance
Red Indian lubricating oil
Oil of Olay beauty liquid
It can help you look young-
er, too
Oil of Orange
There is no finer
The oil that goes farther, fast-
er, safer
Pennzoil motor oil
Oilray Safety Heater, Inc.
Comfortable heat when you
want it, at a price you
can afford
Okaze denture cleaner
Okaze deodorizes your plates
as it cleans them
Okaze your plates, okaze
your breath
Okaze deodorizes your plates as
it cleans them
Okaze denture cleaner
Okaze your plates, okaze your
breath
Okaze denture cleaner
Oklahoma's greatest newspaper
Tulsa World
Old. See also: Auld
Old Anchor Beer

It's smooth sailing with
Old Anchor Beer
Smooth sailing with Old
Anchor Beer
Old Briar pipe tobacco
The aristocrat of pipe
tobacco
Its blend is our secret,
its fragrance your de-
light
Old Bushmill's Irish Whiskey
Individuals have poured
this smooth mellow
whiskey since 1608
Mellow as old Bourbon
One of the world's great
whiskeys
Robust as old rye
Tangy as old Scotch
Whiskey that has every-
thing
The world's oldest whiskey
You can tell a lot about an
individual by what he
pours into his glass
Old Chum tobacco
The tobacco of quality
Old Colony Brewing Co.
Be ale-wise
Old Colony Envelope Corp.
Where quality is traditional
Old Crow whiskey
Famous. Smooth. Mellow
The greatest name in bour-
bon
Those in the know ask for
Old Crow
A truly great name among
America's great whis-
kies
Old Dutch Cleanser
All is not new that glitters
Chases dirt
Doesn't scratch
It zips me through my
cleaning
Old England's finest chocolates
Cadbury's, Ltd.
Old English lawn seed
Old English lawn seed
makes better lawns
Old English lawn seed makes
better lawns
Old English lawn seed
Old English No Rubbing Wax
Gleaming armor for your

floors
Old English Powdered Cleaner
Melts dirt away
Old English Scratch Removing
Polish
Scratches disappear as you
polish
Old Export beer
Mountain water makes the
difference
Old-fashioned goodness in every
piece
Mary Lincoln Candies, Inc.
Old Fitzgerald whiskey
Your key to hospitality
Old floors look new in six to
nine minutes
Aerowax
Old Forester bourbon whiskey
There is nothing better in
the market
You can taste the truth of
this famous claim
Old Gold cigarettes
If you want a treat instead
of a treatment, smoke
Old Golds
Not a cough in a carload
The smoothest cigarette
Why be irritated? Light an
Old Gold
The world's smoothest cigar-
ette
Old Grand-Dad whiskey
Head of the bourbon family
114 barrel proof: so smooth
some people won't go
anywhere without the
barrel
Slightly more portable by
the bottle
That taste's always in season
Old Homestead Bread
Old Homestead Bread makes
little bodies gain
Old Homestead Bread makes little
bodies gain
Old Homestead Bread
Old Mac Coal
A thrifty fuel
Old ocean at its best
Southern Pacific steamship
cruises
Old Overholt whiskey
As different as day and
night

Its good taste always stands
out
Old Poindexter whiskey
The peak of perfection
Old Reliable Coffee
Always the same, always
good
The old reliable since 1891
Life Insurance Company of
Georgia
An old responsible house
American Bond & Mortgage
Co.
The Old South's treasure now
all America's pleasure
Maxwell House Master
Blend Coffee
Old Spice lotion
The man's spice so many
women love
Old Spice shaving mug refill
More practical than ever
Old Sunny Brook whiskey
Cheerful as its name
Old Taylor whiskey
Of topmost choice
Signed, sealed and deli-
cious
The sportsmen's whiskey
Old Thompson whiskey
Wed in the wood
Old-time. See also: Oldtyme
An old-time soup hits an all-
time high
Campbell's condensed soups
Old York cereal
The right road to health
Olde English Household Cleaner
Wipes off dirt and grease,
as easy as dusting
The oldest and largest tree
saving service in the
world
Davey Tree Expert Co.
The oldest domestic electric
refrigeration
Kelvinator refrigerator
The oldest farm paper in Amer-
ica
Southern Planter
Oldest in permanent type wall
coverings
Frederic Blank & Co.,
Inc.
The oldest mail order house is
today the most pro-

gressive
Montgomery Ward & Co.
The oldest, most complete and
highest quality line in
America
Devoe & Reynolds paint
The oldest name in pipes
House of Comoy
The oldest name in Scotch
Somerset Importers, Ltd.
Oldfield tires
The most trustworthy tires
built
Olds & Whipple
The ideal complete plant food
It costs more because it
lasts longer
The properly balanced or-
ganic plant food
The season-long plant food
Oldsmobile automobile
The car ahead? It's Olds-
mobile
The car that has everything
Escape from the ordinary
Get more go from every
gallon
Have one built for you
Here's riding at its level
best
Look to Olds for the new
Oldsmobile for safety first
The rocket action car
Seen in the smartest places
where the smartest car
belongs
640 trips to the moon
Stops are few and far be-
tween; Olds need little
gasoline
We've had one built for
you
Oldsmobile for safety first
Oldsmobile automobile
Oldsmobile Toronado automobile
As unique as the person
who drives one
Oldtyme. See also: Old-time
Oldtyme Distillers
The whiskey that speaks
for itself
The whiskey with no re-
grets
Oleg Cassini, Inc.
Finer seamless stockings
Olga Co.

Behind every Olga there
really is an Olga
Olin Mathieson Chemical Corp.
Don't say it can't be done
... talk to Olin
Oliver farm equipment
Sturdy is the word for
Oliver
Oliver typewriter
A finer typewriter at a
fair price
The standard visible writer
Olivetti Corporation of America
The world's best designed
products, inside and
out
Olsen & O'Brien
Goods well displayed are
half sold
Olsten Temporary Services
Good people
Olympene medicine
Athletes know it's best
Olympia electronic typewriters
Precision typewriters
Quality that improves the
quality of life in your
office
Your key to the electronic
office
Olympia Self-Playing Music Box
Plays over a thousand
tunes
There is no "Just as Good"
Olympic paints and stains
One strong finish after
another
Olympic Radio and Television
Div., Lear Siegler,
Inc.
From the space age labor-
atories of Olympic
Omaha Public Power District
The land of elbow room
and elbow grease
We've got coal to burn
(And nuclear fuel,
too)
Omar cigarettes
Smoke Omar for aroma
Omega Oil
The great penetrative
liniment
Omega watch
First name in time, last
word in watch styling

For a lifetime of proud pos-
session
Omni
The classic magazine of the
space age. Join us in
the future ... now!
The omnibus company
Greyhound Corporation
Omnicare Dental Services
The dental concept of the
future
On a pedestal
Gold Stripe stockings
On every spare a Johnson Lock
to keep it there
Johnson tire lock
On rearing children from crib
to college
Parents Magazine
On the air and everywhere
Philip Morris cigarettes
On the bench since 1850
Prentiss Vise Co.
On the job wherever a client's
interest is at stake
Marsh & McLennan, Inc.
On the range
Williams Gun Sight Co.
On the skill of a mechanic may
depend your life
Multibestos brake lining
On the spot when you need us
Bank of America
On the well-dressed head
Stetson hats
On-time-delivery is our #1 con-
cern
Reading Railroad
On time every day is the Bur-
lington way
Chicago, Burlington and
Quincy Railroad
On top of the problem, part of
the solution
Cities Service Company
On your wrist, off your mind
Croton watch
Onan products
Power and light for every
need
The once a month fabric softener
Free 'n' Soft fabric softener
Once a Pioneer, always a Pioneer
Pioneer Lacquer
The once a year car polish
Nu Finish automobile polish

Once again the answer is AIG
The AIG Companies
Once in a lifetime
New Jersey Zinc Co.
Once it leaves your hands it
never leaves our net-
work
DHL Worldwide Courier
Once tried, always satisfied
Golden Virginia tobacco
Once you know the story behind
them you'll know why
so many Americans are
purchasing them
The Gold Coins of Mexico
Once you try it you'll love the
difference
Dr. Pepper soft drink
One-A-Day vitamins
Look for the label with the
Big Red "1"
The 1½ calorie breath mint
Tic Tac
The one and only
Hammond organ
The one and only cocktail gum
Warren's Chewing Gum
The one bed frame people ask
for by name
Harvard Mfg. Co.
One best temperature as an in-
vestment
Tagliabue Mfg. Co.
One bolt turns the trick
Kaplan Wheel Co.
One Canadian stands alone
Windsor Canadian whiskey
One chord is worth a thousand
words
Sohmer piano
The one cigarette for everyone
who smokes!
Kent cigarettes
The one cigarette sold the world
over
Melachrino cigarettes
One coat covers all surfaces
Elliott Paint & Varnish
One corporation covers a world
of energy
Pioneer Corporation
One delicious flavor in two
delicious forms
Grape-Nuts cereal and
Grape-Nuts Flakes
One drop for your beauty, two

drops for a beau, three
drops for romance, it's
Frolic, you know
Frolic Perfume
The one for kids
Kool-Aid soft drink mix
One good cup deserves another
Beechnut coffee
One good idea after another
AMFAC Hotels (Dallas/Fort
Worth)
One good ton deserves another
Doughtridge Fuel Co.
One great idea after another
Quasar television sets
The one great name in valves
The Lunkheimer Co.
The ONE great name that identi-
fies fine cars exclusively
Pierce-Arrow automobile
One hot dish and no hot kitchen
Campbell's condensed soups
One Hour Martinizing
Certifies the most in dry
cleaning
The most in dry cleaning
104 shaves in the big tube
Listerine shaving cream
114 barrel proof: so smooth
some people won't go
anywhere without the
barrel
Old Grand-Dad whiskey
The 100 largest foreign invest-
ments in the U. S.
Consolidated Gas Fields Ltd.
100% cotton. The fiber you can
trust
National Cotton Council
100% guaranteed temporary office
help
Kelly temporary office help
services
100% Pennsylvania at its best
Veedol motor oil
100% pure
Baker's Breakfast Cocoa
162 brushings in the 40¢ tube
Listerine toothpaste
103 Degree Incubator Co.
Hen's only rival
A 100-year start on tomorrow
Kodak photocopiers
One hundred years young
Youth's Companion
One if by day, two if by night

Sofa-Niter sofa

One investment firm you'll be
    glad to hear from
    Dean Witter Reynolds in-
    vestments

One look proves they are styled
    right, one step proves
    they are made right
    W. L. Douglas Shoes

One look to know they are
    styled right, one step
    to prove they are made
    right
    W. L. Douglas Shoes

One luxury all can enjoy
    Piel's beer

The one-man, one-hand shingle
    Bird and Son, Inc.

One management, ship and shore
    Canadian Pacific Steamship
    & Railroad Co.

One moist and delicious meal
    in every can
    Fancy Feast Gourmet cat-
    food

The one-man gang
    Towmotor Corp.

One name in furniture every-
    body knows
    Kroehler Mfg. Co.

One of America's best
    Lancaster tires

One of America's fastest-growing
    quality brands
    Breidt beer

One of America's fine watches
    Harvel watches

One of America's great mealtime
    drinks
    Instant Postum

One of America's great weeklies
    Railway Age

One of America's most distin-
    guished motor cars
    Nash automobile

One of nature's most perfect
    foods
    Quaker Oats

One of the banks that define
    banking
    Mellon National Bank

One of the everlasting kind
    Lowenberg golf bags

One of the family
    Pillsbury's Health Bran

One of the good things in life

Kaywoodie pipe

One of the good things in life
    that never varies
    Dewar's Blended Scotch
    Whiskey

One of the great watches of our
    time
    Waltham watches

One of the many distinctive
    faultless loose-leaf books
    Stationers Loose Leaf Binder

One of the many fine products
    that come from 40 years
    of thinking new
    Gold Bond building mate-
    rials

One of the many quality home
    improvement products
    made by J. M.
    Johns-Manville Corporation

One of the Old South's finest
    traditions
    Maxwell House Master
    Blend Coffee

One of the oldest in the business
    Tharp Heating and Air Con-
    ditioning, Inc.

One of the oldest names in tex-
    tiles ... for the newest
    development in syn-
    thetics
    Conmark Plastics Div.,
    Cohn-Hall-Marx Co.

One of the oldest names in the
    business
    Minnesota Mining & Manufac-
    turing Co.

One of the west's great newspa-
    pers
    Oakland Tribune

One of the world's great hotels
    Bellevue Stratford Hotel,
    Philadelphia, Pa.

One of the world's great whiskeys
    Old Bushmill's Irish Whiskey

One of two might be you
    National Safety Council

One pictograph tells more than
    a thousand words
    Pictograph Corp.

One picture tells more than a
    thousand words
    Pictograph Corp.

One policy, one system, univer-
    sal service
    American Telephone & Tele-

graph Co.

One proven design throughout
the line builds greater
value into every engine
Detroit Diesel Engine Div.,
General Motors Corpor-
ation

One purpose rooms make houses
too big
Murphy in-a-door bed

The one really comfortable
garter
Shir Gar garter

The one right oil for Ford cars
Ivaline motor oil

One service from forests to finished product
General Box Company

One source, one standard--
nationwide
Kelly temporary office help
services

One step ahead
Michelob beer

One step ahead of a changing
world
W. R. Grace & Co.

The "one stop" creative lighting
source
Petelco Div., Pyle-National
Co.

One strong finish after another
Olympic paints and stains

One switch controls everything
Philco Socket Power radio
receiver

One taste invites another
Angelus Marshmallows

One taste is all it takes
New Mill Kluski Egg Noodles

One taste is worth a thousand
words
MacFarlane candies

One taste will tell you why
National Distillers

The one that lasts
Echo chain saw
Echo grass trimmer

The one that won't bind
E-Z garters

One third of your life is spent
in bed
Simmons Company

1000 different products to make
business work
Curtis 1000

1006 lotion
Your face never had it so
clean!

The one to crunch when you
want to munch
Planters Sesame Nut Mix

The one to watch for new de-
velopments
Goodrich-Gulf Chemicals,
Inc.

The one toy that holds fun for
years
Richter's Anchor Blocks

One-Up tobacco case
Dignifying the pipe

One well-placed idea after
another
Amfac Hotels (Dallas/Fort
Worth)

One whiff and they're stiff
Flit insecticide

The one white shirt that's different
Van Heusen shirts

Oneida, Ltd.
Mark of excellence

Oneida motor truck
Uncommon carriers

O'Neil Oil Co.
Pour smoothness into your
motor

Oneita Elastic Ribbed Union
Suits
No buttons down the front

Ones that last a lifetime
Union Metal Mfg. Co.

Only a good cracker is fit to
eat
Biscuit & Cracker Mfrs.
Assn.

The only brush worth using is
the best brush you can
buy
Baker paint brush

The only chocolate milk with no
sugar added
Alba dry milk product

The only complete low-priced
car
Chevrolet automobile

The only cooler for milk, lemonade, mead and all
summer drinks
Jewett New Era water cooler

The only daily banking newspaper

American Banker
Only dependability brings suc-
    cess
    Pandora shoes
The only discount broker to of-
    fer complete discount
    commodity service
    Haas Securities Corporation
The only dual automatic refrig-
    erator
    Westinghouse refrigerator
Only Eastman makes Kodak cam-
    eras
    Kodak cameras
Only Eastman makes Kodak film,
    the film in the familiar
    yellow box
    Kodak cameras
Only Eastman makes the Kodak
    Kodak cameras
Only Eastman makes the Kodak
    camera
    Kodak cameras
Only Elgin gives you Engineer-
    ing
    Elgin Softener, Inc.
The only flag that fits all cars
    Fullerton-Kearney funeral
    flag
The only global daily newspaper
    International Herald Tribune
Only half as thick as the ordin-
    ary watch, yet guar-
    anteed accurate and
    even more durable
    Gruen Verithin Watch
Only her hairdresser knows for
    sure
    Clairol, Inc.
Only Hydromatic is completely
    automatic
    Hydromatic Transmission
The only instant coffee that's
    caffeine-free
    Sanka Brand decaffeinated
    coffee
The only iron that banishes
    ironing fatigue forever
    Proctor electric iron
Only master key to the master
    market
    Radio station KDKA, Pitts-
    burgh
The only name for both fuel and
    water pumps
    Airtex Products, Inc.

The only name you need to re-
    member
    Western Union Video Con-
    ferencing, Inc.
Only natural flavors last longer,
    naturally
    Topp's Chewing Gum
The only natural remedy
    Royal Victoria Sleep Pro-
    ducer
The only new idea in shaving
    since the safety razor
    Vaniva Shaving Cream
The only nicer water comes from
    the clouds
    Servisoft Div., Water Treat-
    ment Corp.
The only 100% coverage line for
    cars, trucks, tractors,
    stionary engines
    Victor Manufacturing and
    Gasket Co.
Only one magazine edited for
    rural women exclusively
    The Farmer's Wife
The only perfect cycle seat
    Automatic Cycle Seat
Only quality endures
    Brown Friar whiskey
The only real shaving soap
    Williams' Shaving Soap
The only refill shaving stick
    Colgate's refill shaving
    stick
Only 6 mg. Yet rich enough to
    be called de luxe. Open
    a box today
    Benson & Hedges 100's De
    Luxe Ultra Lights cig-
    arettes
The only "stay-on" stable blanket
    Burlington "Stay-on" horse
    blanket
Only the best is ever labeled
    Phillips Delicious
    Phillips Delicious Soups
Only the fairest get the squeeze
    Sunkist oranges
Only the Hunter Mills between
    the wheat field and
    your bakery
    Hunter Mills
Only the rich can afford poor
    windows
    Andersen Corporation
The only thing you give up is

calories
7UP soft drink
Only think! One soap for all
uses!
Frank Siddalls Soap
The only tissue that pops up
Kleenex tissue
The only truck bodies built like
a trailer
Fruehauf Corporation
The only tuna packed in natural
spring water
Star-Kist canned tuna fish
The only 12-year-old Canadian
whiskey
Grand Award Canadian whis-
key
Only Viceroy has this exclusive
filter
Viceroy cigarettes
The only way to fly
Western Air Lines, Inc.
The only way to get everything
that a Remington cash
register provides is to
buy a Remington
Remington cash register
The only wheel with a cold
tapered disc
Budd truck wheels
Only when the finest is good
enough
Globe Steel Products Corp.
The only whole-wheat food with
a delicious flavor!
Kellogg's Krumbles
Onongaga Pottery Co.
True to its tone
Ontario, Canada, Dept. of
Tourism and Informa-
tion
Friendly, familiar, foreign
and near
Ontario single pack hearing aid
Hear more, carry less
Onyx Hosiery
Constantly imitated--never
equalled
Opel-Kadette automobile
The mini-brutes
Operadio radio receiver
The original self-contained
radio
Oppenheimer Investor Services,
Inc.
It pays to join hands with

Oppenheimer
Optimo cigars
Best of the best
Oragel CSM canker sore medicine
For on-the-spot relief
The pain reliever that works
immediately and lasts
for hours
Oral Hygiene
The Printer's Ink of the
dental profession
Oralgene chewing gum
Chew with a purpose
Orange Crush soft drink
Flavor sealed in the brown
bottle
The orange line, one quality
control from hide to
loom
Graton & Knight Co.
Orchard flavor in every sip
Greystone Fruit Wines
Orchids ... naturally
Thomas Young Orchids, Inc.
Oregon City Woolen Mills
Woven where the wool is
grown
Oregon Highway Department
State of excitement
Orient hosiery
Chosen for lasting loveli-
ness
Oriental Cream
Beauty's master touch
The original
Kellogg's toasted corn flakes
The original air deodorant
Sweet-Avie
The original and largest-selling
in the world
Holland House cocktail
mixes
The original baby food for baby
chicks
Pratt Food Co.
The original chocolate laxative
Ex-Lax laxative
The original corn flakes
Kellogg's toasted corn flakes
The original department store of
artist's materials
Art Brown artist's supplies
The original drawer type freezer
Portable Elevator Mfg. Co.
The original iodized salt
Morton's salt

The original masonry wall
    reinforcement with
    the truss design
    Dur-O-Wal masonry
The original penetrating Stainwax
    finish
    Stainwax
The original Plaster and Stucco
    Fabric
    Addington Mfg. Co.
The original polyethylene coated
    freezer wrap
    Poly Wrap
The original reel spotlight
    Appleton Electric Co.
The original reinforced plastic
    hose
    Supplex Co.
Original research serving the
    physician
    Sandoz, Inc.
The original self-adhesive pin-
    feed labels
    Avery Label Co.
The original self-contained radio
    Operadio radio receiver
The original skin softener
    Campana Italian Balm
The original tooth paste for gums
    and teeth
    Forhan's tooth paste
The original whole milk cheese
    food
    Pabst-ette
The original Worcestershire
    Lea & Perrin's Sauce
Originator and perfecter of the
    garbage disposer
    In-Sink-Erator Manufactur-
    ing Co.
Originator and pioneers of all-
    steel stamping press
    operation
    Verson Allsteel Press Co.
Originator and world's largest
    builder of narrow aisle
    trucks
    Raymond Handling Equip-
    ment, Ltd.
The originator of cultured pearls
    K. Mikimoto, Inc.
Originators and designers of
    ultrasonic sealing
    equipment
    Ultra Sonic Seal, Inc.
The originators of constant

    chassis lubrication
    Bijur Lubrication Co.
Originators of prefinished hard-
    wood flooring
    The Cromar Co.
Originators of radio home-study
    training
    National Radio Institute
Originators of reinforced rubber
    flooring
    Stedman Products Co.
Originators of the world-famous
    Utility ball pen
    Lindy Pen Co., Inc.
Orkin insect exterminators
    Call in the Orkin army
Orlando Morning Sentinel
    Inland Florida's greatest
    newspaper
Orphos toothpaste
    The correct toothpaste
    Dentally different
Orrin Tucker's orchestra
    The danciest band in the
    land
Orthopedic Shoes
    For tired, tender feet
Orvis sportsman's clothing
    A sporting tradition since
    1856
Osborn paint brush
    A better-wearing brush for
    every use
Oscar Mayer wieners
    The wiener the world
    awaited
Oscar Schmidt International, Inc.
    Making music possible for
    everyone
Osco drug stores
    Save the Osco way
OSCO motors
    Men who know back OSCO
Oshkosh, b'gosh
    Oshkosh Overall Co.
Oshkosh Overall Co.
    Oshkosh, b'gosh
    They must make good or
    we will
Osmose Wood Preserving Co.
    Nature's method of wood
    preservation
Osteo-path-ik shoes
    You walk on cushions when
    you walk in Osteo-path-
    iks

349

Ostermoor mattress
America's quality mattress
Beddy bye, but no shut-
eye
Built for sleep
Proven best for rest during
73 years test
Sleep to the sleepless, rest
to the restless
O'Sullivan rubber heel
America's No. 1 heel
Repair 'em and wear 'em
Tough and springy
Otard Cognac
Born where a king of
France was born
The other big "R" in truck
leasing
Rollins Truck Leasing
The other computer company
Honeywell, Inc.
Otis Elevator Company
The budget sets the pace
From pit to penthouse
If you want better service
Instant elevatoring
Morning uplift
Otis, the world's word for
elevator safety
The world's word for ele-
vator safety
Otis, the world's word for
elevator safety
Otis Elevator Company
Otto Stahl meat products
Made with home care
An ounce of prevention for
everybody, every day
Post's Bran Flakes
Our ads neither coax nor hoax
Philip Morris cigarettes
Our ambition: ideal telephone
service for Michigan
Michigan Bell Telephone
Co.
Our business is electrifying
ideas
Crouse-Hinds Company
Our business is going to the
dogs
Champion Animal Food Co.
Our business is helping business
grow
CIT Financial Corporation
Our business is helping other
businesses grow

Management Assistance, Inc.
Our business is sound
Sound Engineering Co.
Our business is the intelligent
use of computers
Electronic Data Systems
Our business works so people
can
Goodwill Industries, Inc.
Our coffees have a national
reputation representing
the finest grown
Chase and Sanborn coffee
Our concern is people
Aetna Insurance Co.
Our construction products are
getting the job done
St. Regis Paper Company
Our future: enhanced computer
solutions
United Telecommunications,
Inc.
Our hand has never lost its
skill
Schaefer beer
Our highest quality
Reid, Murdoch & Co.
Our integrity is your security
American Warehousemen's
Association
Our leases are as individual as
you are
National Truck leasing sys-
tem
Our major is you
Saint Francis College
Our name means moving
Mayflower Moving Agency
Our name says it all
Sears U. S. Government
Money Market Trust
Our partners work with you.
That's why they work
with us
Laventhol & Horwath, Certi-
fied Public Accountants
Our products are your protection
Schwab Safe Co., Inc.
Our readers manage the country
Successful Farming
Our reputation is your protec-
tion
Belyea generators
Our savings are your profits
American Mutual Liability
Insurance Co.

Our second century of service
Mutual Life Insurance Co.
Our sign is our bond
Lehn & Fink
Our success is unheard of
Genstar Corporation
Our teachers mold the nation's
future
The Advertising Council
Our word of honor to the public
Hammermill Paper Co.
Our work is child's play
Fisher-Price Toys, Inc.
Our wounded friends, the trees
Davey Tree Expert Co.
Our wurst is the best
Mickleberry's Sausage
The out-door overhead crane
Street Bros. Crane
Out front. Pulling away
Goodyear Tire & Rubber
Co.
Out front. World wide
Goodyear Tire & Rubber
Co.
Out of the blue comes the whit-
est wash
Reckitt's Bluing
Out of the reels come real
stories
Royal Pictures
Out of this world, into your
heart
Packard automobile
Out-sells because it out-shoots
Western Cartridge Co.
Out-speed and out-last all oth-
ers
Dunne skates
Outboard Marine Co. See:
Cushman Motors Div., Out-
board Marine Co.
Evinrude Motors Div., Out-
board Marine Co.
Johnson Motors Div., Out-
board Marine Co.
Outcleans other leading powders
on tough, greasy, oily
dirt
All detergent
Outcleans, outpulls, outlasts
Firestone tires
Outdoor clothes
Rugged as the West
Outdoor Lifer shirts
Wash without worry

The outdoor plywood
Harbor Plywood Corp.
Outdoor Recreation
The magazine that brings
the outdoors in
The outdoors blanket of America
Pendleton Woolen Mills
Outer beauty, inner worth
Tober-Saifer shoes
Outfitters for the home grounds
Rosedale Nurseries
Outfitters for the rugged in-
doorsman
Gingiss Formalwear
Outgrow toenail pain remedy
Relieves ingrown toenail
pain in minutes
Outlast the factory
Kreolite floors
Outlook
An illustrated weekly of
current life
Outpulls, outperforms, outsaves
General Motors Corporation,
Truck Division
Outselling all others ... by far
Ernest Holmes Co.
Outsells. See: Out-sells
Outstanding--and they are mild
Pall Mall cigarettes
Outstanding performance is not
by chance but by plan
Washburn's Seeds
The outstanding scenic way west
Missouri Pacific Railroad
Outward sign of inward quality
Calvert Litho. Co.
Ovaltine
Builds body, brain and
nerves
Builds brain, nerves and
body
Get all your vitamins in
food
The Swiss food drink, now
made in the U. S. A.
The tonic food beverage
Oven-tempered for flexible
strength
Reynolds aluminum foil wrap
Over a million used by millions
Bobrick soap dispensers
Over 50 years of building well
Gardner automobile
Over $9 billion of assets under
management

Fidelity Group
Over 96 varieties
Vlasic pickles
Over one billion dollars annually
to industry
Walter E. Heller & Co.
financial services
Over 60 years of financing for
commerce and industry
The Finance Company of
America
Over the Atlantic and across
the world
British Overseas Airway
Corp.
Overcome skidding, nerve strain
and muddy roads
American Chain Co.
Overhead economy
Stetson hats
Overhead handling reduces
handling overhead
American Mono-Rail Co.
Overland automobile
It pleases everybody!
The working partner of a
million Americans
Overland Trading Company
Purveyors of first class
footwear for men and
women
The overnight wonder
Ex-Lax laxative
Owen Magnetic Motor Car
The car of a thousand
speeds
Designed for touring com-
fort
Two years ahead
Owens-Corning Fiberglas Corp.
Verified insulation per-
formance
Your partner whose actions
speak louder than
words
Owens hair brushes
Guardians of good groom-
ing
Owens-Illinois Glass Co.
Admits light, retards heat
It takes more than adver-
tising to make a good
product
Light the modern way
O-I takes many shapes to
serve you

We have what it takes
Owens Yacht Co.
Missing the boat? Own an
Owens
Owen's. See: Dr. Owen's Body
Battery
Owl Fumigating Corp.
The guardian of your grove
Own your share of American
business
New York Stock Exchange
Members
Owner. See: Ohner
Oxford. See also: Lord Oxford
cigarette lighter
Oxford Filing Supply Co.
First name in filing
Oxford Paper Co.
Lasting impressions begin
with Oxford papers
Oxides Div., Cabot Corp.
Where flame technology
creates new products
Oxo
It's meat and drink to you
Oxy 10 Skin Salve
Don't play games with your
pimples
Oxydol laundry detergent
Complete household soap
Oxydol. With a white that
compares to new
Rougher on dirt, easiest on
clothes
Roughest on dirt, easiest
on clothes
Sparkling white, sparkling
bright, sparkling clean
Oxydol. With a white that com-
pares to new
Oxydol laundry detergent
Oxydonor cure-all medicine
Enjoy perfect health by
using Oxydonor
Oyster Growers & Dealers Assn.
The last word in sea food
Oyster Growers of North America
Your best food from the
sea
Ozark Air Lines, Inc.
The airline that measures
the midwest in minutes
Ozark Fisheries, Inc.
Remember the Ozarks for
better goldfish
Where better goldfish are

grown
Ozite carpets
   There is only one Ozite,
     look for the name

-P-

P-A-G Div., W. R. Grace & Co.
   The successful ones
P-A-G Div., W. R. Grace & Co.
   See also: W. R. Grace
   & Co.
P. A. Geier Co.
   Gets all the dirt by air
     alone
   The thorough electric
     cleaner
P. A. means Pipe Appeal
   Prince Albert pipe and
     cigarette tobacco
P and D Mfg. Co.
   Ignition starts with P and
     D
P and O Lines
   Life at sea is like nothing
     on earth
   Run away to sea with P
     and O
P. J. Harvey Shoe Co.
   The shoes you order are
     the shoes you get
P. M. whiskey
   For Pleasant Moments
   If it isn't P. M., it isn't
     an evening
   Rich perfection that only
     nature rivals
P. N. Corsets
   Changes those bulges into
     curves
PN-700 washing powder
   Makes water wetter
P. O. N. beer
   Gentlemen, be treated
PPG: a concern for the future
PPG Industries, Inc.
PPG Industries, Inc.
   The fiberglass for finer
     fabrics
   PPG: a concern for the
     future
   PPG makes the glass that
     makes the difference
   When you start with metal
     ... finish with

Duracron!
PPG Industries, Inc. See also:
   Chemical Div., PPG Indus-
     tries, Inc.
   Fiber Glass Div., PPG In-
     dustries, Inc.
PPG makes the glass that makes
   the difference
   PPG Industries, Inc.
P. R. Mallory and Co., Inc.
   It's good business to do
     business with Mallory
P. S. And it's especially great
   as a hand lotion
   Dermassage
P.S.--Personal service
   Aetna Insurance Co.
P. S. The last word in "auto-
     matic control" is still
     Robertshaw
   Robertshaw Controls Com-
     pany
P. W. Eastham & Co.
   The good coffee folks
Pabco linoleum
   Soft-sealed linoleum
   Styled in California, ap-
     plauded by all America
Pabst Blue Ribbon beer
   The best tonic
   The brew of quality
   The brew that brings back
     memories
   Brewery goodness sealed
     right in
   For keener refreshment
   Good taste for 100 years
   It's blended, it's splendid
   It's the blend that betters
     the beer
   The maker's name proclaims
     its quality
   The real taste of beer
   Refresh! Rejoice! Remem-
     ber! Pabst gets the
     call
   Thirst prize
   33 fine brews blended into
     one great beer
Pabst-ette
   The delicious cheddar
     cheese food
   The most talked-about food
     in America
   The original whole milk
     cheese food

Pabst ginger ale
Ginger ale with the long-
life bubble
Pace setting engineered systems
to control materials in
motion
The Louis Allis Co.
The pacemaker in paints
Glidden paints
The pacemaker of gasolines
Texaco, Inc.
Pacemakers in flexible package-
makers
Mira-Pak, Inc.
Pacemakers of aviation progress
Bell Aircraft Corp.
Pacer Sock
Why a million men put their
foot in it
Pacific Brewing & Malting Co.
A taste sells a case
Your first taste tells you
and sells you
The Pacific Coast magazine of
motoring
Motor Land
Pacific Egg Producers
Fresh as dewy dawn
Pacific Electric Railway
Ride the big red cars
Pacific fabrics
Look to the fabric first
Look to the fabric first,
buy Pacific
They resist wear
When your sailor goes to
see
Pacific Knitting Mills
Sweethearts in swim suits
Pacific Northern Airlines
The Alaska flag line
A great name in aviation
Pacific Northwest Fruits, Inc.
An apple a day is Doc
Apple's way
Good to the core
Pacific Sheets
So cool and caressing and
swoony
Pacific Wines, Inc.
The wine with the cham-
pagne taste
Pacific worsted
Be pert in a skirt
Package Machinery Co. See:
National Baker Div.,

Package Machinery Co.
Packaged metal engineering
Grammes & Sons, Inc.
Packages delivered around the
world in three days or
less
International Express Mail
Service
Packages prefer United Air Ex-
press
United Air Express Service
Packaging headquarters to Amer-
ican industry
Millprint, Inc.
Packaging Industries, Ltd., Inc.
The world's largest manu-
facturer of blister
packaging machinery
Packaging materials for American
industry
Cellu-Craft Products Co.
Packaging that builds and holds
sales
Alton Box Board Co.
Packard automobile
Ask the man who owns one
From the speedway comes
their stamina, from the
skyway their style
Get the plus of a Packard
Out of this world, into
your heart
The restful car
Socially, America's first
motor car
Style, like ambition, is a
good servant, but a
poor master
Packard electric shaver
Below skin level shave
Skin level shave
Packed to attract
Hinde & Dauch Paper Co.
Packed with fresh ideas for
business
Altos computer systems
Packed with good taste
Clark's Teaberry Gum
Packed with peanuts Snickers
really satisfies
Snickers candy bar
Packed with the wiggle in its
tail
New England Fish Co.
Packed with the zest of the sea
Chicken of the Sea tuna

Packer's Tar Soap
  Long ago distanced all
    competitors
Packs the power
  Peters bullets
The pad that's kind to your
    hands
  Handy Mandy
Page. See also:
  Paige
  Thomas Page Mill Co.
  W. H. Page Boiler Co.
Page Steel and Wire Div., Amer-
    ican Chain and Cable
    Co.
  The source for answers to
    wire problems
Page Steel and Wire Div.,
    American Chain and
    Cable Co. See also:
    American Chain & Cable
    Co.
Paige automobile
  Built to win, without,
    within
  Commands respect on any
    road
  The most beautiful car in
    America
  The new-day car for new-
    day needs
  Paige, the master of the
    highway
Paige, the master of the highway
  Paige automobile
Pain is the test that Bayer
    meets best
  Bayer aspirin
The pain reliever that works
    immediately and lasts
    for hours
  Oragel canker sore medi-
    cine
The pain stops here
  Bufferin pain reliever
Paine Furniture Co.
  Enchantment that endures
Paine Webber, Jackson & Curtis
  Thank you, Paine Webber!
Painless. Effectual. Worth a
    guinea a box
  Beecham's Pills
Paint & Varnish Assn.
  Save the surface and you
    save all
Paint-box colors in tissue-light

Foundettes
  Foundettes foundations
Paint comes first
  Truscon Laboratories
The paint for all interiors
  Luminal paint
Paint for profit instead of ex-
    pense
  Nason Paint Co.
Paint is at its best only when it
    is properly mixed
  Springfield Tool Co.
Paint it with New-Skin and for-
    get it
  New-Skin Liquid Court
    Plaster
Paint Logic
  The spokesman for the in-
    dependent paint dealer
Paint saves the surface, zinc
    saves the paint
  New Jersey Zinc Co.
The paint that does it right
  Valentine's Valspar
Paint thieves into a corner
  Ion-Guard Security paint
Paint with pencils
  Eberhard Faber, Inc.
Paint with Pettit and see what
    service means
  Pettit paints
Paint with the two bears, it
    wears
  Baer Bros. paint
Paint your cheeks from the in-
    side
  Alamite Dairy
Paint your house to stay painted
  Carter White Lead Co.
Paint yourself a new house
  Pittsburgh Paints
Painter Carpet Mills, Inc., Div.
    Collins and Aikman
  Artistry in carpets
Paintex Products Corp.
  The new fabric paint
Paints and disinfects, dries
    white
  Carbola Chemical Co.
Paints that are different
  Wilbur & Williams paints
Paire Bros. shoe laces
  Lucky for boots
Pakistan International Airlines
  Great people to fly with
  Great people to ship with

355

Pal hollow ground has the
"edge"
Pal razor blades
Pal razor blades
Different because they're
different
Has the "edge" five ways
Pal hollow ground has the
"edge"
Palace Hotel
In San Francisco, it's the
Palace
Palatable as milk
Scott's Emulsion
Palizzio, Inc.
Any Palizzio is better than
no Palizzio
Pall Mall cigarettes
I'm particular
Outstanding--and they are
mild!
A shilling in London, a
quarter here
Wherever particular people
congregate
Palm Beach Times
Devoted to the best inter-
ests of South Florida
Palm Bros. Decalcomania Co.
Bonded pigments
Palmolive cares for more com-
plexions than any other
soap in the world
Palmolive soap
Palmolive dishwashing liquid
Softens hands while you do
dishes
Palmolive soap
Doctors prove Palmolive's
beauty results
For proved beauty results
Keep that schoolgirl com-
plexion
Lovelier skin in 14 days
No soap but Palmolive
Palmolive cares for more
complexions than any
other soap in the
world
Pampers diapers
Helps keep a little baby a
lot dryer
Protects your baby against
wetness right down to
his toes
Pan. See also: Peter Pan

Pan Am makes the going great
Pan American World Airways,
Inc.
Pan-American Coffee Bureau
The friendly drink from
good neighbors
Get more out of life with
coffee
Pan-American Life Insurance Co.
Dollar wise group insurance
Pan American World Airways, Inc.
An airline that goes to the
world's most prestigious
places
America's airline to the
world
First in Latin America
First on the Atlantic
First on the Pacific
First 'round the world
Pan Am makes the going
great
Say hello to Pan Am
We fly the world the way
the world wants to fly
World's largest air cargo
carrier
The world's most experi-
enced airline
You can't beat the experi-
ence
You're better off with Pan
Am
Panagra Airline
World's friendliest airline
Panasonic Company, Video Sys-
tems Division
Panasonic. Just slightly
ahead of our time
Panasonic. Just slightly ahead
of our time
Panasonic Company, Video
Systems Division
Panasonic microcassette recorder
Just slightly ahead of our
time
Panasonic radio receivers
Today's leader in tomor-
row's look
Panasonic video systems
Just slightly ahead of our
time
Pandick Press, Inc.
The financial printer
Pandora shoes
Only dependability brings

success
Panels of permanence
   Harbor Plywood Corp.
Panorama
   The magazine to watch
Pantasote upholstering material
   Exactly resembles Morocco
     leather
Paper Center, Inc.
   Paper engineering
   Paper for every use
Paper Cup & Container Institute
   A clean service for every
     customer
   A clean service for every
     customer every time
Paper engineering
   Paper Center, Inc.
Paper for every use
   Paper Center, Inc.
Paper for the printer who puts
   quality first
     S. D. Warren Co. Div.,
     Scott Paper Co.
Paper is part of the picture
   Strathmore Paper Co.
Paper Machine Co.
   The cutter that does not
     clog
Paper makers of America
   The Mead Corp.
The paper people
   Brown Company
The paper that blazes trade
   trails
   New York Commercial
The paper that IS England
   Punch
Paper Trade Journal
   Magazine of the paper in-
     dustry
Pape's diapepsin
   Upset? Pape's diapepsin
     will put you on your
     feet
Paquins hand cream
   For "dream hands" cream
     your hands
Par-X Vegetables
   The mark of excellence
Parade Magazine
   You ought to be in pic-
     tures
Parade of Stars
   National Broadcasting Co.
Parade of the immortals

Kellogg Co.
Paradise Shoes
   Step into paradise with
     these perfectly heavenly
     shoes
Paragon Oil Co.
   Not just a gallon of oil, but
     a gallon of oil service
   Peak of perfection
Paramount Pictures Corp.
   If it's a Paramount picture,
     it's the best show in
     town
   A king can have no more
Paramount Seeds
   The peak of perfection
Pard dog food
   Ask your veterinarian
   Pard made a pard of my
     dog
Pard made a pard of my dog
   Pard dog food
Parents Magazine
   On rearing children from
     crib to college
Paris. See also: Anita of Paris
     perfume
Paris approves the colors, Amer-
   ica perfects the wear
   Cutex nail polish
Paris Garters
   A gift with a lift
   Look to Paris to look your
     best
   No metal can touch you
   Quality without compromise
   The support of a nation
Paris Nights
   A brisk magazine of Parisian
     life
Paris shoes
   Keep in step with Paris
Park. See also: Parke
Park & Tilford candy
   An American institution
     since 1840
   The talk of the town
   Wherever good candies are
     sold
Park & Tilford has a treat in
   reserve for you
   Park & Tilford whiskey
Park & Tilford whiskey
   America's luxury whiskey
   The blend of experience
   Park & Tilford has a treat

in reserve for you
Quality tells
A whiskey for every taste
and purse
Park Central Hotel, New York
City
A home away from home
Parkay Margarine
The flavor touch they like
so much
Taste Parkay Margarine.
The flavor says "butter"
Parke. See also: Park
Parke, Davis and Co.
Better medicines for a bet-
ter world
Makers of medicines pre-
scribed by physicians
Medicamenta vera
Parker. See also:
Jane Parker Fruit Cake
Jane Parker Rolls
Parker 51 Pen
51 writes dry with wet ink
Jewels of Pen-dom
The world's most wanted
pen
Parker House
Boston's most famous hotel
Parker Pen Co.
It's a mark of distinction
to own a Parker pen
Maker of the world's most
wanted pens
Rivals the beauty of the
scarlet tanager
Visible ink supply
Parker's. See: Mother Parker's
Tea
Parks. See: H. G. Parks,
Inc. sausage packers
Parsons and Whittemore, Inc.
World leaders in the de-
velopment of pulp and
paper mills for the use
of local fibers
Part of the American scene
Maxwell House Master Blend
Coffee
Particular people prefer Hamil-
ton
Hamilton Watch Co.
Partner of light
Barreled Sunlight paint
Partners in progress around
the world

First National City Bank
Partners in providing
J. I. Case earth moving
machines
Partola
The doctor in candy form
Parts. See: A. P. Parts Corp.
mufflers
Pasco Packing Co.
World's largest citrus plant
Pass the salt for better livestock
Sterling Salt
The pass word of the road
Sun Oil Company
The password is Kools
Kool cigarettes
Pasteurized for purity
Kraft Foods Div., Kraftco
Corp.
Pat & Wop
Pat it on the face, wop it
on the body
Pat it on the face, wop it on the
body
Pat & Wop
Patcraft Mills, Inc.
Carpets of distinction
First in fashion
Patent Scaffolding Co.
Safe scaffolding for every
purpose
Patents make jobs
National Patent Council,
Inc.
Pathfinder
Pathfinder is the Ford of
the advertising field
Pathfinder is the Ford of the
advertising field
Pathfinder
Pathfinders in pipedom
M. Linkman & Co.
The Patio restaurant, San Ra-
fael, Calif.
Be our guest
Dream your dreams at the
wishing well
Patou. See: Joy de Jean Patou
The pattern people
Simplicity Pattern Co.,
Inc.
Paul Jones whiskey
A blend of all straight
whiskies
First of all, for flavor
A gentleman's whiskey since

1865
The very best buy is the
whiskey that's dry
Paul Masson wines
Paul Masson will sell no
wine before its time
Paul Masson will sell no wine
before its time
Paul Masson wines
Paul Pendarvis' dance orchestra
When you hear the violin,
that's Paul Pendarvis
Paul's. See: Mrs. Paul's fish
fillets
The pause that refreshes
Coca Cola soft drink
The pavement that outlasts the
bonds
National Paving Brick
Mfrs.
The paving that's saving
Kreolite floors
Pay as you ride!
Maxwell automobile
Pays for itself by what it saves
Iron Fireman
Pays for itself in the money it
saves
Multistamp Co.
Peach Bloom Mineral Corp.
The natural beautifier
A peach of a bleach
Fleecy White Laundry
Bleach
Peachy soft drink
The drink that tastes like
real fruit
Peacock. See: C. D. Peacock
The peak of beer flavor
Trommer's beer
Peak of perfection
Paragon Oil Co.
The peak of perfection
Old Poindexter whiskey
Paramount Seeds
Peak of quality
Apex vacuum cleaner
Peak of quality for more than
30 years
Apex vacuum cleaner
The peak of Swiss watchmaking
perfection
Rado Watch Co.
Pearce Hygienic Fleeced Under-
wear
No irritation--does not

shrink
Pearl. See also: Pearls
Pearl Grit Corp.
Pearl Grit for grinding, for
bone, for shell
Pearl Grit for grinding, for bone,
for shell
Pearl Grit Corp.
Pearl Top lamp chimneys
The best chimneys in the
world
Pearline Detergent
Pearline is the greatest
known detergent
Pearline is the greatest known
detergent
Pearline Detergent
Pearls. See also: Pearl
Pearls in the mouth
Sozodont toothpaste
Pears' Soap
Good morning! Have you
used Pears' Soap?
The purest and most durable
toilet soap, hence the
best and cheapest
Pearson. See: Ben Pearson,
Inc.
Pease. See: C. F. Pease Co.
Pebeco toothpaste
Brush your teeth twice a
day and see your den-
tist twice a year
Have you "Acid Mouth,"
the forerunner of tooth
destruction?
Keeps the mouth glands
young
Pecan. See: O. C. Pecan
Fudge
Pecco unit heaters
They keep the whole place
warm
Pediforme shoes
Designed for going places
in style, in comfort
Pedigreed Pennsylvania products
Conawanga Refining Co.
Peel a bite of health
Fruit Dispatch Co.
The peer of beers
Rubsam & Horrmann
Peerless Electric Co.
The silent four
Peerless marks practically every-
thing best

Peerless Roll Leaf Co.
Peerless Plumbers Corp.
   Are you annoyed by a
      drip?
Peerless Roll Leaf Co.
   Peerless marks practically
      everything best
Peerless Tube Co.
   The Tiffany tube of Amer-
      ica
Peerless Unit Ventilation Co.
   Pioneers in unit ventilation
Peggy Sage
   The manicure everyone knows
Pellon Corp.
   Keeps the shape
Pemco glass colors
   Always begin with a good
      finish
Pen. See also: Penn
A pen for every purpose and a
   point for every hand
   W. A. Sheaffer Pen Co.
A pen is only as good as its
   point
   C. Howard Hunt Pen Co.
Pen Metal Co., Inc.
   A name to remember
The pen that fills itself
   Conklin Pen Co.
The pen that writes like a pen-
   cil
   Inkograph
The pen with the clip-cap
   Waterman's Ideal Fountain
   Pen
The pen with the red-headed
   filling pump
   Dunn-Pen
The pencil of the pros
   Scripto pencil
Pencil Specialty Co.
   Advertise and realize
The pencil that works
   Autopoint pencil
Pendarvis'. See: Paul Pen-
   darvis' dance orchestra
Pendleton Woolen Mills
   Always virgin wool
   The outdoors blanket of
   America
Penetrates deep for a dynamite
   clean
   Dynamo laundry detergent
Penetrates, lubricates, cuts
   grease, prevents

rust, will not gum
   American Grease Stick Co.
Penetro
   The salve with a base of
      old-fashioned mutton
      suet
Penflex tubing
   Tight as pipe, but flexible
Penn. See also:
   Pen
   William Penn whiskey
Penn Electric Switch Co.
   Furnace freedom
Penn Fishing Tackle Mfg. Co.
   The reels of champions
Penn Maryland whiskey
   Rich as a symphony
Penn Mutual Life Insurance Co.
   Back of your independence
      stands the Penn Mutual
Penn Mutual Underwriter Insur-
   ance
   Your life plan deserves ex-
      pert guidance
Penn Square Mutual Fund
   Explore our objectives
Penney. See:
   J. C. Penney and Co.
   J. C. Penney Auto Center
   Pennies
   Penny
Pennies. See also:
   J. C. Penney and Co.
   J. C. Penney Auto Center
   Penny
Pennies more in cost ... worlds
   apart in quality
   J & B Rare Scotch whiskey
Pennsylvania
   The birth state of the na-
      tion
   The keystone of your vaca-
      tion
Pennsylvania Knit Coat Co.
   Springs right back into
      shape
Pennsylvania Power and Light
   Co.
   The heart of the market
Pennsylvania Railroad
   Hauls more freight and
      handles more passengers
      than any other railroad
      in the world
   Serving the nation
Pennsylvania Tires

Know them by the jet
black tread
Ton tested
Pennwalt Corporation
For 130 years we've been
making things people
need--including profits
Penny. See also:
J. C. Penney & Co.
J. C. Penney Auto Center
Penney
Pennies
A penny a night for the finest
light
Coleman Co., Inc.
Pennzoil Company
A national resources com-
pany
Pennzoil motor oil
Flows fast, stays tough
Gives your engine an extra
margin of safety
Goes farther safer
The oil that goes farther,
faster, safer
Protection and Pennzoil;
get them together in
your car
Quality in every extra
mile
Quality protection. Ask
for it
Sound your Z
People building transportation
to serve people
General Motors Corporation
People caring for people
Hospital Corporation of
America
People committed to making tech-
nology work
Exxon Office Systems Co.
People have faith in Reader's
Digest
Reader's Digest
People have trusted Murphy's for
75 years
Murphy's Oil Soap
The people movers
The Budd Company
People profit when a business
prospers
General Motors Corporation
People put their trust in us
CIT Financial Corporation
People think of us when

they're in the market
Nabisco, Inc.
People trust Seiko more than any
other watch
Seiko Time Corp.
The people who bring you the
machines that work
International Harvester Co.
The people who care about peo-
ple who move
Fernstrom Storage and Van
Co.
People who don't like Chex Cere-
als have never tried
Chex Cereals
Corn Chex Cereal
People who fly for a living
choose United
United Air Lines, Inc.
The people who invented a nicer
way to cruise
Holland-American Line
The people who keep improving
flame
Ronson cigarette lighters
People who know buy Bigelow
Bigelow-Sanford, Inc.
People who talk about good food
talk about General
Foods
General Foods Corporation
People you can count on
Mutual of Omaha Insurance
Co.
People you can depend on to
power America's pro-
gress
Investor-Owned Electric
Light and Power Com-
panies
Peoples Energy Corporation
Managing energy is our
business
Peoples Fire Insurance Co.
Safe and sound
Peoples Gas Company
Diversified energy for Mid-
America
People's Popular Monthly
The home craft magazine
People's Trust & Guaranty Co.
People's Trust is the peo-
ple's bank
People's Trust is the people's
bank
People's Trust & Guaranty

Co.
Pep Cereal
 Vitamins for pep, Pep for
  vitamins
Pep for your pup
 Min-A-Gro Corp. pet food
Pep spark plug
 Your money back if you'll
  take it
Pepper. See: Dr. Pepper soft
 drink
Pepperell sheets
 The beautiful sheets with
  wear woven in
 Guest-room luxury for
  every bed in your
  house
 Sheet music to sing about
Peppermint that is peppermint
 Clark's Teaberry Gum
The Peppy Bran Food
 Kellogg's Pep-Bran Flakes
Pepsi-Cola soft drink
 Come alive!
 The drink with quick food-
  energy
 For those who think young
 Have a Pepsi day
 Hits the spot
 Let your taste decide ...
  take the Pepsi chal-
  lenge!
 Nickel drink worth a dime
 Pepsi's got your taste for
  life
 Taste that beats the others
  cold
 Tops for quality
 You're in the Pepsi genera-
  tion
Pepsi's got your taste for life
 Pepsi-Cola soft drink
Pepsodent antiseptic
 Keeps breath pure and
  sweet 1 to 2 hours
  longer
Pepsodent Decoater toothbrush
 The new era toothbrush
Pepsodent toothpaste
 For a come-closer smile
 For the safety of your
  smile
 The new-day dentifrice
 Removes the dingy film
 Use Pepsodent twice a
  day, see your dentist

twice a year
 You'll wonder where the
  yellow went when you
  brush your teeth with
  Pepsodent
Pepsodent tooth powder
 The professional tooth pow-
  der for daily home use
Pepto-Bismol
 Eats by the clock, pays for
  it in time
 The gripes of wrath
 Never an upset stomach
 Never upset an upset stomach
Pequot sheets
 First in wear, first in peace
 Made stronger, last longer
 So good-looking, so long-
  wearing
Percy Kent bags
 Always something new
Perdue Farms, Inc.
 It takes a tough man to
  make a tender chicken
The perfect anti-freeze
 Prestone anti-freeze
The perfect candy for smart
  entertaining
 Brach's candies
The Perfect chair
 It rests the back
The perfect cigarette
 Marlboro cigarettes
Perfect Circle piston rings
 Smoke behind means trouble
  ahead
The perfect cold cream
 Daggett & Ramsdell cold
  cream
Perfect fit not only in the cup,
  but all around the torso
 La Trique brassiere
The perfect gift
 Puritan Chocolate Co.
The perfect gift for her
 Lady Remington electric
  shaver
The perfect gift, to give, to
  get
 Better Homes & Gardens
The perfect glass
 Ballantine ale
The perfect gum
 Wrigley's chewing gum
Perfect host to a host of friends
 Budweiser beer

The perfect laundry starch
Linit laundry starch
A perfect machine for business
purposes or home use
The Sun Typewriter
A perfect mayonnaise
Premier Salad Dressing
The perfect pencil
Koh-I-Noor Pencil Co.
Perfect phonograph record
America's fastest selling
record
The perfect pickle
Aunt Jane's Pickles
The perfect plant food
Loma Plant Food
Perfect platemates, Treet and
tomatoes
Armour's Treet
The perfect raincoat that mil-
lions of mothers have
been seeking
Esquire raincoat
The perfect reading light
American Gas Machine Co.
A perfect salt, a natural tonic
Worcester Salt Co.
The perfect servant
Copeland refrigeration
A perfect set-up for a set up
that is perfect
Baltimore Salesbook Co.
The perfect shave
Schick electric shaver
A perfect skin and toilet soap,
made without fats,
grease or dangerous
alkali
Hyomei Antiseptic Skin Soap
Perfect Sleeper mattress
Words to go to sleep by
You sleep on it ... not in
it!
The perfect sour milk biscuit
flour
Thomas Page Mill Co.
Perfect Spread Stoker
Won't clog on wet coal
Perfect start to a lasting finish
Simoniz
A perfect trench at one cut
Buckeye Traction Ditcher
Co.
The perfect tube
Gold Seal radio tube
The perfect under-arm pro-

tective
Perstik
Perfect Voice Institute
Your voice can be improved
100%
A perfected flow control instru-
ment
Thermotron
Perfected wood pencils
Scripto pencil
Perfection Belting
No speed too high, no pul-
ley too small
Perfection bread
It's the lowest calorie bread
you can buy
A mighty good thought
Perfection Burial Vault
The thicker the metal, the
longer the protection
Perfection Clothes
The kind real boys wear
Perfection for new cars; protec-
tion for old cars
Veedol motor oil
Perfection in a confection
Snacks candy
Perfection in projection since
1909
Da-Lite Screen Co., Inc.
Perfection in rust-free protection
Ruud water heaters
The perfection of natural tone
in radio
Lyradion radio receivers
The perfection of Scotch whiskey
Teacher's Highland Cream
Scotch whiskey
Perfection oil heaters
As reliable as grandfather's
clock and as portable
as the cat
Chases chills from cold
corners
Perfolastic girdle
It ventilates
Performance as great as the
name
Edison-Splitdorf spark
plugs
The performance company
Phillips Petroleum Co.
Performance controls the air
Pump Eng. Service Corp.
Performance counts
Mack trucks

Performance insurance
    CaPac automobile parts
The performance line
    HPM Div., Kohlring Co.
Performance points to Pesco
        first
    Pump Eng. Service Corp.
The performance-minded fuel
        saver
    Gulfstream Commander 980
        aircraft
The perfume of romance
    Chanel No. 22 perfume
Perfume that spins a moment
        into a memory
    Charbert's Perfume
Perhaps we can help you
    Hercules Powder Co.
Periphonics Corporation
    Periphonics ... letting your
        imagination work
Periphonics ... letting your
        imagination work
    Periphonics Corporation
Perk floor finish
    Perk up your no-wax floors
        with Perk
Perk up your no-wax floors with
        Perk
    Perk floor finish
Perma-grip bristle can't come
        out
    Pro-Phy-Lac-Tic toothbrush
Perma-Lift brassiere
    The lift that never lets you
        down
Permanence for economy
    Dura-Sheen Signs
Permanent as the pyramids
    Higgins drawing ink
Permanently identifies your
        property
    Ion-Guard Security paint
Permatex Co., Inc.
    Made for the professional!
Permits daylight speed at night
    Saf-De-Lite headlights
Permutit water treatment
    It's good business to begin
        with good water
    Safe with soft water
    Take all the hardness out
        of water
    Velvet water
Perrier table water
    The champagne of table

        waters
Perrine fishing tackle
    Pick a Perrine today!
Perry Davis' Pain Killer
    Will cure your cough or cold
Perry-Fay Co. See: Manatool
        Div., Perry-Fay Co.
Perrymen radio receiver
    Distance without distortion
The personal bathroom scale
    Detecto
A personal blend
    Mother Parker's Tea
The personal computer
    Apple computers
Personal Finance Co.
    The company that likes to
        say YES
The personal service bank
    Anglo-California Trust Co.
The personal writing machine
    Corona typewriter
Personalized cosmetic services
    Luzier, Inc.
Personalized home study training
    Markus-Campbell Co.
A personalized service that comes
        to your home
    Avon cosmetics
Personalized service that makes
        the big difference
    A. L. Mechling Barge
        Lines, Inc.
Perstik
    The perfect under-arm pro-
        tective
Pert shampoo
    Bouncin' and behavin'--
        that's Pert
Pertussin cough medicine
    Safe for every cough
Pervel handkerchiefs
    Why carry a cold in your
        pocket?
Pestolite. See also: Prest-O-
        Lite
Pestolite insect repellant
    Bug-free, buzz-free, bite-
        free
Pestroy insecticide
    Bringing the marvels of
        science to your farm
Pet milk
    Gives cream and butter
        flavor
    Milk at its best

No matter how diluted, it
is never skimmed milk
The pet of the petite
Betty Rose Clothing
Petalpoint Motif brassiere
For beauty to have and to
hold
Petelco Div., Pyle-National Co.
The "one stop" creative
lighting source
Peter Cailler Kohler Swiss Choco-
late Co.
High as the Alps in quality
Peter J. Schweitzer Div., Kim-
berly-Clark Corp.
Whenever good impressions
count, rely on carbon-
izing papers by
Schweitzer
World's largest manufacturer
of fine carbonizing pa-
pers
Peter J. Schweitzer Div., Kim-
berly-Clark Corp. See
also: Kimberly-Clark
Corp.
Peter Pan
Fashion begins with your
fabric
Peter Pan brassiere
The secret's in the circle
Peters bullets
Packs the power
Peters Shoe Co.
The leather is there in
every pair
Peterson, Howell and Heather
Car plan management and
leasing specialists
Petit. See also: Pettit
Petit Point brassieres
The young girl's best
friend
Petroleum services and equip-
ment worldwide
NL Industries, Inc.
Petti sportswear
Magic word in junior
sportswear
Pettit. See also: Petit
Pettit paints
Paint with Pettit and see
what service means
Peugeot automobile
The automobile that wants
for nothing

Progress, not compromise
Pfanstiehl Chemical Co.
Great name in science
Pfeffer. See: N. Pfeffer
Pfister Associated Growers
The corn with husk ability
The corn with stand ability
The corn with yield ability
Feels better, too
Genuine Pfister hybrids
Man, that's corn
More acres of corn, more
corn per acre
More corn, less cob; it's
bred that way
More shelled corn per ear,
per acre, per farm 8
out of 10 times
Shells out better, too
Tops at shelling time
Win 8 out of 10 times
Pfizer Pharmaceuticals
Chemicals for those who
serve man's well-being
Pharmaceuticals. A partner
in healthcare
Science for the world's well-
being
Pfleuger fishing tackle
A great name in tackle
Pharmaceuticals. A partner in
healthcare
Pfizer Pharmaceuticals
Phelps Dodge Corporation
The copper people from
Phelps Dodge
Philadelphia & Reading Railway
Travel on the Reading
Philadelphia Brand cream cheese
Look for this famous name
in the oval
Nothing else is made like it
Philadelphia Bulletin
Dominant Philadelphia
In Philadelphia nearly every-
body reads the Bulletin
Philadelphia's newspaper
Philadelphia Carpet Co.
Quality since 1846
Since 1846, the quality of
elegance underfoot
Philadelphia Gas Works Co.
Gas, the comfort fuel
Philadelphia Inquirer
Tell it in the morning, tell
it in the Philadelphia

Inquirer
Philadelphia Record
  Always reliable
Philadelphia Seed Co.
  Puregrain Seeds, 100% pure
    grain
  Quaker Brand seeds, the
    finest of the crop
Philadelphia whiskey
  A heritage to remember
  The heritage whiskey
Philadelphia's newspaper
  Philadelphia Bulletin
Philco. See also: Filko
Philco portable radio receiver
  You CAN take it with you
Philco radio receiver
  Famous for quality the
    world over
  I tank I go home, I have
    a Philco there
  A musical instrument of
    quality
  When there's a choice, it's
    Philco
Philco Socket Power radio re-
    ceiver
  One switch controls every-
    thing
Philip. See also: Phillips
Philip Morris cigarettes
  Always better, better all
    ways
  America's finest cigarette
  Call for Philip Morris!
  The flavor's all yours
  Good people make good
    things
  If every smoker knew what
    Philip Morris smokers
    know, they'd all change
    to Philip Morris
  It takes art to make a
    company great
  On the air and everywhere
  Our ads neither coax nor
    hoax
Philip Morris cigarettes. See
    also: Horace Heidt
    and his Musical Knights
    orchestra
Philippine Airlines
  First class on Asia's first
    airline
Phillips. See also: Philip
Phillips cocoa

It beats the Dutch
Phillips Cream
  Be your age, but look
    younger
Phillips Delicious Soups
  Only the best is ever
    labeled Phillips Delicious
Phillips-Jones collars
  The world's smartest collar
Phillips-Jones shirts
  They fit royally
Phillips' Milk of Magnesia
  America's true blue friend
  In the best of regulated
    families
  So gentle for children, so
    thorough for grown-ups
  Stay fit for fun with Phil-
    lips
  To fly high in the morning,
    take Phillips at night
Phillips' Milk of Magnesia tablets
  No water needed
Phillips Petroleum Co.
  The performance company
Phillips Research Laboratories
  Trust in Phillips is world-
    wide
Phillips 66 gasoline
  Go first class ... go Phil-
    lips 66
Phillipson Rod Co.
  World's finest
Phin, Inc.
  Innovators in the design
    and manufacture of
    quality labeling equip-
    ment
Phinney Walker automobile
    clocks
  Time before your eyes
Phoenix hosiery
  Long Mileage Hosiery
  Something has happened to
    hosiery
  You're sure of yourself in
    Phoenix
Phoenix of Hartford Insurance
    Companies
  Restituimus--"We restore"
    ... since 1854
Phone power in action
  Bell Telephone System
The phonograph of marvelous
    tone
  Vitanola phonograph

The phonograph with a soul
    Edison phonograph
Photographers Assn. of America
    Photographs live forever
    Photographs live forever in
        loving hearts
    Photographs tell the story
    Say it with pictures, often
    Snapshots, often, are all
        that remain after your
        dear ones go
    Snapshots remain long after
        you go
Photographs live forever
    Photographers Assn. of
        America
Photographs live forever in lov-
    ing hearts
    Photographers Assn. of
        America
Photographs of distinction
    Bachrach, Inc.
Photographs tell the story
    Photographers Assn. of
        America
Photoplay
    The magazine of the fifth
        estate
    The national guide to motion
        pictures
    Predominant with the 18 to
        30 age group
Photos never forget
    Kodak photographic paper
Photoswitch Div., Electronics
    Corp. of America
    New ideas in automation
        control
Physical Culture
    To build a stronger nation
A piano is the soul of the home
    Musette piano
The piano of international fame
    Steinway piano
Pick a Perrine today!
    Perrine fishing tackle
The pick o' the pines
    Western Manufacturers As-
        sociation
The pick o' the season fruit
    club
    Pinnacle Orchards
The pick of pickles
    Crosse & Blackwell pickles
The pick of the field
    Herschell-Spillman Motor

Co.
The pick of the pack
    Polar Frosted Foods
The pick of the pack, picked at
    the peak of perfection
    Polar Frosted Foods
The pick of the portables
    RCA Victor radio receiver
Pick the polka dot package
    Swift's Premium meats
A pick-up for a let-down
    Lime Cola
Picked at the fleeting moment of
    perfect flavor
    Green Giant Peas
Picked sweet. See: Pictsweet
Picked with pride, packed with
    skill since 1869
    Welch's grape juice
Pickering and Co., Inc.
    For those who can hear the
        difference
    The world's largest and
        most experienced manu-
        facturer of magnetic
        pickups
Pickford. See: Mary Pickford
    Cosmetics
Pictograph Corp.
    One pictograph tells more
        than a thousand words
    One picture tells more than
        a thousand words
Pictorial Review
    The really perfect printed
        pattern
    They almost talk to you
Pictsweet Canned Corn
    Plump and buttersweet
The picture of health
    Pine Tree Soap
Pictures that satisfy or a new
    roll free
    Agfa-Gavaert, Inc.
Piedmont Airlines
    The up and coming airlines
Piel's beer
    Delicious, deLIGHTful, de-
        mand it
    One luxury all can enjoy
Pierce-Arrow automobile
    America's finest motor car
        for America's finest
        families
    The ONE great name that
        identifies fine cars

exclusively
Pierce watch
  Watches of tested accuracy
Pike's Toothache Drops
  Pike's Toothache Drops cure
    in one minute
Pike's Toothache Drops cure in
    one minute
  Pike's Toothache Drops
A pillow for the body
  Sealy Mattress Co.
Pillsbury's cake mix
  How sweet it is!
Pillsbury's dotted circle, symbol
    of reliability
  Pillsbury's flour
Pillsbury's flour
  Balanced for perfect baking
  Best baking prize is a de-
    lighted husband
  The farm-fresh spread bet-
    ters any bread
  A lift for the lunch box
  Pillsbury's dotted circle,
    symbol of reliability
  You bake your best with
    Pillsbury's best
  You don't "knead" the
    dough
Pillsbury's Health Bran
  One of the family
Pillsbury's pancake flour
  How to make a man's face
    glow on a dark morning
Pilot Precise ball liner pen
  The rolling ball pen that
    revolutionizes thin
    writing
Pilot Radio Corp.
  Unquestionably the world's
    finest stereophonic
    console
Pilsner Beer
  Often imitated but never
    duplicated
Pin-up favorites since 1900
  Moore Pins
A pinch is all it takes
  Copenhagen chewing tobacco
  Happy Days chewing tobac-
    co
  Skoal chewing tobacco
Pinch Scotch whiskey
  An inch of Pinch, please
Pine Tree Shampoo
  It puts the sunshine in

your hair
Pine Tree Soap
  The picture of health
Pinettes
  Eliminate sewing on shank
    buttons
Pinkerton. The most famous
    name in security and
    investigation
  Pinkerton's, Inc. detective
    agency
Pinkerton's, Inc. detective
    agency
  Pinkerton. The most famous
    name in security and
    investigation
  We never sleep
Pinkham's. See: Lydia E.
    Pinkham's Vegetable
    Compound
The pinnacle of perfection in
    fruit
  Pinnacle Orchards
The pinnacle of performance
  Acme motor truck
Pinnacle Orchards
  From famous orchards of
    the great west
  The fruit of connoisseurs
  Most-a-pound-a-piece
  The pick o' the season fruit
    club
  The pinnacle of perfection
    in fruit
  Superba Fruit Basket
  Year 'round Fruit Club
Pioneer and pacemaker in essen-
    tial fields of industry
  Firestone Tire and Rubber
    Co.
Pioneer Box Co.
  Delivers the goods
Pioneer builders of American
    sixes
  Stevens-Duryea automobile
Pioneer chain saw
  It's one Hulluva chain saw
Pioneer Corporation
  One corporation covers a
    world of energy
A pioneer in claim services
  GAB Business Services,
    Inc.
Pioneer in easier ironing
  Proctor electric iron
Pioneer in powder and molten

metallurgy
Firth Sterling, Inc.
Pioneer in the development and
construction of electric
industrial trucks
Elwell-Parker Electric Co.
A pioneer in the leasing field
Emkay, Inc.
Pioneer Lacquer
Once a Pioneer, always a
Pioneer
Pioneer Laser Disc
If you really care about
picture and sound, you
have no choice
Pioneer makers of modern steel
windows
David Lupton's Sons
Pioneer manufacturers of elec-
tric control apparatus
Cutler-Hammer, Inc.
Pioneer Mints
A breathless sensation
The pioneer of low fares to Eu-
rope
Icelandic Airlines
Pioneer process plate makers
Electro-Tint Engraving Co.
Pioneer railroad of the southwest
Missouri-Kansas-Texas Rail-
road
Pioneer Rubber Mills
Tain't gwine rain no mo'
Pioneer Suspender Co.
The easiest belt a man ever
felt
For men who care what they
wear
Your shoulders will thank
you
Your wait will thank you
Pioneer Video, Inc.
Stereo you can see
Television you can learn
from
Pioneered the continuous extru-
sion process in 1880
John Royle and Sons
Pioneering better guns and
greater values since
1864
Stevens arms
Pioneering in ideas for industry
United States Gypsum Co.
The pioneering spirit keeps
America's pipelines

flowing
United Energy Resources,
Inc.
Pioneers in automated lithography
H. S. Crocker Co., Inc.
Pioneers in banking
Indiana National Bank
Pioneers in colored glass technol-
ogy
Houze Glass Corp.
Pioneers in energy
United Energy Resources,
Inc.
Pioneers in hydride chemistry
Metal Hydrides, Inc.
Pioneers in plastics
Flex-O-Film, Inc.
Hopp Plastics Div., Hopp
Press, Inc.
Pioneers in pneumatic bar feed-
ing
Lipe-Rollway Corp.
Pioneers in polycoatings
H. P. Smith Paper Co.
Pioneers in precision
Leeds and Northrup Co.
Pioneers in recording achieve-
ment
Recordisc Corp.
Pioneers in the radio industry
All-American Radio Corp.
Pioneers in unit ventilation
Peerless Unit Ventilation Co.
Pioneers of disposers dedicated
to quality
National Commercial Dispos-
ers
A pip of a chip
Jay's potato chips
The pipe of distinction
L & H Stern Co.
The pipe that everybody knows
Kaywoodie pipe
The pipe that sidetracks moisture
Smokemaster pipe
The pipe that's broken in
M. Linkman & Co.
Pipeliners of energy
Texas Eastern Transmission
Corp.
Pipelines. Energy. And the
experience to go from
there
Midcon Corporation
Piper Aircraft Corporation
Look to the leader for good

safe planes you can af-
ford to buy and fly
More airplane for the dollar
More people have bought
Pipers than any other
plane in the world
Piper-Heidsieck champagne
Pop goes the Piper
Piperazine W-a-t-e-r
The most powerful uric
acid solvent known
A pipe's best friend is fragrant
Heine's Blend
Heine's Blend smoking
tobacco
A pippin of a drink
Virginia Fruit Juice Co.
Pit and Quarry
Editorial excellence in ac-
tion
Pitman. See: J. C. Pitman
and Sons, Inc.
Pitney-Bowes mail handling
machines
We can lighten your paper
weight
World leader in mailing sys-
tems
Pittsburgh Brewing Co.
Every taste a treat
Finer than the finest
First for flavor
Pittsburgh Garter Co.
It lox the sox
Pittsburgh Paints
Paint yourself a new house
Pittsburgh Plate Glass Co.
A little extra glass means
a lot of extra charm
Mark of good plate glass
Pittsburgh Reflector Co.
Something better has come
to light
The place to go
Spanish National Tourist
Office
The place to make friends for
your company
Reader's Digest
The place where you keep your
checking account
Foundation for Commercial
Banks
Planetary Pencil Pointer
Not a toy but a machine
Planters cheese balls

More MMM MM after every
crunch
Planters is the word for peanuts
Planters salted peanuts
Planters peanut oil
Not only light but deliciously
light
Planters salted peanuts
The name for quality
The nickel lunch
Planters is the word for
peanuts
The snack that makes or-
dinary occasions special
Planters Sesame Nut Mix
The one to crunch when you
want to munch
Plants like human hands
Hayes Pump & Planter Co.
Plastic Industries, Inc.
America's foremost leg spe-
cialists
Plastic Sheeting Div., Eastman
Chemical Products, Inc.
Look to Eastman to look
your best!
Plastic Sheeting Div., Eastman
Chemical Products, Inc.
See also: Eastman
Chemical Products, Inc.
The plastic wrap professionals
use
Reynolds plastic wrap
PlastiCraft motor boat
It's a winner
Plastics Div., Seiberling Rubber
Co.
Seilon, world's broadest
line of thermoplastic
sheet materials
Plastics Div., Seiberling Rubber
Co. See also: Seiber-
ling tires
Plastics that fit the job
Durez plastics
Plate Glass Mfrs. of America
Nothing else is like it
Plato. Changing how the world
learns
Control Data Corporation
Platts Bros., Ltd.
The first name in textile
machinery
Play off your fat!
Wallace Reducing Records
Play-Poise shoes

Biggest news in infants'
   shoes
Play safe with Wilco
   Wilco float coat
Play the best you can play
   Ben Hogan golf clubs
Play to win with Wilson
   Wilson Sporting Goods Co.
Player cigarettes
   It's the tobacco that counts
Plays all records, natural as
   life
   Vitanola phonograph
Plays over a thousand tunes
   Olympia Self-Playing Music
   Box
Playtime pals for the nation's
   kiddies
   Coronet toys
The Plaza pleases
   Hotel Plaza, New York City
Pleasant way to reduce
   Marmola
Please! Only you can prevent
   forest fires
   The Advertising Council
The pleasure is back
   Barclay cigarettes
Pleasure is where you can find
   it
   Viceroy cigarettes
Pleasure pirate pilgrimage
   United American Lines
Plenty of juice pork and spicy
   "down east" sauces
   B & M Baked Beans
Pliofilm
   Primer of packaging per-
   fection
Plop, plop! Fizz, fizz! Oh,
   what a relief it is!
   Alka-Seltzer
Plug in, I'm Reddy
   Reddy Kilowatt
Plumb tools
   Quality comes first; Plumb
   is first in quality
The plumbing and heating weekly
   Domestic Engineering
Plump and buttersweet
   Pictsweet Canned Corn
Plus extra energy
   Welch's marmalade
The plus food for minus meals
   Kellogg's All-Bran
Plus packaging

Ekco Containers, Inc.
Plus values
   Chemical Div., General
   Mills, Inc.
Pluto Water
   America's physic
   When nature won't, Pluto
   will
Plylock
   Wood that's stronger than
   wood
Plymouth automobile
   The American way to get
   your money's worth
   Facts show it, owners know
   it
   Invest in the car that stands
   up best
   It's a short street without a
   Plymouth
   Let yourself go ... Plymouth
   Look what Plymouth's up to
   now
   New driving feel that's slick
   as silk
   Plymouth builds great cars
   Ride and know
   Sets the pace
   World's safest low-priced
   car
Plymouth builds great cars
   Plymouth automobile
Plymouth Cordage Co.
   The rope you can trust
   Rope you can trust because
   it is engineered for
   YOUR job
Plymouth Golf Ball Co.
   World's largest exclusive
   manufacturer of golf
   balls
Plymouth Rock Pants Co.
   Do you wear pants?
Pneumatics. See: Numatics,
   Inc.
Pocket Books, Inc.
   Kind to your pocket and
   pocket BOOK
Pocket-paying dividend prices
   Champ-Items, Inc.
The point of penetration to the
   shoe market
   Boot and Shoe Recorder
Polar Frosted Foods
   The pick of the pack
   The pick of the pack,

picked at the peak of
perfection
Polar Ice Laboratories
Cleanses the pores and
softens the skin
Polaroid Sun Glasses
Don't make "glaring" mis-
takes
Polaroid SX-70 Sonar
The world's finest instant
camera
Poli-grip denture cream
Keeps food out, dentures
in
The policy back of the policy
Hardware Mutual Casualty
Co.
A policy for every purse and
purpose
Home Life Insurance Co.
The policy makers
Crum & Forster Insurance
Companies
Polident denture cleaner
Keeps plates and bridges
odor-free
Polident green gets tough
stains clean
Recommended by more den-
tists than any other
denture cleaner
The safe modern way to
clean plates and
bridges
You can't "brush off" den-
ture breath
Polident green gets tough stains
clean
Polident denture cleaner
Polident toothpaste
Recommended by dentists
surveyed 9 to 1 over
all toothpastes combined
Polish Duco with Duco polish
Duco automobile polish
Polishes all metals
Dura-Gilt polish
Poll Parrot shoes
Pre-tested shoes for boys
and girls
Polly-Flex Housewares
Always first with the best
Woman's best friend
Poly Wrap
The original polyethylene
coated freezer wrap

Polyvinyl Chemicals, Inc.
Specialists in high polymers
Pomiac gasoline
Full powered
Pompeian beauty products
Windblown through silk
Pompeian massage cream
Clears the skin
Don't envy a good com-
plexion; use Pompeian
and have one
Don't envy beauty, use
Pompeian
Easy to use
Your drug store has it.
Use it regularly at home
Pompeian talcum powder
A new talc with a new odor
Ponderosa Mouldings, Inc.
Chief of the mouldings
Ponderosa steak restaurants
Biggest little steakhouse in
the U. S. A.
Pontiac automobile
America's lowest-priced fine
car
Chief of the sixes
A fine car made finer
A fine new value and a fine
old name
Finest of the famous "Silver
Streaks"
Good to be in, good to be
seen in
Is THAT all Pontiac costs?
The most beautiful thing on
wheels
Pontiac for pride and per-
formance
Pontiac moves to the head
of the class
Satisfy yourself with some-
thing better; buy a
Pontiac
There's no substitute for
experience
We build excitement
Wide-track
Pontiac for pride and perform-
ance
Pontiac automobile
Pontiac moves to the head of the
class
Pontiac automobile
Pool products from a name you
know--Purex

Purex cleaning materials
Pop goes the Piper
Piper-Heidsieck champagne
Pope and Talbot, Inc.
Products of wood technology
for construction and
industry
Pope-Toledo automobile
Be sure the name "Pope" is
on your automobile
The popular aluminum
Viko aluminum kitchenware
Popular as music itself
Winter piano
Popular at contract or auction
games
American Chewing Products
Corp.
Popular for flavor, taste, price
Deerfoot Farm Sliced Bacon
Popular Mechanics
Written so you can under-
stand it
Porcelain cleaner
A wipe and it's bright
Porcelain top, no shocks, no
burns
Trico Fuse Mfg. Co.
A poreless-as-porcelain com-
plexion
Revlon face makeup
Porosknit
The active man's summer
underwear
Porsche and Audi automobiles
Nothing even comes close
Port Authority of the City of
St. Paul
Make the capital choice
The portable clothes closet
Atlantic Products Corp.
Portable Elevator Mfg. Co.
The original drawer type
freezer
Portable phonographs of dis-
tinction
Caswell Mfg. Co.
Portable pony power
Johnson Iron Horse gas
engine
Portable power for progress
Battery Div., Sonotone
Corporation
Porter. See: H. K. Porter
Co., Inc.
Portland Cement Assn.

Concrete for permanence
Porto-Red shoes
Look smart, feel fresh
The post everlasting
Long-Bell Lumber Co.
Post Toasties
Stay crisp in milk or cream
Tops in taste, low in price,
rich in food
The post with the steel backbone
American Steel & Wire Co.
Postman's gloves
Postman's, the gloves Milady
loves
Postman's, the gloves Milady
loves
Postman's gloves
Post's Bran Chocolates
A delicious health confection
Post's Bran Flakes
America's favorite bran
flakes
Life is swell when you keep
well
An ounce of prevention for
everybody, every day
She who prizes beauty must
obey Nature's law!
Post's Raisin Bran
The fruit and cereal lover's
cereal
Postum. See also: Instant
Postum
Postum Cereal Co., Inc.
Now you'll like bran
Pot-luck or full dress
Shefford cheese
Potash Co. of America
The salt of the earth
The potato is man's greatest
food
Maine Development Commis-
sion
Potent essence of desire to touch
White Shoulders perfume
Potlatch Forests, Inc.
Depend on Potlatch for
everything in quality
lumber
Symbol of quality
We grow the working trees
Potosi Brewing Co.
The beer for good cheer
The beer that made the
nineties gay
Quality brew since 1852

The poultry authority
Poultry Tribune
Poultry Tribune
The poultry authority
Pour Glenmore, you get more
Glenmore whiskey
Pour smoothness into your motor
O'Neil Oil Co.
Pour these down your shirt front
Arrow neckties
Pour yourself an apple pie
Comstock pie-sliced apples
Powdered perfume for the com-
plexion
Velveola Souveraine Face
Powder
Powell. See also: The Wm.
Powell Co.
Powell Muffler Co.
Built stronger to last longer
Power across land and sea
ASEA Electric, Inc.
Power and light for every need
Onan products
Power and light with the quiet
Knight
Willys-Knight automobile
The power behind the dough
KC Baking Powder
Power behind the leading prod-
ucts
Bodine Electric Co.
Power Boating
America's leading power
boat magazine
Power Farming
Power farming is profit
farming
Power farming is profit farming
Power Farming
Power for progress
Consolidated Edison Com-
pany
Southern Company
Power from the world leader
Briggs & Stratton Corpora-
tion
Power House candy bar
They don't call it Power
House for nothing
The power is within your reach
Timex computers
Power
To energize your sales
crew, put Power
behind it

The power of balance
Avco Corporation
The power of ingenuity
Bendix Corporation
The power of technology is the
power to create
United Technologies Corpor-
ation
The power that lights and moves
Alabama
Alabama Power Co.
Power that stays
Monarch automobile batteries
The power tiller of a hundred
uses
Rototiller
The power to please!
Florida Power Corporation
Power to spare
Eveready flashlights and
batteries
U. S. L. batteries
The power-wise group their
drives
American Pulley Co.
Power without powder
Crosman Arms Co.
Powered by Howard
Howard Industries, Inc.
Powerful as the nation
Continental automobile
A powerful part of your life
Westinghouse Electric Corp.
Powermatic, Inc.
Today's ideas ... engineered
for tomorrow
Powers. See: John Robert
Powers Products Co.
Practical feeds for practical
feeders
Dietrich & Gambrill
Practical in design. Dependable
in action
New Holland Div., Sperry
Rand Corporation
The practical poultry paper for
practical poultry people
American Poultry Advocate
Praise dog food
Dogs love Praise
Pratt & Lambert paint
What good is paint if it's
not good paint?
Pratt & Lambert varnish
Heelproof, marproof and
waterproof

Hit it with a hammer
Shows only the reflection
Test it with a hammer
The world walks on '61
You may dent the wood but
    the varnish won't crack
Pratt Food Co.
    The original baby food for
    baby chicks
Pre-cize girdle
Fits to precision
Pre-tested shoes for boys and
    girls
Poll Parrot shoes
A precious bit more than a
    laxative
Alonzo
Precious little aids to beauty
Sta-Rite Hair Pin
Precise banking worldwide
Citibank, New York City
Precisely right, in time, in
    design
Telechron Electric Clock
Precision-built, water-tight
Johnson sea-worthy boats
Precision engineering applied
    to the end of a wire
Aircraft Marine Products
Precision Fastener Div., Stand-
    ard Pressed Steel Co.
    UNBRAKO costs less than
    trouble
Precision first ... to last
Triplett tube tester
Precision fishing reels since
    1883
Martin Reel Co.
The precision line
Fellows Gear Shaper Co.
Precision machinery since 1880
Warner and Swasey Co.
Precision typewriters
Olympia electronic type-
    writers
Precision Valve Corp.
Leaders by design
The precision watch, America's
    choice
Gruen watch
Precisioneered by Edelmann
E. Edelmann and Co.
Predominant with the 18 to 30
    age group
Photoplay
Preference for Ediphone per-

sists
Ediphone Dictograph
Preferred by particular people
    for more than a century
Rigby brushes
The preferred corrective shoe
Fairy Foot shoe
Preferred; easily acquired; in-
    stant liquidity
Tanqueray Distilled English
    Gin
Preferred for America's most dis-
    tinguished homes
Romweber Industries
Preferred for its flavor, praised
    for its price
Quaker Maid salad dressing
Rajah Salad Dressing
Preferred ... for mellow moments
Hamm's beer
Preferred for quality
Trico Fuse Mfg. Co.
Preferred Hotels
    We accept only one standard.
    Yours
Preferred in fine homes for many
    years
Hawes Floor Wax
Preferred position before a pre-
    ferred audience
United States Daily
Preflex auto mirror
    Night or day it safens the
    way
Prell shampoo
    New Prell puts the ooooo
    in shampoo
Prelude to adventure
Gay Diversion Perfume
A premium motor oil at regular
    price
Gulflube motor oil
Premier automobile
    The aluminum six with mag-
    netic gear shift
Premier clean is REALLY clean
Premier vacuum cleaner
Premier Salad Dressing
    Makes every meal an event
    A perfect mayonnaise
Premier vacuum cleaner
    Premier clean is REALLY
    clean
Premier Warm Air Heater
    Indoor weather as you want
    it, with a weatherator

Instant hot water
THE premium beer
    Barbarosa Beer
Premium Catnip
    Makes cats playful!
Prentice slide fastener
    You call it a "zipper"; its
        real name is Prentice,
        the dependable slide
        fastener
Prentiss Vise Co.
    On the bench since 1850
    The third hand with a
        mighty grip
Preparation H hemorrhoid oint-
        ment
    Relieves pain and itch--even
        helps reduce swelling
Prepares for college or business
        while touring the world
    Nautical Preparatory School
Prescription for your teeth
    Listerine toothpaste
Prescription medicines around
        the world
    Eli Lilly and Co.
The present with a future
    West Branch cedar hope
        chest
Preserve with refined cane sugar
    The Sugar Institute
Preserve your horse's feet
    Collins Eureka Pad
Press it from steel instead
    Youngstown Pressed Steel
        Co.
Press, it's lit; release, it's out
    Ronson cigarette lighters
The pressing service that shapes
        your clothes
    U. S. Hoffman Machinery
        Corp.
Pressroom efficiency depends on
        electrical control
    Cutler-Hammer, Inc.
The pressure cooker people
    National Presto Industries,
        Inc.
Prest-O-Lite
    The battery with a kick
    The fastest growing battery
        business in America
Prest-O-Lite. See also: Pesto-
    lite
Presteline
    The electric range with

    the safety top
Presto FryDaddy deep fryer
    Quality that makes it last
        and last
Prestone anti-freeze
    Costs more by the gallon,
        less by the winter
    Deep inside trust Prestone
    Does not boil away
    The perfect anti-freeze
    Won't boil off; contains no
        alcohol
    You're safe and you know it
The prettiest thing on two feet
    Carlisle Shoe Co.
Prevent schoolroom slouch
    American Seating Co.
Prevents stoppages, cleans and
        purifies
    Ross Mfg. Co.
Price. See also:
    Rowe Price Growth Stock
        Fund
    Rowe Price Prime Reserve
        Fund, Inc.
    Rowe Price Tax-Free Income
        Fund, Inc.
The price of a Moon is an appeal
        to your reason
    Moon automobile
Price--the only sensation
    Reo automobile
Priced from mill to Milady
    Admiration nylon stockings
The priceless ingredient, Squibb
        quality
    Squibb Beech-Nut, Inc.
Priceless ingredient of every
        product is the honor
        and integrity of its
        maker
    E. R. Squibb
Price's. See: Dr. Price's
    vanilla
Pride of Cognac since 1724
    Rémy Martin cognac
The pride of the pantry
    Military Brand Camembert
        Cheese
Pride without prejudice
    French S. S. Line
Priestley's Nor-East
    Aristocrat of summer suits
Prim Miss brassieres and girdles
    The boast of the town
    The smart set

Primatene Mist
   The asthma reliever doctors
      recommend most
Prime Soap
   The complete first suds de-
      tergent
Prime source for weighing equip-
      ment and technology
   Toledo Scale Co.
Primer of packaging perfection
   Pliofilm
Primo del Rey cigars
   Primo del Rey never forgets
      tobacco must be as fine
      as the hands that shape
      it
Primo del Rey never forgets
      tobacco must be as fine
      as the hands that shape
      it
   Primo del Rey cigars
Primrose face powder
   A shiny nose is a thorn
      in the heart of charm
Primrose foundations
   A "fitting" tribute to the
      feminine figure
Prince. See also: Prints
Prince Albert pipe and cigarette
      tobacco
   The national joy smoke
   No other tobacco is like it
   P. A. means Pipe Appeal
Prince Gardner Co.
   Distinctive designs in
      leather accessories
   The royalty of leatherware
The prince of ales
   Busch Pale Dry ale
The prince of pales
   Busch Pale Dry ale
Prince of soles
   Alfred Hale Rubber Co.
Princesses de Conde Chocolates
   A gift to remember
Printed proof on Barrett Port-
      able
   Barrett Portable adding
      machine
The Printers' Ink of the dental
      profession
   Oral Hygiene
Printing and typography are
      related
   Nala Press
Printing Machinery Co.

A familiar name of national
      fame
   Foundation blocks of profit-
      able printing
Printing Magazine
   News and management month-
      ly of the graphic arts
Printing with a personal appeal
   Advertising Supply Co.
Printing with a plus
   Francis Emory Fitch, Inc.
Prints. See also: Prince
Prints from type
   Addressograph-Multigraph
      Corp.
Prints the news, tells the truth
   The Signal
Pritikin Longevity Center
   Pritikin: the better way
Pritikin: the better way
   Pritikin Longevity Center
The private insurance broker.
      We answer only to you
   Johnson & Higgins
Prized of writing perfection
   Stratford pens
The pro in projectors
   Kodak Carousel projectors
The pro line
   Roberts Div., Rheem Mfg.
      Co.
Pro-Phy-Lac-Tic toothbrush
   Be good to your gums
   A clean tooth never decays
   The green cleans in-between
      ... the white polishes
      bright
   No other has round-end
      bristle
   Perma-grip bristle can't
      come out
Pro-tek-tiv. See also: Protec-
      tive
Pro-tek-tiv shoes
   For normal foot growth
Probing deeper to serve you
      better
   Ford Motor Company Re-
      search Laboratories
The problem-solver people
   Champ-Items, Inc.
The problem solvers
   E-Systems
   General Electric Company
Procrastination is the highest
      cost of life insurance.

It increases both your
premium and your risk
The Union Central Life In-
surance Co.
Proctor & Gamble Co.
Good soap is good business
Products for the home since
1837
Save yourself two rubs out
of every 3
The soap of beautiful women
Proctor electric iron
Banishes ironing drudgery
The only iron that banishes
ironing fatigue forever
Pioneer in easier ironing
You never have to lift or
tilt it
You never lift or tilt it
Proctor toaster
Merry crispness
TOAST for every TASTE
Prodex Div., Koehring Co.
In design and performance,
always a year ahead
Producers of all basic urethane
chemicals
Allied Chemical Corp.
Producers of quality steel for
industry and construc-
tion
Laclede Steel Co.
Producers of zinc for American
industry
St. Joseph Lead Co.
Product Engineering
The No. 1 buy in the de-
sign field
Product of Cuban soil and
Cuban sun
La Primadora cigars
The product with the pluses
Dodge Manufacturing Corp.
Production for sleep and rest
Englander mattress
The productivity bankers
First National Bank of
Chicago
Products for the home since
1837
Proctor & Gamble Co.
Products made to measure
Daniel Orifice Fitting Co.
Products of wood technology
for construction and
industry

Pope and Talbot, Inc.
Products that extend and protect
man's physical senses
American Optical Co.
Products that think
JS&A Group, Inc.
Products you can depend on ...
day in ... day out
NVF Co.
Products you can trust from
people you know
Will Ross, Inc.
The professional calculators that
never call it quits
Canon electronic calculators
Professional cosmetics for lovelier
hair color
Roux Labs, Inc.
The professional in home security
Nutone Security System
The professional moving system
for the amateur mover
Jartran Truck Rental
The professional nail enamel you
can use at home
Revlon nail enamel
Professional relationship banking
in over 100 countries
through a mature net-
work of branches and
affiliates
Chase Manhattan Bank
The professional tooth powder
for daily home use
Pepsodent tooth powder
The professionals
Bekins Van and Storage
Co.
Profit from Austin's management
consulting expertise
The Austin Company
The Profit Line
The Shaler Company
The profit line in wine
Greystone Fruit Wines
Profit with Wissco products
Wickwire Spencer Steel Co.
Progress begins with digging
Marion Power Shovel Co.
Progress for industry worldwide
Combustion Engineering,
Inc.
Progress in the world of time
Westclox Div., General Time
Corp.
Progress is our most important

378

product
General Electric Company
Progress, not compromise
Peugeot automobile
Progress through precision
Torrington Co.
Progressive Farmer
The farm weekly of largest
circulation and most
influence
The magazine that moves
the men who move the
merchandise
The Progressive Grocer
The national magazine of
the grocery trade
A progressive past. A golden
future
Wilson Sporting Goods Co.
Progressive products for fluid
control
Manatool Div., Perry-Fay Co.
Progressive products thru chem-
ical research
Hysol Div., Dexter Corp.
Promise her anything but give
her Arpege
Arpege perfume
Promise tooth paste
For relief of sensitive teeth
Promotes a tan while it protects
your skin
Dorothy Gray suntan oil
Promoting high standards in the
public interest
New York Stock Exchange
Members
Pronounced by all who have
used it to be the best
Dog Food in the market
Austin's Dog Bread
The proof is in the listening
Motorola radio receiver
The proof is in the pad
Stri-Dex skin cleanser
The proof is in the wearing!
Damart Thermolactyl under-
wear
Proofread your typing before
it's typed
Brother Electronic Office
Typewriter
Proofs of leadership
Lawrence Leather Co.
The propeller with a brain for
your private plane

Aeromatic Koppers
Proper moistening is essential to
good sealing
Hummel gummed paper mois-
tener
The properly balanced organic
plant food
Olds & Whipple
Prophet Co.
The good food service
Proprietary pharmaceuticals made
to ethical standards
Contac nasal decongestant
Prospect foundations
Keep in touch with Prospect
Prosperity follows the plow
Agricultural Publishers
Assn.
Protect horsepower; that's horse
sense
Mobilgas
Protect the records you can't
insure
Art Metal Construction Co.
Protect what you have
Insurance Co. of North
America
Protect your family
Smith & Wesson revolver
Protect your investment with
Kendall confidence
Kendall motor oil
Protect yourself against the mid-
dleman
Aladdin prefabricated houses
Protected where the wear comes
Holmes & Edwards silver-
plate
Protecting the American home
National Life Insurance Co.
of Vermont
Protecting the nation--through
hometown agents
Great American Insurance
Cos.
Protecting the nation's hand-
power
Boss work gloves
Protecting the new in your
pneumatics
Wilkerson Corp.
Protection and Pennzoil; get
them together in your
car
Pennzoil motor oil
Protection for employer and

employee
American Mutual Liability
Insurance Co.
Protection in a new light
Monumental Life Insurance
Co.
Protection in depth
Liberty Mutual Insurance
Company
Protection you can see through
Cellophane
Protective. See also: Pro-tek-
tiv
Protective service
Seiberling tires
Protects teeth beautifully
Teel mouthwash
Protects you at all times
Union Life Insurance Co.
Protects you handsomely
Lakeland Sportswear
Protects your baby against wet-
ness right down to his
toes
Pampers diapers
Protects your garden, and you
Ever Green Garden Spray
Protein-rich foods cats crave
Crave catfood
Proud bird with the golden tail
Continental Air Lines, Inc.
Proud of our past and com-
mitted to your future
Fort Wayne National Bank
A proud paper for a proud in-
dustry
Tavern Weekly
The proudest name in shoes
Keith Highlanders
Proved and improved for 55
years
Kelly-Springfield Tire Co.
Proved by proofs
Indiana Truck Corp.
Proved throughout industry for
over 40 years
Rust-Oleum Corp.
Proven best by government test
Colt revolver
Proven best for rest during 73
years test
Ostermoor mattress
Proven by the test of time
Habirshaw Electric Cable
Co.
Proven performance systems

Gates Learjet Corporation
Provide through Providence
Provident Mutual Life Insur-
ance Co. of Philadelphia
Provident Life and Accident In-
surance Co.
The home of human security
Provident plans for provident
people since 1887
Provident Mutual for stability,
safety, security
Provident Mutual Life Insur-
ance Co. of Philadelphia
Provident Mutual Life Insurance
Co. of Philadelphia
Low rate--low cost
Provide through Providence
Provident Mutual for stabil-
ity, safety, security
Tighten your grip on the
future
Provident plans for provident
people since 1887
Provident Life and Accident
Insurance Co.
Prudential has the strength of
Gibraltar
Prudential Life Insurance
Co. of America
Prudential Life Insurance Co. of
America
The future belongs to those
who prepare for it
Get a piece of the rock
Nothing else like it
Prudential-planned protec-
tion
Prudential has the strength
of Gibraltar
The strength of Gibraltar
Prudential-planned protection
Prudential Life Insurance
Co. of America
The prune juice with the fruit
juice appeal
Del Monte prune juice
Prunes give you so much for so
little
Del Monte prunes
The public appreciates quality
Horn & Hardart automat
restaurants
The public be dined
Knickerbocker Grill, New
York City
A public-minded institution

General Motors Corporation
Public policy advertising
National Geographic
Public Service Electric & Gas
  Co.
  The energy people are en-
    vironmental people too!
  Nuclear power cuts oil im-
    ports
Public Service of Indiana, Inc.
  Industry's friendliest climate
Publicity Clock Co.
  Let time tell your story
Published in the heart of Amer-
    ica: most prosperous
    district of the world
  Kansas City Post
Publisher's Central Bureau
  We bring the world to your
    mailbox
Puregrain Seeds, 100% pure
    grain
  Philadelphia Seed Co.
The Puerto Rican mountain rum
  Bon Merito rum
Puerto Rican rums
  Aged for smoothness and
    taste
  The world's best climate
    makes the world's best
    rum
Puerto Rico
  The ideal second home for
    American business
Puffer-Hubbard cabinet
  The mark of a good case
Puffs tissue
  Softer is the better buy
Pull-U-Out Hoist
  The wonderful new hoist
Pullman sleeping car
  The safest, most comfort-
    able way of going
    places fast
  The safest way to go and
    the sure way to go
    there
  Sleep going to keep going
  Two people sleep when one
    goes Pullman
  Whatever the weather, Pull-
    man gets you there
Pulsar watches
  Accuracy to seconds a
    month
Pulvex Flea Powder

Kills them off and keeps
  them off
Pump Eng. Service Corp.
  Performance controls the
    air
  Performance points to Pesco
    first
The pump of compulsory accuracy
  Milwaukee Tank Works
The pump that is self-adjusting
    for wear, famous bucket
    design
  Blackmer Pump Co.
The pump that oils itself
  Coe-Stapley pump
The pump with the flexible im-
    peller
  Jabsco Pump Co.
The pump with the rubber im-
    peller
  Jabsco Pump Co.
The Pumpernickel you'll like
  Stuhmer's Pumpernickel
The pumportation people
  Gray Co., Inc.
Punch
  The paper that IS England
Punch and power at point of
    purchase
  Transit Advertisers, Inc.
Pure, always pure
  Dainty Flour
A pure and natural product for
    over 130 years
  Arm & Hammer baking soda
Pure as the mountain air
  Clark candy bar
The pure beef brand
  Mighty Dog dog food
Pure brewed in God's country
    slowly and naturally
  Heilmann's beer
Pure country milk with the cream
    left in
  Borden's condensed milk
Pure, natural, unsweetened
  Del Monte pineapple
The Pure Oil Co.
  Be sure with Pure
Pure Quill gasoline
  Try a tankful, you'll notice
    the difference immedi-
    ately
Pure, soft, absorbent
  Interlake bathroom tissue
The purest and most durable

toilet soap, hence the
best and cheapest
Pears' Soap
The purest iron made
American Rolling Mill Co.
Purex cleaning materials
Nowadays Purex quality
makes even more sense
Pool products from a name
you know--Purex
The symbol of value
You'll find the woman's
touch in every Purex
product
Purina. See also: Ralston
Purina Co.
Purina Cat Chow
Depend on Purina Cat Chow
The good for your cat cat-
food
The most trusted name in
pet food
Now! Tastes better than
ever
Purina Dog Chow
The great American dog
food
The most trusted name in
pet food
Purina poultry feed
If Purina chows won't make
your hens lay, they
are roosters
Life and growth for baby
chicks
Puritan Chocolate Co.
The perfect gift
Puritan cooking oil
Puritan wants you to win
Puritan Malt
It's all quality because
it's all barley
Puritan paper cups
A long-established name in
cups
Puritan Soap Co.
The last word in auto wax
Puritan Stationery Co.
The first name in American
stationery
Puritan wants you to win
Puritan cooking oil
Purity Cheese Co.
The king of cheese
Purity flour
Best for all your baking

Purity liquid tile
Tough as they make them
Purity Oats Co.
Famed for flavor
Totally different
Purity salt
Rain or shine, it will al-
ways run
Purolator filter
Covers all filtration prob-
lems
Purox wire
To be sure it's pure, be
sure it's Purox
You'll never tire of Purox
wire
Purposeful growth in power
transmission
Diamond Chain Co.
Purposely made for every purpose
Lucas paints
Purveyor to America's finest eat-
ing establishments
since 1893
Stock Yards Packing Co.
Purveyors of first class footwear
for men and women
Overland Trading Company
The push-out bottom
Kleen Kup
Push the button and run
Diebold Safe & Lock Co.
Push the button back--recline
Royal Easy Chair Co.
Pussywillow face powder
Sifted through silk
Put a Burke where they lurk!
Burke fishing lures
Put a little weekend in your
week
Michelob beer
Put a roof on costs
Cooley Roofing Systems
Put a smile on your taste
Long John Silver's seafood
restaurants
Put a tiger in your tank
Enco Div., Humble Oil and
Refining Co.
Put Alliance in your appliance
The Alliance Mfg. Co., Inc.
Put an overcoat on that chilly
house
Capital Insulation
Put Corroon & Black at the helm
Corroon & Black insurance

brokers
Put Corroon & Black on the job
    Corroon & Black insurance
    brokers
Put it up to men who know
    your market
    Federal Advertising Agency
Put on a new Windex shine
    Windex glass cleaner
Put one on, the pain is gone
    Zono Pads
Put muscle in your heat transfer
    applications
    Young Radiator Company
Put quality first and everything
    follows
    Fuji Electric Co., Ltd.
Put your best face forward,
    every day
    Coronet vibrator
Put your eyes at ease
    United Optical Co.
Put your feet on Comfort Street
    in Wolverines
    Wolverine Work Shoes
Put your feet on easy street
    Weyenberg Shoe Mfg. Co.
Put your heating plan on a
    budget
    Williams Oil-O-Matic Heating
    Corp.
Put your key in your own front
    door
    Sargent door locks
Put your lighting up to Whiting
    H. S. Whiting Co.
Put your money on Nettleton
    shoes, they win in a
    walk
    Nettleton shoes
Put your money where the mar-
    ket is
    Modern Machine
Put your money where your
    heart is
    U. S. Savings bonds
Put your sweeping reliance on a
    Bissell appliance
    Bissell carpet sweeper
Put your throat on N'ice
    N'ice cough lozenges
Puts air to work
    Sturtevant Co.
Puts its quality in writing
    Eberhard Faber, Inc.
Puts pep in your step

Kalak Water Co.
Puts sunshine in your wash,
    even on rainy days
    Rinso
Puts the "go" in ignition!
    Tungsten Ignition, Tungsten
    Contact Mfg. Co.
Puts the right bearing in the
    right place
    SKF Industries, Inc.
Puts the steady hum in motordom
    Carter carburetors
Puts the YOU in irresistible
    YOUth
    Irresistible Lipstick
Puts wings on your car
    Tydol gasoline
Puts you ahead in offset dupli-
    cating
    Kodak Ektalith
Puts you in the game
    Activision video games
Puts your best figure forward
    Francette corsets
Putting ideas into picture form
    Retlaw Visualizations
Putting ideas to work ... in
    machinery, chemicals,
    defense, fibers and
    films
    FMC Corp.
Putting insurance risks into per-
    spective
    Corroon & Black insurance
    brokers
Putting knowledge to work
    Special Libraries Association
Putting the "push" in America's
    finest aerosols
    Genetron aerosol
Putting you first, keeps us first
    Chevrolet Motor Div., Gen-
    eral Motors Corporation
Pyle-National Co. See: Petelco
    Div., Pyle-National Co.
Pyorrhea attacks 4 out of 5
    Forhan's tooth paste
Pyorrhocide Powder
    Keeps the gums healthy
Pyraglass Products, Inc.
    Welded on wood
Pyrene fire extinguisher
    Fortify for fire fighting
    Kills fire, saves life
Pyrex glassware
    Better baking with less fuel

For better and faster bak-
ing
For better and faster cook-
ing
Pyrofax
Burns like city gas, not a
liquid fuel
Pyrograph Advertising Sign
Corp.
Bright by day, light by
night

-Q-

Q. See: Don Q Rum
Q-B-Q Gloves
Take your cue--"Q-B-Q"
Gloves--Quality beyond
question
Q. D. corset clasp
A boon to woman
Q for Quality
Q-Tips cotton swabs
QT suntan lotion
Get a tan in one day
Q-Tips cotton swabs
Just the thing
Q for Quality
The safe swab
Quaint Inn, Indianapolis, Ind.
Cooked the way you like
it
Quaker Brand seeds, the finest
of the crop
Philadelphia Seed Co.
Quaker Halfsies cereal
Half the sugar of most
sugar-coated cereals
Quaker Maid Candies
Make the greeting sweeter
Quaker Maid salad dressing
Preferred for its flavor,
praised for its price
Quaker Oats
America's popular year
'round breakfast
Eat it all the year
For bracing up digestion,
nerves and appetite
One of nature's most per-
fect foods
The richest oats made
delicious
World's best-tasting break-
fast food

Quaker Oats Company
Maker of America's number 1
cat food
Shot from guns
Quaker Puffed Rice
Food shot from guns
Shot from guns
Quaker Puffed Wheat
Food shot from guns
Quaker Rubber Corp.
If there is a way to get it
done, Quaker will do it
Quaker Sparkies
Wheat shot from guns is
elegant eatin'
Quaker State Oil Refining Corp.
Engine life preserver
An extra quart of lubrica-
tion in every gallon
The first choice of experi-
ence
It's a lucky day for your
car when you change to
Quaker State motor oil
Trust your car to the oil
of character
We put it in writing. No
one else does
Quaker stockings
Legs are young in Quaker
stockings
Legs look young in Quaker
stockings
Quaker White Oats
The easy food. Easy to
buy, easy to cook,
easy to digest
Qualities to the last impression
Standard Ink & Color Co.
Quality above all
Solar capacitors
Quality all the way
The Hobart Mfg. Co.
The quality alternative to high-
cost inflatable boats
Sea Eagle boats
Quality always maintained
Hood rubbers
Quality and productivity through
employee participation
in management
Motorola, Inc.
Quality at its best
Ebling beer
Quality at low cost
Chevrolet automobile

Quality at modest cost
   International Shoe Co.
Quality at your feet
   Brown Shoe Company
Quality beyond the call of duty
   Nunn-Bush Shoe Co.
Quality brew since 1852
   Potosi Brewing Co.
Quality built into the car
   Bock Bearing Co.
Quality clear through
   Stroh's beer
Quality comes first; Plumb is
      first in quality
   Plumb tools
Quality costs no more
   Frederick Nelson Dry Goods
Quality electrical protective
      devices and specialties
   Trico Fuse Mfg. Co.
Quality electronic components
   Allen-Bradley Co.
The quality equipment line
   Bishman Manufacturing Co.
Quality fastening products for
      industry
   Simmons Fastener Corp.
Quality first ... from America's
      first penmaker
   Esterbrook Steel Pen Co.
Quality foods
   John Sexton Co.
A quality for every purse and
      purpose
   Thomaston sheets
Quality goes clear through
   Dort automobile
The quality goes in before the
      name goes on
   Zenith television sets
Quality Ice Cream
   It's still smart to be
      healthy
Quality in every drop
   Canada Paint
Quality in every extra mile
   Pennzoil motor oil
Quality in tires is the key to
      safety
   U. S. Royal tires
Quality is demonstrated by their
      performance
   Stockham Pipe & Fittings
The quality is higher than the
      price
   Juvenile Shoe Corp.

Quality is in the limestone
   Woodville Products Co.
Quality is Job 1
   Ford Motor Company
Quality is not accidental
   Goldenrod Ice Cream Co.
Quality is paramount to price
   Johnson & Johnson
Quality is standard equipment
   Mosler Safe Co.
Quality is the best policy
   Castrol motor oil
Quality is the best tradition
   Allen-Bradley Co.
Quality leaves no regrets
   Haserot Company
The quality line
   Wagner Electric Corp.
The quality line since eighty-nine
   Ruud water heaters
The quality line that's easy to
      find
   Dorman Products, Inc.
A quality loaf for quality folks
   Baby Bear Products Corp.
Quality made by Illinois Shade
   Illinois Shade Div., Slick
      Industrial Co.
The quality magazine of the boat-
      ing field
   Yachting
The quality magazine of the radio
      industry
   Radio Broadcast
The quality mark to look for
   Libbey-Owens-Ford Co.
Quality motor control
   Allen-Bradley Co.
The quality name in air condi-
      tioning and refrigera-
      tion
   York Corporation
A quality name in forest prod-
      ucts
   Long-Bell Lumber Co.
Quality never goes out of style
   Levi jeans
The quality of being special
   Sakowitz mail order service
Quality papers for industry
      since 1889
   Sonoco Products Co.
Quality part of every partition
   Upson Co.
Quality parts for auto makers
      and owners

385

Holley Carburetor Co.
Quality perpetuates preference
  Wooster paint brush
The quality pipe tobacco
  Sir Walter Raleigh tobacco
A quality product for every
    chocolate use
  Baker's Breakfast Cocoa
Quality products for home and
    family
  Scott & Fetzer Company
Quality products for quality
    living
  Mirawal Co.
Quality products known through-
    out the world for engi-
    neered quality
  Bastien-Blessing Co.
Quality protection. Ask for it
  Pennzoil motor oil
The quality razor of the world
  Gillette safety razor
Quality requires no apology
  Red Head Brand clothing
Quality, reliability, service,
    support and available
    software
  Hewlett-Packard Co.
Quality seals build the reputa-
    tion of professional
    mechanics
  Chicago Rawhide Mfg. Co.
Quality. Security. Simplicity
  Firestone Mechanically
    Fastened Pneumatic
    Tires
Quality shows through
  Drew Furniture Co.
Quality since 1846
  Philadelphia Carpet Co.
The quality slide fastener
  Talon slide fastener
Quality takes wing
  Mitsubishi Aircraft Inter-
    national, Inc.
Quality tells
  Park & Tilford whiskey
  Vat 69 whiskey
Quality tells, economy sells
  Red & White Food Stores
Quality that improves the qual-
    ity of life in your
    office
  Olympia electronic type-
    writers
Quality that makes friends,

  service that keeps them
  Borden Stove Co.
Quality that makes it last and
    last
  Presto FryDaddy deep fryer
Quality ... the best economy of
    all
  Sun Oil Company
Quality through craftsmanship
  The Hallicrafters Co.
Quality toys with a purpose
  Tinkertoy
Quality trucks always cost less
  Chevrolet trucks
Quality turns on Timken
  Timken Roller Bearing Co.
Quality without compromise
  Paris Garters
Quality you can taste
  Adohr Creamery Co.
Quality you can trust
  Crown Central Petroleum
    Corp.
Quality you can trust. Value
    you can recognize
  Iona Mfg. Co.
Quantas Airline
  The Australian airline
  Australia's round-the-world
    jet airline
  Quantas. What a name for
    an airline!
Quantas. What a name for an
    airline!
  Quantas Airline
A quarter says you're gonna love
    it
  Caffeine-Free Diet 7UP soft
    drink
A quarter turn to unseal, a
    quarter turn to seal
  American Metal Cap Co.
Quasar television sets
  For quality and depend-
    ability, shouldn't you
    have a Quasar?
  Nobody offers you more
    than Quasar
  One great idea after another
  The solid state service
    miser
Queen Lily Soap
  You can't keep a good soap
    down
The queen of all slot machines
  Maley's slot machines

386

Queen of distinctive cigarettes
  Helmar cigarettes
Queen Quality shoes
  Famous shoes for women
  Favored footwear of Her
    Majesty, "Queen for
    a Day"
Queen slide fastener
  Fit for a queen
Queen's Health salt
  It's as good as the best
    and better than the
    rest
Queenston Limestone
  Building for the ages
Quell household deodorant
  Checks odors instantly
Quest deodorant
  A winner with women
Quick. See also:
  Kwik
  Quik
The quick and gentle way to
    end a corn
  Blue-Jay corn plaster
The quick brown fox
  Smith-Corona typewriters
Quick Cooking Oats
  The quickest hot cereal
Quick, Henry, the Flit
  Flit insecticide
The quick kind you cook up
    fresh
  Kraft Foods Div., Kraftco
    Corp.
Quick relief for sunburn, too!
  Absorbine Jr.
Quick starts, long life
  Willard battery
Quick to start. Quiet on the
    go
  Lawn-Boy lawn mowers
Quick-Way Household Paste
    Cleaner
  The new slick way to chase
    dirt
The quicker picker upper
  Bounty absorbent towels
The quickest hot cereal
  Quick Cooking Oats
The quickest way to duplicate
  Ditto duplicating machine
Quickly kills garden pests
  Snarol
The quiet company
  Northwestern Mutual Life

Insurance Co.
Quik. See also:
  Kwik
  Quick
Quik chocolate milk additive
  You can't drink it slow if
    it's Quik
Quix foot pads
  It's cheaper to buy good
    pads than new hose
  Will not ruin hose
The quiz show with a heart
  Strike It Rich
Quonset huts
  America's busiest buildings

-R-

R. A. Flatt Tire Co.
  Lots of Flatt tires running
    around
R. A. Johnston Co.
  Eat Johnston Cookies, the
    taste that thrills
  Famous for biscuits
  Taste the difference
R and K Originals, Inc.
  America lives in R and K
    Originals
RCA American Communications
  The solution that beats the
    system
RCA Corp.
  The fountain head of mod-
    ern tube development
    is RCA
  The greatest music the world
    has known
  His master's voice
  The most trusted name in
    electronics
  The most trusted name in
    television
  The music America loves
    best
  The music you want
  The music you want when
    you want it
  A symbol of technical excel-
    lence
  A tradition on the move
  The world's most broadly
    based electronics com-
    pany
RCA is making television better

and better
RCA television sets
RCA Radiotron Co.
The heart of your radio
RCA Telephone Systems
The future is calling
RCA television sets
RCA is making television
better and better
RCA Victor radio receiver
The pick of the portables
RC Cola soft drink
Drink RC--for quick, fresh
energy
R. I. Tool Co.
The Tiffany of the bolt
and nut business
R. J. Gold chewing tobacco
The mild chewing plug in
a pouch
The R. T. French Co.
Canaries, the only pets that
sing
Don't feed your canary a
diet of dust
Give a canary for companion-
ship
Good things to eat come
from 1 Mustard Street
Lopsided diet may ruin your
canary's song
A song in every seed
This plus in his diet puts
song in his heart
Your canary may be over-
fed, yet undernour-
ished
Racine tires
Remember the horse-shoe
tread
Racing planned for pleasure
Garden State Racing Assn.
Radak radio receiver
You turn the knob; Radak
does the rest
Radi-Oven
Everybody appreciates the
finest
The radiant name in radio
Magnavox radio receiver
Radio. See also: Rado
Radio Age
The magazine of the hour
Radio Broadcast
The quality magazine of
the radio industry

Radio builds for the years to
come
All-American Radio Corp.
Radio built for the years to
come
All-American radio receiver
Radio Cooking School of America
Broadcasts as she bakes
Radio Corporation of America.
See: RCA
Radio Digest
The national broadcast au-
thority
Radio Guide
The national weekly of pro-
grams and personalities
The radio in America's finest
homes
Freed-Eisemann Radio Corp.
A radio in every room, a radio
for every purpose
Crosley radio receivers
Radio-ize your phonograph
Magnavox radio receiver
Radio Merchandising
The magazine of the radio
trade
Radio Retailing
The business magazine of
the radio industry
Radio School of the Bible
Moody Bible Institute of
Chicago
Radio Shack
The biggest name in little
computers
Radio station KCMO
Expanded coverage for
E-X-P-A-N-D-I-N-G
Mid-America
Radio station KDKA, Pittsburgh
Only master key to the
master market
Radio station KMPC, Beverly
Hills, Calif.
KMPC, the station of the
stars
Radio station KWK, St. Louis,
Mo.
St. Louis' own and St.
Louis owned
Radio station WJR
Michigan's greatest adver-
tising medium
Radio station WKW, St. Louis
At the right of your dial

Radio station WLW
 The nation's station
 The sports voice of the
  Midwest
Radio station WMC, Memphis,
 Tenn.
 The station most people
  listen to most
Radio station WMT
 The voice of agriculture
 The voice of Iowa
Radio station WNEW
 Entertaining New York and
  New Jersey 24 hours a
  day
 Selling New York and New
  Jersey 24 hours a day
 Serving New York and New
  Jersey 24 hours a day
Radio station WSIX, Nashville,
 Tennessee
 The voice of Tennessee's
  capital city
A radio that you can play
 Eckhardt radio receiver
The radio used by the broad-
 casting stations
 Day-Fan Electric Co.
The radio with the big plus
  value
 G. E. radio receiver
Radiola radio receiver
 Take it wherever you go
 There's a Radiola for every
  purse
 This symbol of quality is
  your protection
Radiolite watch
 Tells time in the dark
 There's no Radiolite but
  the Ingersoll Radiolite
Radio's best batteries
 French batteries
Radio's motive power since 1915
 Cunningham radio tube
Radio's richest voice
 Sparton radio receiver
Radio's richest voice since 1926
 Sparton radio receiver
Radium Dial Co.
 Luma, the radium luminous
  compound
Rado. See also: Radio
Rado Watch Co.
 The peak of Swiss watch-
  making perfection

Radway's Ready Relief
 Warmth works wonders
The rag-content loft-dried paper
  at the reasonable price
 Eastern Mfg. Co.
Rag Content Paper Mills
 Your letterhead is the voice
  of your business
Ragu Home Style spaghetti sauce
 Tastes like homemade be-
  cause it's made like
  homemade
 That's Italian!
Raid insecticide
 Raid kills bugs dead
Raid kills bugs dead
 Raid insecticide
Raid tomato and vegetable fogger
 Kills garden bugs dead.
  Naturally
The railroad of "Creative Crews"
 Milwaukee Road
The railroad of planned progress
  ... geared to the na-
  tion's future
 Rock Island Lines
The railroad that runs by the
  customer's clock
 Nickel Plate Railroad
The railroad that's always on the
  move toward a better
  way
 Santa Fe System Lines
The railroad timekeeper of
  America
 Hamilton Watch Co.
Railway Age
 One of America's great
  weeklies
The railway is the right way
 French National Railroads
The railway system that gives a
  green light to innova-
  tions
 Southern Railway Co.
The railway to everywhere in
  Canada
 Canadian National Railway
Rain & Hail Insurance Bureau
 Insure today to save tomor-
  row
 A man who can't remember
  his last hailstorm is
  likely to get one he
  will never forget
Rain or shine, it will always run

Purity salt
Rainbow fresh
   Yes detergent
A rainbow of distinctive flavors
   Hiram Walker's cordials
A rainbow of flavors
   Skittles candies
The rainy day pal
   Reflex slicker
Raise profits
   Euclid Crane & Hoist Co.
Raise your hand if you're Sure
   Sure anti-perspirant
Raisin Grape Nuts
   Crunchycheweynuttysweet
Raisinets candy
   Hooray for Raisinets!
   The movie time candy
Rajah Salad Dressing
   Preferred for its flavor,
      praised for its price
Raleigh. See also: Sir Walter
   Raleigh tobacco
Raleigh cigarettes
   It's moisturized
   The taste is richer, yet
      the smoke is milder
Raleigh Lights cigarettes
   Take the road to flavor in
      a low tar cigarette
Ralph A. Miele, Inc.
   If it's chairs ... it's
      Miele!
   If Miele doesn't have it ...
      no one has!
Ralston Purina Co.
   Health and growth for boys
      and girls
Ralston Purina Co. See also:
   Shredded Ralston
Ralston's puts the B-1 in Break-
   fast
   Shredded Ralston
Ramada Inns, Inc.
   Luxury for less
   We're changing right before
      your eyes
   We've got a new world for
      you
Rambler automobile
   America's best fleet buy
Rand dress shields
   Light as a breeze, soft as
      a cloud
   They last longer
   You'll never know you're

      wearing 'em
Rand McNally and Co.
   Serving America's schools,
      homes, commerce and
      industry
Rand shoes
   Comfortable as old carpet
      slippers
The range with a reputation
   Majestic Range
The range with the Centra-cook
   top
   Roberts & Mander Corp.
Ranger shoes
   For men of action
The ranges that bake with fresh
   air
   Estate Stove Co.
Ranier automobile
   America's smartest car
Ransome concrete
   If it calls for concrete, it
      calls for Ransome
Rap-I-Dol beauty aids
   Drafted for beauty
Rap-I-Dol hair coloring
   The master hair coloring
Rapala Div., Nordic Enterprises,
   Inc.
   World's most wanted lure
Rapid Electrotypes
   The largest plate makers
      in the world
Rapid Mfg. Co.
   The light that never fails
Rapid Thermogas Co.
   City convenience ... RFD
Rapids-Standard Co., Inc.
   It's wise to conveyorize
Raquel, Inc.
   A marvelous new perfume
Rare Taste. Ask for it by name
   J & B Rare Scotch whiskey
Raritan truck tires
   Meets today's requirements,
      sets tomorrow's stand-
      ard
Rath sausages
   Finer flavor from the Land
      O' Corn
   Smoked with hickory
Rauchbach-Goldsmith luggage
   Luggage you will love to
      travel with
   The name that means every-
      thing in luggage

Rauh house slippers
   Best for rest
Rawlings Corp.
   The finest in the field
Rawlplug Co.
   Rawlplugs hold screws fast
Rawlplugs hold screws fast
   Rawlplug Co.
Rax sandwich restaurants
   I'd rather Rax
Ray Ban bans rays
   Ray Ban sunglasses
Ray Ban sunglasses
   Ray Ban bans rays
Ray has been first from the very
      first
   Ray Oil Burner Co.
Ray-O-Vac batteries
   The ABC of radio satisfac-
      tion
   Big name in batteries
   Buy spares, they stay fresh
   Stay fresh for years
Ray Oil Burner Co.
   First, from the very first
   Ray has been first from
      the very first
Raybestos-Manhattan, Inc.
   America's best-selling brake
      lining
   The complete brake lining
      service
   It's "packed with satisfac-
      tion" when you use
      R/M
   Means safety made certain
   Reliability in rubber, as-
      bestos, sintered metal,
      specialized plastics
   Your best friends for high-
      way safety
Raybestos-Manhattan, Inc. See
      also: Grey-Rock Div.,
      Raybestos-Manhattan,
      Inc.
Rayette-Faberge, Inc.
   For twenty-five years, first
      in professional hair care
Raymond Handling Equipment,
      Ltd.
   Originator and world's
      largest builder of
      narrow aisle trucks
Raynorshyne
   Keep your car beautiful
      always

Keep your floors beautiful
   always
Keep your furniture beauti-
   ful always
Keep your leather goods
   beautiful always
Keep your shoes beautiful
   always
Raytheon Co.
   Excellence in electronics
   The most complete line of
      electronic ovens
Raytheon radio tubes
   For better reception
   The heart of reliable radio
      power
   You can't go wrong with
      Raytheon
Rayve Shampoo
   Makes him love every hair
      of your head
The razor with 1000 new edges
   Super razor
Reach for a Lucky instead of a
      sweet
   Lucky Strike cigarettes
Reach for a Sprite
   Sprite soft drink
Reach for Campbell's. It's right
      on your shelf
   Campbell's condensed soups
Reach for Ideal
   Ideal dog food
Reach for Sunbeam bread instead
   Sunbeam bread
Reach for the sun in the dairy
      case
   Azteca tortillas
Reach, heat and eat
   Morton's chicken giblets
Reach her when home is on her
      mind
   American Home
Reach out and touch someone
   Bell Telephone System
Reach the affluent in Forbes
   Forbes
Reaches the mother through her
      child
   Child Life
Reaching influential America
   United States Daily
Read. See also:
   Red
   Reed
Read and preferred by construc-

391

tion men
Construction Methods and
 Equipment
Read by everybody, everywhere
 All Fiction Field
Read Time and understand
 Time
Reader's Digest
 People have faith in Read-
  er's Digest
 The place to make friends
  for your company
 World's best seller
 The world's most-read
  magazine
Reading & Bates
 The diversified energy com-
  pany
Reading anthracite
 Naturally superior
Reading Industrial Loom
 An institution of service
Reading Railroad
 On-time-delivery is our #1
  concern
Ready. See also: Reddy
Ready to eat
 Wheaties cereal
Ready to ride right now!
 The Budd Company
Reagan bread
 For goodness sake, eat
  Reagan bread
Real bacon. No fakin'
 Hormel Bacon Bits salad
  dressing
A real bargain
 Clorox bleach
A real cigarette
 Camel cigarettes
Real farm sausage from a real
  Wisconsin farm
 Jones Dairy Farm
Real-form girdles
 Girdles of grace
Real gusto in a great light beer
 Schlitz beer
Real juices for real taste
 9-Lives cat food
The real magazine of the small
  towns
 American Woman
A real magnetic horn
 North East Electric Co.
Real or reel, Royal is best
 Royal Pictures

A real razor, made safe
 Durham-Duplex razor
Real restful rest on steel feathers
 Hercules bed springs
A real safe, not a pretense
 Taylor safes
Real Silk Hosiery
 From mill to millions
 The utmost in luxury at
  moderate prices
The real taste of beer
 Pabst Blue Ribbon beer
The real thing from Florida
 Florida Citrus Commission
The real thing in noodle soup
 Barker Food Products
The real voice of radio
 Bendix radio receiver
The really perfect printed pat-
  tern
 Pictorial Review
Really starts your engine
 Startzer automobile starter
Rebbor Candies
 Candy has energy and taste
Reckitt's Bluing
 Out of the blue comes the
  whitest wash
Reckless drivers are seldom
  wreckless long
 National Safety Council
Recoat with Spracote
 Spracote Products Corp.
Recognized as a standard
 Harrisburg couplings
Recommended by dentists sur-
  veyed 9 to 1 over all
  toothpastes combined
 Polident toothpaste
Recommended by moms like me
  who care about teeth
 Trident Sugarless Gum
Recommended by more dentists
  than any other denture
  cleaner
 Polident denture cleaner
The record is trouble-free
 Kelvinator refrigerator
Record systems that talk facts
  fast
 Diebold Safe & Lock Co.
Recordak Corp.
 First and foremost in micro-
  filming since 1928
Recorder
 The "time clock" for

machinery
Recordings for the connoisseur
    Vanguard Recording Society, Inc.
Recordio
    The world's finest home
        recording instrument
Recordisc Corp.
    Pioneers in recording
        achievement
Red. See also:
    Big Red chewing gum
    Read
    Reed
Red and blue make white
    Gilbert Paper Co.
Red & White Food Stores
    Quality tells, economy sells
Red apples for red cheeks
    Hood River Apple Growers
        Assn.
Red Book. See: Redbook
Red Brand fencing
    Your fence for keeps with
        Red Brand
Red by chance and read by
        choice
    Redbook
Red Cedar Shingle and Hand-
        split Shake Bureau
    The crowning touch of
        quality
Red Cross. See also: American
        Red Cross
Red Cross mattress
    Worthy of its name
Red Cross Shoes
    Beauty treatment for your
        feet
    Bends with your foot
    Half the fun of having feet
    The most salable shoe in
        America
    The most salable shoe in
        America today
Red Cross spaghetti
    So good it tastes good all
        alone
Red Cross towels
    I got rid of kitchen jitters
Red Devil enamel
    Covers with one coat
    No brush marks
Red Devil Glass Cutter
    It's all in the wheel
Red Devil, Inc.

World's largest manufac-
        turer of painters' and
        glaziers' tools--since
        1872
Red Devil Pliers
    Fingers of steel
    Leads the way
Red Goose shoes
    Action shoes for boys and
        girls
Red Gum dentifrice
    The toothsome paste
Red Head Brand clothing
    Quality requires no apology
Red Heart dog food
    3-flavor dog food
Red Indian lubricating oil
    The oil of endurance
Red Jacket Coal Sales Co.
    The aristocrat of smokeless
        coals
    Chief of West Virginia high
        volatile coals
    For 40 years the standard
        of West Virginia
    Justly famous
    Looks clean, is clean, stays
        clean
    More heat per dollar
    The new smokeless coal from
        Old Virginia
    Rugged as the Rockies
Red Lobster seafood restaurants
    For the seafood lover in you
Red Man chewing tobacco
    Get more out of it
    Satisfaction
The red nylon ring of reliability
    Elastic Stop Nut Corp. of
        America
Red Rock cheese
    You'll like Red Rock
Red Rose Tea
    Red Rose Tea is good tea
Red Rose Tea is good tea
    Red Rose Tea
Reda Pump Co.
    The best pump. The best buy
Redbook
    The magazine of a re-made
        world
    Red by chance and read
        by choice
Reddy. See also: Ready
Reddy Kilowatt
    Cook electrically and enjoy

the difference
Live electrically and enjoy
    the difference
Plug in, I'm Reddy
Work electrically and enjoy
    the difference
Your cheapest helper
Your electrical servant
Your power-ful worker
Redfern corsets
    The standard of corset
    fashion
Reduce or increase your weight
    Annette Kellermann health
    studios
Reduce the cost but not the heat
    Victor-American Fuel Co.
Reduces friction to a fraction
    Cellophane
Redwood City, Calif.
    Climate best by government
    test
Reece. See: Rees
Reed. See also:
    Read
    Reed
Reed & Barton sterling silver
    It's smart to choose the
    finest sterling
    Solid happiness
The reels of champions
    Penn Fishing Tackle Mfg. Co.
Re-equip/equip and profit
    Ammco Tools, Inc.
Re-equip/equip and profit with
    Bear
    Bear Mfg. Co.
Rees jack
    The jack that saves your
    back
Refined protection for motor
    cars
    Hershey locks
Refinite water softener
    Rival of the clouds
Reflecto Letters, Inc.
    Never a dull moment
Reflects good housekeeping
    Mirro Aluminum Co.
Reflects good taste
    Equitable Paper Bag
Reflex Ignition Co.
    Keep the car on the go
Reflex slicker
    The rainy day pal
Refresh! Rejoice! Remember!

    Pabst Blue Ribbon beer
Pabst Blue Ribbon beer
Refresh, revive that sleepy skin
    Dorothy Gray suntan oil
Refresh yourself
    Coca Cola soft drink
Refreshing as fresh fruit
    Beechnut Packing Co.
Refreshing as the rising sun
    American Chewing Products
    Corp.
The refreshing grape flavored
    chewing gum
    Val chewing gum
Refreshing, invigorating, strong;
    the last word in Grade
    A
    Challenge milk
Refrigeration is our business ...
    our only business
    Norcold, Inc.
The refrigerator you hear about
    but never HEAR
    Electrolux Refrigerator
Refrigerators for all purposes
    McCray Refrigerator Corp.
A refuge in time of storm
    National Reserve Life Insur-
    ance Co.
A regal guy deserves a Regal
    Tie
    Regal Neckties
Regal Neckties
    A regal guy deserves a
    Regal Tie
Regal salt
    Free running
Regal scent to center attention
    on lovely you
    Anita of Paris perfume
Regal shoes
    From maker to wearer
Regatta yacht paints
    First on the finish
Regens cigarette lighter
    If it's a Regens, it lights
Regent cigarettes
    The milder, better-tasting
    cigarette
    They cost no more
Register socially
    Hotel Delmonico, New York
    City
The registered symbol of quality
    since 1908
    Garfield Manufacturing Co.

Regular as clockwork
  Nujol laxative
A regular camel for ink
  Dunn-Pen
Reichardt Cocoa & Chocolate
  Co.
  The cup that cheers
  Even a child can tell the
    difference
Reid, Murdoch & Co.
  Our highest quality
Reis underwear
  Change to Reis
  They're cut to fit to fight
    fatigue
Reiss-Premier Pipe Co.
  You can't get a drink from
    a drinkless pipe
Relax and enjoy
  Nehi soft drink
Reliability in rubber, asbestos,
    sintered metal, spe-
    cialized plastics
  Raybestos-Manhattan, Inc.
Reliability: we count on being
    counted on
  Beech Aircraft Corp.
A reliable doll
  Cuddles doll
Reliable dolls
  The heart's desire for
    every youngster
Reliance Electric and Engineer-
    ing Co.
  Builders of the tools of
    automation
  Motor drive is more than
    power
Reliance State Bank
  Better banking, better
    service. Better join
    us
Relief is just a swallow away
  Alka-Seltzer
Relieve the strains of coupling
    trains
  Ohio Brass Co.
Relieves ingrown toenail pain in
    minutes
  Outgrow toenail pain remedy
Relieves itching of dry scalp
  Kreml shampoo
Relieves pain and itch--even
    helps reduce swelling
  Preparation H hemorrhoid
    ointment

Relieves the daily grind
  Keystone Emery Mills
Relieves twelve cold symptoms
  Dristan
Rely on lead
  Lead Industries Assn., Inc.
Rely on T I
  Texas Instruments, Inc.
Rely on us
  Louisville and Nashville
    Railroad
Rely on your brakes instead of
    your horn
  Noise Abatement Comm.
Remar bread
  Four hours fresher
  REMARkable fed with
    REMARkable bread
REMARkable fed with
  REMARkable bread
  Remar bread
The remarkable new carpet
    that's flooring the
    country!
  Densylon carpets
Rembrandt pipe
  "Heart of the root" briar
Remember, for better reading
    it's "Circle 12" books
  Circle 12 books
Remember: no one is paid to
    play Titleist
  Titleist golf balls
Remember Ronrico, best rum,
    bar none
  Ronrico rum
Remember the horse-shoe tread
  Racine tires
Remember the name, Folger's;
    you'll not forget the
    taste
  Folger's ground coffee
Remember the name, it signifies
    locker satisfaction
  Durabilt steel locker
Remember the name, you'll never
    forget the taste
  Rubsam & Horrmann
Remember the Ozarks for better
    goldfish
  Ozark Fisheries, Inc.
Remember what ARCO did
  ARCO Atlantic Richfield
    Co.
Remington. See also: Lady
  Remington electric

shaver

Remington cash register
The only way to get everything that a Remington
cash register provides
is to buy a Remington

Remington cutlery
Famous for their razor-
sharp edges

Remington Office Systems Div.,
Sperry Rand Corpora-
tion
The automated answer to
the paper explosion
The first name in business
systems
The hallmark of a system,
the symbol of accuracy
Methods that keynote the
future of business

Remington shells
For clean hits and clean
barrels
If it's Remington it's right

Remington typewriter
It writes. It adds. It
subtracts
A machine for every pur-
pose
To save business time
Works swiftly. Wears
slowly

Remoulade
New Orleans' most famous
sauce

Removes cause of tooth decay
Colgate's dental cream

Removes the dingy film
Pepsodent toothpaste

Removes the film of dirt and
smudge
Keyspray

Remy Electric Co.
The Remy standard is ex-
cellence

Rémy Martin cognac
The first name in cognac
since 1724
The centaur ... your
symbol of quality
Pride of Cognac since
1724

The Remy standard is excellence
Remy Electric Co.

Renault automobile
The car company of France

A twentieth century expression of the French civil-
ization

Renee brassiere
Next to my heart

Rengo Belt
No name in corsetry is better known

Rennus luggage
Built to last through every
trip

Rennus time clock
Time hurries in every factory

Renowned 'round the world
American Wine Co.

Rensie watches
Engineered for accuracy
Exquisite as America's
beauties
'til the end of time

Rent a born-again car
Rent-a-Wreck Auto Rental

Rent-a-Wreck Auto Rental
Rent a born-again car

Reo automobile
The car that marks my
limit
A combination not found in
any other car
The gold standard of value
Not one American car lasts
as long as Reo, not
one
Price--the only sensation
There is no other car like
Reo--not at any price
You cannot match this car

Reo-Form slips
You're always in good form
with Reo-Form

Reo lawn and garden equipment
Reo Reliables ... the powerful performers

Reo Reliables ... the powerful
performers
Reo lawn and garden
equipment

Repair 'em and wear 'em
O'Sullivan rubber heel

The repeat order truck
Fulton truck

Repetition makes reputation
Emil Brisacher & Staff

Replace fear with cheer. Send
Christmas cards this

year
Greeting Card Association
Replace utensils that wear out
with utensils that
WEAR-EVER
Wear-Ever aluminum
The reproducer supreme
Magnavox radio receiver
The reproducer with the movable
coil
Magnavox radio receiver
Republic Airlines
Nobody serves our republic
like Republic Airlines
Republic Bank, Dallas
We know no limits
Republic Brass Co.
The modern plumbers'
trade magnet
Republic Steel Corp.
In stainless, too, you can
take the pulse of
progress at Republic
Serves the world
You can take the pulse of
progress at Republic
Steel
Republic truck
More trucks in use than
any other
Research belting's double plus
Graton & Knight Co.
Research-Cottrell
It takes energy to control
the future
Research in the service of medi-
cine
G. D. Searle and Co.
A residential hotel of refinement
The Greystone, New York
City
Resilent as a reed
Wyler Incaflex shockproof
watch
Resilient floors for every need
Bonded Floors Co.
Resina Automatic Machinery
Co., Inc.
"Cap" Resina tops them
all
Resins that fit the job
Durez resins
Resistol self-conforming hats
The most comfortable hat
made
Resists fire and rot

California Redwood Associa-
tion
Resists heat and moisture
Neptolac quick drying enamel
Resists rust
Armco Steel Corp.
The resourceful company
Diamond Shamrock Corpora-
tion
The responsibility of being the
best
Wild Turkey bourbon whiskey
The responsiveness of a well
trained servant
North East Electric Co.
Rest assured
Manzelle brassiere
Marshall mattress
Times Square Hotel, New
York City
A rest cure for tired faces
Yardley's Face Cream
The rest is easy
Simons nightwear
The rest-pause that refreshes
Coca Cola Co. of Canada
The restful car
Packard automobile
Restituimus--"We restore" ...
since 1854
Phoenix of Hartford Insur-
ance Companies
The retailer's daily newspaper
Women's Wear
The retailer's line
National Blank Book Co.
Retains all the esters
Buckeye Producing Co.
Rethinking property conserva-
tion from the ground up
Allendale Mutual Insurance
Company
Retire in our sleepers instead
of retiring to your car
Baltimore & Ohio Railroad
Retlaw Visualizations
Putting ideas into picture
form
Revco, Inc.
Leader in the manufacture
of custom built-in re-
frigeration
Reveals the hidden beauty of
your hair
Halo shampoo
Reveals what it seals

397

Cellophane
Revelation pipe tobacco
    It's mild and mellow
Revere Copper and Brass, Inc.
    First and finest in copper
      and brass. Fully inte-
      grated in aluminum
Revere movie camera
    In pursuit of happiness,
      Revere adds to your
      pleasure
Revere-Wollensack Div., Minne-
    sota Mining & Manufac-
    turing Co.
    What you want is a Wollen-
      sack
Revere-Wollensack Div., Minne-
    sota Mining & Manufac-
    turing Co. See also:
    Minnesota Mining &
    Manufacturing Co.
Revive tired colors
    Sanitone Cleaners
Revlon face makeup
    A poreless-as-porcelain
      complexion
    Sorcery in a single second
Revlon, Inc.
    From the world's most re-
      nowned cosmetic re-
      search laboratories
Revlon lipstick
    It looks like you just put
      it on when you didn't
      just put it on
Revlon lipstick and nail enamel
    For matching lips and
      fingertips
Revlon nail enamel
    The nail enamel your mani-
      curist recommends
    The professional nail enamel
      you can use at home
The revolutionary copiers that
    are winning over big
    business
    Savin copiers
Rex Chainbelt, Inc.
    The chains that have grown
      up with the oil fields
    Industry's helping hand
Rex tees
    King of all tees
Rexall Drug Stores
    King of them all
    Rexall for reliability

There is one near you
You can always save with
    safety at your Rexall
    store
Rexall for reliability
    Rexall Drug Stores
Rexall "93" Hair Tonic
    Eradicates dandruff--pro-
      motes hair growth
Reyner & Bros., Inc.
    That good Pittsburgh candy
Reynolds aluminum foil wrap
    The aluminum foil you can
      count on
    The good food wrap
    Oven-tempered for flexible
      strength
    Spanning the spectrum of
      packaging
Reynolds Aluminum Supply Co.
    Service that never sleeps
Reynolds ball point pen
    Write on the ball
Reynolds lifetime aluminum
    Never before utensils like
      these
    Triple thick bottoms
Reynolds Metals Company
    Conserving our resources
      and energy. Aluminum
      can and Reynolds does
    If you see rust, you'll know
      it's not aluminum
    Where new ideas bring you
      better packaging
    Where new ideas take shape
      in aluminum
Reynolds plastic wrap
    The plastic wrap profes-
      sionals use
Reynolds Shingle Co.
    Built first--to last
Rheem air conditioners
    The air of quality
Rheem Mfg. Co.
    Making houses into homes
    World's largest manufactur-
      er of steel shipping
      containers
Rheem Mfg. Co. See also:
    Roberts Div., Rheem
    Mfg. Co.
Rheingold Beer
    Get that golden glow with
      Rheingold
    It's beer as beer should

taste
My beer is the dry beer
Rhinelander Refrigerator Co.
Made a little better than
seems necessary
Rhino enamel
Tough as the hide of a
rhinoceros
Rho-Jan plastic compacts
Light as foam, yet holds
oceans of powder
Rhode Island
A great state in which to
live and work
Rhymes with increase
Cantrece
Rhythm Step shoes
More miles per gal
More than just beautiful
shoes
Ribaux watches
America appreciates good
time
The ribbon of 1000 uses
Allpeece Corp.
Rice-A-Roni prepared rice
The San Francisco treat
Rice Council
Easy, delicious ... ver-
satile, nutritious...
Rich. See also: Louis Rich
preserved meats
Rich as a symphony
Penn Maryland whiskey
Rich as butter, sweet as a nut
Franz Butter-Nut Bread
Rich coffee always tastes better
Dwight Edwards Coffee
Rich full-bodied jam, clear
sparkling jelly
Welch's grape jelly and
grapelade
Rich in flavor
Richardson root beer
Rich in strength
Enterprise Flour
The rich low "tar"
Viceroy cigarettes
The rich milk chocolate melts in
your mouth, not in
your hand
M & M milk chocolate
Rich perfection that only na-
ture rivals
P. M. whiskey
Richard Ginori china

Finest china since 1735
Richard Hudnut Sportsman
Spirited new scent of the
sixties
Richard Hudnut toilet specialties
To know them is to love
them
Your wish fulfilled
Richards. See: Caryl Richards,
Inc.
Richardson & Boynton Co.
The heating sensation of
the century
Richardson & Robbins plum pud-
ding
America's supreme dessert
Richardson Ranger boat
The cruiser of tomorrow
Richardson root beer
Rich in flavor
Richardson's Mints
For entertaining royalty or
royally
They're pure
Richer. And, of course, costlier
Hennessy cognac
Richer juice, finer flavor
Sunkist oranges
Richest in cream
Nestle's Milk Chocolate Bar
The richest oats made delicious
Quaker Oats
Richlee elevator shoes
Elevators. Quality leather
footwear that will make
you almost 2" taller
Richmond Piston Rings
Guaranteed for the life of
the motor
Richter's Anchor Blocks
The one toy that holds fun
for years
Ricoh Copiers
Finally, a copier that gives
you an original
We respond
Ride a bicycle
Cycle Trades of America
Ride and know
Plymouth automobile
Ride like a feather in your
pocket
Rumpp Wallets
Ride the big red cars
Pacific Electric Railway
Ride the path of satisfaction

Atlas Plycron tire
Ride the road of satisfaction
Atlas Plycron tire
Rider. See: Ryder
Ridgeways Tea
Safe-Tea First
Ridpath's History of the World
The work of the century
Riegel Paper Corp.
The merchant-minded mill
with variety and reli-
ability
Rigby brushes
Preferred by particular
people for more than a
century
Right. See also:
Rite
Wright
Write
The right angle in advertising
Collin Armstrong, Inc.
The right bearing for every car
Bearing Co. of America
The right business form for
every form of business
Moore Business Forms, Inc.
The right choice for the right
time
Harvel watches
The right clean at the right
price
Spic & Span cleaning powder
Right combination, world's best
tobaccos properly aged
Chesterfield cigarettes
Right for cool comfort
Stetson hats
Right for Sunday morning
Stetson hats
RIGHT from the cyprus casks
of Goebel
Goebel beer
Right from the start
A & P Coffee
Right Guard anti-perspirant
The more protection you
need, the more protec-
tion you get
The right hand of production
Industrial Distributors,
Ltd.
The right hat for real men
Langenberg Hat Co.
The right hoist for every
application

Harnischfeger Corp.
Right in the mixing bowl, light
from the oven
Clabber Girl Baking Powder
A right kind for every purpose
Montauk Paint Mfg. Co.
The right mix at the right time
Internorth
Right on the floor
Jewel Paint & Varnish Co.
The right paper for the purpose
American Writing Paper Co.
The right point for the way you
write
Esterbrook Steel Pen Co.
The right road to health
Old York cereal
The right Scotch when all is
said and done
Johnnie Walker Red Label
Scotch whiskey
The right shoes on time
B. Friedman Shoe Co.
The right softener for the right
machine
Bounce fabric softener
The right spirit
Teacher's Highland Cream
Scotch whiskey
Right time since 1817
New Haven Clock & Watch
Co.
Right to the point
Conklin Pen Co.
Wallace Pencil Co.
Yankee tools
The right tool for painting
Wagner power painter
The right tool for the right job
True Temper Corp.
The right way to weigh right
Stimpson Computing Scale
Co.
Rightly put together to fight
both time and weather
Ohio Brass Co.
Rigid as an oak
Sturdee Folding Ironing
Table
Riker's Compound Sarsparilla
The best blood purifier
in the world
The Ring
World's outstanding boxing
magazine
Rinsenvac rug cleaner

I did it myself
Rinso
    Grease just vanishes from
        pots, pans, dishes
    Puts sunshine in your wash,
        even on rainy days
    Rinso gives suds thick as
        whipped cream
    Rinso is the only soap
        recommended by 33
        washers
    Rinso white!
Rinso gives suds thick as
    whipped cream
    Rinso
Rinso is the only soap recom-
    mended by 33 washers
    Rinso
Rinso white!
    Rinso
Ripe 'n' ready for smokin'
    steady
    Dr. Grabo pipes
The rising BARometer of whiskey
    preference
    Three Feathers whiskey
Rising higher and higher in
    public esteem
    Gardner automobile
Rising Paper Co.
    Ask your printer, he knows
        papers
Risk control means cost control
    Commercial Union Insurance
        Companies
Risk management is essential
    to sound financial
    management
    Fred S. James & Co., Inc.
Risky to pay less, needless to
    pay more
    National Printing Co.
Risqué Shoes Div., Brown Shoe
    Company
    Look Risqué from the ankles
        down
Risqué Shoes Div., Brown Shoe
    Company. See also:
    Brown Shoe Company
Rit dyes
    Don't miss the magic of
        Rit
    Dyeing with Rit is fast,
        fun, almost foolproof!
    Fast colors without slow
        boiling

The finest dye that money
    can buy
Never say dye, say Rit
You'll have better luck with
    Rit
Rite. See also:
    Right
    Wright
    Write
Rite-Grade shingles
    The roof of ages
Rite-Way Milker
    More milker for less money
Ritespoons
    The true shape of table
        silver
Rittenhouse Hotel, Philadelphia,
    Pa.
    Convenient to everywhere
Ritz-Carlton Hotel, Atlantic
    City, N. J.
    America's smartest resort
        hotel
Ritz-Carlton Hotel, Washington,
    D. C.
    A hotel so luxurious no
        other name would do
Ritz crackers
    The cracker that makes a
        thousand other things
        taste better
    He's stone deaf until you
        say RITZ
    I'm always stopping at the
        Ritz
    Nothing tastes as good as
        Ritz, but RITZ
    They just don't wilt
Rival Mfg. Co.
    It's fun to own a gift by
        Rival
Rival of the clouds
    Refinite water softener
Rival Pet Foods Div., Associated
    Products, Inc.
    When it comes to cooking
        for dogs--Rival has no
        rival
Rivaled only by reality
    Federal Radio Corp.
Rivals the beauty of the scarlet
    tanager
    Parker Pen Co.
River brown rice
    As nature made it
The river-runt does the stunt

401

Heddon fishing tackle
Rivet-Grip Steel Co.
    The most dependable joint
      known
The road of a thousand wonders
    Southern Pacific Co.
The road of planned progress
    Rock Island Lines
Road of the daily streamliners
    Union Pacific Railroad
Road of travel luxury
    Illinois Central Railroad
Road proven by millions of
      motorists
    Kendall motor oil
Road to the future
    New York Central System
Roar. See also: Rohr
Roar with Gilmore
    Gilmore Oil Co.
Roar with silence
    Gilmore Oil Co.
The roast beef king
    McGinnis restaurants
Roaster-fresh coffee made in
      the cup
    Nescafe instant coffee
Robbins. See also: Robins
Robbins & Myers. See also:
    Hunter Div., Robbins
    & Myers, Inc.
Robbins & Myers electric fan
    Use cool judgment, buy a
      good fan
Robert Burns cigar
    The aristocrat of cigars
    Have you tried one lately?
    It started me smoking
      cigars
    Take a tip from Robert
      Burns
Roberts & Mander Corp.
    Fitted flame burners
    The range with the Centra-
      cook top
    Tailored heat from the fitted
      flame
Roberts Company
    Roberts keeps you years
      ahead
    Roberts value keeps you
      years ahead
Roberts Div., Rheem Mfg. Co.
    The pro line
Roberts Div., Rheem Mfg. Co.
    See also: Rheem

Mfg. Co.
Roberts keeps you years ahead
    Roberts Company
Roberts value keeps you years
    ahead
    Roberts Company
Robertshaw Controls Company
    The energy control company
    The name that means tem-
      perature control
    P. S. The last word in
      "automatic control" is
      still Robertshaw
Robertson. See also: H. H.
    Robertson Co.
Robertson Factories, Inc.
    The most beautiful curtains
      in America
Robin Hood Flour
    Makes more loaves of better
      bread
Robin Hood Rapid Oats cereal
    Best because it's pan-
      dried
Robins. See also:
    A. H. Robins Co.
    Robbins & Myers electric
      fan
Robins conveyor belt
    For material help in mate-
      rial handling it's
      Robins
Robox emergency auto control
    Guardian of highway safety
Robust as old rye
    Old Bushmill's Irish Whiskey
Rock Bit Div., Timken Roller
      Bearing Co.
    Your best bet for the best
      bits
Rock Bit Div., Timken Roller
      Bearing Co. See also:
    Timken Roller Bearing
    Co.
Rock Flint Co.
    For the shave that never
      fails
Rock Island Lines
    The railroad of planned
      progress ... geared to
      the nation's future
    The road of planned pro-
      gress
Rock of Ages
    Standard Granite Quarries
Rock of Ages Corp.

The flawless Barre Granite
The rocket action car
Oldsmobile automobile
Rocktite
For longer-lasting beauty,
stucco paint
Rockwell-Collins Communications
Systems
The latest words in com-
munications: Rockwell-
Collins
Rockwell International
Where science gets down to
business
Rockwood Sprinkler
Water engineered by Rock-
wood cools, confines,
smothers
The rod of champions
True Temper Corp.
The rod with the fighting heart
Heddon fishing tackle
Roebling mining cables
A century of confidence
Roebuck. See: Sears Roebuck
& Co.
Roehlen Engraving Works
Where engraving is still an
art
Rogan & Co.
California investments of
greater stability
Roger & Gallet face powder
I'll cling to the powder
that clings to me
Rogers. See: William Rogers
& Co. silverware
Rohr Corp.
Dedicated to the pursuit of
excellence
Roi-Tan Little Cigars
The cigar that breathes
Man to man, Roi Tan, a
cigar you'll like
New taste enjoyment, new
smoking convenience
... anywhere, anytime
Rolaids pain reliever
How do you spell "relief"?
"Rolaids" spells 100% relief
"Rolaids" spells 100% relief
Rolaids pain reliever
Roll on rubber
Chicago Rollor Skato Co
Roll south into summer this
winter

Greyhound Corporation
The roll specialists
Eastern Specialties Co., Inc.
A roller rolls and there's ice
Norge refrigerator
The roller skate with three lives
Chicago Roller Skate Co.
Rollfast bicycles
As sturdy as they are
beautiful
Made to last
Styled for beauty
Styled for beauty, made to
last
Rollfast roller skates
Styled for beauty, made to
last
Rollin. See also: Rollins
Rollin automobile
America's only motor car
designed originally for
both 4-wheel brakes
and balloon tires
The rolling ball pen that revo-
lutionizes thin writing
Pilot Precise ball liner pen
Rollins. See also: Rollin
Rollins answers the gift question
Rollins Hosiery Mills
Rollins-Burdick-Hunter insurance
brokers
A specialist for each line
Straight talk, in any lan-
guage
Rollins Hosiery Mills
Rollins answers the gift
question
They do things for your
legs
Rollins Truck Leasing
The other big "R" in truck
leasing
Rollit pen
Writes better--always
Rolls razor
The world's largest razor
Rolls-Royce aircraft engines
Staying ahead in the race
to tomorrow
Rolls-Royce automobile
The heart and soul of a
masterpiece
A Rolls-Royce is a Rolls-
Royce
A Rolls-Royce is a Rolls-Royce
Rolls-Royce automobile

The Rolls-Royce of coaster
   wagons
      Burnham Mfg. Co.
Rollway Bearing Co.
   Engineered to the job
   Think straight ... think
      Rollway
Roma champagne
   To make a golden moment
      live forever
Roma wines
   From the heart of California
   The greatest name in wine
   Made in California for en-
      joyment throughout the
      world
   Selected from the world's
      greatest reserves of
      fine wines
   Your best buy in good
      taste
Roman. See: Martin L. Roman
Romance Readers' Guide
   A monthly review of ro-
      mance novels
Rome kitchen ware
   The aristocrat of the kitchen
   The heirloom of the future
   Rome polished copperware
      makes cooking easy for
      the home
   To bring you permanent
      cooking satisfaction
   Worthy to become heirlooms
Rome polished copperware makes
   cooking easy for the
   home
      Rome kitchen ware
Rome Wire Co.
   From wire bar to finished
      copper wire
Romweber Industries
   Furniture of timeless beauty
   Preferred for America's
      most distinguished
      homes
Rondo radio receiver
   Smart and new from every
      view
Ronnoco Coffee Co.
   You can't describe it until
      you've tried it
Ronrico, a rum to remember
      Ronrico rum
Ronrico rum
   Remember Ronrico, best

rum, bar none
   Ronrico, a rum to remember
Ronson cigarette lighters
   Automatically better
   The lighter side of business
   The people who keep im-
      proving flame
   Press, it's lit; release, it's
      out
   World's greatest lighter
   Yes, there IS a difference
Ronsonol lighter fuel
   Best for all wick type
      lighters
A roof for every building
      Bird and Son, Inc.
The roof of ages
      Rite-Grade shingles
The roof that's requested by
      name
      Carlisle single-ply roof
Rookie Cookies
   Easy to take, quick to make
Room for 5 toes!
      Educator shoe
The roomier ride
      Northwest Orient Airlines
Rooties soft drink
   Buy a rack of Rooties
The rope that endures
      Whitlock Cordage Co.
The rope you can trust
      Plymouth Cordage Co.
Rope you can trust because it
      is engineered for YOUR
      job
      Plymouth Cordage Co.
Rosa Aroma cigars
   With the aroma of the rose
Rose. See also: Betty Rose
      Clothing
Rose & Company discount brokers
   Do business with a leader
   Don't sell our discount
      short
   We provide quality broker-
      age service
Rosedale Nurseries
   Outfitters for the home
      grounds
Rosenberg Bros. & Co.
   The world's foremost dried
      fruit packers
Rosicrucians
   Truths ageless as time
Ross. See also:

404

Betsy Ross spinet piano
Will Ross, Inc.
Ross Mfg. Co.
Easily distinguished by the
yellow back
Easily identified by the
yellow back
Prevents stoppages, cleans
and purifies
Stop that leak in the toilet
tank
Ross Steering Gear
Doubles your ability to
handle your car
Easier steering, less road
shock
Handles your car like an
invisible giant
Leverage gives control
Rossville alcohol
The spirit of the nation
Rotair Burner Corp.
Silent as a coal fire, clean
as gas
The Rotarian
The magazine of service
Rotation Diet Center
Here's the diet you can live
with!
Rothschild Bros. Hat Co.
All the new ones all the
time
Roto-Rooter Corp.
And away go troubles down
the drain
Rototiller
The power tiller of a hun-
dred uses
Rough-on-rats rat poison
They'll die outside
Rougher on dirt, easiest on
clothes
Oxydol laundry detergent
Roughest on dirt, easiest on
hands
Oxydol laundry detergent
Roughneck refuse container
We build it so rugged it
loves abuse!
'Round and 'round and over
and over
Whirlpool clothes washer
Round the calendar comfort
Lennox Industries, Inc.
Round-The-Clock stockings
They fit

A 'round the year coat
Alligator raincoats
The round tire that rolls 3,000
miles further
Atlas Plycron tire
The rounded shredded wheat
Muffets
Rouse Woodcock Commodities
Brokers
The more you know about
commodities the more
you'll like RW
Where your futures become
our most precious com-
modities
The route of the Black Diamond
Lehigh Valley Railroad
Route of the Diesel-power stream-
liners
Baltimore & Ohio Railroad
Route of the incomparable empire
builder
Great Northern Railway
Route of the Vista-Dome North
Coast limited
Northern Pacific Railway
Roux Labs, Inc.
Professional cosmetics for
lovelier hair color
Rowe Price Growth Stock Fund
Like wine, a company's
future value will depend
on how well it ages
Rowe Price Prime Reserve Fund,
Inc.
Compare yields
Rowe Price Tax-Free Income
Fund, Inc.
The biggest mouth you feed
is your tax bite
Royal. See also:
Royl
U. S. Royal tires
Royal Baking Co.
The thoroughbred of breads
Royal Baking Powder
Absolutely pure
Royal Banquet whiskey
Aristocrat of blended
Scotch-type whiskey
Welcomed in the best homes
Royal Blend Coffee
Always in good taste
Morning's first thought
A "Royal Blue" broom adds life
to the rug in your

room
American Broom & Brush
Co.
Royal Crown Cola
Best by taste test
Take time for a "quick-up"
with Royal Crown
Royal Crystal fuse plug
Instantly known when blown
Royal Duke pipe
Cooler on the draw
Royal Dutch Airlines
The airline of the interna-
tional business traveler
Royal Easy Chair Co.
Push the button back--
recline
Royal Enfield bicycle
Made like a gun
Royal family of home fashions
Cannon Mills, Inc.
The royal family of motordom.
See:
Cadillac and LaSalle auto-
mobiles
LaSalle and Cadillac auto-
mobiles
Royal Flush toiletries
As masculine as the trade-
mark
Royal Gelatin
It's a matter of good taste
The tender-textured gelatin
Royal Imperial Florsheim shoes
We make them for only one
man out of every 100
Royal Imperial Florsheim shoes.
See also:
Florsheim Shoe Co.
Royal is loyal to American democ-
racy
Royal Pictures
Royal Naugahyde
The finest in expanded
vinyl fabric
The finest in vinyl uphol-
stery
Royal Pictures
Motion pictures are the
nation's relaxation
Movies make many merry
moments
Movies mean many merry
moments
Out of the reels come
real stories

Real or reel, Royal is best
Royal is loyal to American
democracy
Royal releases release your
worries
Royal portable typewriter
Give your child a career for
Christmas
How to make a bright child
brighter
Royal releases release your wor-
ries
Royal Pictures
Royal Salute Scotch whiskey
What the rich give the
wealthy
Royal Scarlet Foods
Sunny by nature
Royal Tourist automobile
Most economical in upkeep
Royal Trust Co.
No estate too small for our
administration
Royal typewriter
End the day with a smile
Every year, more Royal
typewriters are bought
in America than any
other brand
Everybody wants one
Most modern of lightweight
typewriters
The standard typewriter in
portable size
They do run easier
You can pay more but you
can't buy more
Royal vacuum cleaner
Leads the world for value
Royal Victoria Sleep Producer
The only natural remedy
Royal Worcester Corset Co.
As modern as tomorrow
Fashioned each season to
fit each season's
fashions
Royalist cigar
The friendly smoke
Royalty in slips
Aristocrat slips
The royalty of lamps
The Stiffel Co.
The royalty of leatherware
Prince Gardner Co.
The royalty of radio
Kennedy radio receiver

The royalty of radio since
 1920
 Air King radio receiver
Royl. <u>See</u>:
 John Royl and Sons
 Royal
Royledge Shelving
 The life of the pantry
Royson auto signals
 The little extra that makes
  it better
Royster. <u>See</u>: F. S. Royster
 Guano Co.
Rub 'em, tub 'em, scrub 'em,
 they come up smiling
 Jack Tar Togs
Rub your cold away
 Mistol rub
Rubberized Products Co.
 For modern bathrooms
Rubbermaid, Inc.
 Rubbermaid means better
  made
Rubbermaid means better made
 Rubbermaid, Inc.
The rubbers of a gentleman
 Everstick invisible rubber
Rubberset paint brush
 The brush with the per-
  manent wave
Rubberset shaving brush
 The bristles can't come out
Rubberset toothbrush
 The first <u>safety</u> toothbrush
Rubee. <u>See also</u>: Ruby
Rubee Furniture Mfg. Corp.
 It's the very finest be-
  cause it's Rubee
Ruberoid Company
 Fine flooring
Rubifoam dentifrice
 It cleanses, preserves, and
  beautifies the teeth so
  perfectly
Rubsam & Horrmann
 The peer of beers
 Remember the name, you'll
  never forget the taste
 Staten Island beer
 Taste the difference
Ruby. <u>See also</u>: Rubee
Ruby Lighting Corp.
 America's largest manu-
  facturer of lighting
  reproductions
Rudley's Food Stores

The best for less
Rudofker's Sons
 America's first name in for-
  mal wear
Rudy Vallee's Connecticut Yankees
 dance orchestra
 Heigh-ho, everybody!
Ruffles potato chips
 The champion chip
Rugged as the Rockies
 Red Jacket Coal Sales Co.
Rugged as the West
 Outdoor clothes
Rugged luggage
 There is only one "old faith-
  ful"
Rugs, carpets since 1825
 Bigelow-Sanford, Inc.
Rules the waves
 Venida hair net
RumBRA
 For a figure to remember
Rumford Baking Powder
 Triply protected for oven-
  time freshness
Rumpp Luggage
 The sterling of leatherware
Rumpp Wallets
 Ride like a feather in your
  pocket
Run away to sea with P and O
 P and O Lines
Runkel Bros. cocoa
 The all-purpose cocoa
 The cocoa with that choco-
  laty taste
Runs accurately without winding
 Croton watch
Runs in, will not run out
 American Grease Stick Co.
Runs like a bicycle
 Stearns Ball-Bearing Mower
Runstop Hosiery
 The vital ¼ of your costume
Ruppert's beer
 The beer that made the old
  days good
 The brews that satisfy
 The friendly beer for
  friendly people
 Make mine Ruppert
 Slow aged for finer flavor
 Some things can't be hur-
  ried
Rusco windows
 Always one step ahead of

the weather
Rush jobs are a special delight
    Big Six Press
Russ Morgan's dance orchestra
    Music in the Morgan manner
Russel Motor Axle Co.
    Master of road and load
Russell brake lining
    Engineered brake service
    Engineered sets
Russell, Bursdall Bolts
    Making strong the things
        that make America strong
Russwin-Emhart Corp.
    Unlocking new concepts in
        architectural hardware
        since 1839
Rust Craft greeting cards
    Birthday greeting cards of
        character
    Christmas greeting cards of
        character
    Easter greeting cards of
        character
    Everyday greeting cards of
        character
    Greeting cards of character
Rust-Oleum Corp.
    Any metal worth painting
        is worth protecting
    Distinctive as your own
        fingerprint
    Proved throughout industry
        for over 40 years
    Rust-Oleum quality runs
        deep
    Stops rust!
Rust-Oleum quality runs deep
    Rust-Oleum Corp.
Rust Sash & Door Co.
    Built to weather the years
Ruud water heaters
    Buy once, buy wisely, buy
        Ruud
    Perfection in rust-free
        protection
    The quality line since
        eighty-nine
Ry-Krisp
    Good for you and good to
        you
    Good to eat and good for
        you
    More pillow-y than
        willow-y
Ryder Truck Rental, Inc.

If your trucks are eating
    you alive, lease a Ryder
Rylard varnish
    The world's best varnish

-S-

S & H Green Stamps
    This year Santa's wearing
        green
S & W Fine Foods
    Better coffee every time
        with S & W
S. C. Johnson & Son
    The floor finishing author-
        ities
S. D. Warren Co. Div., Scott
        Paper Co.
    Better paper, better print-
        ing
    Constant excellence of
        product
    Paper for the printer who
        puts quality first
S. D. Warren Co. Div., Scott
        Paper Co. See also:
        Scott Paper Co.
SKF Industries, Inc.
    Puts the right bearing in
        the right place
    When you've got to be right
S. L. Allen & Co.
    Grow what you eat
S. O. S. detergent
    Cuts grease quicker
S. O. S. Magic Scouring Pads
    Clean up with S. O. S.
        It's easy
    X marks the spot where
        S. O. S. shines
SPC Communications
    The leading alternative to
        the phone company
SST Freight Carriers
    Tomorrow's freight savings
        plan--today!
STP oil additive
    Fight motor oil breakdown
SW--Symbol of excellence
    Stewart-Warner Corporation
Saab automobile
    The most intelligent car
        ever built
Saab-Fairchild 340 aircraft
    Built to be the best turbo-

prop in the world
Sabena Belgian World Airways
  Europe's most helpful airline
Sack. See also: Saks
A sack of satisfaction
  Bewley's flour
Saegertown Mineral Water Co.
  The aristocrat of ginger
    ales
Saf-De. See also:
  Safe-T
  Safe-Tea
  Safety
Saf-De-Lite headlights
  Divides the road in half
  Permits daylight speed at
    night
The safe and gentle way to end
    a corn
  Blue-Jay corn plaster
Safe and sound
  Peoples Fire Insurance Co.
The safe-and-sure deodorant
  Etiquet
The safe antiseptic
  Listerine mouth wash
The safe antiseptic with the
    pleasant taste
  Listerine mouth wash
Safe as sunshine
  Dietz lanterns
The safe bonfire
  Cyclone Catch-All Basket
Safe-Cabinet Co.
  The world's safest safe
Safe driving is a frame of mind
  Lee tires
Safe for every cough
  Pertussin cough medicine
The safe, gentle polish
  Silvo
The safe investment
  Gary Safe Co.
The safe modern way to clean
    plates and bridges
  Polident denture cleaner
The safe nursing bottle
  Hygeia Nursing Bottle Co.
Safe scaffolding for every pur-
    pose
  Patent Scaffolding Co.
Safe, sure, instant
  Stearns' Electric Rat and
    Roach Paste
The safe swab
  Q-Tips cotton swabs

The safe, swift, silent "lift"
  Turnbull Elevator Co.
Safe-T. See also:
  Saf-De
  Safe-Tea
  Safety
Safe-T Cone, the official Coneing
    cone
  Illinois Baking Corp.
Safe-Tea. See also:
  Saf-De
  Safe-T
  Safety
Safe-Tea First
  Ridgeways Tea
The safe way is the Welch way
  Welch's grape juice
The safe way out
  Von Duprin Div., Vonnegut
    Hardware Co., Inc.
Safe with soft water
  Permutit water treatment
SAFECO Insurance Co. of Amer-
    ica
  Surety bonds: the right
    cement between owner
    and contractor
Safeguard soap
  The smallest soap in the
    house
Safeguards liquid assets
  The Liquidometer Corp.
Safest, fastest and finest trains
    in America
  Baltimore & Ohio Railroad
The safest, most comfortable way
    of going places fast
  Pullman sleeping car
The safest package of milk you
    can buy
  Dacro Metal Coverall Caps
The safest thing on wheels
  Servicycle Western Corp.
Safest to use the best
  Agricultural Publishers
    Assn.
The safest way to go and the
    sure way to go there
  Pullman sleeping car
Safety. See also:
  Saf-De
  Safe-T
  Safe-Tea
Safety after dark
  Arrow headlights
Safety and conservation, our

409

aim and policy
Federal Bond & Mortgage
Co.
Safety first, friendliness, too
Association of American
Railroads
Safety first railroad
Southern Pacific Co.
Safety is always the first con-
sideration, nothing else
is so important
New York Life Insurance
Co.
Safety lies in Weed Chains
Weed tire chains
Safety on the road. Security
in space
Irving Air Chute Co.
Safety Poise Cycle Seat
The invention of a medical
expert
Safety with saving
Mutual Union Auto Insur-
ance Co.
Saflight means safety in flight
Aircraft Accessories Cor-
poration
Safticycles, Inc.
A better buy, by any com-
parison
Smooth, easy, "floating"
ride
Very TOPS in low-cost
motorized transporta-
tion
Sage. See: Peggy Sage
Saginaw Steering Gear Div.,
General Motors Corpor-
ation
Tilt the odds in your favor
Saginaw Steering Gear Div.,
General Motors Corpor-
ation. See also: Gen-
eral Motors Corporation
Sail a happy ship
Holland-American Line
Sail with the British tradition
wherever you go
Cunard Steamship Lines
Sailing the South Pacific Skies
UTA French Airlines
Saint Francis College
Our major is you
St. Joe Minerals Corporation
Discover us
St. Joseph Lead Co.

Die casting is the process
... zinc, the metal
Producers of zinc for Amer-
ican industry
St. Joseph, Mich.
Where life is complete
St. Louis Globe-Democrat
St. Louis' largest daily
St. Louis' largest daily
St. Louis Globe-Democrat
St. Louis, Mo.
Ship from the center, not
from the rim
St. Louis' own and St. Louis
owned
Radio station KWK, St.
Louis, Mo.
St. Louis Post-Dispatch
Fileworthy
St. Louis-San Francisco Railway
Co.
Call your man on the Frisco
St. Louis Star
Don't say "paper," say
"Star"
St. Paul. See also: Port Au-
thority of the City of
St. Paul
The St. Paul Insurance Cos.
Serving you around the
world ... around the
clock
St. Regis Paper Company
The nation's printing pa-
pers
Our construction products
are getting the job done
St. Regis. Serving man
and nature
St. Regis. Serving man and
nature
St. Regis Paper Company
Sainthill Levine uniforms
Uniformly good
Sakowitz mail order service
The quality of being spe-
cial
Saks. See also: Sack
Saks Shoe Corp.
If it's new, Saks has it
Sal Hepatica
For the smile of health
The mineral salt laxative
Salable to the last pair
Stanley Dutenhofer Shoe
Co.

The salad and cooking oil
Mazola vegetable oil
Salada tea
For particular people
Fresh from the gardens
Salem cigarettes
For a taste that's Spring-
time fresh
Salem softness freshens
your taste
Salem Slim Lights cigarettes
Slim in looks. Low in tar.
Refreshing Salem taste
in one beautiful box
Salem softness freshens your
taste
Salem cigarettes
Sales Affiliates, Inc.
Zephyr-screened face pow-
der
Sales specialists in every market
area
National Food Brokers Assn.
Sales through the air with the
greatest of ease
National Broadcasting Co.
Blue Network
Salesman extraordinary to your
biggest consumers
Country Life Insurance Co.
The salient six
Stephens automobile
Salomon Brothers, Inc.
Innovation plus performance
The salt cellar of America
Barton Salt Co.
The salt dentifrice
Bleachodent dentifrice
A salt for every purpose
International Salt Co.
Salt Lake City Tribune
The West's great paper
Salt Lake City, Utah
The center of scenic
America
The salt of the earth
Morton's salt
Potash Co. of America
Salt of the earth, the sub-
scribers to Needle-
craft, over one
million of them
Needlecraft Magazine
The salt that's all salt
Diamond Crystal Salt
Salted just right

June Dairy Products Co.
Saltine dentifrice
To keep teeth clean use
Saltine
Salty tang of the sea
Walker's oysters
Salvage. See: Selvage
Salvation Army
Help others help themselves
Sharing is caring
The salve with a base of old-
fashioned mutton suet
Penetro
Sam. See also: Uncle Sam
Sam Bonnart, Inc.
A hat for every face
Samaritan Sacred Songs
We do not sell our publica-
tions, they belong to
God
Same great whiskey today as
before the war
Four Roses whiskey
Sammy Kaye's dance orchestra
Swing and sway with Sammy
Kaye
Samson folding table
Strong enough to stand on
Samson irons
Whatever YOUR speed,
dial the heat YOU need
Samson shoes
Better shoes for less money
Samson tires
From out of the West
No claim is ever made
about Samson tires that
cannot be proven
Single line wear in pas-
senger car tires
Stage line wear in pas-
senger car tires
Samsonite Corp.
Business case that knows
its way around the
world
The luggage that knows
its way around the
world
The luggage that sets the
pace for luxury
The more living you do,
the more you need
Samsonite
Samuel Katz
The largest immediate de-

livery fur house
San Antonio Municipal Information Bureau
    Vacationing in San Antonio
      is a family affair
San Antonio, Texas
    The winter playground of
      America
San Francisco, Calif.
    The city that knows how
San Francisco Call
    San Francisco's leading
      evening newspaper
San Francisco Convention and
    Visitors Bureau
    You can't get the whole
      picture in just a day
      or two
San Francisco discovers a
    Golden Gait
    Chrysler automobile
San Francisco Examiner
    Monarch of the Dailies
San Francisco peninsula
    Find your place in the sun
The San Francisco treat
    Rice-A-Roni prepared rice
San Francisco's leading evening
    newspaper
    San Francisco Call
Sana-bestos Tiles
    Floor of beauty, economy
      and durability
Sana-Wall makes tile and paint
    old-fashioned
    Sana-Wall plastic wall cov-
      ering
Sana-Wall plastic wall covering
    Sana-Wall makes tile and
      paint old-fashioned
Sanat Refrigerating Co.
    Ice that never melts
Sanatogen
    The Food-Tonic
Sancho. See: Tio Sancho
    Mexican food flavorings
Sander loud speaker
    Covers the whole range
Sanders, Colonel, Kentucky
    fried chicken. See:
    Kentucky fried chicken
Sandoz, Inc.
    Original research serving
      the physician
    Sandoz thinks ahead with
      textiles

Sandoz thinks ahead with textiles
    Sandoz, Inc.
Sands Level & Tool Co.
    Sands levels tell the truth
Sands levels tell the truth
    Sands Level & Tool Co.
The sandwich spread of the na-
    tion
    Underwood's Original Deviled
      Ham
Sane toys for healthy kids
    Lionel Toy Corporation
Sanek folded tissue strips
    The sign of a smart shop
Sanford Mfg. Co.
    The ink that never fades
Sanford Truss, Inc.
    World's largest roof truss
      system
Sanforized cloth
    Fabric shrinkage held to
      mere 1%
    Sanforized, the checked
      standard of shrinkage
Sanforized, the checked stand-
    ard of shrinkage
    Sanforized cloth
Saniflush Toilet Bowl Cleaner
    The meanest chore is a
      chore no more
    Works like the others can't
Sanitarium Equipment Co.
    The health builder keeps
      you fit
The sanitary cold cream remover
    Kleenex tissue
Sanitas wall covering
    Styles for every room in
      the house
    Wash off the dirt
    The washable wall covering
    Wipe off the dust
Sanitize your dishes sparkling
    clean!
    Frigidaire Div., General
      Motors Corporation
Sanitone Cleaners
    Dry cleaning gets clothes
      cleaner
    Revive tired colors
Sanka Brand decaffeinated
    coffee
    Drink it and sleep
    Enjoy your coffee and en-
      joy yourself
    For people who love coffee

but not caffeine
Good coffee that makes
good sense. Anywhere
97% caffeine-free
The only instant coffee
that's caffeine-free
That fresh perked taste
You can drink it and sleep
Sanpeck fabric
The featured brand through-
out the land
The mark of distinction
Santa Fe all the way
Santa Fe System Lines
Santa Fe cigars
Ten to one it's a Santa Fe
Watch his smoke
Santa Fe Industries
Working to foil energy
shortages
Santa Fe System Lines
Have fun, be gay on the
Santa Fe
The railroad that's always
on the move toward a
better way
Santa Fe all the way
Sapolio
A clean nation has ever
been a strong nation
Sapphire hosiery
Lasting loveliness
Sara Lee coffee cake
Nobody doesn't like Sara
Lee
Sara Lee puts the "M-M-M"
in your morning
Sara Lee puts the "M-M-M" in
your morning
Sara Lee coffee cake
Sarah Coventry, Inc.
Fine fashion jewelry
Leading direct sellers of
fine fashion jewelry
Sarasota, Fla.
Where summer stays and
the nation plays
Saratoga, N. Y.
The spa that was inevitable
Saratoga Vichy Spring Co.
Feel fine, go alkaline
Sargent door checks
Gently as a whisper
Sargent door locks
Put your key in your own
front door

Sargeant's. See: Sergeant's
Sasieni pipe
The world's premier pipe
Satin cigarettes
Spoil yourself with Satin
Satin-finish lipstick; petal-
finish face powder
Tangee lipstick and face
powder
Satinwax
Spreads like good news
Satisfaction
Red Man chewing tobacco
Satisfaction guaranteed or your
money back
Sears Roebuck & Co.
Satisfies best
Kent cigarettes
Satisfy yourself with something
better; buy a Pontiac
Pontiac automobile
Saturday Evening Post
An American institution
Sau-Sea shrimp cocktail
Don't wait to order a shrimp
cocktail--open one
Saunders. See: Clarence
Saunders retail grocery
stores
The sausage with the just-right
seasoning
Swift's Brookfield sausage
Savabrush cleaner
Makes old paint brushes
new
Savage Arms Div., Emhart Corp.
A demonstration is a reve-
lation
For a lifetime of hunting
Largest manufacturer of
shotguns in the world
The most complete line of
firearms in the world
Ten shots quick
World's most complete line of
sporting arms and ac-
cessories
Savage Ironer
As simple as touching the
space bar of a type-
writer, quick as the
action of a piano key
Savage tires
Built to excel
Savarin coffee
The coffee served at the

Waldorf-Astoria
The coffee-er coffee
So good you want a second
cup
Save. See also: Shave
Save a place for wild life
National Wildlife Federation
Save from the bottom up
Cat's Paw rubber heel
Save the easy, automatic way;
buy U. S. Bonds
U. S. Savings Bonds
Save the Osco way
Osco drug stores
Save the surface and you save
all
Paint & Varnish Assn.
Sherwin-Williams Co.
Save the wheels that serve
America
Chevrolet automobile
Save time and space
American Tool & Machine
Co.
Save two ways
National Paint Co.
Save wandering and wondering.
Give Walnut this
Christmas
Walnut tobacco
Save with safety; shave with
safety
Gem razor
Save your eyes
Ideal Sight Restorer
Save your money, time and
shoes; read Missoula
Shopping News
Missoula Shopping News
Save yourself 2 rubs out of
every 3
Proctor & Gamble Co.
Saves a business day
DeLuxe Golden State Lim-
ited, Southern Pacific
Co.
Saves food, chills water
Illinois Refrigerator Co.
Saves shaving seconds and
second shavings
Durex Razor Blades
Saves time, labor, patience
Enterprise raisin and
grape seeder
Saves your nerves
Kaffee Hag

Savin copiers
The revolutionary copiers
that are winning over
big business
The saving flour, it goes farther
Hecker H-O Co., Inc.
The saving place
K mart Stores
Saving ways in doorways since
1895
Kinnear Corp.
The Savings and Loan Founda-
tion, Inc.
Savings and Loans. We're
the biggest little busi-
ness in America
Where you save does make
a difference
Savings and Loans. We're the
biggest little business
in America
The Savings and Loan
Foundation, Inc.
Savings Bank Association
Be SURE you save at a
savings bank
Savogran painters' supplies
Start with Savogran
The saw most carpenters use
Disston saws
Sawyer Biscuit Co.
Better biscuits made the
better way
Sawyer-Massey Co.
The imperial line of road
machinery
Saxon automobile
A good low priced car
Say hello to Pan Am
Pan American World Air-
ways, Inc.
Say it again
Virginia Dare wines
Say it with flowers
Society of American Florists
Say it with flowers, by wire
Florists Telegraph Delivery
Assn.
Say it with pictures
Commercial Photo Service
Co.
Stereopticon Lantern Slides
Say it with pictures, often
Photographers Assn. of
America
Say Seagrams and be sure

Seagram's Distillers Corp.
Seagram's Seven Crown
whiskey
Say Seagram's and be sure of
pre-war quality
Seagram's Distillers Corp.
Say Shefford for fine cheese
Shefford cheese
Say Skinless when you say frank-
furters
Visking Corp. skinless
frankfurters
Saylor's. See: Miss Saylor's
Chocolates
Scandia means craftsmanship
Scandia Packaging Machinery
Co.
Scandia Packaging Machinery Co.
Scandia means craftsmanship
Scarfe paint
Surface satisfaction
Scatter sunshine with greeting
cards
Greeting Card Association
The scenic line of the world
Denver & Rio Grande West-
ern Railroad
The scenic route
New York Central System
Schaefer beer
The finest beer we ever
brewed
Our hand has never lost
its skill
Scheirich. See: H. J.
Scheirich Co.
Schell's seeds
To grow the best, plant
the best; use Schell's
seeds
The scheme is in the seam
Way Never-Spread Mattress
Schenley Distillers Corp.
As natural as nature
The best in the house is
Schenley
First in quality
Schenley's the "buy" word
for '40
The taste it takes four
states to make
There's a difference worth
knowing
When day is done, you de-
serve the best
Schenley's the "buy" word

for '40
Schenley Distillers Corp.
Schiaparelli beauty creams
Creates essentials of beauty
Schick Electric, Inc.
The mark of quality
Schick electric shaver
By the beards of three mil-
lion prophets
The civilized way of shaving
Give him Schick's appeal
Nice work, and you CAN
get it
The perfect shave
Shave the surface and you
shave all
Schick injector razor
Morning upsetting exercises
The shave of your life for
the rest of your life
You can change these blades
in the dark
Schick Super II razor blades
Get macho close
Schickerling radio tubes
Win preference by perform-
ance
Schilling. See also: Shilling
Schilling Div., McCormick and
Co., Inc.
It's no secret ... Schilling
flavor makes all the dif-
ference in the world!
Schilling Div., McCormick and
Co., Inc. See also:
McCormick and Co.,
Inc.
Schlitz beer
The beer that made Mil-
waukee famous
The drink that made Mil-
waukee famous
Just the kiss of the hops
Real gusto in a great light
beer
Schlosser Paper Co.
For your paper needs
Schlumberger, Ltd.
Leads in automatic log
computation
Schmidt. See: Oscar Schmidt
International, Inc.
Schneider lenses
Classics of optical precision
Schneider-Mittenzwei
Homes of the better sort

Scholl's. See:
    Dr. Scholl's arch supporters
    Dr. Scholl's bunion pads
Schrader products
    Makes tires last longer
Schrader's. See: A. Schrader's
        Son
Schrafft's chocolates
    Designed for giving
Schwab. See also: Charles
        Schwab & Co., Inc.
Schwab Safe Co., Inc.
    Our products are your
        protection
Schwabacher Bros.
    The coffee of inspiration
    The coffee that's "always
        good"
    The inspiration coffee
Schwabacher-Frey stationery
        store
    It pays you to buy at
        Schwabacher-Frey
    Office supplies to business-
        like buyers
    Where departments unite
        to make service right
Schwartz Bros. Dress Co.
    Learn about little women
        from us
Schweitzer. See: Peter J.
        Schweitzer Div., Kim-
        berly-Clark Corp.
Schweppes Tonic Water
    The taste-maker
Schwobilt clothing
    Suits the South
Science for the world's well-being
    Pfizer Pharmaceuticals
Science, guardian of quality
    BerNARdin metal closures
Scientific American
    We reach the people who
        make the future happen
Scientific Anglers, Inc.
    Think system
    World's largest exclusive
        fly line manufacturer
The scientific corn-ender
    Bauer & Black
Scientific lubricants for sci-
        entific lubrication
    Swan & Finch Co.
Scientific pest control
    California Spray-Chemical
        Corp.

The scientific system of water
        treatment for all
    National Aluminate Corp.
Scientifically correct shoes for
        juveniles
    H. W. Merriam
Scoldy Lox bobby pins
    Never let your hair down
Scope breath deodorant
    Fights bad breath, doesn't
        give medicine breath
The Scotch that circles the globe
    Continental Distilling Corp.
The Scotch with a following of
        leaders
    Cutty Sark Scotch whiskey
The Scotch with character
    Black and White Scotch
        whiskey
The scotchman who KILT high
        prices, awful fresh
        MacFarlane
    MacFarlane candies
Scott. See also: C. M. Scott
        and Co.
Scott & Fetzer Company
    More growth, more balance
        and more ahead
    Quality products for home
        and family
Scott makes it better for you
    Scott Paper Co.
Scott Paper Co.
    Scott makes it better for
        you
Scott Paper Co. See also:
        S. D. Warren Co. Div.,
        Scott Paper Co.
Scott Testers, Inc.
    The sure test ... Scott
ScotTissue
    The absorbent soft white
        toilet tissue
    Do not ask for toilet paper,
        ask for ScotTissue
    For use once by one user
    Made strong to work hard
    New ScotTissue is softer
        than ever
    ScotTissue is soft as old
        linen
    Soft as old linen
    Softness for comfort,
        strength for security
ScotTissue is soft as old linen
    ScotTissue

Scott's. See also:
  Dr. Scott's Electric Flesh
    Brush
  Dr. Scott's Electric Foot
    Salve
  Dr. Scott's Electric Tooth-
    brush
Scott's Emulsion
  The cod liver oil with the
    plus value
  Palatable as milk
Scours the pan, not your hands
  Glo Soapy Scouring Pads
Scouts of the world, building for
    tomorrow
  Boy Scouts of America
Scovill Mfg. Co.
  Does a lot for you
Scranton & Lehigh Coal Co.
  The fuel that satisfies
Scratches disappear as you polish
  Old English Scratch Remov-
    ing Polish
Screens out burn and makes you
    brown
  Dorothy Gray suntan oil
Scripps-Howard newspapers
  Give light and the people
    will find their own
    way
Scripto erasable pen
  Behind every happy thumb
    there's a Scripto
Scripto pencil
  The pencil of the pros
  Perfected wood pencils
  Your write-hand man
Scudder Cash Investment Trust
  Invest in a quality name
  You get high interest with
    no strings attached
Sea Eagle boats
  The quality alternatives to
    high-cost inflatable
    boats
Sea Island Mills
  The aristocrat of shirtings
Sea Pines Plantation
  America's favorite vacation
Sea-Seald Cod Liver Oil
  Ocean fresh
See the difference
  Eveready radio batteries
Seaforth deodorant
  The finishing touch you
    can't afford to forget

How to get further with
    father
  Seaforth for men
  Stay shower-fresh all day
    long
  Step forth with Seaforth
Seaforth for men
  Seaforth deodorant
Seagram's Distillers Corp.
  Designed for your pleasure
    today, tomorrow and
    always
  Drinking and driving do not
    mix
  For a man who plans beyond
    tomorrow
  Just that much better
  Say Seagram's and be sure
  Say Seagram's and be sure
    of pre-war quality
  The seal of assurance
  Think before you drink, say
    Seagram's and be sure
  Time works wonders
  You're sure of genuineness
Seagram's Seven Crown whiskey
  Easy listening stirs with
    Seven and Seven
  Good times stir with Seven
    and Coke
  Say Seagram's and be sure
Seagram's V. O. whiskey
  Enjoy our quality in moder-
    ation
  It's smart to say Seagram's
    V. O.
  Known by the company it
    keeps
  The standard of giving
  The symbol of imported
    luxury
  Treat yourself like company
Seal in oil, seal out trouble
  National Motor Bearing Co.
The seal mechanics see most,
    use most
  Chicago Rawhide Mfg. Co.
The seal of assurance
  Seagram's Distillers Corp.
The seal of certainty upon an
    insurance policy
  Hartford Fire Insurance
    Co.
The seal that endures is the
    seal that insures
  Norwalk Vault

Seal the cylinders. Save oil
  Sealed Power piston rings
Sealastic paint brush
  The bristles are sealed, the
    brush will last
Sealastic toothbrush
  Cleans teeth all around
Seale-Lilly Ice Cream Co.
  You eat it with a smile
Sealed Power piston rings
  Best in new cars; best in
    old cars
  Long the ring leader! Now
    the line leader
  Seal the cylinders. Save
    oil
  The world rides on Sealed
    Power
Sealpax underwear
  Step thru, button two
  Two buttons on the shoulder,
    none down the front
Seals flavor in and grease out
  Golden Dipt breading
Sealtest ice cream
  Ice cream parlor taste at
    supermarket prices
Sealtex
  The bandage that breathes
Sealy Mattress Co.
  Like sleeping on a cloud
  A pillow for the body
  Sleeping on a Sealy is like
    sleeping on a cloud
  Your morning is as good
    as your mattress
The seam that sells the garment
  Willcox & Gibbs Sewing
    Machine Co.
The search ends at Wellington
    Sears
  Wellington Sears textiles
Searle. See: G. D. Searle and
  Co.
Sears. See also: Wellington
    Sears textiles
Sears Roebuck & Co.
  Satisfaction guaranteed or
    your money back
  Shop at Sears and save
  The store that never closes
  Straight talk, good values
    and satisfaction
  You can count on Sears
  You can't do better than
    Sears

Sears Roebuck & Co. electric
    typewriters
  Correcting your mistakes
    now costs less at Sears
Sears Roebuck jeans
  Take Sears back to school
Sears U. S. Government Money
    Market Trust
  Our name says it all
The season-long plant food
  Olds & Whipple
The seasoned traveler goes by
    train
  Union Pacific Railroad
The seasoning supreme
  Tabasco pepper sauce
The season's best and the best
    of seasoning
  Heinz ketchup
The season's eatings bring sea-
    son's greetings
  Dole Pineapple
The seat of the in house
  Magnolia Products, Inc.
Seattle Cedar
  'Twont krinkle, 'twont
    krack, 'twont krawl
Seattle First National Bank
  We've got all the right
    components to be one
    of your major banks
Seattle Post Intelligencer
  Seattle's only morning news-
    paper
Seattle's only morning newspaper
  Seattle Post Intelligencer
The second best nurser in the
    world
  Eveready Nurser
Secord. See: Laura Secord
    Candy
Secrets
  Actual stories of actual
    people
The secret's in the circle
  Peter Pan brassiere
Sectional Steel buildings
  Made by the mile, sold by
    the foot
Secure as the bedrock of New
    York
  New York Title & Mortgage
    Co.
Secure, fore and aft
  Multinational Insurance Brok-
    ers

418

Security is our business
    United of Omaha
Security is the keynote today,
        and every day
    Northern Insurance Co.
Security Pacific Bank
    If it has anything to do
        with money, anywhere
        in the world, we can
        help
Security since 1859
    Brink's armored car service
See America best by car
    American Petroleum Institute
See America first
    Great Northern Railway
See it all by train
    Associated British Railways
See it made
    Sunkist Fresh Fruit Drinks
See Norge before you buy
    Norge electric range
    Norge refrigerator
The SEE story of the year
    Fisher automobile bodies
See that hump
    Hump hairpin
See that name is on the box
        and brush
    Dr. Scott's Electric Tooth-
        brush
See the Americas first
    American Republic Line
See the FIRST of America first
    Chesapeake and Ohio Rail-
        way
See the First Trust first
    First Trust & Deposit Co.
See this world before the next
    Canadian Pacific Steamship
        & Railroad Co.
See twice as much for half as
        much
    Southern Pacific Co.
See what air can do for you
    Gardner-Denver Co.
See what air-conditioning is do-
        ing now
    Gardner-Denver Co.
See what happens when you start
        using American ingen-
        uity
    Standard Oil Div., Ameri-
        can Oil Co.
Seeds of satisfaction
    Associated Seed Growers

Seeds that grow in sales
    Associated Seed Growers
Seeds that satisfy
    Dominion Seed House
Seeds you can trust
    Ferry-Morse seeds
Seeger. See: Karl Seeger
Seeing is believing
    Oculens sun glasses
Seems to work like magic
    Magic-Keller Soap Works
Seen in the best company
    Vanity hats
Seen in the smartest places
        where the smartest car
        belongs
    Oldsmobile automobile
Sego evaporated milk
    Cream's rival
Seiberling air-cooled tires never
        wear smooth
    Seiberling tires
Seiberling Rubber Co. See:
        Plastics Div., Seiber-
        ling Rubber Co.
Seiberling tires
    Bites deep, stays clean,
        like a plow
    It lasts longer because it
        runs cooler
    Protective service
    Seiberling air-cooled tires
        never wear smooth
    Self-sealing, self-cementing
    So much more in quality for
        so little more in price
Seidenberg cigar
    No finer-tasting cigar at
        any price
    Smart smokers smoke Seid-
        enberg
Seiko Time Corp.
    Modern masters of time
    People trust Seiko more
        than any other watch
Seilon, world's broadest line of
        thermoplastic sheet
        materials
    Plastics Div., Seiberling
        Rubber Co.
Selas Corp. of America
    Worldwide in heat and fluid
        processing
Selby. See also: Shelby
Selby Shoe Co.
    Compare and you'll wear

Holds your foot like a
gentle hand
Use your head about your
feet
World's Fair feet
Seldom equalled, never excelled
Hyde Park beer
Select building insulation and
sound control material
Flax-li-num Insulating Co.
Select the right pencil for your
use
Eberhard Faber, Inc.
Selected from the world's greatest
reserves of fine wines
Roma wines
Selectivity--Distance--Volume--
and Ease of Operation
Atwater Kent radio receiver
Self-adjusting for wear
Blackmer Pump Co.
Self-polishing wax
Johnson's wax
Sell it in the all-day home news-
paper
New York Sunday American
Sell protection, not policies
America Fore Insurance &
Indemnity Group
Self-conforming hats
Resistol self-conforming
hats
Self reliance. It's one of our
strengths
United States Steel Corp.
Self-sealing, self-cementing
Seiberling tires
Selig Manufacturing Co., Inc.
In a word ... it's Selig
Sell at the decision level
Business Week
Sell Simpson and be sure
Simpson Timer Company
Sell the man who talks to the
farmer just before the
sale
Farm Store Merchandising
Selling and advertising to busi-
ness and industry
Industrial Marketing
Selling New York and New Jer-
sey 24 hours a day
Radio station WNEW
Sells easy ... sells fast ...
makes resales
Insulite Div., Minnesota

and Ontario Paper Co.
Sells for three cents and is worth
it!
New York Tribune
Sells hard wherever hardware
sells
Hardware Age
Selvage will tell if made by
Migell
Migell fabrics
Selznick Pictures Corp.
Create happy hours
Semet-Solvay Co. coke
The fuel without a fault
Senate beer
The brew that holds its
head high in any com-
pany
The brew with the small
bubble carbonation
Send it to the dry cleaner
American Laundry Machinery
Co.
Send it to the laundry
American Laundry Machinery
Co.
The send-off breakfast of flavor-
packed whole wheat
Shredded Ralston
Send Trend to a friend
Trend apron
Send your tax bite to bed ...
hungry
Tax-Free Income Fund, Inc.
Senour. See: Martin Senour
Co.
The sensation of radio
Thermiodyne radio receivers
The sensational new oatmeal skin
beauty treatment that
softens, whitens and
protects the complexion
Lavena beauty preparation
A sensible cigarette
Fatima cigarettes
Sensible protection, fore and
aft
American Chain Co.
The sensible spectaculars
American Motors Corp.
Sentry Insurance Co.
Looks out for you
The small business that got
big serving small busi-
ness
Serendipity mail order services

Share the distinctive touch
of Serendipity
Sergeant's. See also: Sargent
Sergeant's flea collar
Works like a powder and a
spray
Works harder when it gets
hotter
Sergeant's flea powder
Wipe 'em out, don't stir
'em up
Sergeant's pet products
Better products for man's
best friend
Sero Shirtmakers
The last of the great shirt-
makers
Serutan is Natures spelled
backwards
Serutan laxative
Serutan laxative
Be as regular as a clock
Serutan is Natures spelled
backwards
Servants for the home
Hotpoint Div., General
Electric Company
Serve summer's most delicious
drink
Welch grape juice
Serve the drink, save the bottle
Lily-Tulip Cup Corp.
Serve the meats your butcher
eats
Felin's fresh sausage
Serve the world's industries
A. P. Green Fire Brick
Co.
Serve this feast for four in a
thrifty jiffy
Armour's Treet
Served by modern hostesses
American Chewing Products
Corp.
Servel refrigerator
The boss is a different
man since we changed
to silence
The flame that freezes
Ice by wire
Men like the quiet type
Stays silent, lasts longer
Serves all Chicago
Yellow taxicabs
Serves all the West
Union Pacific Railroad

Serves in conservation
Johns-Manville Corporation
Serves the world
Republic Steel Corp.
Serves you first
Independent Insurance
Agent
Service-backed shop equipment
Snap-On Tools Corp.
Service beneath the surface
Todd Shipyards
Service beyond the contract
Dan River sheets
Haas & Howell
Service first
Houston Lighting and Power
Co.
Service guaranteed for life!
The Garcia Corp.
SERVICE, in the broadest sense
is the difference
Century Electric Co.
Service in years sells Marathon
gears
Ohio Brass Co.
Service insurance for your
machinery
Humble Oil and Refining
Co.
Service is the difference
Century Electric Co.
The service magazine
Architecture
Service motor truck
Builder of business
Service, not promises
Gulf Engineering Co.
The service railroad of America
Chicago & Eastern Illinois
Railroad
The service shop authority
Motor Service
Service that never sleeps
Reynolds Aluminum Supply
Co.
Service that saves
Norwood tires
Service that's as good as Atari
Atari television repair
service
Service through science
U. S. Royal tires
Service to industry
Fairmont Coal Bureau
Service to investors
E. F. Hutton & Co., Inc.

Service to medicine
  Wyeth Laboratories Div.,
    American Home Products
    Corp.
Service with a style
  Ford motor trucks
Servicycle Western Corp.
  The safest thing on wheels
Serving American business for
    65 years
  Victor business products
Serving America's billionarea
  Northwest Airlines, Inc.
Serving America's great builders
  Lonestar Industries, Inc.
Serving America's schools, homes,
    commerce and industry
  Rand McNally and Co.
Serving human progress through
    photography
  Kodak cameras
Serving industry constructively
    since 1902
  Miller Freeman Publications
Serving industry from A to Z
  American Rope Co.
Serving industry which serves
    mankind
  Monsanto Company
Serving man's need for knowl-
    edge ... in many ways
  McGraw-Hill, Inc.
Serving New York and New
    Jersey 24 hours a day
  Radio station WNEW
Serving the big river region
  Texas Gas Transmission
    Corp.
Serving the businessman in the
    blue denim suit
  Master Mix feed
Serving the fishermen's needs
    for over 100 years
  Fish Net & Twine Co.
Serving the golden empire
  Southern Pacific Co.
Serving the heart of industrial
    America
  Erie Railroad
Serving the investment field
    since 1931
  Arnold Bernhard & Co.,
    Inc.
Serving the nation
  Pennsylvania Railroad
Serving the nation's health

and comfort
  American Standard, Inc.
Serving through science
  U. S. Royal tires
Serving with distinction
  Har-tru tennis courts
Serving you
  Bell Telephone System
Serving you around the world
    ... around the clock
  The St. Paul Insurance
    Cos.
Serving you through science
  U. S. Rubber Co.
Servisoft Div., Water Treatment
    Corp.
  The only nicer water comes
    from the clouds
Sesamee combination padlocks
  Sesamee: resets in seconds
Sesamee: resets in seconds
  Sesamee combination pad-
    locks
Sessions clocks
  Dependable time
Set it and forget. it
  Kelvinator range
  Kelvinator refrigerator
  Silex Coffeemaker
Seton Mfg. Corp.
  America's best cartons
Sets a new braking standard
  Manhattan brake lining
Sets performance standards
  Aerospatiale Helicopter
    Corporation
Sets the pace
  Plymouth automobile
Sets the pace in valves
  O I C valves
Sets the style
  De Soto automobile
Setting new standards in sound
  Electro-Voice, Inc.
The Seven Aces--all eleven of
    them
  The Seven Aces Orchestra
The Seven Aces Orchestra
  The Seven Aces--all eleven
    of them
Seven cents a glass
  La Vor jelly
The seven course meal
  Ideal dog food
Seven good coffees in one
  Del Monte Coffee

Seven leagues ahead
  Thermadore Electrical Mfg.
    Co. Div., Morris In-
    dustries, Inc.
Seven Seas slacks
  Not the biggest--but the
    best!
  Trimness for men, slimlines
    for ladies
7UP soft drink
  Don't you feel good about
    7UP?
  Fresh-up with 7UP
  Keyed to family harmony
  No caffeine. Never had it.
    Never will
  The only thing you give up
    is calories
  7UP, the "fresh-up" drink
  7UP your thirst away
  The uncola
  You like it, it likes you
7UP soft drink. See also:
  Caffeine-Free Diet 7UP
    soft drink
7UP, the "fresh-up" drink
  7UP soft drink
7UP your thirst away
  7UP soft drink
A sewed shoe that will not rip
  W. L. Douglas shoe
Sexton. See: John Sexton Co.
Seymour blanket
  A blanket invitation to
    sleep
A shade better than the rest
  Superior Hat Co.
A shade is only as good as its
    rollers
  Stewart Hartshorn Co.
Shaft-Pierce Shoe Co.
  Double welt means double
    wear
  Keeps children's feet as
    nature made them
  Specialists in children's
    good shoes since 1892
Shake 'n' Bake coating mix
  The sit down dinner
Shake the salt habit
  No-Salt salt substitute
Shakeproof Lock Washer Co.
  It's the twisted teeth that
    lock
Shakes the flask, not the
    building

Flotex Foundry Shakeout
Shakey's, Incorporated
  Don't stand still for the 80's
The Shaler Company
  The Profit Line
Shameless--for the modern Eve
  Shameless perfume
Shameless perfume
  Shameless--for the modern
    Eve
Shamrock clothes hamper
  When it's a Shamrock,
    you've got the best
Shane Co. direct diamond im-
    porters
  Now you have a friend in
    the diamond business
Shane Uniform Co.
  Look smarter, wear better
Shaped to conform to nature's
    laws
  Si-wel-clo water closet
Shaped to fit like your stockings
  Foot Saver Shoes
Shapemakers to the world's most
    beautiful women
  Treo Co., Inc.
Shar-Loo Slips
  The slip that can't slip
Share the cost of living
  American Cancer Society
Share the distinctive touch of
    Serendipity
  Serendipity mail order
    service
Share the load and save the ex-
    pense
  Chessie System Railroads
Sharing greatly in America's
    growth
  General Telephone & Elec-
    tronics Corp.
Sharing is caring
  Salvation Army
Sharing the responsibilities of
    modern medicine
  Stanlabs, Inc.
Sharon Steel Corp.
  America's foremost producer
    of custom steels
Sharp Electronics Corp.
  From Sharp minds come
    Sharp products
Sharp-Moore Meat Co.
  Smoked meats that are
    treats

Sharp PC-1500 computer
  The colorful portable computer
Sharp's. See: Hal Sharp's Golden Bears dance orchestra
Shave. See also: Save
Shave and save with Marlin blades
  Marlin razor blades
Shave electrically. A close shave in minutes without cutting
  Vibro-Shave electric razor
The shave is better when the lather stays wetter
  Lifebuoy Shaving Cream
The shave of your life for the rest of your life
  Schick injector razor
The shave that clicks
  King Razor Co.
Shave the surface and you shave all
  Schick electric shaver
Shave with a smile
  Durham-Duplex razor
Shaw-Walker steel filing cabinets
  Built like a skyscraper
  Free-coasting files
  Lifetime office equipment
She drives a Duesenberg
  Duesenberg automobile
She gave me bride ideas
  Kleenex tissue
She has it made
  Clairol, Inc.
She likes the fragrance
  Henry Sutliff Tobacco Co.
She merely carried the daisy chain ... yet she has "Athlete's Foot!"
  Absorbine Jr.
She walks in beauty
  Brauer Bros. Shoe Co.
She was beautiful in her sleep because her skin was wide awake
  Woodbury's Cold Cream
She who prizes beauty must obey Nature's law!
  Post's Bran Flakes
Sheaffer. See also:
  Sheffer
  W. A. Sheaffer Pen Co.
Sheaffer Eaton

It helps treasurers budget their time
  Shearson/American Express
The flagship of the financial world
Sheath the leg in loveliness
  Cameron nylon stockings
Sheer makeup for sheer beauty
  Houbigant
A sheer veil of scented mist
  Cheramy perfume
Sheet music to sing about
  Pepperell sheets
Sheffer. See also: Sheaffer
The Sheffer Corp.
  Sheffer, the muscles of automation
Sheffer, the muscles of automation
  The Sheffer Corp.
Shefford cheese
  Pot-luck or full dress
  Say Shefford for fine cheese
  Zest at its best
Shelby. See also: Selby
Shelby bicycle
  America's quality bicycle
  Best bicycle buy
  Best bike to sell
  Care for your bike and you'll never hike
Shell gasoline
  The fuel of the future
  Try a tankful of research genius
Shell motor oil
  Does four jobs at once
Shell Oil Company
  Come to Shell for the answers
  Finer fuels for the age of flight
  Horizons widen through Shell research
  Sign of a better future for you
  You can be sure of Shell
Shells out better, too
  Pfister Associated Growers
Shelter Life Insurance Co.
  All the shield you'll ever need
Shelvador refrigerator
  This much more in a Shelvador
Shephard Niles Crane and Hoist

Corp.
Giving industry a lift since
1878
The most widely used elec-
tric hoist in America
Shepp Ranch (Idaho)
The ultimate vacation re-
sort
Sheriff's. See: Shirriff's
Sherwin-Williams Co.
All you need to know about
paint
Coatings, colors and chem-
icals for industry
Save the surface and you
save all
Cover the earth
She's sure--are you?
Odorono deodorant
Shift your gears from the steer-
ing wheel
C-H magnetic gear shift
Shilling. See also: Schilling
A shilling in London, a quarter
here
Pall Mall cigarettes
A shine in every drop
Black Silk stove polish
A shine is the sign of a healthy
shoe
Shinola
The shine of approval
Mr. Clean cleaning fluid
The shine won't crack off
Johnson's self-shining shoe
polish
Shines aluminum fast
Brillo Cleanser
Shines as it dries
Simoniz
Shines more than windows!
Windex glass cleaner
A shiny nose is a thorn in the
heart of charm
Primrose face powder
Shinola
America's home shoe polish
A shine is the sign of a
healthy shoe
Ship from the center, not from
the rim
St. Louis, Mo.
Ship 'n Shore, Inc.
Lead the Ship 'n Shore life
Ships of the air can't stop for
repair

Wolf's Head motor oil
The ships that serve Hawaii,
South Seas and Aus-
tralia
Matson Navigation Co.
Shir Gar garter
The one really comfortable
garter
Shirriff's Lushus jelly
The flavor is sealed in the
flavor bud
Shirriff's marmalade
Made from a rare old recipe
Makes better breakfasts
To bid you good morning
Shirriff's vanilla
Less than a cent's worth
will flavor a cake
Sho. See also: Show
Sho-Lite, Inc.
The combination pilot light
and switch
A glass arm conveys the
light
You know when a light is
on, you know when a
light is off
The shock absorber that shifts
gears
Struthers Mfg. Co.
The shoe everybody knows, and
almost everybody wears
Melville Shoe Corp.
The shoes of champions
Keds
The shoe that holds its shape
W. L. Douglas shoes
The shoe that's different
Field & Flint Co.
The shoe that's standardized
Educator shoe
The shoe with a memory
Johnson & Murphy shoe
A shoe with a talking point
Teeple Shoe Co.
The shoe with the beautiful fit
Naturalizer shoes
The shoe with the mileage
W. H. Walker & Co.
The shoe with the youthful feel
Air Step shoe
Shoes for all the family
Ground Gripper shoes
Shoes of character
Vollman Lawrence Co.
Shoes of worth

Nettleton shoes
The shoes you order are the shoes
    you get
    P. J. Harvey Shoe Co.
Shop at Sears and save
    Sears Roebuck & Co.
Shop early and easily
    Bell Telephone System
Shop with people of taste
    B. Altman & Co.
Short lengths, easy to eat
    Mueller's macaroni
Short on work, long on flavor
    Del Monte fruits
Shorter days mean longer odds
    --against you
    National Safety Council
The shortest distance between
    two hearts
    Indiscreet Perfume
The shortest route to the mail
    chute
    Dictaphone Corp.
The shortest word for longest
    mileage
    General tires
Shot from guns
    Quaker Oats Company
    Quaker Puffed Rice
Shout detergent
    Shout it out
Shout it out
    Shout detergent
The shovel with a backbone
    Union Fork & Hoe Co.
Show. See also: Sho
"Show-How" is know-how in
    action
    Greenfield Tap & Die Corp.
Show off your hair, not the
    itching dandruff
    Head and Shoulders sham-
    poo
Show your colors; live with the
    symbol of liberty
    Flag Products, Inc.
Shower yourself with skin care
    Liqua 4 Skin Cleansing
    System
Shows good form in the stretch
    Lastex swim suit
Shows only the reflection
    Pratt & Lambert varnish
Shows the way!
    Masonite Corp.
Shows what it protects

Cellophane
Shredded Ralston
    Bite size
    Ralston's puts the B-1 in
    Breakfast
    The send-off breakfast of
    flavor-packed whole
    wheat
    Spirits soar, energy zooms
    when you help yourself
    to Shredded Ralston
Shredded Ralston. See also:
    Ralston Purina Co.
Shredded Wheat
    All the meat of the golden
    wheat
    The cereal you can serve a
    dozen ways
    A full meal in two biscuits
    Health insurance for the
    family
    I have a new man for a
    husband
    It's mother who guards the
    family's health
    The national breakfast
Shredded Wheat. See also:
    Kellogg's Shredded
    Mini-Wheat cereal
Shredded wheat that's fun to
    eat
    Kellogg's Shredded Mini-
    Wheat cereal
Shrimply. See also: Simply
Shrimply delicious
    Long John Silver's seafood
    restaurants
Shur. See also:
    Shure
    Sure
Shur-Gro fertilizer
    For the land's sake use
    Shur-Gro
Shur-Stop automatic fire ex-
    tinguisher
    The automatic fireman
    The automatic fireman on
    the wall
Shure. See also:
    Shur
    Sure
Shure Brothers, Inc.
    High fidelity phone cart-
    ridges ... world stand-
    ard wherever sound
    quality is paramount

426

Si-wel-clo water closet
Shaped to conform to nature's laws
Siddalls. See: Frank Siddalls Soap
Sierra Candy Co.
For the lady of your heart
Sierra Pine Soap
Where complexions are fine there's always pine
Sifted through silk
Hanley & Kinsella Spices
Pussywillow face powder
Sigmor Corporation
We have the momentum
Sigmund Ullman & Co.
After all, ink makes the picture
Sign of a better future for you
Shell Oil Company
The sign of a better job
Frank Adam Electric Co.
The sign of a good cigar
United Cigar Stores
The sign of a health mouth
Amerdent mouthwash
The sign of a lifetime
W. A. Sheaffer Pen Co.
The sign of a new prosperity in agriculture
H. Ferguson Farm Equipment
The sign of a smart shop
Sanek folded tissue strips
The sign of better taste
Mott's Apple Juice
The sign of extra service
Esso gasoline
Sign of good cooking
Gravy Master
The sign of good taste
Distillers & Brewers Corp. of America
Sign of happy travel
Downtowner Corporation
The sign of paint success
Acme White Lead & Color Works
The sign of precision
Skan Exposure Meter
Sign of the leader in lawn/ garden equipment
Wheel Horse Products, Inc.
Sign of the right time
Zodiac Watch Co.
The sign of tomorrow ...

today
General Tire & Rubber Co.
The sign the nation knows
Socony Vacuum Oil Co.
The Signal
Prints the news, tells the truth
A signal for every traffic need
American Gas Accumulator Co.
Signal safety with O-B bonds
Ohio Brass Co.
Signal with a smile
Aermore exhaust horn
Signed, sealed and delicious
Old Taylor whiskey
Signs of long life
Artkraft Sign Co.
Silent as a Christmas candle
Electrolux Refrigerator
Silent as a coal fire, clean as gas
Rotair Burner Corp.
Silent as the rays of the sun
Silent Glow Oil Burner
Silent as the sun
Silent Glow Oil Burner
Silent Automatic Corp.
The noiseless oil burner
The silent drapery track
Silent Gliss, Inc.
The silent four
Peerless Electric Co.
Silent Gliss, Inc.
Manufacturers of quality drapery hardware since 1903
The silent drapery track
Silent Glow Oil Burner
Silent as the rays of the sun
Silent as the sun
The silent grey fellow
Harley-Davidson motorcycle
Silent partners in famous foods
Stange seasonings
Silent refrigeration at low cost
National Refrigerating Co.
The silent servant
National Refrigerating Co.
The silent servant with a hundred hands
Hoosier Mfg. Co.
Silex Coffeemaker
Set it and forget it
Silex makes "Merry Christmas" last all year

Silex makes "Merry Christmas"
last all year
Silex Coffeemaker
Silhouette smooth
Sitroux hair net
Silk stockings that wear
Gotham silk hosiery
Silks for every purpose
Belding Bros.
Silks of enduring quality
Belding Bros.
Silvaire aircraft
Ask the pilot who flies Sil-
vaire
First in all-metal personal
planes
Silver Buckle Coffee
The kind to buckle to
Silver King food mixers
The best mixers
Silver Spray soft drink
It was inevitable
Silver with a past, a present
and a future
International Silver Co.
Silverglo lamps
Daylight's only rival
Eye-ease at the snap of a
switch
The lamp that chases gloom
and glare
The light that lightens
labor
The modern genie of the
lamp
Silver's. See: Long John Sil-
ver's seafood restau-
rants
Silvo
The safe, gentle polish
Simmons. See also: Symons
Simmons Chains
Always "correct" in style
Simmons Company
Built for sleep
Makers of the world's only
electronic blanket
Nature's sweet restorer
One third of your life is
spent in bed
World's largest mattress
maker
Simmons Fastener Corp.
Quality fastening products
for industry
Simmons gloves

Fit all hands and all purses
Simon Bros. shoes
The walk of the town
Simon Bros. straw handbags
Nationally recognized as the
"straw pioneer"
Tropical masterpieces
Where technicolor comes to
life
Simon Manges and Son, Inc.
We care about color
Simoniz
Keeps car new
Motorists wise Simoniz
Motorists wise Simoniz;
housewives do likewise
Perfect start to a lasting
finish
Shines as it dries
Simons nightwear
The rest is easy
The simple car
Gas-au-lec automobile
Simple in operation--startling
in efficiency
C-H magnetic gear shift
Simple--Sturdy--Accessible.
Absolutely prevents
stalling
Dyneto-Entz automobile
starter
The simplest electric refrigerator
Electro-Kold Corp.
Simplex electronic time calculator
An American tradition, grow-
ing with time
Simplex Ironer
It is a mark of intelligent
housekeeping to possess
a Simplex Ironer
Simplex piston rings
The velvet power piston
ring
Simplex shoes
Keep young feet young
Keep your feet young
Simplicity and a Strathmore
paper
Strathmore Paper Co.
Simplicity davenport sofa bed
Handsome and doubly use-
ful
Simplicity Pattern Co., Inc.
The pattern people
Simplicity--Reliability
Westinghouse automobile

electric systems
The simplified electric refrigerator
ElectrICE refrigerator
The simplified travel guide
Motor Trips
Simplify the business of homekeeping
Fuller brushes
Simply. See also: Shrimply
Simply brilliant
Canon AP-500 electronic typewriter
Simply brush it on
Kyanize paints
Simply say Delco
Delco storage batteries
Simpson Timer Company
Sell Simpson and be sure
Since 1720, a family heritage of careful boat building
C. P. Leek and Sons, Inc.
Since 1808, a tradition in factoring and financing
William Iselin and Co., Inc.
Since 1833 ... better vision for better living
American Optical Co.
Since 1846, the quality of elegance underfoot
Philadelphia Carpet Co.
Since 1847 the trusted and authoritative name in dictionaries
G. and C. Merriam Co.
Since 1857 ... the standard of excellence in men's footwear
Foot-Joy shoes
Since 1867 maker of watches of the highest character
Longines-Wittnauer Watch Co.
Since 1867 ... the first name in materials handling
The Louden Machinery Co.
Since 1874 stringed instrument house of the masters
William Lewis and Son
Since 1876, the servant of the well-dressed woman
White Sewing Machine
Since 1877, America's first bicycle
Columbia bicycles
Since 1886 ... scientifically

designed for practical use
John Blue Co., Inc.
Since 1900, America's hardest working truck
Mack trucks
Since 1904 fine plumbing fixtures
Eljer Plumbingware Div., Wallace-Murray Corp.
Since 1910, America's No. 1 scratchproof wood finish
Stainwax
Since 1921 ... the engine builders source!
Muskegon Piston Ring Co.
Since 1922, leader in motivating people
E. F. MacDonald Co.
Since 1928--industry leadership in heating and air conditioning
Fraser and Johnston Co.
Sinclair gasoline
Liquid dynamite under control
Sinclair Oil Corp.
For every machine of every degree of wear there is a Sinclair oil to suit its speed and seal its power
A great name in oil
Keeps your motor clean as a whistle
Sing out for Jay's, a pip of a chip
Jay's potato chips
Singapore Airlines
A great way to fly
Singer Co. See: Friden Div., Singer Co.
Singer sewing machine
Make it yourself on a Singer
Singer sewing machine oil
A specially prepared lubricant for household sewing machines
Singing
The aristocrat of music magazines
Single line wear in passenger car tires
Samson tires
A single match is your year's kindling
Bryant Heater Co.

429

The single six
  Hartman radio receiver
Sioux tools
  The Sioux way is the better
    way
The Sioux way is the better way
  Sioux tools
Sip-It cough remedy
  Nip it with Sip-It
Sir Walter Raleigh tobacco
  The quality pipe tobacco
  Sooner or later, your favor-
    ite tobacco
Sirrine. See: J. E. Sirrine &
  Co.
The sit down dinner
  Shake 'n' Bake coating mix
Sitroux hair net
  The hair net that sits true
  Silhouette smooth
Sitroux tissue
  The box with the bow on
    top
Six and a half billion dollars of
    protection for our
    policyholders
  Great-West Life Assurance
    Co.
Six delicious flavors--Strawberry,
    raspberry, cherry,
    orange, lemon and lime
  Jell-O gelatin dessert
Six good companions
  Kaywoodie pipe
640 trips to the moon
  Oldsmobile automobile
Sixteen skin lotion
  Must clear your skin
The 60-second workout
  Vitalis hair tonic
60,000 owners drove it to suc-
    cess
  Mercury automobile
Sizzling is silly
  Duo-Therm Oil Burner
Skaggs. See: O. P. Skaggs
  Food Stores
Skan Exposure Meter
  The sign of precision
The skate with a backbone
  Winchester Repeating Arms
    Co.
Skelgas gasoline
  For quality you can
    depend on ... depend
    on Skelgas

Skelly Oil Co.
  The best of miles
  There is no substitute for
    quality
  The utmost in lubrication
Ski Industries America
  Authentically ski
The skier's tailor since 1927
  White Stag Mfg. Co.
Skil Corp.
  Go with the pick of the pros
  Skil makes it easy
Skil makes it easy
  Skil Corp.
The skill is in the can
  Bradley & Vrooman Co.
A skilled hand in chemistry ...
    at work for you
  Nopco Chemical Co.
Skin level shave
  Packard electric shaver
The skin you love to touch
  Jergens Lotion
  Woodbury's Facial Soap
Skinner garment linings
  Look for the name in the
    selvage
  A matter of pride, pleasure
    and good, plain sense
Skin's greatest guardian
  Frostilla
Skip the rest and drive the best
  Federal tires
Skippy peanut butter
  If you like peanuts, you'll
    like Skippy
  It's hard to beat Skippy
Skittles candies
  A rainbow of flavors
Skoal chewing tobacco
  A pinch is all it takes
Skol suntan oil
  If you look like a lobster,
    you'll act like a crab
  Skol tan keeps you "outdoor
    lovely"
Skol tan keeps you "outdoor
    lovely"
  Skol suntan oil
Skookum Packers Assn.
  Famously good
Sky-high style, down to earth
    comfort
  Winthrop shoes
Skylark fragrance
  Gay and spirited as young

430

laughter
It's all in fun
Slate--consider its uses
National Slate Association
Slays all insects
Slazol
Slazengers, Inc.
Covers a world of sports
Slazol
Slays all insects
Sleep. See also: Edward Sleep
Tire Sales
A sleep-aid for the eighties
Nytol
Sleep beautifully on Dan River
sheets
Dan River sheets
Sleep electrically and enjoy the
difference
Collins electric blanket
Sleep going to keep going
Pullman sleeping car
Sleep like a kitten, arrive fresh
as a daisy
Chesapeake and Ohio Rail-
way
Sleep like a log, wake like a
lark
Telechron Electric Clock
Sleep on Spring-Air
Spring-Air mattress
Sleep to the sleepless, rest to
the restless
Ostermoor mattress
Sleep under a Kenwood for the
rest of your life
Kenwood Blankets
Sleeping on a Sealy is like
sleeping on a cloud
Sealy Mattress Co.
Sliced sunshine, straight from
the tropics
Del Monte pineapple
Slick Airways
Freight by air
Slide Fasteners, Inc.
The favorite home-sewing
notion of the nation
Slides over the face like skis
over snow
Gillette Blue Blades
Slightly more portable by the
bottle
Old Grand-Dad Whiskey
Slim in looks. Low in tar.
Refreshing Salem

taste in one beautiful
box
Salem Slim Lights cigarettes
Slim-Mint gum
The best friend your will-
power ever had
The modern aid to appetite
control
Slingerland. See also: J. H.
Slingerland
Slingerland Drum Co.
The foremost in drums
Slip into a Bradley and out-of-
doors!
Bradley bathing suit
Slip into something tan. Copper-
tone
Coppertone sun tan lotion
The slip that can't slip
Shar-Loo Slips
Slipper-free where the foot bends
Bates Shoe Co.
Slippers of merit
Kozy Komfort slippers
Sloan's Liniment
As comfortable as a kitchen
before a fireplace
The family liniment
Famous name in pain relief
Keep it handy
Kills pain
The world's liniment
Sloat & Scanlon
Depression spells opportun-
ity for the real investor
Slow aged for finer flavor
Ruppert's beer
Sly. See: W. W. Sly Mfg. Co.
The small business that got big
serving small business
Sentry Insurance Co.
Small cost for great richness
Algoma Panel Co.
Small enough to mount on a
stamp
Engel Art Corners
Small in size, great otherwise
J. H. Williams & Co.
The small lathe for the big job
Dalton lathe
The smaller fine car
Allen automobile
The smallest soap in the house
Safeguard soap
Smart. See also: Bob Smart
Shoe Co.

Smart and new from every view
　　Rondo radio receiver
Smart enough for sleepwalking
　　Textron Pajamas
Smart people, smart money
　　American Credit Indemnity
　　　Company
Smart Set
　　True stories from real life
The smart set
　　Prim Miss brassieres and
　　　girdles
Smart shoes for beautiful feet
　　Julian & Hokenge Co.
Smart smokers smoke Seidenberg
　　Seidenberg cigar
Smart, smooth, sensibly priced
　　Gilbey's vodka
Smart to be seen in, smarter to
　　buy
　　Studebaker automobile
The smart way to plan
　　Morris Plan
Smarter shoes for natural walk-
　　ing
　　Natural Bridge Shoemakers
The smartest cool suit, the
　　coolest smart suit
　　Haspel seersucker
The smartest thing on two feet
　　Esquire sock
The smartest thing on wheels
　　Lyon Whitewall Tires
Smartest togs on the beach
　　Asbury Mills
The smartest zippers are fabric
　　covered
　　Waldes-Kover Zip
The Smead Mfg. Co.
　　Your one-source solution to
　　　every film problem
Smells better in the pouch;
　　smokes better in the
　　　pipe
　　Model tobacco
Smile at miles
　　Lee tires
A smile in every glass
　　Hazel-Atlas Glass Co.
A smile in every spoonful
　　Stokeley's baby foods
Smile while you can, and can
　　while you smile
　　Kerr Fruit Jar Co.
Smilen Bros.
　　Fruiterers of distinction

In the garden today, on
　　your table tomorrow
Smirnoff vodka
　　The greatest name in vodka
　　It leaves you breathless
　　Smirnoff vodka leaves you
　　　breathless
　　Smirnoff vodka leaves you breath-
　　　less
　　Smirnoff vodka
Smith. See also:
　　Edwin C. Smith and Co.,
　　　Inc.
　　H. P. Smith Paper Co.
　　J. P. Smith Shoe Co.
　　Kate Smith radio greeting
　　Kenneth Smith
　　Lew Smith Beads
Smith & Wesson revolver
　　Protect your family
Smith Brothers cough drops
　　The cheapest health insur-
　　　ance in the world
　　A cough is a social blunder
　　Drop that cough
　　Famous since 1847
Smith-Corona typewriters
　　The quick brown fox
　　Think ahead--think SCM
Smith-Douglass Div., Borden
　　Chemical Co.
　　You can depend on the in-
　　　tegrity and quality of
　　　Smith-Douglass
Smith glass cutter
　　It's all in the wheel
Smith water heaters
　　Guardian of the nation's
　　　health
Smithfield Meat
　　For those who really like to
　　　eat
Smithfield Meat Spread
　　It's joy in a jar
Smitty builds walls for keeps
　　Edwin C. Smith and Co.,
　　　Inc.
Smokador Mfg. Co.
　　The ashless ashstand
Smoke all 7
　　Viceroy cigarettes
Smoke all you like, like all you
　　smoke
　　L & H Stern Co.
Smoke behind means trouble
　　ahead

Perfect Circle piston rings
Smoke Omar for aroma
   Omar cigarettes
Smoke that never varies from
   fires that never die
   Swift's Premium meats
The smoke with a smile
   Briggs pipe mixture
Smoked meats that are treats
   Sharp-Moore Meat Co.
Smoked with hickory
   Rath sausages
Smokemaster pipe
   The pipe that sidetracks
   moisture
The smoker's friend
   Bost toothpaste
The smoker's toothpaste
   ToPol toothpaste
Smokes fresher--and tastes bet-
   ter than any other
   menthol cigarette
   Newport cigarettes
Smooth as a kitten's ear
   Hammond Cedar Co.
Smooth as a love song, modern
   as jive
   Corinthia Lipstick
Smooth as silk but not high hat
   Kessler's blended whiskey
Smooth as silk, strong as steel
   J. Dixon Crucible Co.
Smooth, easy, "floating" ride
   Safticycles, Inc.
Smooth 'n' easy-going
   Lazy Joe Casuals Shoes
Smooth sailing with Old Anchor
   Beer
   Old Anchor Beer
The smooth toothpaste
   Chlorax toothpaste
The smooth way to rough it
   Coleman Co., Inc.
Smoother faces
   Gem razor
Smoother, lighter, richer than
   ever
   Three Feathers whiskey
Smoother than velvet
   McCormick and Co., Inc.
Smoothest "afloat"
   Dodge automobile
The smoothest cigarette
   Old Gold cigarettes
Smoothest smoking tobacco
   Velvet Tobacco

Smoothing industry's pathway for
   nearly half a century
   Messinger Bearings, Inc.
Smooths the healing right in
   Vaseline Intensive Care Lo-
   tion
The snack that makes ordinary
   occasions special
   Planters salted peanuts
Snacks candy
   It's butter rich
   Perfection in a confection
Snap back with Stanback
   Stanback Headache Powders
Snap-On Tools Corp.
   Choice of better mechanics
   For all industry
   Service-backed shop equip-
   ment
The snap with the turtle back
   So E-Z snap fastener
Snapper lawn mower
   Discover the difference
Snapshots, often, are all that
   remain after your dear
   ones go
   Photographers Assn. of
   America
Snapshots remain long after
   you go
   Photographers Assn. of
   America
The snapshots you'll want tomor-
   row, you must take
   today
   Kodak cameras
Snarol
   Quickly kills garden pests
Snickers candy bar
   Packed with peanuts,
   Snickers really satisfies
Snider's. See also:
   Snyder
   Snyder's
Snider's tomato products
   Adds zest
   If the Snider folks put it
   up, it tastes like home
Snug as a mother's hug
   Merrichild Sleepers
Snugtex
   Keeps shirts smooth and
   trousers snug
Snyder. See:
   H. P. Snyder Mfg. Co.
   Snider's tomato products

Snyder's confections
Snyder's confections
    I can't make all the candy
      in the world, so I just
      make the best of it
So advanced it's simple
    Canon camera
So beautifully practical
    Jenn-Air Corp.
So comfortable anything goes
    Hush Puppies shoes
So cool and caressing and swoony
    Pacific Sheets
So E-Z snap fastener
    The snap with the turtle
      back
So easy a child can steer it
    Cleveland tractor
So easy to choose, so sure to
    please
    Cannon Mills, Inc.
So gentle for children, so thor-
    ough for grown-ups
    Phillips' Milk of Magnesia
So glamorous you have to be
    told they're hypo-
    allergenic
    Almay cosmetics
So good it tastes good all alone
    Red Cross spaghetti
So good-looking, so long-wearing
    Pequot sheets
So good you can cook with it
    Sunnybank Oleomargarine
So good you want a second cup
    Savarin coffee
So high in fashion ... so light
    in weight
    Ventura Travelware, Inc.
So little never bought so much
    Buskens shoes
So long as the rig is on the
    location
    Drilling
So many times a telegram means
    so much
    Western Union Corporation
So much more in quality for so
    little more in price
    Seiberling tires
So new! So right! So ob-
    viously Cadillac!
    Cadillac automobile
So powerful yet absolutely safe
    to tissues
    Zonitors suppository

So round, so firm, so fully
    packed, so free and
    easy on the draw
    Lucky Strike cigarettes
So sheer, so sleek, so smooth
    fitting
    Mojud hosiery
So soft ... it comes in a tub
    Chiffon margarine
So squeezably soft
    Charmin bathroom tissue
So you won't miss the good
    things
    Contac nasal decongestant
The soap of beautiful women
    Proctor & Gamble Co.
The soap that agrees with your
    skin
    Sweetheart Soap
Soaping dulls hair, Halo glorifies
    it
    Halo shampoo
Soapitor Co., Inc.
    Cuts the cost of clean hands
Socially, America's first motor
    car
    Packard automobile
Society Brand Clothes
    For young men and men who
    stay young
    Soft and silky as a kitten's
    purr
Society for Electrical Develop-
    ment
    A better way of living
    Electric refrigeration, a way
    to better living
    Electrical refrigeration, a
    way to better living
Society Girl foundations
    Fit as a fiddle
Society of American Florists
    Say it with flowers
    A true expression of heart-
    felt sympathy
Society's town car
    Detroit Electric automobile
The sock America wears to work
    Nelson Knitting Co.
Socony Vacuum Oil Co.
    America's No. 1 gasoline
    A grade for each type of
    motor
    The inside track to profits
    It's standard
    The sign the nation knows

Sodiphene antiseptic
　　First aid for all the family
Sofa-Niter sofa
　　The convertible sofa with
　　　accordion action
　　One if by day, two if by
　　　night
Soft and silky as a kitten's purr
　　Society Brand Clothes
Soft and sweet like big drops of
　　　honey
　　Green Giant Peas
Soft as a butterfly wing
　　Hampden face powder
Soft as a kitten's ear
　　Hews & Potter belts
Soft as a mist
　　Mistere cold cream
Soft as kitten's ears
　　Melbroke ties
Soft as old linen
　　ScotTissue
Soft Lite Lens Co.
　　Keepers of the light
Soft-sealed linoleum
　　Pabco linoleum
Soft shoes for hard wear
　　Jumping Jacks
Soft shoes for tender feet
　　J. J. Grover's Sons Co.
Soft-Weve bathroom tissue
　　Cleansing tissue soft,
　　　toilet tissue firm
The soft whiskey
　　Calvert "Extra" whiskey
The soft you can't get from
　　　soap
　　Caress bath oil
Softens hands while you do
　　　dishes
　　Palmolive dishwashing
　　　liquid
Softens the beard at the base
　　Colgate's shaving cream
Softer is the better buy
　　Puffs tissue
Softness for comfort, strength
　　　for security
　　ScotTissue
Softness is Northern
　　Northern bathroom tissue
Softness you can feel and see
　　Northern bathroom tissue
Softol cuticle remover
　　The cuticle vanishes
Softwash Cleaner

Gets at the core of every
　　　cleaning chore
The softwear company
　　Management Science America,
　　　Inc.
Sohio gasoline
　　For a change, try Sohio
Sohio motor oil
　　Motors cry for it
Sohmer piano
　　Made by our family for
　　　yours
　　One chord is worth a thou-
　　　sand words
Soilax
　　Your biggest bargain in
　　　cleanliness
Soiled clothes that are not
　　　spoiled clothes
　　The Thoro Products Co.
Solar capacitors
　　Quality above all
Solar Electric Corp.
　　Nothing better has come to
　　　light
　　There's a new light in your
　　　life
Sold American!
　　American Tobacco Company
Sold by more dealers than any
　　　other brand
　　A. P. Parts Corp. mufflers
Sold by the carload, used by the
　　　drop
　　Mrs. Stewart's Bluing
Sole idea
　　Neolite shoe soles
Sole makers of Acousticon since
　　　1903
　　Acousticon hearing aid
Sole of fashion
　　Neolite shoe soles
Sole owner of my name
　　Clarence Saunders retail
　　　grocery stores
Sole-satisfying comfort
　　Freeman Shoe Corp.
Solex lamp
　　The lamp with the 1500-
　　　hour guarantee
Solid comfort seating
　　Hampden Specialty Products
　　　Co.
Solid happiness
　　Reed & Barton sterling
　　　silver

Solid silver where it wears
  Holmes & Edwards silver-
    plate
The solid state service miser
  Quasar television sets
Solitaire Coffee
  Learn the economy of qual-
    ity in Solitaire Coffee
Solo: deep-down clean; Fluffed-
    up soft
  Solo detergent
Solo detergent
  Solo: deep-down clean;
    Fluffed-up soft
  Solo gets clothes deep-down
    clean
Solo gets clothes deep-down
    clean
  Solo detergent
Solovox piano attachment
  Made by the makers of the
    Hammond organ
The solution that beats the sys-
    tem
  RCA American Communica-
    tions
A solvent for stone in the blad-
    der
  Buffalo Lithia Water
Solves the problem at once
  Springfield Portable House
Sombre silver dulls more than
    the dinner
  Wright's silver cream clean-
    er
Sombre silver dulls the dinner
  Wright's silver cream clean-
    er
Sombrero for south-bound
    señoritas
  Sombrero Sun Lotion
Sombrero Sun Lotion
  Sombrero for south-bound
    señoritas
Some day you will drive a Velie
  Velie automobile
Some things. See also: Some-
    thing
Some things can't be hurried
  Ruppert's beer
Some things speak for them-
    selves
  Michelob beer
Somebody did it right
  Toyota trucks
Someone's always looking at

  your luggage
  Amelia Earhart luggage
Somerset Importers, Ltd.
  The oldest name in Scotch
Something. See also: Some
    things
Something better has come to
    light
  Pittsburgh Reflector Co.
Something entirely new! The
    aesthetic taste gratified!
  Carpenter Library Organ
Something from the jeweler's is
    always something special
  Jewelry Industry Council
Something has happened to hosi-
    ery
  Phoenix hosiery
Something more than a beer, a
    tradition
  Budweiser beer
Something more than sweetness
  Honey Scotch Candy
Something new
  Dr. Scott's Electric Foot
    Salve
Sometimes it takes forever to get
    to the green
  Walter E. Heller & Co.
    financial services
Sominex, simply faster
  Sominex sleeping pills
Sominex sleeping pills
  Better sleep, 38% faster
  Sominex, simply faster
Sommers Brass Co., Inc.
  Exacting standards only
A song in every seed
  The R. T. French Co.
Sonny. See: Sunny
Sonoco Products Co.
  Quality papers for industry
    since 1889
Sonora phonograph
  Clear as a bell
  It's in her home where he
    plans his
Sonotone Corporation. See:
  Battery Div., Sonotone
    Corporation
Sony Corp. of America
  For a big choice there's
    only one choice
  Machines that understand
    people
  The tapeway to stereo

Sony Superscope
　　You never heard it so good
Sooner or later, your favorite
　　tobacco
　　Sir Walter Raleigh tobacco
The sooner the better
　　Ivaline motor oil
Soothes. Cleanses. Refreshes
　　Murine eye drops
Soothing, healing, pain-relieving
　　Mecca Ointment
Sophisticute dresses
　　Debutante Originals
The sophistocrat of cigars
　　General Cigar Co.
Sorcery in a single second
　　Revlon face makeup
Sorg Printing Company
　　When it comes to financial
　　　　printing, come to Sorg
Sorry, all you other airlines.
　　　　We just beat you to it.
　　　　Again
　　Jet American Airlines
Sorry, Charlie!
　　Star-Kist canned tuna fish
The sound approach to quality
　　Kenwood Electronics, Inc.
Sound Engineering Co.
　　Our business is sound
The sound investment
　　Baldwin pianos
Sound your Z
　　Pennzoil motor oil
A soup in search of an appetite
　　Campbell's condensed soups
Soup is good food
　　Campbell's condensed soups
The soup most folks like best
　　Campbell's condensed soups
The soup Mother gave up mak-
　　ing
　　Campbell's condensed soups
The soup that eats like a meal
　　Campbell's Chunky Soup
A soup that makes meal-planning
　　easy
　　Campbell's condensed soups
Source fiber
　　Source, the creating fiber
The source for answers to wire
　　problems
　　Page Steel and Wire Div.,
　　American Chain and
　　Cable Co.
Source Securities Corp.

The broker for experienced
　　investors
Source, the creating fiber
　　Source fiber
The source you can build on
　　ITT Grinnell Corporation
South Bend Tackle Co., Div.
　　Gladding Corp.
　　Creating world-famed fish-
　　　　ing tackle since 1893
　　Fishing tackle for every
　　　　kind of fishing
South Bend watch
　　The watch with the purple
　　　　ribbon
South Dakota Dept. of Highways
　　Friendly land of infinite
　　　　variety
Southern Agriculturist
　　The giant of the South
Southern Biscuit Works
　　Southern cakes for southern
　　　　tastes
Southern cakes for southern
　　tastes
　　Southern Biscuit Works
Southern Candy Co.
　　The famous Southern Praline
Southern Comfort liquor
　　Discover the difference
　　Everyone needs a little
　　　　Comfort
　　The grand old drink of the
　　　　South
Southern Comfort Mattress
　　For the best in rest
Southern Company
　　Power for progress
　　The Southern electric sys-
　　　　tem
Southern Cotton Oil Co.
　　For making good things to
　　　　eat
Southern Cypress Mfrs. Assn.
　　The wood eternal
The Southern electric system
　　Southern Company
Southern fertilizers for the
　　southern farmer
　　The Barrett Co.
Southern Ohio's greatest news-
　　paper
　　Cincinnati Post
Southern Pacific Co.
　　Four great routes of trans-
　　　　continental travel

The road of a thousand
wonders
Safety first railroad
See twice as much for half
as much
Serving the golden empire
We're making tracks for the
future
Your main line to sunshine
Southern Pacific Co. See also:
DeLuxe Golden State
Limited, Southern
Pacific Co.
Southern Pacific steamship
cruises
Old ocean at its best
Southern Pine Association
The supreme structural
wood of the world
The wood of service
Southern Planter
The oldest farm paper in
America
Southern Railway Co.
Innovations that squeeze
the waste out of dis-
tribution
Look ahead, look South
The railway system that
gives a green light to
innovations
Southern serves the South
Southern's accent is on
you
We have the energy for the
long haul
Southern Rice Sales Co.
It's air washed
Southern serves the South
Southern Railway Co.
Southern's accent is on you
Southern Railway Co.
The South's fastest-growing
newspaper
Dallas Times-Herald
The South's greatest newspaper
Birmingham News
Memphis Commercial Appeal
The South's most famous con-
fection
Creole Pralines
The South's oldest maker of fine
furniture
White Furniture Co.
The South's standard newspaper
Atlanta Constitution

The South's supreme hotel
Atlanta Biltmore Hotel, At-
lanta, Ga.
Southwest Sun Country Assn.
Now's the time to get away
to it all!
Sozodont toothpaste
Men go wild about splendid
teeth
Pearls in the mouth
Sozonian metal vaults
A lasting tribute of modern
interment
The spa that was inevitable
Saratoga, N. Y.
Space economizer
Diebold Safe & Lock Co.
Spalding. See: A. G. Spalding
& Bros.
Spam. See also: Deviled Spam
Spam prepared meat
Cold or hot, Spam hits the
spot
Extra! Extra! News that's
hot; Spam 'n' pancakes
hit the spot
A winner for dinners
The Spam that's ready to spread
Deviled Spam
Spandex
Nothing but Spandex makes
you look so female
Spanish National Tourist Office
The place to go
Spanning the spectrum of packag-
ing
Reynolds aluminum foil wrap
Spans the world
Canadian Pacific Railway
Sparhawk flavors
The stilled breath of nature
The spark of genius
Autolight spark plugs
Spark Plug. See: A. C. Spark
Plug Div., General
Motors Corporation
Spark plugs are the pulse of
your engine
Champion spark plugs
SparkLin Ale
Taste tells the tale
Sparkling Grenay
The malt beverage that
looks and tastes like
a champagne
Sparkling hair that thrills men

Lustre-Cream shampoo
Sparkling white, sparkling
    bright, sparkling clean
Oxydol laundry detergent
Sparta Herald
    Wisconsin's greatest com-
    munity newspaper
Sparton radio receiver
    Radio's richest voice
    Radio's richest voice since
    1926
Sparton refrigerator
    Cold and silent as a winter
    night
¡Speak Spanish like a diplomat!
    Audio-Forum Foreign Service
    Institute
The speaker that speaks for it-
    self
    Jaynell radio speaker
Speakman plumbing fixtures
    If it's Speakmen, it's qual-
    ity
    If it's Speakman, it's un-
    surpassed
    It eliminates the noise that
    annoys
Special chemicals for industry
    Carlisle Chemical Works,
    Inc.
Special Libraries Association
    Putting knowledge to work
Special skills for special needs
    Allegheny International
A specialist for each line
    Rollins-Burdick-Hunter
    insurance brokers
Specialist in enamel papers/
    printing paper
    Consolidated Paper Co.
The specialist in plate steels
    Lukens Steel Co.
Specialists in children's good
    shoes since 1892
    Shaft-Pierce Shoe Co.
Specialists in digital technology
    California Computer Prod-
    ucts, Inc.
Specialists in farmstead me-
    chanization
    New Holland Div., Sperry
    Rand Corporation
Specialists in filing supplies and
    equipment since 1894
    The Weis Mfg. Co.
Specialists in financing

Associates Investment Co.
Specialists in fluid power control
    Waterman Hydraulics Corp.
Specialists in frozen food packag-
    ing
    Iceland Products, Inc.
Specialists in high polymers
    Polyvinyl Chemicals, Inc.
Specialists in international jet
    service to Texas or
    South America
    Braniff Airways, Inc.
Specialists in making water be-
    have
    Anderson Chemical Co.,
    Inc.
Specialists in process and energy
    control
    The Foxboro Company
Specialists in seating--and seat-
    ing only--since 1927
    Harter Corporation
Specialists in skin care
    Chap Stick Co.
Specialists in solving unusual
    heating problems
    Glas-Col Apparatus Co.
Specialists in the application of
    adhesives
    The Brown-Bridge Mills,
    Inc.
Specialized lubrication
    Alemite automobile lubrica-
    tion system
A specially prepared lubricant
    for household sewing
    machines
    Singer sewing machine oil
Specialty chemicals for industry
    Carlisle Chemical Works,
    Inc.
Specialty products for diversified
    markets
    Stauffer Chemical Company
Specialty Salesman Magazine
    The national inspirational
    monthly for men and
    women who sell
The specialty shop of origina-
    tions
    Bonwit Teller & Co.
The specialty steel company
    Latrobe Steel Company
Specify Spicer
    Spicer Div., Dana Corp.
Speed Nuts

The mark of total reliability
Speed. Simplicity. Versatility
　Dura Corporation
Speed stick deodorant
　The wide stick
Speed with economy
　Barney-Ahler Construction
　　Co.
　Yale Express System, Inc.
Speed with safety
　Northern Texas Traction
　　Co.
Speedaway detachable rowboat
　motor
　Why don't you get your
　　family a Speedaway?
Speedbird service
　British Overseas Airway
　　Corp.
Speedwriting Company
　Speedwriting, the natural
　　shorthand
Speedwriting, the natural short-
　hand
　Speedwriting Company
The speedy cleanser that "hasn't
　scratched yet"
　Bon Ami cleanser
Speedy is its middle name
　Alka-Seltzer
Speidel Corp. watch bands
　It S-T-R-E-T-C-H-E-S and
　　springs back
　Jewelry for years to come
　Never fasten or unfasten
　　it
　Tomorrow on every wrist
　Watches out for your watch
Spencer. See also:
　Sponsor
　Wickwire Spencer Steel Co.
Spencer Chemical Div., Gulf Oil
　Corporation
　Don't just fertilize ...
　　Spencerize
　In plastics, it's Spencer ...
　　for action
Spencer Chemical Div., Gulf Oil
　Corporation. See also:
　Gulf Oil Corporation
Spencer-Kellogg linseed oil
　The life of paint
Spend the difference
　Ford automobile
Spendable everywhere
　American Express traveler's

checks
Sperry Flour Co.
　In every home
Sperry footwear
　Sticks like a barnacle
Sperry Rand Corporation
　The computer people who
　　listen
　The first computer
　Making machines do more so
　　man can do more
　Univac is saving a lot of
　　people a lot of time
　We understand how impor-
　　tant it is to listen
　We're synergistic
Sperry Rand Corporation. See
　also: New Holland
　Div., Sperry Rand
　Corporation
Spic & Span cleaning powder
　The big job cleaner
　The right clean at the right
　　price
Spice to taste
　Stickney & Poor Spice Co.
Spicer Div., Dana Corp.
　Specify Spicer
The spirit of the Czar
　Wolfschmidt vodka
The spirit of the nation
　Rossville alcohol
Spirited new scent of the sixties
　Richard Hudnut Sportsman
Spirits soar, energy zooms when
　you help yourself to
　Shredded Ralston
　Shredded Ralston
Splendid for children--fine for
　men
　Mulsified Cocoanut Oil
　　Shampoo
Splendid nursery stock of all
　kinds
　L. W. Hall Co.
Splitdorf Cigalite
　A cigarette container that
　　lights 'em for you
Spode, Inc.
　Don't wait to inherit Spode
Spoil yourself with Satin
　Satin cigarettes
The spokesman for the inde-
　pendent paint dealer
　Paint Logic
Sponsor

440

The magazine of broadcast
advertising
Sponsor. See also: Spencer
Sponsored group travel
Hayes-Hamilton, Inc.
Sport-Tights
The fit-from-any-angle,
patented pantie girdle
A sporting tradition since 1856
Orvis sportsman's clothing
Sportleigh's briefer coat
A "must" for every ward-
robe
Sportlife
The national magazine of
sports and recreation
Sportmart athlete's shoes
For sport it's Sportmart
Sports Illustrated
America's sports news-
weekly
Each week the facts add
up to success
Sports isn't just fun and
games
Sports isn't just fun and games
Sports Illustrated
The sports voice of the Midwest
Radio station WLW
Sportsman pipe mixture
The blend of a perfect day
Champion of blends
Champion of pipes
The sportsman's car
BMW automobile
Sportsmen grooming essentials
Considered essential by
considerate men
The sportsmen's whiskey
Old Taylor whiskey
Sportster Moccasins
Like strolling on a cloud
Sportswear for sportsmen
Jantzen, Inc.
Spot Bottle whiskey
Needs no chaser
Spot it by the dot
W. A. Sheaffer Pen Co.
The spotlight car of the year
Studebaker automobile
Spotlite handbags
Always on the beam
Spracote Products Corp.
Recoat with Spracote
Spray 'n' Wash
America's No. 1 stain

remover
Spray that cleans windows with-
out water
Windex glass cleaner
Sprays on, stays on
Arco paint
The spread that betters your
bread
Wilson's Oleomargarine
Spreads like backyard news
Golden Harvest wheat paste
Spreads like good news
Satinwax
Spree Togs for children
For those frisky years
Spring-Air mattress
America's finest mattress
Controlled comfort
If you'd walk without a
care do your sleeping
on Spring-Air
The mattress that feels so
good
Sleep on Spring-Air
When experts buy, they
demand Spring-Air
The spring damps out the shock
Falk couplings
Spring step shoes
Murphy & Saval
Springfield Portable House
Solves the problem at once
Springfield Tool Co.
Paint is at its best only
when it is properly
mixed
Springfoot socks
For boys from six to sixty
Springmaid sheets
A buck well spent on a
Springmaid sheet
We love to catch them on a
Springmaid sheet
Springs right back into shape
Pennsylvania Knit Coat Co.
Sprite soft drink
Reach for a Sprite
Spry shortening
Try Spry, here's why
You'll be a better cook
with Spry
Spud menthol cigarettes
Enjoy their smoothness and
give your throat a rest
Finer taste and after-taste
Menthol-cooled

Millions of Spud smokers
can't be wrong
Spuds are soothing
Switch to Spuds
Spuds are soothing
Spud menthol cigarettes
Spun to a cream
Bradshaw & Sons honey
Spur soft drink
Zip in every sip
Square. See also: Crosby
Square Shoes
Square and Compass
A chronicle of current
Masonic events
Square D Co.
Where quality is a tradi-
tion ... and an obliga-
tion
Wherever electricity is dis-
tributed and controlled
Square deals revolve on Marmon
wheels
Marmon automobile
A square meal from a square can
Broadcast Redi-Meat
The squeezing gets you; the
softness keeps you
Charmin bathroom tissue
Squibb. See also: E. R.
Squibb
Squibb Beech-Nut, Inc.
A leader in dental research
A name you can trust
The priceless ingredient,
Squibb quality
Squibb toothbrush
Bent like a dentist's mir-
ror to reach more
places
New angle on brushing
teeth
Squibb toothpaste
Action keeps on longer
after the brushing
stops
The alkaline dental cream
As long as the danger
line keeps healthy,
you needn't fear
pyorrhea
A name you can trust
You can taste cool April
in your mouth
Squirt! It's in the public's
eye

Squirt soft drink
Squirt soft drink
Grapefruit drink that gives
you GO
Squirt! It's in the public's
eye
A sweet-tart of a drink
Sta. See also: Stay
Sta-Neet hair cutting set
The family barber
Stability based on progress
J. Walter Thompson Co.
Stacomb hair dressing
Keeps the hair in place
Stacy Adams shoe
The last fits, the fit lasts
Not the price per pair but
the cost per mile
Stadium clothes
Help build personality
Stage line wear in passenger
car tires
Samson tires
Stahl. See: Otto Stahl meat
products
Stainwax
Modern, yet proved by
centuries of use
The original penetrating
Stainwax finish
Since 1910, America's No.
1 scratchproof wood
finish
Stakmore Co., Inc.
The chair that stands by
itself
The folding furniture with
the permanent look
Staley stock feed
Hits the mark
Stampede of power
Exide storage batteries
Stamps
A weekly magazine of
philately
Stan Kenton's dance orchestra
Artistry in rhythm
Stanback Headache Powders
Snap back with Stanback
Stand by, America, for Amer-
ica's stand-out buy
Studebaker automobile
Stand out in a crowd, be figure
proud
Life brassiere
Standard Accident Insurance

Co.
Burglars know no season
Cheaper insurance is easier
    to purchase but harder
    to collect
Standard & Poor's investment
    service
There is only one thought-
    ful choice
Standard batteryless radio re-
    ceivers
Just plug in, then tune in
The world at your finger-
    tips
Standard Brewing Co.
Always in good company
Any time is STANDARD
    time
Standard Chartered Bank, Ltd.
Standard Chartered helps
    you throughout the
    world
Standard Chartered helps you
    throughout the world
Standard Chartered Bank,
    Ltd.
Standard Cigar Co.
Man alive! Two for five
Standard Diary Co.
Give memory insurance
Invest in memory insurance
Standard Electric Stove Co.
Change work to play three
    times a day
Standard Envelope Mfg. Co.
The envelope is the first
    impression
Standard for accuracy
Starrett steel tapes
Standard Four Tire Co.
Chief of the tire tribe
Standard Granite Quarries
Rock of ages
Standard in rubber goods for
    nearly half a century
Kleinert Rubber Co.
Standard Ink & Color Co.
Qualities to the last im-
    pression
Standard Kid Mfg. Co.
The leather for fine shoes
Standard Life Insurance Co.
Make tomorrow pay,
Standard Man today
The standard of accuracy
Marsh Gauges

The standard of comparison
Buick automobile
The standard of corset fashion
Redfern corsets
The standard of giving
Seagram's V.O. whiskey
Standard of perfection
Logan County Coal Corp.
Standard of quality the whole
    world over
McCormick and Co., Inc.
The standard of reception
Andrea radio receiver
Standard of reliability since 1935
Northill anchor
Standard of the globe
Bunnell telegraph equipment
Standard of the industry
Hughes Tool Co.
Mohawk Rubber Co.
Standard of the mechanical world
Brown & Sharpe hardware
Standard of the plotting industry
California Computer Prod-
    ucts, Inc.
Standard of the world
American Blower Co.
Bull Durham tobacco
Cadillac automobile
The standard of value in auto-
    matic coal firing equip-
    ment
Iron Fireman
Standard of value in shale face
    brick
Streator Brick Co.
Standard Oil Co. of California
The chevron--the sign of
    excellence
Standard Oil Co. of Indiana
You expect more from a
    leader
Standard Oil Div., American Oil
    Co.
As you travel ask us
Call the man who puts the
    farmer first--your
    Standard Oil Farm Man
See what happens when you
    start using American
    ingenuity
We take better care of your
    car
You expect more from Stand-
    ard and you get it
The standard packing of the

world
Garlock Packing Service
Standard Paper Mfg. Co.
For the illustrated side, a
coated paper, for the
letter side, a bond pa-
per
More mental impressions
from each printing im-
pression
Standard plasters of the world
Allcock's Porous Plasters
Standard Pressed Steel Co.
See: Precision Fastener
Div., Standard Pressed
Steel Co.
Standard Products Co.
Where your sealing is un-
limited
Standard railroad of the South
Atlantic Coast Line Railroad
The standard road guide of
America
Automobile Blue Book
The standard Southern news-
paper
Atlanta Constitution
Standard Tool and Mfg. Co.
Better products at a lower
cost through better
methods
Standard Triangle Tubs
Step into America's newest
bath thrill
The standard typewriter in port-
able size
Royal typewriter
The standard visible writer
Oliver typewriter
Standards are set by Triplett
Triplett tube tester
Standby. See: Stand by
Stands the oven test
Fant Milling Co.
Stands up fine
Valentine's Valspar
Stange seasonings
In seasoning, it's Stange
Silent partners in famous
foods
Stanlabs, Inc.
Sharing the responsibilities
of modern medicine
Stanley Dutenhofer Shoe Co.
Salable to the last pair
Stanley Home Products, Inc.

Where the nicest people
meet the nicest things
Stanley Shave Cream
For a better shave
Stanley Steemer
The carpet cleaning company
women recommend
Stanley Tool Div., The Stanley
Works
The tool box of the world
The Stanley Works
Helps you do things right
Leading the do-it-yourself
industry
Stanton Home Safe Co.
The bank behind the book
Stanwood Corporation
More steam with less coal
Star Ale
Good food tastes better with
Star Ale
The Star is Kansas City and
Kansas City is the Star
Kansas City Star
Star-Kist canned tuna fish
The only tuna packed in
natural spring water
Sorry, Charlie!
The tender tuna with the
delicate taste
Star Razor Blades
Next to mine I like your
face
Starburst Fruit Chews
A burst of refreshing fruit
flavor
Starcraft Company
America's most popular boats
The Starcraft wide world of
recreation
The Starcraft wide world of rec-
reation
Starcraft Company
Stardust Hotel and Golf Club
Where your "resort dollar"
buys more
Starflite Luggage
For people who travel ...
and expect to again and
again
Starrett steel tapes
Standard for accuracy
Stars for your kitchen
Foley Mfg. Co.
The stars who make the hits are
on Victor records

Victor phonograph records
Start. See also: Fresh Start
    laundry detergent
The start that's bowls apart
    Total cereal
Start the day the American way
    Toastmaster toaster
Start the day with style, end it
    with a smile
    Florsheim Shoe Co.
Start the day with Yale Coffee
    Yale Coffee
Start with Savogran
    Savogran painters' supplies
Start with--stay with Knox
    Knox Gelatine, Inc.
Start with the finish
    Laucks paints
Start with the "heart" where
    farmers are worth 2
    for 1
    Successful Farming
Start with us. Stay with us
    Exxon Office Systems Co.
The starter that is built to order
    Wagner Electric Corp.
The starter that starts her
    Startzer automobile starter
Startex Mills, Inc.
    King of the kitchen
Starts from the seat without
    cranking
    Winton Six automobile
Starts--stops--regulates--
    controls
    Cutler-Hammer, Inc.
Starts the day in Detroit
    Detroit Free Press
Starts with a quarter turn
    Elto Outboard Motor
Startzer automobile starter
    Really starts your engine
    The starter that starts her
Stat-Tab Computer Services
    The action company
State Farm. See also: Home
    State Farm
State Farm Insurance Co.
    The friendly hands people
    The good hands people
    Like a good neighbor,
        State Farm is there
State of excitement
    Oregon Highway Depart-
    ment
Staten Island beer

Rubsam & Horrmann
The state's greatest newspaper
    Arizona Republican
The station most people listen to
    most
    Radio station WMC, Memphis,
    Tenn.
Stationers Loose Leaf Binder
    The binder that grows with
        your business
    One of the many distinctive
        faultless loose-leaf books
Staude Mak-a-Tractor
    America's most useful farm
        implement
Stauffer Chemical Company
    Specialty products for diver-
        sified markets
Stay. See also: Sta
Stay brighter longer
    General Electric Mazda Lamp
Stay crisp in milk or cream
    Post Toasties
Stay fit for fun with Phillips
    Phillips' Milk of Magnesia
Stay fit. Unwind tense nerves.
    Have more energy
    Battle Creek Manufacturers,
    Inc.
Stay-Free maxipads
    Comfort without compromise
    Comfort you can count on
    The full-sized pads filled
        with freshness
Stay fresh for years
    Ray-O-Vac batteries
Stay on the Breidt side
    Breidt beer
Stay on the right side
    Breidt beer
Stay pretty in the sun
    Elizabeth Arden suntan oil
Stay put
    Tweedie Boot Top Co.
Stay-Rite Hair Pin
    Precious little aids to beauty
The stay-satisfactory range
    Malleable Iron Range Co.
Stay shower-fresh all day long
    Seaforth deodorant
Stay sweet with Hush
    Hush deodorant
Stay warm with someone you
    know
    Sunbeam kerosene heaters
Stay young as you grow old

Abbey Effervescent Co.
Staying ahead in the race to
    tomorrow
    Rolls-Royce aircraft engines
Staynew Filter Corp.
    World's greatest motor ne-
        cessity
Stays alive
    Hoffman club soda
Stays dustless until the last
        shovelful
    Giese Bros. Coal Co.
Stays on till you take it off
    Coty 24 hour lipstick
Stays silent, lasts longer
    Servel refrigerator
Staze denture products
    Staze stays stronger,
        LONGER
Staze stays stronger, LONGER
    Staze denture products
Steady as she goes
    Gorton-Pew Fisheries, Inc.
Stearns automobile
    This is the envied car
    The ultimate car is the
        Stearns
    The White Line radiator
        belongs to the Stearns
Stearns Ball-Bearing Mower
    Runs like a bicycle
Stearns Coal & Lumber Co.
    It's always coal weather
    Stearns coal is solid heat
    Stearns coal, the famous
        portable climate coal
Stearns coal is solid heat
    Stearns Coal & Lumber
        Co.
Stearns coal, the famous port-
        able climate coal
    Stearns Coal & Lumber
        Co.
Stearns' Electric Rat and Roach
        Paste
    Safe, sure, instant
Stedman Products Co.
    Originators of reinforced
        rubber flooring
Steel and Tube Div., Timken
        Roller Bearing Co.
    The men who make it make
        the difference
Steel and Tube Div., Timken
        Roller Bearing Co.
    See also: Timken

Roller Bearing Co.
    The steel backbone for concrete
        American Steel & Wire Co.
Steel Barrel Institute
    Steel barrels endure
Steel barrels endure
    Steel Barrel Institute
Steel strengthened plastering
    North Western Expanded
        Metal Co.
Steelcase, Inc.
    Design/plus
Steelcraft boat
    You're safer in a Steelcraft
The steels with Indian names
    Ludlum Steel Co.
Steero bouillon cubes
    A cube makes a cup
Steger & Sons Piano Co.
    The finest reproducing
        phonograph
    If it's a Steger it's the
        most valuable piano in
        the world
    The most valuable piano in
        the world
Steinmetz Elec. Motor Car Corp.
    Cuts down delivery costs
SteinRoe Inc.
    Don't put your assets on
        ice
Steinway piano
    As intimate as firelight,
        as infinite as the stars
    The instrument of the im-
        mortals
    The piano of international
        fame
StenoCord Dictation Systems
    World's easiest-to-use dic-
        tating machines
A step ahead of tomorrow
    Zurn Industries, Inc.
Step forth with Seaforth
    Seaforth deodorant
Step inside and make yourself
        comfortable
    Thom McAn shoes
Step into a Fortune, your key
        to a wealth of satisfac-
        tion
    Fortune shoes
Step into a private realm where
        cares cannot trespass,
        where moss-soft towels
        wrap you in colorful

caress
  Cannon Mills, Inc.
Step into America's newest bath
    thrill
  Standard Triangle Tubs
Step into paradise with these
    perfectly heavenly shoes
  Paradise Shoes
Step out with a Stetson
  Stetson hats
Step thru, button two
  Sealpax underwear
A step to distinction
  Crosby Square Shoes
Step up to Wheel Horse
  Wheel Horse Products, Inc.
Step up with Hupp
  Hupmobile automobile
Step up your business with Nix-
    dorf
  Nixdorf computer
Stephens. See also: Stevens
Stephens automobile
  The salient six
Stereo you can see
  Pioneer Video, Inc.
Stereopticon Lantern Slides
  Say it with pictures
The Steril-Sil Co.
  Leadership through quality
Sterizol Co.
  I'm well. You well?
Sterling Faucet Co.
  Where quality is produced
    in quantity
The sterling of cooking wear
  Nesco utensils
Sterling of lasting good taste
  Lunt silverware
The sterling of leatherware
  Rumpp Luggage
Sterling Photo Co.
  Your snapshots look better
    enlarged
Sterling Salt
  Pass the salt for better
    livestock
Sterling Silversmiths of America
  It is sterling, more cannot
    be said
Sterling tires
  Super size, super service
Stern. See: L & H Stern Co.
Sterno
  The clean, convenient fuel
Stetson hats

Are you true to your type?
Born in America. Worn
  round the world
The mark of the world's
  most famous hat
On the well-dressed head
Overhead economy
Right for cool comfort
Right for Sunday morning
Step out with a Stetson
Styled for young men
You look your best in a
  Stetson
Stetson Shoe Co.
  More by the pair, less by
    the year
  They've got to be Stetson
    to be snappy
Stevens. See also:
  J. P. Stevens and Co.,
    Inc.
  Stephens automobile
Stevens arms
  Pioneering better guns and
    greater values since
    1864
Stevens-Duryea automobile
  Nearly a quarter-century of
    leadership
  Pioneer builder of American
    sixes
Stewart Hartshorn Co.
  A shade is only as good as
    its rollers
Stewart Iron Works Co.
  World's greatest iron fence
Stewart starter for Ford cars
  Always starts your engine--
    and pumps your tires
Stewart-Warner bumpers
  All steel and a car wide
Stewart-Warner Corporation
  Fluid handling is Stewart-
    Warner's business
  SW--Symbol of excellence
  Twelve million people are
    today using Stewart-
    Warner products
Stewart-Warner radio receiver
  Great thrill in radio by the
    pioneers of short-wave
    radio
Stewart-Warner Speedometer
    Corp.
  Brackets of steel that never
    break

Stewart's. See: Mrs. Stewart's Bluing
Stickney & Poor Spice Co.
  Spice to taste
Sticks like a barnacle
  Sperry footwear
Sticks most everything
  Casco cement
Sticks on its job
  Monite Waterproof Glue
Sticks with a touch
  Texcel Tape
The Stiffel Co.
  The royalty of lamps
Stihl chain saw
  The world's largest selling chain saw
Still the most underpriced message service in the world
  Western Union Telex Network
Still the shortest route to your man's heart
  Heinz ketchup
The stilled breath of nature
  Sparhawk flavors
Stimson Computing Scale Co.
  Insure your profits, use Stimson products
  The right way to weigh right
  The weight to profits
Stinson aircraft
  America's most useful personal planes
  Easy to buy, easy to fly
A stitch in time service
  Delco Heat
Stock Yards Packing Co.
  Purveyor to America's finest eating establishments since 1893
Stockham Pipe & Fittings
  Quality is demonstrated by their performance
The stocking beautiful
  La France Hosiery
Stockings of matchless beauty
  Hoover Sales Corp.
Stokely-Van Camp, Inc.
  America's first, finest, and favorite pork and beans
  Color is nature's way of saying flavor. Stoke-

ly is your way of getting it
  Finest way to make a pick-up supper super
  How to give a budget supper a banquet air
Stokely-Van Camp, Inc. See also: Van Camp
Stokeley's baby foods
  A smile in every spoonful
  The strained foods baby really likes
Stolichnaya Russian voda
  The vodka
Stop and start on Multibestos
  Multibestos brake lining
Stop baking risk, use Bisquick
  Bisquick flour
Stop cheating yourself
  Graves Timing Device Co.
Stop excusing your life away
  American Cancer Society
Stop-Fire extinguisher
  The fire extinguisher anyone can use
Stop playing lady-in-waiting to lazy drains
  Drano drain cleaner
Stop tearing your hair
  Gayla Curlers
Stop that leak in the toilet tank
  Ross Mfg. Co.
Stop that skid before it starts
  Weed tire chains
Stop that tickle
  Bunte Brothers cough drops
A STOP to thirst, a STEP to health
  Campbell's tomato juice
Stop window washing
  Whiz mirror and glass cleaner
Stops are few and far between; Olds needs little gasoline
  Oldsmobile automobile
Stops B. O.
  Lifebuoy Soap
Stops pain instantly ... ends corns completely
  Blue-Jay corn plaster
Stops rust!
  Rust-Oleum Corp.
Stops that tickle!
  Frog in Your Throat
Stops toothache instantly

448

Dent's Toothache Gum
A store a woman should look into
  Hoffritz for Cutlery
Store more ... better ... at less
  cost
  Vidmar, Inc.
The store that never closes
  Sears Roebuck & Co.
The stores of friendly service
  H. C. Bohack
Storkline baby carriage
  Storkline thinks of every-
  thing
Storkline thinks of everything
  Storkline baby carriage
Storm Hero umbrella
  A new frame if the wind
  breaks it
Stormy leather
  Florsheim Shoe Co.
Stormy leather; when it rains,
  it scores
  Florsheim Shoe Co.
Story and Clark Piano Co.
  Instruments of quality by
  one family for 100
  years
  The world's most beautiful
  organs
Story Dairy
  You can whip our cream
  but you can't beat our
  milk
A story-telling pictorial of stage,
  art, screen, humor
  American Beauties
Stotler & Co. stock brokers
  Trade the market instead
  of stocks
Stouffer hotels
  The executive decision
  Where you stay says a lot
  about where you're go-
  ing
Stout women dress fashionably--
  look slender
  Lane Bryant stores
The stove with focused heat
  Florence Stoves
Stow and Davis Furniture Co.
  Distinguished furniture
  for distinguished of-
  fices
Stradivara phonograph
  Known for tone
Straight talk, good values

and satisfaction
  Sears, Roebuck & Co.
Straight talk, in any language
  Rollins-Burdick-Hunter in-
  surance brokers
The straight-talk tire people
  B. F. Goodrich Tire Co.
The strained foods baby really
  likes
  Stokley's baby foods
Strained for babies, chopped for
  young children
  Clapp's Baby Foods
The strapless bra that stays up
  Daring brassiere
Strapping Div., Signode Corp.
  Let's find better ways ...
  we'll follow through
The strategic middle route
  Union Pacific Railroad
Stratford Clothes
  Custom tailored throughout
Stratford pens
  Prized of writing perfection
Strathmore nail polish
  Good to your finger tips
Strathmore Paper Co.
  The new way to do prestige
  advertising
  Paper is part of the picture
  Simplicity and a Strathmore
  paper
Strawberry Shortcake cereal
  Berry delicious
A streak of good luck
  Marmon automobile
"Streamlined acting" motor fuel
  Blue Sunoco gasoline
Streator Brick Co.
  Standard of value in shale
  face brick
Street Bros. Crane
  The out-door overhead
  crane
  The Street Cub, a bear
  for work
The Street Cub, a bear for
  work
  Street Bros. Crane
Streit Slumber Chair
  For the REST of your life
Strength ... in a glass by it-
  self
  Guinness ale
Strength in every length
  Ajax Rope Co.

Strength is the foundation of
    all good baking
    Enterprise Flour
The strength of Gibraltar
    Prudential Insurance Co.
    of America
Strength, permanence and stabil-
    ity
    Fireman's Fund American
    Insurance
Strength, safety, style and
    speed
    Hudson automobile
Strength, safety, style and
    speed, Terraplane
    meets every need
    Terraplane automobile
Stri-Dex skin cleanser
    The proof is in the pad
Strictly conFOODential
    Three Feathers whiskey
Strike It Rich
    The quiz show with a heart
The string will not pull out
    Tension envelope
Stroh's beer
    America's only fire-brewed
    beer
    Looks like a Strohlight
    night
    Quality clear through
Stromberg-Carlson radio receiv-
    ers
    There is nothing finer than
    a Stromberg-Carlson
Strombos Air Whistle
    Most powerful of all signals
The strong arm of industry
    Electric Hoist Mfrs. Assn.
Strong as its name
    Hercules umbrellas
Strong as leather
    Mansfield wheat flour
The strong bankers
    AmeriTrust Bank, Cleve-
    land, Ohio
Strong, Cobb & Co.
    The mint within your reach
Strong enough to stand on
    Samson folding table
Strong for wear
    Jobbers Overall Co.
Strong for work
    Jobbers Overall Co.
Strong-Scott Mfg. Co.
    Everything for every mill

and elevator
Strong where strength is needed
    Athol Machine & Foundry
    Co.
Stronger than dirt
    Ajax laundry detergent
Stronger than wood, enduring
    as the rock
    Monite Waterproof Glue
The strongest ally of the glass
    container
    Anchor Cap & Closure
    Corp.
Strongest at the base where
    strength is needed
    Maag gears
Strops, shaves, cleans without
    detaching blade
    AutoStrop safety razor
Structo toys
    Make men of boys
Struthers Mfg. Co.
    The shock absorber that
    shifts gears
Struthers Thermo-Flood Corp.
    Leaders in thermal engi-
    neering design
Strutwear nylon stockings
    Try them on for sighs
Stuart. See:
    Stewart
    Stewart's
Studebaker automobile
    The automobile with a
    reputation behind it
    The car of the year in eye
    appeal and buy appeal
    Drive down your driving
    costs
    First by far with a postwar
    car
    It's an eager-to-go, low,
    long, lovely melody in
    metal
    Largest vehicle manufac-
    turers in the world
    A long, low, lovely "melody
    in metal"
    Low-swung, new-look, soft-
    sprung, new-ride
    Smart to be seen in, smart-
    er to buy
    The spotlight car of the
    year
    Stand by, America, for
    America's stand-out buy

Take the Studebaker third
degree road test
Studebaker trucks
Builder of trucks you can
trust
Stuhmer's Pumpernickel
Fresh to the last slice
Ideal for any meal
It tastes good to the last
crumb
The Pumpernickel you'll like
Sturdee Folding Ironing Table
Rigid as an oak
Sturdy is the word for Oliver
Oliver farm equipment
Sturdy to the last
H. W. Merriam
Sturtevant Co.
Puts air to work
Styl-eez shoes
Compare and you'll wear
Styl-eez
Style and wear in every pair
Hosiers, Ltd.
Style authority in wrought iron
Lee L. Woodward Sons,
Inc.
A style for any taste, a fit for
any foot
Florsheim Shoe Co.
The style leader
Lincoln Zephyr automobile
Style leaders of the world
Butterick patterns
Style, like ambition, is a good
servant, but a poor
master
Packard automobile
Style-Mart suit
Do something for you
Does something for you
Style that goes to your head
Champ Hats
The style that makes 'em look
at your car
Cincinnati Ball Crank Co.
Style that stays
Commonwealth Shoe & Leath-
er Co.
Styled for a figure, not for an
age
Georgiana frocks
Styled for a party, but pow-
ered for a thrill
Buick automobile
Styled for beauty

Rollfast bicycles
Styled for beauty, made to last
Rollfast bicycles
Rollfast roller skates
Styled for the stars
Grantly sun glasses
Styled for tomorrow to enjoy to-
day
Hart Schaffner & Marx men's
clothing
Styled for young men
Stetson hats
Styled in California, applauded
by all America
Pabco linoleum
The styled shoe built on a real
chassis
Wright Arch Preserver
shoes
Styled to comfort
Fashion Eze shoes
Jordan-Williams shoes
Styled to prevent twisting or
riding
Corette slip
Styleplus Clothes
America's only known-
priced clothes
The big name in clothes
Styles for every room in the
house
Sanitas wall covering
Stylish Stout corset
Without the shadow of a
stout
Suave hair dressing
Suave makes you look as
though you spent a
fortune on your hair
Suave makes you look as though
you spent a fortune on
your hair
Suave hair dressing
Subaru automobile
Inexpensive. And built
to stay that way
The substance shows
Mercury Marquis automobile
Subtract all our acquisitions
and the numbers still
look good
Northwest Industries, Inc.
The Suburban Seven
Jordan automobile
Success refrigerator
Is your refrigerator a

Success?
Successful Farming
    The farmer's service station
    Greatest concentration in
        the world's richest farm
        region
    Made to order for America's
        business farmer and his
        wife
    Our readers manage the
        country
    Start with the "heart" where
        farmers are worth 2 for
        1
    There's a difference in farm
        papers
    Tips for table tops
    To sell SUCCESSFUL farm-
        ers buy Successful
        Farming
The successful ones
    P-A-C Div., W. R. Grace
        & Co.
Successor to the binder
    All-Crop Harvester
The successor to the sink
    Hydrocrat plumbing fixture
Such popularity must be de-
    served
    Chesterfield cigarettes
Suchard chocolate bars
    Love at first bite
The sucker with a heart o' gum
    Fleer's chewing gum
Sudden death to moths
    Expello
Suddenly, it's the obvious choice
    Diners Club credit card
Suds fast, and the suds last
    Swan Soap
Suds in a jiffy
    Jif soap flakes
Sue sings before seven
    Colgate's dental cream
Sugar Information, Inc.
    Sugar's got what it takes
The Sugar Institute
    Preserve with refined cane
        sugar
Sugar Pops are tops
    Kellogg's Sugar Pops cereal
Sugar's got what it takes
    Sugar Information, Inc.
Suits the south
    Schwobilt clothing
Suits your land

Farmers Cotton Oil Co.
The sum-total of smoking pleasure
    Chesterfield cigarettes
The summer route you'll brag
    about
    Burlington Northern Railroad
Sumptuously built
    White Town Car automobile
Sun Ball fruit juices
    Get on the ball with Sun
        Ball juices
    Keep on the ball with Sun
        Ball juices
Sun Electric Corp.
    A new high in auto test
        equipment ... a new
        high for you!
Sun Insurance Co.
    Everyone needs the Sun
    Fire insurance is as old as
        the Sun
Sun-Maid raisins
    Had your iron today?
    How young will you be at
        50?
The sun never sets on Hammond
    tanks
    Hammond Iron Works
Sun Oil Company
    The distilled motor oil
    The pass word of the road
    Quality ... the best economy
        of all
Sun Spot Co. of America
    Bottled sunshine
The Sun Typewriter
    A perfect machine for busi-
        ness purposes or home
        use
Sun Valley, Idaho
    Winter fun under a "summer
        sun"
Sun Varnish Co.
    Defies weather and wear
Sunbeam bread
    Reach for Sunbeam bread
        instead
Sunbeam Corporation
    Built with integrity, backed
        by service
Sunbeam Ironmaster electric iron
    First, by choice
Sunbeam kerosene heaters
    Stay warm with someone
        you know
Sunbrite cleanser

Cleans easier, works faster,
won't scratch
Double action, single cost
Sunbrite, the cleanser with
a spotless reputation
You're safe with Sunbrite,
it has a spotless repu-
tation
Sunbrite, the cleanser with a
spotless reputation
Sunbrite Cleanser
Sundial Shoes
Time will tell, wear Sundial
Shoes
Suni-Citrus Products
They moo for more
Sunkist Fresh Fruit Drinks
Good vibrations!
See it made
Sunkist lemons
Buy them by the dozen for
their many uses
First thing on arising
Keep regular this healthful
way
Lemon in water, first thing
on arising
The way the best lemons
sign their names
When you take cold, take
lemons
Sunkist marmalade
The new American marma-
lade
Sunkist oranges
Best for juice and every
use
Bursting with juice
Charm that attracts others
comes from within
If you could see inside
oranges, you'd buy
Sunkist every time
Only the fairest get the
squeeze
Richer juice, finer flavor
Uniformly good
Uniformly good oranges
Sunlane cruises to Europe
American Export Isbrandt-
sen Lines, Inc.
Sunlite Sunflower Cooking Oil
From the seed of the sun-
flower
Sunny by nature
Royal Scarlet foods

Sunny magic for simple meals
Niblets canned corn
Sunny Monday clothes dryer
The Louden Machinery Co.
Sunny Smile dentifrice
Tooth powder in paste form
Sunnybank Oleomargarine
So good you can cook with
it
Sunoco. See: Blue Sunoco
gasoline
Sunray DX Oil Company
America's most customer-
minded oil company!
Known by the customers we
keep
Sunroc electric water cooler
There's nothing like a cool
drink of water
Sunset
Dedicated to serving the
families of the West and
Hawaii ... no one else
The magazine of Western
living
The West's great national
magazine
Sunset lines
America's finest fish lines
Sunshine belt to the Orient
Dollar Steamship Lines
Sunshine biscuits
Look for this Sunshine bis-
cuit rack
Made in the bakery of a
thousand windows
Sunshine Bread
Have a slice of Sunshine
You need sunshine every
day; we knead Sunshine
every day
Sunshine drain pipe cleaner
Eats everything in the pipe
Sunshine Ice Co.
Keeps things to eat good to
eat
The sunshine of the night
Coleman Co., Inc.
Sunsweet marches on!
Sunsweet prunes
Sunsweet prunes
Add sparkle to your break-
fast and sparkle to your
day
For every day in some way
Full of sunshine and good

health
Make Sunsweet your daily
good health habit
Sunsweet marches on!
They must be good
Sunworthy Wallpapers
Dare you move your pic-
tures?
Super-Cyclone
The biggest name in little
engines
Super-moisturizes dry skin zones
instantly!
Dermassage
Super razor
A $5 razor with 1000 new
edges
The razor with 1000 new
edges
Super service
T. I. M. E. Freight, Inc.
The Super-Six
Hudson automobile
Super size, super service
Sterling tires
Super-X piston rings
Announcing a new RING
champ
Superba Fruit Basket
Pinnacle Orchards
The superfine small car
Templar automobile
Superflash photolamp
It's a snap with Superflash
The superior brake fluid
Wagner Electric Corp.
Superior Hat Co.
A shade better than the
rest
Superior Industries, Inc.
Where big ideas turn into
aluminum extrusions
The superior interior
Upson Co.
Superior performance through
design simplicity
Triangle Package Machinery
Co.
A superior quality chewing gum
Topp's Chewing Gum
Superior Uniform Cap Co.
National headquarters for
uniform caps
The superstar in rent-a-car
Hertz credit card
Supersuds

Floods o' suds for dishes
and duds
Supertron radio tube
The tube with the sensible
guarantee
Supima Association of America
World's finest cottons
Supple's milk
Backed by a century of
confidence
Supplex Co.
The original reinforced plas-
tic hose
The support of a nation
Paris Garters
The Supreme Authority
Webster's International Dic-
tionary
Supreme in the laundry industry
Laundry Age
The supreme structural wood of
the world
Southern Pine Association
Sure. See also:
Shur
Shure
Sure allure for the more mature
Life brassiere
Sure anti-perspirant
Raise your hand if you're
Sure
Sure protection for frozen foods
Nepco locker paper
A sure sign they're good
Hood rubbers
The sure test ... Scott
Scott Testers, Inc.
Sure to be tender
Visking Corp. skinless
frankfurters
Sure to delight your appetite
Haserot Company
A sure winner
American Chewing Products
Corp.
Surety bonds: the right cement
between owner and
contractor
SAFECO Insurance Co. of
America
A surety of purity
O. P. Skaggs Food Stores
Surface satisfaction
Scarfe paint
Surpass Leather Co.
It takes on added beauty

454

in the shoe
Surprise brassiere
    Uplift that stays up
The surprise of Formica products
    Formica Corp.
The surprising state
    Washington State
Surround your life with fragrance
    Mary Chess perfume
Surrounds and protects the beverage industry
    United Beverage Bureau
Sussman & Wormser Co.
    Win favor with a flavor,
      serve S & W fine foods
Sustained quality
    Associated Oil Co.
Sutliff. See: Henry Sutliff
    Tobacco Co.
Sutra lotion
    Filters sun, speeds tan
Swaberg Mfg. Co.
    The balanced pencil
Swagelok fittings
    You can't afford to be
      without Swagelok
Swan & Finch Co.
    Scientific lubricants for
      scientific lubrication
Swan is different, Swan is better
    Swan Soap
Swan Soap
    No over-soaped feeling
    Suds fast, and the suds
      last
    Swan is different, Swan is
      better
Swank jewelry
    I am valet to millions
    Jewelry of tradition for
      the contemporary man
Swankies Shoes
    Your eyes say style, your
      feet say comfort
Swan's Down cake flour
    Bake a better cake with
      Swan's Down
    Easy on the sugar, the
      arm, the eye
    Makes fine, better cakes
Swanson's cooking just for you
    Swanson frozen dinners
Swanson frozen dinners
    Swanson's cooking just for
      you
    To get more that's good

... trust Swanson
A sweater is better if it's a
    Huddlespun
    Huddlespun sweater
Swedish American Line
    The white viking fleet
A sweet among sweets
    Kerr's butterscotch
Sweet as a kiss, honest as Mother
    Earth
    Kounty Kist Peas
Sweet-Avie
    The original air deodorant
Sweet Caporal cigarettes
    Ask Dad, he knows
Sweet dreaming from yawn to
    dawn
    Cohler pajamas
Sweet magic
    O. P. Bauer Confectionery
    Co.
Sweet Message Chocolates
    Untouched by human hands
Sweet-tart. See also: Sweet-
    heart
A sweet-tart of a drink
    Squirt soft drink
Sweeten it with Domino
    Domino sugar
Sweeter as the years go by
    Kaywoodie pipe
The sweetest music this side of
    heaven
    Guy Lombardo's Royal Cana-
      dians orchestra
The sweetest pipe in the world
    Wm. Demuth & Co.
The sweetest story ever sold
    Life Savers candy
Sweetheart. See also: Sweet-
    tart
The sweetheart of a "chewsey"
    world
    Tootsie Rolls candy
The sweetheart of the corn
    Kellogg's toasted corn flakes
Sweetheart Soap
    The soap that agrees with
      your skin
Sweethearts in swim suits
    Pacific Knitting Mills
Sweetose syrup
    The EXTRA-sweet corn
      syrup
    It's really sweet
Swerl

The magic suds
Swift and Co.
   Food purveyors to the nation
   In industry world-wide
Swift as the swallow, relief
   Neo-Syn Pills
Swift relief follows the swallow
   Neo-Syn Pills
Swift's bacon
   Traditionally preferred
     throughout our land
   With that sweet smoke taste
Swift's Brookfield cheese
   The cheese most people like
Swift's Brookfield sausage
   Millions favor that Brookfield flavor
   The sausage with the just-right seasoning
Swift's ham
   It's just ham unless it's Swift's
   No parboiling. It's oven-ized
Swift's Premium frankfurter sausage
   Naturally smoked. Delicately seasoned
Swift's Premium meats
   Better beef and it's branded
   Good to the last luscious left-over
   The meat makes the meal
   Pick the polka dot package
   Smoke that never varies from fires that never die
   Try it a week. You'll use it for life
   The two most trusted names in meat
   You can trust the man who sells this brand
Swing and sway with Sammy Kaye
   Sammy Kaye's dance orchestra
Swingline stapler
   If speed is what you need, get a Swingline
   It staples, it tacks, it pins
   It's an "open and shut" case
   World's largest manufacturer of staplers for

home and office
   World's speediest stapler
Swiss Air Transport Co., Ltd.
   Swisscare. Worldwide
   Swiss-care world-wide on the privately owned airline of Switzerland
Swiss-care world-wide on the privately owned airline of Switzerland
   Swiss Air Transport Co., Ltd.
The Swiss food drink, now made in the U. S. A.
   Ovaltine
Swisscare. Worldwide
   Swiss Air Transport Co., Ltd.
Switch to Dodge and save money
   Dodge automobile
Switch to Spuds
   Spud menthol cigarettes
Sylvania Electric Products, Inc.
   Experts know these lamps
   A flair for elegance
   A full package of light
   Total communications from a single source through Sylvania
Symbol of accuracy since 1870
   Marlin Firearms Co.
Symbol of excellence
   Tokheim Corp.
Symbol of excellence in West German optics
   Carl Zeiss, Inc.
The symbol of imported luxury
   Seagram's V. O. whiskey
Symbol of quality
   Potlatch Forests, Inc.
The symbol of quality in radio since 1915
   Magnavox radio receiver
Symbol of security since 1817
   Fire Association Group
Symbol of service
   Consumers Power Company
A symbol of technical excellence
   RCA Corp.
The symbol of value
   Purex cleaning materials
Symbols of sentiment
   Brock Jewelry Co.
Symons. See also: Simmons
Symons Mfg. Co.
   More savings with Symons

Syn-Kro Mills
Fresh feeds are best
Freshness is the first food
law of nature
Synchronics electronic equipment
Ingenious electronics in
step with the times
Synergistic Financial Services,
Ltd.
Unbiased financial planning.
There's a lot more to it
than meets the eye
Synthane Corp.
You furnish the print ...
we'll furnish the part
Synthetic or natural, we can
help fashion the pro-
cessing system you need
The Foxboro Company
Synthetics Finishing Corp.
You can rely on America's
oldest and most experi-
enced custom finisher
Syracuse China Corp.
The beginning of taste
Syroco div., Dart Industries, Inc.
America's foremost manufac-
turer of decorative ac-
cessories since 1890
System
The magazine of business
System/360, the computer with
a future
International Business Ma-
chines Corp.
Systems. See also: E-Systems
Systems for business
Monroe calculators
Systems that work together now
Datapoint Corporation

-T-

TIE/communications, Inc.
When it's a tie, you win
T. I. M. E. Freight, Inc.
Super service
T. S. Hanseatic German
Atlantic Line
Just for the sun of it
"T" stands for Tetley's--Tetley
stands for finest
TEA
Tetley's Tea
TV. See also: Television

TV Guide
American reads TV Guide
America's biggest selling
weekly magazine
The magazine with America's
largest primary audience
More ... for less
TV Guide helps you decide
TV Guide puts it all together
TV Guide: The way to
reach your intermarket
TV Guide helps you decide
TV Guide
TV Guide puts it all together
TV Guide
TV Guide: The way to reach
your intermarket
TV Guide
TV station WGN, Chicago
America's No. 1 sports sta-
tion
TV station WJZ-TV, New York
City
Channel 7 for what's worth
watching
For what's worth watching
Tab soft drink
Great taste, one calorie
How can just 1 calorie taste
so good!
Tabasco pepper sauce
The seasoning supreme
There are imitations--be
sure the brand is
Tabasco
Tables are the costume jewelry
of the home
Mersman Tables
Tabu perfume
The "forbidden" fragrance
Taft Broadcasting Company
Informing and entertaining
the American family
The tag always gets 'em
Narco rayon
Tag them for good
Gospel Pencil Co.
Tagliabue Mfg. Co.
One best temperature as an
investment
Tailor. See also: Taylor
Tailor-made toiletries
Mem toiletries
Tailored heat from the fitted
flame
Roberts & Mander Corp.

Tailored men's toiletries
  Mem toiletries
Tailored to fit
  Formfit Brassiere
Tailored to taste
  Genesee Cream Ale
Tailored to the needs of the
    brake
  Multibestos brake lining
Taint gwine rain no mo'
  Pioneer Rubber Mills
Tak-hom-a-biscuit
  It splits in two
Take a bit e out of crime
  McGruff Crime Prevention
    Coalition
Take a gander
  Gander Publishing Co.
Take a tip from Robert Burns
  Robert Burns cigar
Take Aim against cavities
  Aim toothpaste
Take all the hardness out of
    water
  Permutit water treatment
Take control of your investments
  Dow Jones News Retrieval
Take good care of yourself; have
    an Ocean Spray
  Ocean Spray cranberry
    juice
Take it easy
  Neo-Syn Pills
Take it easy and breezy
  Walk-Over Koolies shoes
Take it wherever you go
  Radiola radio receiver
Take off your hat to the Myers
  F. E. Myers & Bro., Inc.
Take Sears back to school
  Sears Roebuck jeans
Take the dread out of night
    driving
  Autolight Control Co.
Take the road to flavor in a
    low tar cigarette
  Raleigh Lights cigarettes
Take the rough spots out of the
    road
  Lovejoy shock absorbers
Take the sheltered route to
    Europe
  Canadian Pacific Steamship
    & Railroad Co.
Take the slant out of hills
  McQuay-Norris Mfg. Co.

Take the Studebaker third de-
    gree road test
  Studebaker automobile
Take time for a "quick-up" with
    Royal Crown
  Royal Crown Cola
Take to water like a duck
  Adler socks
Take two, pain's through
  Neo-Syn Pills
Take your cue--"Q-B-Q" Gloves
    --Quality beyond ques-
    tion
  Q-B-Q Gloves
Take your travel lightly
  Horn luggage
Takes grease out of your way
  Dawn dishwashing liquid
Takes the burns out of broiling
  Moore's Hi-Lo Broiler
Takes the guessing out of dress-
    ing
  Wembley neckties
Takes the "lug" out of luggage
  Karry-Lite luggage
Takes the odor out of perspira-
    tion
  Mum deodorant
Takes the simmer out of summer
  Horton Pilsener
Takes the WEEP out of
    SweepING, making it
    SING
  Wagner Sweepers
Takes TOIL out of toilet cleaning
  Globe Laboratories
Talk facts fast
  Diebold Safe & Lock Co.
The talk of the town
  Park & Tilford candy
Talk things over, get things
    done ... by long dis-
    tance!
  Bell Telephone System
Talk to the right people in the
    right places
  Time
Talk with the microfilm systems
    people
  Minnesota Mining & Manu-
    facturing Co.
Talk with Tilo, there's a
    MATERIAL difference
  Tilo Roofing Co.
The talked-about jewelry
  Castlecliff, Inc.

The talking machine up to
    date
    Columbia Graphophone
Talking Machine World
    The big book with the orange
    cover
The Tall-One Co.
    Hey! Give me a tall one
    It's as cool as it's tall, and
    it's good for you
Tally Ho
    Good dogs deserve good
    food
Talon slide fastener
    The quality slide fastener
Tampa Daily Times
    Florida's great home daily
Tampa Elec. Co. sight meter
    It will tell your eyes be-
    fore your eyes tell you
Tampa electric range
    The modern bed of coals
Tampax, Inc.
    Invented by a doctor--now
    used by millions of
    women
    Look of the month
    No belts, no pins, no pads,
    no odor
    You feel so cool, so clean,
    so fresh...
Tan with Jan
    Jan suntan oil
The tang of good old ale
    Haffenreffer Ale
Tang orange drink
    If the glass is empty it
    must be Tang
Tangee lipstick
    Ends that painted look
Tangee lipstick and face powder
    Satin-finish lipstick; petal-
    finish face powder
Tangy as old Scotch
    Old Bushmill's Irish Whiskey
Tank II toilet bowl cleaner
    Cleans without scrubbing
The tank with a reputation
    W. E. Caldwell Co.
Tanks for the world
    Columbian Steel Tank Co.
Tanners Council of America
    Kid flatters the foot
Tanqueray Distilled English
    Gin
    Preferred; easily acquired;

    instant liquidity
The tape that tackles everything
    Mystik adhesive products
The tape that won't hurt coming
    off
    Micropore adhesive tape
The tapeway to stereo
    Sony Corp. of America
Tappan Company
    You cook better automatically
    with a Tappan
    You live better automatically
    with a Tappan
Tareyton cigarettes
    Us Tareyton smokers would
    rather fight than switch!
    There's something about
    them you'll like
Tartan lets you TAN, never burn
    Tartan suntan oil
Tartan suntan oil
    Tartan lets you TAN, never
    burn
Tarter, Webster and Johnson
    Div., American Forest
    Products Corp.
    For quality western lumber
    products, look to T,
    W and J
Taste and compare
    Trommer's beer
Taste as good as they make you
    feel
    Tums
Taste B4U buy
    MacFarlane candies
The taste beyond 12-year-old
    Scotch
    The Glenlivet Scotch whis-
    key
Taste champ of the colas
    Nehi soft drink
Taste, chew and enjoy--curb
    hunger
    Ayds diet confection
The taste dogs love
    Bonz dog food
Taste how rootie it is
    Krueger beer
The taste is best
    Heinz food products
The taste is richer, yet the
    smoke is milder
    Raleigh cigarettes
The taste it takes four states
    to make

459

Schenley Distillers Corp.
The taste-maker
Schweppes Tonic Water
A taste of "June in January"
Campbell's condensed soups
The taste of the nation
Brewery Corp. of America
Taste Parkay Margarine. The
flavor says "butter"
Parkay Margarine
A taste sells a case
Pacific Brewing & Malting
Co.
The taste tells
Cudahy Packing Co.
Taste tells the tale
SparkLin Ale
Taste test proves the quality
Bokay soda
Taste test winner
Nehi soft drink
Taste that beats the others
cold
Pepsi-Cola soft drink
The taste that sets the trend
Harper's Bazaar
Taste the difference
Chase Candy Co.
Durkee's Seasoned Salt
E. A. Johnston Co.
Rubsam & Horrmann
Taste the taste
Underwood's Original Deviled
Ham
Taste the thrill of Atari at Mc-
Donald's
McDonald's fast food rest-
aurants
Taste what experience can do
for a wine
Almadén Vineyards, Inc.
Taste without waist
Black Label beer
The taste you wouldn't trade
for just anything
Velveeta cheese slices
Tastes better than any other
menthol cigarette!
Newport cigarettes
Tastes good
Wheatena cereal
Tastes great. Not greasy
Crisco shortening
Tastes great ... tastes mild
Chesterfield King cigar-
ette

Tastes great ... yet it smokes
so mild
Chesterfield cigarettes
Tastes like a million, millions
love its taste
5th Ave. Candy Bar
Tastes like fine imported beer
Trommer's beer
Tastes like homemade because
it's made like homemade
Ragu Home Style spaghetti
sauce
Tastes like you squeezed it
Minute Maid Orange Juice
Tastes so good and so good for
you
Cream of Rice
Tastes so good cats ask for it
by name
Meow Mix catfood
Tastes twice as good as ever be-
fore
Jell-O gelatin dessert
Tasting is believing
Cold Spring Brewing Co.
Tasty. See also: Taystee
Tasty filling in every crispy
nugget
Combos candy bar
Tastykake
All the good things wrapped
up in one
Tate industrial uniforms
Tate-made is Rite-made
Tate-made is Rite-made
Tate industrial uniforms
Tater Flakes
They're smackin' good
Tavern Weekly
A proud paper for a proud
industry
Tax free bonds. Ask the man
who owns them
Multi-Vest Securities, Inc.
Tax-Free Income Fund, Inc.
Send your tax bite to bed
... hungry
Taxpaying servant of a great
state
New Jersey Public Service
Electric and Gas Co.
Taylor. See also: Tailor
Taylor Business Institute
Get needed
Taylor has what America rents!
Taylor Rental Corporation

Taylor Instruments
    Accuracy first in home and
        industry
    Taylor instruments mean
        accuracy first
    There's a Tycos or Taylor
        Thermostat for every
        purpose
    World-wide competence in
        control
Taylor instruments mean accuracy
        first
    Taylor Instruments
Taylor Rental Corporation
    America for rent!
    Taylor has what America
        rents!
Taylor safes
    A real safe, not a pretense
Taystee. See also: Tasty
Taystee Bread
    For fresher bread tomorrow,
        buy Taystee Bread to-
        day
Tea & Coffee Trade Journal
    The Blue Book of the trade
Tea in the finest tradition
    Canterbury Tea
Teaberry   See: Clark's Tea-
        berry Gum
Teacher's Highland Cream Scotch
        whiskey
    The answer is in the bottle
    It's the flavor
    No Scotch improves the
        flavor of water like
        Teacher's
    The perfection of Scotch
        whiskey
    The right spirit
Teaching a native to avoid
        severe colds
    Vick's Vapo-Rub
Teaching kids business is our
        business
    Junior Achievement, Inc.
Teaching the millions to buy
    Millis Advertising Co.
Teak toilet goods
    What Scandinavian men
        have
Team it up with your corporate
        jet
    Bell helicopter
A team of specialists
    Cameron Machine Co.

Teamed up for you since '82
    Western Electric Co.
Tecate beer
    America's largest-selling
        imported beer
    The blond beer with the
        body
    Eastern beer flavor, local
        beer prices
Tech beer
    Too good to forget
Technicolor Corp.
    Greatest name in color
The technology for the job at
        hand
    Grumman Corporation
Technology. Fundamental to
        Crane's growth
    Crane Company
Teco Pancake Flour
    It's the buttermilk that
        does it
Tectrol Div., Whirlpool Corpora-
        tion
    Total environmental control
Tectrol Div., Whirlpool Corpora-
        tion. See also: Whirl-
        pool Corporation
Teel mouthwash
    Gentle dental care
    Protects teeth beautifully
    There's beauty in every
        drop
Teele Soap
    It smells so clean
Teeple Shoe Co.
    Mighty good shoes for boys
    A shoe with a talking point
Teeth whiten 3 shades in 3 days
    Kolynos dental cream
Teflon
    No-stick cooking with no-
        scour clean-up
Tegrin shampoo
    Works between shampoos
Tek toothbrush
    Lovely to look at, pleasant
        to use
    The modern toothbrush
    Now clean the tartar zone
Telechime
    No home's complete without
        a telechime
Telechron Electric Clock
    Give them ALL a good time
    Nobody ever had enough

time
Precisely right, in time, in
design
Sleep like a log, wake like
a lark
These are exciting times
Telephone appointments prevent
disappointments
Bell Telephone System
The telephone of tomorrow
Automatic Electric Co. tele-
phones
Teletone radio speakers
Built like a violin
Teletype Corp.
Machines that make data
move
Where the data movement
started and startling
moves are made
Television. See also: TV
Television you can learn from
Pioneer Video, Inc.
Tell 'em Groucho sent you!
De Soto automobile
Tell it in/the morning, tell it in
the Philadelphia Inquirer
Philadelphia Inquirer
Tell it to the Marine
Marine Midland Bank
Tell the millions in their own
homes
National Broadcasting Co.
Teller. See: Bonwit Teller &
Co.
Tells time in the dark
Radiolite watch
Tells time, saves time
Hawkeye Clock Co.
Temperature made to order
Harrison radiators
Templar automobile
The superfine small car
Tempo antacid
Made soft to work hard
Tempt lazy summer appetites
Armour and Co.
Ten shots quick
Savage Arms Div., Emhart
Corp.
Ten to one it's a Santa Fe
Santa Fe cigars
Ten to one ... it's Guinness
time
Guinness ale
Tender Leaf Tea. See: In-

stant Tender Leaf Tea
The tender-textured gelatin
Royal Gelatin
Tender Touch
The light moisturizing bath
oil for dry skin
The tender tuna with the delicate
taste
Star-Kist canned tuna fish
Tendermint Gum
It's different, naturally
Tenneco, Inc.
Building business is our
business
From natural gas and oil
... heat, power petro-
chemicals that mean
ever wider service to
man
That's Tenneco today:
growing in energy ...
and more
Tennessee Dept. of Conservation
America's most interesting
state
Tennessee Furniture Corp.
Made by the makers of fine
furniture
More than a cedar chest, a
piece of fine furniture
Tension envelope
The string will not pull out
Terraplane automobile
Strength, safety, style and
speed, Terraplane
meets every need
Test-and-farm-proved
Goodyear Auto Tire
Test drive total performance '65
Ford Motor Company
Test it with a hammer
Pratt & Lambert varnish
The test that tells
American Distilling Corp.
Tested goodness
Gulden's mustard
Tested in the waters of the
world
Valentine's Valspar
The tested treatment
Listerine mouthwash
Testor Cement Co.
The house of adhesives
Tetley Teas please
Tetley's Tea
Tetley's Tea

Its flavor wins favor
Makes good tea a certainty
"T" stands for Tetley's--
  Tetley stands for finest
  TEA
Tetley Teas please
Texaco, Inc.
  Keep on saving as you
    drive
  Localized for you
  Lubrication is a major factor
    in cost control
  The pacemaker of gasolines
  Texaco star power for car
    power
  Time makes good things
    better
  Trust your car to the man
    who wears the star
  Trust your car to the prod-
    ucts with the star
  We're working to keep your
    trust
  You can trust your car to
    the products with the
    star
  Your ticket to the Met for
    over forty years
Texaco restrooms
  Clean across the country
Texaco star power for car power
  Texaco, Inc.
Texas Eastern Transmission
  Corp.
  Pipeliners of energy
Texas Gas Transmission Corp.
  Serving the big river
    region
Texas Instruments, Inc.
  Creating useful products
    and services for you
  Rely on T I
  We put computing within
    everyone's reach
Texas National Bank of Com-
  merce of Houston
  All the bank you'll ever
    need in Texas
Texas' oldest newspaper
  Galveston News
Texcel Tape
  Sticks with a touch
The text book of the confec-
  tionery trade
  Candy and Ice Cream
Textile Div., Monsanto Company

Nothing but nylon makes
  you feel so female
Textile Div., Monsanto Company.
  See also: Monsanto
  Company
Textile Machinery Div., Crompton
  and Knowles
  Between today's knowledge
    and tomorrow's looms
  First in fabric forming
    equipment
Textile World
  Largest paid net circulation
    in the textile field
  The world's textile authority
Textilene
  The better backbone of
    modern rugs
Textron
  From yarn to you, it's
    Textron all the way
  That's Textron, making
    strong companies
    stronger
Textron, Inc. See: Gorham
  Div., Textron, Inc.
Textron Pajamas
  Smart enough for sleepwalk-
    ing
Textron Slip
  A white-white slip of soft-
    falling, ice-smooth rayon
    crepe, frosted with deli-
    cate madeira embroidery
Textron Summer Blouses
  Gay as May
Thai Airlines
  How man was meant to fly
Thank goodness for Banquet
    cooking bag foods
  Banquet frozen foods
Thank goodness for Banquet
    frozen foods
  Banquet frozen foods
Thank you, Paine Webber!
  Paine Webber, Jackson &
    Curtis
Thank your Bear man for your
    accident that didn't
    happen
  Bear Safety Device
Thanks for using Coast Line
  Atlantic Coast Line Railroad
Thanks to you it works for all
    of us
  The United Way

Thanks to you it's working
    The United Way
Tharp Heating and Air Condi-
        tioning, Inc.
    One of the oldest in the
        business
That "always fresh" look
    Woodbury's Cold Cream
That Bright Eyes look
    Bright Eyes cat food
That Bud ... that's beer!
    Budweiser beer
That Chancellor taste
    Chancellor cigars
That cushiony feeling lasts
        longer with Marfak
    Marfak motor oil
That eyes may see better and
        farther
    Bausch & Lomb Optical Co.
That finished look
    Venus foundations
That fresh perked taste
    Sanka Brand decaffeinated
        coffee
That frosty mug sensation
    A & W Root Beer
That good Pittsburgh candy
    Reyner & Bros., Inc.
That Kruschen feeling
    Kruschen salts
That makes the difference
    Ferguson Tractor
That marvelous mixer
    Waukesha mineral water
That old-time ale with the old-
        fashioned flavor
    Aetna Brewing Co.
That ole southern flavor
    Abilene Flour Mills
That pleasing cigar
    Muriel cigar
That Red Horse outpaces them
        all
    Mobilgas
That reminds me
    Ever Ready calendars
That South American thrill
    Don X carbonated beverage
That taste's always in season
    Old Grand-Dad whiskey
That they may rest in peace
    Clark Metal Grave Vault
        Co.
That we may ride in comfort
    McGraw tires

That's a Butler building?
    Butler Manufacturing Co.
That's all you need to know about
        stockings
    Mojud hosiery
That's Clayton class
    Clayton Inn, St. Louis, Mo.
That's Italian!
    Ragu Home Style spaghetti
        sauce
That's my bank
    Fort Wayne National Bank
That's my meat
    Kingan & Company
That's putting it MILDLY
    Country Doctor pipe mix-
        ture
That's Tenneco today: growing
        in energy ... and more
    Tenneco, Inc.
That's Textron, making strong
        companies stronger
    Textron
That's the Total difference
    Total vitamin and iron sup-
        plement cereal
That's why, where quality counts,
        calfskin spins the yarn
    Lawrence Leather Co.
The theatre in your home
    U. S. Television Mfg. Co.
Their. See also: There
Their tails will wag if you feed
        them Flag
    Flag Pet Food Corp.
Thematic advertising
    Grey Advertising Agency
Theme-inspired beauty for bud-
        get brides
    Mohawk rugs and carpets
Theobald Industries
    Meals without meat are in-
        complete
There. See also: Their
There are breath mints and
        there's Läkerol
    Läkerol
There are imitations--be sure
        the brand is Tabasco
    Tabasco pepper sauce
There are imitations, of course
    Viyella-International, Inc.
There are many advance styles,
        but there is only one
        Advance pattern
    Advance Pattern Co.

464

There are no dudes in our
    duds
    Man-O-West trousers
There are no easy answers
    ARCO Atlantic Richfield
    Co.
There are no finer shoes
    Nettleton shoes
There can be no compromise
    with safety
    American Chain Co.
There has never been a bad time
    to make a good invest-
    ment
    Gulfstream American execu-
    tive jet airplanes
There is. See also: There's
There IS a difference in hearing
    aids
    Western Electric hearing
    aids
There is a Maidenform for every
    type of figure
    Maidenform brassieres
There is a use for Celotex in
    every building
    Celotex Corp.
There is as much satisfaction in
    the brewing of a good
    beer as in the drinking
    of it
    Blatz beer
There is beauty in every jar
    Ingram's Milkweed Cream
There is no better place to eat
    Lennox Hotel, St. Louis,
    Mo.
    Mayfair Hotel, St. Louis,
    Mo.
    Mayfair House, New York
    City
There is no compromise with
    quality at Longchamps
    Longchamps Restaurants,
    New York City
There is no equal
    Lowerator Div., American
    Machine and Foundry
    Co.
There is no finer
    Oil of Orange
There is no finer solid silver
    than National
    National sterling silver
There is no "Just as Good"
    Olympia Self-Playing

Music Box
There is no Kodak but the East-
    man Kodak
    Kodak cameras
There is no other car like Reo--
    not at any price
    Reo automobile
There is no ration on letters
    Eaton Paper Corp.
There is no saturation point for
    honest value
    Dodge automobile
There is no substitute for ex-
    perience
    Kelvinator refrigerator
There is no substitute for Kalak
    Kalak Water Co.
There is no substitute for marble
    National Association of
    Marble Dealers
There is no substitute for quality
    Skelly Oil Co.
There is no substitute for the
    best
    Jewett superspeaker radio
    loudspeaker
There is no warmer underwear
    made!
    Damart Thermolactyl under-
    wear
There is nothing better in the
    market
    Old Forester bourbon whis-
    key
There is nothing finer than a
    Stromberg-Carlson
    Stromberg-Carlson radio
    receivers
There is one best in everything
    Johns-Manville Corporation
There is one near you
    Rexall Drug Stores
There is only one Fly-Tox
    Fly-Tox insecticide
There is only one Heatrola, Es-
    tate builds it
    Estate Stove Co.
There is only one in-a-door
    bed--the Murphy
    Murphy in-a-door bed
There is only one Jockey
    Jockey Menswear Div.,
    Cooper's, Inc.
There is only one "old faithful"
    Rugged luggage
There is only one Ozite, look

for the name
Ozite carpets
There is only one thoughtful
    choice
    Standard & Poor's invest-
    ment service
There may still be places on
    earth where Grand
    Marnier isn't offered
    after dinner
    Grand Marnier Liqueur
There should be a Lee in your
    future
    Lee Machinery Corp.
There's. See also: There is
There's a Colonial salt for every
    purpose
    Colonial Salt Co.
There's a Corbin behind every
    Corbin
    Corbin Ltd. Tailoring
There's a difference in farm
    papers
    Successful Farming
There's a difference worth know-
    ing
    House of Tre-Jur perfumes
    Schenley Distillers Corp.
There's a Ford in America's fu-
    ture
    Ford automobile
There's a Ford in your future
    Ford automobile
There's a future for YOUR figure
    in Foundettes
    Foundettes foundations
There's a good future with
    Mobil
    Mobil Oil Corp.
There's a Hotpoint electric range
    for every purse and
    purpose
    Hotpoint Div., General
    Electric Company
There's a Jewel for every use
    Jewel Paint & Varnish Co.
There's a Lee for every job
    H. D. Lee Co., Inc.
There's a meal in every Muffet
    Muffets
There's a Merton cap or hat
    for every sport
    C. S. Merton & Co.
There's a need-keyed billfold
    for you
    Amity Leather Products

    Co.
There's a new light in your life
    Solar Electric Corp.
There's a picture ahead
    Kodak cameras
There's a Radiola for every purse
    Radiola radio receiver
There's a reason
    Grape-Nuts cereal
There's a reason for Grape-Nuts
    Grape-Nuts cereal
There's a Tycos or Taylor
    Thermometer for every
    purpose
    Taylor Instruments
There's a world of difference in
    Webster dictionaries
    G. and C. Merriam Co.
There's always a thirst time
    Zimba Cola soft drink
There's an Ingersoll for everyone
    Ingersoll flashlight
There's art to the fit of Artemis
    Artemis slips
There's beauty in every drop
    Teel mouthwash
There's lemon and orange in
    every bite
    Trix cereal
There's magic in La Mode
    La Mode foundations
There's many a castle built out
    of cigarette smoke
    Bonded Tobacco Co.
There's more hard cash ahead
    Welch's grape juice
There's more than one white
    tissue but only one
    White Swan
    White Swan bathroom tissue
There's more to it
    India Tea Bureau
There's never been a low "tar"
    with richer taste
    Viceroy cigarettes
There's no better time
    Big Ben Westclox alarm
    clock
There's no hurt like forgetting
    Whitman's Chocolates
There's no obligation ... except
    to those you love
    Metropolitan Life Insurance
    Co.
There's no place like Hilton
    Hilton Hotels Corp.

There's no place like this
  showplace!
  Chicago Merchandise Mart
There's no Radiolite but the
  Ingersoll Radiolite
  Radiolite watch
There's no substitute for exper-
  ience
  Florsheim Shoe Co.
  Pontiac automobile
There's none better
  White House evaporated
  milk
There's not a cleaner like it
  Monarch Cleaner
There's nothing like a cool drink
  of water
  Sunroc electric water cooler
There's nothing like it under the
  sun
  Nestea
There's nothing too good for men
  in service
  Mennen's talcum powder
There's only one Imperial
  Imperial Margarine
There's only one way to play it
  Kool cigarettes
There's quality about a home
  with Henredon
  Henredon Furniture Indus-
  tries, Inc.
There's quality written all over
  Bradley-Vrooman un-
  usual paint
  Bradley & Vrooman Co.
There's simply no better way to
  automate your office
  Wang Laboratories, Inc.
There's something about them
  you'll like
  Fleurette Frocks
  Tareyton cigarettes
There's style and wear in every
  pair
  Wear-Right Gloves
Therm-O-Disc, Inc.
  Leadership through accom-
  plishment
Therm-O-Disc, Inc. See also:
  Thermo
Thermadore Electrical Mfg. Co.
  Div., Norris Indus-
  tries, Inc.
  Seven leagues ahead
Thermasol, Ltd.

We're changing the way the
  world bathes
Thermiodyne radio receivers
  If it's in the air Thermiodyne
  will get it
  The sensation of radio
Thermo. See also: Therm-O-
  Disc, Inc.
Thermo anti-freeze
  Fill up before you freeze
  up
Thermo King Corp.
  World leader in transport
  refrigeration
Thermogas, Inc.
  America's fastest growing
  fuel
Thermoid brake lining
  For short stops and long
  service
  Install confidence ... install
  Thermoid
  The lining that gives you
  the brakes
  "Longer-life" line for heavy
  duty service
Thermolath
  The greatest recent advance
  in building and heating
  economy
Thermopane glass
  Where there's a window ...
  there's a place for
  Thermopane
Thermotron
  A perfected control instru-
  ment
These are exciting times
  Telechron Electric Clock
These names assure you the best
  in pneumatic, hydraulic
  and electronic compo-
  nents
  Bellows-Valvair Div., Inter-
  national Basic Economy
  Group
They all speak well of it
  De Witt Clinton Hotel, Al-
  bany, N. Y.
They almost talk to you
  Pictorial Review
They always eat better when you
  remember the soup
  Campbell's condensed soups
They are. See also: They're
They are the largest-selling

cigarette in America
Camel cigarettes
They better your aim
Lyman Gun Sight Corp.
They can rest assured
Nashua blankets and sheets
They cost more because they're
worth more
Autocar truck
They cost no more
Regent cigarettes
They cure the tickle
Dean's Mentholated Cough
Drops
They do run easier
Royal typewriter
They do things for your legs
Rollins Hosiery Mills
They don't call it Power House
for nothing
Power House candy bar
They express success
Cutler desks
They finish the day for the sun
Coleman Co., Inc.
They fit
Round-The-Clock stockings
They fit better because they
are better fitted
Enna Jettick shoes
They fit royally
Phillips-Jones shirts
They give you the sweetest and
most tender moments
of their lives, the
fleeting moment of per-
fect flavor
Green Giant Peas
They have a tone that's all their
own
New Departure Bicycle
Bells
They help keep babies dry
Huggies diapers
They hit good from anywhere
Ben Hogan golf clubs
They just don't wilt
Ritz crackers
They keep a-running
Century Electric Co.
They keep the springs like new
Houde Engineering Corp.
They keep the whole place
warm
Pecco unit heaters
They kill them all

Wilson's fly pads
They last forever
Jamestown Panel Co.
They last longer
A. P. Green Fire Brick Co.
Eveready flashlights and
batteries
Eveready radio batteries
Hercules tanks and heaters
National Fiberstock Envelope
Co.
Rand dress shields
They level the road as you go
American Chain Co.
They look real
Arcade toys
They moo for more
Ashcraft-Wilkinson cotton-
seed meal
Suni-Citrus Products
They must be good
Sunsweet prunes
They must make good or we will
Oshkosh Overall Co.
They neither crimp your roll
nor cramp your style
Bob Smart Shoe Co.
They pull you through
Bethlehem spark plug
They reign in the rain
Follmer umbrellas
They resist wear
Pacific fabrics
They respect your throat
Alligator cigarettes
They rise to the occasion
Knockdown bleachers
They satisfy
Chesterfield cigarettes
They satisfy and yet they're
mild
Chesterfield cigarettes
They self-adjust to whatever
your day is like
Ultra Ban deodorants
They show when they blow
Trico Fuse Mfg. Co.
They stay brighter longer
General Electric Mazda
Lamp
They still don't ouch me
Curad bandages
They take every trick
Grand Slam golf clubs
They tie well, they wear well
Cheney Cravats

They walk with you
  Melville Shoe Corp.
They walked the roads to glory
  U. S. National Guard
They will. See: They'll
They win your feet
  United Shoe Manufacturers
They won't fall out
  Hairlainers hairpins
They work while you sleep
  Cascarets laxative
They'll die outside
  Rough-on-rats rat poison
They're. See also: They are
They're better because they're
  seamless
  Godfrey rollers
They're cobwebby wonders
  Cannon nylon stockings
They're cool and easy as an off-
  shore breeze
  Bostonian shoes
They're cut to fit to fight fatigue
  Reis underwear
They're milder; they taste better
  Chesterfield cigarettes
They're pure
  Richardson's Mints
They're smackin' good
  Tater Flakes
They're tops for the bottoms
  Musebeck Shoe Co.
They're walk-fitted to fit right,
  feel right
  Bostonian shoes
They're wear-conditioned
  Monmouth Hosiery Mills
They're worth asking for by
  name
  American Express traveler's
  checks
They've got to be Stetson to be
  snappy
  Stetson Shoe Co.
Thick thirsty thrifty Dundee
  towels
  Dundee towels
The thicker the metal, the long-
  er the protection
  Perfection Burial Vault
Thilmany Pulp and Paper Co.
  Functional papers
The thin man in leather
  Knight wallet
Things go better with Coke
  Coca Cola soft drink

Things look bright with Colfanite
  Colfanite finishing material
The things we'll do to make you
  happy
  Trans World Airlines, Inc.
Think
  International Business
  Machines Corp.
Think ahead--think SCM
  Smith-Corona typewriters
Think before you drink, say Sea-
  gram's and be sure
  Seagram's Distillers Corp.
Think big, think United
  United Air Lines Cargo
  Service
Think copper
  American Brass Co.
Think of it first
  Ideas, Inc.
Think once, write once, at once
  Ediphone Dictograph
Think original, think Dellinger
  Dellinger, Inc.
Think straight ... think Rollway
  Rollway Bearing Co.
Think system
  Scientific Anglers, Inc.
Think what we can do for you
  Bank of America
Thinking capital
  First Boston Bank
The third dimension pattern
  Advance Pattern Co.
The third hand with a mighty
  grip
  Prentiss Vise Co.
Thirst come, thirst served
  Erlanger Brewery
  Goody Root Beer
Thirst prize
  Pabst Blue Ribbon beer
33 fine brews blended into one
  great beer
  Pabst Blue Ribbon beer
33 million tins sold in 1883
  Anglo-Swiss Milk Food
34% stronger points
  Eagle Pencil Co.
A thirty minute ride will win you
  Essex automobile
This Bud's for you
  Budweiser beer
This hotel is for those who ap-
  preciate the difference
  Beverly-Wilshire Hotel,

Los Angeles, Calif.
This is a new influence in radio
    Atwater Kent radio receiver
This is for keeps
    Community silverplate
This is living ... this is Mar-
        riott
    Marriott hotels
This is the answer to the high
        cost of horse delivery
    Maxfer Truck
This is the best $3. shoe in the
        world
    W. L. Douglas shoe
This is the best watch for bi-
        cyclers
    Waterbury watch
This is the center of industrial
        America
    Ohio Edison Power
This is the dream you can be--
        with Maidenform
    Maidenform brassieres
This is the envied car
    Stearns automobile
This is the last word in fountain
        pen convenience
    Camel fountain pen
This is the open world of LOF
        glass
    Libbey-Owens-Ford Co.
This is the way to run a rail-
        road
    Northern Pacific Railway
This mark means good light at
        low cost
    General Electric Mazda
        Lamp
This much more in a Shelvador
    Shelvador refrigerator
This one means business
    DH125 airplane
This plus in his diet puts song
        in his heart
    The R. T. French Co.
This symbol of quality is your
        protection
    Radiola radio receiver
This year Santa's wearing
        green
    S & H Green Stamps
Thom McAn shoes
    Step inside and make
        yourself comfortable
    Your friend
Thom McAn socks

Knit to fit
Thomas Laughlin Co.
    Fist grip clips
Thomas Page Mill Co.
    The perfect sour milk biscuit
        flour
Thomas Young Orchids, Inc.
    Orchids ... naturally
Thomaston sheets
    A quality for every purse
        and purpose
Thomasville Furniture Industries,
    Inc.
    By design ... furniture
        distinguished for value
        since 1904
Thompson. See also:
    J. Walter Thompson Co.
    Norm Thompson mail order
        service
    Thomson
Thompson Bros. Boat Mfg. Co.
    The greatest name in out-
        board boats
Thompson's Double Malted Milk
    If it's Thompson's, it's
        double malted
Thomson. See also: Thompson
Thomson McKinnon Securities,
    Inc.
    A brokerage house you can
        bank on
Thor clothes iron
    It isn't child labor, it's
        child's play
Thor clothes washer
    Get more with Thor
The Thoro Products Co.
    Soiled clothes that are not
        spoiled clothes
The thorough electric cleaner
    P. A. Geier Co.
A thoroughbred air in every
        pair
    Grewen gloves
The thoroughbred of breads
    Royal Baking Co.
The thoroughbred radio
    Freed-Eisemann Radio
        Corp.
Thorpe awnings
    Just a "shade" better
Thorpe Fire Proof Door Co.
    Every room a separate
        building
Those heavenly carpets by Lees

James Lees and Sons Co.
Those in the know ask for Old
    Crow
    Old Crow whiskey
Those who really know drink
    Falstaff
    Falstaff beer
Those who think are proud to
    drink--Hires
    Hires' Improved Root Beer
Thoughtful men make the hap-
    piest husbands
    Whitman's Chocolates
Thoughtfully designed with a
    woman in mind
    Bowlene cleaner
A thousand miles of travel, a
    thousand thrills of
    pleasure
    Canadian Steamship Lines,
    Ltd.
A thousand tender words in one
    Gruen watch
A thousand things may happen
    in the dark
    Eveready flashlights and
    batteries
The three-cent quality medium
    of America's greatest
    market
    New York World
Three Feathers whiskey
    At its pre-war best
    Choice of good judges
    First among fine whiskies
    The rising BARometer of
    whiskey preference
    Smoother, lighter, richer
    than ever
    Strictly conFOODential
3-flavor dog food
    Red Heart dog food
3-in-1 oil
    The finest oil that man
    produces, suited for
    a thousand uses
    The high quality household
    oil
3M hears you...
    Minnesota Mining & Manu-
    facturing Co.
3M 9600 Digital Facsimile Trans-
    receiver
    The twenty-second delivery
    service
Three magazines in one

McCall's
Three Minute Cereals
    Makes kids husky
Three Minute Oats
    Triple-treat breakfast with
    get-up and go
Three minutes of chewing makes
    the difference
    Feen-a-Mint
Three Musketeers candy bar
    The bar that gives you lots
    more of what you buy
    chocolate for
Three point presses
    Kidder Press Co.
Three seals to safety
    Universal Pressure Cooker
Three Sixty Five
    The year-round oil
Three steps to safety
    Grey-Rock Div., Raybestos-
    Manhattan, Inc.
The thriftiest of baking powders
    Calumet Baking Powder
A thrifty fuel
    Old Mac Coal
Thrifty Rent-a-car System Inc.
    The off-airport car rental
    centers
    We take less so you can
    have more
Thrill for breakfast
    Grape-Nuts Flakes
Thrill of a pipetime
    Kirsten Pipe Co.
Thrive catfood
    Nutrition at its best
Through every "storm" since
    1845
    New York Life Insurance
    Co.
Through pictures to inform
    Life
Thundering power in the eye of
    the market
    Metalworking News
Tia Maria liqueur
    Jamaica's legendary liqueur
Tiara vermouth
    America's most distinguished
    vermouth
Tic Tac
    The 1½ calorie breath mint
Tide laundry detergent
    America's favorite
    Claim your spot. Tide gets

it clean
The extra action in Tide
   means dirt can't hide
Tide's in ... dirt's out
Women just won't give up
   the clean they get
   from Tide
Tide's in ... dirt's out
   Tide laundry detergent
Tie. See: Thai
Tiecrafters
   For a narrow point of view
Tiffany & Co.
   Time-Honored Quality
The Tiffany of the bolt and nut
   business
   R. I. Tool Co.
The Tiffany tube of America
   Peerless Tube Co.
Tiffin Products, Inc.
   Candies of distinctive qual-
   ity
Tight as pipe, but flexible
   Penflex tubing
Tighten your grip on the future
   Provident Mutual Life In-
   surance Co. of Phila-
   delphia
'til. See also: Until
'til the end of time
   Rensie watches
Tillamook Cheese
   Look for Tillamook on the
   rind
Tillyen lenses
   Accurate to the very edge
   Clear to the very edge
Tilo Roofing Co.
   Talk with Tilo, there's a
   MATERIAL difference
Tilt the odds in your favor
   Saginaw Steering Gear
   Div., General Motors
   Corporation
Timbertone Decorative Co., Inc.
   First with the finest in
   wallcoverings ... al-
   ways!
Time
   America's #1 news magazine
   More goes into it
   The most colorful coverage
   of the week
   The most important maga-
   zine to the world's
   most important people

Read Time and understand
Talk to the right people in
   the right places
Time: The news magazine
   for the internationally
   minded
The weekly news magazine
World trade UNITES nations
Time before your eyes
   Phinney Walker automobile
   clocks
Time Brewing, Inc.
   Timed to perfection
The "time clock" for machinery
   Recorder
Time for a lifetime
   Gotham watch
Time for a lifetime and longer
   Gotham watch
Time has branded it best
   White Horse whiskey
A time-honored name in scales
   Fairbanks-Morse scales
Time-Honored Quality
   Tiffany & Co.
Time hurries in every factory
   Rennus time clock
Time in sight, day or night
   Gilbert radium dial clock
Time is money--24 hours a day
   Deutsche Bank
Time makes good things better
   Texaco, Inc.
The time-tested laxative
   Espotabs laxative
Time: The news magazine for
   the internationally
   minded
   Time
Time to Re-tire? (Buy Fisk)
   Fisk tires
Time to rejoice
   Walthem watches
Time will tell, wear Sundial
   Shoes
   Sundial Shoes
Time works wonders
   Seagram's Distillers Corp.
Timed to perfection
   Gunther Brewing Co.
   Time Brewing, Inc.
Timed to the stars
   Elgin watches
Timely Clothes, Inc.
   Balanced tailoring
   Balanced tailoring makes

Timely Clothes look better
--longer
Times Square Hotel, New York
City
Rest assured
Times Square Trust Co.
For you--every banking
service
Timex computers
The power is within your
reach
Timex watches
We make technology beauti-
ful
Timken Roller Bearing Co.
All there is in bearings
All work and no play
Can speed the nation's
freight
Dual duty
Quality turns on Timken
Timken Roller Bearing Co.
See also:
Rock Bit Div., Timken
Roller Bearing Co.
Steel and Tube Div., Tim-
ken Roller Bearing Co.
Tin keeps it better
Keekin cans
Tinactin
Get a jump on athlete's
foot with Tinactin
No. 1 recommended for
athlete's foot
Tinkertoy
Quality toys with a pur-
pose
Tinnerman Products, Inc.
Look for the Tinnerman
"T," the mark of total
reliability
Tintex dye
Tintex tints in the rinse
Tintex tints in the rinse
Tintex dye
Tiny Arcadians
Arcade toys
Tio Sancho Mexican food flavor-
ings
I make it easy. You make
it delicious
Tips for table tops
Successful Farming
Tire Rebuilders News
The trade magazine for
independents

The tire with the gum-weld
cushions
India tire
Tirenew rubber tire preservative
Makes tires look new and
last longer
Tires
The trade paper of the tire
industry
Tires with nine lives
Kelly-Springfield Tire Co.
Tirometer Valve Corp.
Adds miles to tire life
'Tis. See also: It is
'Tis a feat to fit feet
Dalsimer shoes
Titchener. See: E. H. Titchen-
er Co.
A title on the door rates a Bige-
low on the floor
Bigelow-Sanford, Inc.
Titleist golf balls
Remember; no one is paid
to play Titleist
Titanox paint
Beauty through whiteness
To be opened at Christmas and
every day thereafter
Kelvinator refrigerator
To be sure it's pure, be sure
it's Purox
Purox wire
To be sure you're right ...
insist on Merriam-
Webster
G. and C. Merriam Co.
To bid you good morning
Shirriff's marmalade
To bring you permanent cooking
satisfaction
Rome kitchen ware
To build a stronger nation
Physical Culture
To earn more, learn more
International Correspondence
Schools
To energize your sales crew,
put Power behind it
Power
To feel new power, instantly,
install new Champions
now and every 10,000
miles
Champion spark plugs
To fly high in the morning,
take Phillips at night

473

Phillips' Milk of Magnesia
To get a letter, write a letter
    Eaton Paper Corp.
To get more that's good ...
        trust Swanson
    Swanson frozen dinners
To get there, try the air
    California Growers Air Ex-
        press
The greater vision through op-
        tical science
    Bausch & Lomb Optical Co.
To grow healthy hair, keep
        your scalp clean
    Jeris hair tonic
To grow the best, plant the
        best; use Schell's seeds
    Schell's seeds
To heat right, burn our anthra-
        cite
    Anthracite Mining Assn.
To increase value is to enrich
        life
    General Motors Corpora-
        tion
To keep happy, keep well
    Kellogg's All-Bran
To keep teeth clean use Saltine
    Saltine dentifrice
To kill that odor just NIL that
        odor
    Nil deodorant
To kindle love, light up your
        type
    Woodbury's Cold Cream
To know them is to love them
    Richard Hudnut toilet
        specialties
To lighten the burden of wom-
        ankind
    Crystal washing machine
To look well and feel well,
        sleep well
    Chatham blankets
To make a golden moment live
        forever
    Roma champagne
To measure is to economize
    Brown pyrometers
To patch a hole, or build a
        home
    Western Wallboard Co.
To promote the American way
        of life, depend on the
        railroad
    Baltimore & Ohio Railroad

To protect the unborn and the
        newborn
    March of Dimes
To rid your car of motor "bugs"
        install a set of Champion
        plugs
    Champion spark plugs
To save business time
    Remington typewriter
To save gasoline keep your spark
        plugs clean
    Champion spark plugs
To see your way clear
    Anco windshield washing
        equipment
To sell millions, tell millions
    National Transitads, Inc.
To sell more shoes, buy Moore
        shoes
    Moore Shoe Co.
To sell SUCCESSFUL farmers
        buy Successful Farming
    Successful Farming
To serve investors more effi-
        ciently
    Barron's
To serve something fancy start
        with something fancy
    Flav-R-Pac canned goods
To skid or not to skid
    Fisk tires
To talk little, to hear much
    International Magazine
To "test with the best"
    Imperial-Eastman Corp.
To the victor goes the crown
    Victor Sporting Goods Co.
To trim you, slim you, to give
        you more swing, more
        zing, for Spring
    Jantzen bathing suits
To unburn sunburn
    Unguentine ointment
To uphold your sox, trousers
        and dignity
    Barrthea garters and sus-
        penders
TOAST for every TASTE
    Proctor toaster
The toast of the Coast
    Aztec Brewing Co.
The toast to good taste
    Hires' Improved Root Beer
Toast to your taste, every time
    General Electric toaster
The toaster you've always

474

wanted
Waters-Center toaster
Toastimonials
Tostmaster toaster
Toastmaster cooking equipment
The complete line of electric cooking equipment
Toastmaster toaster
Famed from toast to toast
For your taste in toast
Keep the home fires burning, but not the toast
No watching, no burning, no turning
Start the day the American way
Toastimonials
Tobacco is our middle name
American Brands, Inc.
The tobacco of quality
Old Chum tobacco
Tober-Saifer shoes
Outer beauty, inner worth
Today is history. Tomorrow is Barron's
Barron's
Barron's Current Corporate Reports
Today's anti-friction path for power
Diamond roller chain
Today's best looking building values
Butler Manufacturing Co.
Today's finest designed for tomorrow's needs
Charles Beseler Co.
Today's high peak in motor car value
Ford automobile
Today's high yields. Plus U. S. Government security
Fidelity U. S. Government Reserves
Today's ideas ... engineered for tomorrow
Powermatic, Inc.
Today's leader in tomorrow's look
Panasonic radio receivers
Today's most scientific shoes
W. B. Coon Co.
Today's need for tomorrow is life insurance
Western Life Insurance Co.

Today's trucking industry. It works for America
American Trucking Associations, Inc.
Todd Shipyards
Service beneath the surface
Toddy
A meal in a glass
Together, we can change things
American Red Cross
Tokheim Corp.
Symbol of excellence
Told on the petals of a rose
Listerine Luster-Foam
Toledo Scale Co.
No springs. Honest weight
Prime source for weighing equipment and technology
Toledo Trust Co.
Everything you want a bank to be
Tom Keen cigar
The cigar made with good judgment
Tomatoes, plump, firm, ruddy and ready
Campbell's tomato juice
Tomorrow is a friend of Dunbar
Dunbar Furniture Corp.
Tomorrow on every wrist
Speidel Corp. watch bands
Tomorrow you can be anywhere
Boeing aircraft
Tomorrow's body today
Tuxedo Hat Body Corp.
Tomorrow's car today
Durant Star automobile
Tomorrow's cellular system today
Motorola, Inc.
Tomorrow's citizens
Juvenile Group Foundation
Tomorrow's energy since 1882
Kansas City Power and Light Company
Tomorrow's freight savings plan--today!
SST Freight Carriers
Tomorrow's medicines from today's research
Nupercainal
Tomorrow's skin care--today
Coty cosmetics
Tomorrow's style today
De Soto automobile
Tomorrow's styles today

Advance Pattern Co.
Tomorrow's way to deliver goods
today
White truck
Ton tested
Pennsylvania Tires
The tone heard 'round the world
Wm. S. Haynes Co.
Tone the sunlight with window
shades just as you tone
the electric light with
lamp shades
Columbia window shades
Toni. See also: Tony
Toni Home Permanent
The creme cold wave
The tonic food beverage
Ovaltine
The tonic fruit
American Cranberry Ex-
change
Tonight at bedtime
Lee's Magnesia
Tonight let it be Löwenbräu
Löwenbräu beer
Tonight show, featuring Johnny
Carson
Heeeeeere's Johnny!
Tons of comfort
Denver Hanna coke
Tony. See also: Toni
Tony Canzoneri's Country Club,
Marlboro, N. Y.
A champion resort
Too good for words
O. C. Pecan Fudge
Too good to forget
Tech beer
Too late for Herpicide
Herpicide hair tonic
The tool box of the world
Stanley Tool Div., The
Stanley Works
A tool for modern times
IBM personal computer
The Tool Holder People
Armstrong Bros. Tool Co.
The tools in the plaid box
American Saw & Mfg. Co.
Tools you can sell with con-
fidence
Marion Tool Works
Toolmaker to the master me-
chanic
Millers Falls Co.
Tooth powder in paste form

Sunny Smile dentifrice
The toothsome paste
Red Gum dentifrice
Tootsie Rolls candy
The chocolated candy bar
that lasts a long time
Making the world sweeter
The sweetheart of a "chew-
sey" world
The TOP in roofing values
Fischer Lime & Cement Co.
Top Job cleaning liquid
Holds up even better under
water
The top name in cordials is at
the bottom of the bottle
Bardinet Cordial
Top of the morning
Cream of Wheat
Top quality for 50 years
General Tire & Rubber Co.
Top Secret pet disinfectant
Keeps litter odors top
secret
The top that sells the bottom
since 1838
Collins & Wright salt shaker
tops
ToPol toothpaste
The smoker's toothpaste
The topping that's too good to
stop with one plop
Dover Farms topping
Topp's Chewing Gum
Only natural flavors last
longer, naturally
A superior quality chewing
gum
Tops at shelling time
Pfister Associated Growers
Tops everything for lasting
beauty
Nevamar plastic
Tops for quality
Pepsi-Cola soft drink
Tops in preference because it's
tops in performance
G. E. refrigerator
Tops in taste
Nehi soft drink
Tops in taste, low in price,
rich in food
Post Toasties
Torfeaco bedding
Warm as sunshine, light
as floating clouds

Torginol of America, Inc.
    A generation of worldwide
        acceptance
Toro power mowers
    Famous for power mowers
        for over 50 years
    If all lawn mowers look the
        same to you maybe
        you're not looking close
        enough
Toronto-Dominion Bank
    Where people make the dif-
        ference
Torrington Co.
    The innovators
    Progress through precision
Toshiba America, Inc.
    The best of two worlds
    In touch with tomorrow
    The international one
Toshiba desktop copier
    Everything's getting smaller
        but performance
Total capability in fire protec-
    tion
    Grinnell Corp.
The total car
    Ford LTD automobile
Total cereal
    The start that's bowls
        apart
Total communications from a
    single source through
    Sylvania
    Sylvania Electric Products,
    Inc.
The total controls company
    Johnson Controls, Inc.
Total environmental control
    Tectrol Div., Whirlpool
    Corporation
Total modal transportation ... a
    sound concept to invest
    in
    Transway International
    Corporation
Total performance
    Ford Motor Company
The total sports network
    ESPN television broadcast-
    ing system
Total transportation
    Fruehauf Corporation
Total vitamin and iron supple-
    ment cereal
    That's the Total difference

Totally different
    Purity Oats Co.
Toto mechanical lawn mowers
    We believe in making things
        better
Touch his heart with smooth,
    soft hands
    Jergens Lotion
A touch of Faultless adds that
    faultless touch
    Faultless laundry starch
The touch of tomorrow in office
    living
    The Globe-Warnicke Co.
Touchable shine
    Favor furniture polish
A tough act to follow
    Northwestern Mutual Life
    Insurance Co.
Tough and springy
    O'Sullivan rubber heel
Tough as a rhino
    Cupples tires
Tough as the hide of a rhinoceros
    Rhino enamel
Tough as they make them
    Purity liquid tile
The tough breed of tire
    B. F. Goodrich Tire Co.
Tough, but oh so gentle
    Hastings piston rings
Tough enough to overstuff
    Hefty Steel Sak trash bag
Tough on dirt even in cooler
    water
    Cheer detergent
Tough on your beard, not on
    your face
    Norelco Rototrack Shaver
The tough pumping problems go
    to Aldrich
    Aldrich Pump Co.
Tougher than elephant hide
    Continental tires
Tougher than the world's tough-
    est roads
    Isuzu trucks
The toughest job you'll ever love
    U. S. Peace Corps
Tourist
    The world's only tourists'
    magazine
A tower of strength
    Bankers Trust Company
The tower of strength in Dixie
    Lamar Life Insurance Co.

Towmotor Corp.
    The one-man gang
Toyota automobile
    Built tough for you
    Get your hands on a
        Toyota ... you'll never
        let go
    It's a good feeling to buckle
        up for safety
    Make the jump to Toyota
    O, what a feeling!
Toyota trucks
    If you want the right
        truck, buy Toyota
    Somebody did it right
Toys that are genuine
    A. C. Gilbert Co.
The trade authority
    Automobile Topics
The trade magazine for inde-
        pendents
    Tire Rebuilders News
The trade mark known in every
        home
    Universal kitchen utensils
The trade paper of the home
    Modern Priscilla
The trade paper of the tire in-
        dustry
    Tires
Trade the market instead of
        stocks
    Stotler & Co. stock brokers
Trade the market without buy-
        ing stock
    Bache stock brokers
Trade Wind ventilating hood
    The name that means
        quality
The trademarked sugar that
        F-L-O-W-S
    Flo-Sweet
A tradition of leadership in ad-
        vanced state of the art
        technologies
    Motorola, Inc.
A tradition on the move
    RCA Corp.
Traditional clothing for less
    Huntington Clothiers
Traditionally preferred through-
        out our land
    Swift's bacon
A trailer for every load
    Warner trailers
The trailer that leads

Nutting Truck Co.
Trailer Train Co.
    Border to border ... coast
        to coast!
Trailways bus system
    Trailways serves the nation
        at "scenery level"
Trailways serves the nation at
        "scenery level"
    Trailways bus system
Train. See also: Trane
Train & McIntyre Scotch whiskey
    Gentle as a lamb
    A noble Scotch
Train your trucks and save
    CSX Corporaton
The trains that railroad men buy
        for their boys
    Lionel electric trains
Trane. See also: Train
Trane Co.
    For any air conditioning
Tranolane hemorrhoid remedy
    Works better
Trans-Canada Telephone System
    In the twinkling of an eye
Trans-Lux Corporation
    Communications specialists
        since 1920
Trans Union Corp.
    Eight companies running
        hard
Trans World Airlines, Inc.
    Nationwide, worldwide de-
        pend on ...
    The things we'll do to make
        you happy
    Up up and away
    You're going to like us
Transamerican Freight Lines,
        Inc.
    Vital link in America's
        supply line
Transcontinental & Western Air-
        lines
    The airline run by flyers
    Nature made it, TWA flies
        it, the sunny Santa Fe
        Trail
Transformer Corp. of America
    It speaks for itself
Transit Advertisers, Inc.
    The eyes have it
    Punch and power at point
        of purchase
Transo Envelope Co.

Transos envelope the world
Transos envelope the world
Transo Envelope Co.
Transway International Corpora-
tion
Total modal transportation
... a sound concept to
invest in
Transway's going places to
bring you products
that serve your needs
Transway's going places to bring
you products that serve
your needs
Transway International Cor-
poration
Traung Label & Lithograph Co.
An institution that sticks
to its last
Travel Adventures
Go as a travel adventurer
Travel begins with Everwear
Everwear trunks
Travel follows good food routes
National Restaurant As-
sociation
Travel light, travel right
Val-A-Pak luggage
Travel on the Reading
Philadelphia & Reading Rail-
way
Travel strengthens America
U. S. Travel Bureau
Travel with Everwear; Everwear
travels everywhere
Everwear trunks
The Travelers Insurance Cos.
For all kinds of insurance
in a single plan, call
your Travelers man
Insure in the Travelers
The largest multiple life
organization in the
world
You can get all types of
insurance under the
Travelers umbrella
The traveler's world
Venture
Trax shoes
We're building a great
name
Tre-Jur. See: House of
Tre-Jur perfumes
A treasure for eating pleasure
Country Gardens canned

vegetables
Treasured American glass
Viking Glass Co.
Treat. See also: Armour's
Treet
Treat the cloth and starve the
moth
Larvex
Treat your home like an old
friend
Dutch Boy White Lead
Treat your water right and it
will treat you right
Chicago Chemical Co.
Treat yourself like company
Seagram's V. O. whiskey
Treat yourself to the best
Mail Pouch chewing tobacco
The tree-growing company
Weyerhaeuser Company
Tree Top frozen apple juice
Many are picked. Few are
frozen
Treet. See:
Armour's Treet
Treat
Treganowan. See: Ernest
Treganowan
Trend apron
Send Trend to a friend
The trend is to Mutual
Central Manufacturers Mutu-
al Insurance Co.
The trend to Dictaphone swings
on
Dictaphone Corp.
Treo Co., Inc.
Shapemakers to the world's
most beautiful women
Trevira
The extraordinary fiber
Tri. See also: Try
Tri-Lok steel flooring
King of the walk
Tri-sure the world over
American Flange & Mfg.
Co., Inc.
Triangle Package Machinery Co.
Superior performance through
design simplicity
Tricks. See: Trix
Trico Fuse Mfg. Co.
Dependability in the field
... safety for the
operator
It's a real fuse, built for

real service
A lifetime of safety-first
service
Porcelain top, no shocks,
no burns
Preferred for quality
Quality electrical protective
devices and specialties
They show when they blow
Try Trico today
Trico windshield wiper blades
Don't wait 'til it storms
Trident Sugarless Gum
Recommended by moms like
me who care about
teeth
Trimble Nurseryland Furniture,
Inc.
Making the world safe for
baby
Trimness for men, slimlines for
ladies
Seven Seas slacks
Trims the ankle, slims the leg
Velva Leg Film
Trio. See: Treo
Triple thick bottoms
Reynolds lifetime aluminum
Triple-treat breakfast with get-
up and go
Three Minute Oats
Triplett tube tester
Precision first ... to last
Standards are set by
Triplett
Triply protected for oven-time
freshness
Rumford Baking Powder
Triumph Ice Machine Co.
True in the long run
Trix cereal
There's lemon and orange
in every bite
Trommer's beer
Beer flavor at its peak
Better because brewed
solely of malt and hops
Brewed solely of malt and
hops
Buy the Big Boy
It's two ways light
Light after you drink it
Light as you drink it
Light beer of Broadway
fame
Made like, tastes like fine

imported beer
The peak of beer flavor
Taste and compare
Tastes like fine imported
beer
Trommer's the malt beer
Trommer's the malt beer
Trommer's beer
Tropical commercial roofing
Commercial roofing systems
for roofs that stay
watertight
Tropical masterpieces
Simon Bros. straw handbags
Tropical Radio Telegraph Co.
The voice of the Americas
The tropical suit that "breathes"
fresh air
Northcool suits
Troster Singer Stevens Rothchild
Corp. stock brokers
Keep your eye on Troster
The trousseau house of America
Grand Maison de Blanc
Troy Engine & Machine Co.
Dependable power, absolute
safety
Tru (tru). See also: True
The tru brew
Young Brewing Co.
Tru-Lax
The true chocolate laxative
Tru-Taste Mayonnaise
Halves the cost and doubles
the satisfaction
Tru-Val shirts
America's smartest buy
Dollar for dollar, your best
buy
The truck of continuous service
Maccar truck
The truck of proved units
Acme motor truck
Truck of value
General Motors Corporation,
Truck Division
The truck stops here
American Trucking Associ-
ations, Inc.
Trucks. See also: Tucks
Trucks are what we're all about
General Motors Corporation,
Truck Division
Trucks for every purpose
Mack trucks
Trucks that can handle America's

problems because they're
built to handle the
world's
Magirus diesel trucks
Trucks you don't steer, you aim
White truck
True. See also: Tru (tru)
True
The massive men's market
in print
The true chocolate laxative
Tru-Lax
True cigarettes
True, the enjoyable low tar.
And that's the truth
True, ultra low tar enjoy-
ment that's smiles ahead
of the rest
You found it
A true expression of heartfelt
sympathy
Society of American Florists
True in every sound
Victor phonograph records
True in the long run
Triumph Ice Machine Co.
The true old-style Kentucky bour-
bon
Early Times bourbon whiskey
True salesmanship in print
Lord & Thomas
True Shape Hosiery
All that its name implies
The true shape of table silver
Ritespoons
True stories from real life
Smart Set
True Story
The necessary two million
True Temper Corp.
Adds science to fishermen's
luck
The right tool for the right
job
The rod of champions
True, the enjoyable low tar.
And that's the truth
True cigarettes
True to its name
Novelty Shoe Co.
True to its tone
Onongaga Pottery Co.
True to our aim
Fleetwood radio products
True, ultra low tar enjoyment
that's smiles ahead of

the rest
True cigarettes
True Value hardware stores
More than just a name. It's
our way of doing busi-
ness
Truhn silk
If it's Truhn, it's washable
A truly great name among Amer-
ica's great whiskies
Old Crow whiskey
The trumpet you hear on the
phonograph
Buescher trumpet
The trunk with doors
Winship trunk
Trunks may come and trunks may
go, but Everwear goes
on forever
Everwear trunks
Truscon Laboratories
Paint comes first
Trushay
The beforehand lotion
Trust Cadillac to lead the way
Cadillac automobile
Trust Company of Georgia
Where banking is a pleasure
Trust in Phillips is worldwide
Phillips Research Labora-
tories
Trust the Midas Touch
Midas muffler and brake
shops
Trust Tylenol--hospitals do
Tylenol pain reliever
Trust your car to the man who
wears the star
Texaco, Inc.
Trust your car to the oil of
character
Quaker State Oil Refining
Corp.
Trust your car to the products
with the star
Texaco, Inc.
The trusted and authoritative
name in dictionaries
G. and C. Merriam Co.
The trusted name in household
products since 1917
Gem, Inc.
A trusted name ... proved by
medical research and
the experience of mil-
lions

Niagara Cyclo Massage
Trustworthy Hardware Stores
    We're the problem solvers
A trustworthy name in electrical
    protection
    Buss fuses
Truth in advertising
    Advertising Federation of
    America
The truth without courting favor
    or fearing condemnation
    Kansas City Post
Truths ageless as time
    Rosicrucians
Try. See also: Tri
Try a tankful of research genius
    Shell gasoline
Try a tankful, you'll notice the
    difference immediately
    Pure Quill gasoline
Try Hollycourt. Why? The bowl
    stays dry
    Hollycourt pipes
Try it a week. You'll use it for
    life
    Swift's Premium meats
Try it ... and show the family
    the smile they love to
    see!
    Valet Auto-Strop Razor
Try on a pair of Jarmans today,
    let the shoe horn be the
    judge
    Jarman shoes
Try Spry. Here's why
    Spry shortening
Try the new "free-stride"
    Modess sanitary napkins
Try them on for sighs
    Strutwear nylon stockings
Try Trico today
    Trico Fuse Mfg. Co.
Trying harder makes Avis second
    to none
    Avis automobile rentals
The tube that lasts and l-a-s-t-s
    Listerine shaving cream
The tube to buy to satisfy
    Magnavox radio tube
The tube with the sensible
    guarantee
    Supertron radio tube
Tubize Artificial Silk Co.
    Artificial silk at its highest
    point of perfection
    Wears longer because it's

    stronger
Tucker Pharmacal Co.
    Hypnosis without Narcosis
Tucker's. See:
    Mrs. Tucker's Shortening
    Orrin Tucker's orchestra
Tucks. See also: Trucks
Tucks hemorrhoid remedy
    For more relief than creams
    or ointments alone
Tudor Press, Inc.
    From design to distribution
Tufraw luggage
    Luggage of distinction
Tulsa World
    Oklahoma's greatest news-
    paper
Tums
    For the tummy
    Taste as good as they make
    you feel
Tune in your favorite tempera-
    ture
    Adolphus Hotel, Dallas,
    Texas
Tune the meal and tone the sys-
    tem
    Florida Citrus Exchange
The tuned car
    Buick automobile
Tung-Sol lamp
    Let Tung-Sol light the way
Tung-Sol radio tube
    The long life radio tube
Tungsten Ignition, Tungsten
    Contact Mfg. Co.
    Puts the "go" in ignition!
Turchin glass
    American artistry in glass
Turn a circle without a wrinkle
    Bias Fold tapes
Turn a frown to a grin with
    Anacin
    Anacin pain reliever
Turn a little meat into a big
    treat
    Herbox Bouillon Cubes
Turn your switch and get Cuba
    or Seattle
    Mu-Rad radio receivers
Turnbull Elevator Co.
    The safe, swift, silent
    "lift"
Turner Construction Co.
    Turner for concrete
Turner for concrete

Turner Construction Co.
Turner microphone
    It magnifies your perform-
      ance
Turns bristles into blotters
    Benex brushless shave
Turns sidewalks into soft carpets
    Air Step shoe
Turtle Wax automobile polish
    The impossible is now pos-
      sible
Tussy cosmetics
    For that young, young look
Tussy deodorant
    Tussy really cares about
      people who care
    Tussy really cares about the
      sorcery of scent
Tussy really cares about people
    who care
    Tussy deodorant
Tussy really cares about the
    sorcery of scent
    Tussy deodorant
Tuxedo Feeds
    The feeder's silent partner
Tuxedo Hat Body Corp.
    Tomorrow's body today
Tuxedo tobacco
    I envy men the pleasant
      puffing of their pipes
    It's good because it's fresh
    Your nose knows
    Your nose quickly knows
    Your nose quickly knows
      the difference
'Twas. See also: It was
'Twas the bite before Christmas
    Jane Parker Fruit Cake
Tweedie Boot Top Co.
    Stay put
12 kinds--better than most people
    make
    Heublein cocktails
Twelve million people are today
    using Stewart-Warner
    products
    Stewart-Warner Corporation
The 12-year-old Scotch well worth
    looking for
    Cutty 12 Scotch whiskey
12-year-old unblended Scotch.
    About $20 the bottle
    The Glenlivet Scotch whis-
      key
A twentieth century expression

of the French civilization
    Renault automobile
Twenty-eight day concrete in 24
    hours
    Atlas Luminite Cement Co.
The 21st century company
    Gulf and Western Indus-
      tries, Inc.
Twenty-five years of record
    growth and progress
    have led us to this
    moment--the threshold
    of a new era
    Occidental Petroleum Cor-
      poration
25 hour protection
    Odorono deodorant
Twenty-four years of tested
    service
    Central Trust & Savings
      Co.
21 kinds--12¢ per can
    Campbell's condensed soups
The twenty-second delivery
    service
    3M 9600 Digital Facsimile
      Transceiver
22% faster
    Underwood typewriter
Twice a day
    Listerine mouthwash
Twice a day, and before every
    date
    Colgate's Ribbon Dental
      Cream
Twice a day we bridge the
    bay
    Bay Cities Transportation
      Co.
Twice as good because it's pork
    and beef
    Hygrade Food Products Co.
Twice as much fun
    Loco-Builder electric trains
Twilight zone
    Diebold Safe & Lock Co.
The "Twin Formula" head cold
    tablet
    Vicks Tri-Span
Twin names in quality towels
    Fairfax and Martex towels
    Martex and Fairfax towels
Twinplex razor
    For smooth shaves
Twix candy bars
    The chocolate candy with

the cookie crunch
Two buttons on the shoulder,
none down the front
Sealpax underwear
Two feet of comfort in every
step
W. H. Walker & Co.
200 extra miles of lubrication
Union Oil Company
Two layers of softness ... and
one is purest white
Aurora bathroom tissue
2,000,000 people fighting cancer
American Cancer Society
Two mints in one
Certs
The two most trusted names in
meat
Swift's Premium meats
Two people sleep when one goes
Pullman
Pullman sleeping car
Two Scotches of exceptional
character
Black and White Scotch
whiskey
Two years ahead
Owen Magnetic Motor Car
'Twont. See also: It won't
'Twont krinkle, 'twont krack,
'twont krawl
Seattle Cedar
Tydol gasoline
The economy gasoline
Puts wings on your car
Tylenol pain reliever
Trust Tylenol--hospitals do
We've worked hard to gain
your trust. We'll work
even harder to keep it
You can trust our good
name
You can't buy a more potent
pain reliever without a
prescription
Tyler Corp.
Boost profits with the com-
petitive edge
Tyler Refrigeration Div., Clark
Equipment Company
World leader in commercial
refrigeration
Tyler Refrigeration Div., Clark
Equipment Company.
See also: Clark
Equipment Company

Typewriter leader of the world
Underwood typewriter
Tyracora
Continuous filament textured
nylon

-U-

U must try me on
Heart Throb Dresses
U. See also: You
UCO Quality Foods
Like a garden in your pan-
try
UMC Industries, Inc. See:
Universal Metal Prod-
ucts Div., UMC Indus-
tries, Inc.
U. S. See also: United States
U. S. Air Force
The wings of America
U. S. Airmail
Wing it there via the air
U. S. Army Recruiting Service
Army. Be all you can be
A good job for you
It takes more than brains
to go to college
U. S. B. Electric Bicycle Lamp
It works
U. S. Brewers Assn.
America's beverage of mod-
eration
U. S. Brewers Foundation
Beer belongs, enjoy it
U. S. Chain & Forging Co.
Better block chains in the
red band bag
U. S. Coast Guard
Help others. Help yourself
U. S. Deck Paint
Dries hard overnight
U. S. Electrical Tool Co.
The good mechanic's choice
U. S. Gaytees rubbers
Fashion over-the-shoe
U. S. Gloves
Double wear in every pair
The U. S. Government securities
specialist
Aubrey G. Lanston & Co.,
Inc.
U. S. Gypsum Co.
The fireproof sheathing
The fireproof wallboard

U. S. Hoffman Machinery Corp.
  The pressing service that
    shapes your clothes
U. S. L. batteries
  Power to spare
U. S. Life Corporation
  Life is a family affair
U. S. National Bank
  The kind of a bank you will
    enjoy doing business
    with
U. S. National Guard
  They walked the roads to
    glory
  With tools of war they
    fashion peace
U. S. Navy Recruiting Service
  The navy needs you!
    Don't READ American
    history--MAKE IT!
U. S. News and World Report
  America's only un-sugar-
    coated news magazine
  News of consequence for
    people of consequence
U. S. Peace Corps
  The toughest job you'll ever
    love
U. S. Postal Service Express
    Mail
  Next day service
  We make you look good for
    less
U. S. Radiator Corp.
  Guaranteed heating
U. S. Royal tires
  Better tires for every farm
    need
  Quality in tires is the key
    to safety
  Service through science
  Serving through science
  U. S. Tires are good tires
U. S. Rubber Co.
  Serving you through sci-
    ence
U. S. Savings bonds
  Put your money where your
    heart is
  Save the easy, automatic
    way; buy U. S. Bonds
U. S. Television Mfg. Corp.
  The theatre in your home
  Window to the world
U. S. tires are good tires
  U. S. Royal tires

U. S. Travel Bureau
  Travel strengthens America
U. S. Van Lines, Inc.
  Dedicated to people on the
    move
  Moving up
UTA French Airlines
  Sailing the South Pacific
    skies
Uajustit Car
  The car that grows with
    the child
Ullman. See:
  Martin Ullman Studios
  Sigmund Ullman & Co.
The ultimate car is the Stearns
  Stearns automobile
The ultimate cigar
  Macanudo cigar
The ultimate driving machine
  BMW automobile
The ultimate in fine corsetry
  The Corselette
The ultimate in radio reception
  MacLaren radio receiver
The ultimate motor home
  Blue Bird Wanderlodge
The ultimate vacation resort
  Shepp Ranch (Idaho)
Ultra Ban deodorants
  They self-adjust to whatever
    your day is like
Ultra-Lite replacement windows
    and doors
  You're always right with
    Ultra-Lite
The ultra-refined British gin
  Boodles London Dry Gin
Ultra Sense panty hose
  Wherever no nonsense is
    sold
Ultra Sonic Seal, Inc.
  Originators and designers
    of ultrasonic sealing
    equipment
Unaware of underwear
  Hanes underwear
The unbeatable way to jet home
  Western Air Lines, Inc.
Unbiased financial planning.
    There's a lot more to
    it than meets the eye
  Synergistic Financial
    Services, Ltd.
UNBRAKO costs less than trou-
  ble

Precision Fastener Div.,
Standard Pressed Steel
Co.
Unchallenged for quality
Cadillac automobile
Unchanged since 1824
The Glenlivet Scotch whis-
key
Uncle Ben's, Inc.
Each grain salutes you
Measure of quality
Uncle Ben's, the rice people
Uncle Ben's, the rice people
Uncle Ben's, Inc.
Uncle Sam Bond
For good business stationery
Uncle Sam wants you!
World War I recruiting post-
er drawn by James Mont-
gomery Flagg
The uncola
7UP soft drink
Uncommon carriers
Oneida motor truck
The unconventional business
computer
Cado computer
Underfeed furnace and boiler
stoker
Cut coals bills 1/2 to 2/3--
guaranteed with the
Underfeed
Underwood portable typewriter
The write gift for Christ-
mas
Underwood speeds the world's
business
Underwood typewriter
Underwood typewriter
The gift that continues to
give
The machine you will
eventually buy
22% faster
Typewriter leader of the
world
Underwood speeds the world's
business
Willing keys bring writing
ease
Underwood's deviled meats
Devilicious!
Underwood's Original Deviled
Ham
Branded with the devil but
fit for the gods

The sandwich spread of the
nation
Taste the taste
Uneeda. See also: You need a
Uneeda Biscuit
National Biscuit Co.
Unequaled for use in livery, ex-
press and private
stables
Frank Miller's Harness
Dressing
Unequalled for speed, accuracy
and durability
Crandall Type-Writer
Unexcelled accuracy
Giddings & Lewis Machine
Tool Co.
Unexcelled for grinding and
polishing
Keystone Emery Mills
Unforgettable Hawaii, no land so
hard to bid adieu
Matson Navigation Co.
Unguentine ointment
The first thought in burns
To unburn sunburn
The unhurried whiskey for un-
hurried moments
Kinsey whiskey
Uniform mileage
Miller tires
Uniformly good
Sainthill Levine uniforms
Sunkist oranges
Uniformly good oranges
Sunkist oranges
Union Barge Line Corp.
When distribution is the
question UBL has the
answers
Union brass faucet
We took the splash out of
the kitchen
Union Camp Corporation
Growing in more ways than
one
Union Carbide Corp.
The discovery company
The Union Central Life Insur-
ance Co.
Procrastination is the high-
est cost of life insur-
ance. It increases both
your premium and your
risk
Union Fork & Hoe Co.

The shovel with a back-
bone
Union Life Insurance Co.
Protects you at all times
Union Metal Mfg. Co.
Ones that last a lifetime
Union Oil Company
America's fifth freedom is
free enterprise
Finest anti-knock non-
premium gasoline ever
offered at no extra cost
Go with the spirit--the
spirit of '76
200 extra miles of lubrica-
tion
Union Pacific Railroad
Be specific, route Union
Pacific
Be specific ... say "Union
Pacific"
Gateway to and from the
booming west
Gateway to and from your
world markets
Road of the daily stream-
liners
The seasoned traveler goes
by train
Serves all the West
The strategic middle route
The wheels of transporta-
tion help turn the
wheels of industry
Union smoking tobacco
Best in the Union, in pocket
tins
The Unique Hair Crimper
The best in the world.
None can equal it
Unique in all the world
Ford Thunderbird auto-
mobile
Unique luggage
Creators of distinctive lug-
gage
Unique, worldwide
Irving Trust Company
Uniroyal, Inc.
Chemical, rubber and
plastic products world-
wide
World's largest manufac-
turer of industrial
rubber products
Uniroyal tires

We give you more to go on
Unisom
Fall asleep faster
The No. 1 sleep aid in
America
Unit banking speeds business
Manufacturers Trust Co.
The Unit-Wall Construction
Bishopric Mfg. Co.
United Air Express Service
Packages prefer United Air
Express
United Air Lines Cargo Service
Think big, think United
United Air Lines, Inc.
Choose your vacation from
the entire nation
The extra care airline
Fly the friendly skies of
United
Known for extra care
The main line airway
The nation's largest airline
People who fly for a living
choose United
Welcome aboard
United American Lines
Across the Atlantic
Pleasure pirate pilgrimage
The voyage of your dreams
United Audio Products, Inc.
Dual's the finest ... the
record proves it since
1900
United Beverage Bureau
Surrounds and protects the
beverage industry
United California Bank
The bankers who do a little
more for you
United Cigar Stores
Largest in the world be-
cause we serve the
people best
The sign of a good cigar
United Electric vacuum cleaner
Cleans without beating and
pounding
United Energy Resources, Inc.
The pioneering spirit keeps
America's pipelines
flowing
Pioneers in energy
United Jewish Appeal
Give them life and make
it worth living

United Mink Producers Assn.
  World's finest mink
United moves the people that
    move the world
  United Van Lines, Inc.
United Negro College Fund
  A mind is a terrible thing
    to waste
United of Omaha
  Security is our business
United Optical Co.
  Put your eyes at ease
United Retail Candy Stores
  Happiness in every box
United Shoe Machinery Corp.
  Makes any good shoe better
United Shoe Machinery Corp.
      See also: B. B. Chem-
      ical Div., United Shoe
      Machinery Corp.
United Shoe Manufacturers
  They win your feet
United States. See also: U. S.
United States Cartridge Co.
  Hits where you aim
  A load for every purpose
    and a shell for every
    purse
United States Daily
  All the facts, no opinion
  All the flexibility of a news-
    paper with the coverage
    of a national magazine
  Preferred position before a
    preferred audience
  Reaching influential America
United States Gypsum Co.
  The greatest name in build-
    ing
  Pioneering in ideas for in-
    dustry
United States Lines, Inc.
  Luxury and comfort with
    utmost safety
United States Shoe Co.
  Fits the foot in action or
    repose
  Flexible where you want it,
    rigid where you need
    it
United States Steel Corp.
  Nothing equals stainless
    steel
  Self reliance. It's one of
    our strengths
  Where the big idea is

  innovation
  You can't beat steel for
    bathrooms
United States Trust Company of
    New York
  When you do something very
    well you simply cannot
    do it for everyone
United States Worsted Corp.
  From fleece to fabric
United Technologies Corporation
  The power of technology is
    the power to create
United Telecommunications, Inc.
  A clear, distinctive voice
    in the Information Age
United Van Lines, Inc.
  Moving with care ... every-
    where
  United moves the people
    that move the world
The United Way
  Care to share
  Thanks to you it works for
    all of us
  Thanks to you it's working
Unitron
  A new flush mounted unit
    cooler
Univac is saving a lot of people
    a lot of time
  Sperry Rand Corporation
Universal Boring Machine Co.
  Where accuracy counts, we
    win
The universal car
  Ford Model T automobile
Universal Cooler Corp.
  Fills a universal need
Universal electric blanket
  With the exclusive slumber
    sentinel
Universal kitchen utensils
  The trademark known in
    every home
The universal mender
  LePage's glue
Universal Metal Products Div.,
    UMC Industries, Inc.
  Leads the industry in qual-
    ity and dependability
Universal motors
  Above all, dependable
Universal Oil Products Co.
  Better ideas from UOP
  Where research is planned

with progress in mind
The universal packing
　　Vulcabeston
The Universal Pad and Tablet
　　Corp.
　　The finest pads have purple
　　bindings
Universal pajamas
　　We put the world to sleep
Universal Paper Products Co.
　　You save with paper
The universal pipe
　　Wm. Demuth & Co.
Universal Pressure Cooker
　　Three seals to safety
Universal university
　　International Correspondence
　　Schools
Universal washer
　　A beauty for double duty
Universal Winding Co.
　　Getting the most from wind-
　　ing
University of the night
　　International Correspondence
　　Schools
Univis glasses
　　Life looks brighter
Unless it has a red wheel it is
　　not a Lorain
　　Lorain stove
Unlocking new concepts in archi-
　　tectural hardware since
　　1839
　　Russwin-Emhart Corp.
Unmistakably ... America's
　　premium quality beer
　　Falstaff beer
Unparch that throat
　　Cliquot Club ginger ale
Unquestionably the world's finest
　　stereophonic console
　　Pilot Radio Corp.
Unrivaled in tone. Elegant in
　　finish. Reasonable in
　　price
　　Estey organ
The unseen giant of the brakes
　　American Asbestos Co.
The "unstoppables"
　　Jeep automobile
Unsurpassed to help motors last
　　Kendall motor oil
Unsurpassed to help your car
　　last
　　Kendall motor oil

Until. See also: 'til
Until Friendly Fives were made,
　　good shoes were expen-
　　sive
　　Jarman shoes
Untouched by human hands
　　Chock Full O' Nuts restaur-
　　ants
　　Sweet Message Chocolates
Unusual reliability and service
　　... the usual at Kopp
　　Glass
　　Kopp Glass, Inc.
Unwind your way to Europe
　　Italian Line
Unwise and unfortunate is the
　　man who tries to shave
　　without Williams' soaps
　　Williams' Shaving Soap
The up and coming airlines
　　Piedmont Airlines
The up-draft lighter
　　Lord Oxford cigarette light-
　　er
Up to your neck in fruity good
　　taste
　　Yoplait Yogurt
Up up and away
　　Trans World Airlines, Inc.
Uplift that stays up
　　Surprise brassiere
Upon reflection, the best
　　Dewar's White Label Whiskey
Upset? Pape's diapepsin will put
　　you on your feet
　　Pape's diapepsin
Upson Co.
　　Quality part of every parti-
　　tion
　　The superior interior
The urge to instant action
　　North East Electric Co.
Urshelime
　　The fat of the lime is
　　Urshelime
Us Tareyton smokers would
　　rather fight than
　　switch!
　　Tareyton cigarettes
Use BOST and get a good paste
　　in the mouth
　　BOST toothpaste
Use cool judgment, buy a good
　　fan
　　Robbins & Myers electric
　　fan

Use 'em yourself to sell 'em
American Chain Co.
Use-engineered for cleaning, pro-
tecting and processing
DuBois Chemical Div., W.
R. Grace & Co.
Use face brick, it pays
American Face Brick Asso-
ciation
Use it as a dentifrice
Forhan's toothpaste
Use Pepsodent twice a day, see
your dentist twice a
year
Pepsodent toothpaste
Use redwood, it LASTS
California Redwood Associ-
ation
Use the Bell to sell
Bell Telephone System
Use the mails to increase your
sales
Martin L. Roman
Use the spark plug engineers
use
Champion spark plugs
Use the Sweetheart Skin Diet
Manhattan Soap Sales Corp.
Use the wheat and spare the
meat
Fisher Flouring Mills
Use your head about your feet
Selby Shoe Co.
Use your head to save your heels
Bell Telephone System
Used and preferred by all
Allcock's Porous Plasters
Used as a skirt supporter and
dress looper they have
no equal
Clinton Nickel Safety Pins
Used by gymnasts and acrobats
Arabian Joint Oil
Used by more men today than
any other hair tonic
Vaseline Hair Tonic
Used by skilled craftsmen every-
where
Empire levels
Used everywhere in beautiful
homes
Columbia window shades
Used where performance counts
Grant Oil Tool Co.
Used while you sleep
Vapo-Cresolene

Useful facts in advertising
Industrial Equipment News
Useful products for family living
Hamilton Cosco, Inc.
Users know
Garford motor truck
Usol Fly Spray
Keeps cows contented from
sunrise to sunset
Usol Mite Killer
Keeps mites out of hen
houses for one year
Utah Power & Light Co.
Coal lights our nights and
brightens our future
Utica sheets
The feel of silk, the
strength of linen
Fine combed, fine count
percale sheets
The utility business paper
Hammermill Paper Co.
Utley paint
Weathers our weather
The utmost in cigarettes
Egyptian Deity cigarettes
The utmost in lubrication
Skelly Oil Co.
The utmost in luxury at moder-
ate prices
Real Silk Hosiery
The utmost in rope value
Whitlock Cordage Co.
Utmost security, minimum cost
Chicago lock
Utz & Dunn Co.
The easiest shoe for women

-V-

V-8 vegetable juice drink
A basket of garden fresh-
ness in every can
Drink a glass of "summer-
time" sometime every
day
Drink V-8 every day for
vegetables the tasty
way
I could have had a V-8!
Wow! I'm gonna have a
V-8!
A vacation in itself
Atlantic City Steel Pier
The vacation way to Hawaii

Matson Navigation Co.
Vacation where you please
　　Karriall trailers
Vacationing in San Antonio is a
　　family affair
　　San Antonio Municipal Infor-
　　mation Bureau
Vacuette non electric vacuum
　　cleaner
　　It's easy to vacuum clean
　　without electricity
Vacuum-packed to preserve the
　　flavor
　　Hanley & Kinsella Coffee
Val-A-Pak luggage
　　Travel light, travel right
Val chewing gum
　　Everybody's chewing it
　　The refreshing grape
　　flavored chewing gum
Valentine's Valspar
　　The paint that does it right
　　Stands up fine
　　Tested in the waters of the
　　world
　　The varnish that won't turn
　　white
　　Weather armor for homes
Valet Auto-Strop Razor
　　Try it ... and show the
　　family the smile they
　　love to see!
Vallee's. See: Rudy Vallee's
　　Connecticut Yankees
　　dance orchestra
Valspar. See: Valentine's
　　Valspar
Value-engineered papers from
　　the mills of Mosinee
　　Mosinee Paper Mills Co.
Value engineering favors zinc
　　American Zinc Institute
"Value" is a good word for
　　Benefit Trust Life
　　Benefit Trust Life Insur-
　　ance Co.
Value ... it runs in the family!
　　Hi Dri paper towels
Valvoline motor oil
　　Be thrifty, buy quality
　　Everything you need in a
　　motor oil
　　It's a life insurance policy
　　for your engine
　　It's life insurance for your
　　engine

It's not just for winning
　　races
　　World's first--world's finest
Van Camp. See also: Stokely-
　　Van Camp, Inc.
Van Camp Sea Food Co.
　　Better, naturally
Van Camp's pork and beans
　　Easy as opening a book
　　A feast for the least
　　Heat, eat, enjoy
Van Dorn & Dutton Co.
　　Gear craftsmen for over a
　　quarter century
Van Dorn Iron Works Co.
　　Master craftsmanship in
　　steel
Van Duyn chocolates
　　The chocolates of good
　　taste
Van Ess Liquid Scalp Massage
　　Costs nothing unless we
　　grow hair
Van Heusen shirts
　　Give his neck a break
　　Magic sewmanship
　　The one white shirt that's
　　different
　　Younger by design
Van Raalte hosiery
　　Because you love nice
　　things
Vanadium-Alloys Steel Co.
　　Metallurgy is our business
Vanadium Corp. of America
　　For strength, toughness
　　and durability
Vanguard Recording Society,
　　Inc.
　　Recordings for the connois-
　　seur
The vanishing breed
　　De Lorean automobile
Vanity Fair Mills, Inc.
　　All is vanity ... all is
　　Vanity Fair
Vanity foundation
　　Every woman needs a little
　　Vanity
Vanity hats
　　Seen in the best company
Vaniva. See also: Venida
Vaniva Shaving Cream
　　The only new idea in shav-
　　ing since the safety
　　razor

Vano
  If you're not using Vano,
    you're working too hard
Vantage Products, Inc.
  The jeweler's quality watch
Vantage Ultra Lights menthol
    cigarettes
  New fresh taste. Only 5
    mg.
  Your best decision in ultra
    low tar
Vantine shaving cream
  Good for its face value
Vapo-Cresolene
  Used while you sleep
Varco-Pruden Buildings
  When you know who we are
    you won't build any
    other way
Variety box of exquisite gift
    candies
  Norris, Inc.
The varnish invulnerable
  Morgan varnish
The varnish that won't turn
    white
  Valentine's Valspar
Varo Optical, Inc.
  Mastery of precision optics
Varsity
  The young man's magazine
Varvella artificial pearls
  The loveliest pearls made
    by man
Vaseline
  The handiest thing in the
    house
Vaseline hair tonic
  For double care, both scalp
    and hair
  Used by more men today
    than any other hair
    tonic
Vaseline Intensive Care Lotion
  Smooths the healing right
    in
Vat 69 whiskey
  Quality tells
Vaughan & Bushnell Mfg. Co.
  It pays to use good tools
Veedol motor oil
  Diving or driving, you've
    got to beat heat
  The film of protection
  100% Pennsylvania at its
    best

Perfection for new cars;
    protection for old cars
Veg-All Larsen Co.
  A fresh vegetable garden
    in every can
  A vegetable garden in a
    can
Vegemato cocktail
  Drink a salad
A vegetable garden in a can
  Veg-All Larsen Co.
Vel
  Mar-VEL-ous for dishes,
    stockings, lingerie,
    woolens
Velamints candy
  Great taste that only hap-
    pens here
Velchek Tool Co.
  Keep mechanics good tem-
    pered
Velie automobile
  The name insures the qual-
    ity
  Some day you will drive a
    Velie
Velon
  The fabric of tomorrow on
    the looms of today
Velva Leg Film
  Trims the ankle, slims the
    leg
Velveeta cheese slices
  Digestible as milk itself
  The taste you wouldn't
    trade for just anything
Velveola Souveraine Face Powder
  Powdered perfume for the
    complexion
The velvet power piston ring
  Simplex piston rings
"Velvet-Suds"
  Ivory soap
Velvet Tobacco
  Aged in the wood
  Smoothest smoking tobacco
  When a miss makes a hit
Velvet water
  Permutit water treatment
Venida. See also: Vaniva
Venida hair net
  Rules the waves
  Venida rules the waves
Venida rules the waves
  Venida hair net
Veno's cough medicine

The first sip sooths it
Ventilated straw hats
Caradine Hat Co.
Ventura Travelware, Inc.
So high in fashion ... so
light in weight
Venture
The traveler's world
Venus foundations
That finished look
Venus pen
Every pen pre-tested for
instant touch and go
When you buy, compare--
the pen and the price
Verified insulation performance
Owens-Corning Fiberglas
Corp.
Verner's ginger ale
Flavor-mellowed in wood for
years
Vernonware
Fine dinnerware
The versatile desiccant
W. A. Hammond Drierite
Co.
Verson Allsteel Press Co.
Originators and pioneers of
allsteel stamping press
operation
Very. See also: Berry
The very best buy is the whis-
key that's dry
Paul Jones whiskey
The very best in floor care
products
Eureka Williams Co.
The very best in temporary help
Manpower, Inc.
Very cooly yours
Coronado clothes
Very effective, yet harmless to
a baby
Arabian Eye Lotion
Very elegant. Very exclusive.
Very Fifth Avenue
Chrysler New Yorker auto-
mobile
The very good washer
Whirlpool clothes washer
Very individually yours
Hickock Buckles
Very TOPS in low-cost motor-
ized transportation
Safticycles, Inc.
Vesta Accumulator Co.

Costs less per month of
service
Vesta Battery Corp.
Vesta for vitality
Vesta for vitality
Vesta Battery Corp.
Vestpok Dry Shaver
The greatest invention
since the face
Veteran reel for veteran fisher-
men
Meiselbach Mfg. Co., Inc.
Vi-lets
The chewing gum bon bon
Vibro-Shave electric razor
New Vibro-Shave stops the
old drudgery of scrap-
ing it off
Shave electrically. A close
shave in minutes with-
out cutting
Viceroy cigarettes
Discover Viceroy satisfac-
tion
The filter for the taste
that's right!
For the taste that's right
The mark of quality in
tobacco products
Only Viceroy has this ex-
clusive filter
Pleasure is where you can
find it
The rich low "tar"
Smoke all 7
There's never been a low
"tar" with richer
taste
Viceroy's got the deep-
weave filter and the
taste that's right
Your smoke comes clean
Viceroy's got the deepweave
filter and the taste
that's right
Viceroy cigarettes
Vicks Tri-Span
The "Twin Formula" head
cold tablet
Vick's Vapo-Rub
At first sneeze, Vick's
Vapo-Rub
Helping a nation to avoid
severe colds
Just rub it on
Just rub it on, inhale the

vapors
Never let a cold get a start
Now over 21 million jars
used yearly
Teaching a nation to avoid
severe colds
World's most widely used
brand of cold's medica-
tion
Victor-American Fuel Co.
Reduce the cost but not the
heat
Victor bicycle
Why not ride the best?
Victor business products
Serving American business
for 65 years
Victor Comptometer Corp. See:
Daisy/Heddon Div.,
Victor Comptometer
Corp.
Victor Insulators
The mark of good insulators
Victor Manufacturing and Gasket
Co.
The only 100% coverage line
for cars, trucks, trac-
tors, stationary engines
Victor phonograph records
His master's voice
The stars who make the hits
are on Victor records
True in every sound
The world's greatest artists
are NATURALLY yours
on Victor records
Victor Sporting Goods Co.
To the victor goes the
crown
Victor tires
Mileage hogs
Victory Bobbie Pins
Victory sets the headlines
of the world
Victory Metal Mfg. Co.
The world's largest manu-
facturer of reach-in
refrigerators and
freezers
Victory sets the headlines of
the world
Victory Bobbie Pins
Victrola talking machine
Dancing to the music of
the Victrola is the
favorite pastime

The gift that keeps on giv-
ing
His master's voice
Look for the dog
The matchless tone of the
"Golden Throat"
Vidmar, Inc.
Store more ... better ...
at less cost
Vigoro Plant Food
The lazy way to a lovely
lawn
Vigorous flavor
Folger's ground coffee
Viking Glass Co.
Treasured American glass
Viking of Minneapolis, Inc.
Your assurance of quality
in tape components
Viking tires
Will do you many a good
turn
Viko aluminum kitchenware
The popular aluminum
Viko Furniture Corp.
Carefree furniture
Vincent Lopez' dance orchestra
Hello, everybody! Lopez
speaking
Vinylite plastics
You know it's right if it's
Vinylite
Violets. See: Vi-lets
Vip medicine
Keeps you vibrantly healthy
Virginia. See also: Golden
Virginia tobacco
Virginia Dare wines
Finest American wines
since 1835
Say it again
Virginia Dept. of Conservation
and Economic Develop-
ment
Birthplace of the nation
Mix fun and history in
Virginia
Virginia Fruit Juice Co.
A pippin of a drink
Virginia Horticultural Society
Eat more apples, take less
medicine
Virginia Maid Hosiery
Background of beauty
Virginia Mirror Company
A heritage of quality,

craftsmanship, service
Virginia Slim Lights cigarettes
    You've come a long way,
        baby
Visa credit card
    The Visa emblem, symbol of
        worldwide acceptance
    You deserve the best.
        We'd like to help
    The Visa emblem, symbol of
        worldwide acceptance
    Visa credit card
The visible guarantee of invisible
        quality
    Kimble glass
Visible ink supply
    Parker Pen Co.
Visine eye drops
    The allergy medicine made
        for your eyes
    Visine gets all the red out
Visine gets all the red out
    Visine eye drops
Visit him in snapshots
    Kodak cameras
Visit your man in the service
        with snapshots
    Kodak cameras
Visitors welcome, customers
        pleased
    Marmon automobile
Visitrips
    Baltimore & Ohio Railroad
Visking Corp. skinless frank-
        furters
    Say Skinless when you say
        frankfurters
    Sure to be tender
Vita-Fluff shampoo
    The world's finest shampoo
Vita Glass Corp.
    Make your windows avenues
        of health
    Vita Glass, growing panes
    Vita Glass, the glass of
        life
Vita Glass, growing panes
    Vita Glass Corp.
Vita Glass, the glass of life
    Vita Glass Corp.
Vita-Lux
    The whiter enamel
Vital link in America's supply
        line
    Transamerican Freight
        Lines, Inc.

The vital $\frac{1}{4}$ of your costume
    Runstop Hosiery
Vitalbrush hair brush
    Be fair to your hair
Vitalis hair tonic
    For handsome hair, come
        sun, wind, water
    Keeps your hair healthy
        and handsome
    The 60-second workout
Vitality shoes
    You're twice as smart with
        Vitality Shoes
Vitalized ventilation
    ILG Electric Ventilating Co.
Vitamin-protected
    Welch's tomato juice
Vitamins for pep, Pep for vita-
        mins
    Pep Cereal
Vitamins for the millions
    Harmony vitamins
Vitamins you can trust
    Benefax
Vitanola phonograph
    The phonograph of marvel-
        ous tone
    Plays all records, natural
        as life
Vitrified pottery is everlasting
    Franklin Pottery
Viviani's beauty products
    In Viviani's the value is
        in, not on the package
Viyella-International, Inc.
    There are imitations, of
        course
Vlasic pickles
    America's favorite pickles
    Now that's the best tasting
        pickle I ever heard
    Over 96 varieties
The vodka
    Stolichnaya Russian vodka
Vogan Candy Co.
    Mellow as moonlight
Vogel-Peterson Co.
    The coat rack people
Vogt. See: Henry Vogt
        Machine Co.
Vogue foundations
    Everything is under con-
        trol
The voice at her fingertips
    Edison phonograph
Voice-O-Graph voice recorder

Don't write, Voice-O-Graph
The voice of agriculture
Radio station WMT
The voice of Iowa
Radio station WMT
Voice of quality
Martin Senour Co.
The voice of Tennessee's capital
city
Radio station WSIX, Nash-
ville, Tennessee
The voice of the Americas
Tropical Radio Telegraph
Co.
The voice of the cathedrals
Liberty carillon
Voice of the dairy farmer
American Dairy Association
The voice of the master barber
Barber's Journal
The voice with a smile
Bell Telephone System
The voice with the smile wins
American Telephone & Tele-
graph Co.
The voice with the smile wins the
world over
American Telephone & Tele-
graph Co.
Volkswagen automobile
Compare features, compare
quality, compare per-
formance, compare price,
compare value: you'll
buy a Volkswagen
The exception to the law of
diminishing returns
Nothing else is a Volkswagen
Vollman Lawrence Co.
Shoes of character
Volvo automobile
A car you can believe in
Haven't you waited long
enough?
Volvo diesel automobile
Longer between fill-ups.
Longer between cars
Volvo 760 GLE automobile
The closest thing yet to a
perfect car
Volvo trucks
Now we're building our best
in the U. S. A.
We're making it in America
Von Duprin Div., Vonnegut
Hardware Co., Inc.

The safe way out
Vornadofan
For the finest in air circula-
tion
Vose & Sons Piano Co.
We challenge comparison
Voss o'clock am sure 9 o'clock
Voss washing machines
Voss washing machines
Voss o'clock am sure 9
o'clock
The voyage of your dreams
United American Lines
Vulcabeston
The universal packing
Vulcan Golf Co.
Clubs of character for every
golfer
Vulcan-Hart Corp.
The world's finest the world
over
Vulcanizers Material Co.
Keep the home tires turning

-W-

W. A. Hammond Drierite Co.
The versatile desiccant
W. A. Sheaffer Pen Co.
Always writes all ways
A pen for every purpose and
every hand
The sign of a lifetime
Spot it by the dot
Your assurance of the best
W. B. Coon Co.
Made-to-measure fit in
ready-to-wear shoes
Today's most scientific
shoes
W. C. Hamilton & Sons
Good papers for good busi-
ness
W. E. Caldwell Co.
The tank with a reputation
W. H. Page Boiler Co.
The distinguished service
line
W. H. Walker & Co.
The shoe with the milage
Two feet of comfort in
every step
W. J. Hagerty and Sons, Ltd.,
Inc.
The world's finest name in

silver care
W. L. Douglas shoes
America's best-known shoes
Best in the world
The hand of a master
craftsman is behind this
trusted trademark
One look proves they are
styled right, one step
proves they are made
right
One look to know they are
styled right, one step
to prove they are made
right
A sewed shoe that will not
rip
The shoe that holds its
shape
This is the best $3. shoe
in the world
W. M. Chace Co.
It bends with the heat
W. R. Grace & Co.
One step ahead of a chang-
ing world
W. R. Grace & Co. See also:
DuBois Chemical Div., W.
R. Grace & Co.
P-A-G Div., W. R. Grace
& Co.
W. T. Grant Co.
Known for values
W. W. Kimball Co.
Instruments worthy of the
masters since 1857
W. W. Sly Mfg. Co.
Lift DUST out of inDUSTry
Wabash Appliance Corp.
The modern light condition-
ing bulb
Wachovia Bank & Trust Co.
For every financial need
Wagner aluminum ware
From generation to genera-
tion
Wagner Electric Corp.
The quality line
The starter that is built to
order
The superior brake fluid
Wagner electric fan
Come on, breeze, let's
blow!
Wagner power painter
The right tool for painting

Wagner Sweepers
Takes the WEEP out of
SweepING, making it
SING
Wak counters
You can count on Wak
counters
The wake tells the story
Kirsten photo-electric cell
Wake up lazy gums with Ipana
and massage
Ipana toothpaste
Wake up refreshed
Nashua blankets and sheets
Wake up to music
G. E. radio receiver
Wake up your liver
Carter's pills
Wakefield Coffee
Heavenly aroma that hangs
like a fragrant halo
'round your coffee pot
Wakefield searchlight
The double duty search-
light
Wakes up food flavor
Accent food flavor stimulant
Wakes up your hair
Admiration soapless shampoo
Walco phonograph needles
A needle for every need
Waldes-Kover Zip
The smartest zippers are
fabric covered
Waldorf is the smart shopper's
towel
Waldorf paper towel
Waldorf paper towel
Waldorf is the smart shop-
per's towel
The walk of the town
Simon Bros. shoes
Walk on air
Weyenberg Shoe Mfg. Co.
Walk-Over Koolies shoes
Take it easy and breezy
Walk with comfort
Modess sanitary napkins
Walker. See:
Hiram Walker bourbon
whiskey
Hiram Walker Ten High
whiskey
Johnnie Walker Black Label
Scotch whiskey
Johnnie Walker Red Label

Scotch whiskey
Phinney Walker automobile
clocks
W. H. Walker & Co.
Walker's. See also: Hiram
Walker's cordials
Walker's Deluxe bourbon whiskey
The elegant 8 year old
Nothing else quite measures
up
Walker's oysters
Salty tang of the sea
Wall Street Journal
All the business news you
need. When you need
it
It works
Wall Street Journal. See also:
Asian Wall Street
Journal Weekly
Wallace & Co.
Candies of character
Wallace-Murray Corp. See:
Eljer Plumbingware Div.,
Wallace-Murray Corp.
Wallace Pencil Co.
Right to the point
Wallace Reducing Records
Play off your fat!
You can get thin to music
Wallace Silversmiths Div., The
Hamilton Watch Co.
The choice you make once
for a lifetime
Grows more beautiful with
use
Wallace Silversmiths Div., The
Hamilton Watch Co.
See also: Hamilton
Watch Co.
Wallis tractor
America's foremost tractor
Walnut tobacco
Save wandering and wonder-
ing. Give Walnut this
Christmas
Walter E. Heller & Co. financial
services
Over one billion dollars
annually to industry
Sometimes it takes forever
to get to the green
Working funds for industry
Walter Hagen Golf Equipment
Co.
You don't have to be a

millionaire to play like
one
Waltham Vanguard watch
The world's finest railroad
watch
Waltham watches
The first American watch
One of the great watches
of our time
Time to rejoice
The world's watch over
time
Walworth valves
It's all worth, if Walworth
The wandering minstrel of today
Crosley radio receivers
Wang Laboratories, Inc.
The office automation com-
puter company
There's simply no better
way to automate your
office
Wanted: future Faradays and
Curies
Westinghouse Electric Corp.
Ward. See:
Johnson's Pie Co. Div.,
Ward Foods, Inc.
Montgomery Ward & Co.
Nimrod Ward Mfg. Co.
Warm as sunshine, light as
floating clouds
Torfeaco bedding
Warm toes in Fox River Hose
Fox River Hose
Warms you and your motor
Francisco Auto Heater
Warmth without waste
La Salle Coke Co.
Warmth works wonders
Radway's Ready Relief
Warner and Swasey Co.
Precision machinery since
1880
Warner Auto-Meter
Avoid a trip to the police
court
Warner Bros. corsets
Be sure our name is on
the box
Warner-Lambert Pharmaceutical
Co.
Another clinical-strength
medication from
Warner-Lambert
Warner radiator cleaner

A famous name in automobile history
Warner trailers
A trailer for every load
Warren. See also: S. D. Warren Co. Div., Scott Paper Co.
Warren Handle Works Co.
The mallet with the oval handle
Warren telechron
Accurate beyond comparison
Washington time from the light socket
Warren's Chewing Gum
The one and only cocktail gum
Wash easier, dry faster, absorb more, wear longer
Curity diapers
Wash off the dirt
Sanitas wall covering
Wash them any way you like, we guarantee the size
Adler socks
Wash without worry
Outdoor Lifer shirts
Washable shoes
Keds
The washable wall covering
Sanitas wall covering
Washburn Crosby flour
Eventually, why not now?
Washburn's beans
Naturally finer
Washburn's Seeds
Outstanding performance is not by chance but by plan
The washer of tomorrow is the Barton of today
Barton clothes washer
Washes and dries without a wringer
Laundryette Mfg. Co.
Washes more clothes faster
Easy Washer
Washes windows without water
Windex glass cleaner
Washington. See also: G. Washington Coffee
Washington Lumber Co.
Builders wise use our supplies
Washington Powder
Cuts dishpan time in half

Washington Shoe Mfg. Co.
Fashion's favored footwear
Washington State
Nature's paradise, man's opportunity
The surprising state
Washington State Apple Commission
An apple a day
Washington time from the light socket
Warren telechron
Wassmuth-Endicott kitchen cabinet
Let the "kitchen maid" be your kitchen aid
Waste management, a concept for today ... and tomorrow
Waste Management, Inc.
Waste Management, Inc.
Waste management, a concept for today ... and tomorrow
The watch dog of your battery
Western Electrical Instrument Co.
The watch for busy men
Harvel watches
Watch his smoke
Santa Fe cigars
Watch Hughson ... for progress through creative research
Hughson Chemical Div., Lord Corp.
The watch of railroad accuracy
Hamilton Watch Co.
The watch that made the dollar famous
Ingersoll dollar watch
The watch that times the airways
Benrus watch
The watch that times the stars
Harvel watches
Watch the buyers go Ford
Ford automobile
Watch the Fords go by
Ford automobile
Watch the wear
Carter overalls
The watch with the purple ribbon
South Bend watch
The watch word of elegance and efficiency
Elgin watches
Watch your children thrive on it

Borden's chocolate malted
milk
Watch your feet
Dr. Scholl's arch supporters
The watchband that was taken
from history is now mak-
ing history
Golden Knight watchband
The watchdog of your gasoline
dollar
Wayne Pump Co.
Watches of tested accuracy
Pierce watch
Watches out for your watch
Speidel Corp. watch bands
Watches your weight
Jarcons Bros. scales
Watchful of the time
Hawkeye Clock Co.
Water by fire
Everite Pump
Water engineered by Rockwood
cools, confines,
smothers
Rockwood Sprinkler
Water level route, you can sleep
New York Central System
The water of health
Mount Zircon Spring Water
Co.
Water-proofed against sogginess
Dr. West's Miracle Tuft
Toothbrush
Water Treatment Corp. See:
Servisoft Div., Water
Treatment Corp.
Waterbury watch
Ask your jeweler for it
This is the best watch for
bicyclers
Waterman Hydraulics Corp.
Specialists in fluid power
control
Waterman's Ideal Fountain Pen
All write with a Waterman's
All write with a Waterman's
Ideal Fountain Pen ...
all wrong if you don't
Daddy of them all
The first and last word in
famous pens
For out-of-doors writing
Makes its mark around the
world
No other pen writes like
a Waterman's

The pen with the clip-cap
Waterproofs everything
Atlantic Drier & Varnish
Co.
Waters-Center toaster
No watching, no turning,
no burning
The toaster you've always
wanted
Watkins Cocoanut Oil Shampoo
Beauty insurance
Makes your hair look its
best
Watkins Products, Inc.
First in home service
Watson Mfg. Co., Inc.
The company of specialists
Watson sterling silver
Modern silver with the
beauty of old master-
pieces
Watts Regulator Co.
The name that protects
your name
Waukesha mineral water
That marvelous mixer
Waukesha Motor Co.
Builders of heavy duty
engines for over twenty
years
Wausau Motor Parts Co.
The free-running ring with
the safety center unit
Wax makes housework click like
clockwork
Johnson's wax
Waxtex wax paper
A good habit
Way Never-Spread Mattress
The scheme is in the seam
The way the best lemons sign
their names
Sunkist lemons
The way to a man's heart
Log Cabin Syrup
The way to get there
Iberia Air Lines of Spain
The way we make it is making
us famous
Famous Recipe chicken
The way we put it all together
is what sets us apart
International Business
Machines Corp.
Wayne feeds
Builders of tomorrow's

feeds ... today!
Wayne Pump Co.
It can't under-measure, it
can't over-charge
The watchdog of your gaso-
line dollar
World's largest manufacturer
of gasoline pumps and
service station equipment
We accept only one standard.
Yours
Preferred Hotels
We aim to humanize the science
of insurance
Manufacturers Liability In-
surance Co.
We are. See also: We're
We are advertised by our loving
friends
Mellin's Food
We are driven
Datsun automobile
We behave responsibly as a cor-
porate citizen
Xerox Corporation
We believe in making things bet-
ter
Toro mechanical lawn mow-
ers
We bring comfort to inner space
Kero-Sun portable heaters
We bring good things to life
General Electric Company
We bring the world to your
mailbox
Publisher's Central Bureau
We build excitement
Pontiac automobile
We build it so rugged it loves
abuse!
Roughneck refuse container
We build our machines better
than they have to be
Ingersoll-Rand Company
We build our products to weather
the worst of conditions
Ingersoll-Rand Company
We build them better than we
have to. We have to
Falcon Jet Corporation
We can help you build your
dreams
Canfield Lumber & Supply
Co.
We can help you do business a
whole new way

Westinghouse Credit Corp.
We can lighten your paper weight
Pitney-Bowes mail handling
machines
We cannot stay when West begins
to spray
West Disinfecting Co.
We can't wait for tomorrow
Aluminum Company of
America
We care about color
Simon Manges and Son, Inc.
We care about you
Lassus Bros. retail gasoline
stations
We carry nothing but the best
Wirthmore Grain
We challenge any business jet
to match it
Canadair Challenger jet
aeroplane
We challenge comparison
Vose & Sons Piano Co.
We challenge the world to produce
its equal
Lovell All-Clamp Roller
Skate
We change people into couples
Arthur Murray dance
studios
We change the way the world
thinks
Digital Equipment Corpora-
tion
We cover the earth with drugs
of worth
Meyer Bros. Drug Co.
We did it our way
Airbus Industrie of North
America
We do business as if we had
only one customer.
You
J. C. Bradford & Co.
We do chicken right
Kentucky Fried Chicken
We do it right or we don't do it
Bob Evans Farms meat
products
We do not sell our publications,
they belong to God
Samaritan Sacred Songs
We do the planning, you have
the fun
Greyhound Corporation
We don't fit the mold. We

501

break it
Newsweek
We engineered the anxiety out
of computers
Data General Corporation
We evolved the styles that the
world admires
Ideal Leather Case Co.
We exist to earn profits
Xerox Corporation
We flag the nation
Dettra Flag Co.
We fly the world the way the
world wants to fly
Pan American World Airways,
Inc.
We fool the sun
Indianapolis Tent & Awning
Co.
We give it our best
Indiana & Michigan Electric
Company
We give you a better look
Chicago Tribune
We give you more
Mexicana Airlines
We give you more to go on
Uniroyal tires
We grew up with the Old West
Anaconda Company
We grow the working trees
Potlatch Forests, Inc.
We hand craft the world's finest
shoes for men
Allen-Edmonds shoes
We have. See also: We've
We have a daily interest in you
Fort Wayne National Bank
We have more ways to lend
money
Barclay's American Busi-
ness Credit
We have the energy for the long
haul
Southern Railway Co.
We have the momentum
Sigmor Corporation
We have to earn our wings every
day
Eastern Air Lines, Inc.
We have what it takes
Owens-Illinois Glass Co.
We help discover oil
NL Industries
We help people manage money
Investors Diversified

Services, Inc.
We help to light and power the
world
Diesel Motors Corp.
We help you here and now.
Not just hereafter
John Hancock Variable Life
Insurance Co.
We know no limits
Republic Bank, Dallas
We know values
American Appraisal
We know what we CAN 'cause we
can what we grow
Donald Duck orange juice
We know where we're growing
Boise Cascade Corporation
We know where you're going
Air France
We lend you their ears
Don Lee Broadcasting Sys-
tem
We like it here
Wisconsin Div. of Economic
Development
We love to catch them on a
Springmaid sheet
Springmaid sheets
We made it low in sugar and
kids made it No. 1
Cheerios cereal
We make a brand to suit your
land
Farmers Cotton Oil Co.
We make for "America's royalty"
Wells Bedding
We make it simple
Honda automobile
We make it, we guarantee it
Norfolk Paint & Varnish Co.
We make technology beautiful
Timex watches
We make them for only one man
out of every 100
Royal Imperial Florsheim
shoes
We make you feel at home in
Milwaukee
Milwaukee River Hilton
hotel
We make you feel at home in
the Twin Cities
Minneapolis Hilton Inn
We make you look good for less
U. S. Postal Service Ex-
press Mail

We make you safe. You make
us famous
Frank B. Hall & Co. insur-
ance brokers
We make your good people even
better
Lanier typewriter
We make your hiring job easier
Dunhill National Personnel
System
We mass produce quality!
Atlas Bradford Co.
We mean business
Diners Club International
We might not be known on the
street, but we're
famous in the field
NL Industries
We move families, not just furni-
ture
Allied Van Lines, Inc.
We need more Calgon!
Calgon laundry detergent
We never sleep
Pinkerton's, Inc. detective
agency
We never stop widening our
horizons
Farrell Lines, Inc.
We offer more kinds of insurance
than anyone else in the
business
The AIG Companies
We outperform our competition to
help you outperform
yours
Gates Learjet Corporation
We pamper passengers throughout
mid-central U. S. A.
Lake Central Airlines, Inc.
We print it before it happens
Clancy Publications, Inc.
We promote excellence
Hilti, Inc.
We provide quality brokerage
service
Rose & Company discount
brokers
We put America on radials
Michelin tires
We put computing within every-
one's reach
Texas Instruments, Inc.
We put data systems where the
action is
Norand data systems

We put it in writing. No one
else does
Quaker State Oil Refining
Corp.
We put our heads together to
cut your drilling costs
Kingsbury Machine Tool Co.
We put the "care" back in "eye
care"
Nu Vision
We put the world to sleep
Universal pajamas
We reach the people who make
the future happen
Scientific American
We redesign the conventional to
create the exceptional
M.A.N. Truck and Bus
Corp.
We require satisfied customers
for success
Xerox Corporation
We respond
Ricoh Copiers
We roast it, others praise it
Big Horn Coffee
We run forums for corporate
America
Chase Manhattan Bank
We run rings around the com-
petition
M&F Case Co.
We seek to serve
Ohio Fuel Supply Co.
We set the table for America
Anchor Hocking Glass Co.
We shelter the world from sun
and rain
Follmer umbrellas
We smile at miles
Airplane transport
We soak the clothes, not the
public
Morin Wet Wash Laundry
We speak technology
Bendix Corporation
We still believe in promises
Whirlpool Corporation
We tackle the tough ones
First National Bank of
Boston
We take better care of your car
Standard Oil Div., Amer-
ican Oil Co.
We take less so you can have
more

Thrifty Rent-a-car System,
Inc.
We teach success
Xerox Learning Systems
We teach wherever the mails
reach
International Correspondence
Schools
We took the splash out of the
kitchen
Union brass faucet
We treat you right
Dairy Queen confectionery
restaurants
We try harder
Avis automobile rentals
We understand how important it
is to listen
Sperry Rand Corporation
We use technology to develop
product leadership
Xerox Corporation
We value our employees
Xerox Corporation
We walk and like it
Bostonian shoes
We want to keep you safe and
sound
American Mutual Insurance
Companies
We want you to hear more music
Harmon Kardon, Inc.
We went, we saw, we listened
to ... silence
Electrolux Refrigerator
We win with quality
Hauser-Stander Tank Co.
We won't steer you wrong
J. C. Penney Auto Center
We work to keep you safe
Liberty Mutual Insurance
Company
A wealth of value in Fortune
shoes
Fortune shoes
Wear-conditioned stockings
Monmouth Hosiery Mills
Wear-Ever aluminum
Made of the metal that cooks
best
Nature made aluminum
friendly to food
Now, more WEAR than
EVER
Replace utensils that wear
out with utensils that

WEAR-EVER
Wear Kayser, you owe it to your
friends
Kayser hosiery and under-
wear
Wear longer
Davenport Hosiery Mills
Wear-Right Gloves
There's style and wear in
every pair
Wear tested for your comfort
Jarman shoes
Wear the bra that gives you
bravada
Exquisite Form Brassiere
Wears longer because it's
stronger
Tubize Artificial Silk Co.
Weather armor for homes
Valentine's Valspar
Weather makers to the world
Carrier Corporation
The weather-weight champ
Dutch Boy White Lead
Weatherbee raincoat
The name to remember in
rainwear
Weathers our weather
Utley paint
Weaver fried chicken
Nobody knows chicken like
the folks at Weaver
Weavers of the world's finest
netting
Fish Net & Twine Co.
Weavewood-Ware
Beautiful on the table.
Carefree in the kitchen
Webb. See also: B. Webb
Company
Webb Coffee
The winning cup
Webber. See also: Paine
Webber, Jackson &
Curtis
Webber Supercharger
Functions when the engine
breathes
Weber Marking Systems, Inc.
Mark it for market ... the
Weber way
Webster. See also: Daniel
Webster whiskey
Webster cigar
Ask him why he smokes a
Webster

504

Executive America's top
cigar
Webster Rubber Co.
Look for the cured-in Red
"W"
Webster's International Diction-
ary
A grand investment
Like sending your family to
college
The Supreme Authority
Webster's Tomato Juice
From juice-heavy beauties
Wed in the wood
Old Thompson whiskey
We'd rather point to character
than chromium
Ford automobile
Weed Chain-Jack
The Jack for Jill
Weed tire chains
Every Weed is guaranteed
Safety lies in Weed Chains
Stop that skid before it
starts
Weigh your family against
a set of Weed tire
chains
Weedone weed killer
Kill lawn weeds without
killing grass
World's number one weed
killers
A weekly for the whole family
Liberty Magazine
The weekly journal of the elec-
trical industry
Electrical World
A weekly magazine of philately
Stamps
The weekly news magazine
Time
A weekly newspaper of insurance
National Underwriter
Weeks'. See: Anson Weeks'
dance orchestra
Weep no more, my ladies
Little's Onion Flakes
Weigh the loads and save the
roads
The Black & Decker Mfg.
Co.
The weigh to profits
Stimpson Computing Scale
Co.
Weigh your family against a

set of Weed tire chains
Weed tire chains
The Weis Mfg. Co.
Specialists in filing supplies
and equipment since
1894
Weiss & Klau Co.
Creators of fashion in oil-
cloth
It's tops for kitchen tops
World's largest oilcloth
distributors
Welch Grape Juice Co.
Welch's energy-packed foods
Welch's energy-packed foods
Welch Grape Juice Co.
Welch's grape jelly and grape-
lade
Great grapes, what a flavor
Rich full-bodied jam, clear
sparkling jelly
Welch's grape juice
Drink a bunch of quick
energy
Fagged? Drink a bunch
of quick energy
For pleasure and energy,
too
For PURE enjoyment
It's wonderful, it's Welch's
The national drink
Picked with pride, packed
with skill since 1869
The safe way is the Welch
way
Serve summer's most deli-
cious drink
There's more hard cash
ahead
Welch's marmalade
Because it's sweet, not
bitter
For PURE enjoyment
Hey, Mom, this marmalade
is different
Plus extra energy
Young America spreads it
on thick
Welch's tomato juice
Luxury in quality, not in
price
Vitamin-protected
Welcome aboard
United Air Lines, Inc.
The welcome partner
American Chewing Products

505

Corp.

Welcome the prodigal sun
  Bartlay & Crown Rayon
Welcome to the Suite life
  Granada Royale Hometels
Welcome to the Sweet Life!
  Equal low-calorie sweetener
Welcomed in the best homes
  Royal Banquet whiskey
Welded on wood
  Pyraglass Products, Inc.
Welk's. See: Lawrence Welk's
  dance orchestra
A well-built car
  E.○ar automobile
Well dressed/wool dressed
  American Wool Council
We'll give you a taste of old-
  time country goodness
  Hickory Farms of Ohio
We'll give you the full picture
  GK Technologies
We'll help. Will you?
  American Red Cross
We'll help you get your money's
  worth
  Better Business Bureau
We'll Lava ya clean
  Lava soap
We'll make you believe in signs
  Frederick Advertising &
  Display Co.
We'll make your business tele-
  phones pay dividends
  General Dynamics Communi-
  cations Company
We'll rest our case on a case
  Liebman Breweries
We'll wait
  Grant's Scotch whiskey
Wellington Sears textiles
  The search ends at Welling-
  ton Sears
Wells Bedding
  We make for "America's
  royalty"
Welsbach Junior gas mantle
  Don't economize on light--
  economize on lighting
  bills
Wembley neckties
  The aristocrat of polyester
  neckwear
  The "color guide" tie
  Takes the guessing out of
  dressing

World famous for quality
  Wenatachee District Co-op Assn.
  Nature's chosen apple land
Wendy's fast food restaurants
  Aint no reason to go any-
  place else
  You're Wendy's kind of
  people
We're. See also: We are
We're a total communications
  company
  General Telephone & Elec-
  tronics Corp.
We're all esteemed up
  Carstairs White Seal whiskey
We're American Airlines doing
  what we do best
  American Airlines, Inc.
We're as basic to America as a
  summer vacation
  Greyhound Corporation
We're as basic to America as the
  4th of July
  Greyhound Corporation
We're as basic to America as the
  Sunday funnies
  Greyhound Corporation
We're Beechnut nuts
  Beechnut chewing tobacco
We're building a great name
  Trax shoes
We're bullish on America
  Merrill Lynch, Pierce, Fen-
  ner & Smith, Inc.
We're careful of your comfort
  Koppers Co., Inc.
We're changing right before
  your eyes
  Ramada Inns, Inc.
We're changing the way people
  feel about work
  Digital Equipment Corpora-
  tion
We're changing the way the
  world bathes
  Thermasol, Ltd.
We're fighting for your life
  American Heart Association
We're finding new growth in
  some of America's
  newer growth fields
  Keene Corporation
We're going to be your favorite
  hotel
  Harley Hotel, New York
  City

We're investing in a healthier
America
American Council of Life
Insurance
We're making it in America
Volvo trucks
We're making tracks for the fu-
ture
Southern Pacific Co.
We're more than 100,000 people
working on energy
Exxon Corporation
We're not giving in. We're going
on
International Harvester Co.
We're out to change America's
tires
Kelly-Springfield Tire Co.
We're synergistic
Sperry Rand Corporation
We're the bank for business
American National Bank and
Trust Co. of Chicago
We're the best GM ever
General Motors Corporation
We're the problem solvers
Trustworthy Hardware
Stores
We're there when you need us
The Bank of New York
We're with you
Mercantile Bank, St. Louis,
Mo.
We're working to keep your
trust
Texaco, Inc.
We're worth watching in the 80's
The Williams Companies
Wertheim & Co.
Investment services under
the same name for 55
years
The West Bend Co.
New ideas for happier
homemaking
West Branch cedar hope chest
The present with a future
West Disinfecting Co.
We cannot stay when West
begins to spray
West Palm Beach, Fla.
Where summer spends the
winter
West Point men's toiletries
West Point stands for good
grooming

The West Point of Christian
service
Moody Bible Institute of
Chicago
West Point-Pepperell, Inc. See:
Industrial Fabrics Div.,
West Point-Pepperell,
Inc.
West Point stands for good
grooming
West Point men's toiletries
Westab, Inc.
World's largest manufacturer
of school supplies and
stationery
Westab, Inc. See also: Montag,
Inc., Div., Westab,
Inc.
Westclox Div., General Time
Corp.
America's "wake-up" voice
Progress in the world of
time
Westcott automobile
The car with a longer life
Western Air Lines, Inc.
The jet with the extra en-
gine
The only way to fly
The unbeatable way to jet
home
Western Auto Supply Co.
More than 125 stores in
the west
Why pay bridge tolls to save
at Western Auto?
Why pay tolls to save at
Western?
Western Cartridge Co.
The choice of champions
Out-sells because it out-
shoots
When you get a shot, you
get a duck, with Super
X
World's champion ammuni-
tion
Western Electric Co.
Equipment for every elec-
trical need
Teamed up for you since
'82
Western Electric fans
Greatest breeze with the
least current consump-
tion

Western Electric hearing aids
  There IS a difference in
    hearing aids
Western Electrical Instrument Co.
  The watch dog of your bat-
    tery
Western Life Insurance Co.
  Enduring as the mountains
  Today's need for tomorrow
    is life insurance
Western Manufacturers Associa-
    tion
  The pick o' the pines
Western Newspaper Union
  Where the sun never sets
    on an unfilled order
Western toothbrush
  Cleans inside, outside and
    between the teeth
Western Union Corporation
  Don't write, telegraph
  Obviously it must be Western
    Union
  So many times a telegram
    means so much
  Western Union: The fastest
    way to get the word
    around
Western Union International, Inc.
  All around the world
Western Union Telex Network
  Instant. In writing. In-
    expensive
  Still the most underpriced
    message service in the
    world
  Western Union: The fastest way
    to get the word around
    Western Union Corporation
Western Union Video Confer-
    encing, Inc.
  The only name you need to
    remember
Western Wallboard Co.
  To patch a hole, or build
    a home
Westgate fabrics
  Gateway to the world of
    fabrics
Westinghouse automobile electric
    systems
  Simplicity--Reliability
Westinghouse Credit Corp.
  We can help you do busi-
    ness a whole new way
Westinghouse Electric Corp.

Guaranteed by the name
Lamps for see-ability
Light your house with West-
    inghouse
The name that means every-
    thing in electricity
The name you know in lamps
A powerful part of your life
Wanted: future Faradays
    and Curies
You can be sure if it's West-
    inghouse
Westinghouse Electric Corp. See
    also: Canadian West-
    inghouse Company
Westinghouse electric oven
  No more cooking by guess
Westinghouse radio receiver
  And when you listen you'll
    buy this Westinghouse
  Listen and you'll buy
    Westinghouse
Westinghouse refrigerator
  The only dual automatic
    refrigerator
The Westminster, New York City
  A homey hotel for home
    folks
Westminster sock
  You're asking for a good
    sock
  You're asking for a good
    sock when you ask for
    Westminster
West's. See also: Dr. West's
    Miracle Tuft Toothbrush
The West's great national maga-
    zine
    Sunset
The West's great paper
    Salt Lake City Tribune
Westvaco Corp.
  Westvaco inspirations lead
    to new value in paper
    and packaging
Westvaco inspirations lead to
    new value in paper
    and packaging
    Westvaco Corp.
We've. See also: We have
We've already done your home-
    work
    Maduff & Sons, Inc. com-
    modities trading ad-
    visors
We've been making happy birth-

days even happier since
1842
Whitman's Sampler candy
We've been Wright for more than
100 years
Wright Arch preserver shoes
We've done it. We can do it for
you
First National Bank of Bos-
ton
We've got a new world for you
Ramada Inns, Inc.
We've got all the right components
to be one of your major
banks
Seattle First National Bank
We've got coal to burn (And
nuclear fuel, too)
Omaha Public Power District
We've got your number
Esterbrook Steel Pen Co.
We've had one built for you
Oldsmobile automobile
We've just begun to grow
Keene Corporation
We've just made your production
line 300,000 miles long
American Railroad Founda-
tion
We've made a deep impression
J. I. Case earth moving
machines
We've matched our strength to
your needs
Bankers Trust Company
We've matched our strengths to
your needs
Lanier Business Products,
Inc.
We've put it all together
Asian Wall Street Journal
Weekly
We've worked hard to gain your
trust. We'll work even
harder to keep it
Tylenol pain reliever
Weyenberg Shoe Mfg. Co.
Cushion every step
Feel the air cushion
Give your feet young ideas
Like walking on air
A man's first choice
Put your feet on easy
street
Walk on air
Weyerhaeuser Company

The tree-growing company
The whale for work
Maxfer Truck
What a delicious difference Cap-
tain Morgan Spiced Rum
makes!
Captain Morgan Spiced Rum
What a difference Midol makes
Midol
What a whale of a difference just
a few cents make
Fatima cigarettes
What America needs is less bull
and more Bulldog
Mack trucks
What are your teeth saying about
you today?
Listerine toothpaste
What Chicago makes, makes Chi-
cago
Chicago Chamber of Com-
merce
What Eagle shows, goes
Eagle clothes
What fine fresh fruit flavor for
five cents!
Life Savers candy
What gives a girl most "flair?"
Lovely, gleaming lus-
trous hair
Drene shampoo
What good is paint if it's not
good paint?
Pratt & Lambert paint
What is. See: What's
What more could a man ask?
Four Roses whiskey
What next from Alcoa!
Aluminum Company of
America
What Scandinavian men have
Teak toilet goods
What soda is to Scotch, Hoffman
rye mixer is to rye
Hoffman rye mixer
What the rich give the wealthy
Royal Salute Scotch whiskey
What we have we hold
Kino Petrol hair tonic
What you want in work clothes
Big Yank work clothes
What you want is a Wollensack
Revere-Wollensack Div.,
Minnesota Mining &
Manufacturing Co.
Whatever the towel, it's a top

value if the label says
Cannon
Cannon Mills, Inc.
Whatever the weather, Pullman
gets you there
Pullman sleeping car
Whatever you do, eat Krumbles
Kellogg's Krumbles
Whatever YOUR speed, dial the
heat YOU need
Samson irons
What's happening in business--
to business
Nation's Business
What's new? Ask Cutler
Cutler-Hammer, Inc.
What's your "eye-cue?"
Formfit Underwear
Wheat. See also: Shredded
Wheat
Wheat for your bread, wealth
for the nation
Caterpillar Tractor Co.
Wheat shot from guns is elegant
eatin'
Quaker Sparkies
Wheatena cereal
The delicious whole wheat
cereal
Tastes good
Wheaties cereal
The breakfast of champions
Had your Wheaties today?
Ready to eat
Wheatlet
All the wheat that's fit to
eat
Wheel Horse Products, Inc.
Sign of the leader in lawn/
garden equipment
Step up to Wheel Horse
Wheelbarrow economy but Pull-
man pleasure
Ford automobile
Wheeler, Osgood Co.
The door that stands the
famous soaking test
Wheeling Metal & Mfg. Co.
A Leadclad roof is lightning
proof
Wheels, Inc.
Business moves better with
Wheels!
Wheels of fortune
Chicago Wheel & Mfg. Co.
The wheels of transportation

help turn the wheels of
industry
Union Pacific Railroad
The wheels that go everywhere
American Trucking Associ-
ations, Inc.
When a feller needs a friend
Briggs pipe mixture
When a miss makes a hit
Velvet Tobacco
When a Studio Girl enters your
home a new kind of
beauty brightens your
life
Helene Curtis Industries,
Inc.
When all is said and done, serv-
ice makes the difference
Joy Manufacturing Co.
When all soaps fail, Flash cleans
Flash
When better automobiles are
built, Buick will build
them
Buick automobile
When day is done, you deserve
the best
Schenley Distillers Corp.
When distribution is the question
UBL has the answers
Union Barge Line Corp.
When E. F. Hutton talks, peo-
ple listen
E. F. Hutton & Co., Inc.
When experts buy, they demand
Spring-Air
Spring-Air mattress
When it absolutely, positively
has to be there over-
night
Federal Express Corpora-
tion
When it comes to color, come to
Cyanamid
American Cyanamid Co.
When it comes to cooking for
dogs--Rival has no
rival
Rival Pet Foods Div., As-
sociated Products, Inc.
When it comes to financial
printing, come to Sorg
Sorg Printing Company
When it comes to insurance,
come to the leader
Marsh & McLennan, Inc.

When it comes to linens, come
     to Baker
     Baker Linen Co.
When it comes to making your
     savings earn more, the
     Citi never sleeps
     Citibank, New York City
When it rains it pours
     Morton's salt
When it writes, it whispers
     Noiseless typewriter
When it's a Shamrock, you've
     got the best
     Shamrock clothes hamper
When it's a tie, you win
     TIE/communications, Inc.
When it's an Exide, you start
     Exide storage batteries
When it's Domino sugar, you're
     sure it's pure!
     Domino sugar
When it's hot it's Vericool
     Manhattan Vericool shirts
When it's time to change, get a
     Glenwood range
     Glenwood Range Co.
When it's wet it's dry
     Worcester Salt Co.
When life needs a lift
     Maxwell House Master Blend
     Coffee
When Marriott does it, they do
     it right
     Marriott hotels
When mosquitoes sing the aria
     from malaria
     Black Flag insect spray
When nature forgets, remember
     EX-LAX
     Ex-Lax laxative
When nature won't, Pluto will
     Pluto Water
When only the best will do
     Butterball turkeys
When others run out we keep
     going
     Gala absorbent towels
When performance counts, call
     on Cyanamid
     American Cyanamid Co.
When quality counts most, most
     men count on Flor-
     sheim quality
     Florsheim Shoe Co.
When radio called, Eveready
     was ready

Eveready radio batteries
When she knocks, use Dox
     Dox motor remedy
When so much depends on a
     valve ... so many de-
     pend on LimiTorque
     LimiTorque Corp.
When something happy happens--
     it's Bulova time
     Bulova watches
When taste desires cooling flavor
     try refreshing Lime
     Life Saver
     Life Savers candy
When the fire starts, the water
     starts
     Grinnell Corp.
When the market moves, you
     should too
     Index and Option Market
When the mercury soars, keep
     happy
     Arctic electric fan
When the name says Gorham, the
     gift says everything
     Gorham Div., Textron, Inc.
When the sun goes down
     Berkeley Square clothes
When there's a choice, it's Philco
     Philco radio receiver
When you buy Beloit, you buy
     more than a machine
     Beloit paper-making ma-
     chinery
When you buy, compare--the pen
     and the price
     Venus pen
When you care enough to send
     the very best
     Hallmark greeting cards
When you crave good candy
     Milky Way candy bar
When you do something very
     well you simply cannot
     do it for everyone
     United States Trust Com-
     pany of New York
When you get a shot, you get a
     duck, with Super X
     Western Cartridge Co.
When you get a talking machine
     get a Graphophone
     Columbia Graphophone
When you grow, we grow
     Diamond International
     Corporation

When you have a service prob-
lem think of Champ-
Items
Champ-Items, Inc.
When you hear the violin, that's
Paul Pendarvis
Paul Pendarvis' dance
orchestra
When you know who we are you
won't build any other
way
Varco-Pruden Buildings
When you land at Atlanta we'll
be waiting with a smile
Coca Cola soft drink
When you make a very good
paint it shows
Glidden paints
When you make your move--make
sure it's a planned
move
Central Illinois Light Co.
When you mix with CinZano you
mix with the best
CinZano vermouth
When you need radials come up
to Goodyear
Goodyear radial tires
When you pay for quality, why
not get the finest?
Florsheim Shoe Co.
When you re-tire, go to Sleep
Edward Sleep Tire Sales
When you see the "REAL" seal,
you know it's real
American Dairy Association
When you shoot for perfection
Hasselblad cameras
When you start with metal ...
finish with Duracron!
PPG Industries, Inc.
When you substitute price for
quality, everyone loses
Arrow Head Steel Products
When you take cold, take
lemons
Sunkist lemons
When you think of asbestos,
think of Johns-Manville
Johns-Manville Corporation
When you think of sweetness
Honey Scotch Candy
When you think of writing,
think of Whiting
Whiting stationery
When you think wire rope,

think Bethlehem
Bethlehem Steel Company
When your energy takes a dive,
drink Horlick's and re-
vive
Horlick's Malted Milk Corp.
When your lips take a "weather-
beating"
Gaby anti-chap lotion
When your picture moves, it
lives
Cine Kodak
When your sailor goes to see
Pacific fabrics
When you're out to beat the
world
Converse Rubber Co.
When you've got to be right
SKF Industries, Inc.
Whenever a recipe calls for
gelatine, think of Knox
Knox Gelatine, Inc.
Whenever good impressions
count, rely on carbon-
izing papers by Schweit-
zer
Peter J. Schweitzer Div.,
Kimberly-Clark Corp.
Wherever the recipe calls for
milk
Borden's condensed milk
Whenever you need it Midol has
the strength
Midol
Where accuracy counts, we win
Universal Boring Machine
Co.
Where advertising pays it stays
--and grows
Boston Herald
Where AVCO leads, confidence
follows
AVCO Corporation
Where banking is a pleasure
Trust Company of Georgia
Where beautiful young ideas
begin
Helene Curtis Industries,
Inc.
Where beauty is material
The Masland Duraleather
Co.
Where better goldfish are grown
Ozark Fisheries, Inc.
Where big ideas turn into
aluminum extrusions

Superior Industries, Inc.
Where big things are happening
Kentucky
Where bold new ideas pay off for
profit-minded farmers
New Idea Farm Equipment
Co.
Where buyer and seller meet
Association of North American Directory Publishers
Where complexions are fine
there's always pine
Sierra Pine Soap
Where departments unite to make
service right
Schwabacher-Frey stationery
store
Where efficiency is demanded, the
Conlon is preferred
Conlon electric washers
Where engraving is still an art
Roehlen Engraving Works
Where every carpet is custom
made
Dellinger, Inc.
Where everything is done in
plastics
American Insulator Corp.
Where experience guides exploration
Dow Corning Corporation
Where face fitness starts
Williams' Shaving Cream
Where flame technology creates
new products
Oxides Div., Cabot Corp.
Where food grows finest, there
Libby packs the best
Libby, McNeill and Libby
Where Ford planes fly
Ford Tri-Motor airplane
Where free enterprise is still
growing
Indiana Dept. of Commerce
Where friend meets friend
Chevrolet automobile
Where good cheer abides
Hotel Touraine, Buffalo,
N. Y.
Where good government is a
habit
North Carolina Dept. of
Conservation
Where great ideas are meant to
happen

Arvin Industries, Inc.
Where ideas unlock the future
Bendix Corporation
Where important people turn to
say important things
American Magazine
Where inches count
Acme National Refrigeration
Co.
Where innovative engineering,
essential equipment and
energy add up to growth
Ingersoll-Rand Company
Where life is complete
St. Joseph, Mich.
Where modern WP began. Where
modern WP is going
Lexitron Corp. word processors
Where nature helps industry
most
Los Angeles, Calif.
Where new ideas bring you better packaging
Reynolds Metals Company
Where new ideas take shape in
aluminum
Reynolds Metals Company
Where only the best will do
Hanley & Kinsella Coffee
Where only the plane gets more
attention than you
Iberia Air Lines of Spain
Where outstanding performance
is standard
New York Shipbuilding
Corp.
Where people and ideas create
security for millions
Connecticut General Life
Insurance Co.
Where people make the difference
Toronto-Dominion Bank
Where performance must be
measured by results
Hewlett-Packard Co.
Where politics and economics
converge ... the
Financial Times excells
Financial Times
Where pride of craftsmanship
comes first
Empire Furniture Corp.
Where private enterprise is
making possible a
better kind of hospital

Humana, Inc.
Where progress is a daily practice
    Oil Center Tool Div., FMC
    Corp.
Where quality counts
    Luce Packing Co.
Where quality counts most
    Ladish Drop Forge Co.
Where quality is a family tradition
    Gehl Bros. Mfg. Co.
Where quality is a tradition
    Bismarck Hotel, Chicago,
    Ill.
    Dierks Forests, Inc.
Where quality is a tradition ...
    and an obligation
    Square D Co.
Where quality is built in, not
    added on
    American Motors Corp.
Where quality is produced in
    quantity
    Sterling Faucet Co.
Where quality is traditional
    Old Colony Envelope Corp.
Where quality is the constant
    factor
    Canon electronic calculators
Where quality makes sense
    House Beautiful
Where research and development
    make exciting ideas
    General Tire & Rubber Co.
Where research is planned with
    progress in mind
    Universal Oil Products Co.
Where sales and service meet
    Marmon automobile
Where science gets down to business
    Rockwell International
Where short stays are long remembered
    Alameda Plaza Hotel, Kansas
    City, Mo.
Where softness begins
    Monchel bath soap
Where Southern hospitality
    flowers
    Atlanta Biltmore Hotel,
    Atlanta, Ga.
Where style begins
    Buddy Lee men's suits
Where summer spends the winter
    West Palm Beach, Fla.

Where summer stays and the
    nation plays
    Sarasota, Fla.
Where sunshine spends the winter
    El Paso, Texas
Where technicolor comes to life
    Simon Bros. straw handbags
Where telling the world means
    selling the world
    Life International
Where the action is!
    Zebco fishing tackle
Where the best costs less
    Hotel New Yorker, New
    York City
Where the big idea is innovation
    United States Steel Corp.
Where the brightest ideas come
    to light
    General Electric Company
Where the data movement
    started and startling
    moves are made
    Teletype Corp.
Where the guest is always right
    Hotel Statler, New York
    City and elsewhere
Where the newest in packaging
    is happening today
    Millprint, Inc.
Where the nicest people meet the
    nicest things
    Stanley Home Products, Inc.
Where the summer spends the
    winter
    Miami, Fla.
Where the sun never sets on an
    unfilled order
    Western Newspaper Union
Where the world comes for energy solutions
    McDermott International,
    Inc.
Where there's a window ...
    there's a place for
    Thermopane
    Thermopane glass
Where there's life ... there's
    Bud
    Budweiser beer
Where today's theory is tomorrow's remedy
    Merck, Sharp and Dohme
    Div., Merck and Co.,
    Inc.
Where tradition works wonders

514

Drake Hotel, Chicago, Ill.
Where were you last week?
New Yorker
Where what you want to know
comes first
Columbia Broadcasting System, Inc.
Where what's happening gets its
start
Amoco Chemicals Corp.
Where winners rent
Hertz automobile rentals
Where you are always number
one
The Glen Falls Group
Where you save does make a
difference
The Savings and Loan
Foundation, Inc.
Where you see obstacles, we may
see paths
Dresdner Bank
Where you stay says a lot about
where you're going
Stouffer hotels
Where your advertising earns
extra interest
American Banker
Where your dollar works harder
... grows bigger!
Insured Savings and Loan
Associations
Where your fiscal fitness begins
Cessna Aircraft Co.
Where your futures become our
most precious commodities
Rouse Woodcock Commodities
Brokers
Where your "resort dollar" buys
more
Stardust Hotel and Golf
Club
Where your sealing is unlimited
Standard Products Co.
Wherever electricity is distributed and controlled
Square D Co.
Wherever fruit grows, our
machinery goes
Elliott Mfg. Co., Inc.
Wherever good candies are sold
Park & Tilford candy
Wherever it must be the best
Dayton Engineering Laboratories

Wherever metals are cast you'll
find The Foundry
The Foundry
Wherever money is handled or
records are kept
National Cash Register Co.
Wherever no nonsense is sold
Ultra Sense panty hose
Wherever particular people
congregate
Pall Mall cigarettes
Wherever piping is involved
Grinnell Corp.
Wherever quality counts most
Ladish Drop Forge Co.
Wherever reliability counts most
Ladish Drop Forge Co.
Wherever the mails reach, there
we teach
International Correspondence
Schools
Wherever wheels turn or propellers spin
Delco storage batteries
Wherever you cruise you'll find
a Matthews
Matthews boat
Wherever you go, go Jolly
Jolly cabs
Wherever you go, there it is!
Hiram Walker bourbon
whiskey
Wherever you go you look better
in Arrow
Arrow shirts
Wherever you go you'll find
Buffalo
Buffalo sausage machines
Wherever you look ... you see
Budd
The Budd Company
Whether you look or listen, it's
perfect both ways
Crosley radio-phonograph
While other magazines are looking at today this one is
looking at tomorrow
Next
While there is Life there is hope
Life
Whippet Bond paper
Fast running
Whirlpool clothes washer
Built like the finest automobile
It tumbles the clothes as

it circulates them
'Round and 'round and over
and over
The very good washer
Whirlpool Corporation
Making your world a little
easier
We still believe in promises
Whirlpool Corporation. See also:
Tectrol Div., Whirlpool
Corporation
A whiskey for every taste and
purse
Park & Tilford whiskey
The whiskey of the gourmet
Kentucky Tavern whiskey
The whiskey that grew up with
America
Alexander Young Distilling
Co.
Whiskey that has everything
Old Bushmill's Irish Whiskey
The whiskey that speaks for itself
Oldtyme Distillers
The whiskey with no regrets
Oldtyme Distillers
The whiskey you feel good about
Golden Wedding whiskey
Whisper sheer
Hudson Hosiery
White & Wyckoff Mfg. Co.
For every occasion of social
correspondence
For those letters you owe
Makes writing easier
The write gift
Writing paper that welcomes
the pen
White Cloud bathroom tissue
Little things mean a lot
White Consolidated Industries
Inc.
The best of two worlds
White Construction Co., Inc.
Let White build it of con-
crete
White Cross malted milk
If it's AA-grade malted
milk, it's White Cross
White Frost refrigerators
Keeps food pure and sweet
White Furniture Co.
The South's oldest makers
of fine furniture
White Horse whiskey
Time has branded it best

White House evaporated milk
Mother's first thought for
every milk need
There's none better
White is right
The Lufkin Rule Co.
White King Soap
Easy on your clothes, easi-
er still on your pocket-
book, that's White King
Soap
It takes so little
It takes so little for every
household use
Nothing washes like soap,
and there is no soap
like White King
The white line is the Clorox line
Clorox bleach
The White Line radiator belongs
to the Stearns
Stearns automobile
White Motor Co.
World leader in heavy duty
trucks
White paint that stays white
New Jersey Zinc Co.
White Rock club soda
America's finest mixer
Bottled only at the springs
Brisk as a breeze
Keeps YOU sparkling, too
The world's best table
water
White Sewing Machine
Since 1876, the servant of
the well-dressed woman
White Shoulders perfume
Potent essence of desire to
touch
White Stag Mfg. Co.
The skier's tailor since
1927
White Swan bathroom tissue
There's more than one
white tissue but only
one White Swan
White Town Car automobile
Sumptuously built
White truck
Tomorrow's way to deliver
goods today
Trucks you don't steer,
you aim
The white viking fleet
Swedish American Line

The white white lead
    Carter White Lead Co.
A white-white slip of soft-
        falling, ice-smooth rayon
        crepe, frosted with
        delicate madeira em-
        broidery
    Textron Slip
The white wine in the black bot-
        tle
    Black Tower wine
Whitecraft, Inc.
    The name for fine rattan
        furniture
The whiter enamel
    Vita-Lux
Whiter, finer, softer, Carter
    Carter White Lead Co.
Whitey Research Tool Co.
    For exacting service
    Matchless valves for exact-
        ing service
Whiting. See also: H. S.
    Whiting Co.
Whiting & Davis mesh bags
    Hand in hand with fashion
Whiting stationery
    When you think of writing,
        think of Whiting
Whitlock Associates, Inc.
    First in quality conveyers
        and driers for the
        plastics industry
Whitlock Cordage Co.
    The rope that endures
    The utmost in rope value
Whitman's Chocolates
    How to put the lovelight in
        her eyes
    It's the thoughtful thing to
        do
    Love does not live by cal-
        endars
    Love lives on little things
    There's no hurt like forget-
        ting
    Thoughtful men make the
        happiest husbands
Whitman's Instantaneous Choco-
        late
    Every family should have
        it
    The greatest invention of
        the age
Whitman's Sampler candy
    Give Whitman's Chocolates,

it's the thoughtful thing
    to do
Her Easter token
We've been making happy
    birthdays even happier
    since 1842
A woman never forgets the
    man who remembers
Whitten Machine Works
    The best way to better
        yarns
Whiz candy bar
    Best nickel candy there
        iz-z-z
Whiz insect killer
    98% kill-power
Whiz mirror and glass cleaner
    Stop window washing
Who can resist a Guinness?
    Guinness ale
Who changed it?
    H. K. Porter Co., Inc.
Who we serve proves how we
        serve
    Fishback and Moore, Inc.
The whole bowl cleaner
    Lysol Disinfectant
Whole wheat, deliciously differ-
        ent because hammered
    Educator Thinsies
Whole wheat--ready to eat!
    Kellogg's Krumbles
Wholesale floor coverings of dis-
        tinction
    Manuel Feldman Co., Inc.
Wholesome sweets for children
    Laura Secord Candy
Why a million men put their foot
        in it
    Pacer Sock
Why be a servant to your re-
        frigerator?
    Norge refrigerator
Why be irritated? Light an Old
        Gold
    Old Gold cigarettes
Why build to burn?
    Gyproc wallboard
Why carry a cold in your
        pocket?
    Pervel handkerchiefs
Why don't you get your family
        a Speedaway?
    Speedaway detachable row-
        boat motor
Why drive a car?

Jeep automobile
Why drown your soul in a greasy
    dishpan?
    Conover electric dishwasher
Why look like the deuce when
    you can look like a king?
    Wildroot Cream Oil
Why not be a nurse?
    Chicago School of Nursing
Why not ride the best?
    Victor bicycle
Why not smoke the finest?
    Dunhill cigarettes
Why pay bridge tolls to save at
    Western Auto?
    Western Auto Supply Co.
Why pay more for less?
    Blatz beer
Why pay more? Why accept less?
    Chevrolet automobile
Why pay tolls to save at Western?
    Western Auto Supply Co.
Why struggle for a sparkle?
    Bon Ami cleanser
Why the 1980's look brighter in
    Florida than in other
    states
    Barnett Bank
Why wait when you don't have
    to?
    Federal Express Corporation
Wichita Beacon
    Wichita's only evening news-
    paper
Wichita's only evening newspaper
    Wichita Beacon
Wick Narrow Fabric Co.
    The band with the little
    hooks
Wickwire Spencer Steel Co.
    Profit with Wissco products
Widdicomb. See: John Widdi-
    comb Co.
The wide-cabin airline
    Northwest Orient Airlines
Wide range of therapeutic use-
    fulness
    Donnatol medicine
The wide stick
    Speed stick deodorant
Wide-track
    Pontiac automobile
Wide world of entertainment
    American Broadcasting
    Co.
Widen your circle of influence

Harris Publications
Widget cutting tool
    It's perfect for scores of
    chores
Wieland's Beer
    Wieland's extra pale is al-
    ways extra good
Wieland's extra pale is always
    extra good
    Wieland's Beer
The wiener the world awaited
    Oscar Mayer wieners
Wiggletoe shoes
    The best for the purpose
Wilbur & Williams paints
    Paints that are different
Wilco float coat
    Play safe with Wilco
Wilcox & Gibbs sewing machine
    The machine that makes
    production
Wild Turkey bourbon whiskey
    The responsibility of being
    the best
Wild Turkey liqueur
    America's first great liqueur
Wildroot Cream Oil
    Why look like the deuce
    when you can look like
    a king?
Wile. See: Julius Wile Sons
    and Co., Inc.
Wilkerson Corp.
    Protecting the new in your
    pneumatics
Will bring peace of mind to you
    and your family
    The Guardian Life Insur-
    ance Co. of America
Will cure a cold in one night
    Carter's Compound Extract
Will cure your cough or cold
    Perry Davis' Pain Killer
Will do you many a good turn
    Viking tires
Will not kink
    Milo Hose
Will not ruin hose
    Quix foot pads
Will not shrink, swell or warp
    Laminex doors
Will Ross, Inc.
    Products you can trust
    from people you know
Willard battery
    Last longer, crank faster,

don't let you down
Quick starts, long life
Years ahead in life and
power
Willcox & Gibbs Sewing Machine
Co.
The seam that sells the gar-
ment
Wm. Demuth & Co.
The insured pipe
The sweetest pipe in the
world
The Universal pipe
Wm. H. Jackson Co.
Everything for the fireplace
since 1827
William Iselin and Co., Inc.
Since 1808, a tradition in
factoring and financing
William Lewis and Son
Since 1874 stringed instru-
ment house of the
masters
William Penn whiskey
The measure of perfection
The Wm. Powell Co.
Men who know valves know
Powell
World leader of the valve
industry since 1846
William Rogers & Co. silverware
The best at the price
Wm. S. Haynes Co.
The tone heard 'round the
world
Williams. See also:
Eureka Williams Co.
J. H. Williams & Co.
Williams and Humbert dry sack
World-famous Spanish sher-
ries
The Williams Companies
The fertilizer, energy and
metals company
We're worth watching in the
80's
Williams Gun Sight Co.
On the range
Williams Oil-O-Matic Heating
Corp.
It budgets the oil
Measured heat
Put your heating plan on
a budget
Williams Sealing Corp.
The cap with the little

lever
Williams' Shaving Cream
It's quick wetting
Where face fitness starts
Williams' Shaving Soap
The only real shaving soap
Unwise and unfortunate is
the man who tries to
shave without Williams'
soaps
Williamson. See: Ault Williamson
Shoe Co.
Willing Keys bring writing ease
Underwood typewriter
Willmark Service System
Builders of business
Willsonite sun glasses
For everything "under the
sun"
Willys-Knight automobile
For those who want the
finest
Power and light with the
quiet Knight
With an engine you'll never
wear out
Willys-Overland automobile
Makers of America's most
useful vehicles
Wilson & Co., Inc.
If this gold seal is on it--
there's better meat in
it
The Wilson label protects
your table
Wilson Bros. shirts
The easiest name for a
man to remember
The Wilson label protects your
table
Wilson & Co., Inc.
Wilson Sporting Goods Co.
It's Wilson today in sports
equipment
Play to win with Wilson
A progressive past. A
golden future
Wilson, that's haul
Wilson truck
Wilson truck
Wilson, that's haul
Wilsonite sun glasses
Always right with Wilsonite
An eye for comfort
Eyes right
Wilson's fly pads

They kill them all
Wilson's Oleomargarine
    The spread that betters
        your bread
Wilton. See also:
    Winston
    Winton
The Wilton Company
    Elegant. Yet so practical
Wilts whiskers
    Mennen's shave cream
Win 8 out of 10 times
    Pfister Associated Growers
Win favor with a flavor, serve
        S & W fine foods
    Sussman & Wormser Co.
Win preference by performance
    Schickerling radio tubes
Win the smile of perfection
        through Forhan's pro-
        tection
    Forhan's tooth paste
Win their way by their play
    Hunt phonograph sound
    boxes
Win yourself a halo for these
        heavenly meals
    Armour and Co.
Winchester cigarettes
    Blended right
Winchester flashlight
    Give long-lasting light,
    bullet-fast
Winchester Repeating Arms Co.
    The balanced load shells
    The skate with a backbone
Windblown through silk
    Pompeian beauty products
Windex glass cleaner
    Get brighter windows quick-
    er with Windex
    Get brighter windows with
    Windex
    Gets windows brighter
    quicker
    Put on a new Windex shine
    Shines more than windows
    Spray that cleans windows
    without water
    Washes windows without
    water
Window beauty is Andersen
    Andersen Corporation
Window to the world
    U. S. Television Mfg.
    Corp.

Windsor Canadian whiskey
    One Canadian stands alone
Windsor loudspeaker console
    Keeping radio in its place
Wine Advisory Board
    As friendly as a letter from
    home
    Be considerate, serve wine
The wine that tastes as good as
    it looks
    Cresta Blanca wine
The wine with the champagne
    taste
    Pacific Wines, Inc.
Wines of California since 1882
    Christian Brothers wines
Wing it there via the air
    U. S. Airmail
The wings of America
    U. S. Air Force
The wings of man
    Eastern Air Lines, Inc.
Wings of steel
    Nestor Johnson ice skates
Wings Shirts
    Are you pensioning your
    shirts too soon?
A winner for dinners
    Spam prepared meat
A winner wherever it's sold
    Fruit Bowl Drink
A winner with women
    Quest deodorant
Winning and holding good will
    Oakland automobile
The winning cup
    Webb Coffee
Winship trunk
    The trunk with doors
Winston. See also:
    Wilton
    Winton
Winston cigarettes
    Finer filter. Finer flavor
    The men. The cigarette.
    Nobody does it better
    Winston tastes good like a
    cigarette should
    Winston tastes good like a cig-
    arette should
    Winston cigarettes
Wint-o-Green
    The candy with a hole
The winter brew for brew
    drinkers
    Hoffman Beverage Co.

Winter enchained in silent
service
Copeland refrigeration
Winter fun under a "summer sun"
Sun Valley, Idaho
Winter piano
Popular as music itself
The winter playground of America
San Antonio, Texas
Winthrop puts you on Easy
Street
Winthrop shoes
Winthrop shoes
Always first with all that's
new
Sky-high style, down to
earth comfort
Winthrop puts you on Easy
Street
Winton. See also:
Wilton
Winston
Winton bicycle
The Winton is a winner on
road or in race
The Winton is a winner on road
or in race
Winton bicycle
Winton Six automobile
Starts from the seat without
cranking
The Winton Six is the best
purchase on the market
The Winton Six is the best pur-
chase on the market
Winton Six automobile
A wipe and it's bright
Porcelain cleaner
The wipe-clean wall covering
Columbus-Union Oil Cloth
Co.
Wipe 'em out, don't stir 'em up
Sergeant's flea powder
Wipe off the dust
Sanitas wall covering
Wipes off dirt and grease, as
easy as dusting
Olde English Household
Cleaner
Wire for industry
Keystone Steel & Wire Co.
The wire rope with the service
record
Leschen & Sons Rope Co.
The wire that remembers
Lear plane radio

Wirebound Box Manufacturer's
Association
It gets there right in Wire-
bounds
Wirthmore Grain
We carry nothing but the
best
Wisconsin Div. of Economic De-
velopment
We like it here
Wisconsin Gas Company
Wisconsin won't run out of
gas
Wisconsin Knife Works, Inc.
Engineers to the woodwork-
ing industry
Wisconsin Motor Corp.
World's largest builder of
heavy-duty air-cooled
engines
Wisconsin Vacation and Travel
Service
The land that was made
for vacations
Wisconsin won't run out of gas
Wisconsin Gas Company
Wisconsin's greatest community
newspaper
Sparta Herald
The wise investor knows when to
invest
International Gold Bullion
Exchange
Wise men seek wise counsel
Employers Liability Assur-
ance Corp.
Wise Rubber Products
Be wise, buy Wise
Wish Bone salad dressings
Flavor so delicious only
your figure knows
they're low calorie
Wishbone incubator
The Wishbone is the money
making mammoth
The Wishbone is the money
making mammoth
Wishbone incubator
Wisk gets ring around the col-
lar and your whole
wash clean
Wisk laundry detergent
Wisk laundry detergent
Gets your whole wash
clean!
Wisk gets ring around the

collar and your whole
wash clean
Wiss shears
The easiest line to sell
Never a dull moment
With a heart of steel
Michigan Seating Co.
With all the grace and beauty of
its name
Gulbransen piano
With an engine you'll never wear
out
Willys-Knight automobile
With Crest your kids could have
even fewer cavities than
you did
Crest tooth paste
With everything American, tomor-
row is secure
American Insurance Co.
With Graflex the payoff is in the
picture
Graflex, Inc.
With Grecian Formula you'll play
longer
Grecian Formula hair dress-
ing
With hair-conditioning action
Drene shampoo
With men who know tobacco
best, it's Luckies 2 to 1
Lucky Strike cigarettes
With oodles of noodles and
chicken, too
Heinz chicken-noodle soup
With pleasure, sir!
General Cigar Co.
With real root juices
Hires' Improved Root Beer
With that hand-made look
Faerie undergarments
With that sweet smoke taste
Swift's bacon
With the aroma of the rose
Rosa Aroma cigars
With the better taste
Mueller's macaroni
With the exclusive slumber
sentinel
Universal electric blanket
With the fragrance men love
Cashmere Bouquet soap
With the pistol grip and trig-
ger switch
The Black & Decker Mfg.
Co.

With the wire part for the part
of beauty
Foremost foundations
With tools of war they fashion
peace
U. S. National Guard
Without chemicals, life itself
would be impossible
Monsanto Company
Without it you don't have the
power
Napa power storage battery
Without the shadow of a stout
Stylish Stout corset
Withstands the test of time
Barber Asphalt Co.
Wits End stationery
For pen-tied or pen-clever
people
Witter. See: Dean Witter Rey-
nolds investments
Wittliff Furniture Brace Co.
Makes good beds better
Wix Corp.
The gold standard
Wizard of the wash
Maid-Easy Cleansing Prod-
ucts Corp.
WoHeLo
Campfire Girls
Wohl shoes
Every inch has style, every
foot has comfort
Wolff Tailoring
If you think clothes don't
make a difference, try
walking down the street
without any
Wolf's Head motor oil
It pays to be particular
about your oil
Ships of the air can't stop
for repair
Wolfschmidt vodka
The spirit of the Czar
Wollensack Optical Co.
Let the user judge
Wolthausen hats
Hatter to gentlemen for
over half a century
Wolverine Work Shoes
Put your feet on Comfort
Street in Wolverines
A woman never forgets the
man who remembers
Whitman's Sampler candy

The woman of tomorrow guards
today's beauty
Elizabeth Arden cosmetics
The woman who uses it, knows
E-Z Polish
The womanly way to remove hair
El Rado Depilatory
Woman's best friend
Polly-Flex Housewares
Woman's Digest
The best of the world's
press
Woman's Home Companion
Intimate as her diary, per-
sonal as a back-fence
chat
The woman's razor
Curvfit razor
Women just won't give up the
clean they get from
Tide
Tide laundry detergent
Women's Wear
The retailer's daily news-
paper
Won its favor through its flavor
Kellogg's toasted corn flakes
Wonder bread
Helps build strong bodies
12 ways!
The wonder city of America
Miami, Fla.
The wonder fuel
Blue Sunoco gasoline
The wonder-healing salve
Kleerex
The wonder rug of America
Karastan Rug Mills Div.,
Field Crest Mills, Inc.
Wonder white bread
Good nutrition doesn't have
to be whole wheat
Wonderform corsets
In silver it's sterling, in
corsetry it's "Wonder-
form"
The wonderful new hoist
Pull-U-Out Hoist
Won't boil off; contains no al-
cohol
Prestone anti-freeze
Won't clog on wet coal
Perfect Spread Stoker
Won't shrink woolens
Lux soap
Won't stretch in wearing or

shrink in dry cleaning
Bur-Mil suiting
Wood and Hogan
America's most distinguished
source for fine English
furniture
The wood eternal
Southern Cypress Mfrs.
Assn.
The wood of service
Southern Pine Association
Wood that weathers every storm
National Oak Lumbermen's
Assn.
Wood that you always prefer
National Oak Lumbermen's
Assn.
Wood that you would and should
use
National Oak Lumbermen's
Assn.
Wood that's stronger than wood
Plylock
Woodbury College
Executive training for busi-
ness leadership
Woodbury's Cold Cream
All through your beauty
sleep your skin must
stay awake
"Beauty Glo" cleansing
She was beautiful in her
sleep because her skin
was wide awake
That "always fresh" look
To kindle love, light up
your type
Woodbury's face powder
Film-finish powder
Gleaming silver on your
gown, but no shine on
your nose
Woodbury's Facial Soap
The bedtime way to loveli-
ness
Does 20 years experience
count for anything?
For now-and-forever-after
loveliness
The skin you love to touch
Woodcock. See: Rouse Wood-
cock Commodities
Brokers
Woodcraft tools
Make an heirloom
Woods automobile

523

The Gas-Electric Car
Woodville Products Co.
Quality is in the limestone
Woodward. See: Lee L. Wood-
ward Sons, Inc.
Woody Herman's orchestra
The band that plays the
blues
Wool Carpets of America
The answer is wool ... it
costs less in the long
run
Wool drest is best drest
Woolen Corp. of America
Woolen Corp. of America
Wool drest is best drest
Woolworth. See: F. W. Wool-
worth Co.
Wooster paint brush
If it's worth painting it's
worth a Wooster brush
Quality perpetuates prefer-
ence
Worcester Salt Co.
It takes the best to make
the best
A perfect salt, a natural
tonic
When it's wet it's dry
The word for champagne
Mumm's champagne
Word to the wives is sufficient
Carey Salt Co.
Words to go to sleep by
Perfect Sleeper mattress
The Work Boat
The authority of the water-
ways
Work clothes that fit and look
like dress clothes
Kast-Iron Work Clothes
Work clothing that conquers hard
wear
Cowden work clothing
Work electrically and enjoy the
difference
Reddy Kilowatt
Work horse of the world
Jeep automobile
Work in the state that works for
you
Massachusetts
The work machine
Bolens tractor
The work of the century
Ridpath's History of the

World
Working for America's property
owners
National Association of
Realtors
Working for the day kids won't
know what a cavity
feels like
Crest toothpaste
Working for today, planning for
tomorrow
Norge refrigerator
Working funds for industry
Walter E. Heller & Co. fi-
nancial services
The working partner of a million
Americans
Overland automobile
Working smarter
Bethlehem Steel Company
Working to foil energy shortages
Santa Fe Industries
Working to hold your insurance
costs down
Allstate Insurance Co.
Working Woman
The magazine for women
who expect to be taken
seriously
Working wonders with wire
E. H. Titchener Co.
Workmen's Circle Call
The Jewish market at its
best
Works best under pressure
Hydro-Line Mfg. Co.
Works better
Tranolane hemorrhoid reme-
dy
Works between shampoos
Tegrin shampoo
Works harder when it gets hotter
Sergeant's flea collar
Works like a powder and a spray
Sergeant's flea collar
Works like magic
Amorall automobile polish
Works like the others can't
Saniflush Toilet Bowl
Cleaner
Works of art in leather
Krucraft Leather Co.
Works swiftly. Wears slowly
Remington typewriter
Works while you sleep
Cascarets laxative

Works with you--works for you
    Battle Creek Manufacturers,
        Inc.
Works wonders
    Goblin soap
World Airways, Inc.
    World's largest charter air-
        line
    The world's largest inde-
        pendent airline
World Almanac
    America's greatest reference
        book
The world at your fingertips
    Standard batteryless radio
        receivers
World Book encyclopedia
    The world is yours with the
        World Book
World champions of worth!
    Hesston Corp.
The world-famed effervescent
        salt
    Eno effervescent salt
World famous for quality
    Wembley neckties
World-famous Spanish sherries
    Williams and Humbert dry
        sack
World Fire and Marine Insurance
        Co.
    Get the best in the world
The world is going our way
    Northwest Orient Airlines
The world is small when you fly
        a Beechcraft
    Beech Aircraft Corp.
The world is yours with the
        World Book
    World Book encyclopedia
The world knows no better
        Scotch
    Haig & Haig Scotch whiskey
World leader in commercial re-
        frigeration
    Tyler Refrigeration Div.,
        Clark Equipment Com-
        pany
World leader in energy technol-
        ogy
    Combustion Engineering,
        Inc.
World leader in filtration
    Great Lakes Carbon Corp.
World leader in heavy duty
        trucks

White Motor Co.
World leader in luxury cigars
    Gold Label cigars
World leader in mailing systems
    Pitney-Bowes mail handling
        machines
World leader in packaged power
    ESB, Inc.
World leader in recorded sound
    Command records
World leader in temporary help
    Manpower, Inc.
World leader in transport re-
        frigeration
    Thermo King Corp.
World leader of the valve indus-
        try since 1846
    The Wm. Powell Co.
World leader on highway and
        speedway
    Monroe Auto Equipment Co.
The world leaders in duplicat-
        ing supplies since 1906
    Frankel Manufacturing Co.
World leaders in the development
        of pulp and paper mills
        for the use of local
        fibers
    Parsons and Whittemore,
        Inc.
World money for world travelers
    Bank of America travelers
        cheques
The world moves, so do we
    O. K. Storage & Transfer
        Co.
A world of difference
    CBS Evening News TV
        broadcast
A world of different voices
        where freedom speaks
    Gannett newspapers and
        broadcasting systems
A world of engineering experi-
        ence
    Globe Hoist Company
A world of experience
    Collins Radio Co.
A world of furniture made in a
        way that makes a world
        of difference
    Kroehler Mfg. Co.
A world of profits awaits the
        well informed
    Dow Theory Forecasts,
        Inc.

The world over
    Mothersill's Seasick Remedy
The world over, it's Everlast
    Everlast sporting goods
World peace through world trade
    International Business Ma-
    chines Corp.
World renowned for perfection in
    sound
        James B. Lansing Sound,
        Inc.
The world rides on Sealed Power
    Sealed Power piston rings
World standard
    Bell helicopter
World trade UNITES nations
    Life
    Time
The world walks on '61
    Pratt & Lambert varnish
World War I recruiting poster
        drawn by James Mont-
        gomery Flagg
    Uncle Sam wants you!
World-wide. See also: Worldwide
World-wide building service
    H. H. Robertson Co.
World-wide competence in control
    Taylor Instruments
World-wide engineering, manu-
        facturing and construc-
        tion
    Dorr-Oliver, Inc.
World-wide favorite
    Johnson sea-horse motor
World-wide reception
    De Forest-Crosley radio re-
    ceivers
A world-wide reputation for
        high-tension insulation
    Ohio Brass Co.
World-wide suppliers of the fin-
        est ball pen inks
    Formulabs, Inc.
World-wide voice writing service
    Ediphone Dictograph
The world-wide water condition-
        ing people
    Culligan, Inc.
The world's best climate makes
        the world's best rum
    Puerto Rican rums
The world's best designed prod-
        ucts, inside and out
        Olivetti Corporation of
        America

World's best seller
    Reader's Digest
The world's best table water
    White Rock club soda
World's best-tasting breakfast
    food
    Quaker Oats
The world's best varnish
    Rylard varnish
The world's best way to own
        gold
    Krugerrand gold coins
World's biggest seller!
    Honda motorcycle
World's champion ammunition
    Western Cartridge Co.
The world's coolest shave
    Ingram's shaving cream
World's easiest-to-use dictating
        machines
        StenoCord Dictation Sys-
        tems
World's Fair feet
    Selby Shoe Co.
The world's fastest cook stove
    American Gas Machine Co.
World's fastest shine
    Bixby's Jet Oil shoe polish
The world's fastest way to rent
        a car
    Hertz automobile rentals
World's finest
    Autocar truck
    Garrard phonograph record
        changer
    J. A. Baldwin Mfg. Co.
    Phillipson Rod Co.
The world's finest
    Goya Guitars, Inc.
World's finest automatic record
        changer
    Garrard phonograph record
        changer
The world's finest bourbon
        since 1795
    Jim Beam whiskey
The world's finest cigarette
        paper
    Ecusta Paper Corp.
World's finest cottons
        Supima Association of Amer-
        ica
The world's finest gas range
    Chambers Corp.
World's finest golf clubs and
        accessories

Bristol Pro-Golf, Inc.
The world's finest home record-
ing instrument
Recordio
The world's finest instant camera
Polaroid SX-70 Sonar
World's finest mink
United Mink Producers Assn.
The world's finest motor oil
Gulf Oil Corporation
The world's finest name in silver
care
W. J. Hagerty and Sons,
Ltd., Inc.
World's finest petrochemical
products
Gulf Oil Corporation
The world's finest railroad watch
Waltham Vanguard watch
World's finest reproductions
Deltah pearls
The world's finest shampoo
Vita-Fluff shampoo
The world's finest the world over
Vulcan-Hart Corp.
World's first and largest manu-
facturer of deep fat
frying equipment
J. C. Pitman and Sons, Inc.
The world's "first family" of
changers and tape decks
BSR (USA), Ltd.
World's first family of jets
Boeing aircraft
World's first mass produced
tractor
Ford Tractor Div., Ford
Motor Company
World's first--world's finest
Valvoline motor oil
The world's foremost dried fruit
packers
Rosenberg Bros. & Co.
World's foremost heavy-duty
ignition line
Blue Streak
World's foremost rebuilders of
automotive parts
Kimco Auto Products, Inc.
World's friendliest airline
Panagra Airline
The world's greatest artists are
NATURALLY yours on
Victor records
Victor phonograph records
The world's greatest Catholic

monthly
Extension Magazine
The world's greatest industrial
paper
Iron Age
World's greatest iron fence
Stewart Iron Works Co.
World's greatest lighter
Ronson cigarette lighters
World's greatest motor necessity
Staynew Filter Corp.
The world's greatest newspaper
Chicago Tribune
The world's greatest table mak-
ers
Imperial Furniture Co.
The world's greatest travel
publication
Golfer's Magazine
World's greatest travel system
Canadian Pacific Steamship
& Railroad Co.
World's greatest value in depend-
able refrigeration
Copeland refrigeration
World's largest air cargo carrier
Pan American World Air-
ways, Inc.
The world's largest airline
Air France
The world's largest and finest
Lindsay Ripe Olive Co.
The world's largest and most
experienced manufac-
turer of magnetic pick-
ups
Pickering and Co., Inc.
World's largest builder of
heavy-duty air-cooled
engines
Wisconsin Motor Corp.
World's largest builder of organs
and pianos
Wurlitzer Company
The world's largest business
training institute
La Salle Extension Univer-
sity
World's largest charter airline
World Airways, Inc.
World's largest citrus plant
Pasco Packing Co.
World's largest commercial oven
manufacturer since
1888
Middleby-Marshall Oven Co.

World's largest creator of pre-
school toys
Fisher-Price Toys, Inc.
World's largest exclusive fly line
manufacturer
Scientific Anglers, Inc.
World's largest exclusive manu-
facturer of electrical
industrial trucks
Lewis-Shepard Co.
World's largest exclusive manu-
facturer of golf balls
Plymouth Golf Ball Co.
The world's largest independent
airline
World Airways, Inc.
World's largest maker of fan belts
Gates Rubber Co.
World's largest maker of small
radios
Emerson radio receiver
World's largest maker of tufted
carpets and rugs
E. T. Barwick Industries,
Inc.
World's largest maker of V-belts
Gates Rubber Co.
The world's largest makers of
furniture
Kroehler Mfg. Co.
The world's largest manufacturer
and designer
Bead Design Studio
The world's largest manufacturer
of blister packaging
machinery
Packaging Industries, Ltd.,
Inc.
World's largest manufacturer of
fine carbonizing papers
Peter J. Schweitzer Div.,
Kimberly-Clark Corp.
The world's largest manufacturer
of fine kitchen cabinets
Colonial Products Co.
World's largest manufacturer of
gasoline pumps and
service station equip-
ment
Wayne Pump Co.
World's largest manufacturer of
glass tableware
Anchor Hocking Glass Co.
World's largest manufacturer of
industrial rubber
products

Uniroyal, Inc.
World's largest manufacturer of
mirrors
Carolina Mirror Corp.
World's largest manufacturer of
painters' and glaziers'
tools--since 1872
Red Devil, Inc.
The world's largest manufacturer
of reach-in refrigerators
and freezers
Victory Metal Mfg. Co.
World's largest manufacturer of
school supplies and
stationery
Westab, Inc.
World's largest manufacturer of
staplers for home and
office
Swingline stapler
World's largest manufacturer of
steel shipping contain-
ers
Rheem Mfg. Co.
World's largest manufacturer of
ventilating louvers
Louver Mfg. Co., Inc.
World's largest mattress maker
Simmons Company
World's largest newspaper
Los Angeles Times
World's largest oilcloth distri-
butors
Weiss & Klau Co.
World's largest producers of
automotive wheels, hubs
and drums
Kelsey-Hayes Co.
World's largest producer of bath
scales
The Brearley Company
World's largest producer of com-
mercial heavy-duty truck
drive axles
Axle Division, Eaton Manu-
facturing Co.
World's largest producer of non-
powder guns and ammo
Daisy/Heddon Div., Victor
Comptometer Corp.
The world's largest razor
Rolls razor
World's largest retailer of hats
Kaufman Hats, Inc.
World's largest roof truss system
Sanford Truss, Inc.

World's largest selling air
  conditioners
    Fedders Corp.
The world's largest selling chain
  saw
    Stihl chain saw
World's largest selling tea
    Lipton's tea
World's largest ski maker
    Northland Ski Mfg. Co.
World's largest specialized pub-
  lisher
    Gulf Publishing Co.
World's leading direct-by-mail
  vitamin and drug com-
  pany
    Hudson National, Inc.
World's leading manufacturer of
  plastic products for 35
  diversified industries
    Colorite Plastics, Inc.
World's leading padlock manufac-
  turers
    Master Lock Co.
World's leading supplier of
  diamonds for industry
    De Beers Consolidated Mines,
    Ltd.
The world's liniment
    Sloan's Liniment
World's liveliest bait
    Live-Lure
The world's most beautiful china
    Meakin & Ridgeway
    Minton, Inc.
The world's most beautiful organs
    Story and Clark Piano Co.
World's most beautiful stockings
    Canadian Silk Products, Ltd.
The world's most broadly based
  electronics company
    RCA Corp.
The world's most "carefree"
  watch
    Croton watch
The world's most comfortable
  mattress
    Beautyrest mattress
World's most complete fishing
  tackle line
    Horrocks-Ibbotson Co.
World's most complete line of
  sporting arms and
  accessories
    Savage Arms Div., Emhart
    Corp.

World's most complete transportation system
    Canadian Pacific Railway
World's most dependable air
  freight service
    Airborne Freight Corp.
The world's most distinctive digging machines are Davis
    Davis Manufacturing, Inc.
The world's most efficient business jet. Now building
  our second 1000
    Gates Learjet Corporation
The world's most experienced
  airline
    Pan American World Airways,
    Inc.
World's most experienced detergent engineers
    Ing. Mario Ballestra & Co.
World's most experienced ski
  maker
    Northland Ski Mfg. Co.
The world's most honored hands
  wear the world's most
  honored watch
    Longines-Wittnauer Watch
    Co.
The world's most honored watch
    Longines-Wittnauer Watch
    Co.
The world's most luxurious low-
  priced automobile
    Chevrolet automobile
World's most perfect high fidelity
  components
    Empire Scientific Corp.
The world's most popular gold
  coin
    Krugerrand gold coins
The world's most precious simu-
  lated pearls
    Majorica
The world's most-read magazine
    Reader's Digest
The world's most respected ac-
  cordion
    Nunziola accordion
World's most wanted lure
    Rapala Div., Nordic Enter-
    prises, Inc.
The world's most wanted pen
    Parker 51 pen
World's most widely used brand
  of cold's medication
    Vick's Vapo-Rub

The world's most wonderful
    phonograph
    Aeolian-Vocalion
The world's motor car unique
    American automobile
World's number one weed killers
    Weedone weed killer
World's oldest and largest manu-
    facturer of electric
    blankets
    Northern Electric Co.
The world's oldest whiskey
    Old Bushmill's Irish Whiskey
The world's 100,000 mile durabil-
    ity champion
    Mercury Comet automobile
The world's only tourists' maga-
    zine
    Tourist
World's outstanding boxing maga-
    zine
    The Ring
The world's outstanding small
    boat
    Gibbs boat
The world's premier pipe
    Sasieni pipe
World's safest low-priced car
    Plymouth automobile
The world's safest safe
    Safe-Cabinet Co.
World's second largest manufac-
    turer of cameras and
    films
    Agfa-Gevaert, Inc.
The world's smartest collar
    Phillips-Jones collars
The world's smoothest cigarette
    Old Gold cigarettes
The world's smoothest drink
    Bacardi rum
World's speediest stapler
    Swingline stapler
The world's standard for zinc
    products
    New Jersey Zinc Co.
The world's standard of quality
    New York Central System
World's strongest padlocks
    Master Lock Company
The world's supreme travel ex-
    perience
    American President Lines
The world's textile authority
    Textile World
The world's watch over time

Waltham watches
The world's word for elevator
    safety
    Otis Elevator Company
World's worst beauty soap.
        World's best hand soap
    Lava soap
Worldwide. See also: World-wide
Worldwide electronics telecom-
    munications
    International Telephone &
    Telegraph Corp.
Worldwide in heat and fluid
    processing
    Selas Corp. of America
Worn with pride by millions
    Freeman Shoe Corp.
Worsted-Tex clothing
    Clothes that enhance your
    public appearance
Wortendyke gummed tape
    It sho sticks
Worth a guinea a box
    Beecham's Pills
Worth behind the name
    Worthington Pump & Ma-
    chinery Corp.
Worth changing brands to get
    Firebird gasoline
Worth Cologne
    Worth knowing, worth re-
    membering
Worth it's WAIT in gold
    Admiral refrigerator
Worth knowing, worth remem-
    bering
    Worth Cologne
Worth more. See: Wirthmore
    Grain
Worth their WAIT in gold
    Darling Metal Fixtures
Worthington Pump & Machinery
    Corp.
    Blue brutes
    Get more worth from air
    with Worthington
    A great team in steam
    Worth behind the name
Worthy of its name
    Red Cross mattress
Worthy of the name
    Gray & Dudley stoves and
    ranges
A worthy product deserves a
    fitting package
    Metal Package Corp.

Worthy to become heirlooms
  Rome kitchen ware
Would you like to see what one
    can do for you?
  Bell helicopter
Wouldn't you really rather have
    a Buick?
  Buick automobile
Woven where the wool is grown
  Oregon City Woolen Mills
Woven with a warp of honesty
    and a woof of skill
  Magee Carpet Co.
Wow! I'm gonna have a V-8!
  V-8 vegetable juice drink
A wower for power
  Ford automobile
Wrangler's ranch togs
  Fashion in action
Wrath. See: Rath
Wren. See: Jenny Wren Co.
The wrench people
  J. H. Williams & Co.
Wright. See also:
  Write
  Right
  Rite
Wright Arch Preserver shoes
  The man's styleful shoe on
    a real chassis
  Men ... perfect fit ... by
    mail! We guarantee it!
  The styled shoe built on a
    real chassis
  We've been Wright for more
    than 100 years
  The Wright selection
The write gift for Christmas
  Underwood portable type-
    writer
Wright Hat
  You know you're right with
    a Wright Hat
The Wright selection
  Wright Arch Preserver shoes
Wright's coal tar soap
  He won't be happy till he
    gets it
Wright's French dressing
  It stays on the salad
Wright's silver cream cleaner
  Sombre silver dulls more
    than the dinner
  Sombre silver dulls the
    dinner
Wrigley's chewing gum

After every meal
  Chew it after every meal
  The flavor lasts
  For beauty exercise
  The gum with the fascinat-
    ing artificial flavor
  It's clean, pure, healthful
    if it's Wrigley's
  Nothing like the flavor
  The perfect gum
Wrigley's Doublemint Gum
  Double your pleasure with
    Doublemint Gum
Wrigley's P. K. chewing gum
  Fine for the breath
Wrigley's Spearmint Gum
  Keeps you hummin'
Wrisley. See: House of Wris-
    ley, Inc.
Write. See also:
  Right
  Rite
  Wright
Write around the world
  Alexander pens and pencils
The write gift
  White & Wyckoff Mfg. Co.
Write often, write cheerfully,
    WRITE!
  Eaton Paper Corp.
Write on the ball
  Reynolds ball point pen
Write! Write with Eversharp!
  Eversharp mechanical pencil
Writer's Monthly
  A journal for all who write
Writes a strong, rich blue
  Carter's ink
Writes better--always
  Rollit pen
Writes dry with permanent ink
  Eversharp pen
Writing paper that welcomes the
    pen
  White & Wyckoff Mfg. Co.
Writing papers that create an
    impression
  Montag, Inc., Div.,
    Westab, Inc.
Written so you can understand
    it
  Popular Mechanics
The wrong shade of powder can
    turn the right man
    away
  Lady Esther face powder

Wrought from solid silver
International Silver Co.
Wurlitzer Company
World's largest builder of
organs and pianos
Wurlitzer means music to
millions
Wurlitzer means music to millions
Wurlitzer Company
Wurlitzer phonograph
Musical fun for everyone
Wyeth Laboratories Div., Amer-
ican Home Products
Corp.
Service to medicine
Wyler Incaflex shockproof watch
Resilent as a reed

-X-

X. See: Don X carbonated
beverage
X marks the spot where S. O. S.
shines
S. O. S. Magic Scouring
Pads
XO Rare Reserve brandy
If you think the best sip-
ping brandy is cognac,
you haven't sipped
America's XO
X-Ray razor
You can shave in a foxhole
with X-Ray
XX. See: Double-X Floor
Cleaner
Xerox Corporation
Now everybody can have
Xerocopies
We behave responsibly as
a corporate citizen
We exist to earn profits
We require satisfied custom-
ers for success
We use technology to de-
velop product leadership
We value our employees
Xerox frees information
Xerox frees information
Xerox Corporation
Xerox Learning Systems
We teach success

-Y-

Yachting
Edited by yachtsmen for
yachtsmen
The quality magazine of the
boating world
Yale and Towne locks
The finest name in locks
and hardware
Locks recommended by the
world's leading lock ex-
perts
Yale marked is Yale made
A Yale battery for every need
Yale Electric Corp.
Yale bicycle
The bike you'll like
Yale Coffee
Start the day with Yale
Coffee
Yale Electric Corp.
A Yale battery for every
need
Yale Express System, Inc.
Speed with economy
Yale marked is Yale made
Yale and Towne locks
Yamaha electric organ
Bringing out the music in
you
Yank
The army weekly
Yankee Toffee
Dandy candy
Yankee tools
Right to the point
Yankee tools make better
mechanics
Yankee tools make better
mechanics
Yankee tools
Yankiboy Play Clothes
Make the children happy
A yard near you
Comfort Coal-Lumber Co.
Yardley's Face Cream
A rest cure for tired faces
Yardley's Old English soap
The gay-hearted fragrance
The luxury soap of the
world
Young beauty, clear as the
chime of bells
The yarn with the "crepe" built
in

Enka Crepeset yarn
The yarn you love to use
Bear Brand Yarn
Yawman & Erbe steel filing
cabinets
Built like a safe
Ybry perfume
The jewel of perfumes
Year in, year out, the perfect
servant
Copeland refrigeration
A year of sunshine in every sip
Citrus Hill orange juice
Year 'round fruit club
Pinnacle Orchards
The year-round-oil
Three Sixty Five
The year-round pantie
Chafe-O-Tex
Years ahead in life and power
Willard battery
Years ahead in the science of
flight
Lockheed Aircraft Corpora-
tion
Years from now you'll be glad
it's Norge
Norge refrigerator
Years of wear in every yard
Congoleum-Nairn floor cov-
erings
Yeast builds resistance
Fleischmann's Yeast
The yellow pencil with the red
band
Eagle Pencil Co.
Yellow taxicabs
Every driver an escort
A Newark institution
Serves all Chicago
Yes detergent
Cleans--softens--controls
static
Rainbow fresh
Yes, he's used to the best
Everess sparkling water
Yes, I know ... Marie Brizard
Marie Brizard liqueurs
The yes people
McDonnell-Douglas Finance
Corporation
Yes, there IS a difference
Ronson cigarette lighters
Yes Tissues
The new tender touch
tissues

Yesterday's vision. today's
achievement
Carrier Corporation
Yield with every step
Massagic Air Cushion shoes
Yodora
The gentler cream deodorant
Yoplait Yogurt
Up to your neck in fruity
good taste
York Chemical Co.
A better yield in every
field
York cigarettes
The first new no-filter
cigarette in years
York Corporation
The quality name in air
conditioning and re-
frigeration
You. See also: U
You adjust it. See: Uajustit
You always pay more for the
best
Celo Co. of America
You and your clothes can depend
on it
Ban deodorant
You are. See also:
Your
You're
You are reading through its in-
visible sheerness
Griffin Hosiery Mills
You are secretary of the interior
Campbell's condensed soups
You are the main component
Citibank, New York City
You bake your best with Pills-
bury's best
Pillsbury's flour
You bet it's good--it's a Brent-
wood
Brentwood sportswear
You bet your Life Savers
Life Savers candy
You buy the best when you buy
the Bessemer
Bessemer Gas Engine Co.
You call it a "zipper"; its real
name is Prentice, the
dependable slide fasten-
er
Prentice slide fastener
You can always save with safety
at your Rexall store

Rexall Drug Stores

You can bank on a Frank
Frank trumpet

You can bank on Bankers
Bankers Accident Insurance
Co.

You can be sure if it's Westinghouse
Westinghouse Electric Corp.

You can be sure of Shell
Shell Oil Company

You can change these blades in
the dark
Schick injector razor

You can cook it better with
Magic Chef
Magic Chef gas range

You can count on Continental to
take care of you
Continental Steel Corp.

You can count on Kemper care
under the Kemper flag
Kemper Insurance Co.

You can count on Sears
Sears Roebuck & Co.

You can count on Wak counters
Wak counters

You can DEPEND on Esso farm
products
Esso farm products

You can depend on it
National Oil Fuel Institute,
Inc.

You can depend on the integrity
and quality of Smith-
Douglass
Smith-Douglass Div., Borden
Chemical Co.

You can depend on the name
Borden's condensed milk

You can do better in Frederick
Frederick, Maryland

You can do it better with gas
American Gas Association,
Inc.

You can drink it and sleep
Sanka Brand decaffeinated
coffee

You can enjoy eight months of
June
Libbey-Owens-Ford Co.

You can expect it from B. F.
Goodrich
B. F. Goodrich Tire Co.

You can feel it when you drive
Bridgestone tires

You can get all types of insurance under the Travelers
umbrella
The Travelers Insurance
Cos.

You can get thin to music
Wallace Reducing Records

You can go a long way with the
fleet leader
Chevrolet trucks

You can have your cake and
drink it, too
Guittard Chocolate Co.

You can pay more but you can't
buy more
Royal typewriter

You can put them on in a moment
American Chain Co.

You can rely on America's oldest
and most experienced
custom finisher
Synthetics Finishing Corp.

You can see the difference at
harvest
Lasso fertilizer

You can shave in a foxhole with
X-Ray
X-Ray razor

You CAN take it with you
Philco portable radio re-
ceiver

You can take the pulse of progress at Republic Steel
Republic Steel Corp.

You can taste cool April in your
mouth
Squibb toothpaste

You can taste the truth of this
famous claim
Old Forester bourbon whiskey

You can tell a lot about an individual by what he
pours into his glass
Old Bushmill's Irish Whiskey

You can trust our good name
Tylenol pain reliever

You can trust the man who sells
this brand
Swift's Premium meats

You can trust today's Cheer
Cheer detergent

You can trust your car to the
products with the
star
Texaco, Inc.

You can whip our cream but
you can't beat our milk
Story Dairy
You cannot match this car
Reo automobile
You can't afford to be without
Swagelok
Swagelok fittings
You can't afford to miss a minute
Hour Magazine television
program
You can't be optimistic with
misty optics
Meigs Glasses
You can't beat steel for bath-
rooms
United States Steel Corp.
You can't beat the experience
Pan American World Airways,
Inc.
You can't "brush off" denture
breath
Polident denture cleaner
You can't buy a better brake
lining to save your
life!
Grey-Rock Div., Raybestos-
Manhattan, Inc.
You can't buy a more potent
pain reliever without a
prescription
Tylenol pain reliever
You can't buy a Multigraph un-
less you need it
Addressograph-Multigraph
Corp.
You can't describe it until
you've tried it
Ronnoco Coffee Co.
You can't do a man-size job on
a bird-size breakfast
Grape-Nuts cereal
You can't do better than Sears
Sears Roebuck & Co.
You can't drink Folger's coffee
without smiling--try it
and see
Folger's ground coffee
You can't drink it slow if it's
Quik
Quik chocolate milk additive
You can't eat the box
MacFarlane candies
You can't fool the microphone
Lyon & Healy
You can't forget to make a

Colt safe
Colt revolver
You can't get a drink from a
drinkless Kaywoodie
Kaywoodie pipe
You can't get a drink from a
drinkless pipe
Reiss-Premier Pipe Co.
You can't get any closer
Norelco Rototrack Shaver
You can't get the whole picture
in just a day or two
San Francisco Convention
and Visitors Bureau
You can't go wrong with any
"Feist" song
Leo Feist, Inc. music pub-
lishers
You can't go wrong with Ray-
theon
Raytheon radio tubes
You can't keep a good soap
down
Queen Lily Soap
You can't knock the crease out
Digby slacks
You can't mistake the flavor
Beechnut coffee
You can't pay for a Heatrola, it
pays for itself
Estate Stove Co.
You can't ride home on an in-
surance policy
Foamite-Childs Corp.
You can't run 11 successful
companies with just
one man
Northwest Industries, Inc.
You can't wear out their looks
J. P. Smith Shoe Co.
You cook better automatically
with a Tappan
Tappan Company
You couldn't express it better
DHL Worldwide Courier
You couldn't have a sounder
pipe dream
Chase Brass & Copper Co.
You deserve a break today
McDonald's fast food restau-
rants
You deserve National attention
National Car Rental System,
Inc.
You deserve the best. We'd
like to help

Visa credit card

You don't have to be a million-
aire to play like one
Walter Hagen Golf Equipment
Co.

You don't have to be rich to
have MONY
Mutual of New York

You don't have to park your
street car
Northern Texas Traction
Co.

You don't "knead" the dough
Pillsbury's Flour

You don't know what it is to
love a car until you
build one
Fiberfab MG Replica

You don't need caffeine, and
neither does your cola
Like soft drink

You don't stay first unless
you're best
Goodyear Auto Tire

You eat it with a smile
Seale-Lilly Ice Cream Co.

You expect more and get more
from Mallory
Mallory controls

You expect more from a leader
Standard Oil Co. of Indiana

You expect more from Amoco
Amoco Chemicals Corp.

You expect more from Standard
and you get it
Standard Oil Div., American
Oil Co.

You expect the best from Hanson
... and you get it
Henry L. Hanson Co.

You feel so cool, so clean, so
fresh...
Tampax, Inc.

You feel you've had something
worth drinking when
you've had a Guinness
Guinness ale

You found it
True cigarettes

You furnish the print ... we'll
furnish the part
Synthane Corp.

You gave her a ring to be near
her, now give her a
RING when away
Bell Telephone System

You get big, crunchy nuts in a
Mars Bar
Mars candy bar

You get good things first from
Chrysler Corp.
Chrysler Corporation

You get half a chicken in a can
Lynden chicken fricassee

You get high interest with no
strings attached
Scudder Cash Investment
Trust

You get more from American
American Laundry Machine
Industries

You get more out of Hampden
Hampden Brewing Co.

You get more than just a car at
Budget
Budget Rent-a-car

You get more with cable TV
Cable Network, Inc.

You get power, pick-up and pep
Mobilgas

You have a friend at Chase
Manhattan
Chase Manhattan Bank

You have the power to end
H. D.
National Huntington's Dis-
ease Association

You haven't seen your country
if you haven't seen
Alaska
Alaska Travel Div., Dept.
of Economic Development
and Planning

You just know she wears them
McCallum Hosiery Co.

You know it's fresh, it's dated
Dated Mayonnaise, Inc.

You know it's right if it's Vinylite
Vinylite plastics

You know when a light is on,
you know when a light
is off
Sho-Lite, Inc.

You know you're right with a
Wright Hat
Wright Hat

You like it, it likes you
7UP soft drink

You live better automatically
with a Tappan
Tappan Company

You look your best in a
Stetson
Stetson hats
You may dent the wood but the
varnish won't crack
Pratt & Lambert varnish
You may know us by our Skittle
Game
Berea College Student
Crafts Industries
You meet the nicest people on a
Honda
Honda motorcycle
You need a. See also: Uneeda
Biscuit
You need a heavier cream to
shave a tender skin
Molle shaving cream
You need sunshine every day;
we knead Sunshine
every day
Sunshine Bread
You never had coffee like this
before
Borden's Instant Coffee
You never had it this fresh
Bright cigarettes
You never have to lift or tilt it
Proctor electric iron
You never heard it so good
Sony Superscope
You never lift or tilt it
Proctor electric iron
You ought to be in pictures
Parade Magazine
You ought to meet Muriel
Muriel cigar
You pay less for Gem blades be-
cause you need so few
Gem razor
You press the button, we do the
rest
Kodak cameras
You save with paper
Universal Paper Products
Co.
You see what you write as you
write it
New Era Check Protector
You select, we protect
Marmon automobile
You sleep on it ... not in it!
Perfect Sleeper mattress
You taste its freshness
Cuyamaca Water Co.
You trust its quality

Coca Cola soft drink
You turn the knob; Radak does
the rest
Radak radio receiver
You walk on cushions when you
walk in Osteo-path-iks
Osteo-path-ik shoes
You will. See: You'll
You won't find a better value
than Midway Airlines
Midway Airlines
You'll always be glad you bought
a G. E.
G. E. refrigerator
You'll bake it better with Five
Roses
Five Roses Flour
You'll be a better cook with Spry
Spry shortening
You'll be ahead with Chevrolet
Chevrolet automobile
You'll be ahead with Nash
Nash automobile
You'll be lovely, too, in a
Loveable brassiere
Loveable brassiere
You'll fall in love with Jersey
Maid
Jersey Maid Ice Cream Co.
You'll feel softer and silkier
after only one use
Liqua 4 Skin Cleansing
System
You'll find the woman's touch
in every Purex prod-
uct
Purex cleaning materials
You'll go for it when you see
how it goes for you
Chevrolet automobile
You'll have better luck with
Rit
Rit dyes
You'll have better times with
Early Times
Early Times bourbon whis-
key
You'll like it, too
Hanley & Kinsella Coffee
You'll like our krust
Excelsior Baking Co.
You'll like our prices and
you'll love our food
Denny's restaurants
You'll like our style
Kirchner Moore & Company

You'll like Red Rock
　Red Rock cheese
You'll like the taste
　Armour Grain Co.
You'll love the look of your leg
　　in Larkwood
　Larkwood hosiery
You'll never know you're wearing
　　'em
　Rand dress shields
You'll never tire of Purox wire
　Purox wire
You'll take a shine to burnished
　　browns
　Bostonian shoes
You'll wonder where the yellow
　　went when you brush
　　your teeth with Pepso-
　　dent
　Pepsodent toothpaste
Young.　See also:
　Alexander Young Distilling
　　Co.
　Thomas Young Orchids,
　　Inc.
Young America spreads it on
　　thick
　Welch's marmalade
Young & Rubicam advertising
　　agency
　Does Niagara make a noise?
Young beauty, clear as the
　　chime of bells
　Yardley's Old English soap
Young Brewing Co.
　The tru brew
The young girl's best friend
　Petit Point brassiere
Young Hat Co.
　All over town
The young man's magazine
　Varsity
The young point of view in shoes
　Life Stride shoes
Young Radiator Company
　Put muscle in your heat
　　transfer applications
Younger by design
　Van Heusen shirts
Youngstown Pressed Steel Co.
　Press it from steel instead
Your.　See also:
　You are
　You're
Your air commuter service in 12
　　busy states

Allegheny Airlines, Inc.
Your anywhere anything anytime
　　network
　Bell Telephone System
Your assurance of quality in tape
　　components
　Viking of Minneapolis, Inc.
Your assurance of the best
　W. A. Sheaffer Pen Co.
Your assurance that this fabric
　　has been pretested for
　　performance by Celanese
　Celanese Corp.
Your baby's comfort begins with
　　Luvs
　Luvs diapers
Your best bet for the best bits
　Rock Bit Div., Timken
　　Roller Bearing Co.
Your best buy in good taste
　Roma wines
Your best buy in tissue
　Kleenex tissue
Your best decision in ultra low
　　tar
　Vantage Ultra Lights men-
　　thol cigarettes
Your best food from the sea
　Oyster Growers of North
　　America
Your best friends for highway
　　safety
　Raybestos-Manhattan, Inc.
Your best salesman, printing
　　ink
　National Association of
　　Printing Ink Makers
Your best single source for
　　quality drive train re-
　　placement parts
　Borg-Warner Corporation
Your biggest bargain in clean-
　　liness
　Soilax
Your bottom line is our top
　　concern
　Drexel Burnham Lambert
　　Securities
Your buying guide, the classi-
　　fied
　Bell System telephone di-
　　rectory yellow pages
Your canary may be overfed,
　　yet undernourished
　The R. T. French Co.
Your car deserves one

538

Boyce Moto Meter
Your car looks like new when
    you use Carnu
Carnu auto polish
Your cheapest helper
    Reddy Kilowatt
Your closest friend
    Cupid foundation
Your complexion's best friend
    Campana Italian Balm
Your doctor of family finances
    Household Finance Corp.
Your doctor will endorse it
    Automatic Cycle Seat
Your drug store has it. Use it
    regularly at home
    Pompeian Massage Cream
Your druggist is more than a
    merchant
    National Association of Re-
    tail Druggists
Your electrical servant
    Reddy Kilowatt
Your everyday dishes don't look
    everyday
    Joy dishwashing liquid
Your eyes say style, your feet
    say comfort
    Swankies Shoes
Your face never had it so clean!
    1006 lotion
Your feet are worth Fortunes
    Fortune shoes
Your feet are your fortune
    Musebeck Shoe Co.
Your fence for keeps with Red
    Brand
    Red Brand fencing
Your first taste tells you and
    sells you
    Pacific Brewing & Malting
    Co.
Your footprint in leather
    Matrix shoes
Your footprints in leather
    Matrix shoes
Your friend
    Thom McAn shoes
Your friend in the home, on the
    highway, where you
    work
    Liberty Mutual Insurance
    Company
Your friend on the highway
    Liberty Mutual Insurance
    Company

Your gas bills cut in two
    National Automatic Gas Light
Your gateway to business in
    Brazil
    Banco do Brazil
Your Guardian for life
    The Guardian Life Insurance
    Co. of America
Your guide to good liquors
    National Distillers
Your guide to good living
    National Distillers
Your guide to the best in men's
    slippers
    Evans slippers
Your guide to quality in alumi-
    num
    Aluminum Company of Amer-
    ica
Your Hartford agent does more
    than he really has to
    Hartford Insurance Group
Your heart will lose its mind
    Chen Yu Lipstick
Your helping hand when trouble
    comes
    American Mutual Liability
    Insurance Co.
Your home state farm paper
    Montana Farmer
Your hometown agent
    Fireman's Fund American
    Insurance
Your hometown oil company
    Lassus Bros. retail gaso-
    line stations
Your investment success is our
    success
    E. I. DuPont de Nemours
    & Co.
Your job is well powered when
    it's Ford powered
    Industrial Engine Dept.,
    Ford Div., Ford Motor
    Company
Your key to hospitality
    Old Fitzgerald whiskey
Your key to the electronic office
    Olympia electric typewriters
Your kitchen companion since
    1899
    Dazey Products Co.
Your legs will thank you
    Brighton Wide-Web Garters
Your letterhead is the voice of
    your business

539

Rag Content Paper Mills
Your life depends upon the
forgings in your car
Atlas Drop Forge Co.
Your life plan deserves expert
guidance
Penn Mutual Underwriter
Insurance
Your lips are first and last to
touch a Lily cup
Lily-Tulip Cup Corp.
Your main line to sunshine
Southern Pacific Co.
Your mind is burglar-proof
International Correspondence
Schools
Your money back if you'll take it
Pep spark plug
Your money goes farther in a
General Motors car
General Motors Corporation
Your morning is as good as your
mattress
Sealy Mattress Co.
Your NEC computer grows with
you
NEC Information Systems,
Inc.
Your neighbors know New Eng-
land Coke
New England Coke Co.
Your nose knows
Tuxedo tobacco
Your nose quickly knows
Tuxedo tobacco
Your nose quickly knows the
difference
Tuxedo tobacco
Your one-source solution to every
film problem
The Smead Mfg. Co.
Your packaging deserves Crown
quality
Crown Cork & Seal Co.,
Inc.
Your paper problems are in good
hands with Marathon
Marathon Div., American
Can Co.
Your partner in packaging pro-
gress
Ball Brothers Co., Inc.
Your partner in protection
Grange Mutual Insurance
Your partner whose actions speak
louder than words

Owens-Corning Fiberglas
Corp.
Your peace of mind is worth the
premium
National Surety Co.
Your personal pedestal
Adler elevator shoes
Your personal plane is HERE
Aeronca aircraft
Your power-ful worker
Reddy Kilowatt
Your premium's worth
Fireman's Fund American
Insurance
Your printer's performance
starts with fine papers
Crocker Hamilton Papers,
Inc.
Your safety is our business
Hazard Wire Rope
Your shoulders will thank you
Pioneer Suspender Co.
Your skin knows and shows the
difference
Lana Oil Soap
Your skin, wake it up before
you make it up
Cosray skin freshener
Your smile of beauty
Ipana toothpaste
Your smoke comes clean
Viceroy cigarettes
Your snapshots look better en-
larged
Sterling Photo Co.
Your story in pictures leaves
nothing untold
American Photo Engravers
Assn.
Your symbol of quality and
service
Firestone Tire and Rubber
Co.
Your T-zone will tell you
Camel cigarettes
Your teeth are only as healthy
as your gums
Forhan's tooth paste
Your ticket to the Met for over
forty years
Texaco, Inc.
Your unseen friend
Inco Nickel
Your voice can be improved
100%
Perfect Voice Institute

Your waist will thank you
Pioneer Suspender Co.
Your way of life depends upon
your day of work
Morrison tractor
Your wish fulfilled
Richard Hudnut toilet spe-
cialties
Your world of ideas and products
MPA Magazines
Your wrist watch deserves the
best
Hadley watch band
Your write-hand man
Scripto pencil
You're. See also:
You are
Your
You're always in good form with
Reo-Form
Reo-Form slips
You're always right with Ultra-
Lite
Ultra-Lite replacement win-
dows and doors
You're always safe with Baker's
Magdolite
Baker's Magdolite
You're asking for a good sock
Westminster sock
You're asking for a good sock
when you ask for West-
minster
Westminster sock
You're better off with Bostitch
Bostitch stapler
You're better off with Pan Am
Pan American World Airways,
Inc.
You're going to like us
Trans World Airlines, Inc.
You're in good hands with All-
state
Allstate Insurance Co.
You're in style when you step
into a Fortune
Fortune shoes
You're in the Pepsi generation
Pepsi-Cola soft drink
You're miles ahead with B. F.
Goodrich, first in
rubber tires
B. F. Goodrich Tire Co.
You're miles ahead with General
General tires
You're money ahead when you

paint with white lead
Lead Industries Assn., Inc.
You're money ahead with a May-
tag
Maytag laundry washers
You're right with Lufkin
The Lufkin Rule Co.
You're safe and you know it
Prestone anti-freeze
You're safe with Sunbrite, it
has a spotless reputa-
tion
Sunbrite Cleanser
You're safer in a Steelcraft
Steelcraft boat
You're sure of genuineness
Seagram's Distillers Corp.
You're sure of yourself in
Phoenix
Phoenix hosiery
You're the winner with Blatz
quality
Blatz beer
You're twice as smart with Vital-
ity Shoes
Vitality shoes
You're twice as sure with
Frigidaire
Frigidaire Div., General
Motors Corporation
You're Wendy's kind of people
Wendy's fast food restaur-
ants
Yours are the only lips to touch
a Lily cup
Lily-Tulip Cup Corp.
Yours for a good morning
Carnation Albers cereals
Yours for growing satisfaction
Neosho Nurseries
Yours for leisure
Eureka vacuum cleaner
Yours for Victory
Bond's handkerchiefs
Yours, in haste
Heinz spaghetti
Youthline foundation
For the full figure
Youth's Companion
One hundred years young
You've come a long way, baby
Virginia Slims Lights cig-
arettes
You've got a treat ahead of you
Listerine shaving cream
You've got good things going

for you with service by
Investor-Owned Electric
Light and Power Com-
panies
Investor-Owned Electric
Light and Power Com-
panies
You've read about it. Now you
can invest in it
First Index Investment
Trust
Yuban
The guest coffee

-Z-

Zale's diamond store
It's all you need to know
for Christmas
Zapon lacquer finish
The lacquer finish that
stays new
Zapon leather cloth
It wears--and wears--and
wears
Ze dash zat makes ze dish
A-1 Sauce
Zebco fishing tackle
Where the action is!
Zeiss. See: Carl Zeiss, Inc.
Zenith radio receiver
Again a year ahead
Always a year ahead
America's most copied radio
Costs more but does more
Zeniths play where many
fail
Zenith television sets
Built better because it's
handcrafted
The handcrafted T.V.
The quality goes in before
the name goes on
Zenitherm Co.
Looks like stone, works like
wood
Zeniths play where many fail
Zenith radio receiver
Zephyr. See also: Lincoln
Zephyr automobile
Zephyr-screened face powder
Sales Affiliates, Inc.
Zerex anti-freeze
The best anti-freeze since
mink

Zero weather, summer heat,
always creamy fresh
and sweet
Crisco shortening
Zest at its best
American Dairy Association
Shefford cheese
Zest for breakfast, best for
health
Kellogg's All-Bran
Zest soap
The deodorant bar that
leaves no sticky film
Discover the cleaner feeling
of Zest
Get Zest. Feel your best
Ziebart Rust Protection
Ziebart: your rust proof-
ing expert
Ziebart: your rust proofing ex-
pert
Ziebart Rust Protection
Zimba Cola soft drink
There's always a thirst time
Zimmerman-Scher Co.
Furs that reflect youth
Zip hair remover
A dab makes you as dainty
as a deb
It's off because it's out
Zip in every sip
Spur soft drink
The zipper of tomorrow
Crown slide fastener
Zippo Manufacturing Co.
The lighter that made the
world lighter-conscious
The lighter that works
Zodiac Watch Co.
Sign of the right time
Zonite
Zonite meets woman's great
need
Zonite meets woman's great need
Zonite
Zonitors suppository
So powerful yet absolutely
safe to tissues
Zono Pads
Put one on, the pain is
gone
Zoom cereal
A hot weather hot cereal
Zoom 8 camera
The name quality made
famous

Zurn Industries, Inc.
  A step ahead of tomorrow

Zymole Trokeys
  For husky throats